Management Accounting

FIFTH EDITION

Anthony A. Atkinson
University of Waterloo

Robert S. Kaplan
Harvard University

Ella Mae Matsumura
University of Wisconsin–Madison

S. Mark Young
University of Southern California

PEARSON
Prentice
Hall

Upper Saddle River, New Jersey 07458

Library of Congress Cataloging-in-Publication Data
Atkinson, Anthony A.
    Management accounting / Anthony A. Atkinson, Robert S. Kaplan,
    Ella Mae Matsumura, S. Mark Young.—5th ed.
        p. cm.
    Includes index.
    ISBN 0-13-173281-1
    I. Kaplan, Robert S. II. Young, S. Mark. III. Title.

HF5657.4.M328 2007
658.15'11--dc22   2006034277

AVP/Executive Editor: Wendy Craven
VP/Editorial Director: Jeff Shelstad
Manager, Product Development: Pamela Hersperger
Project Manager: Kerri Tomasso
Editorial Assistant: Marybeth Ward
AVP/Executive Marketing Manager: John Wannemacher
Marketing Assistant: Patrick Barbera
Associate Director, Production Editorial: Judy Leale
Senior Managing Editor, Production: Cynthia Zonneveld
Production Editor: Denise Culhane
Permissions Coordinator: Charles Morris
Associate Director, Manufacturing: Vinnie Scelta
Manufacturing Buyer: Diane Peirano
Cover Design: Bruce Kenselaar
Cover Illustration/Photo: Getty Images, Inc.
Director, Image Resource Center: Melinda Patelli
Manager, Rights and Permissions: Zina Arabia
Manager: Visual Research: Beth Brenzel
Image Permission Coordinator: Kathy Gavilanes
Photo Researcher: Rachel Lucas
Composition/Full-Service Project Management: GGS Book Services/
    Andrew Roney
Printer/Binder: RR Donnelley—Willard
Typeface: 10/12 Times

Credits and acknowledgments borrowed from other sources and reproduced, with permission, in this textbook appear on appropriate page within text.

Pearson Education LTD.   Pearson Education Australia PTY, Limited
Pearson Education Singapore, Pte. Ltd   Pearson Education North Asia Ltd
Pearson Education, Canada, Ltd   Pearson Educación de Mexico, S.A. de C.V.
Pearson Education–Japan   Pearson Education Malaysia, Pte. Ltd.

10 9 8 7 6 5 4 3
ISBN-13: 978-0-13-600531-5
ISBN-10: 0-13-600531-4

This book is dedicated to our
parents and families.

Brief Contents

CONTENTS

PREFACE

"Companies need financial professionals who know how to communicate not only what a company spent but also how it consumed that spending and where it provided value and alignment to strategy. The financial skills that are needed are those which allow us to focus on the future as well as the past, with a common thread of creating value."

RALPH W. CANTER
Bearing Point

Intended Audience

This textbook is designed for undergraduate and MBA courses in managerial accounting. *Management Accounting*, Fifth Edition, represents state-of-the-art thinking on all of the major topics in management accounting including activity-based management, the Balanced Scorecard, target costing, and management control system design.

Each of the text authors is both a scholar and a top consultant for *Fortune 500* or smaller companies. As a result, they have a unique focus: to help all students better understand management accounting topics, research, and issues from the perspective of a business manager. Although this text is primarily intended for business students, it is also useful for practicing managers who would benefit from understanding how accounting drives value in organizations.

All Businesses Have the Same Goal

Whether an enterprise intends to earn money for owners and stockholders or is a not-for-profit organization, the goal is the same: creating value. One company may be improving workforce conditions while another may be investing in new product development based on customer feedback. Whatever the strategy, the only management accounting textbook that explains in detail how to use measurement and management systems for value creation is *Management Accounting*, Fifth Edition, by Anthony A. Atkinson, Robert S. Kaplan, Ella Mae Matsumura, and S. Mark Young.

Special Note About the Author Team

Our collaboration has been enhanced with the addition of Ella Mae Matsumura. Ella Mae brings many years of both exceptional teaching and research experience to the book and we are all very pleased to welcome her to the author team.

Other Points of Distinction

- *New* **cases** including cases from Harvard Business School, the Institute of Management Accountants (IMA), and others that require both strategic and interpersonal analysis and make this text an even better fit for upper level undergraduate and MBA courses in Management Accounting.

New to This Edition

- *New* **Harvard Business School cases** that place the student in a managerial role. Four are new:
  - * Sippican (Brand new Harvard case, just developed; integrates time-driven activity-based costing, budgeting, and the Balanced Scorecard.)
  - * Midwest Office Products
  - * Chadwick (abridged)
  - * Domestic Auto Parts
- All of these cases are brief for preparation ease and are accompanied by Instructor Case Notes found in the Instructor resources.
- *New* **Institute of Management Accountants cases**—Two are new and include such topics as:
  - * How Mercedes-Benz used target costing to develop its new SUV.
  - * Improving processes in order entry, with linkages to value-chain ideas (effects on customers, sales representatives, manufacturing, and other internal uses of the order entry information).
- *New* **Chapter Opening Vignettes**—that describe realistic business problems that can benefit from managerial accounting analysis or approaches.
- **Revised Chapter 4**—Robert S. Kaplan is considered the world's leading expert on activity-based costing and the Balanced Scorecard. For this edition, he has revised and reorganized Chapter 4, "Activity-Based Cost Systems". In the fifth edition, Kaplan, cocreator of ABC, integrates the new time-driven ABC approach with the conventional ABC approach. Two new cases help students learn how to build their own time-driven ABC models.
- **Revised Chapter 7**—An extended quantitative example on target costing has been added.
- **Revised Chapter 9**—Kaplan has also revised Chapter 9, "The Balanced Scorecard". This is a comprehensive full-chapter treatment of how to translate a strategy into a strategy map and Balanced Scorecard. Written by the cocreator of this concept as well, the fifth edition also contains two new Harvard Business School cases for students to gain experience with the topic.
- **Revised Chapter 10**—The chapter has been expanded to include a more explicit and detailed treatment of uncertainty in the budgeting process.
- **Revised Chapter 12**—The chapter has been revised to include more detailed material on financial control.
- *New* Improved organization and clarity based on feedback from users of the fourth edition.
- *New* New questions and problems that correspond to new material, and additional problems on "previous" material.

For Instructors:

The following supplements are available to adopting instructors. For detailed descriptions, please visit: www.prenhall.com/atkinson.

- **Instructor's Resource Center (IRC) online:** Login at www.prenhall.com/irc
- **Printed Instructor's Manual**—ISBN: 0-13-198792-5

Each chapter of this comprehensive resource includes a list of the student learning objectives, a chapter outline with teaching tips organized by learning objective, teaching notes for the Harvard Business School Cases, and a chapter quiz. Instructor Excel spreadsheet solution files are available for download from www.prenhall.com/atkinson.

- **Printed Test Item File**—ISBN: 0-13-173716-3
  The Test Item File features over 1,200 questions specifically written for the fifth edition. Multiple-choice, true/false, problems, exercise and essay questions are all linked to specific chapter learning objectives that aid in precise quantitative and qualitative testing.
- **Solutions Manual**—ISBN: 0-13-221622-1
  This manual contains the accuracy-checked solutions for every question, exercise, problem, and all the Harvard Business School Cases in the text.
- **PowerPoint slides**—Visit the IRC for this text.
- **Readings in Management Accounting by S. Mark Young**
  Contains recent business press and academic articles that correlate to the chapter coverage in *Management Accounting*, Fifth Edition. Ideal for additional content reinforcement and for any case-based course, this supplement includes articles from a variety of sources. Readings in Management Accounting can be used with *Management Accounting*, Fifth Edition, or any other management or cost accounting text.

Please visit www.prenhall.com/atkinson for the Instructor's Manual to accompany this book.

Instructor's Resource Center:

Register. Redeem. Login.

www.prenhall.com/irc is where instructors can access a variety of print, media, and presentation resources available with this text in downloadable, digital format. For most texts, resources are also available for course management platforms such as Blackboard, WebCT, and Course Compass.

It gets better. Once you register, you will not have additional forms to fill out, or multiple usernames and passwords to remember to access new titles and/or editions. As a registered faculty member, you can login directly to download resource files and receive immediate access and instructions for installing Course Management content to your campus server.

Need help? Our dedicated Technical Support team is ready to assist instructors with questions about the media supplements that accompany this text. Visit: http://247.prenhall.com/ for answers to frequently asked questions and toll-free user support phone numbers.

For Students:

- www.prenhall.com/atkinson contains valuable resources for both students and professors, including Powerpoint slides.

ACKNOWLEDGMENTS

We would like to acknowledge, with thanks, the individuals who made this text possible. For the fifth edition, these people include the following:

Dr. Paul Copley, James Madison University
Dr. Allan R. Drebin, Northwestern University
Scott Keating, University of Chicago
Danny Litt, UCLA Anderson School
Frederick W. Rankin, Washington University
Dr. Kelly Richmond, University of North Carolina at Greensboro
Dr. Soliman Y. Soliman, Tulane University
Dr. Nathan V. Stuart, University of Florida
Clark Wheatley, Florida International University
Dr. Jennifer Yin, Rutgers University

We would also like to extend a special acknowledgment for those professors and reviewers who worked on previous editions of this text.

We also gratefully acknowledge Professors Shahid Ansari, Jan Bell, Thomas Klammer, and Carol Lawrence for allowing us to use some of their material on Target Costing, and Professor Michael D. Shields for his continuing support of the book.

Of course, another note of appreciation to our team at Prentice Hall. We're glad to have had Kerri Tomasso—who navigates the myriad of issues required from manuscript to book so deftly—on board as project manager for the fifth edition. We also enjoy the steady flow of emails from our editor Wendy Craven. Special thanks to our production team, Denise Culhane, Cindy Zonneveld, Diane Peirano and Charles Morris for leading us through the production process and bringing the book in on time.

The author and product team would appreciate hearing from you! Let us know what you think about this textbook by writing to wendy_craven@prenhall.com. Please include "Feedback about AKYM 5e" in the subject line.

If you have questions related to this product, please contact our customer service department online at www.247.prenhall.com.

Anthony A. Atkinson

Professor in the School of Accountancy at the University of Waterloo. Anthony A. Atkinson received a Bachelor of Commerce and M.B.A. degrees from Queen's University in Kingston, Ontario, and M.S. and Ph.D. degrees in Industrial Administration from Carnegie-Mellon University in Pittsburgh. He is a fellow of the Society of Management Accountants of Canada and has written or coauthored two texts, various monographs, and more than 35 articles on performance measurement and costing. In 1989, the Canadian Academic Accounting Association awarded Atkinson the Haim Falk Prize for Distinguished Contribution to Accounting Thought for his monograph that studied transfer pricing practice in six Canadian companies. He has served on the editorial boards of two professional and five academic journals and is a past Editor of the *Journal of Management Accounting Research*. Atkinson also served as a member of the Canadian government's Cost Standards Advisory Committee, for which he developed the costing principles it now requires of government contractors.

Robert S. Kaplan

Robert S. Kaplan is Baker Foundation Professor at the Harvard Business School. Kaplan joined the HBS faculty in 1984 after spending 16 years on the faculty of the business school at Carnegie-Mellon University, where he served as Dean from 1977 to 1983. Kaplan received a B.S. and M.S. in Electrical Engineering from M.I.T., and a Ph.D. in Operations Research from Cornell University. He has received honorary doctorates from University of Stuttgart and University of Lodz.

Kaplan, a co-developer of both activity-based costing and the Balanced Scorecard, has shown how to design cost and performance management systems for effective strategy implementation and operational excellence. He has authored or co-authored 13 books, 16 Harvard Business Review articles, and more than 120 other papers.

His fourth book co-authored with David Norton, *Alignment*, was published in February 2006. His previous books with Norton include *Strategy Maps*, named as one of the top ten business books of 2004 by Strategy & Business and amazon.com, *The Strategy-Focused Organization*, named by Cap Gemini Ernst & Young as the best international business book for year 2000, and *The Balanced Scorecard: Translating Strategy into Action*, which has been translated into 22 languages and won the 2001 Wildman Medal from the American Accounting Association for its impact on practice. Kaplan's most recent book, on time-driven activity-based costing, was published in March 2006.

Kaplan was inducted into the Accounting Hall of Fame in 2006 and received the Lifetime Contribution Award from the Management Accounting Section of the American Accounting Association in January 2006. He was selected among the top 20 Business Writers/Management Gurus in the Financial Times 2005 CEO Survey. Kaplan received the Outstanding Accounting Educator Award in 1988 from the American Accounting Association (AAA), the 1994 CIMA Award from the Chartered Institute of Management Accountants (UK) for "Outstanding Contributions to the

Accountancy Profession," and the 2001 Distinguished Service Award from the Institute of Management Accountants (IMA) for contributions to the practice and academic community.

Ella Mae Matsumura

Ella Mae Matsumura is an Associate Professor in the Department of Accounting and Information Systems in the School of Business at the University of Wisconsin-Madison, and is affiliated with the university's Center for Quick Response Manufacturing. She received an A.B. in Mathematics from the University of California, Berkeley, and M.Sc. and Ph.D. degrees from the University of British Columbia. Matsumura has won two teaching excellence awards at the University of Wisconsin–Madison and was elected as a lifetime fellow of the university's Teaching Academy, formed to promote effective teaching. She is a member of the university team awarded an IBM Total Quality Management Partnership grant to develop curriculum for total quality management education.

Matsumura has served in various leadership positions in the American Accounting Association, including Secretary–Treasurer and President of the Association's Management Accounting Section. She also chaired or served on numerous Association committees. She served two terms as an Associate Editor of Accounting Horizons and is currently co-editor of the journal. Her past and current research articles focus on decision making, performance evaluation, and compensation issues. She also coauthored a monograph on customer profitability analysis in credit unions.

S. Mark Young

S. Mark Young holds the George Bozanic and Holman G. Hurt Chair in Sports and Entertainment Business and is also Professor of Accounting, Professor of Management and Organization at the Marshall School of Business, University of Southern California and Professor of Communication at the Annenberg School for Communication at USC. Previously, Dr. Young served as the Associate Dean for Academic Planning and Associate Dean and Academic Director of the Marshall MBA (Full-Time MBA) Program. Professor Young received an A.B. from Oberlin College (Economics), an M. Acc. from the Ohio State University, and a Ph.D. from the University of Pittsburgh.

Professor Young has published research in a variety of journals including *The Accounting Review, Accounting, Organizations and Society*, the *Journal of Accounting Research*, the *Journal of Marketing Research*, the *Academy of Management Review* and the *Journal of Research in Personality*. Currently, he is on the editorial board of several major journals and was past Associate Editor for *The Accounting Review*. In 2006, he was a co-winner of the Notable Contribution to the Accounting Literature (with Shannon Anderson) and has won the Notable Contributions to the Management Accounting Literature Award twice—with Frank Selto (1994) and Shannon Anderson (2003). He also received the Jim Bulloch Award for Innovations in Management Accounting Education in 2005.

Dr. Young has extensive executive teaching and consulting experience having taught in executive programs for Daimler- Chrysler, Texas Instruments, Shell Oil, AMGEN and British Airways. Most recently, Young has had consulting or research relationships with the First Data Corporation, the Chrysler Corporation, Texas Instruments and Southwest Airlines. He has won four outstanding teaching awards at the undergraduate and graduate levels, including the Golden Apple Teaching Award and is a Distinguished Fellow in the Center for Excellence in Teaching at USC.

Currently he teaches courses in management accounting and entertainment management, and leads the entertainment management program within the Marshall School at USC. His book, *Entertainment Management—Understanding the Business of Motion Pictures, Television, Music and Games* will soon be published by Prentice Hall.

Professor Young also maintains an interest in popular culture and his paper, "Narcissism and Celebrity," (with Dr. Drew Pinsky) published in the Journal of Research in Personality (October 2006: 463-471) recently received world-wide attention. Young even appeared on Mitch Albom's and Howard Stern's shows to discuss the findings of the research.

Chapter 1

Management Accounting: Information That Creates Value

After reading this chapter, you will be able to:

➤ understand and exploit the differences between management accounting information and financial accounting information

➤ understand how the organization's strategy drives the need for different types of management accounting information

➤ understand how financial accounting information provides an overall measure of the organization's performance

➤ realize how management accountants can develop nonfinancial information that can predict and explain financial results

➤ appreciate the behavioral and ethical issues faced by management accountants

Cabinets by Design

Diane Wilson was the majority share owner, chief executive officer, and chief operating officer of Cabinets by Design (CBD). CBD manufactured kitchen cabinets to customer specifications. Production was on demand—only a customer order could trigger production.

Three cabinet styles were available: country, contemporary, and modern. Each style required a different mix of raw materials, machine time, and hand finishing. The modern style used more metal, glass, laminates, and machine time than either country or contemporary. The country style used wood almost exclusively, used less machine time, and required more hand finishing. The contemporary style was a hybrid of country and modern.

Customers would visit one of CBD's authorized agents who were located across the country and use a computer terminal to choose a style and to propose a cabinet design and size. The computer program checked

Source: Hal Lott/CORBIS.

the proposed design for manufacturability and integrity, and approved acceptable designs. It would immediately schedule production at CBD's sole manufacturing facility and quote the customer a price and a guaranteed delivery date—"On time or it's free." The cabinets were expensive, so customers demanded that quality work be delivered at the delivery time promised.

CBD believed customers valued the look of its cabinets, their durability, the ability to custom design and that they could take delivery at a construction site where the cabinets would be installed.

After 4 years of promoting its products to customers; ironing out kinks in its order-taking, production scheduling, and manufacturing systems, and signing up agents, business at CBD took off. For the next 8 years, profit growth was explosive, increasing at an average compounded rate of more than 32% per year. During this period, Diane garnered many awards, including entrepreneur of the year, for her innovative and successful business.

Then, unexpectedly, profit growth leveled off. Diane's managers assured her that intense competition from new competitors who were grabbing market share by offering huge price discounts was causing the stalled profit growth. The consensus among these managers was that competitors could not sustain their intense price-cutting and, therefore, growth in CBD's profits would resume next year. Satisfied, Diane did not pursue the profit picture further and looked forward to renewed growth in the following year. However, next year, profits growth stalled again, prompting Diane to launch a full-scale investigation.

MANAGEMENT ACCOUNTING INFORMATION

What Is Management Accounting Information?

Management accounting systems provide information, both financial and nonfinancial, to managers and employees inside an organization. Management accounting information is tailored to the specific needs of each decision maker and is rarely distributed outside the organization. **Financial accounting** reports, in contrast, communicate standard format economic information to individuals and organizations that are external to the company, such as shareholders, creditors (bankers, bondholders, and suppliers), regulators, and governmental tax authorities.

Since the needs of decision makers in the organization drive the scope and focus of management accounting, we can predict the scope of management accounting by considering the three broad classes of organization decision making, shown in Exhibit 1-1, which are planning, organizing, and controlling.

Planning includes activities such as product planning (which requires information such as prospective revenues and costs), production planning (which requires information such as resource availability and its use by various products the organization makes), and strategy development (which requires information about the organization's external environment and, in particular, the requirements of target customers). Most planning information is predictive and forward looking, which is an important contrast to financial accounting information, which is historical and backward looking.

Organizing activities focus on developing the organization systems that will develop, produce, and deliver the organization's products (goods or services) and the required infrastructure to support the primary production systems. The information required often focuses on assessing the potential of alternative systems to achieve the organization's objectives, such as prospective product quality and service levels provided to customers. Information required for organizing activities includes items such as the performance potential of different production systems, for example, the efficiency and productivity of different machines that could be used on an assembly line.

Exhibit 1-1
The Roles of
Management

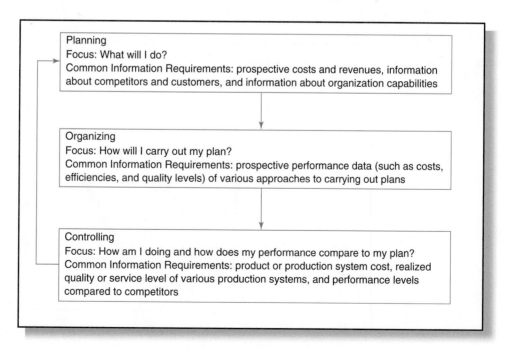

Planning
Focus: What will I do?
Common Information Requirements: prospective costs and revenues, information about competitors and customers, and information about organization capabilities

Organizing
Focus: How will I carry out my plan?
Common Information Requirements: prospective performance data (such as costs, efficiencies, and quality levels) of various approaches to carrying out plans

Controlling
Focus: How am I doing and how does my performance compare to my plan?
Common Information Requirements: product or production system cost, realized quality or service level of various production systems, and performance levels compared to competitors

A good example of prospective information that organizations use in the planning stage is the test market. In test marketing, an organization offers a new product, good, or service in a geographic area that it believes will provide it with a good indication of the product's wider acceptability and sales potential. Marketing personnel scrutinize test market data carefully before deciding whether to release the product for wide distribution.

Controlling activities focus on measuring and evaluating the performance of existing organization systems and entities to identify how each is contributing to achieving the organization's objectives. The information required here includes system performance information, such as the cost of producing a product or operating a process such as a bottling line, achieved product quality levels, an organization unit's profit contribution to organization profitability, and the time taken by a sales management system to respond to a customer's request.

Because contemporary management accounting systems focus on decision makers at all levels in the organization, they must be flexible and pragmatic. As summarized in Exhibit 1-2, decision makers at senior levels of the organization tend to focus primarily on financial performance measures, such as profits and costs. Why? Because senior executives communicate, almost exclusively, using financial information with people outside the organization. As we move down the organization hierarchy, we find that the mix of information required by decision makers includes less financial information and more **nonfinancial information**. Why? Because people at these levels of the organization need to know the performance characteristics of the systems they are monitoring and managing. Because of the differing information needs of managers at different levels of the organization, management accounting systems that used to focus exclusively on financial information have begun to measure and report nonfinancial information, such as product quality, customer satisfaction, and service response rates.

Exhibit 1-2
Information Used and the Organization Level

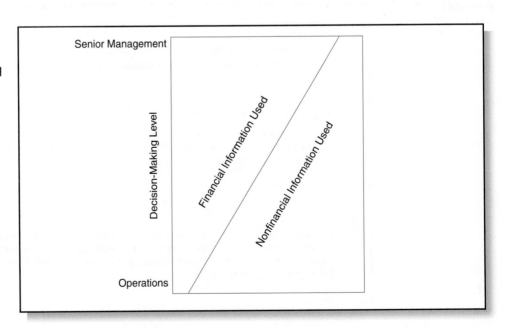

The reported expense of an operating department, such as the assembly department of an automobile plant or an electronics company, is one example of management accounting information. Other examples are the cost of producing a product, the cost of delivering a service, and the cost of performing an activity or business process, such as creating a customer invoice or serving a customer.

Differences Between Management Accounting and Financial Accounting

The International Accounting Standards Board and accounting standards boards in individual countries create and enforce required financial accounting practices. To be consistent in meeting the needs of diverse external users who have unspecified information needs, financial accounting is rules driven, and students of financial accounting study the journal entries, procedures, standards, and regulations for producing the mandated financial statements. In short, financial accounting information is based on historical information and stresses the form in which it is measured, organized, and communicated.

However, companies exercise individual discretion to design management accounting systems that provide information to support internal decision making. Although some management accounting bodies (such as the International Federation of Accountants' International Management Accounting Practice Statements) have suggested management accounting standards, these standards provide only broad guidelines, and organizations are left on their own to develop the management accounting systems that they feel best suit their needs. Exceptions to the voluntary nature of management accounting standards are the management accounting standards developed by various governments, such as the Cost Accounting Standards Board in the United States, that regulate how government contractors will report their costs for contract reimbursement.

To understand how management accounting information helps increase profits, reduce costs, and improve processes, we must focus on the information employees and managers need to make their decisions, not on the information needs of external individuals and organizations. Exhibit 1-3 provides an overview of the basic features of

Exhibit 1-3
Financial and Management Accounting Basic Features

	FINANCIAL ACCOUNTING	MANAGERIAL ACCOUNTING
Audience	*External:* Stockholders, creditors, tax authorities	*Internal:* Workers, managers, executives
Purpose	Report on past performance to external parties; provide a contracting basis for owners and lenders	Inform internal decisions made by employees and managers; feedback and control on operating performance
Timeliness	Delayed; historical	Current; future oriented
Restrictions	Regulated; rules driven by generally accepted accounting principles and government authorities	No regulations; systems and information determined by management to meet strategic and operational needs
Type of Information	Financial measurements only	Financial plus operational and physical measurements on processes, technologies, suppliers, customers, and competitors
Nature of Information	Objective, auditable, reliable, consistent, precise	More subjective and judgmental; valid, relevant, accurate
Scope	Highly aggregate; report on entire organization	Disaggregate; inform local decisions and actions

financial accounting and management accounting and illustrates the contrast between them. In this book, we focus on how companies' management accounting practices can be derived from the information and decision needs of their managers and employees, not from requirements to prepare statements for external constituencies.

A Brief History of Management Accounting

Despite attempts by accounting historians, the origins, cause, and evolution of management accounting systems continue to be difficult to pin down. Historians searching company, university, and government archives continue to uncover evidence to support a new candidate for the title of "oldest documented management accounting system."

Historical evidence suggests that the development and evolution of these management accounting systems were driven by the need for information to promote the organization's success in achieving its objectives—that is, to support the organization's strategy. The type of information evolved over time as organization strategies and therefore information needs changed.

Traditional management accounting systems were called cost accounting systems since they focused on assessing the cost of an important product or activity in the organization. By the late nineteenth century, railroad managers implemented large, complex costing systems that allowed them to compute the costs of carrying the different types of freight, such as coal and steel. This information supported efficiency improvements and pricing in the railroads. The railroads were the first modern industry to develop and use large quantities of financial statistics to assess organizational performance. About the same time, though, Andrew Carnegie developed detailed records of the cost of materials and labor used in his steel mills. Carnegie was ruthless in reducing costs, and he would close mills that he felt were irretrievably inefficient.

The emergence of large, integrated companies, such as DuPont and General Motors, at the start of the twentieth century changed the focus from cost accounting to management accounting. The design of these integrated companies created complex organizations as "modern business enterprise took the place of market mechanisms in coordinating the activities of the economy and allocating its resources. In many sectors of the economy the visible hand of management replaced what Adam Smith referred to as the invisible hand of market forces."[1]

By internalizing what were previously open market transactions, these organizations sought to improve efficiency and therefore profitability by eliminating the costs of transacting with external agents. The rise of these integrated companies created a demand for measuring the performance of individual organizational units, as shown in Exhibit 1-4, to evaluate their performance through comparisons with stand-alone organizations that performed the same task. For example, an automobile company might want to compare the cost performance of a division that makes transmissions with that of an independent supplier. Managers developed ways to measure the profitability and the performance of their units. Today, many organizations continue to use these tools as they evaluate whether to make or buy goods and services that they use—a topic we will consider in chapter 5.

---

[1] Alfred Dupont Chandler, *The Visible Hand: The Managerial Revolution in American Business* (Cambridge, Mass.: Belknap Press, 1977).

Exhibit 1-4
Departments Now
Supplying Inside
the Organization

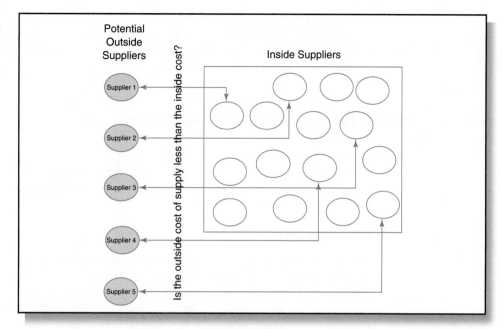

After the late 1920s, the evolution of management accounting practice slowed as senior management and interest focused on developing and preparing financial statements to meet the new regulatory external reporting requirements resulting from stock market failures.

It was only in the 1970s, when American and European companies were under intense pressure from Japanese automobile manufacturers, that interest turned to developing more comprehensive management accounting systems that reported on strategic dimensions such as quality and service rather than simply organization unit cost performance. During the latter part of the twentieth century, innovations in costing and performance measurement systems—the focus of this text—were designed.

In summary, the history of management accounting exhibits two characteristics:

1. In high-performing organizations, innovations in management accounting practice were—and continue to be—driven by the information needs of evolving strategy. When cost control was the strategic imperative, costing systems became more accurate. When the ability of organizations to adapt and change to environmental changes became important, management accounting systems that supported adaptability to environmental changes were developed.

IN PRACTICE
Reviving Open Market Transactions

While most of the twentieth century saw the rise of giant organizations that internalized market transactions by doing everything themselves (the epitome being Henry Ford's River Rouge Plant), the latter part of the twentieth century witnessed a partial reversing of this process. Organizations including for-profit, not-for-profit, and governments, around the world, citing a need to focus on what they did best, began to contract out activities they formerly did themselves to organizations they feel could do a better job.

For example, Magna Steyr built the Jeep Commander and the Chrysler Voyager and Grand Voyager at its plant in Graz, Austria. Mecca relied on a private contractor to collect garbage and keep the city clean. Boeing announced that it would contract out the wing for its new 787 jet to Japan's Mitsubishi Heavy Industries.

2. Management accounting innovations have usually been developed by managers and not professional accountants to address their unique decision-making needs. Management accounting must be pragmatic and must add value to the organization.

DIVERSITY OF MANAGEMENT ACCOUNTING INFORMATION

We will illustrate the different types of management accounting information needed to support organization decision making using Cabinets by Design (CBD).

Financial Information

Financial information pervades our economy. It is the primary means for profit-seeking organizations to communicate with their stakeholders. In order to align internal focus with external requirements, organizations use financial measures internally as a broad indicator of performance. Financial information is also important in not-for-profit and government organizations. In both, financial information provides a means to evaluating organization efficiency, such as the cost to provide a unit of service. Spending authority in governments is conveyed through budgets, and government managers must ensure that spending authorizations are not breached.

For CBD, Diane relies on financial information, such as shown in Exhibit 1-5. Note that sales are increasing through time while profits flattened in the past 2 years. This financial information provides a signal that something is wrong, but not *what* is wrong. As shown in Exhibit 1-6, financial information summarizes the financial effect of underlying activities, but to explain financial results, managers must dig deeper and inevitably focus on the nonfinancial or operating data that explain the performance of the activities that are driving the financial results.

As a first step, Diane asks her accountant to prepare a financial analysis and receives the information shown in Exhibit 1-7.

This new information provides some insight into what is happening to profits. First, CBD's market share has been declining since year 7. Perhaps more important,

Exhibit 1-5
Cabinets by Design

Exhibit 1-6
Underlying
Activities Drive
Financial Results

> Remember, managers cannot manage financial results; they can only manage the activities that create those results. Management observes information about the underlying activities to understand the production function (or processes) that translates those activities into financial results so they can explain, manage, and improve financial results by changing the way the underlying activities are undertaken.

Financial Results
- Costs
- Revenues
- Profits
- Sales

Activities Causing Financial Results
- Developing products
- Making products
- Marketing products
- Selling products
- Delivering products
- Serving customers

return on sales—the ratio of profit to sales, which is a measure of operating efficiency—has been falling since year 7. The expanding market for kitchen cabinets has masked two problems at CBD: a falling market share and a falling return on sales. Again, these are broad indicators of performance; they suggest, but do not identify, the underlying problems. Diane will have to dig deeper to discover what is causing the flattening of profits.

Business-Level Strategy and the Value Proposition

In order to identify why performance is declining, Diane must start by examining her business strategy. Key activities of any organization's business-level strategy are identifying its target customers and delivering what those target customers want. What the organization tries to deliver to customers is called its **value proposition**. Value propositions have four elements:

1. Price: the relative price the customer pays, given the product's features and competitors' product features.

Exhibit 1-7
Cabinets by
Design

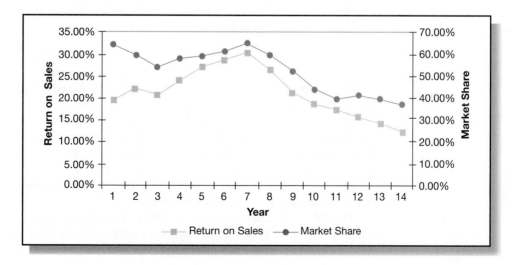

2. Quality: the degree of conformance between what the customer is promised and what the customer receives. For example, high quality is a defect-free automobile that performs as promised by the salesperson.
3. Functionality and features: the performance of the product, such as a meal in a restaurant that provides the diner with the level of satisfaction expected for the price paid.
4. Service: all the other elements of the product relevant to the customer. For example, for an automobile, service might include how the customer is treated as the automobile is purchased and the degree and form of after-sales service.

McDonald's provides an example of a value proposition that includes all four elements. Ray Kroc, who developed McDonald's restaurants into what we recognize as the company today, described the McDonald's value proposition as QSCV—quality, service, cleanliness, and value. Dell Computer's value proposition is building computers to customer requirements quickly and at a low price.

Nonfinancial Information and the Value Proposition at CBD

The value proposition at CBD is flexibility (producing what the customer wants), quality, and service (which means delivery when and where required). CBD's prices are high relative to competitors, but CBD believes that its higher levels of flexibility, quality, and service make the higher price competitive. This perspective on customer requirements provides strategic information. On investigation, Diane discovers the following:

- Contrary to CBD's beliefs, customers are very price sensitive because cabinets are a significant cost in home building or renovation.
- Customers have complained about CBD's product quality. Some cabinet styles have problems relating to condensation and rot.
- Customers have complained that a competitor's design software is easier to use and provides a broader range of style alternatives.
- Although customers value the service promise, CBD has not lived up to its delivery guarantee. The fine print in CBD's service guarantee includes the words "under normal circumstances, if the delivery is late, the product is free." Customers complain that the organization has used this qualification to excuse late deliveries, which occur for about 15% of the orders. Word is circulating that the delivery promise is unreliable and that resulting construction delays have been adding costs to builders and home owners.

This perspective on customer requirements explains why CBD's market share is falling. Competitors are outperforming CBD in meeting customer requirements relating to price, quality, functionality, and service. Because CBD is not tracking how often it meets delivery dates, customer complaints about quality, its prices relative to competitors' prices, or customer satisfaction with its design software, its managers are unaware of these failures and their potential effect on sales. If CBD had been tracking nonfinancial information about quality, the number of times delivery promises were not met, and customer satisfaction with its software, managers would have had advance warning of problems and might have been able to take steps to avoid the company's loss of market share.

The role of an effective management accounting system is to capture, track, and report these value proposition measures, which are the leading indicators of financial performance.

Delivering the Value Proposition

To deliver the value proposition, organizations use processes that they design and manage. McDonald's delivers its value proposition by developing operating procedures that specify precisely how the food is to be prepared, the equipment used to prepare the food, the layout for equipment in the restaurant, the form of the raw materials provided by suppliers, standards for property maintenance and service, and the audit procedures that ensure that franchisees are conforming to these standards.

Dell delivers its value proposition by providing customers easy access to ordering and insisting that suppliers locate close to its assembly facilities. These steps enable Dell to minimize its inventories and minimize the costs of holding inventory and obsolete inventory in a rapidly changing industry.

As Diane investigates the reasons for delivery failures, high prices, quality problems, and noncompetitive software, she will examine process failures that have caused these problems. This process perspective provides insight into why CBD has failed to deliver on its value proposition. Diane needs information about process performance to identify and correct these problems.

On investigation, Diane traces the quality complaints to two causes. First, designs cause condensation to pool on cabinet tops, promoting wet conditions that lead to rot. Second, CBD uses finishes that do not protect the cabinets adequately from water. The solution is simple: provide thin plastic finishes for the problem areas and use a waterproof finish elsewhere. The solution would have been noticed earlier had CBD tracked customer concerns and traced those concerns back to the manufacturing process. Diane makes a note to the controller to develop a system to track quality data and trace those issues back to process problems.

The production scheduler reports to Diane that the delivery failures relate to a small group of cabinet designs that invariably create assembly problems. After convening a meeting between design and production personnel, Diane discovers two possible solutions for these assembly problems: (1) restrict the range of designs so that these cabinets cannot be ordered or (2) develop a template that manufacturing personnel can use during assembly. Diane instructs the group to meet with marketing and to report back to her within 30 days with their choice between these two alternatives.

Diane directs the controller to develop systems to accumulate costs by product type and order and to record the elapsed time of every order through the manufacturing process. This cost and time information will allow production managers to compare actual and planned costs and identify areas and opportunities for process improvement.

Diane's interest in costs reflects her concern about declining margins and reports that some CBD prices, which are determined by marking up costs by 25%, are noncompetitive. The marketing manager argues that there are no market prices that CBD must meet because all production is custom. However, potential customers do compare the ratio of value to price for different products. For example, a consumer might consider whether the added costs of a window's features, including design and functionality, are worth the incremental price over a window without those features. The controller reports that prices are based on what costs are expected to be and do not reflect the actual costs CBD incurs to make the products. Past manufacturing reports suggest that actual costs are higher than planned costs, but no one has studied these cost differences other than to develop a broadly held suspicion in the organization that material costs and rework costs are higher than they should be. Diane instructs the controller to begin a project to compute the costs of two selected products whose prices are higher than competitors' prices. She requests a report showing actual versus planned costs and recommendations for improving efficiency to cut costs.

Many organizations use cause-and-effect diagrams (also called Ishikawa or fishbone diagrams) to identify the causes of process failures. Exhibit 1-8 identifies materials, operator, equipment, process, and management problems that are thought to contribute to poor-quality products in one organization. With this information in hand, the management accountant can develop information systems to track performance on the causes of poor product quality so that they can be monitored and corrected.

**Exhibit 1-8
Cause-and-Effect
Diagram**

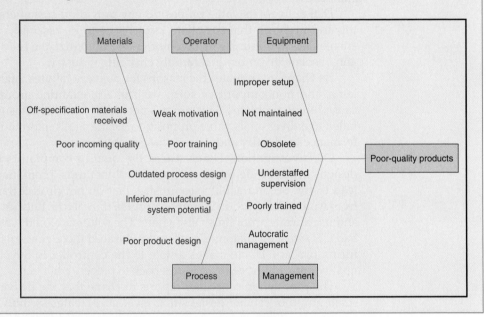

This process perspective illustrates the various types of financial and nonfinancial information that CBD might develop to monitor processes to identify potential problems in delivering the value proposition and to take action before sales are lost. Note also that cost information not only meets the operational purpose of identifying opportunities for process improvement, but also provides information for planning, such as forecasting costs and setting prices.

In summary, CBD needs to develop customer information and process information so that it can monitor how well it is delivering its value proposition (the customer perspective) and the potential for failures (the process perspective). When process improvements are required, CBD will have to rely on the skills, insights, and motivation of its employees to make the changes. This perspective on learning suggests that CBD should monitor its ability, both potential and realized, to develop the motivation and skills employees need to make these changes. CBD can monitor the level of employee skills and the rate of innovation to provide insights into its ability to continuously monitor and improve processes once the diagnostic data discussed here are in place.

MANAGEMENT ACCOUNTING AND CONTROL IN SERVICE ORGANIZATIONS

The major changes in the demand for management accounting and control information experienced by manufacturing companies in recent years also have occurred in virtually all types of service organizations. Service companies have existed for hundreds of years; their importance in modern economies has increased substantially during the twentieth century. See Exhibit 1-9 for examples of service industries and companies.

Service Companies' Demand for Management Accounting Information

Service companies differ from manufacturing companies in several ways. The obvious differences are that service companies do not produce a tangible product or hold inventories. A less obvious difference is that many employees in service companies have direct contact with customers. Thus, service companies must be especially sensitive to the timeliness and quality of the service that their employees provide to customers. Customers of service companies immediately notice defects and delays in service delivery. The consequences of such defects can be severe, as dissatisfied customers usually choose alternative suppliers after an unhappy experience.

Managers in service companies, however, have historically used management accounting information far less intensively than have managers in manufacturing companies. Such a lack of accurate information about the cost of operations probably occurred because many service organizations operated in benign, noncompetitive markets, either highly regulated or government owned (such as national railroads, airlines, postal services, and telecommunications companies). Others, such as local retailers, were subject only to local, not national or global, competition. In these noncompetitive environments, managers of service companies were not under great pressure to lower costs, improve the quality and efficiency of operations, introduce new products that made profits, or eliminate products and services that were incurring losses. Because managers were not making such decisions, they made little or no demand for information to help them make such decisions. Consequently, the management accounting systems in most service organizations were simple. They allowed managers to budget expenses by operating department and to measure and monitor actual spending against these functional departmental budgets.

Exhibit 1-9
Examples of Service Industries and Companies

Service Industries	Service Companies
Financial institutions	Commercial banks, investment banks, mortgage companies, insurance companies, brokerage organizations
Transportation	Railroads, airlines, truckers, bus companies, package delivery, overnight delivery, postal service
Telecommunications	Local phone service, long-distance voice and data communications, wireless services
Merchandising	Supermarkets, department stores, discount stores, wholesalers, warehouse club stores
Professional services	Consulting, public accounting, engineering and software firms
Health care	Physician groups, hospitals, outpatient clinics
Retailing	Grocery chains, department stores, gasoline stations, mass-merchandise discount stores

The competitive environment for both manufacturing and service companies is now far more challenging and demanding than it was even 10 years ago. Today's companies demand better management accounting information.

Manufacturing and Service Companies

Starting in the mid-1970s, manufacturing companies in North America and Europe encountered severe competition from Asian companies that offered higher quality products at lower prices. Together, global networks for raising and disbursing capital, for acquiring and transporting raw materials, and for distributing finished goods made it possible for the best manufacturers anywhere to access local domestic markets throughout the world. No longer was it enough for a company to have cost and quality parity with its domestic competitors. A company could survive and prosper only if its costs, quality, and product capabilities were as good as those of the best companies in the world. Similarly, the deregulation movement in North America and Europe since the 1970s and the switch from centrally controlled socialist economies to free market economies in much of the rest of the world have completely changed the ground rules under which many service companies operate. As in manufacturing companies, managers of service companies now require accurate, timely information to improve the quality, timeliness, and efficiency of the activities they perform, and to make decisions about their individual products, services, and customers.

Government and Nonprofit Organizations

Government and nonprofit organizations, as well as profit-seeking enterprises, are feeling the pressures to improve performance. Citizens are demanding more responsive and more efficient performance from their local, regional, and national governments. In 1990, the U.S. Congress passed the **Chief Financial Officers (CFO) Act**, which requires each major federal agency to have a chief financial officer who is responsible for "the development and reporting of cost information" and "the systematic measurement of performance." The **Government Performance and Results Act (GPRA)** of 1993 requires that each U.S. federal agency

- establish top-level agency goals, objectives, and annual program goals,
- define how it intends to achieve those goals, and
- demonstrate how it will measure agency and program performance in achieving those goals.

In signing the GPRA, President Clinton announced that the act would

- chart a course for every endeavor paid for by taxpayers' money,
- see how well we are progressing,
- tell the public how we are doing,
- stop the things that don't work, and
- never stop improving the things that are worth investing in.

In 1993, Vice President Gore, as part of his National Performance Review to "reinvent government," recommended an action to require the Federal Accounting Standards Advisory Board (FASAB) to issue a set of cost accounting standards for all federal activities. To implement these directives, managers of government agencies will need greatly improved management accounting information. In response to the CFO and GPRA acts, the FASAB issued a document that stated, "In managing federal government programs, cost information is essential in the following five areas:

1. budgeting and cost control,
2. performance measurement,
3. determining reimbursements and setting fees and prices,
4. program evaluations, and
5. making economic choice decisions."

Thus, the demands for cost information in government will be similar to those in for-profit manufacturing and service companies.

Nonprofit organizations are also feeling the pressure for cost and performance measurement. There has been explosive growth in nongovernmental organizations dealing with economic development, the environment, poverty, illiteracy, hunger and malnutrition, and public and private health, plus nonprofit organizations focused on social services and the arts. These organizations compete for funds from governments, foundations, and private individuals. Increasingly, public and private donors are demanding accountability from the organizations they fund, including measures of effectiveness. They are asking whether organizations are achieving their intended purpose and measures of efficiency and whether they are using their resources productively. Managers of nonprofit organizations, of all types, are looking to adapt management accounting procedures, developed in the private sector, to the demands they face for accountability and cost and performance measurement.

Financial and Nonfinancial Information in Government and Not-for-Profit Organizations

Government and not-for-profit organizations can use the process Diane followed at CBD to improve performance. While the primary objective at CBD is profitability, the primary objective for government and not-for-profit organizations is to provide services to citizens or clients (for example, the food provided to the needy by a shelter)—their customers. Thus, the customers' objectives should be the government or not-for-profit organization's objectives. In innovative government and not-for-profit organizations, managers use nonfinancial and financial performance measures to evaluate how well and how efficiently these organizations used their funds to provide services to their customers. Like Diane at CBD, governments and not-for-profits must look at the processes they use to deliver services to their customers to ensure that these processes meet customer requirements at the lowest possible cost. They must ask, for example, what is the best way to approach training for an individual who is chronically unemployed so that the person's needs are met at the lowest cost to society?

BEHAVIORAL IMPLICATIONS OF MANAGEMENT ACCOUNTING INFORMATION

While the role of management accounting information is essential for supporting decisions and solving problems, information is never neutral. The mere act of measuring and informing affects the individuals involved. A famous study conducted in the 1920s at the Hawthorne Plant of the Western Electric Company showed that individuals and groups will alter their behavior when they know they are being studied and their performance is being measured. People react when they are being measured, and they react to the measurements. They focus on the variables and behavior being measured and pay less attention to those not being measured. Some people have recognized this phenomenon by declaring, "What gets measured gets done," or "If I can't measure it, I can't manage it."

Moreover, as managers try to introduce or redesign cost and performance measurement systems, people familiar with the previous systems resist. These people have acquired expertise in the use (and occasional misuse) of the old system and are concerned about whether their experience and expertise will be transferable to the new system. People also may feel committed to the decisions and actions taken on the basis of information an old system has produced. These actions may no longer seem valid based on the information produced by a newly installed management accounting system. Thus, a new management system can lead to embarrassment and threat, a trigger for reactions against change.

Management accountants must understand and anticipate the reactions of individuals to information and measurements. The design and introduction of new measurements and systems must be accompanied by an analysis of the behavioral and organizational reactions to the measurements. Even more important, when the measurements are used not only for information, planning, and decision making but also for control, evaluation, and reward, employees and managers place great emphasis on the measurements themselves. Managers and employees may take unexpected and undesirable actions to influence their score on the performance measure. For example, managers seeking to improve current bonuses based on reported profits may skip discretionary expenditures such as preventive maintenance, research and development, and advertising that may improve performance in future periods.

ETHICS AND THE MANAGEMENT ACCOUNTANT

Ethics is the moral system or set of values that individuals use to regulate their behavior. Despite attempts over many years to develop a universal system of values, none has evolved. Therefore, individuals are guided by different ethical systems. Why is this important? It is important because organizations can be profoundly affected by legal or social sanctions resulting from unethical behavior of their employees. For example, in 2005, the U.S. member firm of KPMG, one of the world's largest public accounting firms, paid almost $500 million in fines and accepted legal sanctions because a handful of its employees had engaged in developing dubious tax shelters for KPMG clients. In 1990, when traces of benzene were found in Perrier bottled water, the company claimed that the contamination resulted from an isolated, nonsystematic incident. Later Perrier issued a 160 million bottle recall of its product and admitted that the benzene was a naturally occurring component of the water at the source that had to be filtered out before the water was bottled. Perrier now claimed that the cause of the product failure was a failure of workers to properly maintain the filters needed to remove the benzene from the source water. The company was heavily criticized for its initial lack of honesty in dealing with the problem and lost 50% of its market share to its competitors.

In short, ethical lapses can have profound implications for organizations and their employees. Therefore, many organizations are developing and instituting ethics control systems to promote ethical behavior by their employees.

For a management accountant working inside an organization, the following ethical systems are particularly relevant: the laws of society, societal standards that are not laws but that reflect expected behavior, corporate values, professional codes of ethics, and personal systems of values.

1. The laws of society define certain decisions as illegal. For example, government safety regulations might rule out certain approaches to undertaking a repair on a piece of machinery that would put an employee in harm's way.

2. Social standards, which often become laws through time, rule out certain types of behavior as unacceptable even though they are not illegal. For example, many people may feel that subcontracting work to an organization in a foreign country that has labor or environmental laws that permit behavior unacceptable in the home country is morally unacceptable.

3. Corporate values come in two forms—boundary systems and belief systems. **Boundary systems** are prescriptive and define behavior that is unacceptable and has direct consequences. For example, public accounting firms protect the privacy of their clients by advising staff that discussing a client's business with an outsider is grounds for immediate dismissal. **Belief systems** are descriptive and identify broad goals for organization behavior, such as honesty, fairness, and equal treatment. We need to be very careful to distinguish between the organization's stated codes of ethics and its practiced codes of ethics. Regrettably, in some organizations the stated code of ethics is simply boilerplate that is used to promote a favorable image and does not reflect the practiced code of ethics. The conflict between the stated and the practiced code of corporate ethics is evidenced by what those who study organizational behavior call the organization's culture.

4. Accounting bodies, like most professional organizations, have codes of conduct. While codes of conduct vary across countries and even across different accounting professions within the same country, there are code-of-conduct items that are common to almost all organizations. They are protecting the client's right to privacy and that the accountants will prepare reports that reflect their informed and unbiased beliefs.

5. Finally, all individuals accumulate personal ethics systems through their family, culture, and religion.

Think of these ethics systems as a set of concentric rings wherein each successive ring allows a smaller set of acceptable decisions. For example, the law may not prohibit something, such as moving production to a Third World country to avoid workplace laws, that would be construed as socially undesirable. Something that is socially acceptable, such as a certain amount of puffery in advertising, may not be viewed as acceptable from the perspective of an organization's code of ethics.

For a management accountant, an ethical conflict arises when behavior that is prohibited by an ethical system higher in the previous list of five systems is acceptable in one that is lower. For example, a management accountant may be asked by a superior to prepare a report that the accountant believes is biased and misleading. In this case, behavior that is permitted in the company's practiced code of ethics is prohibited by the accountant's professional code of ethics. Examples include overstating the potential of a division that is being sold off to enhance its perceived value, overstating the performance of a division so that the division manager can earn a bonus, and manipulating accounting reporting practice to provide an income number that meets a stated management requirement. These types of pressures create a conflict between value system 3 in the previous list and value system 4. In effect, the organization's practiced value

Published versus Practice Codes of Ethics

In a biting article, Michael Miller ("Enron's Ethics Code Reads Like Fiction," *Columbus Business First*, March 29, 2002) identified contradictions between each of the principles supporting Enron's stated code of ethics (respect, integrity, communication, and excellence) and Enron's practiced code of ethics. Events since the collapse of Enron confirm that there were systematic violations of Enron's stated code of ethics and that some of the violations involved criminal behavior. Enron's subsequent decline supports two of the major claims of people who advocate monitoring compliance with the organization's stated code of ethics. First, compliance promotes an unequivocal congruence between the organization's claimed and actual ethical behavior. Second, by providing employees with unambiguous ethical guidelines, monitoring compliance reduces the potential for organization damage resulting from unethical behavior.

system permits asking management accountants to misrepresent their professional judgment. Regrettably, management accountants as part of the finance team in organizations are often the last line of defense in promoting honest behavior and for this reason have stressful relationships in their respective organizations as they come under intense pressure to conform with what their superiors want.

Examples of organizations that do not have clear, enforceable boundary systems often appear on the front pages of newspapers and on television. Violations of ethical norms, society's rules, and the company's own policies may jeopardize an organization's existence. For example, Kidder Peabody, Baring's Bank, and Sumitomo Metals suffered severe penalties and losses when managers and traders took huge unauthorized risks to generate near-term earnings. Managers in other companies may collude with competitors to set prices or allocate market share in clear violation of antitrust laws. When discovered, the company, its employees, and its shareholders suffer losses, such as fines and an impaired corporate image.

Management accountants, when faced with pressure to manipulate or bias reported numbers, will be guided by their own and the organization's norms and values. The organization's values should be communicated through belief systems that inspire individuals about working toward a mission somewhat higher than improving short-term performance. The organization hopes that belief systems will support and reinforce the individual's own inner values to act appropriately. However, belief systems by themselves are insufficient. The management accountant must be aware of the organization's code of conduct, society's laws, and the standards set by his or her professional organization to provide guidance about the behavior and actions that are unacceptable under any circumstances and to develop systems that monitor, promote, and enforce individual behavior that is consistent with the organization's stated code of ethics.

The governance movement, which has gained momentum after the series of corporate frauds and failures reported in the financial press in the late 1990s and early 2000s, represents a reaction to these ethical conflicts that arise so often in organizations.

Corporate governance is concerned with how to promote the achievement of the organization's stated objectives. A key element that is emerging in the modern view of corporate governance is the need for senior management to provide systems of internal control that promote and monitor compliance with the organization's stated code of ethics. Management accountants will increasingly become intimately involved in designing these systems of internal control.

SUMMARY

Management accounting has become an exciting discipline that is undergoing major changes to reflect the challenging new environment that organizations worldwide now face. Accurate, timely, and relevant information about the economics and performance of organizations is crucial to organizational success. This chapter introduced the need for organizations to develop and use appropriate financial and nonfinancial information as they perform their tasks. Such information will do the following:

1. Focus on aggregate—usually financial—measures of performance in for-profit organizations that provide an overall summary of performance and foster the organization's ability to meet its financial objectives. In government and not-for-profit organizations, the focus is on the organization's performance in meeting the needs of its citizens or clients.
2. Focus on the organization's success in meeting its customers' requirements in for-profit organizations so that the organization can react promptly to failures in delivering its value proposition. In public sector and not-for-profit organizations, the focus is on the cost to deliver services to customers to monitor and improve process efficiency.
3. Enable all organizations to identify process improvements needed to improve the organization's ability to deliver its value proposition.

4. Enable all organizations to identify the potential of the organization's members to manage and improve process performance.
5. Enable the for-profit organization to assess the profitability and desirability of continued investment in various entities, such as products, product lines, departments, and organization units.
6. Enable the organization to monitor and detect inappropriate organization behavior.

This book introduces the opportunities for enhancing organizational performance through effective design and use of management accounting systems.

Epilogue

By following up on the price, quality, service, and functionality of CBD's products, Diane will understand how each of these factors drives (affects) market share and margins. By focusing only on financial information, Diane was able to recognize that there were problems but could not identify what they were. By understanding and monitoring the determinants, or drivers, of sales and profits, Diane is now in a position to manage more effectively. She or her staff can take corrective actions before process failures affect sales and profits. By looking at the causes of financial performance, Diane is well on the way to improving CBD's fortunes.

KEY TERMS

Belief systems, 17
Boundary systems, 17
Chief Financial Officers (CFO) Act, 14
Controlling, 4

Financial accounting, 3
Government Performance and Results Act (GPRA), 14
Management accounting systems, 3

Nonfinancial information, 4
Organizing, 3
Planning, 3
Value proposition, 9

ASSIGNMENT MATERIALS

Questions

1-1   What are the three broad classes of organization decision making, and what information requirements are commonly associated with each class? (LO 1)

1-2   Why do a company's operators/workers, managers, and executives have different informational needs than shareholders and external suppliers of capital? (LO 1)

1-3   Why may financial information alone be insufficient for the ongoing informational needs of operators/workers, managers, and executives? (LO 1, 2)

1-4 Why might senior executives need measures besides financial ones to assess how well their business performed in the most recent period? (LO 1, 2)

1-5 How does the role for management accounting systems change as the environment becomes more competitive? (LO 1, 2)

1-6 What are the four generic elements of an organization's value proposition? Define or explain each element. (LO 2)

1-7 What is the relationship between an organization's value proposition and its management accounting system? (LO 2)

1-8 What, if any, are the differences between the management accounting information needed in manufacturing organizations and that needed in service organizations? (LO 2)

1-9 Why is management accounting information important in government and nonprofit organizations? (LO 2)

1-10 How can management accounting information produce behavioral and organizational reactions? (LO 5)

1-11 How can belief systems and boundary systems foster high ethical standards among employees? (LO 5)

1-12 Describe corporate governance and explain how it overlaps with management accounting. (LO 5)

Exercises

LO 1, 2, 3, 4, 5 **1-13** *The role of management accounting* Consider the descriptions of management accounting provided in Exhibit 1-3 and in the remainder of the chapter. Discuss why the associated responsibilities are viewed as "accounting" and how people handling those responsibilities interface with other functional areas in fulfilling the stated responsibilities. What skills and knowledge does one need to fulfill the responsibilities?

LO 1, 2, 3 **1-14** *Different information needs* Consider the operation of a fast-food company with hundreds of retail outlets scattered about the country. Consider the descriptions of management accounting provided in Exhibit 1-3 and in the remainder of the chapter to identify management accounting information needs for the following:
a. The manager of a local fast-food outlet that prepares food and serves it to customers who walk in or pick it up at a drive-through window
b. The regional manager who supervises the operations of all the retail outlets in a three-state region
c. Senior management located at the company's corporate headquarters. Consider specifically the information needs of the president as well as the vice presidents of operations and marketing.
Be sure to address the content, frequency, and level of aggregation of information needed by these different managers.

LO 1, 2, 3 **1-15** *Different information needs* Consider the descriptions of management accounting provided in Exhibit 1-3 and in the remainder of the chapter to identify management accounting information needs for the following:
a. The managers of (1) a patient unit, where patients stay while being treated for illness or while recuperating from an operation, and (2) the radiology department, where patients obtain X-rays and receive radiological treatment
b. The manager of the nursing service who hires and assigns nurses to all patient units and to specialty services, such as the operating room, emergency room, recovery room, and radiology room
c. The chief executive officer of the hospital
Be sure to address the content, frequency, and level of aggregation of information needed by these different managers.

LO 2 **1-16** *The elements of quality* For each of the following products, suggest three measures of quality:
a. television set
b. university course

c. meal in an exclusive restaurant
d. carryout meal from a restaurant
e. container of milk
f. visit to the doctor
g. trip on an airplane
h. pair of jeans
i. novel
j. university textbook

LO 2   **1-17** *Product functionality and service*   For each of the following products, suggest one important element of functionality and features and one element of service:
a. television set
b. university course
c. meal in an exclusive restaurant
d. carryout meal from a restaurant
e. container of milk
f. visit to the doctor
g. trip on an airplane
h. pair of jeans
i. novel
j. university textbook

Problems

LO 1   **1-18** *Differences between financial and managerial accounting*   Many German companies have their management accounting department as part of the manufacturing operations group rather than as part of the corporate finance department. These German companies operate two separate accounting departments. One performs financial accounting functions for shareholders and tax authorities, and the other maintains and operates the costing system for manufacturing operations.

Required

What are the advantages and disadvantages of having separate departments for financial accounting and management accounting?

LO 1   **1-19** *Differences between financial and managerial accounting*   The controller of a German machine tool company believed that historical cost depreciation was inadequate for assigning the cost of using expensive machinery to individual parts and products. Each year, he estimated the replacement cost of each machine and included depreciation based on the machine's replacement cost in the machine-hour rate used to assign machine expenses to the parts produced on that machine. Additionally, the controller included an interest charge, based on 50% of the machine's replacement value, into the machine-hour rate. The interest rate was an average of the 3- to 5-year interest rate on government and high-grade corporate securities.

As a consequence of these two decisions (charging replacement cost rather than historical cost and imputing a capital charge for the use of capital equipment), the product cost figures used internally by company managers were inconsistent with the numbers that were needed for inventory valuation for financial and tax reporting. The accounting staff had to perform a tedious reconciliation process at the end of each year to back out the interest and replacement value costs from the cost of goods sold and inventory values before they could prepare the financial statements.

Required

    a. Why would the controller introduce additional complications into the company's costing system by assigning replacement value depreciation costs and imputed interest costs to the company's parts and products?

    b. Why should management accountants create extra work for the organization by deliberately adopting policies for internal costing that violate the generally accepted accounting principles that must be used for external reporting?

LO 1, 2, 4   **1-20**   *Role of financial information for continuous improvement*   Consider an organization that has empowered its employees, asking them to improve the quality, productivity, and responsiveness of their processes that involve repetitive work. This work could arise in a manufacturing setting, such as assembling cars or producing chemicals, or in a service setting, such as processing invoices or responding to customer orders and requests. Clearly the workers would benefit from feedback on the quality (defects, yields) and process times of the work they were doing to suggest where they could make improvements. Identify the role, if any, for sharing financial information with these employees to help them in their efforts to improve quality, productivity, and process times. Be specific about the types of financial information that would be helpful and the specific decisions or actions that could be made better by supplementing physical and operational information with financial information.

LO 5   **1-21**   *Ethical issues*   You are employed as a senior manager in an insurance organization. One of your responsibilities is to randomly review claims for reimbursement that have been submitted by people who have traveled on the organization's behalf.

    By chance, you have pulled a falsified claim that was submitted by Andrew, one of your closest friends. You decide to confront your friend with your findings. Andrew, knowing you are a friend, replies; "Sure the claim contains false items. Everybody does it, and it is almost expected!"

    Stunned by his confession, you tell him that he has to resubmit an accurate reimbursement claim. Andrew responds; "Look, I don't feel that I get paid enough in this lousy organization, and this is my way of getting a few extra dollars each month. You know how they have been working all of us to death after the layoffs. I'm entitled to this, and I refuse to resubmit the claim."

Required

    a. What do you think of Andrew's argument?

    b. Should you have approached him differently?

    c. What should you do now and why?

    d. How might the company's control system be designed to foster high ethical standards regarding reimbursement claims and other issues?

LO 5   **1-22**   *Ethical issues*   Chris and Pat are discussing labeling for product 121, one of their company's products that will be exported overseas to country C.

    Chris: In the United States, product 121 must be labeled as possibly hazardous to humans. I think the warning is unnecessary, though, because the amounts shown to present a hazard are much higher than people will encounter with normal use of product 121. Given this evidence, country C's laws do not require us to label the product as possibly hazardous to humans.

> Pat: I had a work assignment in country C for 2 years, and I know that its residents would avoid a product with product 121's U.S. labeling. I think we should leave out the cautionary statement. After all, we'll be in compliance with country C's laws.

Required

Taking into account the various parties potentially affected in this situation, discuss reasons for and against putting a cautionary statement on the labels of product 121 that are shipped to country C. What do you recommend?

Cases

LO 1, 2, 3 **1-23 *Different information needs*** Julie Martinez, manager of the new retail outlet of Super Printing, is pondering the management challenges in her new position. Super Printing is a long-established printing company in a major metropolitan area. The new Super outlet, located at the edge of the parking lot for Western Business School, represents Super's attempt to break into the rapidly growing business for retail digital imaging.

The Super retail store provides a range of copying and digital imaging services for the business school's students, faculty, and administrators, plus other retail customers. Super's primary products are black-and-white copies of documents. Variation exists even in this basic product, however, as consumers can choose from a variety of paper colors, sizes, and quality. Super recently purchased a machine that prints color copies from digital input. Color copies also can be produced in a variety of sizes, paper quality, and paper types, including transparencies for overhead projection and photographic-quality reproductions. Other printing products include business cards, laminated luggage tags, and name badges for conferences, executive programs, and students.

In addition to physical printing, the Super center provides fax services by which individuals can both receive and transmit documents. When incoming faxes are received, a store employee calls the recipient, who stops at the outlet to pick up the document. The center also has several personal computers, both Windows-based and Macintosh, that students rent by the hour for basic computer processing, Internet access, e-mail, and preparing presentations and résumés. Each computer is connected to Super's black-and-white and color printers, enabling students to produce paper copies of their presentations and résumés.

Super has other machines that assemble printed pages into bound documents. Two different binding types are available. The store also sells a limited selection of office supplies, including paper, envelopes, paper clips, glue, binders, tabs, pens, pencils, and marking pens.

Currently, about five employees (including Julie) work at the retail outlet during prime hours (8:00 A.M. to 5:00 P.M.) with two to four people working the evening shift (5:00 P.M. to midnight) when walk-in business is much slower. The number of people working during the evening hours is determined by the anticipated backlog of reproduction work that will be performed during these hours.

Prices for the various products and services have been set on the basis of those of competitors, such as FedEx Kinko's and Staples. Julie receives a daily report on total sales, broken down by cash sales, credit card sales, and credit sales to various programs at the business school; however, she currently does not have a report on expenses such as labor, materials, and equipment for each line of business (black-and-white and color printing, computer services, document preparation, fax services, and sales of office supplies). Thus, Julie is unsure whether each line of business is profitable. Julie is also unsure how efficiently the business is run.

Further, the different business lines require different quantities and types of capital: equipment such as copying and printing machines, computers, and facsimile machines; physical capital such as office space; and the different inventories of paper types, colors, grades and sizes, and office supplies.

If the pilot store that Julie is operating is successful, then the parent company will likely try to open many similar outlets near schools and universities throughout the metropolitan area. For this purpose, the parent company wants to know which business lines are the most profitable, including the cost of capital and space required, so that these lines can be featured at each retail outlet. If some business lines are not profitable, then Super probably will not offer those services at newly opened stores unless they are necessary to build retail traffic.

Required

Identify the management accounting information needs for the following:

a. An employee desiring to help serve customers more efficiently and effectively
b. Julie Martinez, the manager of the pilot retail outlet
c. The president of Super Printing

Be sure to address the content, frequency, and level of aggregation of information needed by these different individuals.

LO 1   **1-24 *Information for employee empowerment***   A U.S. automobile components plant had recently been reorganized so that quality and employee teamwork were to be the guiding principles for all managers and workers. One production worker described the difference:

In the old production environment, we were not paid to think. The foreman told us what to do, and we did it even if we knew he was wrong. Now, the team decides what to do. Our voices are heard. All middle management has been cut out, including foremen and superintendents. Management relies on us, the team members, to make decisions. Salary people help us make these decisions; the production and manufacturing engineers work for us. They are always saying, "We work for you. What do you need?" And they listen to us.

The plant controller commented as follows:

In traditional factories, the financial system viewed people as variable costs. If you had a production problem, you sent people home to reduce your variable costs. Here, we do not send people home. Our production people are viewed as problem solvers, not as variable costs.

Required

a. What information needs did the production workers have in the old environment?
b. What information do you recommend be supplied to the production workers in the new environment that emphasizes quality, defect reduction, problem solving, and teamwork?

LO 1, 4   **1-25 *Financial information for continuous improvement***   The manager of a large semiconductor production department expressed his disdain for the cost information he was presently given:

Cost variances are useless to me.[2] I don't want to ever have to look at a cost variance, monthly or weekly. Daily, I look at sales dollars, bookings, and on-time delivery (OTD)—the percent of orders on time. Weekly, I look at a variety of quality reports including the outgoing quality control report on items passing the final test before shipment to the customer, in-process quality, and yields. Yield is a good surrogate for cost and quality. Monthly, I do look at the financial reports. I look closely at my fixed expenses and compare these to the budgets, especially on discretionary items like travel and maintenance. I also watch headcount.

---

[2] We will study cost variances in later chapters. For purposes of working this problem, it is sufficient to recognize that a cost variance represents the difference between the cost actually assigned to a production department and the cost that was expected or budgeted for that department.

But the financial systems still don't tell me where I am wasting money. I expect that if I make operating improvements, costs should go down, but I don't worry about the linkage too much. The organizational dynamics make it difficult to link cause and effect precisely.

Required

Comment on this production manager's assessment of his limited use for financial and cost summaries of performance. For what purposes, if any, are cost and financial information helpful to operating people? How should the management accountant determine the appropriate blend between financial and nonfinancial information for operating people?

LO 1, 2, 3, 4 **1-26 *Comprehensive performance measurement in public and nonprofit organizations*** Organizations in the public and nonprofit sector, such as government agencies and charitable social service entities, have financial systems that budget expenses and monitor and control actual spending. Explain why these organizations should consider developing a comprehensive set of performance measurements (including nonfinancial measures) to monitor and report on their performance. Provide examples of financial and nonfinancial measures that should be included in such a comprehensive set of measurements.

LO 5 **1-27 *Ethical issues, revenue recognition*** Read the article "What's Wevenue?" by Elizabeth MacDonald in the *Wall Street Journal* (January 6, 2000, p. A1). The article states that managers faced aggressive revenue targets and reports testimony about "a dozen or more accounting tricks that various employees, at various levels of management, had deployed to keep the stock buoyant."

Required

a. What revenue recognition or other accounting-related improprieties does the article report?
b. How widely known were the improprieties within the company?
c. Describe the responsibilities and challenges management accountants and others within the organization face with respect to the accounting issues reported in the article and explain how organizational leadership or control systems can help foster high ethical standards and help prevent the problems described in the article.

LO 5 **1-28 *Ethical issues in current events*** Identify articles in the business press or materials from Web pages that describe a recent occurrence of accounting-related improprieties.

Required

a. Summarize the reported improprieties.
b. Describe the responsibilities and challenges management accountants and others within the organization face with respect to the reported accounting issues and explain how organizational leadership or control systems can help foster high ethical standards and help prevent the problems.

LO 5 **1-29 *Ethical belief systems*** Locate Johnson & Johnson's credo at www.jnj.com/our_company/our_credo/index.htm and explore the related links to address the following:

Required

a. To which groups of people does Johnson & Johnson state responsibilities?
b. How has the credo changed since its inception?
c. How does the company evaluate how well it is following its credo?
d. What was the Tylenol® crisis?
e. How did the credo affect the way the company handled the Tylenol® crisis?

Cost Management Concepts and Cost Behavior

After reading this chapter, you will be able to:

➤ explain why the appropriate way to calculate a cost depends on how the cost will be used

➤ understand and be able to exploit the difference between direct and indirect costs

➤ recognize different cost behavior patterns and use that knowledge to predict costs and profits with different sales levels

➤ understand why management accountants and financial accountants use different approaches to classifying costs

➤ show why the concept of opportunity cost is used in short-run decision making and how opportunity cost relates to conventional accounting costs

➤ explain the notions of long-run and short-run costs and how these different costs are used in decision making

➤ explain the modern approach of cost classifications based on activity levels

Lynn's Landscaping Services

Lynn knew that her landscaping business was in trouble. While sales continued to grow at Lynn's Landscaping Services, profits had been in an accelerating freefall for 3 years.

Lynn was perplexed about the decline in profits because she believed that her organization was doing everything right. She was hiring well-trained people and ensuring that their training continued after they joined the firm. For conventional landscaping services, Lynn charged the prevailing market price. For specialized services, she had the market virtually to

Source: Ilene MacDonald/Alamy Images.

herself and seemed to have all the business she could handle at the prices she charged—implying that she was not overcharging for her services.

Most conventional landscaping services were competitive because of the low entry costs. Although many organizations did not last long, Lynn's was one of the dozen or so in the community that was more than 5 years old.

Lynn was a trained horticulturist, and it showed in her work. While other organizations focused on routine landscaping services, including lawn mowing, tree pruning, and applying lawn chemicals, a major part of Lynn's business came from landscape design and planting.

As part of her management studies in college, Lynn had taken two accounting courses. She believed she could identify opportunities to improve profits by developing the product-line income statement that appears in Exhibit 2-1.[1]

Lawn mowing was mostly a contract business. Customers would sign up for the season and pay a quoted rate per cut. The work was straightforward. The lawn was mowed and the edges were trimmed. The landscape designing business consisted of developing a garden and lawn layout for the customer and then installing the approved plan. Other maintenance services included tree pruning and the application of weed control chemicals.

The variable costs associated with each line of business are the costs of the materials and wages of the people who work in that area. The fixed costs, which total $300,000 in this organization, relate to the office costs, such as the salaries of Lynn and her administrative staff, and the equipment costs. Lynn knows that equipment deteriorates with use, so

---

[1] Throughout this book, calculations are shown rounded to the nearest cent or dollar, depending on the situation, but ongoing calculations continue with spreadsheet-level accuracy. Therefore, on occasion an equation might show rounding errors if it is actually computed as stated.

she figures that equipment costs should be allocated in proportion to revenue, which is a measure of use.

The income statement in Exhibit 2-1 is a cause of both frustration and concern for Lynn. Based on an earlier period's income statement similar to this one, Lynn had decided to focus on the landscape design business because it appeared to be the most lucrative and also was subject to the least competition. However, as efforts and sales in the landscape design business continued to increase, profits continued to erode at a greater rate. Lynn wondered why this was happening.

Exhibit 2-1
Lynn's Landscaping Services

PRODUCT LINE INCOME STATEMENTS			
	LAWN MOWING	LAYOUT DESIGN	OTHER MAINTENANCE
Revenues	$230,000	$175,000	$250,000
Variable costs	125,000	56,000	145,000
Fixed costs	105,343	80,153	114,504
Profit	$–343	$38,847	$–9,504

WHAT DOES COST MEAN?

The most common definition of cost is the monetary value of goods and services expended to obtain current or future benefits. Thus, while costs reflect an outflow of resources, such as cash, or a future financial commitment to pay, such as an accounts payable, the outflow leads to benefits such as raw material or machinery that can be used to make a product that can be sold to generate a cash benefit. However, an old adage in management accounting advocates, "Different costs for different purposes." This suggests that there is no universal way to compute the cost of something. The way that a cost will be used defines the way it should be computed. Consequently, we must be very careful when we speak about the "cost" of something. We need to be very specific about what we are talking about and how it was computed.

For example, financial accountants use the historical cost of an asset to keep track of how the organization's funds have been spent—which is a central focus when reporting management's activities to the organization's owners. However, for decision-making purposes, the asset's replacement cost, or its net realizable value (selling price less selling costs), may be more relevant than its historical cost.

Management accountants define and compute costs that reflect identified decision-making needs. For example, after studying Exhibit 2-1, Lynn is thinking about abandoning the Other Maintenance business of Lynn's Landscaping Services because it is unprofitable. While the variable costs associated with this unit of her business would be avoided if the division were shut down, the fixed costs may not be since they reflect the allocation to this business of the costs of resources—such as machinery and personnel that are used in other parts of the business—resources that cannot be sold if the Other Maintenance business is closed down.

We will now look at some different systems for organizing costs. A useful way to consider the different cost organizing systems is whether the cost is needed for external (shareholders, creditors, government, employees) or internal (management) decision making. As we move through these different systems, remember the adage: different costs for different purposes.

HOW THE USE OF PRODUCT COST INFORMATION DEFINES ITS FOCUS AND FORM

As we will soon see, financial accountants and management accountants define and think about costs, particularly **product costs**, very differently. As the adage concerning different costs for different purposes implies, these different product cost definitions reflect the different objectives that financial accountants and management accountants have for cost information. Let's begin with the financial accounting perspective on product cost.

Using Product Cost Information Outside the Organization

Companies prepare financial statements for stakeholders such as employees, creditors, and government. The purpose is to provide outsiders who are interested in the company's operations with a consistent way to evaluate the performance of the company and its management. The key requirements for external users of accounting information are consistent (through time) and comparable (across organizations) reporting of the organization's current performance (the income statement), its stock of assets and liabilities (the balance sheet), and its financing operations (the funds statement).

Since no one knows how the investors, creditors, and other organization stakeholders use the cost numbers in financial statements, **generally accepted accounting principles (GAAP)** that specify the focus, content, and form of financial statements

Financial accountants define the cost of a building as net book value, which is the building's purchase price less any depreciation that has been recognized to date.

Source: EMG Education Management Group.

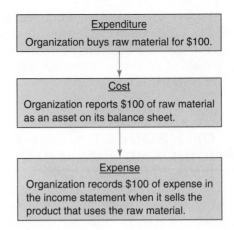

focus on methods for computing costs rather than how they might be best calculated to support a given decision. The intended result of GAAP is that costs be computed consistently through time and across different organizations rather than costs that are necessarily useful for a given decision-making purpose. In general, we can say that costs computed for outside users are historical costs that are computed in a standard way because they follow specific rules.

Expenditures, Costs, and Expenses

An expenditure is the exchange of an asset (such as cash) or a liability (such as a debt) for an asset such as a piece of production machinery. Expenses are the costs of assets that the financial accountant deems have been used up when goods or services are sold. So the cycle is that an expenditure creates an asset that becomes an expense when the asset is sold. Save for a few exceptions, GAAP cost has a very specific meaning—it is the estimated value of the resources that the organization has sacrificed to acquire the asset that is reported on its balance sheet. The focus on financial accounting is on asset valuation—that is, the cost that is reported on the balance sheet. A cost becomes an expense when the asset is sold or used.

Product Costs

In order to compare financial accounting thinking about product costs with management accounting thinking, we need to focus on the financial accounting notion of inventory—that is, goods that are held for sale.

For manufacturing firms, financial accountants include only manufacturing cost in the cost they report for product inventory, and therefore, as the expense they report for the goods sold. Manufacturing costs include three categories of costs: direct materials, direct labor, and manufacturing overhead. Direct materials include the cost of purchased raw materials. Direct labor reflects the wages of the people who work directly on making the product. Manufacturing overhead includes the costs of assets like machinery and other manufacturing facilities that the organization uses to convert purchased raw materials into finished goods. (For retail organizations, product costs include only the costs of items purchased for resale to customers.)

Therefore, in financial accounting, only manufacturing costs are reported when valuing inventory for manufacturing firms—all other product-related costs, such as research and development, design, marketing, and selling, are excluded and charged against income as expenses in the period they are incurred. Consequently, product cost in financial accounting includes only the manufacturing cost of the product. In addition, financial accountants are not directly concerned with the valuation of individual units of inventory—the focus is on the valuation of overall inventory. Therefore, if one type of inventory is overvalued and another is undervalued, that is not a concern to the financial accountant for balance sheet purposes as long as the inventory account in aggregate is valued reasonably. The focus is on valuing the overall stock of inventory assets in order to report on management's responsibility for asset management.

In summary, for a manufacturing firm, product costs reported on the balance sheet include only manufacturing costs and almost always reflect historical costs. This approach reflects the primary mandate of financial accounting, which is to report on management's fiduciary responsibility in managing the organization's assets. As we will now see, management accountants have a very different objective in—and consequently have a very different approach to—measuring product costs.

Using Product Cost Information Inside the Organization

Inside the organization, costs serve many different purposes. These purposes can be divided into two broad categories: planning and evaluation. Examples of planning purposes occur when cost serves as a reference point for determining the selling price of a prospective product—for example, when the pricing formula is cost plus 15% or when the unit cost is used in a budgeting model to forecast total costs under different levels of production and selling activities. Evaluation purposes occur when deciding whether the market price for an existing product makes the product profitable or when evaluating whether a process is efficient compared with the costs of similar internal or external processes. Some organizations base performance bonuses on cost information. For example, the Scanlon Plan, an incentive plan developed in the 1930s, bases workers' rewards on their ability to reduce labor costs below a labor cost standard established in a baseline period.

As we will see later in this book, in their decision making (often called planning) and control roles, management accountants focus on the costs of many different things. For this reason, management accountants have developed the notion of a cost object— something for which the management accountant computes a cost. Examples of cost objects include a product, a product line, or an organizational unit, such as the shipping department of an online retailer. While we will consider other types of cost objects in this book, our focus for the moment will be on product costs in order to compare and contrast the management accounting view with the financial accounting view.

There are two major differences between how financial accountants and management accountants view product costs:

1. In financial accounting, the focus is on determining the total cost of all inventory. In management accounting the focus is usually on the cost of an individual unit of inventory or product. Why?

   a. Because the financial accountant is concerned with the aggregate value of inventory, which helps evaluate how well management has used the organization's resources.

   b. Because the management accountant is often concerned with providing decision makers with information about product costs so that management can make decisions, such as introducing or abandoning a product; redesigning a product; improving a product or process, and, in the special case where the company can set the product price, providing cost information for product pricing.

2. In financial accounting, inventory cost (and therefore product cost) includes only manufacturing cost. In management accounting, product cost will include

all product-related costs, including research and development, marketing, advertising, and selling. Why?

a. Because a guiding principle in financial accounting is the doctrine of conservatism, which requires that financial accountants report assets whose ability to produce future benefits can be estimated in a systematic way. Expenditures like advertising, research and development, and product improvement are seen as too subjective and difficult to estimate, so they are not reported as product costs.

b. Because management accountants provide, for existing and prospective products, information that is needed to estimate the total costs of developing, introducing, making, and supporting a product that is brought to the market so that decision makers can evaluate product profitability.

For these reasons, cost definitions in management accounting are more complex and occasionally more subtle than those in financial accounting. Let's explore some of these cost definitions and why they are important in management accounting.

Understanding Cost Behavior to Predict Costs

Cost behavior analysis is one of the most important topics that you will study in this book. Understanding cost behavior allows the management accountant to develop estimates of product costs and to predict costs for various levels of production activity.

Fundamental to understanding cost behavior is the notion of **flexible resources** and **capacity-related resources**. Flexible resources are resources whose costs are proportional to the amount of the resource used. Examples of flexible resources in a furniture company are raw materials, such as wood and stain, and electricity to run the machines used in the factory. The costs of flexible resources

During halftime of the 1984 Super Bowl, Apple Computer ran a television advertisement to announce the Macintosh computer. This advertisement, depending on the source referenced, cost Apple Computer between $0.6 million and $1.5 million to make and $0.5 million for the 60-second time slot in which it was shown. The advertisement, which was later acclaimed as iconic and one of the best commercials ever made, was never shown again on national television in its original version. Although clearly designed to promote future sales of a new product, conventional financial accounting practice requires that investments such as these be expensed in the periods in which they are incurred.

Source: www.macdailynews.com/1984.php. Anya Major.

are called **variable costs**. Because they are proportional to the amount of resource used, variable costs are also proportional to some underlying activity, such as number of units produced.

For example, consider the Fyfe Company, which requires 4 units of a key raw material for each unit of production. Each unit of raw material costs $15. Exhibit 2-2 shows the relationship between the raw materials costs, which are variable costs, and the number of raw materials units, which are the flexible resources. Underlying or driving the use of the flexible resource units are the units of production. Note the characteristic shape of the variable cost graph. It is linear in relationship to the number of flexible resources used, which in turn are linear in relationship to the underlying activity level—in this case, the number of units produced.

Capacity-related resources are acquired and paid for in advance of when the work is done. The costs associated with capacity-related resources are called **fixed costs** because they vary with the amount of capacity *acquired*—not on the amount of capacity *used*. Most personnel costs and depreciation on machinery and buildings are examples of fixed costs. Therefore, the amount of fixed costs is related to the planned rather than the actual level of activities.

For example, suppose that Fyfe Company manufactures its products on machines that cost $5,000 each and that have a capacity of 10 units.

In Exhibit 2-3, the solid line shows the relationship between the machinery costs and the number of machines acquired. However, the dashed line shows the relationship between the fixed cost and the units of production—the underlying level of activity. This highlights the fact that fixed costs depend on how much capacity an organization acquires, not on how much it uses to complete production. Note how fixed costs differ from variable costs, which are directly proportional to the actual level of activity.

The cost of crude oil used in this refinery is a variable cost—the company pays only for the crude oil that it uses. The cost of the refinery itself is a fixed cost because the cost depends on the refinery capacity and not on the amount of capacity used.

Source: Wes Thompson/CORBIS/Stock Market.

Exhibit 2-2
Variable Cost
Behavior

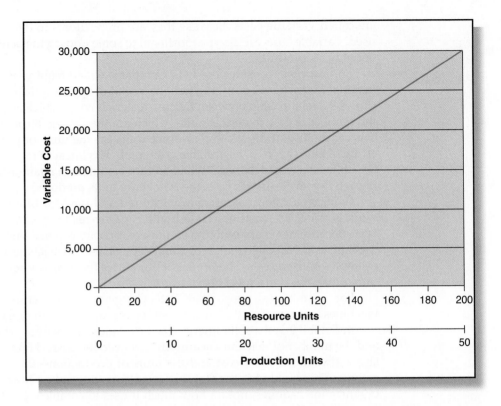

Exhibit 2-3
Fixed Cost
Behavior

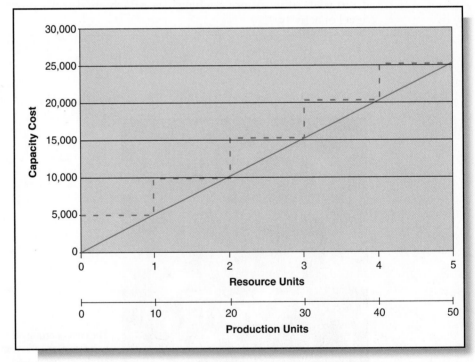

You can now see why understanding cost behavior is crucial for predicting costs. First, the management accountant must determine whether the cost is variable or fixed—this is crucial since cost prediction is usually based on some projected production level. Assuming that all costs are variable will underestimate costs since

Exhibit 2-4
Production Cost
Under Different
Assumptions

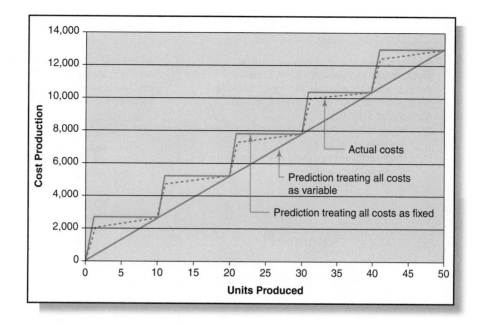

it will not account for the costs of idle capacity (the space between the dashed and solid lines in Exhibit 2-4). Assuming that all costs are fixed will overestimate costs since it will not reflect that the organization will need to pay only for the flexible resources that it uses.

To illustrate, return once again to Fyfe Company. Suppose that variable costs and fixed costs are as indicated in the two examples summarized in Exhibits 2-2 and 2-3. Exhibit 2-4 illustrates how misclassifying costs can lead to over- or underprediction of actual costs.

Second, once the cost is classified, the management accountant must estimate variable cost per unit. In the case of Fyfe Company, the management accountant must estimate the resource cost of $15 per unit of raw material, the use of 4 units of raw material per unit of production, the cost per unit of capacity of $2,000, and the ability to produce 10 units with each unit of capacity. All these are important estimates, as we will see in later chapters when we discuss various costing systems.

Understanding Cost Behavior to Cost Products

So far, we have considered cost concepts and definitions that management accountants use to help identify cost behavior patterns. Now we will turn to consider cost concepts that management accountants use when they compute product costs. Central to the job of product costing in management accounting are the notions of direct and indirect costs.

A **direct cost** is the cost of a resource or activity that is acquired for or used by a single cost object—in other words, it is the cost of a resource that can be associated unequivocally and specifically with a single cost object. For example, if the cost object were a dining room table, one of the direct costs, called a direct material cost, would be the cost of the wood used to make the dining room table. Similarly, if a manager were hired solely to supervise the production of dining room tables, that manager's salary would be a direct cost for the cost object of dining room tables.

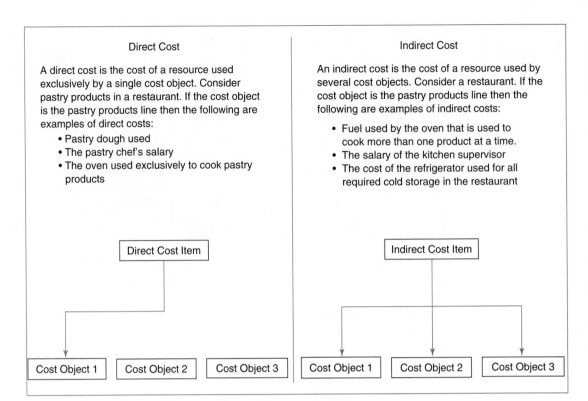

Direct Cost	Indirect Cost
A direct cost is the cost of a resource used exclusively by a single cost object. Consider pastry products in a restaurant. If the cost object is the pastry products line then the following are examples of direct costs: • Pastry dough used • The pastry chef's salary • The oven used exclusively to cook pastry products	An indirect cost is the cost of a resource used by several cost objects. Consider a restaurant. If the cost object is the pastry products line then the following are examples of indirect costs: • Fuel used by the oven that is used to cook more than one product at a time. • The salary of the kitchen supervisor • The cost of the refrigerator used for all required cold storage in the restaurant

An **indirect cost** is the cost of a resource that is used by more than one cost object. For example, the cost of a saw used in a furniture factory is an indirect cost because it is used to make different products, such as dining room tables, china cabinets, and dining room chairs.

Note that a cost classification can vary if the cost object changes. Consider a factory supervisor's salary. If the cost object is a product, the factory supervisor's salary is an indirect cost for the several products made in the factory. If the factory is the cost object, the factory supervisor's salary is a direct cost. While most of the examples we consider in this chapter and in this book use a product as a cost object, the cost object can be any unit of analysis, including product, product line, customer, department, division, geographical area, country, or continent.

Is the salary paid to your accounting instructor a direct or an indirect cost if the cost object is the course? It could be either. If your instructor was hired on a contract to teach only the course you are taking, then his or her salary is a direct cost. If your instructor teaches several different courses, then his or her salary is an indirect cost to the various courses.

When the cost object is a product, variable costs can be direct or indirect. If the variable cost varies in proportion to the number of units produced, then it is a direct cost. Examples include raw materials and power used in a steel mill, tires in an automobile assembly plant, and computer chips used to assemble a computer. However, if the variable cost varies in proportion to some activity that supports several products, then the variable cost will be indirect to the individual products. An example is the fuel in a train that is carrying passengers and freight (assuming that the fuel used is proportional to miles traveled and not weight hauled) and where the cost objects are passenger costs and freight costs.

Fixed costs can be direct or indirect. For example, in the case of a multiproduct firm that acquires a climate-controlled warehouse for the exclusive use of one product,

The cost of the ingredients bottled on this line is a direct cost of the product being made. The cost of the machinery is an indirect cost of the product being made since it can be used to package different products.

Source: AP Wide World Photos.

IN PRACTICE
The Financial Risk of Fixed Costs

"The origins of this long-running dispute (between Airbus and Boeing) lie in the economics of the development and manufacturing of large commercial aircraft. Modern planes sell for between $50 million and $250 million, depending on whether they are 120-seaters or jumbos. . . . A new plane also requires huge upfront R&D spending before the first test flight. The latest Airbus, the A380 double-decker to carry 555 passengers, had cost around $12 billion even before its first test flight a couple of months ago. The new Boeing 787 will probably cost at least $10 billion to develop."

Source: Alastair Miller/Landov LLC.

"Once production starts, the learning curve is steep and difficult. Each doubling of production generally yields a cut of one-fifth in unit cost per plane. Consequently, it takes production of about 500–600 aircraft before a model starts to earn a profit. That would typically amount to around ten years of production. Total industry demand in good years runs around 700–800 planes but is spread across a wide range from short-haul, single-aisle models to long-range and jumbo aircraft. The combination of these factors explains why the industry has a tendency towards natural monopoly."

Source: "Boeing v Airbus Nose to Nose," *The Economist*, June 23, 2005.

that warehouse cost would be fixed and direct to the product that uses it. Alternatively, when the resource provides services to many different products, its cost is indirect.

Labor costs have caused both confusion and controversy in costing circles. Labor costs were originally treated as variable costs because workers were paid in proportion to how much they produced. In fact, some workers are still paid based on the number of hours they work or the number of items they produce (the latter is called a piece-rate system). Scheduling and union considerations have changed most labor costs into fixed costs because, even though they are paid on an hourly basis, many workers' wages are guaranteed to be paid, at least in the short run, regardless of whether or not work is available. For this reason, most organizations now treat labor costs as fixed rather than variable.

Differentiating between direct and indirect costs has a major effect on product cost estimates, as we will see in chapter 4. Many disputes between defense contractors and governments involve whether a cost is appropriately classified as direct or indirect. Why? Because if the contractor is reimbursed for costs plus a profit margin, then classifying a cost as direct will result in all that cost being attributed to the contract. If the cost is classified as indirect, then only part of that cost can be attributed to the contract.

Using Cost Information to Predict Costs and Profits

Many decision makers like to combine information about variable and fixed costs with revenue information to project profits for different levels of volume, a procedure called **cost-volume-profit (CVP) analysis**.

Conventional CVP analysis rests on the assumptions that all organization costs are either purely variable or fixed, that units made equal units sold, and that revenue per unit does not change as volume changes. With these assumptions, an organization that makes a single product can write its profit equation as follows:

$$\text{Profit} = \text{Revenue} - \text{Costs} \tag{2.1}$$

$$\text{Profit} = \text{Revenue} - \text{Variable costs} - \text{Fixed costs} \tag{2.2}$$

$$\text{Profit} = (\text{Units sold} \times \text{Revenue per unit}) - (\text{Units sold} \times \text{Variable cost per unit}) - \text{Fixed costs} \tag{2.3}$$

$$\text{Profit} = [\text{Units sold} \times (\text{Revenue per unit} - \text{Variable cost per unit})] - \text{Fixed costs} \tag{2.4}$$

Managers often like to know the **contribution margin** per unit, which is the product's price less its variable costs. The unit contribution margin measures the contribution that each product sold makes toward covering fixed costs. With the contribution margin definition in hand, we rewrite equation 2.4 as

$$\text{Profit} = (\text{Units sold} \times \text{Contribution margin per unit}) - \text{Fixed costs} \quad (2.5)$$

Equation 2.5 is one that we will exploit in chapter 10 when we discuss budgeting.

Decision makers can use the CVP equation to identify the number of units required to achieve any given level of profit by rearranging equation 2.5 as follows:

$$\text{Units required to earn a target profit} \ = \ \frac{\text{Target profit} + \text{Fixed cost}}{\text{Contribution margin per unit}} \quad (2.6)$$

In the special case when the decision maker wants to know how many sales are required to break even, that is, to just cover fixed costs, equation 2.6 becomes

$$\text{Breakeven unit sales} \ = \ \frac{\text{Fixed cost}}{\text{Contribution margin per unit}} \quad (2.7)$$

Equation 2.7 is usually called the **breakeven equation**.

Some decision makers prefer to express equations 2.6 and 2.7 in terms of the revenue required to break even. In equation 2.6, if we multiply both sides by the revenue per unit, we have

$$\text{Units required} \times \text{Revenue per unit} = \frac{(\text{Target profit} + \text{Fixed cost}) \times \text{Revenue per unit}}{\text{Contribution margin per unit}} \quad (2.8)$$

Dividing the numerator and denominator of the right-hand side of the equation 2.8 by revenue per unit, we get

$$\text{Revenue required} \ = \ \frac{\dfrac{(\text{Target profit} + \text{Fixed cost})}{\text{Contribution margin per unit}}}{\text{Revenue per unit}} \quad (2.9)$$

Management accountants call the ratio of contribution margin per unit to revenue per unit the **unit contribution margin ratio**; which is the fraction of each sales dollar that goes toward covering fixed costs. We can now rewrite equation 2.9 as

$$\text{Revenue required} \ = \ \frac{(\text{Target profit} + \text{Fixed cost})}{\text{Contribution margin ratio}} \quad (2.10)$$

Finally, we can write the revenue required to break even as

$$\text{Breakeven sales revenue} \ = \ \frac{\text{Fixed cost}}{\text{Contribution margin ratio}} \quad (2.11)$$

We can illustrate CVP analysis by considering the operations at Lynn's Landscaping Services that are summarized in Exhibit 2-1. We assume that the variable costs reported in Exhibit 2-1 vary directly with the number of units of service provided. Suppose that

IN PRACTICE

Exploiting CVP Analysis to Predict Profit

Because fixed costs are a large proportion of total costs for airlines, using available capacity is crucial for an airline's success. This explains the intense industry interest in two measures: (1) *passenger yield*, which equals the price (in cents) a passenger pays to fly 1 mile and (2) *load factor*, which is the average proportion of seats filled on an aircraft. Executives, ana-

lysts, and regulators track average yield and load factor for the industry and each airline very carefully.

Here are the passenger yield and load factor data for national and domestic airlines between 1980 and 2005.

Source: Air Transport Association Office of Economics www.airlines.org/econ 8 7/14/2006.

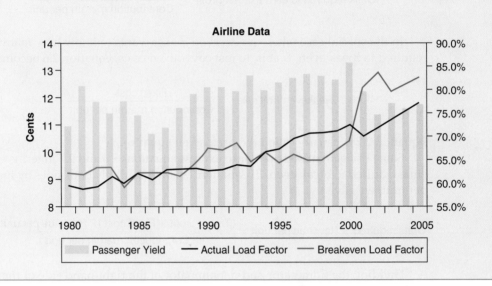

Lynn charges, on average, $50 to mow a lawn. This means that she mowed 4,600 lawns (230,000/50), the variable cost per lawn is about $27.17 (125,000/4,600), the contribution margin per lawn mowed is $22.83 ($50 – $27.17), and the contribution margin ratio per lawn mowed is about 0.4565 (22.83/50.00).

With this information, we can write the profit equation for the lawn mowing operations at Lynn's as follows:

$$\text{Profit of lawn mowing operation} = (\text{Number of lawns mowed} \times \$22.83) - \$105,343 \qquad (2.12)$$

Using equation 2.7, we can compute the breakeven number of lawns mowed as

$$\text{Breakeven number of lawns mowed} = \frac{\text{Fixed cost}}{\text{Contribution margin per unit}}$$
$$= \frac{\$105,343}{\$22.83} = 4,615 \qquad (2.13)$$

Using equation 2.11, we can compute the breakeven lawn mowing revenue as

$$\text{Breakeven sales revenue} = \frac{\text{Fixed cost}}{\text{Contribution margin ratio}}$$

$$= \frac{\$105,343}{0.4565} = \$230,762 \qquad (2.14)$$

In summary, knowledge of the organization's cost behavior allows decision makers to develop equations they can use to model the relationship between activity levels, costs, and profits. This information can be readily displayed in graphical form, as we will now see.

The CVP Chart

Executives, analysts, and regulators track average yield and load factor for the industry and each airline very carefully since small changes in the load factor have large effects on profits (since fixed costs make up most of the total costs, the total cost curve has a small slope) and since most airlines operate near their breakeven load factor as shown in the practice box Exploiting CVP Analysis to Predict Profit.

Decision makers often summarize CVP information in a CVP chart. Exhibit 2-5 summarizes this information for the lawn mowing operations at Lynn's Landscaping Services. The CVP chart provides a graphic and therefore an intuitive and accessible picture of the organization's profit behavior as sales level vary.

The CVP chart provides a convenient way of summarizing the relationship between volumes, revenues, costs, and profits and provides a visual way to display the effect of volume changes on profits. The critical line—the primary focus of attention—is the profit line. Note that the profit line crosses the horizontal axis, which denotes a zero, or breakeven, level of profits at around 4,600 lawns mowed, and that the total revenue line intersects the total cost line at around $231,000.

Exhibit 2-5
Lynn's Landscaping CVP Chart

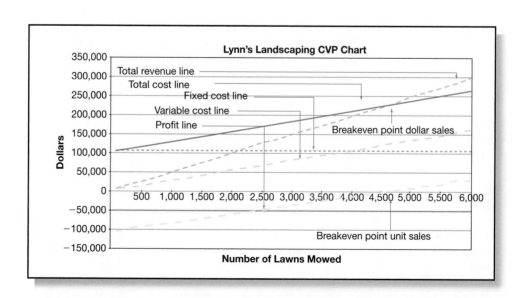

Extending CVP Analysis for Multiproduct Organizations

Business managers developed CVP analysis as a convenient way of modeling profit at a time when computing was done manually. Therefore, this charting approach is quite rudimentary. So, as you study the CVP chart in Exhibit 2-5, it might occur to you that this chart works only for single-product organizations, something that seriously inhibits its value as a practical decision-making tool. To overcome this limitation, analysts developed an extension to the basic CVP analysis that allowed it to be applied to multiproduct organizations. To illustrate this extension, we return to the data in Exhibit 2-1 for Lynn's Landscaping Services.

Suppose that Lynn is wondering what sales levels for each of her services would allow her to break even overall in her business. Many combinations of sales levels for her three products—in fact, an infinite number—would allow her to break even. These can be simulated using an electronic spreadsheet by varying the sales levels of the three products and finding combinations that result in total profits being positive or at least zero. This approach is discussed in chapter 11.

When management accountants did CVP analysis manually, it was impractical to manipulate multiple products simultaneously in order to find a mix of production and sales that would be profitable, so decision makers developed an extension of basic CVP analysis that allowed them to continue to use the basic profit equation and graphing techniques.

That extension was to create a hypothetical average product that was a weighted combination of the organization's products. The weights were determined by estimating the sales mix. For example, if one product made up 30% of the estimated total sales, that product's revenues and variable costs would be weighted 30% in determining the revenues and variable costs of the average product. For Lynn's Landscaping Services, Lynn would construct an average product by weighting each of her company's three real products—lawn mowing, layout design, and other maintenance—by their respective proportions in the estimated product mix. Suppose that further analysis of the data in Exhibit 2-1 yielded the information in Exhibit 2-6.

The next step is to compute each product's share of total sales. Exhibit 2-7 shows each product's proportion of total sales.

The next step is to weight each product's revenue per unit by its proportion of total sales to get a weight. For example, the weight for layout design is 5.65% × $500, or $28.23. Then add the weights for all the products to get the total weighted revenue of $105.65 per unit of the composite product.

Exhibit 2-6
Lynn's Landscaping Services

| | LAWN MOWING | | LAYOUT DESIGN | | OTHER MAINTENANCE | |
	UNIT	TOTAL	UNIT	TOTAL	UNIT	TOTAL
Units sold	4,600		350		1,250	
Revenues	$50.00	$230,000	$500.00	$175,000	$200.00	$250,000
Variable costs	27.17	125,000	160.00	56,000	116.00	145,000
Fixed costs		105,343		80,153		114,504
Profit		−$343		$38,847		−$9,504

Exhibit 2-7
Lynn's Landscaping Services: Composite Product Calculation

	LAWN MOWING		LAYOUT DESIGN		OTHER MAINTENANCE		
	UNIT	% TOTAL	UNIT	% TOTAL	UNIT	% TOTAL	TOTAL ALL
Units sold	4,600	74.193548%	350	5.645161%	1,250	20.161290%	6,200
	UNIT	WEIGHT	UNIT	WEIGHT	UNIT	WEIGHT	TOTAL ALL
Revenues	$50.00	$37.10	$500.00	$28.23	$200.00	$40.32	$105.65
Variable costs	27.17	20.16	160.00	9.03	116.00	23.39	52.58
Contribution margin							$53.06

IN PRACTICE
Exploiting Breakeven Information

Organizations making products for which raw materials costs are a big share of total costs are very sensitive to the price of raw materials and will close down operations when raw materials prices get too high. Consider the following:

"In the South, with very wet weather and distressed red oak prices, some mills are coming up short on logs, as loggers will not bring in logs at prices that allow sawmills to break even. In some instances, mills have shut down for a week or two; others are contemplating short closures in the near future."

Source: Hardwood Review Weekly, August 19, 2005.

Now repeat what you did only with costs to compute the weighted variable cost of $52.58 per unit of the composite product. We now subtract the weighted variable cost from the weighted revenue to get $53.06, the weighted contribution margin per unit of the composite product.

The result of these calculations is a composite fictitious product that reflects the characteristics of the real products—each characteristic weighted in proportion to the underlying products' fractions of total sales. Noting that the total fixed costs at Lynn's Landscaping is $300,000 ($105,343 + $80,153 + $114,504), use the breakeven formula (equation 2.7) to compute the breakeven level of sales for this composite product:

$$\text{Breakeven unit sales} = \frac{\text{Fixed cost}}{\text{Contribution margin per unit}} = \frac{\$300,000}{\$53.06} = 5,654 \quad (2.15)$$

And we can use equation 2.11 to compute the breakeven sales in dollars:

$$\text{Breakeven sales revenue} = \frac{\text{Fixed cost}}{\text{Contribution margin ratio}}$$
$$= \frac{\$300,000}{\dfrac{\$53.06}{\$105.65}} = \frac{\$300,000}{0.502224} = \$597,343 \quad (2.16)$$

Exhibit 2-8
Lynn's Landscaping CVP Chart for Composite Product

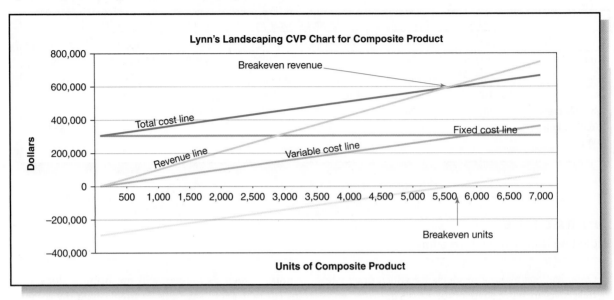

Exhibit 2-9
Lynn's Landscaping Services: Composite Product Calculation

	LAWN MOWING		LAYOUT DESIGN		OTHER MAINTENANCE		TOTAL ALL
	UNIT	TOTAL	UNIT	TOTAL	UNIT	TOTAL	
Units sold	4,194.529		319.149		1,139.818		
Revenues	$50.00	$209,726	$500.00	$159,574	$200.00	$227,964	$597,264
Variable costs	27.17	113,982	160.00	51,064	116.00	132,219	297,264
Fixed costs		105,343		80,153		114,504	300,000
Profit		−$9,598		$28,356		−$18,759	$0

Exhibit 2-8 displays the CVP graph for this composite product. What does this composite product information mean? How do we interpret the breakeven quantity for individual units of production given the computed breakeven level for this average product? We simply reverse the process of computing the average.

With the current sales mix, the required sales levels to break even are as follows:

1. Lawn mowing = 5,653.50 × 4,600/6,200 = 5,653.50 × 0.742 = 4,194.529
2. Layout design = 5,653.50 × 350/6,200 = 5,653.50 × 0.056 = 319.149
3. Other maintenance = 5,653.50 × 1,250/6,200 = 5,653.50 × 0.202 = 1,139.818

Exhibit 2-9 summarizes these calculations and verifies that this mix and level of sales indeed provides a breakeven level of profits for Lynn's Landscaping Services. Note that this breakeven calculation differs from the breakeven calculation computed earlier for the Lawn Mowing group because the latter calculation focuses

"Ken Pedeleose's eyes popped in awe as he plowed through a bill for airplane parts in 1999: $2,522 for a 4½-inch metal sleeve, $744 for a washer, $714 for a rivet, and $5,217 for a 1-inch metal bracket." (David Phinney, "Diminished Oversight Leads to Overpricing," *Federal Times*, April 5, 2004)

Journalists and government auditors routinely pounce on seemingly absurd situations where a government contractor submits a bill for something like a $1,000 hammer. However, suppose it costs $950 to make the mold for this special purpose hammer and only $50 for the material that goes into the hammer.

If the mold has the capacity to make 100 hammers before it expires, it would seem reasonable to attribute a fixed cost of $9.50 ($950/100) to each hammer resulting in a total hammer cost of $59.50 ($50 of materials cost and $9.50 of fixed cost).

However, suppose that this mold has no other conceivable use and will never be used to make another hammer. Does it still make sense of the contractor to bill the government for $59.50?

You may have thought of a very practical way around this problem. The contractor transmits the mold and the single hammer to the government and submits a bill of $950 for the mold and $50 for the hammer. The cost of unique parts or tools has prompted many governments, particularly in defense contracting, to insist that wherever possible, contractors use off-the-shelf parts and tools rather than expensive custom-designed parts or tools.

on breakeven for the overall company, assuming that the product mix remains constant, while the earlier calculation focuses on breakeven for one department. Note also that, according to these calculations, the Lawn Mowing and Other Maintenance operations are losing money.

To summarize, CVP analysis provided decision makers with a handy, flexible, and convenient way to model the relationship between volume and profits. This type of analysis has fallen into disuse with the advent of spreadsheets and powerful personal computers. However, the cost behavior information that lies behind CVP analysis is information that is invaluable in planning, as we will see in chapter 10.

Using Cost Information to Develop Product Costs

We have considered how knowledge of cost behavior patterns helps management accountants predict costs. Now we turn to consider briefly how this knowledge supports product costing, a topic that we will cover in detail in chapters 3 and 4.

If you return to the discussion of Lynn's Landscaping, you will note that we addressed product costing only indirectly. Specifically, we assumed that total variable costs in each of the organization units varied with the number of units of work done. Those variable costs could relate to the cost of fuel, people, and supplies that vary proportionately with the amount of work done in each department. These variable costs are an integral part of product cost. But what about the fixed costs?

Recall that the amount of capacity acquired determines the fixed costs regardless of whether the capacity is used. Fixed costs provide the ability or capacity to do work. There are many issues surrounding fixed costs that we will leave to discussions at the end of this chapter and in later chapters. To continue with the Lynn's Landscaping example, we will assume that all fixed costs in Lynn's Landscaping relate to the supervisors in each department and the machinery used in each department. It would seem reasonable to include the costs of the supervisors and machinery used in each department to compute total product costs. But the question is how to do that. At first glance, this issue of including fixed costs in product costs may seem mundane, but in fact, computing a total product cost has many practical

Exhibit 2-10
Cost per Lawn Mowed

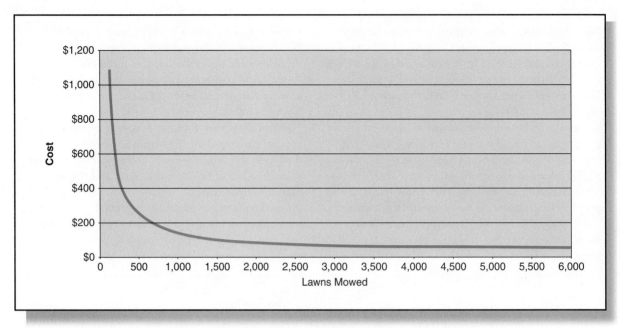

consequences since product cost information can be used for cost-reimbursement purposes in contracting, in inventory valuation for insurance purposes, and in justifying a product cost when the product price must be justified, as in a legal proceeding when the company is accused of dumping—that is, selling its product below cost.

Therefore, we are faced with the problem of how to incorporate fixed costs into a product cost. We will consider only two simple alternatives here. A widely used approach is to divide fixed costs by the number of units actually produced. This has the nice effect of including all the fixed costs in the product costs, but it has the unfortunate effect of increasing the computed cost of a product as demand goes down. For example, returning to the lawn mowing department at Lynn's Landscaping, let's assume that the current fixed costs provide a capacity to mow 6,000 lawns. Exhibit 2-10 shows the computed cost per lawn mowed as the number of lawns mowed varies and assuming that the cost per lawn is computed as the sum of variable cost and fixed cost divided by number of lawns mowed.

Market prices change to align demand with quantity available. However, there is no logical reason to assume that the cost of something should depend on customer demand. Therefore, an approach that results in customer demand affecting computed product cost makes no intuitive sense. Moreover, if the organization uses this approach to cost products and based its prices on costs computed this way, such as cost plus 25%, the organization increases the price as demand falls. This is clearly an absurd practice that would result in a death spiral as the organization goes through the cycle of raising prices and responding to the consequential falling demand by raising prices again.

An alternative approach to including fixed costs in product costs is to divide the fixed cost by the practical level of capacity provided to get a cost per unit of capacity. Then use the computed cost per unit of capacity to charge out capacity to products based on the amount of capacity that each product uses. This seems more sensible than the former approach but has the characteristic of chronically underassigning fixed costs since few organizations operate at capacity.

We will confront the issue of choosing an appropriate base to impound fixed cost in product cost in chapters 3 and 4 as well as considering what to do when fixed costs are incurred at the organization level—for example, head office at Lynn's Landscaping rather than at the department level. We will have a hint of the issues involved in assigning organization level costs to divisions at the end of the chapter when we revisit Lynn's situation.

Cost-Benefit Considerations in Developing Cost Information

We have seen how the format for determining costs for external reporting is prescribed by GAAP, whereas the format for determining costs for internal decision making varies since costs used internally reflect the needs of a particular decision. This means that developing cost information for internal decision making is a matter of choice. Because the organization must pay someone to develop cost information, its expected benefits should exceed its development costs.

You might suspect—and it is generally true—that it is difficult to compute the value of using cost information in a particular decision. Nevertheless, the fundamental principle remains: in the cost-benefit trade-off of developing cost information, the benefit should outweigh the cost.

Consider an example that provides one approach to quantifying the value of cost information. Suppose you are making a product with a price of $20 and you sell 150,000 units per year. You know that your cost system is rudimentary and that, given the estimated cost of $19, the actual cost could be $16 or $22 with either possibility equally likely. Therefore, the expected cost is $19 [(0.5 × $16) + (0.5 × $22)].

The decision here is whether to continue to make and sell the product for the next 2 years or to abandon it now. Given prior beliefs, the expected value of producing is $300,000 [(2 × 150,000) × (20 − 19)].

Now suppose that you can do a cost study that identifies what the actual cost will be. In other words, the information is perfect. If the study reports that the cost will be $22, you will not produce since associated with the $22 cost is a loss of $600,000 [(150,000 × 2) × (20 − 22)]. If the study reports that the cost will be $16, you will produce since associated with the $16 cost is a profit of $1,200,000 [(150,000 × 2) × (20 − 16)]. Since you believe that there is 50% chance that the cost will be $16, your expected gain from making decisions with perfect information is $600,000 ($1,200,000 × 50%). Since your expected gain is $300,000 when making decisions without perfect information, your expected gain from having the information is $300,000 ($600,000 − $300,000) and that is the most you would be willing to pay for the cost study. Exhibit 2-11 summarizes the calculations and the decision steps for the perfect information evaluation.

How Decisions Define the Nature of the Cost Required

The adage concerning different costs for different purposes implies that because cost information is used to guide a decision, that decision will define the nature of the required cost, the way it should be computed, and the value of any cost number. This means that a cost number that is useful for one decision may be useless or perhaps even harmful if it is used for another decision.

Exhibit 2-11
Determining the
Value of Perfect
Cost Information:
An Example

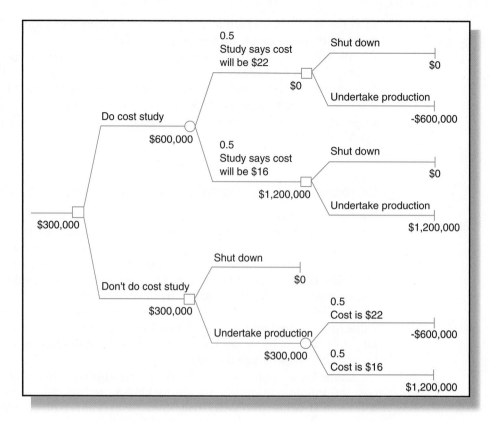

For example, suppose that you were asked to compute the cost of flying one person from London to Zurich. You might start by estimating the cost of the flight, including fuel, depreciation on the aircraft, employee salaries, meals, landing fees, and other related costs. Next, you might consider what other company overhead should be added to these costs to get the total cost of the flight. Finally, you might divide the total cost of the flight by some number (such as the capacity of the aircraft or the number of people on board a particular flight) to get a cost per person. Now suppose you were told that the flight is going to take off as scheduled and that you must compute the cost of adding one more person to the flight. Would you use the same cost? Not likely. In this latter case, you might include only the incremental cost of items such as fuel and meals that are created by adding one more person to the flight.

The point is that the appropriate cost to use is defined by the context of the decision. The full cost might be used for planning to determine the average ticket price the airline will have to charge if it puts a scheduled flight into operation. Airlines that operate with fixed capacity can cut prices toward incremental costs to fill the capacity in the short run. However, this pricing strategy becomes addictive to passengers and the airlines, and soon, as airlines compete to use the capacity they are stuck with, average prices fall below the level required to cover fixed costs.

Using the incremental cost to develop a long-term ticket pricing strategy is a disaster because it ensures the airline's failure. Relying on short-run prices that fill up capacity but do not adequately contribute to fixed costs is the primary cause of poor profit performance in airlines.

As you go through this book and you think about the types of information that decision makers use, always keep in mind that a cost that is suitable for one decision making purpose may be inappropriate for another.

Do Different Costs for Different Purposes Cause Costing Chaos?

At first, you might think it curious or even wrong that cost is not a rigid number calculated according to some formal rules. One challenge of working with costs, however, is that they are used in many different contexts.

As an example that illustrates a range of possible cost alternatives, suppose you are asked to estimate the cost of going to a movie. That task seems somewhat unambiguous until you start digging into the analysis. Should you focus on historical cost (the cost last week at this theater) or some cost that might exist in the future? If the cost of the movie varies by date or time or by movie or theater, should you use average cost or the cost of a specific movie at a specific location and at a specific time? If there are discount periods, such as matinees or Tuesday evenings, should you consider the full rate, the discounted rate, or the average of the two? Are there other costs? For example, if you expect that the attendee will pay to hire a babysitter, to park, and to have a drink and a snack, should those costs be added to the admission cost? They might well be considered elements of the total cost of going to a movie. Finally, are there hidden costs? For example, if Mary goes to the movie, she will be unable to study for her exam, dropping her expected grade from A to B. The cost that Mary assigns to this grade reduction is an implicit cost associated with going to the movie that she would add to the explicit costs associated with the movie.

However, if the question were rephrased as "I promised to pay John's admission to the movie he attended last Thursday. What was the cost?" all ambiguity is resolved, and a specific and relevant cost can be computed. Note that conventional accounting

What is the cost of attending a play?

Source: Niall MacLeod/CORBIS.

for external reporting avoids all these issues because it is understood that reported cost will be the historical cost for a particular transaction that has already occurred.

Opportunity Cost

The implicit cost relating to the impact on Mary's grade of going to the movie is an example of what management accountants call an opportunity cost. An opportunity cost is the sacrifice one makes when using a resource. If Mary has excess time on her hands and going to a movie will not affect her grade, then her opportunity cost is zero. So remember that the opportunity cost of a resource is zero if there is excess capacity of that resource.

To illustrate the idea of opportunity cost, suppose that Mount Pleasant Plastics can use an injection-molding machine with 1,000 hours of capacity to produce two products: a plastic crate for milk or a plastic container to carry soda bottles. Demand is such that Mount Pleasant Plastics can sell all it makes of either product. Exhibit 2-12 summarizes the price and variable cost for each product. The only constraint limiting production is machine time. What would you choose to do?

You are likely to respond, intuitively, to use the machine to make the product that is more profitable. Suppose that the milk crates have a contribution margin of $8 and that the soda containers have a contribution margin of $5. Which one would you make? The milk crate looks more profitable, but suppose you discover that it takes 1 minute to make a milk crate on the machine but only 30 seconds to make a soda carrier. Therefore, the contribution margin per machine minute is $10 if you make soda carriers and $8 if you make milk crates, as shown in Exhibit 2-13. If we use the 1,000 hours of machine time to make 60,000 (1,000 × 60) milk crates, we can generate a total contribution margin of $480,000 ($8 × 60,000). If we use the 1,000 hours of machine time to make 120,000 (1,000 × 60 × 2) soda carriers, we can generate a total contribution margin of $600,000 ($5 × 120,000). The soda carrier is a better product because it maximizes the profit for a given supply of machine time.

We use the concept of opportunity cost that we described earlier to decide which product to make. Since we can sell all the products we can make, we know that machine time, the capacity resource, will be constrained. The opportunity cost of

Exhibit 2-12
Mount Pleasant Plastics Contribution Margins

	MILK CRATE	SODA CARRIER
Price	$12.00	$8.00
Variable cost	4.00	3.00
Contribution margin	$8.00	$5.00

Exhibit 2-13
Mount Pleasant Plastics Capacity Use Decision

	MILK CRATE	SODA CARRIER
Price	$12.00	$8.00
Variable cost	4.00	3.00
Contribution margin	$8.00	$5.00
Minutes of machine time	1.00	0.50
CM/Minute of machine time	$8.00	$10.00

using a minute of the machine time to make milk crates is $10 and to make soda carriers is $8. Choosing the decision that minimizes opportunity costs will maximize profits. So, in this case, we should use the available machine time to produce soda carriers.

Suppose now that Mount Pleasant Plastics can sell only 100,000 soda carriers and 40,000 milk crates. Exhibit 2-14 shows that decision makers would allocate machine capacity first to the soda carriers, which have the highest contribution margin per hour of machine time. However, after 833 hours of machine capacity is allocated to soda carriers, the maximum number of units that can be sold have been produced. Then planners allocate 833 hours of machine capacity to produce 100,000 soda carriers and the remaining 167 of machine hours to produce 10,000 milk crates. In this case, the opportunity cost of capacity is $8, meaning that if another product could be made with an expected contribution margin of more than $8 per machine hour, it would be made and dislodge the production of milk crates.

Finally, suppose that Mount Pleasant Plastics can sell only 50,000 soda carriers and 30,000 milk crates. Exhibit 2-15 shows that planners will allocate 417 hours of machine time to produce the 50,000 soda carriers, leaving 583 machine hours to produce milk crates. The company will use 500 hours to produce the 30,000 milk crates, leaving 83 hours of unused capacity. In this case, the opportunity cost of capacity is $0. The opportunity cost of a resource equals the contribution per unit of that resource made by the next unit of production.

As you can see, opportunity costs are implicit costs because they do not appear anywhere in the accounting records. Nevertheless, they are important in management accounting, and we will be using this notion at several different places in this book.

Exhibit 2-14
Mount Pleasant Plastics: Allocation of Available Capacity Given Initial Demand

PRODUCT	CONTRIBUTION PER MACHINE MINUTE	MAXIMUM SALES UNITS	UNITS MADE AND SOLD	PRODUCT CONTRIBUTION MARGIN	MACHINE HOURS USED	MACHINE HOURS AVAILABLE
Soda carrier	$10.00	100,000	100,000	$500,000	833	1,000
Milk crate	$8.00	40,000	10,000	$80,000	167	167
Idle capacity	$0.00					0

Exhibit 2-15
Mount Pleasant Plastics: Allocation of Available Capacity Given Revised Demand

PRODUCT	CONTRIBUTION PER MACHINE MINUTE	MAXIMUM SALES UNITS	UNITS MADE AND SOLD	PRODUCT CONTRIBUTION MARGIN	MACHINE HOURS USED	MACHINE HOURS AVAILABLE
Soda carrier	$10.00	50,000	50,000	$250,000	417	1,000
Milk crate	$8.00	30,000	30,000	$240,000	500	583
Idle capacity	$0.00					83

Long-Run and Short-Run Costs

Short run is the period over which a decision maker cannot adjust capacity. The level of capacity-related resources, hence of fixed costs, is fixed. Therefore, the only costs that vary in the short run are those that vary in proportion to production or some activity that is related to production. These short-run costs are variable costs. If you think of the example discussed earlier in this chapter about computing the cost of flying someone from London to Zurich, short-run costs are those that change when you add one more person to the flight that was going anyway, such as the incremental fuel costs and the incremental meal costs added by one person. Examples of short-run costs are wood, power, and incidental supplies in a furniture factory; crude oil in an oil refinery; and fuel in an electric generating plant.

Long run is the period over which capacity can be adjusted. Long-run costs are the sum of variable and fixed costs associated with a cost object, which is usually a product. They are important for product planning purposes because they are an estimate of the cost of all resources consumed to make the product. The average price charged for a product must cover its long-run cost for the organization to replace the capacity used to make the product when the capacity deteriorates. Examples of long run costs are buildings and equipment in any manufacturing environment.

In chapter 6, we will consider the importance of the notions of short-run and long-run in product pricing decisions.

HOW ORGANIZATIONS CREATE COSTS: AN EXAMPLE

Let us review the definitions of cost and consider how organizations create costs by considering the activities of Fred's Grocery Services.

Starting Up

Fred Stanford owns and operates a grocery delivery service for a select group of customers. Fred chose his customers using two criteria: First, he knows that they will pay him cash for his services. Second, they are in a geographical area that Fred can serve reasonably.

On Monday of each week, Fred provides his customers with a list of groceries from which they can order. These groceries reflect discounts or bargains that Fred has managed to find at the local farmers' market and through large wholesalers that have excess supply.

Fred's customers value his services because the quality is always high and the prices are low. Fred's customers call in their orders, which Fred delivers at a pre-arranged time on the following day. Since the availability of bargains is limited, Fred's products are offered on a first-come, first-serve basis. Fred usually acquires his products on Saturday and Sunday, and because he has very limited storage space (in a garage that belongs to his parents) and most of the goods he carries are perishable, Fred's objective is to clear his inventory by Friday evening of each week. Fred's costs include printing flyers, acquiring inventory, maintaining a telephone line (which includes a call answer service), and delivering groceries, which includes the cost of gasoline, maintenance, and insurance (he drives an old vehicle with negligible value).

What are Fred's costs in a start-up phase? The cost of the flyers is an advertising cost that accountants call a discretionary cost. The cost of the merchandise may sound

Accountants classify the cost associated with using this advertising space as a period cost. This reflects the conservative assumption that advertising, benefits only current period sales.

Source: Sandra Baker/Getty Images, Inc.–Liaison.

like a variable cost, but think about its nature. There is no evidence in the case that Fred can return unsold inventory to his suppliers. Therefore, the cost of the inventory depends on the amount purchased and not on the amount used (which, in this case, means sold)—a hallmark of fixed costs. This classification choice is confirmed by the observation that Fred's sales are limited by the amount of inventory he acquires: Fred does run out during the week. Note that this fixed cost is a fairly short-run cost, as it is committed only once and only for the week. The following week, Fred can choose a different level of inventory capacity to hold. Think of how this situation would change if Fred were required to buy the same amount each week. That would represent a much longer commitment. The only other cost that Fred incurs is the cost of gasoline for deliveries. This appears to be a variable cost because it depends on the number of deliveries made. An opportunity cost is buried in here. Can you think of what it is? It is the income that Fred forgoes by not working elsewhere.

Early Growth

Word of Fred's reasonable prices and high-quality groceries has spread. The number of Fred's customers has grown, and Fred is facing capacity constraints. He can no longer fit his weekly purchases in his parents' garage, and he has leased a small commercial warehouse. One advantage of the warehouse is its large refrigerated area. Fred leases the warehouse on a monthly basis for $3,000 per month, which includes utilities and taxes.

Fred has decided that his old car is no longer suitable for grocery deliveries because it is too small, unreliable, and inconvenient. Fred has purchased a used cube van for $8,000. Fred figures that the van will last 4 years. The insurance on the vehicle is $1,500 annually, which Fred pays on a monthly basis. With the addition of the van and the warehouse, Fred's business triples.

Fred's cost structure is now changing. In addition to the costs in the start-up phase, Fred now has new costs: the costs of the warehouse, the van, and the insurance on the van. The warehouse cost is a fixed cost since the cost of the warehouse depends not on how much Fred uses it but rather on its size. Similarly, the cost of the van, which would be reflected in its depreciation charges, is a fixed cost because the cost of the van does not vary in proportion to any activity measure but rather is more likely related to its age. The vehicle insurance is a fixed cost because it bears no relationship to any underlying activity measure, such as number of deliveries, number of customers, or level of sales.

Reaching the Boundaries of Existing Capacity

Time passes, and we discover that Fred is having trouble handling order taking because he is spending so much extra time making additional deliveries as his business continues to grow. He hires his sister-in-law Elizabeth to run the office. Elizabeth's duties are to take telephone orders, schedule deliveries, keep the records for the business, and help in handling the inventory in the warehouse. Fred pays Elizabeth $500 each week. Fred is under pressure from some customers to accept credit cards. However, for the moment he is resisting, insisting on cash and no personal checks.

Now Fred has added another fixed cost since Elizabeth's salary does not depend on any underlying activity volume. Since it is the increase in sales that has prompted Fred to hire Elizabeth, you might think that somehow the salary is volume related. However, the definition of fixed cost is a cost whose level depends on the amount of resource acquired, not the amount of resource used. Fred has to pay Elizabeth $500 per week whether she is busy or idle.

Expanding the Product Line and Acquiring More Capacity Resources

Faced with demands from many customers, Fred has expanded his product line, which formerly consisted primarily of produce, to include many types of canned goods. Fred purchases the canned goods in truckload lots from a supplier, thereby receiving a moderate discount. Because of the order size required to earn the discount, Fred is no longer clearing his entire inventory each week and now has a permanent revolving inventory of canned goods. Therefore, Fred has been forced to expand to a larger warehouse. The rent is now $5,000 per month, but instead of paying monthly and leasing month-to-month, Fred must sign a 2-year lease.

Again, Fred is on the move, and the cost structure of his business is changing. The larger warehouse means that his commitment to fixed costs is now $5,000 per month for rent, but the cost is also much longer term since the lease is for 2 years. This creates more risk for Fred since he is committed to paying that amount even if his business slows. Fred also is now holding inventory, which will create inventory-holding costs, such as spoilage and damage, and opportunity costs in the form of money that is tied up in inventory and cannot earn a return elsewhere. The cost of the canned goods is a variable cost, unlike the cost of the produce, because the canned goods can be held until they sell, unlike the produce, which has to be disposed of if it is not sold promptly.

From the perspective of a management accountant the most important development for Fred is the move to multiple product lines. It is likely that Fred will want to compute the profits earned on his two lines of business: produce and canned goods. If he does, the accounting system will create two cost objects, one for the produce and one for the canned goods. When that happens, the costs of the warehouse and the van will be indirect costs and will have to be allocated to each of the product lines using some basis so that each product line bears its appropriate share of the cost of the capacity that it uses. However, not all these costs may be indirect. For example, if a portion of the warehouse is refrigerated and only the produce is stored in that area, all costs relating to refrigeration are related to the produce, and all should be assigned to the produce.

Redefining the Business

Fred is now doing more than $600,000 of business each year. One of Fred's customers remarks, "Hey, Fred, you should start your own grocery store." This comment gives Fred cause for thought. Fred never wanted to operate a grocery business. His value proposition was to provide customer service by delivering high-quality merchandise to the customer without requiring the customer to come to a store. Despite his having hired Grady, a part-time employee, to help Elizabeth, the order-taking business is again a bottleneck.

What kind of cost is Grady's salary? Since this is a part-time position, Grady's salary is variable if he is paid only when work is available and only for the work he does. His salary is an incremental cost in the sense that it is created by the expansion, and it varies with short-term fluctuations in the underlying volume of activity, which creates a need for his services.

Fred starts to think about the Internet. He discovers that a local Internet service provider will design and maintain a Web site for him for $300 per week. The Website will contain the weekly list of products available, complete with pictures. Fred is intrigued with the idea for two reasons: First, he can provide product availability data so that customers know what products are available and in what quantities, and, second, he can change his product list during the week if additional products become available. The Web site opportunity deals with two major complaints that customers have: (1) the difficulty of getting through on the phone to Elizabeth or Grady and (2) the inconvenience of not knowing what products are available before they call.

Fred signs up for the service and tells his customers that prices will be discounted 5% for any items ordered via the Website. Within 4 months, 80% of Fred's business is through the Web site. Fred sells the list of his customers who do not want to move over to the Web to his friend Lamont, who will operate his business the way Fred operated when he was in the start-up phase. With this move, Fred abandons telephone orders and cash and moves exclusively to Web-based orders and credit card sales.

Fred is now committing to a Web site that will add more fixed costs. Unlike the cost of the truck or the warehouse, which ultimately will have to grow as the business grows, the Web site costs will not expand as the business grows. Therefore, this cost might be treated as a business-level or business-sustaining cost that is not allocated to any of the product lines.

Continued Growth

Business is booming. Elizabeth has become a full-fledged office manager with a staff of four; an accountant who handles the books and all sales, which are now strictly credit card sales; a dispatcher who schedules the four drivers needed to handle the volume of deliveries; a purchasing manager who is responsible for finding the best prices for the products stocked; and a warehouse manager. Fred now devotes his time exclusively to making choices about what products to carry. The business is housed in its own building that cost $1 million to purchase. The product line includes produce, packaged meats, many types of household cleaners, and a limited line of dairy items. As always, Fred's value proposition is convenience and costs that are equal to or lower than what is available in the local supermarket.

Note that Fred has now acquired many new fixed costs. These costs create business risk since they are locked in place for an extended period of time. A good example is the cost of the building, which will be reflected in depreciation charges.

Fred's story models the general pattern of business growth, in which variable costs, such as paying people by the hour or renting capacity based on the amount used, gradually evolve into committed or fixed costs because the capacity is acquired and paid for regardless of how much is used.

How cost creation creates the logic for allocating costs to cost objects is discussed further in chapter 4.

COST STRUCTURES TODAY

The composition of manufacturing costs has changed substantially in recent years. In the early 1900s, when many businesses first installed formal cost systems, direct labor represented a large proportion, sometimes 50% or more, of the total manufacturing costs. Direct materials cost was also substantial. As a result, cost accounting systems were designed to focus on measuring and controlling direct labor and materials use, and they served this purpose admirably. Fixed costs (both direct and indirect), which generally represented a small fraction of total manufacturing costs, were usually accumulated in a single pool and allocated to products in proportion to some volume measure, such as the labor or machine hours used by the product.

In today's industrial environment, however, direct labor is often only a small portion of manufacturing costs. In the electronics industry, for example, direct labor cost is often less than 5% of the total manufacturing cost. The cost of direct materials, however, remains important, for it represents about 40% to 60% of the costs in many plants.

The big change in cost structures of manufacturing entities today has been the much higher share of total costs represented by fixed costs. This change has occurred because of the shift toward greater automation, which requires more production engineering, scheduling, and machine setup activities; the emphasis on better customer service; and the increase in support activities required by a proliferation of multiple products. In addition to fixed manufacturing costs becoming more important, both variable and fixed costs associated with design, product development, distribution, selling, marketing, and administrative activities have increased.

This change in cost structure has caused cost systems that used volume measures to allocate indirect costs to become increasingly inaccurate in computing product costs because they were designed for manufacturing activities with high direct labor content. Many costs do not vary proportionally with volume. Therefore, an allocation that is volume based has the potential to distort costs, particularly when the direct costs are a tiny fraction of the fixed costs.

The following example illustrates this idea. Nanticoke Electric has three groups of customers: industrial, commercial, and residential (both single-unit and multiple-unit dwellings). It sells about 1,000,000,000 units of electricity each month to its 455,000 customers. The selling price of the electricity is about $0.50 per unit. A recent costing study has determined that the full manufacturing and distribution cost is

Organizations replace variable costs with fixed costs as they replace hourly paid workers who are paid only when work is available with machines.

Source: Jim Pickerell/The Stock Connection.

IN PRACTICE
The Effect of Changing Cost Structures

Many years ago work in service stations was done with simple and inexpensive tools. The consequence was that the cost of labor and materials comprised virtually all the costs of automobile repair. Therefore, it was reasonable and practical to bury fixed costs in the rate charged for labor—resulting in the so-called shop rate for labor. Today many service stations use expensive and sometimes sophisticated diagnostic equipment to make automotive repairs. However, most service stations continue to use a shop rate to charge labor and

Source: Getty Images, Inc.–Image Bank.

fixed costs to jobs. In the summer of 2005, many British newspapers complained about the high shop rates for labor being charged in the United Kingdom—some of which were in excess of £ 200. The problem is that simple jobs, such as oil changes, were contributing to the recovery of expensive equipment, such as diagnostic computers and wheel alignment machines, that were not used in those jobs. These high rates should drive customers with simple jobs such as oil changes out to businesses that do oil changes only, resulting in lost business for conventional service stations and a need to increase labor shop rates even more.

Exhibit 2-16
Nanticoke Electric Detailed Costing

	Industrial	Commercial	Home	Apartment
Number of customers	1,000	4,000	150,000	300,000
Total demand	875,000,000	80,000,000	30,000,000	15,000,000
Mfg and delivery cost	$262,500,000	$24,000,000	$9,000,000	$4,500,000
Heading and billing cost	$13,000	$52,000	$1,950,000	$3,900,000
Actual cost	$262,513,000	$24,052,000	$10,950,000	$8,400,000
Actual average profit per customer	$174,987.00	$3,987.00	$27.00	−$3.00

about $0.30 per unit. The only other major costs are meter reading costs, which amount to $5 per reading, and billing and processing costs, which amount to $8 per bill. Each customer's meter is read monthly, and bills are prepared monthly. Exhibit 2-16 provides a breakdown of customer types and demand and the costs of supplying each demand on the basis of the data developed in the special costing study.

The manufacturing and delivery cost for each group is computed by multiplying the total demand for that group by the unit cost of $0.30. The reading and billing cost for each group is computed by multiplying the total reading and billing cost of $13 per customer by the number of customers in that group. The actual cost for each group is the sum of the manufacturing and delivery cost and the reading and billing cost for that group.

Now contrast this information with what is prepared by conventional costing systems. The computed cost for each group is calculated using a simplifying cost allocation approach that is common in traditional costing systems. The total reading and billing costs for all groups are accumulated in a single account. This account totals $5,915,000. This sum is then allocated to the three groups based on demand, which is a volume measure. The total demand by all groups is 1,000,000,000 units. Therefore, the rate per unit of demand for reading and billing costs is $0.005915 ($5,915,000/1,000,000,000). The reading and billing cost allocated to each group is the product of this allocation rate of $0.005915 and its total demand. This allocated cost is then added to the manufacturing and delivery cost for each group to get the computed cost for each group. Exhibit 2-17 summarizes this information. Notice the differences between the actual average profit per customer shown in Exhibit 2-16 and the average profit per customer estimated by the costing system shown in Exhibit 2-17.

You might wonder why the costs of reading and billing would be accumulated for all groups and then allocated using a volume measure. Simply, it is an easy and low-cost approach.

Exhibit 2-17
Nanticoke Electrical Conventional Costing

	Industrial	Commercial	Home	Apartment
Number of customers	1,000	4,000	150,000	300,000
Average demand per customer	875,000	20,000	200	50
Total demand this group	875,000,000	80,000,000	30,000,000	15,000,000
Computed cost this group	$267,675,625	$24,473,200	$9,177,450	$4,588,725
Computed average profit per customer	$169,824.38	$3,881.70	$38.82	$9.70

What is the result? The number shown as the actual average profit per customer is the difference between the total revenue for each customer group and the actual cost divided by the number of customers. The number shown as the computed average profit per customer is the difference between the total revenue for each customer group and the computed cost divided by the number of customers.

You can see the effect of treating the reading and billing costs as if they varied with volume. The computed average cost per customer for the home and apartment customers is understated. Why? Because a portion of their costs is allocated to the industrial and commercial customers by the inappropriate allocation basis.

The point is that this type of distortion is common in many costing systems. Such costing systems take costs that did not vary proportionally with volume, accumulate them, and then allocate them using a volume measure.

Because of the change in the mix of factory costs from mainly variable to mainly fixed, and because costs outside the factory, such as those for marketing and selling, are increasing proportionately more rapidly than manufacturing costs, costing systems today can no longer rely on volume-based costing systems and approaches. This has prompted a different way to look at the focus and structure of costing systems—which we will now consider.

Types of Production Activities

Traditionally, accountants classified activities into those that varied with volume (leading to what we have called variable costs) and those that did not (typically leading to supplying capacity and associated committed costs). However, this simple dichotomy does not capture the full richness of the types of activities that take place in organizations. The following hierarchy, developed originally for manufacturing operations, gives a broader framework for classifying an activity and its associated costs:

1. Unit related
2. Batch related
3. Product sustaining
4. Customer sustaining
5. Business sustaining

Unit-Related Activities

Unit-related activities are those whose volume or level are proportional to the number of units produced or to other measures, such as direct labor hours and machine hours that are themselves proportional to the amount of work done. The indirect labor required for quality inspection that checks every item (or 10% or 20% of items) is clearly associated with the number of units produced. Uniform supervision of all activities performed by direct workers requires effort that is associated with the number of direct labor hours. The consumption of lubricating oil by factory machinery, the energy required to operate the machines, and the scheduled maintenance of machines after every 20,000 hours or any other specified amount of use are examples of manufacturing support costs that are proportional to machine hours.

Since both direct labor hours and machine hours increase with the number of units produced or, more generally, with the amount of work done, the use of many activities supporting production increases with the level of production. For example, if machine activity increases proportionately with the level of production, the variable cost of supporting those machines would be unit-related costs. Unit-related activities apply to more than just production activities, however. Loading shipments onto a truck is a unit-related activity, for example, because it is proportional to the volume of shipments.

Batch-Related Activities

In a production environment, batch-related activities are triggered by the number of batches produced rather than by the number of units manufactured. Machine setups, for example, are required when beginning the production of a new batch of products. Once the machine has been set up, no additional setup effort is required whether we produce a batch of 100 units or 1,000 units of the product. If the in-process materials for a batch are moved together from one work center to the next, the cost of materials handling will be associated with the number of batches rather than with the number of units in the batches. Similarly, indirect labor for first-item quality inspections (inspections of only the first unit in each batch) involves testing a fixed number of units for each batch produced rather than a percentage of the entire batch. Therefore, the indirect labor required for such inspections also is associated with the number of batches. The cost of factory floor machinery that is used proportionately with the number of batches (for example, machines used to move batches of production around the factory floor) would be a batch-related cost.

Clerical effort expended to issue purchase orders or to receive materials from suppliers is a support activity associated with the number of purchase orders or with the number of deliveries rather than with the quantity of materials ordered. The support costs of processing the paperwork for purchases depends only on the number of orders rather than the quantity ordered. Production scheduling is also considered a batch-related activity because it is performed for each production run that needs to be scheduled in a plant rather than for each unit produced in a production run.

Similarly, many shipping costs may be batch related. For example, if the organization pays the shipper a charge per container or truckload, that unit of shipment is a batch, and the cost of shipping is a batch-related cost because it depends on the number of batches and not directly on the number or weight of the units shipped.

Product-Sustaining Activities

Product-sustaining activities support the production and sale of individual products. Product-sustaining activities are activities that provide the infrastructure that enables the production, distribution, and sale of the product but are not involved

Operating this kiln is a batch-related activity since it applies to a batch of products that have just been fired.

Source: Tim Thompson/Corbis–NY.

directly in the production of the product. By their nature, these costs are independent of the units of products produced.

Examples of product-sustaining activities include administrative efforts required to maintain product plans, labor, and machine routings for each part; product engineering efforts to maintain coherent specifications, such as the bill of materials for individual products and their component parts and their routing through different work centers in the plant; managing and sustaining the product distribution channel; and the process engineering required to implement engineering change orders. Engineering efforts to design and test process routines for products and perform product enhancements are other examples of product-sustaining activities. The need to expedite production orders also increases as the number of products and customers serviced by a plant increases. Costs of obtaining patents or regulatory approval, such as Food and Drug Administration approval for new pharmaceutical drugs or food products, increase with the number of products introduced. Revising product plans is a product-sustaining activity, and depreciation of a computer-assisted design machine used to make and revise product plans would be a product-sustaining cost.

IN PRACTICE

Product-Sustaining Activities

"Every day, we change 200 CAD models, adjust 150 standards, and update 3,000 drawings.

Nevertheless, we can tell at any time which component has been used in which revision step in production or planning."

Source: Helmut Ritter, *Information Management and Engineering, MAGNA STEYR.*

Customer-Sustaining Activities

Shifting from a production to a marketing and sales environment, customer-sustaining activities enable the company to sell to an individual customer but are independent of the volume and mix of the products (and services) sold and delivered to the customer. Examples of customer-sustaining activities include sales calls and technical support provided to individual customers.

Product- and customer-sustaining activities are easily traced to the individual products, services, and customers for whom the activities are performed. However, the quantity of resources used in these activities is, by definition, independent of the production and sales volumes and independent of the quantity of production batches and customer orders. This richer framework enables many more activities to become directly traceable to cost objects rather than treated as indirect since they are not proportional to the volumes of production or sales.

Beyond unit- and batch-related and product- and customer-sustaining activities are other resource-supply capabilities that cannot be traced to individual products and customers. These are channel-sustaining activities, such as supporting distributors, and business-sustaining activities, such as the cost of a plant manager and administrative staff.

Channel-Sustaining Activities

Channel-sustaining activities are activities that are required to maintain and sustain product distribution channels. Channel-sustaining expenses such as the cost of trade shows, advertising, and catalogs are the costs of channel-sustaining activities. The expenses of product-line facility and channel resources can be assigned directly to the individual product lines, facilities, and channels but should not be allocated to individual products, services, or customers.

Business-Sustaining Activities

Business-sustaining activities are those required for the basic functioning of the business. These core activities are independent of the size of the organization or the volume and mix of products and customers. For example, organizations need only one chief executive officer, regardless of their size, and they need to perform certain basic functions, such as registration or reporting, that also are independent of the size of the organization. Similarly, all factories may need one plant manager, one controller or financial manager, one human resource manager, and minimal amounts of activities for housekeeping, maintenance, landscaping, and security. These business or facility-sustaining activities are unrelated to the number of individual products, the number of production runs, or the number of units manufactured; and their costs, therefore, are not allocated to cost objects.

Other Support Activities

Other support activities go beyond the basic or core level of business-sustaining activities. The costs of these other sustaining activities vary in proportion to the size or complexity of the organization and are allocated to cost objects in a way that reflects their cause.

Using the Cost Hierarchy

The cost hierarchy developed in this section is a model of cost behavior that can be used in two ways: to predict costs and to develop the costs for a cost object such as a product or product line. We will use this hierarchy in chapter 4 when we discuss activity-based costing systems and in chapter 10 when we discuss forecasting and budgeting.

Understanding the Underlying Behavior of Costs

If we understand the underlying behavior of costs, we have means to predict costs and to understand how costs will behave as volume expands and contracts. Consider the operations of Orillia Novelty Plastics, a small manufacturer that makes three novelty products that customers emboss with their names and use as promotional items. Exhibit 2-18 displays its estimated average monthly production and related demands for raw materials and labor for the next 6 months. Machine times are not considered because they are budgeted separately. Plastic costs $0.10 per unit and is purchased as needed. All production workers undertake three tasks: setting up the machinery (a batch-related activity), tending the machinery while it is producing (a unit-related activity), and moving work in process around the factory (a batch-related activity). All factory workers are crosstrained so that they can do either run-time work or batch work. The total cost of a worker, including wages and fringe benefits, is $25 per hour.

    The union contract requires that the number of workers employed can be adjusted only every 6 months. Therefore, Orillia Plastics must make a 6-month commitment to a particular level of worker hours. Based on the projection in Exhibit 2-18, Orillia Plastics has decided to contract for 1,500 labor hours per month for the next 6 months at a total cost of $37,500 (1,500 × $25). The difference of $1,250 between the contracted cost of labor ($37,500) and the amount estimated, on average, to be needed ($36,250) is a projected excess capacity cost.

Exhibit 2-18
Orillia Novelty
Plastics, Estimated
Monthly Demand

| | PRODUCT | | | |
	1	2	3	TOTAL
Units made	25,000	40,000	10,000	
Plastic per unit	2	1	3	
Units of plastic	50,000	40,000	30,000	120,000
Cost of plastic	$5,000.00	$4,000.00	$3,000.00	$12,000.00
Run-time labor per unit	0.01	0.005	0.04	
Total-run time labor hours	250	200	400	850
Units per batch	5,000	4,000	500	
Batches	5	10	20	
Labor hours per batch	10	15	20	
Total batch labor hours	50	150	400	600
Total labor hours	300	350	800	1,450
Total cost of labor used				$36,250.00
Total cost of labor paid				$37,500.00
Cost excess capacity (unused labor cost)				$1,250.00
Total cost				$49,500.00

Exhibit 2-19
Orillia Novelty
Plastics:Estimated
Monthly Demand

| | PRODUCT | | | |
	1	2	3	TOTAL
Units made	26,000	41,000	8,000	
Plastic per unit	2	1	3	
Units of plastic	52,000	41,000	24,000	117,000
Cost of plastic	$5,200.00	$4,100.00	$2,400.00	$11,700.00
Run-time work per unit	0.01	0.005	0.04	
Total-run-time labor hours	260	205	320	785
Units per batch	5,200	4,100	500	
Batches	5	10	16	
Labor hours per batch	10	15	20	
Total batch labor hours	50	150	320	520
Total labor hours	310	355	640	1305
Total cost of labor used				$32,625.00
Total cost of labor paid				$37,500.00
Cost excess capacity (cost of unused labor)				$4,875.00
Total cost				$49,200.00

Exhibit 2-19 summarizes the production activities for the first month of the 6-month contract. Production of item 3 fell, but sales of products 1 and 2 were higher than the average plan. Study Exhibits 2-18 and 2-19 carefully. Note how the use and cost of plastic follow production up and down. This is the nature of a variable cost, which depends on the amount of resource used. Note that the cost of labor is stuck at $37,500 because labor is a committed, or fixed, cost that has been committed for a 6-month period. Like all fixed costs, labor cost depends on the capacity acquired and not on the capacity used. Note also that in this case the demand for labor was less than what was available. If the production of products 1 and 2 had shot up even more, the demand for labor may have exceeded the supply, and production would have been less than the demand.

Suppose after studying Exhibit 2-19, the management at Orillia Plastics undertakes an evaluation of product 3. The cost of the plastic per unit of product 3 is computed as $0.30 (3 units of plastic per unit of product 3 × $0.10 per unit of plastic) and the cost of labor per unit of product 3 as $2 [(0.04 run-time hours + 20/500 batch-time hours) × $25 per labor hour], yielding a total cost of materials and labor of $2.30 per unit. Since the selling price of product 3 is only $2.50, and since the $2.30 cost does not include machine-related costs for the production equipment used to make the products or the customer-related costs of shipping and selling, management has decided that the product is a loser and has abandoned it.

If product 3 is abandoned, what costs will change? Will costs really fall by $18,400 (8,000 × $2.30) when product 3 is eliminated? Exhibit 2-20 projects costs with product 3 gone. Note that the total costs are now projected to be $46,800, which is a decline of $2,400 ($49,200 − $46,800). Why have costs not fallen by the predicted amount of $18,400? Labor costs will remain the same for the life of the 6-month contract regardless of whether labor is used. After 6 months (the long run), labor costs will fall by $16,000 (8,000 × $2) as a result of this decision because at that time, the labor contract can be renegotiated and labor capacity adjusted downward. In the short run, labor costs will remain the same. This illustrates the concept

Exhibit 2-20
Orillia Novelty
Plastics: Drop
Product 3

| | PRODUCT | | | |
	1	2	3	TOTAL
Units made	26,000	41,000	0	
Plastic per unit	2	1	3	
Units of plastic	52,000	41,000	0	93,000
Cost of plastic	$5,200.00	$4,100.00	$0.00	$9,300.00
Run-time work per unit	0.01	0.005	0.04	
Total run-time labor hours	260	205	0	465
Units per batch	5,200	4,100	500	
Batches	5	10	0	
Labor hours per batch	10	15	20	
Total batch labor hours	50	150	0	200
Total labor hours	310	355	0	665
Total cost of labor used				$16,625.00
Total cost of labor paid				$37,500.00
Cost excess capacity (cost of unused labor)				$20,875.00
Total cost				$46,800.00

of abandonment costs, which are the costs an organization incurs when it stops using a resource (such as a mine) or stops making a product. Therefore, in the short run, costs will decline only by the amount of the plastic cost avoided, which is $2,400 ($8,000 × $0.30).

In month 3 of the contract—and recognizing that the labor costs are committed—management decides to expand the production of products 1 and 2. We know from our previous discussion that plastic costs will increase as production of products 1 and 2 increases but that labor costs will remain fixed at the level of $37,500. The only issue facing management is that the demand for labor of scheduled production cannot exceed the 1,500 hours that are available under the contract. Exhibit 2-21 shows that the constraint of 1,500 labor hours is not exceeded. Note that only the cost of plastic has increased to reflect the increased production level. Labor costs have not increased. These are committed costs that will remain unchanged until the end of the 6-month period, when they will be renegotiated.

Does this mean that, for planning purposes, organization decision makers should assume that labor costs are zero for product 1 and product 2? Certainly not. While the incremental costs of increasing the production levels of product 1 and product 2 reflect only the cost of plastic, in the long run when the contract for labor is renegotiated and when organization decision makers are deciding whether to continue making products 1 and 2, the price of these products will have to cover all costs, including the cost of labor. This is the reason why product pricing decisions are based on long-run costs, which include fixed costs, and this also is the reason that product costing must reflect the underlying issue of cost behavior. This issue is explored in chapter 4.

The important message of this example is that there is a clear difference between the cost of acquiring and the cost of using different resources. For some resources, the cost to the organization is proportional to how much is purchased, whether or not it is used. For other resources, the cost to the organization is proportional to how much is consumed. As is shown in chapter 4, for purposes of decision making about products,

	PRODUCT			
	1	2	3	TOTAL
Units made	40,000	80,000	0	
Plastic per unit	2	1	3	
Units of plastic	80,000	80,000	0	160,000
Cost of plastic	$8,000.00	$8,000.00	$0.00	$16,000.00
Run-time work per unit	0.01	0.005	0.04	
Total run-time labor hours	400	400	0	800
Units per batch	5,000	4,000	500	
Batches	8	20	0	
Labor hours per batch	10	15	20	
Total batch labor hours	80	300	0	380
Total labor hours	480	700	0	1180
Total cost of labor used				$29,500.00
Total cost of labor paid				$37,500.00
Cost excess capacity (cost of unused labor)				$8,000.00
Total cost				$53,500.00

costing systems take a long-run perspective and treat all costs as if they are proportional to the amount that is used. This may serve the needs of some decisions, but treating costs this way can be misleading when the same information is used to develop budgets or to evaluate cost performance. This issue is taken up in detail in chapter 10.

Nonmanufacturing Costs as Product Costs

Although we have mentioned nonmanufacturing costs, most of our discussion has focused on manufacturing costs. This preoccupation with manufacturing costs is the legacy of external reporting, which places most of its attention on isolating and classifying product related costs because of their importance in inventory valuation.

The issue is quite different for management accountants. Although manufacturing costs often are the most significant component of total costs, nonmanufacturing costs, such as the costs of research and development, marketing, selling, and logistical activities, are large and growing in many organizations because of the demands that increased competition places on organizations. There is an increasing recognition that the management of nonmanufacturing costs is an important contributor to the organization's financial success.

Like manufacturing costs, nonmanufacturing costs include both flexible and capacity-related components. Traditionally, management accountants have looked at nonmanufacturing costs as a large pool of costs that should be managed by periodic budget appropriations. For example, expenditures on items such as advertising are determined by what we can afford rather than by the mission we have to accomplish with advertising.

The nonmanufacturing costs that have attracted the most attention are customer-related costs. These include the cost of selling the product to the customer, putting the product in the customer's hands, and providing after-sales support to the customer. These costs can be significant, and they can vary widely from customer to customer.

Many organizations have thus begun to undertake what they call **customer accounting** to determine the profitability of dealing with different customers or different types of customers. Customer accounting systems have caused some organizations to abandon certain customers or to provide differential service fees based on the services that customers demand. Because many customer services are proportional to the number of customers rather than the quantity of purchases (recall the billing and meter reading example earlier in this chapter), the effect of replacing traditional costing systems with customer accounting has been to shift costs back from big customers to the smaller customers that create those costs.

Because we need to start somewhere, because manufacturing costs are large, and because we need to avoid overwhelming you with detail, this chapter has focused on manufacturing costs. However, you should remember that nonmanufacturing costs are important and are now attracting considerable attention in many organizations.

EVALUATING PROFIT PERFORMANCE AT LYNN'S LANDSCAPING SERVICES

Returning to Lynn's Landscaping Services, we are now in a position to think about some of the company's problems.

Several hints might suggest the problem. First, Lynn has the layout design business to herself, and her fees are not a problem for potential customers. Since there do not appear to be large barriers to entering this business, a lack of competitors suggests that other landscapers believe that the layout design business is unprofitable at the prices that Lynn is charging. Either Lynn is much more efficient than her competitors, or she is seriously underestimating her costs. So the culprit may be the way allocated costs are being handled, and a careful study of those costs is needed. Suppose that an analysis of allocated costs reveals the information shown in Exhibit 2-22. The costs of $300,000 reflect the general business costs (rent on a building where Lynn stores her equipment, telephone costs, and billing costs) of about $40,000. The rest of the costs are equipment costs. Moreover, it turns out that none of the equipment, except the trucks (which are shared equally by all businesses), is used in more than one segment of the business.

The allocation rates are computed by dividing the activity cost by the capacity. The allocation amount is computed by multiplying the allocation rate by the capacity used.

The analysis of the equipment used in the business identified that the layout design business used some expensive equipment that tended to reduce labor costs in that division at the expense of higher machine costs. In particular, the equipment included a small earthmoving machine and grader, which accounted for the majority of the costs in this division.

Exhibit 2-22
Lynn's Landscaping Services

	RESOURCE USE INFORMATION				
	COST	CAPACITY	RATE	USED	ALLOCATION
Trucks and related costs	$40,000	800	$50	600	$30,000
Lawn mowing equipment	$30,000	1,500	$20	1200	$24,000
Layout design equipment	$120,000	400	$300	400	$120,000
Other maintenance equipment	$70,000	700	$100	500	$50,000

	LAWN MOWING	LAYOUT DESIGN	OTHER MAINTENANCE	TOTAL
Revenues	$230,000	$175,000	$250,000	$655,000
Direct costs	125,000	56,000	145,000	326,000
Margin	$105,000	$119,000	$105,000	$329,000
Cost of used capacity				
•Own equipment	24,000	120,000	50,000	194,000
•Trucks	10,000	10,000	10,000	30,000
Cost of unused own capacity	6,000	0	20,000	26,000
Unit profit	$65,000	−$11,000	$25,000	$79,000
Cost of unused shared capacity				10,000
Business-sustaining costs				40,000
Organization profit				$29,000

With this information, the original profit information can be recast as in Exhibit 2-23. Note that the unit profit numbers do not include the $40,000 of basic business costs and the $10,000 of unused truck capacity costs because there is no practical way of allocating these costs to any one of the three lines of business. They must be covered by the margins created by each of the three business lines.

Now that fixed costs have been properly attributed to each of the three operating businesses, we have a very different picture of this organization. First, we see that cutting back efforts on lawn mowing and other maintenance, as Lynn did, was ill-advised. Both units have unused capacity that continue to create the same level of costs as the activity level declines. The layout design business is a big loser and the major drain on profits in this business. The costs of the specialized equipment are evidently not being reflected in prices charged for this work. This confirms the original suspicion that Lynn's prices are so low that they are encouraging demand and discouraging competition.

Lynn needs to raise prices on the layout design business and increase volume in the high-margin lawn mowing and other maintenance components of her business to better use available capacity.

SUMMARY

This chapter introduced the important idea of "different costs for different purposes." This idea means that there is no one single best way to compute cost. The appropriate cost calculation reflects how a decision maker will use the cost.

Generally accepted accounting principles (GAAP), which provide financial information for people outside the organization, prescribe how costs should be computed for external reporting. GAAP reflects the need for consistency in reporting because we are unsure how people use the cost information in financial reports. Because GAAP treats only manufacturing costs as product costs, it includes no selling, general, or administrative costs in the reported product cost.

Decision makers inside the organization use cost information in many different ways, resulting in many different approaches to computing cost. In cost-volume-profit analysis, which we saw is an approach to financial modeling, the implicit definition of cost is total variable (or variable) cost, which includes the cost of all flexible resources (manufacturing and nonmanufacturing) incurred to make the good or service. This provides a sharp counterpoint to the GAAP notion of cost, which includes only manufacturing costs.

The discussion in the chapter used the example of computing the costs of flying a person from London to Zurich to illustrate the many different uses—and therefore calculations—of cost information. Again, we saw how the context of the decision defines the appropriate definition and calculation of cost.

The chapter introduced the important notion of opportunity cost, which is the opportunity or return that a multipurpose asset forgoes when it is used in a particular project.

The chapter also discussed the ideas of short-run and long-run costs, which parallel the economist's notion of short- and long-run marginal costs. The critical importance of the concept of short-run cost is that it reflects the costs that can be adjusted by decisions made in the short-run. Short-run cost computations exclude fixed costs because they are fixed in place and cannot be changed by decisions in the short-run. However, long-run cost estimates include fixed costs because management accountants assume that, in the long run, all costs are subject to change.

The extended example of Fred's Grocery Services illustrates how organizations create costs and the various definitions of cost provided in the chapter—thereby providing a summary of the cost concepts introduced to that point in the chapter.

The chapter then turned to consider how unit- and batch-related and product-, customer-, and business-sustaining activities related can create organization costs and provided an important introduction to cost behavior that modifies and extends the notions of variable and fixed costs introduced early in the chapter.

KEY TERMS

Batch-related activities, 60
Breakeven equation, 39
Business-sustaining
  activities, 62
Capacity-related resources, 33
Channel-sustaining
  activities, 62
Contribution margin, 39
Cost, 28
Cost object, 31

Cost-volume-profit (CVP)
  analysis, 38
Customer accounting, 66
Customer-sustaining activities, 62
Direct cost, 35
Fixed cost, 33
Flexible resources, 33
Generally accepted accounting
  principles (GAAP), 29
Indirect cost, 36

Long run, 52
Manufacturing costs, 30
Opportunity cost, 50
Product costs, 29
Product-sustaining activities, 60
Short run, 52
  Unit-related activities, 59
Variable costs, 33

ASSIGNMENT MATERIALS

Questions

2-1 What are some different uses of cost information? (LO 1)

2-2 Why do different types of cost information need to be reported to support different managerial purposes and decisions? (LO 1)

2-3 What is a cost object? (LO 1)

2-4 How is it possible to distinguish direct costs from indirect costs? (LO 2)

2-5 Explain the difference between variable costs and fixed costs. (LO 3)

2-6 Are variable costs always direct costs? (LO 2, 3)

2-7 Are fixed costs always indirect costs? (LO 2, 3)

2-8 How are costs in a manufacturing firm classified for external reporting? (LO 1, 4)

2-9 Describe the difference between costs and expenses. (LO 1)

2-10 What are the two principal categories into which manufacturing costs are classified? (LO 1, 2)

2-11 Why do traditional cost accounting systems tend to analyze manufacturing costs in greater detail than they do other functional categories of costs? (LO 1)

2-12 What are two broad purposes for which costs are used inside an organization? (LO 1)

2-13 What does the term *contribution margin per unit* mean? How is the contribution margin used in cost analysis to support managerial decisions? **(LO 3)**

2-14 What does the term *breakeven point* mean? **(LO 3)**

2-15 Explain why you agree or disagree with the following statement: "An organization should have the most accurate and complete cost system possible." **(LO 1)**

2-16 What is an opportunity cost? **(LO 5)**

2-17 What is the distinction between short-run costs and long-run costs? **(LO 6)**

2-18 How has the composition of manufacturing costs changed in recent years? How has this change affected the design of cost accounting systems? **(LO 1, 3, 7)**

2-19 What are the five categories of production activities? Explain the differences among them. **(LO 1, 3, 7)**

2-20 Why have customer-related costs attracted increasing attention in recent years? **(LO 1, 3, 7)**

Exercises

LO 1, 2, 4   **2-21** *Cost classification by function*   Classify each of the following costs as manufacturing or nonmanufacturing:
  a. direct labor
  b. sales commissions
  c. depreciation on delivery trucks
  d. salary and bonus for the chief executive officer
  e. direct materials
  f. product design staff salaries
  g. advertising
  h. property taxes on the corporate headquarters building
  i. gas and electricity for the factory
  j. accounting-office staff salaries
  k. operators of product help lines for customers
  l. customer credit evaluation staff salaries

LO 1, 2, 4   **2-22** *Components of manufacturing costs*   Classify each of the following manufacturing costs as direct or indirect for automobiles:
  a. insurance on manufacturing equipment
  b. cost of steel plates used in making an automobile body
  c. wages of assembly workers
  d. salaries of plant security personnel
  e. cost of tires
  f. overtime premiums paid to assembly workers
  g. depreciation on the factory building
  h. cost of electric power to operate machines
  i. production workers' holiday and vacation pay benefits
  j. wages of materials-handling workers
  k. cost of seats placed in automobiles
  l. quality inspection costs

LO 1, 4, 7   **2-23** *Cost classification by activity type*   Classify the following costs as unit-related, batch-related, product-sustaining, or business-sustaining activity costs:
  a. direct materials
  b. setup labor wages
  c. salaries of plant engineers responsible for executing engineering change orders
  d. corporate office building depreciation
  e. direct labor wages
  f. purchase order clerk wages
  g. product design engineer salaries
  h. rent for plant building
  i. quality inspection of first item produced in each batch
  j. moving materials from one machine to the next

k. accounting

l. sales support for individual products

LO 1, 4, 7   **2-24** *Cost classification by activity type*   Classify the following costs as unit-related, batch-related, product-sustaining, or business-sustaining activity costs:

a. packing labor wages

b. materials-handling labor wages

c. part administrators' salaries

d. plant management salaries

e. production scheduling staff salaries

f. cost of servicing production equipment, based on hours used

g. property taxes for a plant site

h. production expediters' salaries

i. insurance for plant facility

j. plant security

k. production workers' training

l. cost of electricity to run production equipment

LO 3   **2-25** *Classification of variable and fixed costs*   Classify each of the following as a variable or fixed cost with respect to a unit of production:

a. salaries of production supervisors

b. steel used in automobile production

c. wood used in furniture production

d. charges for janitorial services

e. commissions paid to sales personnel

f. advertising expenses

g. salaries of billing clerks

h. gasoline used to deliver products

i. lubricants for machines

j. maintenance for production equipment, based on volume produced

k. maintenance for production equipment, performed every month

LO 3   **2-26** *Classification of variable and fixed costs*   Classify each of the following as a variable or fixed cost with respect to a unit of production:

a. paper used in newspaper production

b. wages of production workers

c. salary of the chief executive officer

d. glue used in furniture production

e. depreciation of factory equipment

f. depreciation of shipping truck

g. electricity used to operate machines

h. boxes used for packing products

i. rent for factory building

j. factory insurance

LO 3, 4   **2-27** *Breakeven analysis for a hospital*   Murillo Medical Institute operates a 100-bed hospital and offers a number of specialized medical services. Murillo's hospital facility and equipment are leased on a long-term basis. The hospital charges $100 per patient day. On the basis of past cost data, Murillo has estimated its variable costs as $45.70 per patient day. Fixed costs are $91,000 per month. The hospital's administrator has estimated that the hospital will average 2,300 patient days per month.

Required

a. How much will the hospital need to charge per patient day to break even at this level of activity?

b. Refer to the original data in the problem. How many patient days must Murillo average each month to earn a target profit of $45,000 per month?

2-28 *Breakeven analysis*   Preston Parkas Company's sales revenue is $30 per unit, variable costs are $19.50 per unit, and fixed costs are $147,000.

Required

a. What is Preston's contribution margin per unit?
b. Determine the number of units Preston must sell to break even.
c. Determine the sales revenue required to earn (pretax) income equal to 20% of revenue.
d. Preston is considering increasing its advertising expenses by $38,500. How much of an increase in sales units is necessary from expanded advertising to justify this expenditure?

LO 3, 4   **2-29** *Income statement, breakeven analysis, target profit*   Last year, Able Co. sold all the goods it produced (it had no finished goods inventories), and sales revenues were $1,260,000. It recorded the following costs for the year:

	Manufacturing Costs	Selling and Administrative Costs	Total
Variable	$420,000	$150,000	$570,000
Fixed	220,500	260,000	$480,500
Total	$640,500	$410,000	$1,050,500

Required

a. Prepare a financial reporting income statement (that is, in the form required under GAAP for U.S. external reporting).
b. Determine income in the manner used in cost-volume-profit analysis (that is, using equation 2.2).
c. At what sales dollar level will Able earn a before-tax target profit of $250,000?
d. At what sales dollar level will Able break even?

LO 3   **2-30** *Multiple-product breakeven analysis*   Florida Favorites Company produces toy alligators and toy dolphins. Fixed costs are $1,290,000 per year. Sales revenue and variable costs per unit are as follow:

	Alligators	**Dolphins**
Sales price	$20	$25
Variable costs	8	10

Required

a. Suppose the company currently sells 140,000 alligators per year and 60,000 dolphins per year. Assuming the sales mix stays constant, how many alligators and dolphins must the company sell to break even per year?
b. Suppose the company currently sells 60,000 alligators per year and 140,000 dolphins per year. Assuming the sales mix stays constant, how many alligators and dolphins must the company sell to break even per year?
c. Explain why the total number of toys needed to break even in (a) is the same as or different from the number in (b).

LO 1, 2, 3, 5   **2-31** *Opportunity cost*   Healthy Hearth specializes in lunches for the health conscious. The company produces a small selection of lunch offerings each day. The menu selections may vary from day to day, but Healthy Hearth charges the same price per menu selection because it adjusts the portion sizes according to the cost of producing the selection. Healthy Hearth currently sells 5,000 meals per month. Variable costs are $3 per meal, and fixed costs total $5,000 per month. A government agency has recently proposed that

Healthy Hearth provide 1,000 meals next month for senior citizens at $3.50 per meal. Volunteers will deliver the meals to the senior citizens at no charge.

Required

a. Suppose Healthy Hearth has sufficient idle capacity to accommodate the government order for next month. What will be the impact on Healthy Hearth's operating income if it accepts this order?

b. Suppose that Healthy Hearth would have to give up regular sales of 500 meals, at a price of $4.50 each, to accommodate the government order for next month. What will be the impact on Healthy Hearth's operating income if it accepts the government order?

LO 1, 3, 7   **2-32 *Customer-related costs*** Nehls Company is concerned about its growing customer-related expenses. The company currently allocates customer fixed support costs on the basis of revenues at a rate of 30% of sales revenue. After discovering that ordering patterns vary quite dramatically across customers, it proposed a more accurate method that would assign costs of $35 per order. Following are the data on two customers:

	Customer 1	Customer 2
Sales	$1,200	$1,200
Cost of goods sold	750	750
Number of orders per year	2	12

Required

a. Compute the customer fixed support costs assigned to customers 1 and 2 under the current system.

b. Compute the customer fixed support costs assigned to customers 1 and 2 under the proposed system.

c. Comment on what the two systems reveal about the profitability of customers 1 and 2.

Problems

LO 1, 2, 5   **2-33 *Cost classification and target profit*** Bart's Woodwork Company makes and sells wooden shelves. Bart's carpenters make the shelves in the company's rented building. Bart has a separate office at another location that also includes a showroom where customers can view sample shelves and ask questions of salespeople. The company sells all the shelves it produces each year. Assume the company keeps no inventories. The following information pertains to Bart's Woodwork Company for the past year:

a. Units produced and sold	50,000
b. Sales price per unit	$70
c. Carpenter labor to make shelves	600,000
d. Wood to make the shelves	450,000
e. Sales staff salaries	80,000
f. Office and showroom rental expenses	150,000
g. Depreciation on carpentry equipment	50,000
h. Advertising	200,000
i. Sales commissions based on number of units sold	180,000
j. Miscellaneous fixed manufacturing overhead (support)	150,000
k. Rent for the building where the shelves are made	300,000

| l. Miscellaneous variable manufacturing overhead (support) | 350,000 |
| m. Depreciation for office equipment | 10,000 |

Required

a. Based on this information, prepare a financial accounting income statement (that is, in the form required under GAAP for U.S. external reporting).

b. For this information, make appropriate assumptions about cost behavior and assume that direct labor costs vary directly with the number of units produced. How many units must the company sell in order to earn a pretax profit of $500,000?

LO 4   **2-34** *Cost-benefit considerations in developing cost information*   JF Company is considering whether to undertake a new project but is unsure of the ultimate cost of the new project. The company estimates that the cost will be $150,000 with probability 0.4 and will be $200,000 with probability 0.6. The estimated revenues from the project are $170,000. JF can hire a consulting company that will identify whether the actual cost will be $150,000 or $200,000. In other words, the information is perfect.

Required

a. If JF does not hire the consulting company to determine the actual cost and would like to undertake the new project only if the expected value of the profit is positive, should the company undertake the project?

b. How much will JF be willing to pay to hire the consulting company to determine the actual cost?

LO 1, 2, 4, 7   **2-35** *Cost classification*   The L.A. Dress Shop produces custom-designed dresses for retail sales on the premises. The shop sold 50 dresses last month. Costs incurred during the last month include the following:

Cost of fabric used in dresses	$60,000
Wages of dressmakers	5,000
Wages of dress designers	4,000
Wages of sales personnel	1,000
Wages of designers who experiment with new fabrics and dress designs	3,000
Wages of the employee who repairs the shop's pattern and sewing machines	2,000
Salary of the owner's assistant	1,200
Cost of the new sign displayed in front of the retail shop	400
Cost of electricity used in the pattern department	200
Depreciation on pattern machines and sewing machines	10,000
Cost of advertisements in local media	800
Cost of hiring a plane and a pilot to fly along the beach pulling a banner advertising the shop	1,400
Cost of insurance for the production employees	2,000
Rent for the building	6,000

Apportion the rent into different categories based on the following facts:

Half of the building's first floor is used for administrative offices.

The other half of it is used for a retail sales shop.

The second floor is used for making dresses and storing of raw material.

Required

a. Classify these costs into one of the following categories: direct materials costs, direct labor costs, indirect manufacturing costs, selling costs, marketing costs, research-and-development costs, and general and administrative costs. What is the total cost for each category?

b. Classify the costs as unit-related, batch-related, product-sustaining, or business-sustaining costs. What is the total cost for each category?

LO 1, 3, 7   **2-36**   *Cost behavior, cost classifications*   Shannon O'Reilly is trying to decide whether to continue to take public transportation to work or to purchase a car. Before making her decision, she would like to compare the cost of using public transportation and the cost of driving a car.

Required

a. What activity measure should Shannon use as she estimates the cost of driving?

b. What should Shannon view as incremental (variable or out-of-pocket) costs of driving from home to work?

c. What are some fixed costs of driving a car?

d. Suppose that if Shannon purchased a car, she would use it to take a 2-week scenic vacation by car. What activity measures might Shannon use to estimate her vacation and lodging expenses?

LO 1, 3, 7   **2-37**   *Single drivers versus multiple drivers*   Eagan Electrical Instruments Company estimates manufacturing support as 950% of direct labor costs. Eagan's controller, Jim Chang, is concerned that the actual manufacturing support activity costs have differed substantially from the estimates in recent months. He suspects that the problem is related to the use of only one cost driver. Jim identified the following three additional cost drivers that reflect support activities: number of material moves, number of setups, and number of machine hours. He developed the following rates to estimate manufacturing support activity costs:

Multiple Cost Driver System

100% of direct labor cost
$200 per move
$300 per setup
$20 per machine hour

Information for 2 recent months includes the following:

Cost and Quantity	May	June
Direct labor cost	$3,000	$4,200
Number of material moves	50	70
Number of setups	30	40
Number of machine hours	1,000	1,200

Required

a. Estimate manufacturing support costs using the single-driver and multiple-driver systems.

b. Why do the two sets of estimates differ?

c. Why will both methods fail to predict accurately the manufacturing support costs? Is one of the two methods likely to be more useful than the other? Explain.

2-38 *Cost classification*   Poker's is a small hamburger shop catering mainly to students at a nearby university. It is open for business from 11:00 A.M. until 11:00 P.M., Monday through Friday. The owner, Chip Poker, employs two cooks, one server, and a part-time janitor. Because there is no space for dining inside the shop, all orders are takeout orders. Poker's sold 10,000 hamburgers last month. The average hamburger requires 1 hamburger bun, 8 ounces of meat, 4 ounces of cheese, one-eighth a head of lettuce, and $0.07 worth of other ingredients. Costs incurred during the last month include the following:

Meat	$5,000
Cheese	1,000
Bread	800
Lettuce	600
Other ingredients	700
Cooks' wages	5,000
Server's wages	1,500
Janitor's wages	600
Utilities	500
Depreciation on cooking equipment	300
Paper supplies (napkins and bags)	200
Rent	600
Advertisement in local newspaper	300

Required

a. Classify these costs into one of the following categories: direct materials, direct labor, indirect support costs, selling costs, and marketing costs. What is the total cost for each category?
b. Classify the costs as unit-related, batch-related, product-sustaining, or business-sustaining costs. What is the total cost for each category?

LO 1, 2, 3, 5   **2-39** *Cost behavior and decisions*   Second City Airlines operates 35 scheduled round-trip flights each week between New York and Chicago. It charges a fixed one-way fare of $200 per passenger. Second City Airlines can carry 150 passengers per one-way flight. Fuel and other flight-related costs are $5,000 per one-way flight. On-flight meal and refreshment costs average $5 per passenger. Flight crew, ground crew, advertising, and other administrative expenditures for the New York-to-Chicago route amount to $400,000 each week.

Required

a. How many passengers must each of the 70 one-way flights have on average to break even each week?
b. If the load factor is 60% on all flights (that is, the flights are 60% full), how many flights must Second City Airlines operate on this route to earn a total profit of $500,000 per week?
c. Are fuel costs variable or fixed?
d. What is the variable cost to Second City Airlines for one additional passenger on a flight if the passenger takes a seat that would otherwise go empty?

LO 3   **2-40** *Breakeven point, competitive contribution margin analysis*   Johnson Company and Smith Company are the two competing firms offering limousine service from the Charlesburg airport. While Johnson pays most of its employees

Exhibit 2-24
Competing
Limousine Service
Bids from
Charlesburg
Airport: Per-Ride
Data

Cost Category	Johnson Company	Smith Company
Selling price	$30	$30
Variable cost	24	15
Contribution margin	6	15
Fixed costs per year	$300,000	$1,500,000

on a per-ride basis, Smith prefers to pay its employees fixed salaries. Information about the cost structures of the two firms is given in Exhibit 2-24.

Required

a. Calculate the breakeven point in the number of rides for both firms.
b. Draw two graphs plotting profit as a function of the number of rides for the two firms.
c. Explain which firm's cost structure is more profitable.
d. Explain which firm's cost structure is riskier.

LO 3   **2-41 *Multiple breakeven points*** In September 2006, Capetini Capacitor Company sold capacitors to its distributors for $250 per capacitor. The sales level of 3,000 capacitors per month was less than the single-shift capacity of 4,400 capacitors at its plant located in San Diego. Variable production costs were $100 per capacitor, and fixed production costs were $200,000 per month. In addition, variable selling and distribution support costs are $20 per capacitor, and fixed selling and distribution support costs are $62,500 per month. At the suggestion of the marketing department, in October 2006, Capetini reduced the sales price to $200 and increased the monthly advertising budget by $17,500. Sales are expected to increase to 6,800 capacitors per month. If the demand exceeds the single-shift capacity of 4,400 capacitors, the plant needs to be operated in two shifts. Two-shift operation will increase monthly fixed production costs to $310,000.

Required

a. Determine the contribution margin per capacitor in September 2006.
b. Determine the sales level in number of capacitors at which the profit-to-sales ratio would be 10% in September 2006.
c. Determine the two breakeven points for October 2006.
d. Determine the sales level in number of capacitors at which the profit-to-sales ratio in October is the same as the actual profit-to-sales ratio in September. Is there more than one possible sales level at which this equality would occur?

LO 1, 2, 3   **2-42 *Commitment and consumption of activity resources*** Capilano Containers Company specializes in making high-quality customized containers to order. Its agreement with the labor union ensures employment for all its employees and a fixed payroll of $80,000 per month, including fringe benefits. This payroll makes available 4,000 labor hours each month to work on orders the firm receives. The monthly wages must be paid even if the workers remain idle because of a lack of work. If additional labor hours are required to complete jobs, overtime costs $30 per labor hour.

Each job requires 4 labor hours for machine setup and 0.05 labor hours per container. Variable costs are $1.60 per container for materials and $8.00

per labor hour for manufacturing support expenses. In addition, the firm must pay $20,000 per month for selling, general, and administrative expenses and $36,000 per month lease payments for machinery and physical facilities. In April, the firm won 90 orders, of which 60 were for 800 containers each and 30 for 1,600 containers each. Determine the total costs for April.

LO 1, 2, 3, 7   **2-43** *Planning activity workloads*   The Abby Corporation, a chain of department stores, estimates the standard workload at its retail outlets in terms of the time required for the activities of (1) hanging new inventory; (2) selling merchandise; (3) handling complaints, inquiries, and returns; (4) taking markdowns; and (5) counting inventory. The following are the estimated average times for each of these five activities:

Activity	Average Time Required
Hanging new inventory	1 minute per piece hanged (HANG)
Selling merchandise	10 minutes per customer (CUST)
Handling complaints and returns	15 minutes per complaint (CMPL)
Taking markdowns	2 minutes per piece marked down (MARK)
Counting inventory	0.5 minutes per piece counted (COUN)

The Abby Corporation uses these workload estimates to plan its staffing levels. Past experience indicates that it needs to provide for about 30% more time than the standard workload estimate to ensure satisfactory customer service. The Abby Corporation has a policy of hiring only full-time sales consultants working 40 hours a week. The following information shows the estimated quantities of the five activities for the 4 weeks in June:

WEEK	HANG	CUST	CMPL	MARK	COUN
1	5,000	4,500	500	400	1,000
2	6,000	5,000	400	300	1,400
3	5,500	4,800	600	500	1,500
4	6,200	5,500	550	600	2,000

Required

Determine the number of full-time equivalent sales consultants needed in each of these 4 weeks.

LO 1, 2, 3, 7   **2-44** *Commitment of activity resources*   Crown Cable Company provides cable television service in the Richfield metropolitan area. The company hires only full-time service persons working 40 hours a week at $18 per hour, including fringe benefits. Service persons handle additional service demand by working overtime at the rate of $24 per hour. The service manager uses standards for estimating the workload and staffing requirements. Each service person can handle an average of six calls in an 8-hour work day. The estimated number of service calls for the first 3 weeks of next month follow:

Week	Service Calls
1	1,280
2	1,340
3	1,200

Required

a. Determine the number of service persons that will be hired in each of these 3 weeks to minimize costs.

b. Estimate the service labor cost for each of the 3 weeks.

c. Suppose that the company cannot change the staffing level from week to week. Estimate the service labor costs, assuming that the same number (38, 39, 40, 41, 42, 43, 44, or 45) of workers is hired for all 3 weeks. How much do costs increase under this restriction?

LO 1, 2, 3, 4, 5   **2-45** *Profitability, opportunity cost*   Dawson Company produces and sells 80,000 boxes of specialty foods each year. Each box contains the same assortment of food. The company has computed the following annual costs:

COST ITEM	TOTAL COSTS
Variable production costs	$ 400,000
Fixed production costs	480,000
Variable selling costs	320,000
Fixed selling and administrative costs	200,000
Total costs	$1,400,000

Dawson normally charges $25 per box. A new distributor has offered to purchase 8,000 boxes at a special price of $22 per box. Dawson will incur additional packaging costs of $1 per box to complete this order.

Required

a. Suppose Dawson has surplus capacity to produce 8,000 more boxes. What will be the effect on Dawson's income if it accepts this order?

b. Suppose that instead of having surplus capacity to produce 8,000 more boxes, Dawson has surplus capacity to produce only 3,000 more boxes. What will be the effect on Dawson's income if it accepts the new order for 8,000 boxes?

LO 1, 2, 3, 4, 5   **2-46** *Capacity level, profitability, opportunity cost*   Wedmark Corporation's Cupertino, California, plant manufactures chips used in personal computers. Its practical capacity is 2,000 chips per week, and fixed costs are $75,000 per week. The selling price is $500 per chip. Production this quarter is 1,600 chips per week. At this level of production, variable costs are $720,000.

Required

a. What will the plant's profit per week be if it operates at practical capacity?

b. If the plant's accounting system allocates fixed cost using a rate based on its practical capacity level as the base, what is the reported cost per unit?

c. Suppose that a new customer offers $480 per chip for an order of 200 chips per week for delivery beginning this quarter. If this order is accepted, production will increase from 1,600 chips at present to 1,800 chips per week. What is the estimated change in the company's profit if it accepts the order?

d. Suppose that the new customer in (c) offered $480 per chip for an order of 600 chips per week and that Wedmark cannot schedule overtime production. Consequently, it would have to give up some of its current sales to fill the new order for 600 chips per week. What is the estimated change in Wedmark's profit if it accepts this order for 600 chips per week?

Cases

2-47 *Flexibility in committing activity resources* Dr. Barbara Benson is the head of the pathology laboratory at Barrington Medical Center in Mobile, Alabama. Dr. Benson estimates the amount of work for her laboratory staff by classifying the pathology tests into three categories: simple routine, simple nonroutine, and complex. She expects a simple routine test to require 2 hours, a simple nonroutine test to require 2.5 hours, and a complex test to require 4 hours of staff time. She estimates the demand for each type of test for June through August to be the following:

Month	Simple Routine	Simple Nonroutine	Complex
June	800	250	450
July	600	200	400
August	750	225	450

Laboratory staff salaries, including fringe benefits, average $3,600 per month. Each worker works 150 hours per month. If the hospital workload exceeds the available staff time, Dr. Benson has the tests performed at a neighboring private pathology laboratory that charges $80 for a simple routine test, $100 for a simple nonroutine test, and $160 for a complex test.

Dr. Benson is thinking of employing 20 to 27 workers. Because of the difficulty in hiring reliable workers, Barrington's chief administrator has instructed her to employ laboratory staff for at least one quarter.

Required

a. Determine how many workers Dr. Benson should employ over the quarter to minimize the costs of performing the tests. What is the minimum cost?
b. Suppose the easy availability of experienced laboratory staff allows Barrington Medical Center to change staffing loads each month. Determine the number of workers Dr. Benson should hire each month in these circumstances to minimize the costs of performing tests. What is the minimum cost?

2-48 *Commitment and consumption of activity resources* Steelmax, Inc., sells office furniture in the Chicago metropolitan area. To better serve its business customers, Steelmax recently introduced a new same-day service. Any order placed before 2:00 P.M. is delivered the same day.

Steelmax hires five workers on an 8-hour daily shift to deliver the office furniture. Each delivery takes 30 minutes on average. If the number of customer orders exceeds the available capacity on some days, workers are asked to work overtime to ensure that all customer orders are delivered the same day. Regular wages are $12 per hour. Overtime wages include a 50% premium in addition to the regular wages.

Steelmax's management has noticed considerable fluctuation in the number of customer orders from day to day over the past 3 months, as shown here:

Day of the Week	Average Number of Orders
Monday	65
Tuesday	70
Wednesday	80
Thursday	85
Friday	95

Steelmax has decided to pursue a more variable hiring policy. It will reduce the number of delivery workers to four on Mondays and Tuesdays and increase the number to six on Fridays.

Required

a. Determine the total and unit delivery cost per day under the old hiring policy when the number of daily customer orders is 70, 80, or 90.

b. For each day of the week, determine the expected total delivery cost per day and the expected delivery cost per customer order based on both the old and the new hiring policy. What is the expected savings per week with the new variable hiring policy?

LO 1, 2, 3, 5 **2-49 Commitment and consumption of activity resources, multiple-product breakeven point** Loren's Lawn and Gardening performs various lawn and garden maintenance activities, including lawn mowing, tree and shrub pruning, fertilizing, and treating for pests. Unlike other lawn and garden businesses in the city, Loren also specializes in landscape design and planting. Loren is pleased that his design specialty is so much in demand. However, he is concerned because profits have been falling, even though sales have been growing over the past few years. In an effort to better understand why profits are falling, Loren prepared the following product-line income statement:

LOREN'S LAWN AND GARDEN PRODUCT-LINE INCOME STATEMENT

	LAWN MOWING	LAYOUT DESIGN	OTHER MAINTENANCE	TOTAL
Revenues	$287,500	$218,750	$312,500	$818,750
Direct costs	$156,250	$ 70,000	$181,250	$407,500
Allocated costs	$131,679	$100,191	$143,130	$375,000
Profit	−$429	$48,559	−$11,880	$36,250

The lawn mowing business involves mowing lawns and trimming edges for customers who generally sign up for the season and pay a flat fee based on the surface area mowed and trimmed. The layout design business involves both designing a garden and lawn layout and installing the design. Other maintenance includes tree and shrub pruning and application of chemicals. The direct costs for each line of business are the costs of the materials and wages of the people who work in that line of business. The remaining costs consist mainly of equipment costs but also include office costs. After some deliberation, Loren decided to allocate the remaining costs of $375,000 on the basis of revenue, reasoning that revenue is a measure of equipment use.

Required

a. Based on this product-line income statement, which business is Loren likely to focus his efforts on? What is the likely result?

A further analysis of the allocated costs produced the information in the following table. General business costs are $50,000, and the remaining $325,000 are equipment costs. The trucks are shared equally by all the segments, but the other equipment is used by only one segment.

	COST	CAPACITY	USED
Trucks and related costs	$50,000	800	600
Lawn mowing equipment	$37,500	1,500	1,200
Layout design equipment	$150,000	400	400
Other maintenance equipment	$87,500	700	500
	$325,000		

b. Prepare a new product-line income statement similar to Exhibit 2-23.

c. What advice do you have for Loren?

d. Suppose Loren currently sells 5,750 units of lawn mowing, 450 units of layout design, and 1,500 units of other maintenance. Assuming the sales mix remains the same, what is Loren's breakeven point in total units of service? Given this breakeven point, what are the associated breakeven points for the individual services?

LO 1, 2, 3, 4, 5   **2-50**   *Value proposition, cost-volume-profit analysis, fixed costs*   Nordstrom, Inc., is an upscale retailer founded in 1901 (see www.nordstrom.com). In Nordstrom's 2001 annual report (p. 7), a sales manager states, "Nordstrom has always been defined by the customer experience—and it's this experience that draws customers in and keeps them coming back." Similarly, an article titled "Nordstrom Accelerates Plans to Straighten Out Business" (*The Wall Street Journal*, October 19, 2001, B4) describes Nordstrom's "glamorous image and highly regarded sales force that once made it a retail success story" but also reports Nordstrom's efforts to battle financial difficulties. Read this article and other sources you can find in order to address the following questions:

a. What is Nordstrom's value proposition as defined in chapter 1 of this textbook?

b. What measures did Nordstrom take to reduce costs? How might these reductions affect Nordstrom's ability to fulfill its value proposition?

c. What fixed costs did Nordstrom incur in hopes of long-term benefits? Can you find reports of Nordstrom enjoying its anticipated benefits?

d. How do Nordstrom's efforts relate to cost-volume-profit analysis?

e. What was Nordstrom's "Reinvent Yourself" campaign, and how successfully did it achieve its objectives? Was any opportunity cost associated with this campaign?

Chapter 3

Traditional Cost Management Systems

After reading this chapter, you will be able to:

➤ determine the difference between direct and indirect costs

➤ understand how job order costing systems work

➤ understand how using job bid sheets is effective for estimating product costs in a job order costing system

➤ use cost driver rates to apply support activity costs to products

➤ discuss why cost systems with multiple cost driver rates give different cost estimates than cost systems with a single rate

➤ evaluate a cost system to understand whether it is likely to distort product costs, explain the importance of recording actual costs, and compare them with estimated costs

➤ appreciate the importance of conversion costs and the measurement of costs in industries using continuous processing

➤ understand the significance of differences between job order costing and multistage process costing systems

➤ understand the two-stage allocation process and service department allocation methods

---

Ken's Auto Service Company

Ken Park started Ken's Auto Service Company in 1983. Over a period of two decades, he built it into a business with more than $1 million in billings each year and a strong reputation for high-quality work. During the past 3 years, however, Ken lost a considerable amount of business to quick-service operations such as Burbank Muffler Company for simple jobs, including exhaust system replacements. Increased competition from companies such as Burbank cut into his sales volume and profit margins, and his take-home income from the business declined precipitously.

Source: Adam Smith/Getty Images.

Ken has expanded his auto shop considerably since its opening. The shop now has five service bays and employs five mechanics, two of whom are highly skilled and trained in doing complex repair jobs. The $60,000 salary and benefits for each expert mechanic exceed the average compensation of the other three mechanics by almost $25,000. The three junior mechanics work primarily on routine repairs, such as brake relinings and muffler replacements.

Ken's accountant, Amy Huang, asked Ken to explain the problem that led to poor financial performance over the past 2 years: "Ken, your net income looks terrible. What has happened to your business?"

Ken responded; "Specialized operators like Burbank Muffler Company have taken away most of my simple repair business with their low prices. How can they price their jobs so low and still make a profit?"

Amy encouraged Ken with this response: "Let me take a look at your job order costing system. I may be able to find the answer to that question." As the consultation with Amy Huang shows, managers today must be able to understand how to calculate the cost of products and services. What costs should be included as part of product costs and why? How should such costs be calculated, accumulated, and reported to decision makers to help them in their planning and operating decisions?

COST MANAGEMENT SYSTEMS

In this and the next chapter, we discuss the topic of cost management systems. Cost management systems have a wide variety of uses, but in these two chapters we focus on their role in measuring the costs of products, services, and customers. Historically, two cost management systems, job order costing and process costing, have been used to cost products and services. Many companies continue to use these two systems. Since the mid-1980s, however, companies have been adopting activity-based costing for product and customer costing. In the past, these three systems have been portrayed as distinct;

however, all cost systems work in essentially the same way. To start, expense categories are developed, and then expenses are matched to service departments, production centers, or activities. In turn, expenses are attached to cost objects. The way these links are made and the activities defined is what really differentiates cost management systems. In this chapter, we focus on the two traditional methods: job order and process costing systems. In chapter 4, we discuss activity-based costing systems.

JOB ORDER AND PROCESS COSTING SYSTEMS

Manufacturing Costs: Direct and Indirect Cost Categories

In traditional manufacturing systems, the costs of producing a product can be broken down into two broad costs: direct and indirect costs. As discussed in chapter 2, a direct cost is a cost of a resource or activity that is acquired for or used by a single cost object, while an indirect cost is the cost of a resource that was acquired to be used by more than one cost object. The most common direct costs are direct materials and direct labor. Indirect costs fall into the category of overhead or support costs.

Direct costs are those that can be easily traced to a cost object, while indirect costs cannot be easily traced to a cost object. Consider a manufacturing facility that produces 100 different types of tin cans. An example of a direct cost in this setting is the amount of tin (direct material) used to produce each can. This amount can be measured and assigned directly to each type of tin can. Contrast this with the salary of a custodian (a support cost) who cleans up the shop floor of the tin can plant. It is extremely difficult (and often infeasible) to determine how much of the custodian's salary should be *assigned* to each type of tin can within the plant. Thus, we call the custodian's salary an indirect cost that has to be allocated to the different types of tin cans.

Allocating overhead or support costs to products is one of the biggest challenges facing organizations today. In the past, many companies simply accumulated all overhead into a single cost pool and allocated it to products on the basis of a single plantwide (single cost driver) rate. Gradually, companies refined this approach and allocated costs on the basis of departmental rates that were more accurate, as the costs of other departments were no longer included in their rates. Finally, in today's manufacturing environment, we see even greater accuracy with an approach called activity-based costing, which we will discuss in chapter 4. As we discuss job order and processing costing systems, we will illustrate how direct and indirect costs are used to determine the unit cost of output and how the choice of cost driver rates is critical for accurate product costing.

A job order costing system estimates the costs of manufacturing products for many different jobs required for specific customer orders. It is applicable in organizations that treat each individual job as a single unit of output. Costs are accumulated and unit costs calculated for each job. For example, a company that makes custom frames to house fine art will use a job order costing system.

In a traditional job order costing system, detailed records are kept of the flow of costs for each job on job cost sheets.[1] The cost flow model essentially uses an

---

[1] There are two traditional forms of product costing known as full absorption and variable costing. Under **full absorption costing,** all production costs, including variable and fixed costs, become product costs. Thus, the cost of a unit of product includes direct labor, direct material, and fixed production costs. In **variable costing**, only variable production costs are included in product costs. Fixed costs are treated as costs of the period and expensed in the period in which they are incurred. Variable costing is also known as marginal costing or direct costing.

inventory concept to track costs, beginning with the raw materials inventory. Over a specific time period, the raw materials are transformed by labor and support resources into work-in-process inventory and then ultimately to finished goods inventory. Work in process represents the costs of the resources for each job not yet completed. Once the goods have been sold, they are accounted for in the expense category known as cost of goods sold. Exhibit 3-1 illustrates the flow of costs in a manufacturing facility.

A process costing system, on the other hand, is applicable when all units produced during a specified time frame are treated as one type of output. All units made during the time period are identical. For example, fiberglass, used for insulation, is produced in large quantities and then cut into individual units. The total amount of fiberglass made during a specified time is the quantity whose overall cost is to be estimated. Individual products that come from the batch produced in that period are then assigned a unit cost. Costs are accumulated by specific departments, and department production reports are the key documents that keep track of costs.

Products may differ in their materials content and the hours of labor and machine time required to make them. Products also may differ in the demand they place on support activity resources (a more traditional term is manufacturing overhead), or in response to special customer needs that may lead to customized production, such as when different product characteristics are targeted for different markets. For example, insulation used in homes in Alaska must, on average,

Exhibit 3-1
Flow of Costs in a Manufacturing Facility

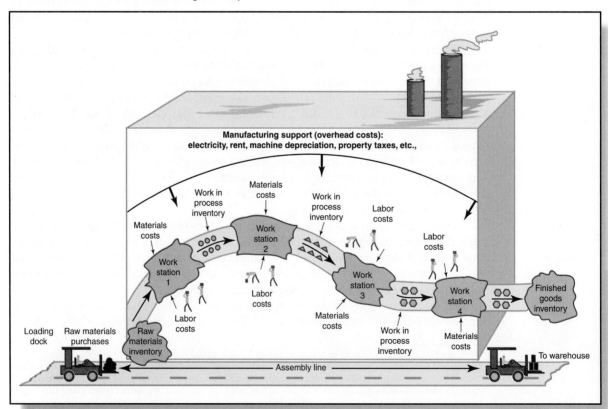

meet more stringent standards than those used in southern California because of climate differences. With such product and customer variety, managers want to understand the costs of individual products so that they can assess product and customer profitability.

Components of a Job Bid Sheet Under Job Order Costing

Many firms are required to bid on jobs before customers decide to place an order with them. To track the flow of costs through a job order costing system, companies use job cost sheets. Costs need to be estimated for each job in order to prepare a bid. Job order costing systems provide the means to estimate these costs.

Exhibit 3-2 displays a job bid sheet, a format for estimating job costs. Famous Flange Company, a manufacturer of a variety of special flanges for several large customers, uses this sheet to bid its jobs. The bid sheet has five distinct panels. Panel 1 identifies the customer, the product, and the quantity of flanges (number of units) required. Panel 2 lists all the materials required to complete the job. For each item of material, the quantity required is estimated on the basis of standard engineering specifications. For example, each unit of flange L181 requires 2.4 pounds of bar steel stock. Therefore, the order for 1,500 units of L181 requires 3,600 pounds of bar steel stock. The current price of $11.30 per pound is obtained from records maintained and updated by the purchasing department. With these inputs, the cost of bar steel stock required for this job can be calculated as $40,680 ($11.30 price per pound $\times$ 3,600 pounds).

Exhibit 3-2
Famous Flange Company: Job Bid Sheet

Panel 1	Bid Number: J4369 Date: July 6, 2006 Customer: Michigan Motors Product: Automobile engine flanges (flange L181) Engineering Design Number JDR-103 Number of Units: 1,500			
	DIRECT MATERIALS	QUANTITY	PRICE	AMOUNT
Panel 2	Bar steel stock	3,600 lb	$11.30	$40,680
	Subassembly	1,500 units	39.00	58,500
	Total direct materials			$99,180
	DIRECT LABOR	HOURS	RATE	AMOUNT
Panel 3	Lathe operators	480	$26.00	$12,480
	Assembly workers	900	18.00	16,200
	Total direct labor	1,380		$28,680
	SUPPORT COSTS			AMOUNT
Panel 4	600 machine hours @ $40 support costs			$24,000
	1,380 direct labor hours @ $36.00 per hour			49,680
	Total support costs			$73,680
	TOTAL COSTS			AMOUNT
Panel 5	Direct materials + direct labor + support costs			$201,540
	Add 25% margin			50,385
	Bid price			$251,925
	Unit cost			$134.36
	Unit price			$167.95

Panel 3 lists the amount of direct labor required for the job. These estimates are obtained from industrial engineering specifications developed on the basis of work and motion studies or by analogy with comparable standard products. As examples, engineering staff at major steel companies study how workers perform each task necessary to make steel to customer specifications so that they can estimate how much time each task requires. Similarly, project managers at software development firms compare new project specifications with projects they have managed previously to estimate the amount of programmer time required to develop new software.

At Famous Flange, industrial engineers have estimated that 0.6 assembly hours are required per flange. Therefore, 900 assembly hours (1,500 units × 0.6 hours per unit) are required for 1,500 flanges. After estimating the direct labor hours required for a job, Famous Flange must determine a separate wage rate for each grade of labor required for the operations performed to manufacture the flanges. The wage rate for assembly workers is $18 per hour, so the 900 assembly hours are estimated to cost $16,200 (900 hours × $18 wage rate per hour).

Panel 4 of the bid sheet contains estimates for cost driver (support) costs. Famous assigns support costs to jobs on the basis of the number of machine hours and direct labor hours expected for the job. For this purpose, Famous uses two cost driver rates, based on the assumption that all manufacturing support costs seem to vary with machines or to direct labor. The company classifies manufacturing support costs into two cost pools, based on whether the costs in the pool appear to increase with the hours the machines are used or the hours of labor that are incurred and computes a separate cost driver rate for each of the two cost pools. (Subsequent sections of this chapter will describe the procedure for calculating cost driver rates in detail.) To obtain the total amount of support costs allocated to the job, an analyst multiplies the number of machine hours (600) and the number of direct labor hours required for the job (1,380) by their respective cost driver rates ($40 per machine hour and $36 per direct labor hour). Then the Famous Flange analyst adds the two estimates to obtain a total of $73,680:

600 machine hours × $40 cost driver rate per machine hour = $24,000
1,380 labor hours × $36 cost driver rate per labor hour   = $49,680
Total   = $73,680

Panel 5 of the job bid sheet shows the total costs estimated for the job, $201,540, obtained by adding the total direct materials, total direct labor, and total support costs ($99,180 + $28,680 + $73,680).

Job Costs and Markup

The total direct material, direct labor, and support costs for the job are the job costs. Most firms mark up the job costs by adding an additional amount, or margin, to make a profit on the job. The total job costs plus the margin equals the bid price. At Famous Flange, the markup rate, or the percent by which job costs are marked up, is 25%. The markup rate depends on a variety of factors, including the amount of support costs excluded from the cost driver rate (e.g., corporate-level costs), the target rate of return (ratio of net income to investment) desired by the corporation, competitive intensity, past bidding strategies adopted by key competitors, demand conditions, and overall product-market strategies. Pricing is discussed thoroughly in chapter 6.

The markup rate may differ for different product groups and for different market segments, depending on local conditions. It also may change over time as conditions change. For example, managers may decide to decrease profit margins when demand is weak and unused production capacity is likely to be available, but may use higher markups to create higher profits when demand is expected to be high and little unused production capacity exists.

Determination of Cost Driver Rates

As discussed, determining realistic cost driver rates has become increasingly important in recent years because support costs now make up a large portion of the total costs in many industries. Notice that allocated support costs in the Famous Flange example ($73,680) are more than twice the direct labor costs ($28,680) and almost as much as direct materials costs ($99,180). In addition, many firms now recognize that support costs are not related to just one or even two factors, such as direct labor hours or machine hours. Rather, several different factors may be driving costs. Firms are now taking greater care when analyzing support costs by identifying which costs should relate to what cost driver. For example, costs identified with the activity of setting up machines are related to the cost driver as setup hours. All costs associated with a cost driver, such as setup hours, are accumulated separately. Each subset of total support costs that can be associated with a distinct cost driver is referred to as a cost pool.

Each cost pool has a separate cost driver rate. The cost driver rate is the ratio of the normal cost of a support activity accumulated in the cost pool to the practical capacity of the cost driver for the activity:

$$\text{Activity cost driver rate} = \frac{\text{Normal cost of support activity}}{\text{Practical capacity of cost driver}}$$

Recall that the normal cost of the support activity is the cost of the resources committed to the particular activity. The practical capacity of the activity cost driver is the long-term average usable capacity made available by the amount of resources committed to a support activity. For example, if 10 setup workers are hired at weekly wages including benefits of $810 each and if each worker has the time to complete 15 setups in a week, then the normal cost for the setup activity is $8,100 per week ($810 × 10 workers). This makes available a capacity for performing 150 setups in a week (15 setups × 10 workers). Then the cost driver rate for the setup activity is $54 per setup ($8,100 normal cost ÷ 150 setup capacity). The normal cost of a support activity, therefore, excludes fluctuations in costs caused by short-term adjustments, such as overtime payments. The practical capacity of the support activity cost driver also excludes short-term variations in demand as reflected in overtime or idle time. Because the ratio shown in the previous equation is based on normal costs and practical capacity cost driver levels, the rate remains stable over time and does not fluctuate as activity levels change in the short run. As a result, this activity cost driver rate does not change simply because of short-run changes in external factors that do not affect the efficiency or price of the activity resources.

Problems Using Fluctuating Cost Driver Rates

Consider the cost driver rate based on machine hours at Famous Flange Company. The cost pool includes machine depreciation, maintenance, power, and other machine-related costs. The normal machine-related costs amount to $900,000 per year; the normal capacity made available is 20,000 machine hours per year, or 5,000 machine hours (20,000 ÷ 4) per quarter. Therefore, the machine-related cost driver rate is $45 per machine hour ($900,000 ÷ 20,000 hours).

The actual machine usage varies each quarter because of fluctuations in demand. Machine hours used are 5,400 in the spring quarter, 4,500 in the summer, 5,000 in the fall, and 3,600 in the winter. The normal capacity of 5,000 machine hours is exceeded in the spring quarter by operating the machines overtime beyond regular shift hours.

Machine-related costs each quarter are $225,000. If the rate for such costs is based on quarterly cost driver levels instead of the normal levels, then the rate increases as the demand for the machine activity falls, and the rate decreases as the demand increases. For example, as the number of machine hours decreases from 5,400 in the spring to 4,500 in the summer, the cost driver rate increases from $41.67 per machine hour for spring to $50 per machine hour for summer (see Exhibit 3-3). In contrast, the cost driver rate based on normal costs and normal activity levels remains fixed at $45 per machine hour ($225,000 ÷ 5,000 hours) throughout the year because costs depend on the machine capacity made available and not on the season.

Determination of cost driver rates based on planned or actual short-term usage results in higher rates in periods of lower demand. In such job costing systems, job costs appear to be higher in time periods when demand is lower. If bid prices are based on estimated job costs, then the firm is likely to bid higher prices during periods of low demand when, in fact, it should be thinking about lowering prices to attract business during slow periods. The higher bid price can further decrease demand, which in turn leads to higher cost driver rates and even higher prices. Thus, the firm can enter an unnecessary death spiral as cost driver rates increase, leading to higher bid prices and ultimately even lower demand for its products. Conversely, cost driver rates can appear low in such a cost system when demand is high and capacity is short. This leads the company to attract additional business just when it should be raising prices to ration demand.

Support activity costs are caused by the level of capacity of each activity that is made available rather than by the level of actual usage of these committed resources. Therefore, the activity cost driver rate should be calculated on the basis of the normal cost per unit of the activity level committed. Determining the cost driver rate by dividing the budgeted or actual cost per unit by the budgeted or actual use of that activity will produce misleading product costs.

Exhibit 3-3
Famous Flange Company Cost Driver Rates and Quarterly Cost Driver Levels

QUARTER	DETAILS[a]	OVERHEAD RATE PER MACHINE
Spring	$\dfrac{\$225,000}{5,400}$	$41.67
Summer	$\dfrac{\$225,000}{4,500}$	50.00
Fall	$\dfrac{\$225,000}{5,000}$	45.00
Winter	$\dfrac{\$225,000}{3,600}$	62.50

[a] Cost driver rate = $\dfrac{\text{Quarterly actual costs}}{\text{Quarterly actual machine hours}}$

Dark Horse Comics, Inc. (DHC), is one of the largest comic book and graphic novel producers in the world. Established in the mid-1980s, by founder and president Mike Richardson, Dark Horse currently produces over thirty titles a month including *Star Wars, Buffy the Vampire Slayer, Spy Boy, Akira, Lone Wolf and Cub,* and *Hellboy.* Dark Horse also produces a vast array of toys and other merchandise that is comic and popular culture-related.

Richardson has penned a number of comics including the *Star Wars Crimson Empire* series and the definitive history of the comic book industry, *Comics Between the Panels,* coauthored by Steve Duin. Richardson is also a movie producer who has a knack for turning his comic properties into movies, most notably, *The Mask* (starring Jim Carrey and Cameron

Diaz, New Line Cinema) and *Hellboy* (featuring Ron Perlman, Sony Pictures).

Producing comics and graphic novels is very specialized work that involves a huge team of highly qualified professionals. A number of costs that go into producing comics and graphic novels including talent costs such as advances and royalties, cover design, interior design, color and lettering, licensing fees, penciling, preproduction, printing, shipping, marketing and other in-house costs, such as editorial costs and company overhead.

According to Neil Hankerson, Executive Vice President and Chief Operating Officer at DHC, the range of costs per comic depending on the title is between $0.85 and $1.25. DHC sells its comics for between $2.50 and $3.99.

Some recent Dark Horse Comic titles.

Source: Data taken from interviews conducted by the authors with Mike Richardson, President and CEO Chief Executive Officer, and Neil Hankerson, Executive Vice President and Chief Operating Officer, Dark Horse Comics, Inc. March, 2005.

KEN'S AUTO SERVICE REVISITED

Let us return to the case of Ken's Auto Service Company. Amy drew up the following description of the cost accounting system used to prepare bids for Ken's customers' jobs (see Exhibit 3-4).

System Description

A cost estimate is prepared for each customer job, as shown in Exhibit 3-4. After initially checking the customer's car, Ken prepares a list of replacement parts required (these are his direct materials). He consults his authorized dealer price book to obtain list prices for the parts. He also consults another manual (his blue book) that tells him what the standard labor hours for the work required to service the car would be. Then he multiplies standard hours by the combined labor, support activities cost, and markup rate of $61.20 per hour. The combined conversion cost rate includes the following:

    Mechanic's wages and benefits
    Shop support activity costs, including tools and machine depreciation
    Markup of 20% to provide a reasonable profit for Ken

The total cost estimate, or bid price, is the sum of the replacement parts cost and the labor cost charged at the combined labor, support conversion, and markup rate.

Ken investigated further how the combined labor, support activities cost, and markup rate of $61.20 per hour were determined. He examined the accounting and operating records in detail to prepare the following summary of costs budgeted for 2006:

Salaries of two expert mechanics ($60,000 each; total of 3,600 billable hours)	$120,000
Salaries of three regular mechanics ($35,000 each; total of 5,400 billable hours)	105,000

Exhibit 3-4
Ken's Auto Service Cost Estimate for Customer Job

Estimate Number:	1732	Date: August 9, 2006			
Customer Name:	Brandon Briggs				
Address:	43 Bridget Blvd.				
	Bounemouth				

	PARTS				
Direct materials	Part	Quantity	List Price	Amount	Total
	Muffler	1	$38.00	$38.00	$38.00
	Tailpipe	1	15.00	15.00	15.00
	Total parts				$53.00

	LABOR		
Direct labor,	Replacement of exhaust systems		
support	2 hours @ $61.20 per hour		$122.40
costs, and	Total labor		$122.40
markup	Total costs		$175.40
	Prepared by Wim Van der Stede		

Fringe benefits	90,000
General and administrative costs	26,000
Depreciation and maintenance on physical facilities, bays, equipment, etc.	64,000
Depreciation and maintenance on special tools and machines (3,600 machine hours)	54,000
Total costs	$459,000

The combined processing cost (labor and support activity) driver rate in dollars is determined by dividing the total costs ($459,000) by the total billable hours (3,600 + 5,400 hours) and then multiplying by 1.20 to represent a markup of 20%:

$$\text{Present cost driver rate} = \$459,000/(3,600 + 5,400) \times 1.20$$
$$= \$61.20 \text{ per labor hour}$$

Amy determined that Ken's company had lost considerable business for simple jobs, such as exhaust system replacement and brake relining, that did not require expert mechanics or specialized tools and machines. The present job costing system was deficient in not distinguishing between the expert and regular types of labor and in not recognizing that some of the support activity costs—$54,000 for depreciation and maintenance—resulted from the availability of special tools and machines. Instead, the costs of expert and regular labor, special tools, and machines were bundled together into a single cost driver rate of $61.20 per labor hour. This type of simple cost system is often referred to as a peanut butter–spreading approach since the cost of all types of resources—different labor skills, different machine types, and different support resources—are allocated across all jobs regardless if a job uses particular resources.

Recommended System Changes

Amy recommended that instead of using a single conversion cost driver rate, Ken should use the following four different cost driver rates:

1. Expert labor wage rate
2. Other labor wage rate
3. Depreciation and maintenance on physical plant
4. Depreciation and maintenance on special tools

The labor and support activity costs should be separated, therefore, into the four cost pools depicted in Exhibit 3-5. To do this, it is necessary first to apportion fringe benefits between the two types of labor costs (expert and regular mechanics) in the ratio of their respective costs. Then the company should determine its labor rates by dividing the total costs for wages and apportioned fringe benefits by the respective billable hours in each labor category and then adding a 20% markup (see Exhibit 3-6). Notice that both support activity costs and markup are included in the labor rate here. In contrast, Famous Flange added markup after determining all product costs—materials, labor, and support activity (see Exhibit 3-2, panel 5). Both methods are common in practice. Ken's method of calculating a combined conversion cost driver rate is used more in service organizations; Famous's method of separating labor from support costs is common in manufacturing and trading establishments.

The machine-related activity rate for special tools and machines is $18 per machine hour: 1.2 markup × ($54,000 costs ÷ 3600 hours). The remaining support activity

Exhibit 3-5
Ken's Auto
Service Proposed
Cost Pools

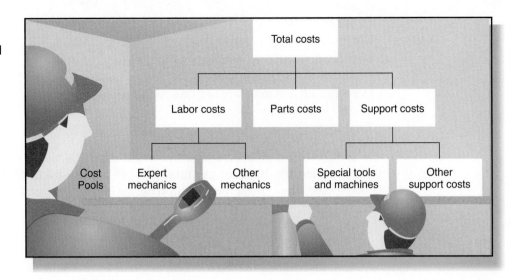

costs, consisting of general and administrative costs and depreciation and maintenance on physical facilities, bays, and equipment, are expected to be related to total labor hours of both types of mechanics. Therefore, the formula to determine the remaining cost driver rate is this:

Cost driver rate = 1.2 markup × ($26,000 general and administrative + $64,000 depreciation and maintenance) ÷ (3,600 expert mechanics' billable hours + 5,400 other mechanics' billable hours) = $12 per labor hour

New Cost Accounting System Illustrated

To illustrate how the new cost accounting system provides better information about job costs, Amy picks two representative jobs. Details of the work requirements for these two jobs appear in Exhibit 3-7. The first job involves the replacement of an exhaust system—a simple job that requires neither expert mechanics nor special tools and machines. The second job is relatively complex and involves rebuilding engine flanges.

Exhibit 3-6
Ken's Auto
Service Labor
Rates

ELEMENTS	EXPERT MECHANICS	OTHER MECHANICS
Wages	$120,000	$105,000
Fringe benefits	48,000[a]	42,000[b]
Total costs	$168,000	$147,000
Markup	20%	20%
Total cost plus markup	$201,600	$176,400
Total billable hours	3,600	5,400
Labor rate per hour	$56,000	$32.67

[a] $$\frac{\$90,000 \text{ benefits} \times \$120,000}{\$120,000 \text{ salaries of expert mechanics} + \$105,000 \text{ salaries of other mechanics}}$$

[b] $$\frac{\$90,000 \text{ benefits} \times \$105,000}{\$120,000 \text{ salaries of expert mechanics} + \$105,000 \text{ salaries of other mechanics}}$$

Exhibit 3-7
Ken's Auto
Service Costs
Under the Old Job
Costing System

Work Description	Job 1732 Replacement of Exhaust System		Job 2326 Rebuilding Engine Flanges
Parts cost		$53	$412
Labor hours:			
Expert mechanic hours	0		4
Other mechanic hours	2		2
Total labor hours		2	6
Special tools and machine hours		0	4

Under the previous system, job 1732 (replacement of the exhaust system) is costed out at $175.40 [$53.00 parts + (2 hours × $61.20) (old support cost driver rate)], including the 20% markup for profit. Under the new system, the cost of the same job is estimated to be $142.34, including the same 20% markup for profit (see Exhibit 3-8). The new system reveals that job 1732 actually costs less than what appeared to be the case under the previous system. The previous system overcosted the job because the single cost driver rate of $61.20 per labor hour wrongly applied a portion of the expert mechanic wages and special tools and machine costs to the job, although this simple job did not use any of these specialized and expensive resources. Thus, with the new cost system, Ken's may be able to win back some of its lost business for simple jobs by lowering the price but not the profit margin.

In contrast, the costs of the more complex job 2326 (rebuilding engine flanges) increase from $779.20 [$412 parts + (6 hours × $61.20) (old cost driver rate)] to $845.34 when the new system is used and the higher costs of expert labor and special tools are recognized (see Exhibit 3-8). Thus, the correct assignment of costs reveal that Ken currently may be underpricing the services of his expert mechanics using special tools. Although this underpricing means that he is getting more complex jobs, he is making much less profit (and perhaps even taking a loss on these jobs) than the present costing system leads him to believe. In addition, he is running out of capacity on the relatively more expensive resources for the complex activities by attracting business that does not cover the costs of these resources.

The difference between the old and the new product costing systems results from the difference in the structure of the cost pools. The new system recognizes two types of labor and support activity costs that include costs of special tools and machines not required for all jobs.

Exhibit 3-8
Ken's Auto
Service Costs
Under the New
Job Costing
System

	Job 1732	Job 2326
Parts cost	$53.00	$412.00
Expert mechanics	0	$224.00 (4 hours × $56 wage rate)
Other mechanics	$65.34 (2 hours × $32.67 wage rate)	$65.34 (2 hours × $32.67)
Special tools support	0	$72.00 (4 hours × $18 cost driver rate)
Other support	$24.00 (2 hours × $12 overhead rate)	$72.00 (6 hours × $12 cost driven rate)
Total costs	$142.34	$854.34

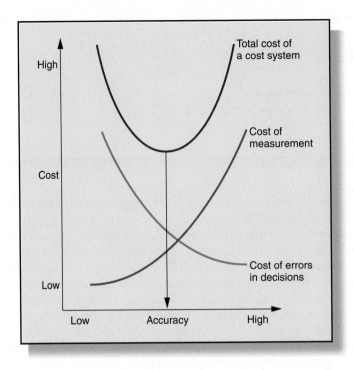

Exhibit 3-9
Trade-Offs in
Choosing the
Accuracy of
a Costing System

Number of Cost Pools

You may ask the question; How many cost pools should there be? The number can vary. Cost accounting systems in many German firms use more than 1,000 cost pools. The general principle is to use separate cost pools if the cost or productivity of resources is different and if the pattern of demand varies across resources. Exhibit 3-9 displays the trade-offs involved in choosing the level of accuracy of a product costing system. The increase in measurement costs required by a more detailed cost system must be traded off against the benefit of increased accuracy in estimating product costs. If cost and productivity differences between resources are small, having more cost pools will make little difference in the accuracy of product cost estimates. In such a case, the benefits of decreasing errors, such as those that resulted in Ken's losing simple jobs, will be relatively small and insufficient to justify the increased cost of more cost pools.

RECORDING ACTUAL JOB COSTS

In addition to preparing bids, job order cost accounting systems also record costs actually incurred on individual jobs as they are produced. This process allows comparison of actual costs with the estimated costs to determine whether unexpected variations occurred in the quantity (efficiency) or prices of the various resources used.

Reconsider job J4369 of the Famous Flange Company in Exhibit 3-2. Once Famous has received the customer order and scheduled production, the company prepares a **materials requisition note** listing materials required to begin production. The materials requisition note M47624 lists the bar steel stock required for initial machining work (see Exhibit 3-10). Famous obtains steel requirements from engineering specifications for part design JDR-103 identified in the customer order. On receipt of the materials requisition note, the stores department issues the bar steel stock and moves the materials to the machining department.

Exhibit 3-10
Famous Flange
Company
Materials
Requisition Note

Materials Requisition Note Number: M47624		Date: August 2, 2006		
From: Machining Department				
Approved by:	Mike Machina	Machining Supervisor		
	Steve Stuart	Stores Supervisor		
Job Number:	J4369			
Engineering Design: JDR-103				

IDENTIFICATION NUMBER	DESCRIPTION	QUANTITY	RATE	AMOUNT
24203	Bar steel stock	720 lbs	$11.50	$8280.00

The 720 pounds of materials issued are for 20% of the total order. The customer requires delivery spread over several months, and Famous Flange schedules production for meeting delivery schedules, a production system called a pull system. This production order is for 300 L181 flanges (20% of the total customer order for 1500 L181 flanges) (see Exhibit 3-2). Each flange requires 2.4 pounds of materials; therefore, 720 pounds (300 flanges × 2.4 pounds per flange) of bar steel stock have been requisitioned. Since the actual price of bar steel is $11.50 per pound, the actual cost of the requisitioned material is $8,280 (720 × $11.50).

IN PRACTICE

Costs and Revenues in the Motion Picture Industry—Comparing *Napoleon Dynamite* to *Stealth*

The costs associated with producing and marketing a movie are in some ways very similar to those required to manufacture and market any other product. According to an AICPA pronouncement, producing and bringing a film to market includes three major costs: production costs, participation costs, and exploitation costs. Much like the manufacturing of products, *production film costs* consist of direct and overhead costs. Direct costs include the costs of securing the script; compensating the cast, directors, producers, and extras; set construction; operations; wardrobe; sound synchronization; rental facilities; and postproduction costs (music, special effects, editing), as well as allocations of production overhead and capitalized interest costs. Production overhead costs consist of costs associated with individuals and departments that have a significant responsibility for the production of the film. Administrative and general expenses are not included in production overhead.

Participation costs are contingent payments to participants involved in the production of the film, such as actors and actresses, writers, and licensors. *Exploitation costs* include marketing, advertising, publicity, promotion, and other distribution expenses.

Studio executives hope to produce a successful movie at the lowest possible cost, with the market rewarding the filmmaker and the movie's participants. Two recent films illustrate how difficult it is to predict whether a movie will be a financial success. In the case of *Napoleon Dynamite* (debuted at the Sundance Film Festival and distributed by Fox Searchlight), an independent film, the total budget for the movie was $400,000. The case consisted largely of unknown actors. The worldwide box office gross (as of October 2005 and excluding ancillary revenues from DVD sales) is just under $46,000,000—a return of close to 5,600%. On the other hand *Stealth* (Sony Pictures) had a budget of $138,000,000, *Stealth* employed several very well-known actors, including Oscar winner Jamie Foxx and Jessica Biel, and it was directed by Rob Coben and produced by well-known producers. And yet *Stealth* had the distinction of being the biggest money loser in motion pictures to date, with worldwide box office revenues of just over $64,000,000—or a loss of 75% based on its initial budget.

With unpredictable results like this, it's no wonder that William Goldman (Adventures in the Screen Trade; New York, Warner Books, 1983), talking about everyone who is involved in the movie industry, exclaimed, "Nobody knows anything."

John Heder and Aaron Ruell as Napoleon and Kip in *Napoleon Dynamite* (Fox Searchlight).
Source: www.images.movie-gazette.com/albums/20041128/napoleon-dynamite-07.jpg.

Jamie Foxx, Jessica Biel, and Josh Lucas in *Stealth*.
Source: Sony Pictures.

Once the machining department receives the materials, the supervisor assigns specific lathe operators to the job. The time the operators spend working on a job is recorded on time cards, as shown in Exhibit 3-11 for machinist Sydney Young (employee number M16). After the completion of machining work, workers either store

Exhibit 3-11
Farnous Flange
Company Worker
Time Card

TIME CARD

Employee Number: M16   Name: Sydney Young
Date: August 2, 2006   Department: Machining
Checked by: Doreen Quan Mane   Machining Supervisor

Job Number	Start Time	Stop Time	Total Hours	Wage Rate	Amount
J4369	6:00	10:00	4	$28.00	$112.00
J4362	10:00	1:00	3	28.00	84.00
J4371	2:00	3:00	1	28.00	28.00
Total			8		$224.00

the machined bars as work in process or move them to the assembly department if they are scheduled for assembly. The just-in-time pull system that Famous Flange uses moves the materials almost immediately to the next department. The assembly department then prepares an additional materials requisition note to have the stores department issue the appropriate subassemblies. The assembly workers also prepare time cards to record the time they spend on job J4369.

Copies of all materials requisition notes and worker time cards are forwarded to the accounting department, which then posts them on a job cost sheet, shown in Exhibit 3-12. Even if time cards are recorded in an integrated computerized information system versus a manual accounting system, job cost sheets are prepared using data obtained from actual materials requisition and actual time card records. The time records may be generated by workers entering data into a computer terminal or by passing an electronic wand over a bar code on the job.

Finally, the system calculates total costs for the portion of the job completed. The structure of the job cost sheet is similar to that of the job bid sheet, except that the direct materials and direct labor costs on the job cost sheet represent actual costs incurred on the job. Direct materials costs include $11,020 for subassemblies, in addition to $8,280 for 720 pounds of bar steel stock recorded in materials requisition note M47624 (see Exhibit 3-10). Referring to Exhibit 3-12, we see that direct labor costs constitute the hours charged by three machinists (M16, M18, M19 lathe operators) and six assembly workers (A25, A26, A27, A32, A34, A35) for this job. (This includes the 4 hours charged for employee number M16 on August 2 as recorded in the time card in Exhibit 3-11.) Support costs are applied to the job on the basis of actual machine hours (117 hours) and direct labor hours (268 hours). The same predetermined support cost driver rates ($40 per machine hour and $36 per direct labor hour) are used as in the job bid sheet because actual total support costs for the plant will not be known until the end of the fiscal period (see Exhibit 3-2, panel 4).

Total costs are determined as before by adding the direct material, direct labor, and support activity costs applied to the job to date. It is now possible to compare these to the costs on the bid sheet. Notice that the actual unit costs of $134.98 ($39,144 total costs ÷ 290 units produced) for the portion of the job completed through August 12, 2006, are higher than the unit costs of $134.36 ($201,540 total cost ÷ 1,500 units) estimated on the job bid sheet (see Exhibit 3-12, panel 5, and Exhibit 3-2, panel 5).

Exhibit 3-12
Famous Flange Company Job Cost Sheet

Panel 1	Job number: J4369 Customer: Michigan Motors Product: Automobile engine valves Engineering design number: JDR-103 Total number of units ordered: 1500				

	MATERIALS REQUISITION NUMBER	DESCRIPTION	QUANTITY	PRICE	AMOUNT
Panel 2	M47624	Bar steel stock	720 lbs	$11.50	$8,280.00
	A35161	Subassemblies	290 units	38.00	11,020.00
	Total direct materials cost				$19,300.00

	DATES	EMPLOYEE NUMBER	HOURS	RATE	AMOUNT
	8/2, 8/3, 8/4, 8/5	M16	24	$28.00	$672.00
Panel 3	8/2, 8/3, 8/4, 8/5	M18, M19	64	26.00	1,664.00
	8/6, 8/7, 8/8, 8/9, 8/10	A25, A26, A27	120	18.00	2,160.00
	8/6, 8/7, 8/8, 8/9, 8/10	A32, A34, A35	60	17.00	1,020.00
	Total direct labor		268		$5,516.00

	SUPPORT COSTS	AMOUNT
Panel 4	117 Machine hours @ $40 per hour	$4,680.00
	268 Direct labor hours @ $36 per hour	9,648.00
	Total support costs	$14,328.00

	Total cost	**$39,144.00**
Panel 5	Number of units produced	290
	Cost per unit	**$134.98**
	Projected unit cost	**$134.36**

MULTISTAGE PROCESS COSTING SYSTEMS

For many plants engaged in continuous processing, such as those in the chemicals, basic metals, pharmaceuticals, grain milling and processing, and electric utilities industries, production flows continuously, semicontinuously (that is, continuously but with a few interruptions), or in large batches from one process stage to the next. At each successive process stage, there is further progress toward converting the raw materials into the finished product. In contrast to a job shop manufacturing establishment, in continuous processing it is necessary first to determine costs for each stage of the process and then to assign their costs to individual products.

The design of product costing systems in such process-oriented plants allows measurement of the costs of converting the raw materials during a time period to be made separately for each process stage. These conversion costs, the sum of direct labor and support resources, are applied to products as they pass through successive process stages. This system for determining product costs, known as a multistage process costing system, is common in process-oriented industries. We also find multistage process costing systems in some discrete-parts manufacturing plants, such as those producing automobile components, small appliances, and electronic instruments and computers.

The common feature in these settings is that the products manufactured are relatively homogeneous. Examples are packaging operations and making newsprint. Few and relatively small differences occur in the production requirements for batches of different products. As a result, it is not necessary to maintain separate cost records for individual jobs. Instead, costs are measured only for process stages, and cost variances are determined only at the level of the process stages instead of at the level of individual jobs.

Take, for example, the process of making fiberglass insulation. In this process, molten glass is pushed very fast through very small holes in a high-speed stream. The fibers that results are drawn very thin and long. They are then collected into a matte to produce insulation.

Comparison with Job Order Costing

Multistage process costing systems have the same objective as job order costing systems. Both types of systems assign material, labor, and manufacturing support resources to products. Some important differences, however, exist between them (see Exhibit 3-13). Note that the factors in column 1 highlight the major points for consideration.

Process Costing Illustrated

Consider the product costing system at the Homebush Glass Company's plant that produces low-cost glass bottles. Raw materials such as sand, soda ash, and limestone are combined with other raw materials, such as cullet, to create the batch mixture. Cullet is crushed recyled glass. As Exhibit 3-14 shows, the raw materials go through a number of stages before they finally emerge as completed glass bottles (or containers as they are referred). During production, labor costs are incurred, as are the support costs of equipment, energy, and supervision for each stage of the process. We refer to the cost of all the activities performed at each stage of the process as the conversion costs for that stage. The total estimated conversion costs for each stage are divided by the corresponding total number of process hours to obtain the estimated conversion cost driver rate per process hour for that stage.

Exhibit 3-13
Differences Between Job Order and Multistage Process Costing Systems

FACTORS	JOB ORDER COSTING SYSTEM	MULTISTAGE PROCESS COSTING SYSTEM
Production	(a) Carried out in many different jobs	(a) Carried out continuously, semicontinuously, or in large batches
Production requirements	(b) Different for different jobs	(b) Homogeneous across products or jobs
Costs	(c) Measured for individual jobs	(c) Measured for individual process stages
Variances	(d) Between actual and estimated direct materials and direct labor costs are determined for individual jobs	(d) Between actual and estimated costs are determined for individual process stages

Exhibit 3-14
Homebush Glass Company

Inside a Glass Plant
This diagram shows a product layout for a glass plant designed to produce high volumes of high quality, low-cast glass bottles. Planners need operating and financial budgets to estimate the operating and financial consequences of their operating plans and to evaluate the implications, both operating and financial, of changing plans.

Source: Ball Corporation.

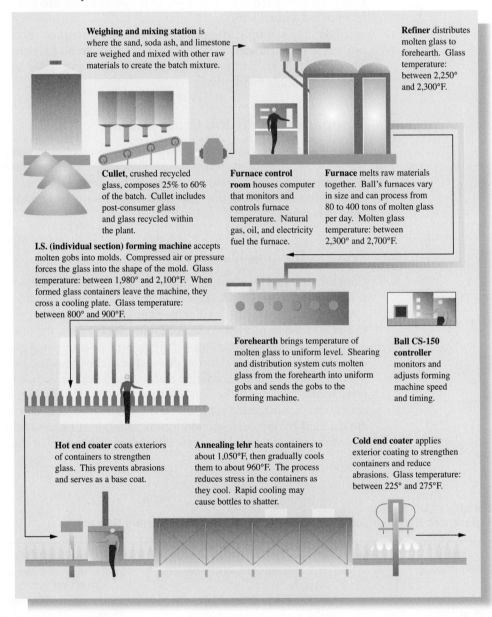

Weighing and mixing station is where the sand, soda ash, and limestone are weighed and mixed with other raw materials to create the batch mixture.

Refiner distributes molten glass to forehearth. Glass temperature: between 2,250° and 2,300°F.

Cullet, crushed recycled glass, composes 25% to 60% of the batch. Cullet includes post-consumer glass and glass recycled within the plant.

Furnace control room houses computer that monitors and controls furnace temperature. Natural gas, oil, and electricity fuel the furnace.

Furnace melts raw materials together. Ball's furnaces vary in size and can process from 80 to 400 tons of molten glass per day. Molten glass temperature: between 2,300° and 2,700°F.

I.S. (individual section) forming machine accepts molten gobs into molds. Compressed air or pressure forces the glass into the shape of the mold. Glass temperature: between 1,980° and 2,100°F. When formed glass containers leave the machine, they cross a cooling plate. Glass temperature: between 800° and 900°F.

Forehearth brings temperature of molten glass to uniform level. Shearing and distribution system cuts molten glass from the forehearth into uniform gobs and sends the gobs to the forming machine.

Ball CS-150 controller monitors and adjusts forming machine speed and timing.

Hot end coater coats exteriors of containers to strengthen glass. This prevents abrasions and serves as a base coat.

Annealing lehr heats containers to about 1,050°F, then gradually cools them to about 960°F. The process reduces stress in the containers as they cool. Rapid cooling may cause bottles to shatter.

Cold end coater applies exterior coating to strengthen containers and reduce abrasions. Glass temperature: between 225° and 275°F.

Exhibit 3-14
Continued

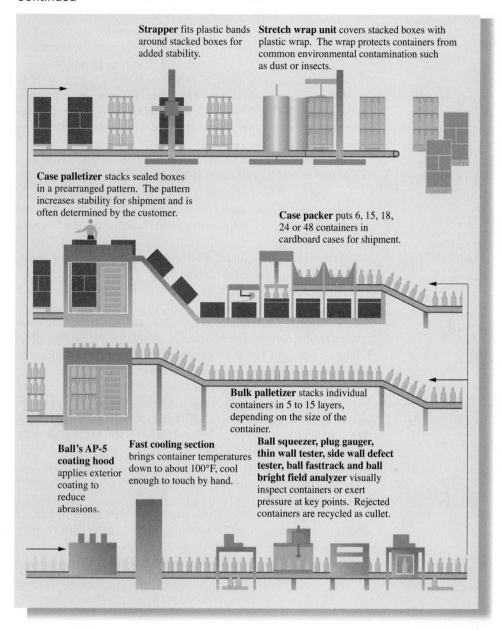

EQUIVALENT UNITS OF PRODUCTION

A key issue that always has to be addressed regarding process costing is the situation that arises at the end of a production period when not all of the product in the manufacturing process has been completed. According to accounting convention, these partially completed units need to be converted mathematically into what are called **equivalent units of production**. As shown in the formula below, calculating equivalent units is accomplished by multiplying the number of partially completed units by how much of the unit has been completed:

$$\text{Equivalent units} = \text{Number of partially completed units} \times \text{Percentage completion}$$

Two different methods are used for computing equivalent units of production: the FIFO (first in, first out) and the **weighted-average method**. Because the weighted average is much more widely used in practice, we illustrate this method here.

The formula used to calculate the equivalent units of production under the weighted-average method is as follows:

$$\begin{array}{c} \text{Equivalent units} \\ \text{of production} \end{array} = \begin{array}{c} \text{Units transferred out to the next} \\ \text{department or to finished goods} \end{array} + \begin{array}{c} \text{Equivalent units in ending} \\ \text{work in process inventory} \end{array}$$

A department's equivalent units of production is the sum of the units transferred to the next department or to finished goods plus the equivalent units in ending work-in-process inventory. To calculate the equivalent units consider the following example for product SMY50. To simplify the example, we assume that 12 containers (bottles) each go into one carton and that the direct materials and conversion costs to complete one carton of containers have averaged $10 and $18, respectively. Thus, the total cost per unit has averaged $28. In the next example, we will see how that cost will change when costs fluctuate in the current period.

In Exhibit 3-15, Homebush Glass Company had 1,000 units or cartons in work-in-process inventory at the beginning of June. These 1,000 units were 40% complete with respect to materials and 30% complete with respect to conversion costs. Thus, 40% of the cost of materials and 30% of the conversion costs had already been incurred. Homebush also started 8,000 new units into production in June. By the end of the month, a total of 7,000 units had been completed, leaving 2,000 units in work-in-process. The 2,000 units were 30% and 25% complete regarding materials and conversion costs, respectively.

Homebush calculates the equivalent units of production for the month of June and finds that a total of 7,600 units are complete with respect to material and 7,500 units are complete with respect to conversion costs (see Exhibit 3-16). This information is then used to calculate the costs per equivalent unit as shown in Exhibit 3-17.

Exhibit 3-15
Homebush Glass Company, June Production Data

| | | PRODUCT SMY50 | |
| | | PERCENT COMPLETED | |
	UNITS (CARTONS)	MATERIALS	CONVERSION
Work in process, June 1	1,000	40%	30%
Units started into production during June	8,000		
Units completed during June and			
transferred to next department	7,000	100%	100%
Work in process, June 30	2,000	30%	25%

Exhibit 3-16
Homebush Glass Company, Equivalent Units of Production: Weighted Average Method

	PRODUCT SMY50	
	MATERIALS	CONVERSION
Units (cartons) transferred to next department	7,000	7,000
Work in process, June 30		
2,000 cartons × 30%	600	
2,000 cartons × 25%		500
Equivalent units of production	7,600	7,500

Exhibit 3-17
Homebush Glass Company, Cost per Equivalent Unit

	TOTAL COST	MATERIALS	CONVERSION	WHOLE UNIT
Cost to be accounted for:				
Work in process, June 1	$9,400	$4,000	$5,400	
Cost added during June	$186,600	$66,000	$120,600	
Total cost to be accounted for (a)	$196,000	$70,000	$126,000	
Equivalent units (b)		7,600	7,500	
Cost per equivalent unit (a) ÷ (b)		$9.21	$16.80	$26.01

Notice that the weighted-average method illustrated earlier combines work that was begun in the previous period with work completed during the current month of June. The rate of $26.01 calculated in Exhibit 3-17 will be used to cost all units that are transferred to finished goods (or the next department, if necessary).

SUMMARY

This chapter begins by discussing the differences between direct and indirect costs. The chapter focuses on how direct and indirect costs are treated in two of the most well-known traditional product costing systems: job order and process costing systems. Both costing systems are used to estimate and then measure actual costs of discrete job orders and products produced in continuous process industries. Although they are described here as two different costing systems, many systems observed in practice exhibit elements of both. Both types of cost systems identify materials and labor costs directly with jobs or products. Both systems also assign the remainder of costs to jobs or products on the basis of predetermined cost driver rates.

The support cost driver rate should be determined as the normal cost per unit of capacity of support activity that is made available. If the cost driver rate is based instead on actual or budgeted activity levels that fluctuate over time, then support activity costs will be understated in periods of high demand and overstated in periods of low demand. If product costing systems do not adequately reflect the systematic differences in prices and productivity of materials and labor resources and of factors driving support activity costs, the resultant job or product costs are likely to be distorted. In particular, if there are several grades of labor with widely differing productivity levels and wage rates but only a single common rate is used for all labor, then product costs are likely to be distorted for products that require different grades of labor in different proportions. Similarly, if support costs are caused by multiple cost drivers but a single cost driver rate is employed to assign all support costs (the peanut butter–spreading approach), then product costs are likely to be distorted for products that require different proportions of the multiple cost drivers.

Appendix 3-1

Service Department Cost Allocations

In this appendix, we discuss three ways that companies allocate service department costs to production departments. The three methods are direct allocation, sequential allocation, and reciprocal allocation. The last two are used when service departments consume services provided by other departments. To begin, we discuss the traditional two-stage cost allocation procedure.

Two-Stage Cost Allocations

Traditional cost accounting systems assign operating expenses to products with a two-stage procedure. First, expenses are assigned to production departments, and then, in the second stage, production department expenses are assigned to the products. Let us begin by discussing how departmental structure influences the first-stage allocation process and then move to examples of the use of specific allocation methods.

The Effect of Departmental Structure on Allocation

Many plants are organized into departments that are responsible for performing designated activities. Departments that have direct responsibility for converting raw materials into finished products are called *production departments*. In a manufacturing plant such as Helping Hand, casting, machining, assembly, and packing are production departments. **Service departments** perform activities that support production, such as machine maintenance, machine setup, production engineering, and production scheduling. All service department costs are indirect support activity costs because they do not arise from direct production activities.

Conventional product costing systems assign indirect costs to jobs or products in two stages. In the first stage, the system identifies indirect costs with various production and service departments, and then all the service department costs are allocated to production departments. In the second stage, the system assigns the accumulated indirect costs for the production departments to individual jobs or products on the basis of predetermined departmental cost driver rates (see Exhibit 3-18).

The Helping Hand plant has four production departments: casting, machining, assembly, and packing. In addition, it has five service departments: machine maintenance, machine setup, production scheduling, production engineering, and general and administrative. The cost accounting system accumulates costs separately for each of these nine departments.

Costs accumulated for the four production departments include supervision, supplies, and machine depreciation costs. Costs for the five service departments include the salaries, wages, and benefits of the engineers and workers who are responsible for these activities as well as the costs of the tools and materials they use. Costs for the general and administrative service department include the salaries and benefits for plant managerial staff, rent, heating and lighting, and janitorial services.

Stage 1 Cost Allocations

Stage 1 allocations involve estimation of the normal manufacturing support costs incurred in each department. The following summary reflects the total support costs for the nine departments, as depicted in Exhibit 3-19.

Because jobs are worked on in production departments, it is relatively easy to identify the number of direct labor and machine hours for individual jobs in each production department. Conventional costing systems are based on the assumption that we cannot obtain direct

Exhibit 3-18
Two-Stage Cost
Allocation System

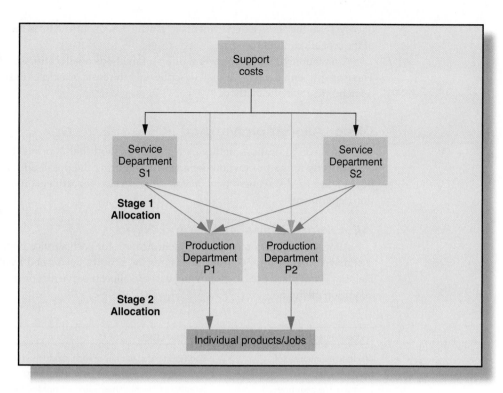

Exhibit 3-19
Helping Hand: Plant Step 1 of Stage 1 Cost Allocation

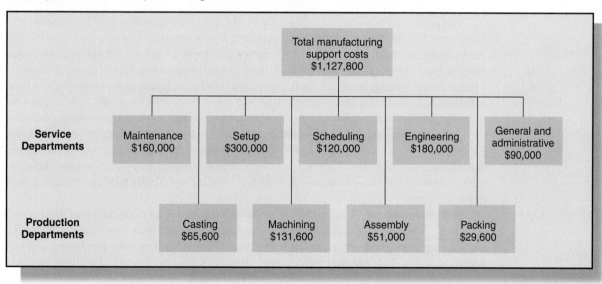

measures of use of service departments' resources on individual jobs as conveniently as we can of production departments' resources because jobs are worked on only in production departments. Therefore, conventional costing systems allocate the service department costs first to the production departments before assigning them to individual jobs. This assignment of costs from the service departments to production departments is the second step in stage 1 of the cost allocation procedure.

As mentioned, there are several different methods of allocating service department costs. These are presented next. We shall describe only the basic principles of stage 1 allocations with reference to a specific method.

Direct Allocation Method

The direct allocation method is a simple method that allocates the service department costs directly to the production departments, ignoring the possibility that some of the activities of a service department may benefit other service departments in addition to the production departments.

Allocation Bases at Helping Hand

Allocation of costs requires the identification for each service department of a basis, or cost driver, that best reflects and measures the activity performed by that department. The Helping Hand plant uses the following bases to allocate service department costs by the direct allocation method.

Service Department	Allocation Basis
Machine maintenance	Book value of machines in each production department
Machine setup	Number of setups in each production department
Production scheduling	Number of machine hours in each production department
Production engineering	Number of direct labor hours in each production department
General and administrative	Number of square feet occupied by each production department

The allocation bases do not always perfectly reflect the activities that generate service department costs. For example, the number of hours of setup work in each production department is a better basis than the number of setups for allocating setup department costs if the time required per setup differs across production departments. Similarly, expected maintenance hours for each department is a better measure for allocating machine maintenance costs than the book value of machines. However, there must be a trade-off between the additional cost of collecting such information against the potential benefits of the greater accuracy that its use may provide. For example, Helping Hand did not believe that the costs of obtaining information about maintenance hours in each department justified the benefit from the greater accuracy it might provide; therefore, the company uses the book value of machines to allocate maintenance costs because this measure is easily available.

It is often difficult to obtain any reasonable measures to allocate the costs of product-sustaining or facility-sustaining activities to production departments. Production scheduling, engineering, and plant administration activities do not benefit specific production departments, although their use may differ across different products. Helping Hand uses machine hours and direct labor hours as the bases to allocate these costs to the production departments. Keep in mind the previous discussion about external financial reporting requirements, such as the valuation of inventory, that have influenced the design of product costing systems in the past. As a result, the objective of most conventional product costing systems, such as the one at the Helping Hand plant, is to assign all manufacturing costs to jobs and products.

Exhibit 3-20 presents the allocation bases and their values for the production departments at Helping Hand. The allocation of normal costs of the service departments to the production departments is made in proportion to their respective allocation basis value.

Exhibit 3-20
Helping Hand: Allocation Bases Values for Production Departments

Allocation Bases	Production Departments				
	Casting	Machining	Assembly	Packing	Totals
Book value of machines	$300,000	$600,000	$180,000	$120,000	$1,200,000
Number of setups	200	400	200	200	1,000
Machine hours	6,000	22,000	9,000	3,000	40,000
Direct labor hours	2,000	11,000	6,000	6,000	25,000
Square feet	6,000	9,000	9,000	6,000	30,000

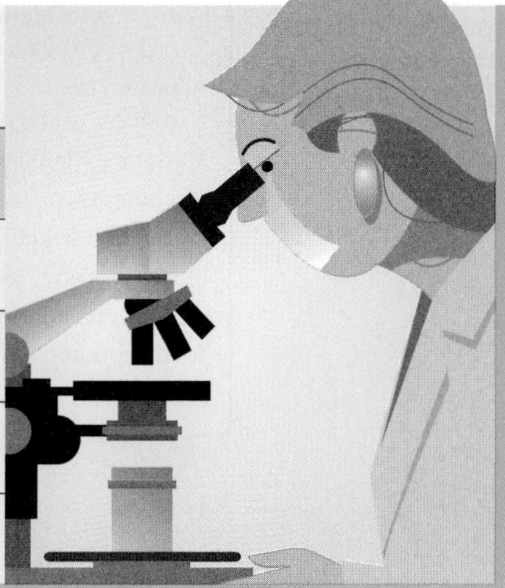

Exhibit 3-21
Helping Hand Allocation Ratios

SERVICE DEPARTMENT	ALLOCATION BASIS	PRODUCTION DEPARTMENTS				
		CASTING	MACHINING	ASSEMBLY	PACKING	TOTALS
Machine maintenance	Book value of machines	0.250	0.500	0.150	0.100	1.000
Machine setups	Number of setups	0.200	0.400	0.200	0.200	1.000
Production scheduling	Machine hours	0.150	0.550	0.225	0.075	1.000
Production engineering	Direct labor hours	0.080	0.440	0.240	0.240	1.000
General and administrative	Square feet	0.200	0.300	0.300	0.200	1.000

To complete the allocation procedure for stage 1, do the following:

1. Obtain the ratio of allocation of machine maintenance service costs to the casting department. To illustrate, consider the ratio 0.250 in the top left corner of Exhibit 3-21. This figure is the ratio of $300,000 (the book value of the machines in the casting department) to $1,200,000 (the total book value of machines in the four production departments):

$$\$300,000 \div \$1,200,000 = 0.250$$

(see Exhibits 3-20 and 3-21)

2. Determine the amount of service department costs allocated to the production department costs by multiplying the allocation ratio by the corresponding service department costs (see Exhibit 3-22). For example, the casting department receives $40,000 of machine maintenance service department costs:

$$0.250 \times \$160,000 = \$40,000$$

(see Exhibits 3-19, 3-21, and 3-22)

Exhibit 3-22
Helping Hand
Allocation
of Service
Department Costs
to Production
Departments

	PRODUCTION DEPARTMENTS			
SERVICE DEPARTMENT COSTS	CASTING	MACHINING	ASSEMBLY	PACKING
Support costs identified directly in step 1 of stage 1 allocations	$65,600	$131,600	$51,000	$29,600
Allocated from service department in step 2 of stage 1:				
Machine maintenance	40,000	80,000	24,000	16,000
Machine setup	60,000	120,000	60,000	60,000
Production scheduling	18,000	66,000	27,000	9,000
Production engineering	14,400	79,200	43,200	43,200
General and administrative	18,000	27,000	27,000	18,000
Total support costs for the production departments	$216,000	$503,800	$232,200	$175,800

3. Add the allocated costs from the service departments to the costs originally identified with the production departments (see Exhibits 3-19 and 3-22). The allocated costs from the service departments to casting are as follows:

$$\$40,000 + \$60,000 + \$18,000 + \$14,400 + \$18,000 = \$150,400$$

This total is added to the $65,600 assigned to casting in stage 1:

$$\$65,600 + \$150,400 = \$216,000$$

Stage 1 of the cost allocation procedure is now complete. The $1,127,800 of both service and production departmental costs for the Helping Hand plant is allocated to the production departments as follows: $216,000 to casting, $503,800 to machining, $232,200 to assembly, and $175,800 to packing (see Exhibit 3-23). During stage 2 of the allocation procedure, these amounts are used to determine the departmental cost driver rates for assignment of these costs to the jobs worked on in each production department.

Stage 2 Cost Allocations

Stage 2 allocations require the identification of appropriate cost drivers for each production department and assign production department costs to jobs and products while they are worked on in the departments. Conventional cost accounting systems use unit-related cost drivers, such as the number of units made, the number of direct labor hours (or direct labor cost), and the number of machine hours. Helping Hand uses machine hours as the cost driver for the casting and machining departments because of their high reliance on machines for the operations performed in these departments. The assembly and packing operations are more labor intensive; therefore, Helping Hand uses direct labor hours as the cost driver in these two departments (see Exhibit 3-24).

Dividing the indirect costs accumulated in each production department by the total number of units of the corresponding cost driver results gives us cost driver rates for each department. To illustrate, the total indirect support costs from stage 1 are $216,000 for the casting department, with total practical capacity machine hours estimated to be 6,000. Therefore, the cost driver rate for the casting department is $36 per machine hour ($216,000 ÷ 6,000).

Support costs are applied to each job as it is worked on in the production department. Exhibit 3-25 presents data on the number of machine and direct labor hours incurred on two representative jobs, J189-4 and J273-2, in each production department. Job J189-4 involves the production of a batch of 12 units of E189, bacterial analysis equipment in the old product line. Job J273-2 is for the production of a batch of 5 units of E273, one of the new products whose sales have been increasing rapidly.

Exhibit 3-23
Helping Hand: Step 2 of Stage 1 of the Allocation Procedure

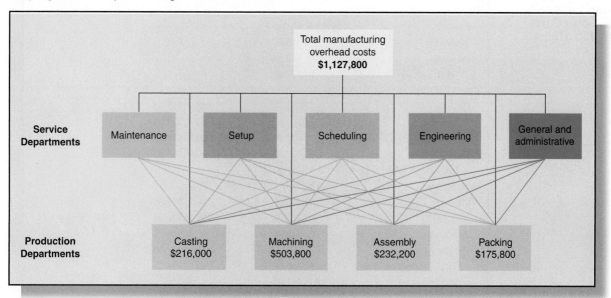

Exhibit 3-24
Helping Hand
Stage 2: Cost
Driver Rates for
Production
Departments

	PRODUCTION DEPARTMENTS			
	CASTING	MACHINING	ASSEMBLY	PACKING
Total support costs (from step 2 of stage 1)	$216,000	$503,800	$232,200	$175,800
Allocation basis	Machine hours	Machine hours	Direct labor hours	Direct labor hours
Total machine hours	6,000	22,000	9,000	3,000
Total direct labor hours	2,000	11,000	6,000	6,000
Allocation rate	$36.00	$22.90	$38.70	$29.30

Exhibit 3-25
Helping Hand
Machine and Labor
Hours for Two
Representative
Jobs

	JOB J189-4 (OLD PRODUCT LINE)	JOB J273-2 (NEW PRODUCT LINE)
Machine hours:		
Casting	40	16
Machining	140	56
Assembly	40	16
Packing	40	16
Direct labor hours:		
Casting	18	7
Machining	70	28
Assembly	40	16
Packing	40	16

Exhibit 3-26
Helping Hand
Application of
Support Costs
to Job J189-4

ITEM	COSTS	CALCULATION DETAILS
Direct materials costs:		
Casting	$2,658.40	
Assembly	1,446.60	
Packing	632.80	
Total materials costs	$4,737.80	
Direct labor costs:		
Casting	$331.20	18 × $18.40
Machining	1,666.00	70 × $23.80
Assembly	632.00	40 × $15.80
Packing	528.00	40 × $13.20
Total direct labor costs	$3,157.20	
Support costs:		
Casting	$1,440.00	40 × $36.00
Machining	3,206.00	140 × $22.90
Assembly	1,548.00	40 × $38.70
Packing	1,172.00	40 × $29.30
Total support costs	$7,366.00	
Total manufacturing costs	$15,261.00	
Number of units	12	
Cost per unit	$1,271.75	

see Exhibit 3-24

Exhibits 3-26 and 3-27 present the costs for direct materials, direct labor, and support costs applied to these two jobs. Recall that direct material costs are identified with the jobs on the basis of requisition notes issued for materials required in the casting department, subassemblies required in the assembly department, and packing materials required in the packing department. Assume for job J189-4 that direct materials costs for casting, assembly, and packing are $2,658.40, $1,446.60, and $632.80, respectively, and that direct materials costs for job J273-2 for casting, assembly, and packing are $1,186.60, $788.80, and $491.40, respectively. Direct labor costs are determined by multiplying the number of direct labor hours by the labor wage rate applicable to each department (see Exhibit 3-25). Assume that direct labor rates for casting, machining, assembly, and packing for jobs J189-4 and J273-2 are $18.40, $23.80, $15.80, and $13.20, respectively. The wage rate is higher in the machining department than in the packing department because more skilled workers are required for machining operations.

To obtain support costs for the jobs J189-4 (Exhibit 3-26) and J273-2 (Exhibit 3-27), multiply the number of machine hours by the departmental cost driver rate for the casting and machining departments and the number of direct labor hours by the cost driver rate for the assembly and packing departments (see Exhibits 3-24, 3-26, and Exhibit 3-27). Notice that the number of machine hours and direct labor hours used for these calculations correspond to the amount of time spent on the job in a particular department rather than on the totals for the job in the entire plant. The total manufacturing costs for each job are the sum of the direct material, direct labor, and support costs. To obtain the manufacturing cost per unit, divide total manufacturing costs for the job by the number of units produced in the job.

Distortions Caused by Two-Stage Allocations

Product costing systems installed in many plants employ the two-stage allocation method just described. The structure of these systems, however, can actually distort product costs. Consider the example on the next page.

Exhibit 3-27
Helping Hand
Application of
Support Costs
to Job J273-2

Item	Costs	Calculation Details
Direct materials costs:		
Casting	$1,186.60	
Assembly	788.80	
Packing	491.40	
Total materials costs	$2,466.80	
Direct labor costs:		
Casting	$128.80	7 × $18.40
Machining	666.40	28 × $23.80
Assembly	252.80	16 × $15.80
Packing	211.20	16 × $13.20
Total direct labor costs	$1,259.20	
Support costs:		
Casting	$576.00	16 × $36.00
Machining	1,282.40	56 × $22.90 see Exhibit 3-24
Assembly	619.20	16 × $38.70
Packing	468.80	16 × $29.30
Total support costs	$2,946.40	
Total manufacturing costs	$6,672.40	
Number of units	5	
Cost per unit	$1,334.48	

Assume that Burbank Company, a company that makes steel valves, has a plant that is organized into three departments: machine setups, which is a service department, and machining and assembly, which are both production departments. Total setup costs of $200,000 are assigned $120,000 to the machining and $80,000 to the assembly departments in proportion to the respective practical capacity setup hours of 480 and 320 in the two production departments.

The plant manufactures two products, labeled A and B, shown in Exhibit 3-28. From the previous information regarding setup costs, the setup activity cost driver is the following:

$$\$200,000 \div (480 + 320 \text{ setup hours}) = \$250 \text{ per hour}$$

Intuitively, it would seem logical to charge products A and B the following for setup costs:

Product A
$$\$250 \times (5 \text{ setup hours} \div 800 \text{ units}) = \$1.5625$$

Exhibit 3-28
Burbank Production
Factors Products A
and B

	Products	
Relevant Factors	A	B
Batch size in number of units	800	200
Setup hours required:		
Machining	3	3
Assembly	2	2
Production in number of units	64,000	16,000
Production in number of batches	80	80

Product B

$$\$250 \times (5 \text{ setup hours} \div 200 \text{ units}) = \$6.2500$$

Let us see now how the two-stage allocation method actually charges setup costs to the products A and B. Stage 2 assigns support costs to products on the basis of machine hours for both production departments at Burbank. Both products require 0.1 machine hours per unit in each department—machining and assembly. Each department has practical capacity of 8,000 machine hours. Therefore, these are the cost driver rates:

Machining Department
$15 per machine hour = $120,000 setup costs ÷ 8,000 machine hours

Assembly Department
$10 per machine hour = $80,000 setup costs ÷ 8,000 machine hours

Both products A and B are charged $2.50 per unit for setup costs:

$$\$2.50 = (0.1 \times \$15) + (0.1 \times \$10)$$

Product A is overcosted because it is charged more than its share of setup costs ($2.50 versus $1.5625). In contrast, product B is undercosted because it is charged less than the costs of resources actually used for setups of product B ($2.50 versus $6.25). Why does the two-stage allocation method distort product costs in this manner?

Reason for Two-Stage Allocation Distortion

The reason for the distortion is the break in the link between the cause for the support activity costs (setup hours) and the basis for assignment of the costs to the individual products (machine hours). Two related factors contribute to these cost distortions:

1. Allocations based on unit-related measures
2. Differences in relative consumption ratios

Both products A and B have the same number of machine hours per unit; therefore, both are assigned the same amount of setup costs ($2.50 per unit). In reality, however, the demand for setup activity is less for product A because it is produced in larger batches. It has been charged the same rate as for product B because of the use of machine hours as the cost driver in the second stage of allocations. Conventional two-stage allocation methods use unit-related cost drivers to allocate support activity costs in the second stage even when the demand for these activities is driven, in fact, by batch-related and product-sustaining cost drivers, such as setups and engineering changes.

Cost distortions are greater when the difference between the relative proportion of the cost driver for the activity (setup hours) and the relative proportion of the basis for second-stage assignment of support costs (machine hours) is greater. Product A needs 0.00625 setup hours per unit (5 ÷ 800) on average, but product B needs more—0.02500 setup hours per unit (5 ÷ 200). Both products need the same number of machine hours per unit. The actual consumption ratio of product A to product B for setup activity is 1:4 (that is, 0.00625 ÷ 0.02500) based on the ratio of the actual cost driver, setup hours; but the apparent consumption ratio used to allocate setup costs is 1:1 based on machine hours (0.1 ÷ 0.1). This difference in the actual cost driver consumption ratio and the unit-level cost drivers used by conventional systems results in overcosting product A and undercosting product B.

Such distortions could be eliminated if we designed a costing system that used the actual cost driver for each support activity to assign costs directly to the products. This logic underlies the development of activity-based costing systems discussed in the following chapter.

Two other traditional methods are used to allocate service department costs. These are presented next.

Sequential and Reciprocal Allocation Methods

Sequential and reciprocal allocation methods are used when service departments consume services provided by other service departments. The sequential allocation method allocates service department costs to one service department at a time in sequential order. The reciprocal allocation method determines service department cost allocations simultaneously. The specifics of each method are described next.

Sequential Allocation Method

Companies use the sequential method under the following condition: There is no pair of service departments in which each department in that pair consumes a significant proportion of the services produced by the other department in that pair. To illustrate this method, consider a plant with two production departments, machining and assembly, and two service departments, power and engineering. Service department costs are allocated on the basis of kilowatt hours and engineering hours, respectively. Exhibit 3-29 displays the directly attributable costs of the four departments and their consumption of the two services.

The sequential allocation method requires that the service departments first be arranged so that a service department can receive costs allocated from another service department only before its own costs have been allocated to other departments. Once a service department's costs have been allocated, no costs of other departments can be allocated back to it.

In this example, the power department does not receive engineering services, but the engineering department uses power. Therefore, in the sequential method, the power department costs are allocated first, followed by allocation of the engineering department costs. The total cost of a service department allocated to other departments equals the amount directly identified with the service department plus the amount allocated earlier to the service department from other service departments.

$$\text{Total costs allocated} = \text{Directly identified costs} + \text{Costs allocated to it}$$

These costs are allocated to the other service and production departments in proportion to their consumption of the service, as detailed in Exhibit 3-29. Therefore, for the allocation of the costs of the power department, the allocation ratios in Exhibit 3-29 are based on the consumption of power by the engineering, machining, and assembly departments. The allocation ratios for the engineering service are based on the consumption by the machining and the assembly departments. Exhibit 3-30 shows the resulting allocations.

Recall that power department costs are allocated first because the power department does not consume any other service. Engineering department costs are allocated next. Allocated costs of $220,000 for engineering are the directly identified costs of $180,000 plus the costs allocated to the engineering department from the power department of $40,000. Notice that no costs are allocated back to the power department.

Exhibit 3-29
Directly Identified Costs and Service Consumption Levels

ITEM	SERVICE DEPARTMENTS		PRODUCTION DEPARTMENTS		
	POWER	ENGINEERING	MACHINING	ASSEMBLY	TOTAL
Directly identified costs	$320,000	$180,000	$120,000	$80,000	$700,000
Consumption of service:					
Kilowatt-hours	0	100,000	480,000	220,000	800,000
Engineering hours	0	0	2,000	2,000	4,000
Allocation ratios:					
Power	0	0.125	0.600	0.275	1.000
Engineering	0	0	0.500	0.500	1.000

Exhibit 3-30
Sequentially
Allocated Costs

	SERVICE DEPARTMENTS		PRODUCTION DEPARTMENTS	
ITEM	POWER	ENGINEERING	MACHINING	ASSEMBLY
Directly identified costs	$320,000	$180,000	$120,000	$80,000
Allocation of power department costs	(320,000)	40,000	192,000	88,000
Allocation of engineering department costs	0	(220,000)	110,000	110,000
Totals	$0	$0	$422,000	$278,000

If both service departments in this example consume each other's services, the reciprocal allocation method is appropriate. The sequential method ignores or suppresses such reciprocal relations.

Reciprocal Allocation Method

The reciprocal allocation method recognizes reciprocal interactions between different service departments. We shall alter the consumption data in Exhibit 3-29 to illustrate this method. Notice that the information in Exhibit 3-31 is the same as that in Exhibit 3-29, except that the power department also consumes 1,000 hours of engineering service.

The sequential method does not work in this situation because when the engineering department's costs are allocated, 20% must be allocated back to the power department, whose costs were already allocated. This would leave unallocated costs in the power department. If we were to allocate this new balance in the power department on the basis of the same allocation ratios as before, we would be left with unallocated costs in the engineering department. In principle, of course, we could repeat these sequential allocations until the unallocated balance of costs became negligible. The same result, however, can be obtained by using the algebraic approach of the reciprocal allocation method.

We shall denote the total costs to be allocated for the power department as P and those for the engineering department as E. Using the equation previously developed, we can find the total costs to be allocated to the power department:

Total costs allocated = Directly identified costs + Costs allocated to it

Because the power department consumes 20% of the engineering services, we have:

$$P = \$320,000 + 0.2E$$

Exhibit 3-31
Directly Identified
Costs and Service
Consumption

	SERVICE DEPARTMENTS		PRODUCTION DEPARTMENTS		
ITEM	POWER	ENGINEERING	MACHINING	ASSEMBLY	TOTAL
Directly identified cost:	$320,000	$180,000	$120,000	$ 80,000	$700,000
Consumption of service:					
Kilowatt-hours	0	100,000	480,000	220,000	800,000
Engineering hours	1,000	0	2,000	2,000	5,000
Allocation rations:					
Power	0	0.125	0.600	0.275	1.000
Engineering	0.200	0	0.400	0.400	1.000

Also, because the engineering department uses 12.5% of the power consumed in the plant, we have:

$$E = \$180{,}000 + 0.125P$$

Both equations thus recognize that the power department's total costs include a 20% share of the engineering department's total costs and that the engineering department's total costs include a 12.5% share of the power department's costs. We can now solve these two equations simultaneously. For this purpose, we shall substitute the expression for E into the first equation for P:

$$
\begin{aligned}
P &= \$320{,}000 + 0.20 \, (\$180{,}000 + 0.125P) \\
&= \$320{,}000 + \$36{,}000 + 0.025P \\
0.975P &= \$356{,}000 \\
P &= \$365{,}128
\end{aligned}
$$

We also can solve for E by substituting this value of P in the second equation:

$$E = \$180{,}000 + 0.125 \, (\$365{,}128) = \$180{,}000 + \$45{,}641 = \$225{,}641$$

Now that we have determined the total costs for the two service departments, we can calculate the amounts to be allocated to the two production departments using the allocation ratios in Exhibit 3-31. These cost allocations appear in Exhibit 3-32. Notice that the allocations are different from those obtained in the earlier illustration for the sequential method because we began with different data. The power department's total costs were higher because it also consumed some engineering services. Because the machining department consumed a relatively larger amount of power, we find that in this case the costs allocated to it are also higher.

We mentioned that the fundamental assumption of the two-stage allocation method is the absence of a strong direct link between the support activities and the products manufactured. For this reason, service department costs are first allocated to production departments in the conventional two-stage allocation methods, using one of the methods described here. As we will see in the next chapter, activity-based costing rejects this assumption and instead develops the idea of cost drivers that directly link the activities performed to the products manufactured. These cost drivers measure the average demand placed on each activity by the various products. Then activity costs are assigned to products in proportion to the demand that the products place on average on the activities. This usually eliminates the need for the second step in stage 1 allocations that allocates service department costs to production departments before assigning them to individual jobs and products.

Exhibit 3-32
Reciprocally
Allocated Costs

ITEM	SERVICE DEPARTMENTS		PRODUCTION DEPARTMENTS	
	POWER	ENGINEERING	MACHINING	ASSEMBLY
Directly identified costs	$320,000	$180,000	$120,000	$ 80,000
Allocation of power departments costs	(365,128)	45,641	219,077	100,410
Allocation of engineering department costs	45,128	(225,641)	90,256	90,256
Totals	$0	$0	$429,333	$270,666

KEY TERMS

ASSIGNMENT MATERIALS

Questions

3-1 Define direct cost and indirect cost and provide an example of each. **(LO 1)**

3-2 Why are costs estimated for individual jobs? **(LO 3, 4)**

3-3 What information is presented in a typical job bid sheet? **(LO 3, 4)**

3-4 What is the source of the information to estimate the cost of materials? **(LO 3, 4)**

3-5 What is the source of the information to estimate the direct labor cost? **(LO 3, 4)**

3-6 How are support cost driver rates determined? **(LO 2, 4)**

3-7 How is support cost estimated for individual jobs? **(LO 2, 4)**

3-8 What is the markup rate? On what factors does it depend? **(LO 3)**

3-9 What are cost pools? How is the appropriate number of cost pools selected? **(LO 4, 5, 6)**?

3-10 What problem arises when cost driver rates are based on planned or actual short-term usage? **(LO 4)**

3-11 Use of a peanut butter–spreading approach of a single cost driver rate when there are multiple cost drivers leads to distortions in job costs. Do you agree with this statement? Explain. **(LO 5)**

3-12 What is the managerial use of tracking actual costs of individual jobs? **(LO 9)**

3-13 Why are predetermined cost driver rates used when recording actual job costs? **(LO 4)**

3-14 What does the term *conversion costs* mean? **(LO7)**

3-15 What is the basic procedure for determining product costs in continuous processing plants? **(LO 7)**

3-16 What are the similarities and differences between job order costing and multistage process costing systems? **(LO 8)**

3-17 (Appendix) What is the difference between production departments and service departments? **(LO 9)**

3-18 (Appendix) What are the two stages of cost allocations in conventional product costing systems? **(LO 9)**

3-19 (Appendix) Why do conventional product costing systems allocate service department costs first to the production departments before assigning them to individual jobs? **(LO 9)**

3-20 (Appendix) What are the different situations for which direct, sequential, and reciprocal allocation methods are designed? **(LO 9)**

3-21 (Appendix) Why are conventional two-stage cost allocation systems likely to systematically distort product costs? **(LO 9)**

3-22 (Appendix) What are two factors that contribute to cost distortions resulting from the use of conventional, two-stage cost allocation systems? **(LO 9)**

Exercises

LO 2, 3, 4 **3-23** *Job order costing, consulting* Mackenzie Consulting computes the cost of each consulting engagement by adding a portion of firmwide support costs to the labor cost of the consultants on the engagement. The support costs are assigned to each consulting engagement using a cost driver rate based on consultant labor costs. Mackenzie Consulting's support costs are $5 million per year, and total consultant labor cost is estimated at $2.5 million per year.
  a. What is Mackenzie Consulting's support cost driver rate?
  b. If the consultant labor cost on an engagement is $25,000, what cost will Mackenzie Consulting compute as the total cost of the consulting engagement?

LO 2, 4 **3-24** *Job order costing, cost driver rates* The Brinker Company uses a job order costing system at its local plant. The plant has a machining department and a finishing department. The company uses machine hours to allocate machining department support costs to jobs and uses direct labor cost to allocate finishing department support costs to jobs. Estimates for 2006 are as follows:

	MACHINING DEPARTMENT	FINISHING DEPARTMENT
Manufacturing support costs	$350,000	$280,000
Machine hours	14,000	1,400
Direct labor hours	3,500	15,400
Direct labor cost	$105,000	$350,000

  a. Determine the cost driver rate for each department.
  b. During September 2006, cost records for job 101 show the following:

	MACHINING DEPARTMENT	FINISHING DEPARTMENT
Direct materials cost	$8,000	$1,400
Direct labor cost	$250	$800
Direct labor hours	7	35
Machine hours	50	6

  Determine the total cost charged to job 101 in September 2006.

LO 4, 5, 6 **3-25** *Single rate versus departmental rates* Western Wood Products has two production departments: cutting and assembly. The company has been using a single predetermined cost driver rate based on plantwide direct labor hours. That is, the plantwide cost driver rate is computed by dividing plantwide support costs by total plantwide direct labor hours. The estimates for support costs and quantities of cost drivers for 2006 follow:

	CUTTING	ASSEMBLY	TOTAL
Manufacturing support	$25,000	$35,000	$60,000
Direct labor hours	1,000	3,000	4,000
Machine hours	4,000	2,000	6,000

a. What was the single plantwide cost driver rate for 2006?

b. Determine departmental cost driver rates based on direct labor hours for assembly and machine hours for cutting.

c. Provide reasons why Western Wood might use the method in (a) or in (b).

LO 5   **3-26** *Fluctuating cost driver rates, effect on markup pricing*   Morrison Company carefully records its costs because it bases prices on the cost of the goods it manufactures. Morrison also carefully records its machine usage and other operational information. Manufacturing costs are computed monthly, and prices for the next month are determined by adding a 20% markup to each product's manufacturing costs. The support activity cost driver rate is based on machine hours, shown below:

MONTH	ACTUAL MACHINE HOURS
January	1,350
February	1,400
March	1,500
April	1,450
May	1,450
June	1,400
July	1,400
August	1,400
September	1,500
October	1,600
November	1,600
December	1,600

Profits have been acceptable until the past year, but Morrison has recently faced increased competition. The marketing manager reported that Morrison's sales force finds the company's pricing puzzling. When demand is high, the company's prices are low, and when demand is low, the company's prices are high. Practical capacity is 1,500 machine hours per month. Practical capacity is exceeded in some months by operating the machines overtime beyond regular shift hours. Monthly machine-related costs, all fixed, are $70,000 per month.

a. Compute the monthly support cost driver rates that Morrison used last year.

b. Suggest a better approach to developing cost driver rates for Morrison and explain why your method is better.

LO 7   **3-27** *Process costs*   Fancy Foods Company produces and sells canned vegetable juice. The ingredients are first combined in the blending department and then packed in gallon cans in the canning department. The following information pertains to the blending department for January:

ITEM	PRICE PER GALLON	GALLONS
Ingredient A	$0.40	10,000
Ingredient B	0.60	20,000
Vegetable juice		27,000
Materials loss		3,000

Conversion costs for the blending department are $0.55 per gallon for January. Determine the cost per gallon of blended vegetable juice before canning.

LO 7 **3-28** *Process costs*   Pitman Chemical Company manufactures and sells Goody, a product that sells for $10 per pound. The manufacturing process also yields 1 pound of a waste product, called Baddy, in the production of every 10 pounds of Goody. Disposal of the waste product costs $1 per pound. During March, the company manufactured 200,000 pounds of Goody. Total manufacturing costs were as follows:

Direct materials	$232,000
Direct labor	120,000
Manufacturing support costs	60,000
Total costs	$412,000

Determine the cost per pound of Goody.

LO 7 **3-29** *Process costing equivalent units*   The information below pertains to July production at Porter Company's paint factory, which produces paints for household interiors:

	GALLONS	MATERIALS	CONVERSION
Work in process, July 1	3,000	30% complete	20% complete
Started in July	7,000		
To account for	10,000		
Completed and transferred out	6,000	100% complete	100% complete
Work in process, July 31	4,000	25% complete	10% complete
Accounted for	10,000		

Using the weighted-average method, determine the number of equivalent units of production for materials and conversion during July.

LO 9 (Appendix) **3-30** *Service department cost allocation, direct method*   San Rafael Company has two production departments, assembly and finishing, and two service departments, machine setup and inspection. Machine setup costs are allocated on the basis of number of setups, while inspection costs are allocated on the basis of number of direct labor hours. Selected information on the four departments follows:

ITEM	DIRECT COSTS	NUMBER OF SETUPS	DIRECT LABOR HOURS
Machine setup	$40,000	0	0
Inspection	15,000	0	0
Assembly	25,000	300	200
Finishing	20,000	100	500

Required

a. Using the direct method, determine the amount of machine setup costs allocated to the two production departments.

b. Using the direct method, determine the amount of inspection costs allocated to the two production departments.

3-31 *Sequential allocation*   Carleton Company has two service departments and two production departments. Information on annual manufacturing support costs and cost drivers follows:

	SERVICE DEPARTMENTS		PRODUCTION DEPARTMENTS	
ITEM	S1	S2	P1	P2
Support costs	$65,000	$55,000	$160,000	$240,000
Direct labor hours	2,000	1,500	2,000	3,000
Number of square feet	800	1,200	2,400	2,600

    The company allocates service department costs using the sequential method. First, S1 costs are allocated on the basis of direct labor hours. Next, S2 costs are allocated on the basis of square footage. The square footage for S1 is assumed to be zero for this purpose. Determine the total support costs allocated to each of the two production departments.

LO 9 (Appendix) **3-32** *Direct, sequential, and reciprocal allocation*   Ming Company has two service departments (S1 and S2) and two production departments (P1 and P2). Last year, directly identified support costs were $300,000 for S1 and $300,000 for S2. Information on the consumption of their services follows:

SUPPLYING	USER DEPARTMENTS			
DEPARTMENT	S1	S2	P1	P2
S1	0%	40%	30%	30%
S2	25%	0%	25%	50%

Required

a. Determine the service department costs allocated to the two production departments using the direct method.
b. Determine the service department costs allocated to the two production departments using the sequential method beginning with the allocation of S1 department costs.
c. Determine the service department costs allocated to the two production departments using the reciprocal method.

Problems

LO 2, 3, 4 **3-33** *Job costing for services*   The Hillman Company sells and services lawn mowers, snow blowers, and other equipment. The service department uses a job order cost system to determine costs of each job, such as oil changes, tune-ups, and repairs. The department assigns conversion costs through a cost driver rate on the basis of direct labor hours. The cost driver rate additionally includes a markup of 25% on the job's conversion costs in order to provide a reasonable profit for Hillman. The customer's invoice itemizes prices for parts and labor, where the stated labor rate is the department's cost driver rate that includes direct labor costs, assigned overhead costs, and the 25% markup on conversion costs. Hillman Company's service department estimated the following information for 2006:

Salaries of mechanics	$120,000
Fringe benefits	54,000
General and administrative	18,000
Depreciation	42,000
Billable direct labor hours	4,500

Required

a. Determine Hillman Company's service department's cost driver rate to be used to assign conversion costs on the basis of billable direct labor hours.

b. Job 254 required $47.40 of materials and 0.7 direct labor hours. Determine the price charged for job 254.

LO 1, 3   **3-34 Job costing**   The Leblanc Company employs a job order cost system to account for its costs. The company has three production departments. Separate departmental cost driver rates are employed because the demand for support activities for the three departments is very different. All jobs generally pass through all three production departments. Data regarding the hourly direct labor rates, cost driver rates, and three jobs on which work was done during June appear below. Jobs 101 and 102 were completed during June, while job 103 was not completed as of June 30. The costs charged to jobs not completed at the end of a month are shown as work in process inventory at the end of that month and at the beginning of the next month:

PRODUCTION DEPARTMENTS	DIRECT LABOR RATE	COST DRIVER RATES
Department 1	$12	150% of direct material cost
Department 2	18	$8 per machine hour
Department 3	15	200% of direct labor cost

	JOB 101	JOB 102	JOB 103
Beginning work in process	$25,500	$32,400	$0
Direct materials:			
Department 1	$40,000	$26,000	$58,000
Department 2	3,000	5,000	14,000
Department 3	0	0	0
Direct labor hours:			
Department 1	500	400	300
Department 2	200	250	350
Department 3	1,500	1,800	2,500
Machine hours:			
Department 1	0	0	0
Department 2	1,200	1,500	2,700
Department 3	150	300	200

Required

a. Determine the total cost of completed job 101.
b. Determine the total cost of completed job 102.
c. Determine the ending balance of work in process inventory for job 103 as of June 30.

LO 1, 3   **3-35 Charging for service activity costs**   Airporter Service Company operates scheduled coach service from Boston's Logan Airport to downtown Boston and to Cambridge. A common scheduling service center at the airport is responsible for ticketing and customer service for both routes. The service center is regularly staffed to service traffic of 2,400 passengers per week: two-thirds for downtown Boston passengers and the balance for Cambridge passengers. The cost to operate this service center is $7,200 per week normally, but it is higher during weeks when additional help is required to service higher traffic levels. The service center costs and number of passengers serviced during the 5 weeks of August follow:

WEEK	COST	BOSTON PASSENGERS	CAMBRIDGE PASSENGERS
1	$7,200	1,600	800
2	7,200	1,500	900
3	7,600	1,650	800
4	7,800	1,700	850
5	7,200	1,700	700

How much of the service center costs should be charged to the Boston service and how much to the Cambridge service?

LO 1, 2, 3   **3-36** *Job cost sheet*   Portland Electronics, Inc., delivered 1,000 custom-designed computer monitors on February 10 to its customer Video Shack; the monitors had been ordered on January 1. The following cost information was compiled in connection with this order:

Direct materials used

Part A327: 1 unit costing $60 per monitor
Part B149: 1 unit costing $120 per monitor

Direct labor used

Assembly: 6 hours per monitor at the rate of $10 per hour
Inspection: 1 hour per monitor at the rate of $12 per hour

In addition, manufacturing support costs are applied to the job at the rate of $5 per direct labor hour. The selling price for each monitor is $350.

Required

a. Prepare a job cost sheet for this job.
b. Determine the cost per monitor.

LO 1, 2, 3   **3-37** *Job cost sheet*   The following costs pertain to job 923 at Becker Auto Shop.

	QUANTITY	PRICE
Direct materials:		
Engine oil	11 ounces	$2 per ounce
Lubricant	2 ounces	3 per ounce
Direct labor	3 hours	15 per hour
Support costs (based on direct labor hours)		10 per hour

Prepare a job cost sheet for job 923.

LO 1, 2, 3, 4, 5   **3-38** *Job cost sheet, markup, single rate versus departmental rates*   Modern Metalworks Company has two departments, milling and assembly. The company uses a job costing system that employs a single, plantwide support cost driver rate to apply support costs to jobs on the basis of direct labor hours. That is, the plantwide cost driver rate is computed by dividing plantwide support costs by total plantwide direct labor hours. The following estimates are for October:

	MILLING	ASSEMBLY
Support costs	$120,000	$160,000
Direct labor hours	8,000	12,000
Machine hours	12,000	6,000

The following information pertains to job 714, which was started and completed during October:

	MILLING	ASSEMBLY
Direct labor hours	10	40
Machine hours	18	8
Direct materials costs	$800	$50
Direct labor costs	$100	$600

Required

a. Prepare a job cost sheet for job 714.
b. Assume next that instead of using a single, plantwide support cost driver rate, the company uses machine hours as the cost driver for the application of support costs in the milling department, and it uses direct labor hours as the cost driver in the assembly department. Prepare a job cost sheet for job 714.
c. Using the costs you computed in (a) and (b), determine the bid price that Modern Metalworks will quote if it uses a 25% markup on total manufacturing cost.
d. Provide reasons why Modern Metalworks might prefer the method in (a) or in (b).

LO 1, 2, 3, 4, 5   **3-39** *Single rate versus departmental rates*   Bravo Steel Company supplies structural steel products to the construction industry. Its plant has three production departments: cutting, grinding, and drilling. The estimated support activity cost, estimated direct labor hours, and estimated machine hours for each department for 2006 follow:

	CUTTING	GRINDING	DRILLING
Support activity cost	$504,000	$2,304,000	$2,736,000
Estimated direct labor hours	60,000	96,000	144,000
Estimated machine hours	960,000	480,000	360,000

The direct labor and machine hours consumed by job ST101 are as follows:

	CUTTING	GRINDING	DRILLING
Direct labor hours	2,000	2,500	3,000
Machine hours	20,000	3,000	2,000

Required

a. Assume that a single, plantwide, predetermined support cost driver rate is computed by dividing plantwide support costs by plantwide direct labor hours. Determine the support cost applied to job ST101.
b. Determine the departmental support cost driver rates and support costs applied to job ST101, assuming that machine hours are used as the cost driver in the cutting department and that direct labor hours are used as the cost driver for the grinding and drilling departments.
c. Explain why Bravo Steel might prefer a plantwide rate or departmental support cost driver rates.

LO 1, 2, 3, 4, 5   **3-40** *Job costing*   The Gonzalez Company uses a job order costing system at its plant in Green Bay, Wisconsin. The plant has a machining department and a finishing department. The company uses two cost driver rates for allocating manufacturing support costs to job orders: one on the basis of machine hours for allocating machining department support costs and the other on the basis of direct labor cost for allocating the finishing department support costs. Estimates for 2006 follow:

	MACHINING DEPARTMENT	FINISHING DEPARTMENT
Manufacturing support cost	$500,000	$400,000
Machine hours	20,000	2,000
Direct labor hours	5,000	22,000
Direct labor cost	$150,000	$500,000

Required

a. Determine the two departmental support cost driver rates.
b. During July 2006, cost records for job 511 show the following:

	MACHINING DEPARTMENT	FINISHING DEPARTMENT
Direct materials cost	$12,000	$2,000
Direct labor cost	$300	$1,200
Direct labor hours	10	50
Machine hours	80	8

Determine the total costs charged to job 511 in July 2006.
c. Explain why Gonzalez Company uses two different cost driver rates in its job costing system.

LO 1, 2, 3, 5   **3-41** *Job costs and bids, comparing actual and estimated costs*   Uyeno Electronic Company manufactures a variety of electronic components. In May 2006, the company received an invitation from Takayama, Inc., to bid on an order of 1,000 units of component C371 that must be delivered by August 16, 2006. The following are the standard (estimated) requirements and prices for 1,000 units of C371:

	QUANTITY	PRICE
Direct material	2,000 units	$10 per unit
Direct labor	1,000 hours	$10 per hour

The cost of support resources is assigned to jobs based on direct labor hours (a single cost driver rate system). The estimated support costs for 2006 are $300,000, and the estimated direct labor hours are 50,000. Uyeno has a policy to add a 20% markup to estimated job costs to arrive at the bid price.

Required

a. Prepare a job bid sheet to determine the bid price for this job.
b. Assume that Takayama, Inc., accepted Uyeno's bid. After producing and delivering the 1,000 units of C371 to Takayama on August 4, Uyeno's management accountants compiled the following information about this job:

	ACTUAL QUANTITY	ACTUAL PRICE
Direct material	2,100 units	$9.75 per unit
Direct labor	1,000 hours	$11.00 per hour

Prepare a job cost sheet to record the actual costs incurred on this job.

c. What are some possible explanations for the differences between the actual and the estimated quantities or costs for the job? Are the differences favorable from Uyeno's point of view?

LO 7 **3-42** *Process costing* Connor Chemical Company's plant processes batches of organic chemical products through three stages after starting with raw materials: (1) mixing and blending, (2) reaction chamber, and (3) pulverizing and packing. Connor Chemical's estimates for the total conversion costs for each of the three processing stages are shown in the table below. These costs include production labor assigned to each stage, support labor performing tasks (such as handling the output of the previous stage and setting up for the new stage), and laboratory testing. Additional materials for packing are needed in the pulverizing and packing stage:

	MIXING AND BLENDING	REACTION CHAMBERS	PULVERIZING AND PACKING
Production labor	$253,000	$1,144,000	$396,000
Engineering support	$22,000	$50,600	$24,200
Materials handling	$19,800	$19,800	$29,700
Equipment maintenance	$11,000	$35,200	$8,800
Laboratory expenses	$22,000	$22,000	$4,400
Depreciation	$44,000	$176,000	$52,800
Power	$35,200	$85,800	$26,400
General and administrative	$17,600	$17,600	$17,600
Total conversion costs	$424,600	$1,551,000	$559,900
Total number of process hours	8,760	35,040	8,760

Required

a. Determine the estimated conversion cost driver rate per process hour for each stage.
b. Consider two of Connor Chemical's representative products, C206 and C208. Both products are derivatives of ethyloleate and at the start of the process require the same basic raw materials. Using the information below, determine the total cost of a batch of C206 and a batch of C208:

	C206	C208
Materials:		
Raw materials, beginning of process	$1,488.00	$1,488.00
Packing materials	$175.20	$280.80
Conversion hours:		
Mixing and blending	6 hours	6 hours
Reaction chamber	24 hours	24 hours
Pulverizing and packing	4 hours	8 hours

LO 7 **3-43** *Process costing equivalent units, product cost* The information below pertains to October production at Zippy Company's bottling plant, which produces and bottles sports drinks. Each unit consists of a case of 12 bottles:

	UNITS	MATERIALS	CONVERSION
Work in process, October 1	2,000	70% complete	60% complete
Started in October	10,000		
To account for	12,000		
Completed and transferred out	8,000	100% complete	100% complete
Work in process, October 30	4,000	40% complete	25% complete
Accounted for	12,000		

Costs, beginning of October	$1,050	$3,240
Added during October	8,200	22,620
To be accounted for	$9,250	$25,860

Required

a. Using the weighted-average method, determine the number of equivalent units of production for materials and conversion during October.

b. Determine the cost per equivalent unit for materials and conversion for October and the total cost per equivalent unit.

c. Determine whether the cost per equivalent unit for materials and conversion increased or decreased from the previous month.

LO 1, 2, 3, 8 **(Appendix) 3-44** *Job bid sheet, direct and sequential allocations* Sanders Manufacturing Company produces electronic components on a job order basis. Most business is gained through bidding on jobs. Most firms competing with Sanders bid full cost plus a 30% markup. Recently, with the expectation of gaining more sales, Sanders dropped its markup from 40% to 30%. The company operates two service departments and two production departments. Manufacturing support costs and quantities of activities for each department are given below:

	SERVICE DEPARTMENTS		PRODUCTION DEPARTMENTS	
ITEM	PERSONNEL	MAINTENANCE	MACHINING	ASSEMBLY
Support costs	$100,000	$200,000	$400,000	$300,000
Number of employees	5	5	5	40
Maintenance hours	1,500	200	7,500	1,000
Machine hours	0	0	10,000	1,000
Direct labor hours	0	0	1,000	10,000

Support costs of the personnel department are allocated on the basis of employees and those of the maintenance department on the basis of maintenance hours. Departmental rates are used to assign costs to products. The machining department uses machine hours, and the assembly department uses direct labor hours for this purpose.

The firm is preparing to bid on job 781, which requires 3 machine hours per unit produced in the machining department and 5 direct labor hours per unit produced in the assembly department. The expected direct materials and direct labor costs per unit are $450.

Required

a. Allocate the service department costs to the production departments using the direct method.

b. Determine the bid price per unit produced for job 781 using the direct method.

c. Assume that the support costs of the service department incurring the greatest costs are allocated first, and allocate the service department costs to the production departments using the sequential method. When allocating personnel costs, assume the maintenance department has 0 employees.

d. Determine the bid price per unit produced for job 781 using the sequential method in (c).

3-45 *Direct, sequential, and reciprocal allocation* Boston Box Company has two service departments, maintenance and grounds, and two production departments, fabricating and assembly. Management has decided to allocate maintenance costs on the basis of machine hours used by the departments and grounds costs on the basis of square feet occupied by the departments. The following data appear in the company's records for last year:

Item	Maintenance	Grounds	Fabricating	Assembly
Machine hours	0	1,500	12,000	6,000
Square feet	3,000	0	15,000	20,000
Support costs	$18,000	$14,000	$45,000	$25,000

Required

a. Allocate service department costs to the production departments using the direct method.
b. Allocate service department costs to the production departments using the sequential method, assuming that the costs of the service department incurring the greatest cost are allocated first.
c. Allocate service department costs to the production departments using the reciprocal method.

LO 1, 2, 3, 8 (Appendix) 3-46 *Job bid price, direct, sequential, and reciprocal allocations* Sherman Company manufactures and sells small pumps made to customer specifications. It has two service departments and two production departments. Data on 2006 operations follow:

| | SERVICE DEPARTMENTS | | PRODUCTION DEPARTMENTS | |
Item	Maintenance	Power	Casting	Assembly
Support costs	$750,000	$450,000	$150,000	$110,000
Machine hours	0	80,000	80,000	40,000
Kilowatt-hours	40,000	0	200,000	160,000
Direct labor hours	0	0	100,000	60,000

Management allocates maintenance department costs using machine hours, and power department costs using kilowatt hours. Separate cost driver rates are determined on the basis of machine hours for the casting department and on the basis of direct labor hours for the assembly department. It takes 1 machine hour to manufacture a pump in the casting department and 0.5 labor hours to assemble a pump in the assembly department. Direct labor and material costs amount to $32 per pump.

A prospective customer has requested a bid on a 2-year contract to purchase 1,000 pumps every month. Sherman Company has a policy of adding a 25% markup to the full manufacturing cost to determine the bid.

Required

a. What is the bid price when the direct method is used?
b. What is the bid price when the sequential method that begins by allocating maintenance department costs is used?
c. What is the bid price when the reciprocal method is used?

Cases

LO 1, 2, 3, 4, 5   **3-47**   *Alternative job costing systems*   Over the past 15 years, Anthony's Auto Shop has developed a reputation for reliable repairs and has grown from a one-person operation to a nine-person operation, including one manager and eight skilled auto mechanics. In recent years, however, competition from mass merchandisers has eroded business volume and profits, leading the owner, Anthony Axle, to ask his manager to take a closer look at the cost structure of the auto shop.

The manager determined that direct materials (parts and components) are identified with individual jobs and charged directly to the customer. Direct labor (mechanics) is also identified with individual jobs and charged at a prespecified rate to the customers. The salary and benefits for a senior mechanic are $65,000 per year, and they are $45,000 per year for a junior mechanic. Each mechanic can work up to 1,750 hours in a year on customer jobs, but if there are not enough jobs to keep each of them busy, the cost of their compensation still will have to be incurred. The manager's salary and benefits amount to $75,000 per year. In addition, the following fixed costs are also incurred each year:

Rent	$40,000
Insurance	7,000
Utilities	7,000
Supplies	10,000
Machine maintenance	9,000
Machine depreciation	23,800
Total costs	$96,800

Because material costs are recovered directly from the customers, the profitability of the operation depends on the volume of business and the hourly rate charged for labor. At present, Anthony's Auto Shop charges $51.06 per hour for all its jobs. Anthony said he would not consider firing any of the four senior mechanics because he believes it is difficult to get workers with their skills and loyalty to the firm, but he is willing to consider releasing one or two of the junior mechanics.

The present job costing system uses a single conversion rate for all jobs. The cost driver rate is currently determined by dividing estimated total labor and support costs by expected hours charged to customers. The eight mechanics are expected to be busy on customer jobs for 95% of the total available time. The price of $51.06 per hour is determined by adding a markup of x% to the cost driver rate, that is $51.06 = [1 + x/100] \times$ cost driver rate. Note that all personnel costs are included in conversion costs at present.

The manager is considering switching to the use of two rates, one for class A repairs and another for class B repairs. Electronic ignition system repairs or internal carburetor repairs are examples of class A repairs. Class A repairs require careful measurements and adjustments with equipment such as an oscilloscope or infrared gas analyzer. Class B repairs are simple repairs, such as shock absorber replacements or exhaust part replacements. Class A repairs can be done only by senior mechanics; class B repairs are done mainly by junior mechanics. Half of the hours charged to customers are expected to be for class A repairs, and the other half are for class B repairs. Because class A repairs are expected to account for all the senior mechanics' time and most of the machine usage, 60% of the total costs (including personnel costs) are attributable to class A repairs and the remaining 40% to class B repairs.

Required

a. Determine the markup of x% currently used.
b. Determine the two new rates, one for class A repairs and another for class B repairs, using the same markup of x% that you determined in (a) above.

c. The following are expected labor hours anticipated for two customer jobs:

Job No.	Class A Repairs	Class B Repairs
101	4.5 hours	1.5 hours
102	None	2.0 hours

Determine the price (in addition to materials) to be charged for each of the two jobs under the present accounting system and under the proposed accounting system.

d. What change in service mix is likely to result from the proposed price change?

e. Provide reasons why Anthony might retain the current costing system or change to the proposed costing system.

Chapter 4

Activity-Based Cost Systems

After reading this chapter, you will be able to:

➤ understand how volume-based cost systems distort product and customer costs

➤ describe why companies producing a more varied and complex mix of products have higher costs than companies producing only a narrow range of products

➤ design a traditional activity-based cost system that links resource costs to the activities the organization performs and then from the activities to cost objects, such as products and customers

➤ use the information from an activity-based cost system to improve operations and to make better decisions about products and customers

➤ understand the importance of measuring the practical capacity of resources and the cost of unused capacity

➤ build a time-driven activity-based cost system that is simpler and that captures more complexity than a traditional activity-based cost system

➤ assign marketing, distribution, and selling expenses to customers

➤ analyze and manage customer profitability

➤ appreciate the role for activity-based cost systems for service companies

➤ discuss the barriers for implementing activity-based cost systems and how these might be overcome

Booth Motors

Jonathan Kellogg, owner and chief executive officer of Booth Motors, was concerned about the recent declines in profitability of his automobile dealership. Booth was a major Ford dealer in the Midwest, and sales of Ford's popular sport utility vehicles and trucks had been excellent. Still, many car models that Jonathan had to stock to display the full product line stayed on his lot for months. Booth Motors was incurring high expenses to lease land to store these vehicles and for the high financial charges on the vehicles.

Source: CORBIS.

In addition to sales of new cars, Booth Motors had four related lines of business: used cars, parts, service, and finance and insurance. With a total of $54 million in annual revenues from all businesses, Kellogg was unsure about the profitability of each line of business. Booth spent $48 million to purchase new cars and trucks, used vehicles, and parts. Dealer operating expenses, including employee compensation, insurance, rent, utilities, taxes, advertising, and interest expense, cost another $5.4 million, leaving Kellogg with a net operating margin of only $600,000. Kellogg felt that as one of the largest auto dealerships in the Midwest, he should be earning much more than a 1% pretax margin on sales. A 1% margin did not adequately compensate him for the capital invested in the dealership. Nor did it compensate him for the risks of purchasing and stocking large quantities of vehicles, many of which had to be sold at significant discounts at the end of the model year.

Kellogg understood that strong tie-ins existed across his five business lines. A new car sale usually involved the purchase of the buyer's current car, financing and insurance fees, and future parts and service business from the new car sale. He still wondered, however, how much each of these business lines contributed to dealership profitability. If any operated at a loss, he was willing to take actions that would enhance dealership profitability, such as adjusting prices, modifying the mix of products and services sold by the dealership, and instituting process improvements. Kellogg was ready to start making tough decisions, both within his dealership and in his negotiations with Ford Motor Company and his financing and insurance suppliers. First, though, he wanted to understand much better the "economic facts" about his dealership. Were all five product lines profitable? Within each product line, especially new vehicle sales, were all products profitable, or were only a few products profitable, with the remainder dragging down profitability?

The existing accounting system at Booth Motors reported the revenues for each of the five product lines and assigned the $48 million in directly attributable costs (that is, purchased vehicles and parts) to each line. The $5.4 million of operating expense, however, was allocated to each department on the basis of sales. Kellogg believed this allocation did not represent the demands that each product line made on Booth's resources. The cost allocation system spread all operating expenses uniformly across everything so that it distorted the cost and profitability of individual product lines and products. Kellogg wondered whether advances in cost measurement and management, especially those that had recently been implemented in the U.S. automobile manufacturing industry, could be applied to his dealership.

TRADITIONAL MANUFACTURING COSTING SYSTEMS

Manufacturing companies operated for many years with the simple job order and process costing systems described in chapter 3. These systems assigned direct labor and direct materials costs to products. The systems also allocated indirect expenses—for operating machines, scheduling, quality control, purchasing, maintenance, supervision, and general factory support (such as building depreciation, insurance, utilities, and housekeeping)—to production departments in simple proportion to the direct labor hours worked in each department, or sometimes through quite complex allocation schemes. The manufacturing cost system then divided the indirect costs at each production department by a simple measure of the volume of activity in the department, such as total direct labor hours or total machine hours worked, to arrive at an overhead allocation rate for the department. This rate was then used to allocate the indirect expenses to the products processed through each production department.

As an example of the problems of simple cost accounting systems, consider the manufacturing plant of the Ericson Ice Cream Company. Historically, Ericson had been the low-cost producer of vanilla and chocolate ice cream and enjoyed profit margins in excess of 20% of sales. Several years ago, Dennis Selmor, the sales manager, had seen opportunities to expand the business by extending the product line into new flavors that earned premium selling prices. Five years earlier, Ericson had introduced strawberry ice cream, which required the same basic production technology but could be sold at prices that were 3% higher than vanilla and chocolate. Last year, the company introduced mocha-almond ice cream, which it could sell at a 10% price premium.

However, Laura Tunney, the controller of Ericson, was disappointed with the most recent quarterly financial results of the factory's operations (see Exhibit 4-1). The new strawberry and mocha flavors were more profitable than the high-volume, commodity vanilla and chocolate flavors as expected, but operating margins overall had decreased, and the company was now operating at a loss. Tunney wondered whether the company should continue to deemphasize the commodity products and keep introducing new specialty flavors.

Exhibit 4-1
Total and Product
Profitability,
Ericson Ice Cream

	VANILLA	CHOCOLATE	STRAWBERRY	MOCHA-ALMOND	TOTAL
Production and sales volume (000)	500	400	90	10	1,000
Unit selling price	$4.50	$4.50	$4.65	$4.95	
Sales (000)	$2,250	$1,800	$418.5	$49.5	$4,518
Material costs (000)	750	600	140.4	16.5	1,506.9
Direct labor (000)	300	240	54	6	600
Overhead at 300% (000)	900	720	162	18	1,800
Total factory expenses (000)	1,950	1,560	356.4	40.5	3,906.9
Gross margin (000)	$300	$240	$62.1	$9	$611.1
Gross margin (%)	13.3%	13.3%	14.8%	18.2%	13.5%
Marketing, selling, distribution, and administrative (MSDA) expenses (000)					$900.0
Operating profit (loss) (000)					($288.9)

Jeffrey Donald, Ericson's manufacturing manager, commented on the how the introduction of the new flavors had changed his production environment:

Five years ago, life was a lot simpler. We produced just vanilla and chocolate ice cream in long production runs, and everything ran smoothly, without much intervention. Difficulties started when we introduced the strawberry flavor. We had to make more changeovers to stop production of vanilla or chocolate, empty the vats, clean out all remnants of the previous flavor, and then start the production of the strawberry flavor. Making chocolate was simple—we didn't even have to clean out the residual from the previous run if we just dumped in enough chocolate syrup to cover it up. For strawberry, however, even small traces of other flavors create quality problems. And because mocha-almond contains nuts, to which many people have severe allergic reactions, we have to do a complete sterilization of the vat after every mocha production run.

We are also spending a lot more time on purchasing and scheduling activities and just keeping track of where we stand on existing, back-logged, and future orders. The new computer system we got last year helped a lot to reduce the confusion. But I am concerned about rumors that even more new flavors may be introduced in the near future. I don't think we have any more capability to handle additional confusion and complexity in our operations.

Ice cream production at the Ericson factory involved preparing and mixing the ingredients for each flavor in large vats. In a subsequent stage, the ice cream mix was packaged into containers using semiautomatic machines. A final packing and ship-ping stage was performed manually.

Each product had a bill of materials that identified the quantity and cost of direct materials and labor required for the product. From this information, it was easy to calculate the direct materials costs and direct labor costs for each flavor. Tunney believed, however, that the assignment of the indirect expenses was probably not accurate. Ericson's indirect expenses (about $1.8 million per quarter) were comprised of the following:

EXPENSE CATEGORY	EXPENSE (000)
Indirect labor	$ 600
Fringe benefits	480
Computer systems	300
Machinery	240
Maintenance	120
Energy	60
Total	$1,800

Because it was a small company that had historically produced only a narrow range of products (vanilla and chocolate ice cream), Ericson used a simple costing system. The plant's indirect expenses ($1.8 million) were allocated to products on the basis of each product's direct labor cost. The cost system's current overhead rate was 300% of direct labor cost. Most people in the plant recalled that not too many years ago, before the new specialty flavors (strawberry and mocha-almond) had been introduced, the overhead rate was only 200% of direct labor cost.

LIMITATIONS OF ERICSON'S TRADITIONAL COST SYSTEM

Ericson's traditional cost system is adequate for the financial reporting role of inventory valuation. It is simple, easy to use and understand, and applied consistently from year to year. When Ericson's management accountants designed the system years ago, production operations were mostly manual, and total indirect costs were less than direct labor costs. Ericson's two products had similar production volumes and batch sizes. Given the high cost of measuring and recording information, the accountants judged correctly that a complex costing system would be more expensive to operate than the company could recoup in benefits from a more detailed assignment of costs.

Ericson's production environment, however, has changed. Because of automation, direct labor costs have decreased and indirect expenses increased. As the custom, low-volume flavors had been added, Ericson needed more scheduling, setup, and quality control people, plus a computer to track orders and product specifications. The cost system that was adequate when indirect expenses were low and product variety was limited could now be giving distorted signals about the relative profitability of Ericson's different products.

The distortions arise because of the way production center costs (both the costs incurred within production departments and the costs allocated to them from production support departments) are allocated to products. Many manufacturing companies, like Ericson, use only unit-level drivers—such as direct labor dollars, direct labor hours, or machine hours—for allocating production center expenses to products. In an environment of high product variety, the exclusive use of unit-level drivers to allocate overhead costs leads to product cost distortion, as illustrated in the example on the next page:

VANILLA FACTORY AND MULTIFLAVOR FACTORY

The Vanilla Factory produces 1 million gallons of ice cream, all the same flavor (vanilla, of course) and all packed in half-gallon containers. The Multiflavor Factory also produces 1 million gallons of ice cream but of many different flavors, recipes, brand names, and package sizes (half-pint, pint, quart, half-gallon, gallon, and two-gallon containers). Multiflavor Factory treats each combination of flavor, recipe, brand name, and package size as a different product (called a stockkeeping unit [SKU]). In a typical year, the Multiflavor Factory produces about 2,500 different SKUs, ranging from specialty flavors and packages, with annual production volumes as low as 50 to 100 gallons per year, up to high-volume standard flavors such as vanilla or chocolate in standard half-gallon packages whose annual production volumes are each about 100,000 gallons per year.

Even though both factories make the same basic product, the Multiflavor Factory requires many more resources to support its highly varied mix. It has a much larger production support staff than the Vanilla Factory because it requires more people to schedule machine and production runs; perform changeovers and setups between production runs in the blending and the packaging line; inspect items at the beginning of each production run; move materials; ship and expedite orders; develop new flavor recipes; improve existing products; negotiate with vendors; schedule materials receipts; order, receive, inspect incoming materials and parts; and update and maintain the much larger computer-based information system. It also operates with considerably higher levels of idle time, setup time, overtime, inventory, rework, and scrap. Because both factories have the same physical output, both have roughly the same cost of materials (ignoring the slightly higher acquisition costs in Multiflavor) for smaller orders of specialty ingredients and flavors and other materials. For actual production, because all gallons of ice cream are about the same complexity, both the Vanilla Factory and the Multiflavor Factory require the same number of direct labor hours and machine hours for actual production (not counting the higher idle time and setup times in Multiflavor). The Multiflavor Factory also has about the same property taxes, security costs, and heating bills as the Vanilla Factory, but it has much higher indirect and support costs because of its more varied product mix and complex production tasks.

Consider now the operation of a traditional cost system, like the one used at Ericson Ice Cream, in these two plants. The Vanilla Factory has little need for a cost system to calculate the cost of a package of half-gallon vanilla ice cream. The financial manager, in any single period, simply divides total expenses by total production volume to get the cost per half-gallon package produced. For a year, divide the factory expenses by the million-gallon capacity to get the cost per gallon (or divide by 2 million to get the cost per half-gallon container produced). For the Multiflavor Factory, the traditional cost system first allocates indirect and support expenses to production cost pools, as described in chapter 3. Once the traceable and allocated support expenses have been accumulated within each production cost pool, the system allocates the pool's costs to products on the basis of the volume cost driver for that cost center: direct labor, machine hours, units produced, or materials quantity processed. On a per-unit basis, high-volume standard half-gallon containers of vanilla and chocolate ice cream require about the same quantity of each cost driver (labor and machine time, number of units, materials quantity) as the very low volume SKUs, consisting of specialty flavors and recipes packaged in a specialty size. Therefore, Multiflavor's overhead costs would be applied to products on the basis of their production volumes. Chocolate and vanilla half-gallon containers, each representing about 10% of the plant's output, would have about 10% of

As at Ericson Ice Cream, setups are done between jobs at the manufacturing company pictured here, and are sometimes time-consuming and therefore, costly. Many production and operations-management techniques can reduce setup times. Data about the cost of such labor form part of an activity-based costing system. *Source*: Will & Deni McInture/Photo Researchers, Inc.

the plant's overhead applied to them. A low-volume product, representing only .01% of the plant's output (100 gallons per year), would have about .01% of the plant's overhead allocated to it. The traditional costing system reports, on a per-gallon basis, essentially identical product costs for all products, standard and specialty, regardless of the relative production volumes of their flavor, recipe, and packaging SKU combination.

Clearly, however, considerably more of the Multiflavor Factory's indirect resources are required (on a per-gallon basis) for the low-volume, specialty, newly-designed products than for the mature, high-volume, standard vanilla and chocolate products. Traditional cost systems, even those with multiple production cost centers, systematically and grossly underestimate the cost of resources required for specialty, low-volume products and overestimate the resource cost of producing high-volume, standard products, such as the half-gallon vanilla and chocolate ice cream SKUs.

Activity-based cost systems have been developed to eliminate this major source of cost distortion. The following section focuses on how activity-based cost systems work.

ACTIVITY-BASED COST SYSTEMS

Activity-based cost (ABC) systems typically use a simple two-stage approach similar to but more general than traditional cost systems. Traditional cost systems use actual departments or cost centers for defining cost pools to accumulate and redistribute costs. ABC systems, instead of using cost centers, use activities for accumulating costs. The design of an ABC system starts by asking what activities are being performed by a department's resources. ABC then assigns the resource expenses to activities on the basis of how much of the resources each activity uses.

Tracing Costs to Activities

Laura Tunney, controller of Ericson Ice Cream, started her analysis of indirect expenses by looking at the fringe benefits paid to employees. She learned that fringe benefits costs amounted to an additional 40% of the wages paid to direct and indirect labor. She applied fringe benefit costs as a simple 40% markup to all direct and indirect labor costs.

Tunney then interviewed department heads in charge of indirect labor and found that the employees in these departments performed three main activities. About half (50%) of indirect labor was involved in scheduling production orders; purchasing, preparing, and releasing materials for the production run; and inspecting the first few units produced each time the process was changed to a new flavor. Tunney aggregated all these tasks into an activity that she called *handle production runs*. Another 40% of indirect labor actually performed the physical changeover from one flavor to another, an activity that she labeled *set up machines*. While interviewing the supervisors, Tunney learned that the time to change over to chocolate was short, only about 2.4 hours, as the previous flavor did not have to be completely washed out. Other flavors required longer changeover times. The mocha-almond flavor required the most extensive changeover time, about 7.6 hours, to flush out the allergen (nuts) and also to meet its demanding quality specification.

For the remaining 10% of the time, indirect labor people maintained records on the four flavors, including making up the bill of materials and routing information, monitoring and maintaining a minimum supply of raw materials and finished goods inventory for each product, improving the production processes, and performing recipe changes for the products. Tunney referred to this activity as *support products*.

As she conducted the interviews, Tunney had performed the first two steps involved in designing an activity-based cost system:

1. Develop the **activity dictionary**—the list of the major activities performed by the plant's resources (both human resources and physical resources)
2. Obtain sufficient information to assign resource expenses to each activity in the activity dictionary (50% of indirect labor to handle production runs, 40% to set up machines, and 10% to support products)

Tunney had followed a good guideline by using verbs—action words such as *handle, set up*, and *support*—to describe activities. Activities should describe what resources, such as people and equipment, were doing.

Tunney next turned her attention to the $300,000 of expenses needed to operate the company's computer system. She interviewed the managers of the data center and the management information system departments and found that scheduling production runs in the factory and ordering and paying for materials for each production run required most of the computer time and software programs. Since each production run was made for a particular customer, the computer time required to prepare shipping documents and to invoice and collect from a customer was also included in this activity. In total, the production run activity consumed about 80% of the computer resource. This expense seemed to relate well to the *handle production runs* activity, already defined.

The remaining 20% of computer resources kept records on the four products, including production process and associated engineering change notice information. Tunney believed that this expense should be assigned to the activity *support products*, which was also already defined in her activity dictionary.

The remaining three categories of overhead expense (machine depreciation, machine maintenance, and the energy to operate the machines) related to the supply of machine capacity to produce ice cream flavors. The machines had a practical capacity of 12,000 hours of productive time for ice cream production. For this work, Tunney added a new entry in the activity dictionary, *run machines*.

Tunney noted that even though she had defined only four activities for Ericson's indirect costs, they represented the three different levels of the manufacturing cost hierarchy:

ACTIVITY	COST HIERARCHY
Run machines	Unit level
Handle production runs	Batch level
Set up machines	Batch level
Support products	Product sustaining

Finding at least one activity for each hierarchy level gave her confidence that the complexity of the manufacturing process could be represented well enough by the activity-based cost system.

At this point, Tunney had completed half the design of the new ABC system and could assign all indirect and support expenses to production activities. She prepared Exhibit 4-2 to summarize her analysis to date. She also drew a diagram of the process she had followed thus far, shown in Exhibit 4-3.

Exhibit 4-2
Ericson Ice Cream:
Activities and
Activity Expenses

	HANDLE PRODUCTION RUNS	SET UP MACHINES	SUPPORT PRODUCTS	RUN MACHINES	TOTAL EXPENSE
Indirect labor (plus 40% fringe benefits)	50%	40%	10%		$840,000
Computer expense	80%		20%		300,000
Machine depreciation				100%	240,000
Maintenance				100%	120,000
Energy				100%	60,000
Activity expense	$660,000	$336,000	$144,000	$420,000	$1,560,000

Exhibit 4-3
Ericson Ice Cream: ABC—Mapping Resource Expenses to Activities

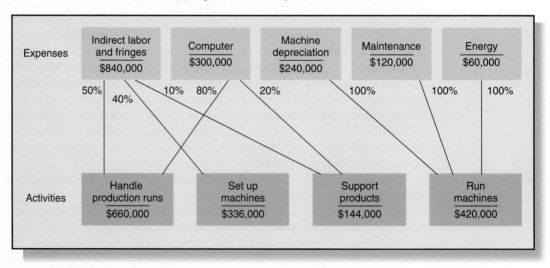

The ABC model was only half completed because while company expenses had been driven down to production activities, the costs had not yet been driven down to individual products. Yet Tunney already had gained some important insights from her analysis. Before, she saw only categories of expenses, such as the company's spending on computers, energy, and indirect labor (the top row in Exhibit 4-3). Now she could see *why* Ericson Ice Cream was incurring expenditures for these resources. In particular, she saw the high expenses of such activities as handling production runs and setting up machines for specialty ice cream flavors (the bottom row in Exhibit 4-2 or 4-3). When Ericson produced only vanilla and chocolate, it had few production runs and consequently little need to continually set up machines; and because half the setups were to make chocolate ice cream, the setup activity had been inexpensive. The introduction of the new specialty flavors had led to high expenses for production run and setup activities.

In the past, industrial engineers at Ericson had studied labor and materials usage closely because these had been the high-cost resources. They were also the primary cost categories featured by Ericson's traditional cost system (which allocated all indirect costs to products using direct labor dollars). The high overhead rate on direct labor seemed to amplify any benefits from the savings in direct labor that the industrial engineers could achieve. Tunney could now see the potential benefits if she could focus the company's industrial engineers on improving the activities of handling production runs and setting up machines.

Tracing Costs from Activities to Products

Once Tunney understood how resources were used to perform activities, she could turn her attention to understanding the quantity required of each activity by each of the four products. This knowledge would permit her to relate the activity costs to each flavor.

Activity cost drivers represent the quantity of activities used to produce individual products. Tunney identified the following activity cost drivers for the activities in her activity dictionary:

Activity	Activity Cost Driver
Handle production runs	Production runs
Set up machines	Setup hours
Support products	Number of products
Run machines	Machine hours

In addition, of course, labor dollars had previously been used as the activity cost driver to assign the cost of fringe benefits to direct and indirect labor employees,

Once the activity cost drivers had been determined, Tunney obtained quantitative information on the total quantity of each activity cost driver and the quantity of cost driver used by each ice cream product. Tunney summarized her findings (see Exhibit 4-4).

Tunney now had sufficient information to estimate a complete ABC model for the Ericson ice cream factory. She calculated the **activity cost driver rate** by dividing the activity expense by the total quantity of the activity cost driver, as shown in Exhibit 4-5. Tunney then multiplied the activity cost driver rate by the quantity of each activity cost driver used by each of the four products, as shown in Exhibit 4-6. Tunney combined the activity expense analysis for each product with their direct materials and labor costs, from Exhibit 4-1, to obtain a new ABC profitability report, shown in Exhibit 4-7.

Exhibit 4-4
Activity Cost Drivers

ACTIVITY COST DRIVER	VANILLA	CHOCOLATE	STRAWBERRY	MOCHA-ALMOND	TOTAL[a]
Direct labor hours/unit	0.02	0.02	0.02	0.02	20,000
Machine hour/unit	0.012	0.012	0.012	0.012	12,000
Production runs	700	650	500	150	2,000
Setup time/run	4	2.4	5	7.6	
Total setup time (hour)	2,800	1,560	2,500	1,140	8,000
Number of products	1	1	1	1	4

[a]The total labor and machine hours are obtained by multiplying the unit amounts by the quantity of each type of ice cream sold (from Exhibit 4-1, these quantities are 500,000 vanilla, 400,000 chocolate, 90,000 strawberry, and 10,000 mocha-almond gallons.

Exhibit 4-5
Calculating Activity Cost Driver Rates

	ACTIVITY EXPENSE	ACTIVITY COST DRIVER	ACTIVITY COST DRIVER QUANTITY	ACTIVITY COST DRIVER RATE
Handle production runs	$660,000	Number of production runs	2,000	$330 per run
Set up machines	$336,000	Number of setup hours	8,000	$42 per setup hour
Support products	$144,000	Number of products	4	$36,000 per product
Run machines	$420,000	Number of machine hours	12,000	$35 per machine hour
Total	$1,560,000			

Exhibit 4-6
Assign Activity Expenses to Products

	ACTIVITY COST DRIVER RATE	ACDQ FOR VANILLA	ACTIVITY EXPENSE: VANILLA	ACDQ FOR CHOCOLATE	ACTIVITY EXPENSE: CHOCOLATE	ACDQ FOR STRAWBERRY	ACTIVITY EXPENSE: STRAWBERRY	ACDQ FOR MOCHA-ALMOND	ACTIVITY EXPENSE: MOCHA-ALMOND
Handle production runs	$330	700	$231,000	650	$214,500	500	$165,000	150	$49,500
Set up machines	$42	2,800	$117,600	1,560	$65,520	2,500	$105,000	1,140	$47,880
Support products	$36,000	1	$36,000	1	$36,000	1	$36,000	1	$36,000
Run machines	$35	6,000	$210,000	4,800	$168,000	1,080	$37,800	120	$ 4,200

Exhibit 4-7
Activity-Based Costing Product Profitability Report (000)

	VANILLA	CHOCOLATE	STRAWBERRY	MOCHA-ALMOND	TOTAL
Sales	$2,250	$1,800	$418.5	$49.5	$4,518
Material costs	750	600	140.4	16.5	1,506.9
Direct labor	300	240	54	6	600
Contribution margin	$1,200	$960	$224.1	$27	$2,411.1
40% fringe on direct labor	120	96	21.6	2.4	240
Handle production runs	231	214.5	165	49.5	660
Set up machines	117.6	65.52	105	47.88	336
Support products	36	36	36	36	144
Run machines	210	168	37.8	4.2	420
Total overhead	714.6	580.02	365.4	139.98	1,800
Gross margin	$485.4	$379.98	($141.3)	($112.98)	$611.1
Gross margin (%)	21.6%	21.1%	(33.8)%	(228.2)%	13.5%
Marketing, selling, distribution, and administrative (MSDA) expenses					$900.0
Operating profit/(loss)					($288.9)

Notice that Exhibit 4-7 contains far more information than the highly aggregated report shown in Exhibit 4-1. In Exhibit 4-1, a single line item, overhead, aggregated (inaccurately) the complex set of activities performed by the company's indirect resources. Now Tunney could see the cost of all the activities performed for each product.

The results from the ABC system were quite different from the results using the traditional cost system shown in Exhibit 4-1. Tunney now understood why the profitability of Ericson had deteriorated in recent years. The two specialty products, which the previous cost system had reported as the most profitable, were in fact the most unprofitable and were losing lots of money. The company had added large quantities of overhead resources—a larger computer system and many more indirect and support employees—to design and produce these products. The incremental revenues from sales of the specialty strawberry and mocha-almond flavors failed to cover the expenses of the additional support resources they required.

The activity-based analysis showed that, contrary to the perspective of the traditional system, Ericson's only profitable products were its mainstay vanilla and chocolate flavors. The actual operating margins on these products exceeded the 20% that the company had enjoyed before the new specialty flavors had been introduced.

Exhibits 4-8a and b compare the costs reported by the traditional and the ABC systems for chocolate and strawberry flavors. The traditional cost system, allocating overhead costs proportional to direct labor costs, assigned too much overhead cost to chocolate, the high-volume simple product, and too little cost to strawberry, the lower-volume and more complex product. In general, not just in the simple example of the Ericson Ice Cream company, a company's production of complex, low-volume products require many more resources per unit produced to perform setups, handle production runs, and design and support.

Exhibit 4-8a
Costing Method
Comparison:
Chocolate

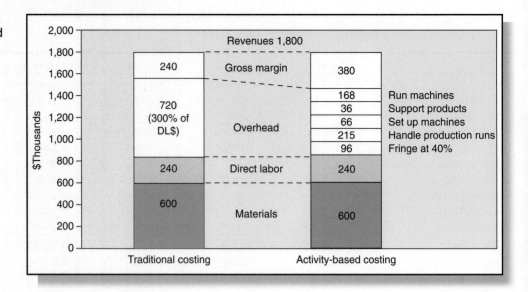

Exhibit 4-8b
Costing Method
Comparison:
Strawberry

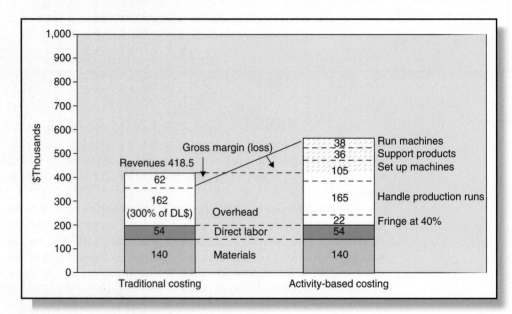

Activity-Based Management

The information in Exhibits 4-7 and 4-8 provides managers with numerous insights about how to increase the profitability of Ericson. **Activity-based management (ABM)** refers to the actions managers take, on the basis of an ABC study, to improve the efficiency of activities and the profitability of products. For example, Dennis Selmor in the sales and marketing department, might try to raise prices for the unprofitable specialty flavors to cover their higher per-unit production and sustaining costs. Currently, the costs for handling production runs and setting up machines for these two flavors are higher than their direct materials and labor costs. Marketing and sales managers can also attempt to expand demand for the profitable chocolate and vanilla flavors.

Other ABM actions aim at improving processes, particularly the processes performing batch and product-sustaining activities. Jeffrey Donald and other manufacturing people at Ericson can redirect their attention from trying to run their production equipment faster (improving the performance of unit-level activities) to learning how to reduce setup times (improving the performance of batch-level activities) so that small batches of the specialty flavors would be less expensive (require fewer resources) to produce. The high cost of the demanding quality specifications for strawberry ice cream—and frequent recipe changes for it—can motivate the technical employees to design new products that are easier to produce and require fewer modifications once introduced, thereby reducing the resource demands by a product-sustaining activity. Another ABM action for transforming loss products into profitable ones is to impose a minimum order size to eliminate short, unprofitable production runs.

The combined impact of process improvements, repricing, sales volume increases, and engineering and design improvements would significantly increase the profitabil-

IN PRACTICE
W.S. Industries Uses ABC Information for Continuous Improvement

W.S. Industries, headquartered in Chennai, India, supplies equipment such as insulators, lightning arrestors, transformers, capacitors, and circuit breakers to companies that transmit and distribute electrical power. As competition intensified in the 1990s, the company could no longer pass on cost increases in the form of higher prices. It had to hold its prices constant or even reduce them. W.S. Industries wanted to protect its strong market position in India, where it was among the top three in market share, while expanding aggressively into international markets in Asia, Europe, Africa, and the United States. Among its primary goals for success was to achieve a "quantum improvement in productivity." It turned to ABC as the primary tool to achieve this business objective.

It formed an ABC project team consisting of middle managers from operations, research and development, quality, information systems, and only one finance representative. W.S. wanted operating people to have ownership of the new system, not to feel that it was developed and mandated by finance. The team mapped all process and activities into a database, classifying each as either value added or non–value added (a non–value-added activity, such as moving parts back and forth into inventory, was one that could be eliminated with no deterioration of product attributes).

Employee teams used the new ABC information to suggest continuous improvement projects (CIPs) that would either eliminate nonvalue adding activities or reduce the cost of performing value-adding activities. For example, one team received approval to break down a wall that was causing excessive quantities of internal movement. The team saw from the ABC analysis that the benefits from reduced material movement costs exceeded the cost of the renovation.

The highly unionized workforce was initially concerned about job loss due to successful improvement projects. The company guaranteed that the benefits from the CIPs would be captured by higher sales growth, not job losses. To reinforce the culture of employee empowerment and informed continuous improvement, the company instituted the following reward program:

- A CIP would be eligible for a reward only if it were successfully implemented by a team and the savings were realized without any adverse side effects.
- Expenses to implement the project would be deducted when calculating the actual savings achieved.
- Employees would receive a fixed proportion of the savings either one-time or annually if savings continued to occur.
- All rewards would be disbursed equally to all team members in an open forum of all employees.

In the first three years, the company completed 56 CIPs yielding savings of Rs. 13.62 million (about U.S. $300,000). More significantly, factory capacity had increased from 9,000 metric tons of product to 11,700 metric tons per year. Material movements dropped by 15,200 metric ton-meters per day; reductions in waste, scrap, and inventory yielded savings of Rs. 10 million per year; and the available time on bottleneck machines increased from less than 85% to more than 95%. On-time delivery to customers had also improved dramatically.

Source: V. G. Narayanan, "Activity-Based Management at W.S. Industries (A)," (HBS Case #101-062).

ity of Ericson without compromising its ability to offer customers both high-volume standard and low-volume specialty flavor products. The ABC system has provided Ericson's managers with many insights that they can exploit to transform their currently unprofitable operations into profitable growth.

Concerns with Activity-Based Costing

In practice, many companies' ABC models are not quite as simple to implement as the example we presented for Ericson Ice Cream. Companies have experienced several problems when they attempt to apply ABC to their complex enterprises. First, the process to interview and survey employees to get their time allocations to multiple activities is time consuming and costly. At one large money center bank's brokerage operation, the ABC model required 70,000 employees at more than 100 facilities to submit monthly surveys of their time. The company had to provide 14 full-time people just to manage the ABC data collection, processing, and reporting. A $20 billion distributor required several months and about a dozen employees to update its internal ABC model. The high time and cost to estimate and maintain an ABC model—through reinterviews and resurveys—has been a major barrier to widespread ABC adoption. And, because of the high cost of continually updating the ABC model, many ABC systems are updated only infrequently, leading to out-of-date activity cost driver rates and inaccurate estimates of process, product, and customer costs.

Managers also question the accuracy of the system since cost assignments are based on individuals' subjective estimates of how they spend their time. Apart from the measurement error introduced by employees' best attempts to recall their time allocations, the people supplying the data—anticipating how it might be used—might bias or distort their responses. As a result, managers often argue about the accuracy of the model's estimated costs and profitability rather than address how to improve the inefficient processes, unprofitable products and customers, and considerable excess capacity that the model has apparently revealed.

Another problem is that traditional ABC models find it difficult to add new activities or add more detail to an existing activity. For example, consider the complexity in an activity, "ship order to customer." Rather than assume a constant cost per order shipped, a company may wish to recognize the cost differences when an order is shipped in a full truck, in a less-than-truckload shipment, using overnight express, or by a commercial carrier. In addition, the shipping order may be entered either manually or electronically, and it may require either a standard or an expedited transaction. Allowing for the significant variation in resources required by each different shipping arrangement requires that new activities be added to the model and personnel reinterviewed to get their time allocations for reassigning aggregate shipping expenses to all the different shipping activity types.

As the activity dictionary expands—either to reflect more granularity and detail about activities performed or to expand the scope of the model to the entire enterprise—the demands on the computer model used to store and process the data escalate dramatically. For example, a company using 150 activities in its enterprise ABC model, applying the costs in these 150 activities to 600,000 cost objects (products or SKUs and customers), and running the model monthly for 2 years requires data estimates, calculations, and storage for more than 2 billion items.

Such expansion has caused many homegrown ABC systems to exceed the capacity of their generic spreadsheet tools, such as Microsoft Excel®, or even their commercial ABC software packages. The systems often take days to process 1 month of data, assuming the solution converges at all. For example, the automated ABC model for a $12 million manufacturer took 3 days to calculate costs for its 40 departments, 150 activities, 10,000 orders, and 45,000 line items.

These data collection, storage, and processing problems have become obvious to many ABC implementers. But a subtle and more serious problem arises from the interview and survey process itself. When people estimate how much time they spend on a list of activities handed to them, invariably they report percentages that add up to 100%. Few individuals report that a significant percentage of their time is idle or unused. Therefore, cost driver rates are calculated assuming that resources are working at full capacity. But, of course, operations at practical capacity are more the exception than the rule. Beyond the distortion caused by assigning unused capacity costs to products, a second-order effect occurs when managers take ABM actions. They can decrease the production of unprofitable products, increase production run sizes, change product mix, and improve process efficiencies. In the short run, these actions increase unused capacity, but unless the cost of the unused capacity is excluded from future cost assignments to products and customers, the apparent gains from these apparently desirable ABM actions get reallocated back to the remaining products, raising their costs and lowering their reported profitability.

In summary, the process of calculating activity expenses through interviews, observation, and surveys requires a time-consuming and costly process to collect the data, an expensive information system to run the model, and a difficult process to update the model in light of changing circumstances. It is also theoretically incorrect by including the cost of unused capacity when calculating cost driver rates.

In the next two sections, we describe how to handle the capacity problem and will introduce, in the third section, a new approach called time-driven ABC (discussed later in this chapter), which enables a much simpler ABC model to capture even highly complex operations.

Measuring the Cost of Resource Capacity

In calculating cost driver rates, such as the cost per production run, Laura Tunney divided the $660,000 of expenses for performing production runs by the 2,000 production runs performed during the period. Suppose, however, that the quantity of indirect labor supplied could have performed 2,400 production runs, even though only 2,000 were scheduled during the quarter. Analysts can obtain a better estimate for the cost of resources required to handle each production run by dividing activity expenses by the practical capacity, not the capacity actually used, of the resources performing the work.

Practical capacity is often estimated as a percentage, say 80% or 85%, of theoretical capacity. That is, if an employee or machine normally can work 40 hours per week (the theoretical capacity), then the practical capacity could be estimated to be 32 hours per week. This estimate allows for 20% of personnel time for breaks, arrival and departure, and communication and reading unrelated to actual work performance. For machines, the 20% represents an allowance for downtime due to maintenance, repair, and scheduling fluctuations.

Knowing practical capacity, the analyst can calculate a more accurate unit cost for an activity, such as handling production runs:

$$\text{Unit cost} = \frac{\text{Cost of capacity supplied}}{\text{Practical capacity of resources supplied}}$$

Cost per production run = $660,000/2,400 runs = $275 per run

This amount is considerably below the $330-per-run estimate Tunney calculated on the basis of the actual work performed. The $330-per-run estimate included not only the cost of resources used for the actual production runs handled but also the cost of unused capacity for this activity. The cost of unused capacity should not be assigned to products produced or customers served during a period. The activity cost driver rate should reflect the underlying efficiency of the process—the cost of resources to handle each production order—and this efficiency is measured better by using the capacity of the resources supplied as the denominator when calculating activity cost driver rates. The numerator in an activity cost driver calculation represents the costs of supplying resource capacity to do work. The denominator should match the numerator by representing the quantity of work the resources can perform.

The cost of unused capacity, however, should not be ignored; it remains someone's or some department's responsibility. Usually one can assign unused capacity after analyzing the decision that authorized the level of capacity supplied. For example, if the capacity was acquired to meet anticipated demands from a particular customer or a particular market segment, the costs of unused capacity due to lower-than-expected demands can be assigned to the person or organizational unit responsible for that customer or segment. Such an assignment is done on a lump-sum basis; it will be treated as a sustaining, not a unit-level, expense.

Unused capacity should not be treated as a general cost; it should be assigned to a product line, a department, or an executive's responsibility. For example, if the unused capacity relates to a particular product line—as when certain production resources are dedicated to individual product lines—the cost of unused capacity is assigned to that product line where the demand failed to materialize. Suppose a division manager knew in advance that resource supply would exceed resource demand but wanted to retain the amount of current unused resources for future growth and expansion. Then that unused capacity could be a division-sustaining cost, assigned to the division making the decision to retain the unused capacity. In making such assignment of unused capacity costs, we trace the costs at the level in the organization where decisions are made that affect the supply of capacity resources and the demand for those resources. The lump-sum assignment of unused capacity costs provides feedback to managers on their supply and demand decisions.

Fixed Costs and Variable Costs in Activity-Based Cost Systems

Even though an ABC system assigns most indirect costs to products, this system does not assume that such costs are "variable" in the traditional sense; that they will increase or decrease with short-term changes in activity volumes. If the company does one less setup or one fewer production run, its overall costs will likely not change, which is why many refer to indirect and support costs as "fixed costs." We prefer, for reasons about to be explained, to refer to such costs as committed, not fixed. Most expenses assigned by an ABC system do represent committed costs, but they can become variable when managers act. (They are only fixed if managers ignore changes in capacity utilization.) Costs become variable through a two-step process. First, demands for the capacity resources change either because of changes in the quantity of activities performed (for example, changes in number of production runs or products supported) or because of changes in the efficiency of performing activities (for example, fewer resources become needed to perform the same quantity of activities). Second, managers make decisions to change the supply of committed resources, either up or down, to meet the new level of demand for the activities performed by these resources.

If activity volumes exceed the capacity of existing resources, the result is bottlenecks, shortages, increased pace of activity, delays, or poor-quality work. Such shortages occur often on machines, but the ABC approach makes clear that shortages can also occur for human resources who perform support activities, such as designing, scheduling, ordering, purchasing, maintaining, and handling products and customers. Companies facing such shortages typically make committed costs variable: They relieve the bottleneck by spending more to increase the supply of resources to perform work, which is why many indirect costs increase over time.

Demands for indirect and support resources also can decline, either intentionally through ABM or inadvertently through competitive or economy-wide forces that lead to declines in sales. Should the demands for batch and product-sustaining resources decrease, few immediate spending reductions will be noticed. Even for many unit-level resources, such as machines and direct labor, reduced demands for work do not immediately lead to spending decreases. People have been hired, space has been rented, and computers, telephones, and furniture have been acquired. The expenses for these resources continue even though there is less work for the resources to perform. The reduced demand for organizational resources does lower the cost of resources used by products, services, and customers, but this decrease is offset by an equivalent increase in the cost of unused capacity.

After unused capacity has been created, committed costs will vary downward if and only if managers actively reduce the supply of unused resources. What makes a resource cost variable downward is not inherent in the nature of the resource; it is a function of management decisions—first to reduce the demands for the resource and second to lower the spending on it.

Organizations often create unused capacity through activity-based management actions, such as process improvement, repricing to modify the product mix, and imposing minimum order sizes on customers. They keep existing resources in place, however, even though the demands for the activities performed by the resources have diminished substantially. They also fail to find new activities that could be done by the resources already in place but not being used. In this case, the organization receives no benefits from its ABM decisions that reduced the demands on its resources. The failure to capture benefits from ABM, however, is not because costs are fixed. Rather, the failure occurs because managers are unwilling or unable to take advantage of the unused capacity they have created, such as by spending less on capacity resources or increasing the volume of work processed by the capacity resources. The costs of these resources is only fixed if managers do not exploit the opportunities from the unused capacity they helped to create.

Thus, making decisions, such as to reduce product variety, solely on the basis of resource usage (the ABC system) may not increase profits if managers are not prepared to reduce spending to align resource supply with the future lower levels of demand. For example, if an action causes the number of production runs to decrease by 10%, no economic benefit will be achieved unless some of the resources previously supplied to perform production runs are eliminated or redeployed to higher-revenue uses. Consequently, before making decisions on the basis of an ABC model, managers should determine the resource supply implications of their decisions.

Having discussed why it is desirable to estimate cost driver rates on the basis of practical capacity, we can now address the other principal problem with implementing activity-based costing: the use of employees' subjective time estimates to assign resource expenses to activities.

Time-Driven Activity-Based Costing

The common approach to activity-based costing assigns many resource expenses to activities on the basis of interviews and surveys. As noted earlier, this approach is time consuming, expensive, often inaccurate, and difficult to update. Companies can now overcome these problems by using time-driven activity-based costing, a new approach for estimating their cost models. The new approach requires that only two parameters be estimated:

1. The unit cost of supplying capacity for each department or process
2. The consumption of capacity (unit times) by each transaction or product

Unit Cost Estimate

Time-driven ABC starts with the same information used by a traditional ABC approach:

- The cost of resources that supply capacity
- The practical capacity of the resources supplied

In the Ericson Ice Cream example, the cost of supplying indirect labor was $840,000, including fringe benefits. To estimate their practical capacity, assume that each of 50 indirect labor employees supplies about 500 hours of work each quarter, or 25,000 hours of labor in total. The practical capacity (at 80% of theoretical) is about 20,000 hours per quarter, leading to a unit cost (per hour) of supplying indirect labor capacity as follows:

$$\text{Indirect Labor Cost per Hour} = \frac{\$840,000}{20,000 \text{ hours}} = \$42 \text{ per hour}$$

The cost of supplying computer capacity was $300,000. Let's assume that the practical capacity is 500 hours per quarter, leading to a unit cost of $600 per hour of computer capacity.

Unit Time Estimate

The second piece of new information is an estimate of the time used on a resource when an activity is performed. Precision is not critical; rough accuracy is sufficient.

Ericson's managers estimate the following unit times for the time required to handle production runs and support products on the indirect labor and computer resources:

RESOURCE	ACTIVITY	UNIT TIME
Indirect labor	Production runs	5 hours per run
	Support products	500 hours per product
Computer	Production runs	0.2 hours per run
	Support products	25 hours per product

The cost driver rate for the activity, *handle production runs*, can now be calculated as the costs of using indirect labor and the computer for each production run:

	UNIT COST	UNIT TIME	COST DRIVER
Indirect labor resource	$42 per hour	5.0 hours per run	$210 per run
Computer resource	$600 per hour	0.2 hours per run	120 per run
Activity cost driver rate			**$330 per run**

We calculate the cost driver rate for the activity *support products* in the same way:

	UNIT COST	UNIT TIME	COST DRIVER
Indirect labor resource	$42 per hour	500 hours per product	$21,000 per product
Computer resource	$600 per hour	25 hours per product	15,000 per product
Activity cost driver rate			**$36,000 per product**

The third activity performed by indirect labor, *set up machines*, is already measured in time units, so we can quickly calculate that each hour of setup uses 1 hour of indirect labor at an hourly cost of $42.

We selected the unit time estimates to correspond to the numbers used in the original Ericson Ice Cream example so that the activity cost driver rates would be identical for the two procedures. Therefore, at first glance, it may be difficult to appreciate the difference between traditional and time-driven ABC; but recall that for the traditional ABC procedure, Laura Tunney and her project team had to interview all the indirect personnel and computer supervisors to get estimates of the percentages of the time each resource spent on its various activities. In practice—and for large organizations—it is this interviewing and surveying procedure that is tedious and subject to considerable estimation error. In the time-driven approach, the ABC project team directly observes the quantity of time required to schedule a production run and to set up machines for different products. The data are easier to obtain and, more important, far easier to validate.

A further advantage is the ease of updating a time-driven ABC model to reflect changes in operating conditions. For example, Ericson's managers may learn that indirect labor performs more than the three activities specified in the original model. They don't have to return to reinterview the personnel in the department. They simply estimate the unit times required for each new activity identified. Managers may also learn that handling production runs or supporting products requires different amounts of effort for each product. They can incorporate the new knowledge by estimating the unit times required for handling production runs and product support for each type of product, easily incorporating more variety into the model.

Managers can also easily update the cost driver rates. Two factors cause the cost driver rates to change. First, changes in the prices of resources supplied affect the hourly cost rate. For example, if indirect labor employees receive an 8% compensation increase, their hourly cost increases from $42 per supplied hour to $45.36 per hour. If new machines are substituted or added to a process, the cost rate is modified to reflect the change in operating expense associated with introducing the new equipment.

Second, the cost driver rates change when there has been a shift in the efficiency of the activity, such as when employees get more efficient at scheduling or performing changeovers. Quality, continuous improvement efforts, and the introduction of new technology all enable the same activity to be done in less time or with fewer resources. When permanent, sustainable improvements in a process have been made, the ABC analyst reduces the unit time estimates—and, hence, the resource requirements—to reflect the process improvements.

Following this procedure, a time-driven ABC model update is triggered by events that require the estimates in the model to be modified. Whenever analysts learn about a significant shift in the costs of resources supplied or about changes in the resources required for the activity, they update the cost rate estimates. Whenever they learn of a significant and permanent shift in the efficiency with which an activity is performed, they update the unit time estimate.

Time Equations

Another advantage of time-driven ABC arises from relaxing the simplifying assumption that all orders or transactions of a particular type are the same, requiring the same amount of time to process. Time-driven ABC does not require this simplification. It accommodates the complexity of real-world operations with time equations, a new feature that enables the model to reflect how particular order and activity characteristics cause processing times to vary. Time equations greatly simplify the estimating process and produce a far more accurate cost model than would be possible using traditional ABC techniques.

Not all transactions or production orders require the same amount of time to perform. Some customer orders arrive over the telephone, others may be faxed in, while many arrive electronically on an automated Web page. Each of these may involve different amounts of time for the company personnel to process. Rather than define a separate activity for every possible combination of order arrival, the time-driven approach estimates the resource demand with a simple equation, as shown next. Suppose that each production order is triggered by a specific customer order. Rather than the standard 5 hours for all the activities required to schedule and execute a production run, the ABC project team might estimate the following time equation for the activity *handle production runs* on the basis of how the order was received:

Indirect labor time to handle production runs = 4 hours + 2 hours (if telephone order)
+ 1 hour (if fax order)
+ 0.2 hours (if electronic order)

The 5 hours per run used earlier in the Ericson Ice Cream example was really an average time across all the different order arrival characteristics. The time equation allows the details of particular orders to be captured simply and incorporated within the model.

As another example, take an activity of getting orders ready for shipment. If the item is already a standard one in a standard package, the operation may take only 0.5 minutes to prepare it for shipment. If the item requires a special package, then an additional 6.5 minutes is required. And if the item is to be shipped by air, an additional 0.2 minutes is required to place it in a special bag. The time equation for the packaging process can be represented as follows:

Packaging time = 0.5 + 6.5 (if special handling required)
+ 0.2 (if shipping by air)

The data for the time equations—order types, method of shipment, and all other production characteristics—are typically already in the company's enterprise resource planning system where the order has been entered. Order-specific data enable the particular time demands for any given order to be quickly calculated with a simple algorithm that tests for the existence of each characteristic affecting resource processing time. In this way, the time-driven ABC model has fewer equations than the number of activities used in any existing traditional ABC system while delivering more accuracy by accommodating more variety and complexity in orders, products, and customers.

In summary, the key elements for time-driven ABC are as follows:

- Estimate the practical capacity of committed resources and their costs
- Estimate unit times for performing transactional activities, including the use of time equations, as needed

The practical capacity should be estimated anyway for doing a valid ABC analysis in which existing products and customers are not burdened with the costs of unused capacity. The unit times need not be estimated to four significant digits. Managers will be using the unit time estimates for making decisions about products, customers, and processes, not to monitor and control the performance of individual employees and equipment. For these purposes, managers need just a rough estimate, generally within 10%, for their ABC model. Gross inaccuracies in unit time estimates will eventually be revealed either in unexpected surpluses or in shortages of committed resources.

MARKETING, SELLING, DISTRIBUTION, AND ADMINISTRATIVE EXPENSES: TRACING COSTS TO CUSTOMERS

Laura Tunney, in her initial ABC model, focused on analyzing the production costs in Ericson Ice Cream's factory. She noticed, however, that the company also had $900,000 in marketing, selling, distribution, and administrative (MSDA) expenses (see Exhibit 4-1). These had contributed to the nearly $300,000 quarterly loss, and she had yet to analyze them. Like many companies, Ericson's MSDA expenses have been increasing rapidly in recent years. As she thought about how to assign these expenses, she realized that many of them do not relate to individual products or product lines. They are incurred to support customers, market segments, and distribution channels. And, like the different demands by products for factory resources, customers differ considerably in their use of MSDA resources.

Take the example of a large mutual fund company. Its cost of marketing products, such as retirement investment programs, directly to companies is very different from the cost of marketing retirement investment programs to millions of dispersed retail customers. The size and revenue of retirement investment accounts also differ substantially between corporate and individual retail customers. Companies need to understand the cost of selling to and serving their diverse customer segments.

Tunney could immediately think of two important customers, Carver and Delta. Both customers were approximately the same size, each with sales revenue of about $320,000 per year. In the past, if someone asked her about customer profitability, she allocated selling and administrative expenses to customers as a percentage of sales revenue. Recently, these expenses had averaged about 35% of total sales. Thus, the customer profitability statements for the two customers were nearly the same:

	CARVER	DELTA
Sales	$320,000	$315,000
Cost of goods sold	154,000	156,000
Gross margin	$166,000	$159,000
MSDA expenses at 35% of sales	112,000	110,250
Operating profit	$54,000	$48,750
Profit percentage	16.9%	15.5%

Both customers seemed highly profitable for the company. Tunney, however, did not believe these two customers were about equal in profitability. She knew that Ericson's account manager for Delta spent a huge amount of time on that account. The customer required a great deal of hand-holding and was continually inquiring whether Ericson could modify products to meet its specific needs. Many technical resources, in addition to marketing resources, were required to service the Delta account. Delta also tended to place many small orders for special products, required expedited delivery, and tended to pay slowly, increasing the demands on Ericson's order-processing, invoicing, and accounts-receivable process. Carver, on the other hand, ordered only a few products and in large quantities, placed its orders predictably and with long lead times, and required little sales and technical support. Tunney believed that Carver was a much more profitable customer for Ericson than the financial statements were currently reporting.

Tunney launched an activity-based cost study of the company's marketing, selling, distribution, and administrative costs. As in the factory cost study, she formed a multi-

Exhibit 4-9
Marketing, Sales, Technical, and Administrative Activities

ACTIVITY	ACTIVITY EXPENSES	ACTIVITY COST DRIVER
Provide marketing and technical support	Salaries and benefits of marketing managers and technical support personnel	Estimated proportion of time spent on each customer
Travel to customers	Salesperson salaries; travel and entertainment expenditures	Actual expenditures
Service customers	Salaries and benefits of customer service representatives	Estimated quantity of time spent on each customer
Handle customer orders	Salaries and benefits of administrative and customer support staff to receive orders and coordinate production to schedule deliveries	Time equation[a]
Ship to customers	Costs of shipping finished goods to customers; some customers required immediate, overnight delivery; others could be serviced using low-cost common carriers	Combination of time equation and actual shipping records

[a]Time equation for order handling is based on order entry method (EDI, Web, phone, or fax), number of line items in order, and time required to process any special packaging, delivery, or payment requirements.

functional project team that included representatives from the marketing, sales, technical, and administrative departments. The team studied the resource spending in the various accounts, identified the activities performed by the resources, and selected activity cost drivers that could link each activity to individual customers (see Exhibit 4-9).

After collecting information about the activity expenses and cost drivers, the team assigned the $900,000 in marketing, selling, distribution, and administrative expenses down to individual customers. The picture of relative profitabilities of Carver and Delta shifted dramatically, as shown here:

ABC CUSTOMER PROFITABILITY ANALYSIS

	CARVER	DELTA
Sales	$320,000	$315,000
Cost of goods sold	154,000	156,000
Gross margin	$166,000	$159,000
Marketing and technical support	7,000	54,000
Travel to customers	1,200	7,200
Service customers	4,000	42,000
Handle customer orders	1,400	26,900
Ship to customers	12,600	42,000
Total MSDA activity expenses	26,200	172,100
Operating profit	$139,800	$(13,100)
Profit percentage	43.7%	(4.2%)

As Tunney suspected, Carver Company was a highly profitable customer. Its ordering and support activities placed few demands on the company's marketing, selling, distribution, and administrative resources, so almost all the gross margin earned by selling to Carver dropped to the operating margin bottom line. Delta Company, in contrast, was now seen to be the most unprofitable customer that Ericson had. While Tunney and other managers at Ericson intuitively sensed that Carver was a more profitable customer than Delta, none had any idea of the magnitude of the difference.

The output from an ABC customer analysis is often portrayed as a whale curve (see Exhibit 4-10), a plot of cumulative profitability versus the number of customers where customers are ranked on the horizontal axis from most profitable to least profitable (or most unprofitable). While cumulative sales follow the usual 20–80 rule—20% of the customers provide 80% of the sales—the whale curve for cumulative profitability typically reveals that the most profitable 20% of customers generate between 150% and 300% of total profits (this is the peak, or hump of the whale above sea level). The middle 70% of customers about break even, and the least profitable 10% of customers lose 50% to 200% of total profits, leaving the company with its 100% of total profits ("sea level" in the whale curve represents the company's actual reported profits). In addition, it is not unusual that some of the largest customers, such as Delta, turn out to be the most unprofitable. The largest customers are either the company's most profitable or its most unprofitable. They are rarely in the middle.

High-profit customers, such as Carver, appear in the left section of the profitability whale curve (Exhibit 4-10). Companies can celebrate the high margins they earn on products and services sold to such customers. These customers should be cherished and protected. Because they could be vulnerable to competitive inroads, the managers of companies serving such customers should be prepared to offer discounts, incentives, and special services to retain the loyalty of these valuable customers, particularly if a competitor were to threaten.

Customers like Delta appear on the right tail of the whale curve, dragging the company's profitability down to sea level with their low margins and high cost to serve. The high cost of serving such customers can be caused by their unpredictable order patterns, small order quantities for customized products, nonstandard logistics and delivery requirements, and large demands on technical and sales personnel.

Exhibit 4-10
Cumulative Profitability by Customers

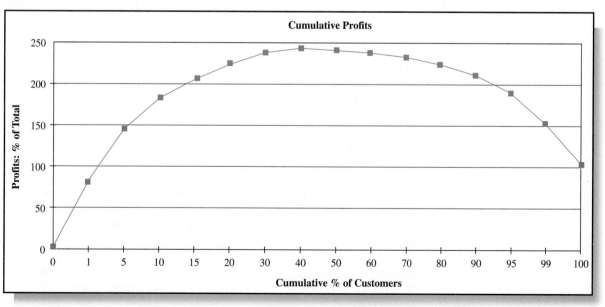

The opportunity for a company to identify its unprofitable customers and then transform them into profitable ones is perhaps the most powerful benefit that a company's managers can receive from an ABC system. Managers have a full range of actions—process improvements, activity-based pricing, and managing customer relationships—for transforming unprofitable customers into profitable ones.

Process Improvements

Managers should first examine their internal operations to see where they can improve their own processes to lower the costs of serving customers. If most customers are migrating to smaller order sizes, companies should strive to reduce batch-related costs, such as setup and order handling, so that customer preferences can be accommodated without raising overall prices. For example, Ericson Ice Cream could strive to become more efficient in handling customer orders by installing greater online capacity and migrating their customers to ordering over the Web. This would substantially lower the cost of processing large quantities of small orders. If customers have a preference for suppliers offering high variety, manufacturing companies can try to customize their products at the latest possible stage as well as use information technology to enhance the linkages from design to manufacturing so that greater variety and customization can be offered without cost penalties.

Activity-Based Pricing

Pricing is the most powerful tool a company can use to transform unprofitable customers into profitable ones. Activity-based pricing establishes a base price for producing and delivering a standard quantity for each standard product. In addition to this base price, the company provides a menu of options, with associated prices, for any special services requested by the customer. The prices for special services on the menu can be set simply to recover the activity-based cost to serve, allowing the customer to choose from the menu the features and services it wishes while also allowing the company to recover its cost of providing those features and services to that customer. Alternatively, the company may choose to earn a margin on special services by pricing such services above the costs of providing the service. Price surcharges could be imposed when designing and producing special variants for a customer's particular needs. Discounts would be offered when a customer's ordering pattern lowers the company's cost of supplying it.

Activity-based pricing, therefore, prices orders, not products. When managers base prices on valid cost information, customers shift their ordering, shipping, and distribution patterns in ways that lower total supply-chain costs to the benefit of both suppliers and customers.

Managing Relationships

Companies can transform unprofitable customers into profitable ones by persuading such customers to use a greater scope of the company's products and services. The margins from increased purchases contribute to covering customer-sustaining costs. Consider a commercial bank with a basic entry-level product: commercial loans. The interest spread on such loans—the difference between the bank's effective borrowing rate and the rate it charges the customers—may be insufficient to cover the bank's cost of making and sustaining the loan because of intense competition and the customer's low use of the lending relationship. However, the bank may make enough profit on other services that the customer uses—for example, investment banking services and corporate money management—that in aggregate the customer is a highly profitable one. Alternatively, however, a small borrower who uses no other commercial banking or investment banking services may be quite unprofitable. In this case, the bank would ask the customer to expand its use of the loan facility (that is, borrow more) and use other and more profitable services offered by the bank's services. If these efforts fail, the bank may then contemplate "firing" the customer by encouraging it to take its demands for a commercial loan to another institution.

Some customers may be unprofitable only because it is the start of the relationship with the company. The company may have incurred high costs to acquire the customer, and the customer's initial purchases of products or services may have been insufficient to cover its acquisition and maintenance costs. No action is required at this point. The company expects and hopes that the customer's purchases of products and services will increase and soon become profitable, including recovering any losses incurred in the start-up years. Companies can afford to be more tolerant of newly acquired unprofitable customers than they can of unprofitable customers they have served for 10 or more years.

IN PRACTICE
Strategic Change at Kemps LLC

Kemps, headquartered in Minneapolis, is a full-line dairy, producing and distributing milk, yogurt, sour cream, cottage cheese, and ice cream products to retailers and distributors as large as Super-Valu and Target and as small as convenience stores. Kemps markets these products under its own branded portfolio along with products sold through private label and copacking contracts. Like most dairies, Kemps was experiencing consolidation in its customer base. It decided to shift from its former customer relationship strategy—willing to do whatever the customer asked—to a lower-total-cost strategy. The new strategy clearly required an accurate understanding of cost by product and customer that Jim Green, chief executive officer of Kemps, would use to instill a "low total cost" culture throughout the organization.

As a critical component of the cost-to-serve model, Kemps implemented a time-driven ABC system so that it could track the costs of changeovers in producing and packaging all its products and the costs of picking, loading, and delivering products to its diverse customer base. The model captured differences in how it entered orders from customers (customer phone call, salesperson call, fax, truck-driver entry, electronic data interchange (EDI), or Internet), how it packaged orders (full stacks of six cases, individual cases, or partial break-pack cases for small orders), how it delivered orders (commercial carriers or its own fleet including route miles), and time spent

by the driver at each customer location. The extra time for changeovers to clean out allergens (nuts, eggs, soy, or wheat) used in certain ice cream products could now be accurately assigned to those products. The model also captured the extra packaging costs for special promotions and customer-specific labels and promotions.

The company soon learned that it was losing money with one of its customers, a chain of specialty high-end shops, because of the low volume and high variety of products ordered and the small just-in-time deliveries it requested. The vice president of sales of Kemps called on the customer, explained the situation, and offered three options: (1) accept a price increase and a minimum order size; (2) eliminate its private-label ice cream, replacing it with the Kemps standard branded product that was already being produced in efficient, high volumes; or (3) find another ice cream supplier. When the customer inquired why Kemps was making the change, the vice president responded that for 25 years, Kemps didn't understand its true manufacturing costs and the impact that specialty production had on its margins. The customer accepted a price increase of 13%, agreed to the elimination of two low-volume products, and agreed to accept full rather than partial truckload orders, thereby eliminating internal storage charges for Kemps. The changes produced immediate benefits of $150,000 per year, and the customer has been a strong profit contributor.

Kemps also used its time-driven ABC model proactively to become the leading dairy supplier to a national customer. Kemps demonstrated that it could identify the specific manufacturing, distribution, and order handling costs associated with serving this customer on the basis of actual order characteristics: DSD (direct store delivery) or shipments to distribution centers, gallon versus pint deliveries, and volume and mix of products. The ABC model facilitated an open, trusting relationship between supplier and customer that differentiated Kemps from its competitors.

Kemps also became aware that some of its smaller convenience store customers had been overordering and returning product when the date code had expired. To save the high cost of these rebates and returns, Kemps offered these retailers a 2% discount if the retailer would manage its own inventory without the return option. In this way, Kemps eliminated 95% of out-of-code returns, generating a net saving of $120,000 per year.

Source: Kemps LLC: Introducing Time-Driven ABC (HBS Case # 106-001).

SERVICE COMPANIES

Although ABC had its origins in manufacturing companies, today many service organizations are obtaining great benefits from this approach. In practice, the actual construction of an ABC model is nearly identical for both types of companies. This should not be surprising since even in manufacturing companies the ABC system focuses on the service component, not on the direct materials and direct labor costs of manufacturing operations. ABC addresses the support resources that serve the manufacturing process—purchasing, scheduling, inspecting, designing, supporting products and processes, and handling customers and their orders.

Service companies in general are ideal candidates for ABC, even more than manufacturing companies. First, virtually all the costs for a service company are indirect and appear to be fixed. Manufacturing companies can trace important components of costs, such as direct material and direct labor costs, to individual products. Service companies have few or no direct materials, and many of their personnel provide indirect, not direct, support to products and customers. Consequently, service companies do not have direct, traceable costs to serve as convenient allocation bases.

The large component of apparently fixed costs in service companies arises because, unlike manufacturing companies, service companies have virtually no material costs—the prime source of short-term variable costs. Service companies must supply virtually all their resources in advance to provide the capacity to perform work for customers during each period. Fluctuations during the period of demand by individual products and customers for the activities performed by these resources do not influence short-term spending to supply the resources.

Consequently, the *variable cost* (defined as the increase in spending resulting from an incremental transaction or customer) for many service industries is close to zero. For example, a transaction at a bank's automatic teller machine requires an additional consumption of a small piece of paper to print the receipt—but no additional outlay. For a bank to add an additional customer may require a monthly statement to be mailed, involving the cost of the paper, an envelope, and a stamp—but little more. Carrying an extra passenger on an airplane requires an extra can of soda pop, two bags of peanuts (for most coach-class U.S. flights these days!), and a minor increase in fuel consumption—but nothing else. For a telecommunications

One of the initial barriers for deploying ABC systems across an enterprise was the lack of data in a centralized location on customer orders and transactions. Now, companies such as Microsoft, Oracle, and SAP have given companies the power to access all customer transaction data even across large numbers of dispersed operations. Microsoft's SQL server provides companies with a robust, secure, fully integrated application for managing and mining their enterprise data.

"Many retailers now use their Microsoft SQL server for two primary functions, online transaction processing (OLTP) and business intelligence," says Rich Johnson, solutions architect for Microsoft consulting services. OLTP lies at the heart of any transactional database application, enabling retailers to retain and manage data on product inventory and sales. These data warehousing capabilities are complemented with business intelligence features, enabling a company to track and interpret patterns in its historical data. The result is valuable information that enables the company to make more knowledgeable business decisions that can lead to reduced operational costs and increased revenue. Johnson states, "A company can closely examine customer buying habits and sales by store and region."

Specialized ABC software providers, such as Acorn System based in Houston, Texas, have customized their programs to sit "on top" of enterprise databases, such as Microsoft's SQL server. This enables companies to run their ABC models on current, accurate, and comprehensive data, giving managers almost real-time visibility into process performance and the profitability of products and customers.

Source: http://www.microsoft.com/industry/retail/products/SQL2005article.mspx#EBAA (accessed February 16, 2006).

company, handling one more phone call from a customer or one more data transfer involves no incremental spending. Therefore, service companies making decisions about products and customers on the basis of short-term variable costs might provide a full range of all products and services to customers at prices that could range down to near zero. In such cases, of course, the companies would get limited to no recovery of the costs of all the committed resources they supplied to enable the service to be delivered to the customer.

Customer Costs in Service Companies

Service companies must focus, even more than manufacturing companies, on customer costs and profitability. Consider a manufacturing company producing a standard product, or widget. Manufacturers can calculate the cost of producing the widget without regard to how their customers use it; thus, the manufacturing costs are *customer independent*. Only the costs of marketing, selling, order handling, delivery, and service of the widget might be customer specific. For service companies, in contrast, customer behavior determines the basic operating costs of products.

Consider a standard product such as a checking account. It is relatively straightforward, using ABC methods, to calculate all costs associated with a checking account. The revenues, including interest earned on monthly balances and fees charged to customers for services, also are easy to attribute to this product. The analysis will reveal whether such a product is, on average, profitable or unprofitable, but such an average look at the product will hide the enormous variation in profitability across customers of this product. One customer may maintain a high cash balance in his checking account and make very few deposits or withdrawals. Another customer may manage her checking account balance very closely, keeping only the minimum amount on hand, and use her account heavily by making many small withdrawals and deposits.

As another example, customers of a telecommunications company can order a basic service unit in several different ways—through a phone call, a letter, or a visit to a local retail outlet. The customer may order two phone lines at once or just one; engineers may have to appear to install the new line, or they may make a change at the local switching center. The customer may make only one request or several and can pay either by direct debit over the Internet, by a telephone banking transfer, by a mailed check, or in person. The cost of each option is quite different. Therefore, measuring revenues and costs at the customer level provides the company with far more relevant and useful information than at the product level.

Service companies need to identify the differential profitability of individual customers, even customers using standard products. The variation in demand for organizational resources is much more customer driven in service organizations than in manufacturing organizations. A service company can determine and control the efficiency of its internal activities, but customers determine the quantity of demands for these operating activities.

Further, a customer may have more than one relationship with a service company. In addition to the basic phone line, a telecommunications customer may have a high-speed data line, a long-distance account, a service contract, and equipment rentals. Therefore, before taking drastic action with a customer who has an unprofitable basic phone line, the company's managers should understand all the relationships it has with the customer and act on the basis of total relationship profitability, not just on the basis of the profitability of a single product.

ABC Model for a Service Company

An activity-based cost system is developed for a service company in the same way it is developed for a manufacturing company: construct the activity dictionary, assign resource expenses to activities, determine activity cost drivers, calculate activity cost driver rates, and drive activity expenses down to products and customers. Exhibit 4-11

Exhibit 4-11
Bank Activities and Activity Cost Drivers

Activity	Activity Cost Driver
Provide ATM service	Number of ATM transactions
Clear debit items	Number of debits processed
Branch operations for debit items	Number of branch counter debits
Issue personal checkbook	Number of books issued
Clear credit items	Number of credits processed
Lending control and security	Number of interventions
Handle customer inquiries	Minutes of telephone call time
Marketing and sales activity	Number of accounts opened
Computer processing	Number of computer transactions
Statements and postage	Number of statements issued
Advise on investments and insurance	Minutes (hours) of advice provided
Process VISA transactions	Number of VISA transactions
Issue VISA statements	Number of VISA statements issued
Open/close accounts	Number of accounts opened/closed
Administer mortgages	Number of mortgages maintained

shows a sample of activities and the associated activity cost drivers used in an ABC study of a British retail bank.[1]

Once the ABC model on product and customer profitability has been obtained, service company managers can contemplate the same set of operational and strategic ABM actions as their counterparts in manufacturing companies. Companies in financial services (banks, insurance companies, and money managers), transportation (airlines, trucking, and railroads), telecommunications, wholesale and retail, healthcare, and even many government agencies are now using ABC analysis to understand and manage the economics of their operations.

IMPLEMENTATION ISSUES

Although ABC has provided managers in many companies with valuable information about the cost of their activities, processes, products, services, and customers, not all ABC systems have been sustained or have contributed to higher profitability for the company. Companies have experienced difficulties and frustrations in building and using ABC and profitability models. We can identify several common pitfalls that have occurred and suggest ways to avoid them.

Lack of Clear Business Purpose

Often, the ABC project is initiated out of the finance or accounting department and is touted as "a more accurate cost system." The project team gets resources for the project, builds an initial ABC model, and then becomes disappointed and disillusioned when no one else looks at or acts on the new ABC cost and profitability information.

To avoid this syndrome, all ABC projects should be launched with a specific business purpose in mind. The purpose could be to redesign or improve processes, to influence product design decisions, to rationalize the product mix, or to better manage customer relationships. By defining the business purpose at the start, the team will identify the line manager or department whose behavior and decisions are expected to change as a consequence of the information. The decision maker could be the manufacturing or operations manager (for process improvement), the engineering manager (for product design decisions), the sales organization (for managing customer relationships), or the marketing department (for decisions about pricing and product mix).

It is also important not to oversell what the ABC system is capable of doing. Some project teams, carried away by their enthusiasm, promise that ABC will solve all the company's problems, at least its costing and financial problems. ABC is a strategic costing system that highlights the costs of processes, products, and customers; it cannot perform the role of operational control, of providing frequent feedback on process and departmental efficiencies and improvements. Many ABC projects were aborted when they did not provide operating managers with frequent feedback on the costs and expenses under their responsibility. These operating managers needed a feedback system, in addition to the ABC system, that could be

---

[1] The time-driven ABC approach, described in this chapter, is perhaps even more powerful for service companies than for manufacturing companies. All service companies sell—whether a hospital, an airline, a bank, or a telecommunications company—is their time, such as to deliver services to customers and to process customer requests. Applying time-driven ABC for service companies requires calculating the cost per hour of each type of resource that delivers services to customers and estimating the time required by each type of customer demand on each resource.

specifically designed for the purpose of providing operational feedback on process efficiencies. Some projects foundered because the company expected its new ABC system model to also be the basis for costing inventory for financial reporting. Such companies failed to realize that their traditional costing system already worked fine for external reporting and did not need to be replaced right away with the ABC system. Companies should allow some experimentation and flexibility with their first ABC system, customizing its design for maximum managerial benefits, before imposing the additional burden of also satisfying external, regulatory reporting.

The primary purpose of the model also should influence the design of the initial model. A model intended primarily for process improvement and process redesign can have a large number of activities but does not have to be concerned with the availability of information about activity cost drivers. Conversely, for decisions about pricing, customer relationships, and product mix, the ABC model should be simpler, using fewer than 50 activities and with data readily available for all the important activity cost drivers. A model intended for product designers and engineers should use activity cost drivers that would be meaningful to them. Drivers such as number of parts placements, number of unique parts, and number of unique vendors are understandable and actionable to product designers.

Lack of Senior Management Commitment

A pitfall related to the first problem arises when the finance department undertakes the project without gaining senior management support and buy-in. When this happens, the rest of the organization views the project as done by and for finance people; as a result, no one outside the finance department pays attention to it. Because the finance department is not empowered to make decisions about processes, product designs, product mix, pricing, and customer relationships, no useful actions are taken that lead to increased profitability.

The most successful ABC projects occur when a clear business purpose exists for building the ABC model and when this purpose is led (or at least understood and fully supported) by senior line managers in the organization. A steering committee of senior managers from various functional groups and business units provides guidance and oversight, meeting monthly to review project progress, make suggestions on how to enhance the model, and prepare for the decisions that will be made once the model has been completed.

Even when the ABC project is initiated from the finance group, a multifunctional project team should be formed. The team should include, in addition to a management accountant or other finance group representative, members from operations, marketing/sales, engineering, and systems. In this way, the expertise from diverse groups can be incorporated into the model design, and each team member can build support for the project within his or her department and group.

Delegating the Project to Consultants

Some projects have failed when they were outsourced to an external consulting company. Consultants may have considerable experience with ABC but not the needed familiarity with a company's operations and business problems. Nor can they build management consensus and support within the organization either to make decisions with the ABC information or to maintain and update the model. Even worse, some companies think they can get an ABC system by buying an ABC software package. The software provides a template to enter, process, and report information, but it cannot provide the thinking required to build a cost-effective ABC model.

One company contemplated the development of an activity-based costing system to assign indirect labor and overhead costs to the five product line units at its Midwest plant. The study was triggered by a major capital expansion for a new product line at the plant. The existing cost system used plantwide overhead rates, so that the cost of the additional equipment and operating expenses raised the costs of the products produced for all five product lines, not just for the unit that installed the new production line. Product managers were beginning to move their production from the Midwest plant to other facilities to avoid the higher charges.

Despite the benefits from more accurate cost attribution, the company decided to delay the development of a more accurate activity-based costing system. It was believed that the new system disturbed the status quo. It would require organizational members to create an agreed-upon ABC methodology and a standardized activity dictionary across different plants. Also, it would change the measure of product line profitability and affect executives' compensation.

ABC would also affect employee behavior, overthrowing some decision models that had worked for years. Senior managers believed it would be difficult for individuals to cast aside a way of thinking that had kept them employed for many years. They believed it would be even more difficult to accept the new system if individuals were poorly motivated to change because they thought that the cause of the immediate problem—the low sales volume on the new product line—might soon correct itself. Some managers believed that the company might decide to eliminate the new product line because it would be unprofitable, once the cross subsidies created by the existing cost system were eliminated. These managers were concerned that the cost of the remaining products would increase, as the overhead previously allocated to the product line would be applied to the remaining product lines. This, perhaps, could lead to eventual closure of the entire Midwest plant.

Others didn't like the complex ABC cost model because they thought the company needed a simpler system that would just point managers in the right direction for decision making. These individuals perceived activity-based costing as a complex solution to a simple problem.

The company decided that implementing ABC was a long-term project. It wanted the new product line to become established before assigning it a full share of activity-based costs. Once the product matures, the company plans to move in incremental steps toward an ABC system, allowing for a more gradual transition to the new paradigm.

Source: Material drawn from R. J. Palmer and M. Vied, "Could ABC Threaten the Survival of Your Company?'" *Management Accounting*, November 1998, 33–36.

ABC consultants and ABC software can play valuable roles for many companies, but they are not substitutes for overcoming the first two pitfalls. Successful ABC projects require top management leadership and sponsorship and a dedicated, multifunctional internal project team. These functions cannot be bypassed just because external consultants and prepackaged software have also been purchased.

Poor ABC Model Design

Sometimes, even with strong management support and sponsorship, the project team gets lost in the details and develops an ABC model that is both too complicated to build and maintain and too complex for managers to understand and act on. In other cases, the model uses arbitrary allocations—frequently percentages, not quantitative activity cost drivers—to map costs from activities to products and customers. The arbitrary allocations create distortions in the model and destroy its credibility among line managers. Often, the model requires other organizational functions to provide new data and information on a regular basis, increasing their workload without providing corresponding benefits. Under the burden of poor design, the ABC system soon collapses under its own weight and neglect.

As noted, ABC model design should be like any design or engineering project: It should be regularly evaluated, with continual appropriate trade-offs to enable the essential function of the system to be accomplished at minimal additional cost. If the ABC project team keeps end users clearly in mind and gets good advice from its senior management steering committee, it should make good cost-effective design decisions along the way. These decisions can help avoid the problem of having an overcomplex system or misidentified causal relationships between cost objects (products and customers), activities, and resources.

Individual and Organizational Resistance to Change

Not all managers welcome technically superior solutions. Individuals often resist new ideas and change, and organizations have great inertia. The resistance to a new ABC model may not be overt. Managers can politely sit through an ABC presentation about product and customer profitability but continue to behave just as they have in the past; or they will ask the project team to reestimate the model, using a more recent period or at another company site. Sometimes, however, the resistance is more overt. Managers may exclaim the company has been successful in the past with its existing cost system; why does it need a new approach? Or, if it has been a finance-led project, they may accuse the finance people of not understanding the complexity of the business or wanting to run the company.

People Feel Threatened

Individual and organizational resistance arises because people feel threatened by the suggestion that their work could be improved. We might not think that a cost model could generate such resistance, but in fact, as we discussed earlier in the chapter, the ABC model could reveal the following:

- Unprofitable products
- Unprofitable customers
- Inefficient activities and processes
- Substantial unused capacity

Managers responsible for these problems could be embarrassed and threatened by the revelation of apparent bad management during their watch. Rather than accept the validity of the ABC model and attempt to rectify the problems (which likely occurred because of inadequacies in the previous cost system, not their own negligence or ineptitude), they may deny the validity of the new approach and question the motives of the people attempting to lead the change. Such defensive behavior will inhibit any effective action.

Chapter 8 includes a discussion of the behavioral issues that arise when implementing new cost control, performance measurement, and management control systems. Resistance is not unique to ABC. It can arise from the introduction of any new measurement or management system or, indeed, any management change initiative. However, as a costing innovation, ABC systems are prime candidates for triggering individuals' and organizations' negative responses to change initiatives. Dealing with such responses requires skills for recognizing and overcoming defensive behavior, skills that fledgling management accountants may not have been taught in their academic studies or in their early job assignments.

SUMMARY

This chapter introduced activity-based cost systems for manufacturing and service companies, including how ABC systems calculate costs more accurately than traditional cost systems, which rely only on unit-level drivers. ABC systems drive the cost of indirect and support resources—manufacturing resources in factories and marketing, selling, distribution, and administrative resources—to the activities they perform and then to the cost objects—the products, services, and customers—that generate the demand for the activities.

To develop an ABC model, management accountants should estimate activity cost driver rates using the practical capacity of the resources supplied. They should also make appropriate trade-offs in the design of the model, balancing the cost of more accurate measurement for more complex models with the benefits from the greater accuracy.

Managers use the information on activity costs to improve profitability. They can identify high-cost and inefficient processes that are prime candidates for operational improvements projects. By driving activity costs down to cost objects, managers identify profitable and unprofitable products, services, and customers. They can make better decisions on pricing, product mix, product design, customer and supplier relationships, and technology that transform unprofitable products and customers into profitable ones. These are examples of activity-based management in action.

Despite the apparent attraction of increased accuracy and managerial relevance from ABC individual and organizational resistance can arise to block the effective use of these systems. Management accountants must be sensitive to the conditions that cause such resistance to arise and devise good countermeasures to overcome them.

Epilogue to Booth Motors

Jonathan Kellogg worked with his controller to develop an ABC model of his automobile dealership. Activities for three of the product lines are as follows:

NEW VEHICLE DEPARTMENT	FINANCE AND INSURANCE (F&I)	SERVICE
Commissions	Commissions	Perform repairs
Interest expense	Sell F&I products	Diagnose problems
Sell new vehicles	Manage lease deals	Generate repair orders
Advertise new vehicles	Manage F&I department	Counter, idle time
Store new vehicles	Administer office	Maintain service area
Prepare new vehicles	Prepare documents	Store vehicles
Manage new vehicle deals	Manage cash and finance deals	Process service documents
Perform billing	Process warranty claims	

ACTIVITY COST DRIVERS INCLUDED	
Number of days on lot	Number of payables processed
Number of cash deals	Number of receipts
Number of new vehicles sold	Number of invoices received
Number of claims processed	Weighted CPU time
Lot square footage	Building square footage
Number of retail leases	Number of warranties processed

The product line ABC analysis showed that the F&I product line was nearly twice as costly as previously thought and that the service product line was 25% more expensive. Even with the higher expenses attributed to the F&I business, however, the ABC analysis showed that the profits from financing and insuring new and used cars accounted for nearly 50% of total dealer profitability. This indicated that the margins from new and used vehicle sales without any financing and insurance tie-ins were barely profitable at best.

The most interesting aspect of the analysis occurred when Kellogg extended the ABC analysis down to individual car line vehicles within the new vehicle product line. Only one of the car lines was profitable; for the remaining lines, financing and space costs exceeded the net margin on sales. The profitable car line had the lowest average days on the lot. Some of the seemingly most popular car lines, the Taurus and Escort, were the most unprofitable. Apparently, competitive pressure had caused margins on these vehicles to fall below dealer operating expenses for them. While the truck line in aggregate was quite profitable, only two of the eight truck lines (Explorer and Windstar) generated all the profits. In fact, the profits from these two lines greatly exceeded the profits from the total truck line since the other six truck lines lost substantial money.

Kellogg is now able to see many opportunities for improving his car and truck purchasing and inventory policies. He will have better information when negotiating with customers, including price concessions if customers were financing and insuring their cars through the dealership. He can also assess the lifetime profitability of a customer by linking the margins from new car sales with profits earned from finance and insurance, service work, and parts sales.

KEY TERMS

Activity-based cost systems, 138
Activity-based management, 144
Activity-based pricing, 156
Activity cost driver, 141

Activity cost driver rate, 141
Activity dictionary, 139
Cost of unused capacity, 148
Practical capacity, 147

Time-driven ABC, 147
Time equations, 151
Whale curve, 155

ASSIGNMENT MATERIALS

Questions

4-1 Why are conventional two-stage cost allocation systems likely to systematically distort product costs? (LO 1, 2)

4-2 Why are conventional product costing systems more likely to distort product costs in highly automated plants? How do activity-based costing systems deal with such a situation? (LO 1, 2, 3)

4-3 "Conventional product costing systems are likely to overcost high-volume products." Do you agree with this statement? Explain. (LO 1, 2, 3)

4-4 What do the terms *activity cost driver* and *activity cost driver rates* mean? (LO 3)

4-5 What major steps must be performed to determine the activity cost driver rates in a traditional activity-based cost system? (LO 3)

4-6 How do activity-based costing systems avoid distortions in tracing batch-related costs to products? (LO 3)

4-7 "Activity-based costing systems yield more accurate product costs than conventional systems because they use more cost drivers to assign support costs to products." Do you agree with this statement? Explain. (LO 3)

4-8 How are cost drivers selected in traditional activity-based costing systems? (LO 3)

4-9 When would you prefer to use the number of setups instead of the number of setup hours as the cost driver measure for the setup activity? (LO 3)

4-10 How can the information from an activity-based costing system guide improvements in operations and decisions about products and customers? (LO 4)

4-11 Why is practical capacity recommended in calculating activity cost driver rates? (LO 5)

4-12 Why might an organization not experience financial improvement even after using activity-based costing to identify and take action on promising opportunities for process improvements and cost reductions? (LO 5)

4-13 What two sets of parameters must be estimated in time-driven activity based costing? (LO 6)

4-14 What advantages does time-driven activity based costing have over traditional activity-based costing? (LO 6)

4-15 Why do conventional product costing systems often exclude selling and distribution costs? (LO 1, 7)

4-16 What recent changes have made it more important to have nonmanufacturing costs assigned to products, product lines, or market segments? (LO 4, 7, 8)

4-17 What are some special considerations in the design of cost accounting systems for service organizations? (LO 9)

4-18 Why might individuals resist implementation of activity-based costing? (LO 10)

Exercises

LO 1, 2, 4 **4-19** *Product costing systems and product profitability* Potter Corporation has gained considerable market share in recent years for its specialty, low-volume, complex line of products, but the gain has been offset by a loss in market share for its high-volume, simple line of products. This has resulted in a net decline in its overall profitability. Advise management about specific changes that may be required in its cost accounting system and explain why the existing system may be inadequate.

LO 3 **4-20** *Revising traditional activity-based cost and time-driven activity-based cost systems* Refer to the Ericson Ice Cream example described in this chapter. Suppose that some unrecorded resource expenses were just discovered at the company. Inspection people costing $150,000 per quarter perform quality inspections at the start of each new production run to ensure that the new color being run meets specifications.

Required

a. Explain how the traditional activity-based cost model should be updated to reflect this newly discovered cost and calculate the resulting costs assigned to all the products.

b. Explain how the time-driven activity-based cost model should be updated to reflect this newly discovered cost and calculate the resulting costs assigned to all the products.

LO 6 **4-21** *Time-driven activity-based costing* Refer to the time-driven activity-based costing analysis of the Ericson Ice Cream example in the chapter.

Required

a. Suppose indirect labor costs have increased by 10% from the original setting but all the other information remains the same. Determine the total time-driven activity-based costs assigned to each of the four products (flavors) after incorporating the 10% increase in indirect labor costs and prepare an income statement similar to Exhibit 4-7.

b. Suppose that in addition to the change in (a), the unit time for handling a production run decreased from 5 hours per run to 4 hours per run. Determine the new total time-driven activity-based costs assigned to each of the four products (flavors) and prepare an income statement similar to Exhibit 4-7 but also showing the total cost of unused capacity.

LO 3, 4, 9 **4-22** *Traditional activity-based costs, service* Friendly Bank is developing an activity-based cost system for its teller department. A task force has identified five different activities: (1) process deposits, (2) process withdrawals, (3) answer customer inquiries, (4) sell negotiable instruments, and (5) balance drawers. By tracing the costs of operating the teller department to these five activities, the task force has compiled the following information regarding support costs and activities for one of its suburban branches:

SUPPORT ACTIVITY	ESTIMATED COST	ACTIVITY COST DRIVER	QUANTITY
Process deposits	$29,630	Number of deposits processed	33,250
Process withdrawals	26,080	Number of withdrawals processed	22,750
Answer inquiries	24,860	Number of customer inquiries	45,000
Sell negotiable instruments	4,860	Number of negotiable instruments sold	1,100
Balance drawers	4,290	Number of drawers balanced	1,300
	$89,720		

Required

   a. Compute the activity cost driver rates for each of the support activities.

   b. The task force has developed the following list of activities for a typical checking account marketed to retired persons:

SUPPORT ACTIVITY	AVERAGE MONTHLY VOLUME
Process deposits	2.3
Process withdrawals	6.0
Answer customer inquiries	2.1
Sell negotiable instruments	0.5

Estimate the total monthly support costs for this checking account product.

LO 3, 4 **4-23** *Traditional activity-based costs* VG Company has identified the following cost pools and cost drivers:

COST POOLS	ACTIVITY COSTS	COST DRIVERS
Machine setup	$360,000	6,000 setup hours
Materials handling	100,000	50,000 pounds of material
Electric power	40,000	80,000 kilowatt-hours

The following information pertains to the production of V203 and G179:

ITEM	V203	G179
Number of units produced	5,000	15,000
Direct materials cost	$25,000	$33,000
Direct labor cost	$14,000	$16,000
Number of setup hours	120	150
Pounds of material used	5,000	10,000
Kilowatt-hours	2,000	3,000

Determine the unit cost for each of the two products using activity-based costing.

LO 3, 4 **4-24** *Traditional activity cost driver rates* Creathon Company's plant in Columbus, Ohio, manufactures two products: BR12 and BR15. Product BR15 has a more complex design and requires more setup time than BR12.

    Setups for BR12 require 2 hours on average; setups for BR15 require 3 hours. Creathon's setup department employs 10 workers whose average wage is $10 per hour; fringe benefits cost 38% of wages. Other costs for setup activities amount to $25 per setup. Creathon plans to use all 10 workers for 40 hours each for the first 3 weeks of the winter quarter. The number of setups for these 3 weeks follow:

	NUMBER OF SETUPS	
WEEK	BR12	BR15
1	85	75
2	90	70
3	80	80

Required

   a. Determine the actual setup activity cost driver rate for each week based on (1) the number of setups and (2) the number of setup hours.

   b. Is either of the two activity cost driver rates or some other rate appropriate in this case? Why?

4-25 *Traditional activity cost drivers* Identify a cost driver for costs for each of the following:

  a. Machine maintenance
  b. Machine setup
  c. Utilities
  d. Quality control
  e. Material ordering
  f. Production scheduling
  g. Factory depreciation
  h. Warehouse expense
  i. Production supervision
  j. Payroll accounting
  k. Custodial service
  l. General and administration
  m. Customer inquiry responses
  n. Customer order processing
  o. Customer representative salaries

4-26 *Capacity costs* Ken's Cornerspot, a popular university eatery in a competitive market, has seating and staff capacity to serve about 600 lunch customers every day. For the past 2 months, demand has fallen from its previous near-capacity level. Concerned about his declining profit, Ken decided to take a closer look at his costs. He concluded that food was the primary cost that varied with meals served; the remaining costs of $3,300 per day were fixed. With demand averaging 550 lunches per day for the past 2 months, Ken thought it was reasonable to divide the $3,300 fixed costs by the current average demand of 550 lunches to arrive at an estimate of $6 of support costs per meal served. Noting that his support costs per meal had now increased, he contemplated raising his meal prices.

Required

  a. What is likely to happen if Ken continues to recompute his costs using the same approach if demand decreases further?
  b. Advise Ken on choosing a cost driver quantity for computing support costs per meal and explain why you advocate your choice of quantity.

4-27 *Assigning marketing, distribution, and selling expenses to customers* Tetra Company's cost system assigns marketing, distribution, and selling expenses to customers using a rate of 33% of sales revenue. The new controller has discovered that Tetra's customers differ greatly in their ordering patterns and interaction with Tetra's sales force. Because the controller believes Tetra's cost system does not accurately assign marketing, distribution, and selling expenses to customers, she developed an activity-based costing system to assign these expenses to customers. She then identified the following marketing, distribution, and selling costs for two customers, Ashton and Brown:

	ASHTON	BROWN
Sales representative travel	$9,000	$42,000
Service customers	15,000	110,000
Handle customer orders	1,000	12,000
Ship to customers	24,000	72,000

The following additional information is available:

	ASHTON	BROWN
Sales	$430,000	$350,000
Cost of goods sold	220,000	155,000

Required

   a. Using the current cost system's approach of assigning marketing, distribution, and selling expenses to customers using a rate of 33% of sales revenue, determine the operating profit associated with Ashton and with Brown.

   b. Using the activity-based costing information provided, determine the operating profit associated with Ashton and with Brown.

   c. Which of the two methods produces more accurate assignments of marketing, distribution, and selling expenses to customers? Explain.

LO 8, 9   **4-28** *Customer profitability*   A credit card company has classified its customers into the following types for customer profitability analysis:

   1. Applies for credit card in response to a low introductory interest rate; transfers balance to new account, but when the low introductory rate expires, the customer transfers the balance to an account with a different credit card company that has offered a low introductory rate.

   2. Charges a large dollar volume of purchases; pays balance in full and on time each month.

   3. Carries a high balance; pays only the minimum required payment but pays regularly with occasional late payment.

   4. Carries a high balance; pays at least the minimum required payment but does not pay in full and always pays on time.

   5. Carries a low balance; pays at least the minimum required payment but does not pay in full and always pays on time.

   6. Does not use the account but does not close the account.

The following facts pertain to the credit card company's operations:

  • Merchants pay the credit card company a percentage of the dollar sales on each credit card transaction.

  • Customers pay no interest on charges for purchases if the balance is paid in full and on time each month.

  • The credit card company charges a late fee if the customer's payment is late.

  • The credit card company incurs costs to send statements to inactive customers.

Required

Given the preceding information, which customer types would you expect to be the most desirable or profitable, the next most profitable, and so on for the credit card company on a long-term basis? Explain your ranking.

LO 10   **4-29** *Activity-based costing implementation issues*   Refer to the situation described in "Barriers to Implementing ABC Systems" (p. 163). What barriers to implementing an activity-based costing system can you identify? How would you respond to the managers' comments?

Problems

LO 1, 3   **4-30** *Cost distortions*   At its manufacturing plant in Duluth, Minnesota, Endo Electronics Company manufactures two products, X21 and Y37. For many years, the company has used a simple plantwide manufacturing support cost rate based on direct labor hours. A new plant accountant suggested that the company may be able to assign support costs to products more accurately by using an activity-based costing system that relies on a separate rate for each manufacturing activity that causes support costs.

After studying the plant's manufacturing activities and costs, the plant accountant has collected the following data for last year:

ITEM	X21	Y37
Units produced and sold	50,000	100,000
Direct labor hours used	100,000	300,000
Direct labor cost	$1,000,000	$4,500,000
Number of times handled	40,000	20,000
Number of parts	12,000	8,000
Number of design changes	2,000	1,000
Number of product setups	8,000	6,000

The accountant has also determined that actual manufacturing support costs incurred last year were as follows:

COST POOL	ACTIVITY COSTS
Handling	$3,000,000
Number of parts	2,400,000
Design changes	3,300,000
Setups	2,800,000
Total	$11,500,000

The direct materials cost for product X21 is $120 per unit, while for product Y37 it is $140 per unit.

a. Determine the unit cost of each product using direct labor hours to allocate all manufacturing support costs.

b. Determine the unit cost of each product using activity-based costing.

c. Which of the two methods produces more accurate estimates of job costs? Explain.

d. Suppose Endo has been setting its product prices by adding a 25% markup to its reported product cost. Compute the product prices on the basis of the costs computed in parts (a) and (b). What do you recommend to Endo regarding its pricing?

e. What product-level changes do you suggest on the basis of the activity-based cost analysis? Who would be involved in bringing about your suggested changes?

LO 1, 3, 4, 5   **4-31** *Product profitability analysis, unused capacity, traditional activity-based costing*   Northpack, Inc., has recently expanded its line of backpacks to include high-quality, lightweight hiker backpacks. This new model uses more expensive material and takes longer to produce. While a basic school backpack can be cut and sewn together in 30 minutes, a hiker backpack takes 45 minutes to cut and sew together. The school model is produced in batches of 1,000 packs, while the hiker model is produced in batches of 100 packs. Each batch of the school model requires 1 hour of inspection time, and each batch of the hiker model requires 2 hours of inspection time. Using direct labor hours to allocate manufacturing support costs (which in this company include ordering and packaging costs), product profitability is analyzed as follows:

ITEM	SCHOOL BACKPACKS	HIKER BACKPACKS
Sales	$15.00	$30.00
Less:		
Direct materials	3.00	10.00
Direct labor	5.00	7.50
Manufacturing support	4.00	6.00
Gross margin	$3.00	$6.50
Selling and administrative	1.00	2.00
Profit	$2.00	$4.50
Sales volume	90,000	6,000

Jens Schmit, the controller at Northpack, believes that activity-based costing may be a more accurate way of measuring the costs of the two models. He has traced manufacturing support costs to the following activity pools and determined the practical capacity levels of the associated activity drivers:

			COST DRIVER UNITS DEMANDED	
ACTIVITY	ACTIVITY COSTS	ACTIVITY DRIVER	SCHOOL MODEL	HIKER MODEL
Cutting machines	$52,000	Machine hours	9,000	1,125
Sewing machines	163,300	Direct labor hours	45,000	4,500
Packaging—order related	8,300	Number of orders	450	200
Packaging—volume related	150,000	Number of items packed	90,000	6,000
Orders	14,000	Number of orders	450	200
Inspections	8,400	Hours of inspections	?	?
Total	$396,000			

Selling and administrative expenses are $102,000 fixed business-sustaining costs. Customers pay actual shipping charges, which are not included in these figures.

Required

a. The method of assigning costs to individual products does not affect the total manufacturing support costs. Only the amounts assigned to individual products change. Explain why Jens should care about how support costs are assigned to individual products.

b. Using activity-based costing, calculate the cost per unit for each of the two models and analyze their profitability.

c. How might managers use the activity-based costing information to enhance the company's profitability? Consider pricing changes and process changes among your suggestions.

d. Suppose that practical capacity remains as described earlier but that demand for the school model is only 85,000 units, while demand for the hiker model remains at 6,000 units. For the school model, the cutting machine hours are now 8,500, and the number of orders is 425. Calculate the cost per unit for each of the two models and prepare an income statement similar to Exhibit 4-7 but also showing the cost of unused capacity for each activity. What actions might management take to deal with the unused capacity highlighted in your analysis?

LO 3   **4-32 Activity cost drivers**   The Simply French Restaurant has identified the following activities performed by its staff:

Set tables	Cook food	Serve dessert
Seat customers	Serve orders	Present and collect bills
Take orders	Take dessert orders	Clean tables

Required

a. For each of these activities, state whether the number of tables served or the number of customers at the tables is a better cost driver.

b. What distortions might result in assigning costs if only one of the two drivers in (a) is used?

LO 3, 4, 5   **4-33 Cost driver rates with practical capacity**   Kohlman Company manufactures two products: K33 and K88. Estimated unit cost and production data follow:

ITEM	K33	K88
Direct materials cost	$30	$45
Direct labor cost ($12 per hour)	$24	$60
Estimated production in units	400,000	150,000

Manufacturing support costs are estimated to be $6,535,000 for the current year. Activity cost pools and cost drivers are as follows:

ACTIVITY	COSTS	ACTIVITY COST DRIVER	PRACTICAL CAPACITY	K33	K88
				COST DRIVER UNITS DEMANDED	
Machine setups	$425,000	Setup hours	6,500	2,000	4,200
Purchase ordering	10,000	Number of orders	100	25	50
Machining	6,000,000	Number of machine hours	75,000	40,000	15,000
Inspection	36,000	Number of batches	1,200	400	600
Packing and shipping	64,000	Number of shipments	1,600	80	1,500
Total	$6,535,000				

Required

a. Estimate the manufacturing cost per unit of each product if support costs are assigned to products using activity-based cost driver rates based on practical capacity.
b. Explain why the unit cost for K33 differs from that for K88.
c. What operational changes might the company take, motivated by analysis of the activity-based cost driver rates?
d. Compute the variance (difference) between the estimated manufacturing support costs and the support costs assigned to the company's products in (a).
e. Interpret the variances (differences) computed in (d) and describe action steps that managers might take to reduce the variances.
f. Should Kohlman base its activity-based cost driver rates on practical capacity or on budgeted usage of the drivers? Explain.

LO 3, 4, 5, 6 **4-34 Traditional activity-based costing and time-driven activity-based costing**
Garber Company uses a traditional activity-based costing system to assign $600,000 of committed resource costs for customer service on the basis of the following information gathered from interviews with customer service personnel:

ACTIVITY	TIME PERCENTAGE	ESTIMATED COST DRIVER QUANTITY
Handle customer orders	75%	8,000 customer orders
Process customer complaints	10%	400 customer complaints
Perform customer credit checks	15%	450 credit checks
	100%	

Required

a. Compute the activity cost driver rates using this system.
b. Suppose instead that Garber uses time-driven activity-based costing to assign the $600,000 of committed resource costs to the three activities. Compute the time-driven activity cost driver rates, assuming 10,000 hours of useful work and the unit time estimates that follow:

ACTIVITY	UNIT TIME (HOURS)
Handle customer orders	0.75
Process customer complaints	3.50
Perform customer credit checks	3.00

c. Suppose that the quantities of activities this period are 8,000 customer orders, 400 customer complaints, and 450 credit checks. Using the information and activity cost driver rates developed in (b), determine the cost assigned to each of the activities and the estimated hours of unused capacity as well as the associated cost. What actions might managers take on evaluating such information?

d. Suppose that in the next time period, the quantities of activities change to 8,500 customer orders, 350 customer complaints, and 500 credit checks. Using the information and activity cost driver rates developed in (b), determine the cost assigned to each of the activities and the estimated hours of unused capacity as well as the associated cost.

e. Explain why the activity cost driver rates computed in (a) are different from the rates computed in (b).

LO 3, 4, 7, 8, 9   **4-35** *Customer profitability analysis*   Kronecker Company, a growing mail-order clothing and accessory company, is concerned about its growing marketing, distribution, selling, and administration expenses. It therefore examined its customer ordering patterns for the past year and identified four different types of customers, as illustrated in the following table. Kronecker sends catalogs and flyers to all its customers several times a year. Orders are taken by mail or over the phone. Kronecker maintains a toll-free number for customers to use when placing orders over the phone. Kronecker prides itself on the personal attention it provides shoppers who order over the phone. All purchases are paid for by check or credit card. Kronecker has a very generous return policy if customers are not satisfied with the merchandise received. Customers must pay return shipping charges, but their purchase price is then fully refunded.

	CUSTOMER 1	CUSTOMER 2	CUSTOMER 3	CUSTOMER 4
Initial sales	$1,000	$1,000	$2,500	$3,000
Number of items returned	0	4	2	24
Dollar value of items returned	0	$200	$500	$1,500
Number of orders per year	1	6	4	12
Number of phone orders per year	1	0	0	12
Time spent on phone placing orders	0.25 hours	0	0	1 hour
Number of overnight deliveries	1	0	0	12
Number of regular deliveries	0	6	4	0

Prices are set so that cost of goods sold is on average about 75% of the sales price. Customers pay actual shipping charges, but extra processing is required for overnight deliveries. Kronecker has developed the following activity cost driver rates for its support costs:

ACTIVITY	ACTIVITY COST DRIVER RATE
Process mail orders	$5 per order
Process phone orders	$80 per hour
Process returns	$5 per item returned
Process overnight delivery requests	$4 per request
Maintain customer relations (send catalogs and respond to customer comments or complaints)	$50 per year

Required

a. Using activity-based costing, determine the yearly profit associated with each of the four customers described.

b. Comment on which customers are most profitable and why.

c. What advice do you have for Kronecker regarding managing customer relationships with the different types of customers represented?

4-36 *Activity cost driver rates, service*   The customer billing department at U.S. West Telecommunication, Inc., currently employs 25 billing clerks on annual contract. Each clerk works 160 hours per month. The average monthly wages of billing clerks, including fringe benefits, amount to $2,800. Other billing-related costs, including stationery and supplies, are $0.50 per billing.

The two types of customers are residential and business. For residential customers, billing takes on average 10 minutes to prepare; each business customer billing requires 15 minutes.

The following information pertains to the estimated number of customer billings for the months of June and July:

	NUMBER OF BILLINGS	
MONTH	BUSINESS CUSTOMERS	RESIDENTIAL CUSTOMERS
June	8,000	12,000
July	6,000	15,000

Required

a. If the expected number of billings each month is used to determine a monthly billing activity cost driver rate, what is the activity cost driver rate for each month based on the expected number of billings?

b. If the expected number of billing labor hours each month is used to determine a monthly billing activity cost driver rate, what is the activity cost driver rate for each month based on the expected number of billing labor hours?

c. Compare the cost driver rates in (a) and (b). Which rate do you recommend? Why?

d. Can you recommend a way to estimate the costs of this activity that is better than using either cost driver rate in (a) or (b)?

4-37 *Activity-based costing in a health care organization*   In computing the cost of patient stays, Riverside General Hospital assigns physician costs and medication costs directly to each patient. Riverside has examined its support costs for patient stays, resulting in identification of 18 account names, related account expenses, and cost drivers for support costs for the most recent fiscal year:

Riverside General Hospital: Operating Costs and Activity Cost Drivers for the Fiscal Year

ACCOUNT NUMBER	ACCOUNT NAME	COST	ACTIVITY COST DRIVER
101	Nursing services	$2,973,154	Nursing hours
102	Nursing administration	1,269,762	Nursing hours
103	Pharmacy	496,629	Number of patient days
104	Laboratory	312,347	Number of tests
105	Medical supplies	482,165	Number of patient days
106	Linen and laundry	358,736	Pounds of laundry
107	Dietary	813,148	Number of meals
108	Employee cafeteria	167,239	Number of nurse days
109	Housekeeping	706,308	Square feet of space
110	Medical records and library	250,345	Number of patients
111	Social services	199,026	Number of patients
112	Patient scheduling and administration	60,238	Number of patients
113	Billing and collection	112,280	Number of patients
114	Plant operations	301,238	Square feet of space
115	Plant maintenance	386,622	Square feet of space
116	Medical equipment operations	496,275	Number of procedures
117	Insurance on hospital property	38,350	Value of property
118	Hospital-related depreciation	960,573	Value of property
	Total operating costs	$10,384,435	

Required

    a. Ana Navarro, Riverside's controller, has suggested using a simpler classification scheme that groups the 18 activities or accounts into unit-related (patient day–related), batch-related (patient-related), and facility-sustaining activity cost pools. Which of the 18 activities should be included in each of these three cost pools?

    b. Ana believes that 45,606 patient days should be used as the cost driver activity level for the unit-related activity cost pool and that 8,367 patients should be used for the batch-related activity cost pool. Using this cost system, what reimbursement from the insurance company is required to cover at least the unit-related and batch-related costs for a patient who stays in the hospital for 14 days?

    c. What advice would you give Riverside regarding choosing between a cost system with the 18 cost drivers initially identified and the cost system described in (b)?

    LO 1, 3, 4   **4-38 Product cost distortions, activity-based management** The Manhattan Company manufactures two models of compact disc players: a deluxe model and a regular model. The company has manufactured the regular model for years; the deluxe model was introduced recently to tap a new segment of the market. Since the introduction of the deluxe model, the company's profits have steadily declined, and management has become increasingly concerned about the accuracy of its costing system. Sales of the deluxe model have been increasing rapidly.

        The current cost accounting system allocates manufacturing support costs to the two products on the basis of direct labor hours. The company has estimated that this year it will incur $1 million in manufacturing support costs and will produce 5,000 units of the deluxe model and 40,000 units of the regular model. The deluxe model requires 2 hours of direct labor, and the regular model requires 1 hour. Material and labor costs per unit and selling price per unit are as follows:

ITEM	DELUXE	REGULAR
Direct materials cost	$45	$30
Direct labor cost	20	10
Selling price	140	80

Required

    a. Compute the manufacturing support cost driver rate for this year.

    b. Determine the cost to manufacture one unit of each model.

    c. The company has decided to trace manufacturing support costs to four activities. Following are the amount of manufacturing support costs traceable to the four activities this year:

				COST DRIVER UNITS DEMANDED	
ACTIVITY	COST DRIVER	COST	TOTAL	DELUXE	REGULAR
Purchase orders	Number of orders	$180,000	600	200	400
Quality control	Number of inspections	250,000	2,000	1,000	1,000
Product setups	Number of setups	220,000	200	100	100
Machine maintenance	Machine hours	350,000	35,000	20,000	15,000
		$1,000,000			

    Compute the total cost to manufacture one unit of each model.

d. Compare the manufacturing activity resources demanded per unit of the regular model and per unit of the deluxe model. Why did the old costing system undercost the deluxe model?

e. Is the deluxe model as profitable as the company thinks it is under the old costing system? Explain.

f. What should the Manhattan Company do to improve its profitability? Consider pricing and product-level changes among your suggestions. Who should be involved in implementing your recommendations?

LO 1, 3, 4   **4-39** *Traditional activity-based costing, activity-based management*   (Adapted from CMA, June 1992) Alaire Corporation manufactures several different types of printed-circuit boards; however, two of the boards account for the majority of the company's sales. The first of these boards, a TV circuit board, has been a standard in the industry for several years. The market for this type of board is competitive and, therefore, price sensitive. Alaire plans to sell 65,000 of the TV boards this year at a price of $150 per unit. The second high-volume product, a PC circuit board, is a recent addition to Alaire's product line. Because the PC board incorporates the latest technology, it can be sold at a premium price; this year's plans include the sale of 40,000 PC boards at $300 per unit.

Alaire's management group is meeting to discuss strategies for this year, and the current topic of conversation is how to spend the sales and promotion dollars for next year. The sales manager believes that the market share for the TV board could be expanded by concentrating Alaire's promotional efforts in this area. In response to this suggestion, the production manager said, "Why don't you go after a bigger market for the PC board? The cost sheets that I get show that the contribution from the PC board is more than double the contribution from the TV board. I know we get a premium price for the PC board. Selling it should help overall profitability."

Alaire uses a standard cost system, and the following data apply to the TV and PC boards:

	PER UNIT	
ITEM	TV BOARD	PC BOARD
Direct materials	$80	$140
Direct labor	1.5 hours	4 hours
Machine time	0.5 hours	1.5 hours

Variable manufacturing support costs are applied on the basis of direct labor hours. This year's variable manufacturing support costs are budgeted at $1,120,000, and direct labor hours are estimated at 280,000. The hourly rates for machine time and direct labor are $10 and $14, respectively. Alaire applies a materials handling charge of 10% of materials cost; this materials handling charge is not included in variable manufacturing support costs. Total expenditures for material this year are budgeted at $10,600,000.

Ed Welch, Alaire's controller, believes that before the management group proceeds with the discussion about allocating sales and promotional dollars to individual products, it may be worthwhile to look at these products on the basis of the activities involved in their production. Welch has prepared the following schedule for the management group:

Costs	Budgeted Cost	Cost Driver	Annual Activity for Cost Driver
MATERIAL SUPPORT COSTS:			
Procurement	$400,000	Number of parts	4,000,000
Production scheduling	220,000	Number of boards	110,000
Packaging and shipping	440,000	Number of boards	110,000
Total costs	$1,060,000		
VARIABLE SUPPORT COSTS:			
Machine setup	$446,000	Number of setups	278,750
Hazardous waste disposal	48,000	Pounds of waste	16,000
Quality control	560,000	Number of inspections	160,000
General supplies	66,000	Number of boards	110,000
Total costs	$1,120,000		
MANUFACTURING SUPPORT COSTS:			
Machine insertion	$1,200,000	Number of machine insertions	3,000,000
Manual insertion	4,000,000	Number of manual insertions	1,000,000
Wave soldering	132,000	Number of boards	110,000
Total costs	$5,332,000		

REQUIRED PER UNIT	TV BOARD	PC BOARD
Parts	25	55
Machine insertions	24	35
Manual insertions	1	20
Machine setups	2	3
Hazardous waste	0.02 pounds	0.35 pounds
Inspections	1	2

"Using this information," Welch explained, "we can calculate an activity-based cost for each TV board and each PC board and then compare it to the standard cost we have been using. The only cost that remains the same for both cost methods is the cost of direct materials. The cost drivers will replace the direct labor, machine time, and support costs in the standard cost."

Required

a. Identify at least four general advantages that are associated with activity-based costing.

b. On the basis of standard costs, calculate the total contribution expected this year for Alaire Corporation's products: (1) the TV board, and (2) the PC board.

c. On the basis of activity-based costs, calculate the total contribution expected this year for Alaire Corporation's two products.

d. Explain how the comparison of the results of the two costing methods may impact the decisions made by Alaire Corporation's management group.

LO 1, 3, 4   **4-40 *Manufacturing support cost driver rates*** (Adapted from CMA, December 1990) Moss Manufacturing has just completed a major change in its quality control (QC) process. Previously, products had been reviewed by QC inspectors at the end of each major process, and the company's 10 QC inspectors were charged as direct labor to the operation or job. In an effort to improve efficiency and quality, a computer video QC system was purchased for $250,000. The system consists of a minicomputer, 15 video cameras, other peripheral hardware, and software.

The new system uses cameras stationed by QC engineers at key points in the production process. Each time an operation changes or there is a new operation, the cameras are moved, and a new master picture is loaded into the computer by a QC engineer. The camera takes pictures of the units in process, and the computer compares them to the picture of a good unit. Any differences are sent to a QC engineer who removes the bad units and discusses the flaws with the production supervisors. The new system has replaced the 10 QC inspectors with two QC engineers.

The operating costs of the new QC system, including the salaries of the QC engineers, have been included as manufacturing support in calculating the company's plantwide manufacturing support cost rate, which is based on direct labor dollars.

Josephine Gugliemo, the company's president, is confused. Her vice president of production has told her how efficient the new system is, yet there is a large increase in the manufacturing support cost driver rate. The computation of the rate before and after automation is shown here:

ITEM	BEFORE	AFTER
Budgeted support costs	$1,900,000	$2,100,000
Budgeted direct labor costs	1,000,000	700,000
Budgeted cost driver rate	190%	300%

"Three hundred percent," lamented the president. "How can we compete with such a high manufacturing support cost driver rate?"

Required

a. Define manufacturing support costs and cite three examples of typical costs that would be included in this category. Explain why companies develop manufacturing support cost driver rates.

b. Explain why the increase in the cost driver rate should not have a negative financial impact on Moss Manufacturing.

c. Explain, in great detail, how Moss Manufacturing could change its accounting system to eliminate confusion over product costs.

d. Discuss how an activity-based costing system may benefit Moss Manufacturing.

LO 1, 3, 4, 7, 9, 10 **4-41** *Traditional activity-based costing for shared services, outsourcing, implementation issues* Smithers, Inc., manufactures and sells a wide variety of consumer products. The products are viewed as sufficiently profitable, but recently some product-line managers have complained about the charges for the call center that handles phone calls from customers about the products. Product lines are currently charged for call center support costs on the basis of product sales revenues. The manager of product X is particularly upset because he has just obtained a report that includes the following information for last year:

	PRODUCT X	PRODUCT Y
Number of calls for information	2,000	4,000
Average length of calls for information	3 minutes	5 minutes
Number of calls registering complaints	200	1,000
Average length of complaint calls	5 minutes	10 minutes
Sales volume	$400,000	$100,000

Product X is simple to use and consumers have little concern about adverse health effects. Product Y is more complex to use and has many health hazard warnings on its label. Smithers currently allocates call center support costs using a rate of 5% of net sales dollars. The manager of product X argues that the current system does not trace call center resource usage to specific products. For example, product X bears four times the call center costs that product Y does, although fewer calls are related to product X, and the calls consume far less time.

Required

a. What activity cost driver would you recommend to improve the current system of assigning call center support costs to product lines? Why is your method an improvement?
b. Suppose Smithers announces that it will now assign call center support costs on the basis of an activity-based cost system that uses minutes of calls (calls for information and calls for complaints) as the activity cost driver. Suppose also that the rate is 70 cents per minute. Compare the call center cost assignments to product X and product Y under the previous system and the new activity-based cost system.
c. What actions can the product managers take to reduce the center costs assigned to their product lines under the previous system and the new system? What other functional areas might help reduce the number of minutes of calls for product Y?
d. Who might resist implementation of the new activity-based cost system? In your response, discuss possible reactions of the call center staff and other staff who might be affected by efforts to reduce minutes of calls.
e. From the company's point of view, how might the activity-based costing system help in the assessment of whether to outsource the call center activities?

Cases

LO 1, 3, 4, 5, 10 **4-42** *Comparison of two costing systems, activity-based management* The Redwood City plant of Crimson Components Company makes two types of rotators for automobile engines: R361 and R572. The old cost accounting system at the plant traced support costs to four cost pools:

Cost Pool	Support Costs	Cost Driver
S1	$1,176,000	Direct labor cost
S2	1,120,000	Machine hours
P1	480,000	—
P2	780,000	—
	$3,556,000	

Pool S1 included service activity costs related to setups, production scheduling, plant administration, janitorial services, materials handling, and shipping. Pool S2 included activity costs related to machine maintenance and repair, rent, insurance, power, and utilities. Pools P1 and P2 included supervisors' wages, idle time, and indirect materials for the two production departments, casting and machining, respectively.

The old accounting system allocated support costs in pools S1 and S2 to the two production departments using direct labor cost and machine hours, respectively, as the cost drivers. Then the accumulated support costs in pools P1 and P2 were applied to the products on the basis of direct labor hours. A separate rate was determined for each of the two production departments. The direct labor wage rate is $15 per hour in casting and $18 per hour in machining.

Direct Labor Hours (DLH)

Department	R361	R572	Total	Direct Labor Costs
Casting (P1)	60,000	20,000	80,000	$1,200,000
Machining (P2)	72,000	48,000	120,000	2,160,000
Total	132,000	68,000	200,000	$3,360,000

Machine Hours (MH)

Department	R361	R572	Total
Casting (P1)	30,000	10,000	40,000
Machining (P2)	72,000	48,000	120,000
Total	102,000	58,000	160,000

Item	R361	R572
Sales price per unit	$19	$20
Sales and production units	500,000	400,000
Number of orders	1,000	1,000
Number of setups	2,000	4,000
Materials cost per unit	$8	$10

Now the plant has implemented an activity-based costing system. The following table presents the amounts from the old cost pools that are traced to each of the new activity cost pools:

	Old Cost Pools				
Activity Cost Drivers	S1	S2	P1	P2	Total
P1-DLH	$120,000	$0	$120,000	$0	$240,000
P2-DLH	240,000	0	0	120,000	360,000
Setup hours	816,000	80,000	240,000	540,000	1,676,000
P1-MH	0	260,000	120,000	0	380,000
P2-MH	0	780,000	0	120,000	900,000
Total	$1,176,000	$1,120,000	$480,000	$780,000	$3,556,000

Setups for R572 are 50% more complex than those for R361; that is, each R572 setup takes 1.5 times as long as one R361 setup.

Required

a. Determine the product costs per unit using the old system. Show all intermediate steps for allocations, including departmental cost driver rates and a breakdown of product costs into each of their components.

b. Determine the product costs per unit using the new system.

c. Explain the intuitive reason that the product costs differ under the two accounting systems.

d. What should Crimson Components do to improve the profitability of its Redwood City plant? Include marketing and product-related changes among your recommendations.

e. Describe how experienced production and sales managers are likely to react to the new product costs.

LO 1, 3, 4   **4-43 *Activity-based costing, service department allocations, activity-based management*** The Fishburn plant of Hibeem Electronics Corporation makes two types of wafers for electronic instruments: W101 and W202. The old cost accounting system at the plant traced support costs to three cost pools:

Cost Pools	Support Costs	Cost Drivers
S	$1,740,000	Machine hours
P1	680,000	—
P2	240,000	—
Total	$2,660,000	

Pool S included all service activity costs at the plant. Pools P1 and P2 included support costs traced directly to the two production departments, photolithography and assembly, respectively.

The old cost accounting system allocated costs in pool S to the two production departments on the basis of machine hours. Then the accumulated costs in P1 and P2 were applied to the products on the basis of direct labor hours. A separate rate was computed for each of the two production departments. The direct labor wage rate is $20 per hour. The following data were compiled from plant records for January:

DIRECT LABOR HOURS (DLH)

Department	W101	W202	Totals
Photolithography (P1)	80,000	20,000	100,000
Assembly (P2)	40,000	20,000	60,000
Total	120,000	40,000	160,000

MACHINE HOURS (MH)

Department	W101	W202	Total
Photolithography (P1)	80,000	30,000	110,000
Assembly (P2)	20,000	15,000	35,000
Total	100,000	45,000	145,000

Item	W101	W202
Sales price per unit	$11.50	$12.25
Sales and production units	600,000	300,000
Number of orders	1,000	1,000
Number of setups	2,000	4,000
Materials cost per unit	$4.00	$5.00

Now the plant has implemented an activity-based costing system. The following table presents the amounts from the old cost pools that are traced to each of the new activity cost pools:

	OLD COST POOLS			
Activity Cost Drivers	S	P1	P2	Total
P1-DLH	$180,000	$140,000	$0	$320,000
P2-DLH	120,000	0	60,000	180,000
Setup hours	900,000	390,000	145,000	1,435,000
P1-MH	400,000	150,000	0	550,000
P2-MH	140,000	0	35,000	175,000
Total	$1,740,000	$680,000	$240,000	$2,660,000

Each W202 setup takes 1.25 times as long as a W101 setup.

Required

a. Determine the product costs per unit using the old system. Show all intermediate steps for allocations, including departmental cost driver rates and a breakdown of product costs into each of their components.

b. Determine the product costs per unit using the new system.

c. Explain the intuitive reason that the product costs are different under the two accounting systems.

d. What should Hibeem Electronics Corporation do to improve the profitability of its Fishburn plant? Include marketing and process changes among your recommendations.

LO 1, 3   **4-44 *Activity-based costing***   Sandra Slaughter, senior vice president for sales for Showman Shoes, Inc., noticed that the company had substantially increased its market share for the high-quality boomer boots (BB) and lost market share for the lower-quality lazy loafers (LL). Sandra found that Showman's prices were lower than the competitors' for BB but higher for LL. She did not understand the reasons for these price differences because all companies used the same production technology and were equally efficient.

The manufacturing process is relatively simple. Showman's manufacturing facility has a cutting department and an assembly department. The high-quality BB is produced in small batches (1,000 pairs of shoes each), and the lower-quality LL is produced in large batches (3,000 pairs each). Sandra has asked you, the company's new controller, to analyze the product costing method to see if the product prices should be changed.

The company currently uses a plantwide cost driver rate based on direct labor hours. The rate is computed at the beginning of the year using the following budgeted data:

Total manufacturing support costs	$1,200,000
Total direct labor hours	49,000
Total machine hours	49,400
Total setup hours	520

Your assistant has provided you with the following additional information about the production of batches of BB and LL:

EACH BATCH OF BB: 1,000 PAIRS

ITEM	CUTTING	ASSEMBLY	TOTAL
Direct labor hours	80	120	200
Machine hours	160	120	280
Setup hours	3	1	4
Direct costs	$7,500	$6,000	$13,500

EACH BATCH OF LL: 3,000 PAIRS

ITEM	CUTTING	ASSEMBLY	TOTAL
Direct labor hours	150	180	330
Machine hours	150	120	270
Setup hours	1	1	2
Direct costs	$9,000	$7,200	$16,200

On further inquiry, your assistant has been able to trace the support costs to the two service departments and the two production departments and to identify the following details for potential cost drivers for the service departments:

ITEM	MAINTENANCE	SETUP	CUTTING	ASSEMBLY	TOTALS
Support costs	$160,000	$400,000	$440,000	$200,000	$1,200,000
Direct labor hours	0	0	21,400	27,600	49,000
Machine hours	0	0	27,800	21,600	49,400
Setup hours	0	0	340	180	520

Your assistant has also collected the following information on activities and their cost drivers:

SUPPORT ACTIVITIES	COST	COST DRIVER
Maintenance	$160,000	Machine hours
Setups	400,000	Setup hours
Cutting supervision	280,000	Setup hours
Cutting depreciation	160,000	Machine hours
Assembly supervision	160,000	Direct labor hours
Assembly depreciation	40,000	Machine hours

Required

a. Using a single, plantwide cost driver rate based on direct labor hours, determine the costs per pair of BB and LL.
b. Determine the costs per pair of BB and LL using departmental cost driver rates based on machine hours for the cutting department and direct labor hours for the assembly department. Allocate service department costs using the direct method.
c. Determine the costs per pair of BB and LL using activity-based costing.
d. Explain why unit costs for product BB are higher when departmental cost driver rates are used than when a single plantwide rate is used.
e. Explain why activity-based costs for product LL are lower than the corresponding costs based on a plantwide rate.

LO 1, 3, 4, 10 **4-45 Product profitability analysis, activity-based management, implementation issues** Petersen Pneumatic Company makes three products. Its manufacturing plant in Petersburg has three production departments and three service departments:

DEPARTMENT	SUPPORT COSTS
Machining (MC)	$40,000
Plating (PL)	50,000
Assembly (AS)	15,000
Purchasing and inventory (PI)	50,000
Setup and scheduling (SS)	120,000
Quality control (QC)	70,000

Support costs are first traced to the six departments. The old cost accounting system allocated the service department costs to the production departments using the following cost drivers:

DEPARTMENT	COST DRIVER
PI	Materials cost (MAT)
SS	Direct labor hours (DLH)
QC	Machine hours (MCH)

The old cost accounting system applied support costs to the three products on the basis of direct labor hours. A different cost driver rate was determined for each department. The direct labor wage rate at the plant is $10 per hour.

		DIRECT LABOR HOURS (DLH)			
DEPARTMENT		GT101	GT102	GT103	MACHINE HOURS (MCH)
MC		7,000	2,800	2,200	5,200
PL		3,500	1,700	1,800	1,900
AS		2,500	1,000	1,000	2,900

	PRODUCT SALES		BATCH-RELATED DRIVERS		MATERIALS COST PER UNIT	
PRODUCT	PRICE	SALES AND PRODUCTION UNITS	ORDERS	SETUPS	MC	PL
GT101	$1.25	500,000	25	110	$0.30	$0.10
GT102	1.20	200,000	10	43	0.25	0.10
GT103	1.30	200,000	40	166	0.28	0.10

The profitability of the Petersburg plant has been declining for the past 3 years despite the successful introduction of the new product, GT103, which has now captured more than a 60% share of its segment of the industry. In an attempt to understand the reasons for its declining profitability, the company has appointed a special task force.

The task force is considering a new cost accounting system based on activity analysis. This system employs five cost drivers: three departmental DLH, setups (SET), and orders (ORD). Each departmental cost pool is divided into homogeneous cost pools identified with a unique driver. The following table presents the percent of the departmental support costs that are put into each of the homogeneous cost pools. The total amounts in the five cost pools are allocated to the three products on the basis of their respective cost drivers:

DEPARTMENT	DLH	SET	ORD
MC	30%	70%	0%
PL	70%	30%	0%
AS	60%	40%	0%
PI	0%	40%	60%
SS	?	?	?
QC	0%	70%	30%

Peter Gamble is the leader of the task force responsible for activity-based cost analysis. He interviewed Nola Morris, who was responsible for the setup and scheduling department, to determine the cost drivers for the departmental support costs:

Gamble: How many people work in the setup and scheduling department?
Morris: I have 12 people who work on setups. Three more are responsible for production scheduling. I spend most of my time supervising them.
Gamble: How do you assign setup workers to production jobs?
Morris: Almost all the time they set up machines in the machining department. The effort depends only on the number of setups.
Gamble: On what does the time spent on scheduling depend?
Morris: It depends on the number of orders.
Gamble: So a large batch or order will require the same amount of setup and scheduling time as a small batch or order.
Morris: Yes, that's right.

Required

a. List the reasons that the old cost accounting system at Petersen Pneumatic may be distorting its product costs.
b. Determine the product cost per unit using both the old and new cost accounting systems. Show all the intermediate steps, including the cost driver rates, amounts in the new cost pools, and a breakdown of product costs into each of their components.

c. Analyze the profitability of the three products. What insight is provided by the new profitability analysis? What should Petersen Pneumatic do to improve the profitability of its Petersburg plant? Include marketing and process changes among your recommendations.

d. Mike Meservy is a veteran production manager, and Shannon Corinth is a marketing manager with considerable experience as a salesperson. Discuss how each is likely to react to your analysis and recommendations. Explain how their expected reactions may affect the way you will present your recommendations.

LO 1, 3, 4, 10 **4-46 *Product profitability analysis, activity-based management, implementa-tion issues*** Pharaoh Phawcetts, Inc., manufactures two models of faucets: a regular and a deluxe. The deluxe model, introduced just 2 years ago, has been very successful. It now accounts for more than half of the firm's profits as evidenced by the following income statement for last year:

ITEM	TOTAL	REGULAR	DELUXE
Sales	$2,400,000	$1,200,000	$1,200,000
Cost of goods sold	1,540,000	771,000	769,000
Gross margin	$860,000	$429,000	$431,000
Selling and administrative expenses	500,000	250,000	250,000
Net income	$360,000	$179,000	$181,000
Number of units	500,000	300,000	200,000

Its manufacturing plant in Phoenix, Arizona, has two production departments: machining and assembly. The cost of goods sold included $720,000 in production support costs. The plant accountant traced $192,000 of the production support costs to the machining department and $168,000 to the assembly department. The balance of $360,000 was attributed to the various service departments, and in the existing cost allocation system, the $360,000 was allocated to the machining and the assembly departments in the proportion of their respective machine hours. Next, separate cost drivers were determined for the two production departments on the basis of their respective direct labor hours to assign the support costs to the two products.

	TOTAL DIRECT LABOR AND MACHINE HOURS		
PRODUCT	MACHINING DEPARTMENT	ASSEMBLY DEPARTMENT	TOTAL
Regular	15,000 DLH	3,000 DLH	18,000 DLH
Deluxe	13,000 DLH	5,000 DLH	18,000 DLH
Total DLH	28,000 DLH	8,000 DLH	36,000 DLH
Total machine hours	52,000 MH	8,000 MH	60,000 MH

The direct labor wage rate is $10 per hour. Direct materials cost is $0.80 per unit for the regular model and $1.10 per unit for the deluxe model. An average customer order for the regular model is for 5,000 faucets, but each order for the deluxe model is for 2,000 units. The machines require a setup for each order. Three hours are required per machine setup for the regular model; the more complex deluxe model requires 5 hours per setup.

Pharaoh Phawcett's profitability has been declining for the past 2 years despite the successful introduction of the deluxe model, which has now captured over a 65% share of its segment of the industry. Market share for the regular model has decreased to 12%. In an attempt to understand the reasons for its declining profitability, the company has appointed a special task force.

The task force is considering a new cost accounting system based on activity analysis. This system employs four cost drivers: two departmental direct labor hours, setup hours, and number of orders. Production support costs are traced to four homogeneous cost pools, each identified with a unique driver as presented in the following table:

ACTIVITY COST DRIVER	COSTS	TRACEABLE NUMBER OF UNITS OF COST DRIVER		
		TOTAL	REGULAR	DELUXE
Machining DLH	$112,000	?	?	?
Assembly DLH	96,000	?	?	?
Setup hours	272,000	?	?	?
Number of orders	240,000	?	?	?
Total manufacturing support costs	$720,000			

The task force also analyzed selling and administrative expenses. These costs included a 5% sales commission on regular models and 10% on deluxe models. Advertising and promotion expenses were $50,000 for the regular model and $90,000 for the deluxe model. The remaining $180,000 of selling and administrative expenses are attributed equally to the two products.

Required

a. Determine the product costs per unit using the existing cost accounting system. Show all the intermediate steps, including the cost driver rates and a breakdown of product costs into each of their components.

b. Determine the product costs and profits per unit using the new activity-based costing system. Show all the intermediate steps, including the cost driver rates and components of product costs.

c. Explain the principal reasons that the old cost accounting system at Pharaoh Phawcetts may be distorting its product costs and profitability. Support your answer with numbers when necessary.

d. Analyze the profitability of the two products. What insight does the new profitability analysis provide? What should Pharaoh Phawcetts do to improve its profitability? What options may be available?

e. Ryan O'Reilley is a marketing manager with considerable experience as a salesperson. Discuss how he is likely to react to your analysis and recommendations.

LO 1, 3   **4-47 Cost distortions** Sweditrak Corporation manufactures two models of its exercise equipment: regular (REG) and deluxe (DLX). Its plant has two production departments, fabrication (FAB) and assembly (ASM), and two service departments, maintenance (MNT) and quality control (QLC). The parts for each model are manufactured in the fabrication department and put together in the assembly department. The maintenance department supports both production departments, and QLC performs all inspections for both production departments. Each unit of both products needs one inspection in each production department. Each inspection takes 30 and 60 minutes for REG and DLX models, respectively. The two production departments have set the following standards for direct material cost, direct labor cost, and machine hours for each unit of product:

ITEM	FABRICATION		ASSEMBLY	
	REG	DLX	REG	DLX
Direct materials cost	$40.00	$80.00	$10.00	$20.00
Direct labor cost	$20.00	$40.00	$20.00	$30.00
Machine hours	2.0	3.0	1.0	2.0

The average wage rate for direct labor is $10 per hour. The following table gives the production volume and support costs for the past 2 weeks:

	PRODUCTION VOLUME		SUPPORT COSTS	
WEEK	REG	DLX	MNT	QLC
45	450	430	$35,000	$6,310
46	450	450	$35,400	$6,350

The present cost accounting system assigns support costs in MNT to the production departments on the basis of machine hours and assigns QLC costs to the two production departments on the basis of the number of inspections. The accumulated costs in FAB and ASM are applied to products based on direct labor hours.

The company is considering implementing an activity-based costing system using machine hours as the cost driver for MNT cost and inspection hours as the cost driver for QLC cost.

Required

a. Using the present cost accounting system, determine the product costs per unit for each product for each of the 2 weeks.

b. Using the proposed ABC system, determine the unit product costs for each product for each of the 2 weeks.

LO 3, 4   **4-48** *Identifying activity costs, activity-based management*   Linda Collins is the manager in charge of cost analysis and planning at Montex Company. Montex makes steel and brass pumps at its four plants located in Minnesota, Indiana, Illinois, and Michigan. Linda first examined the accounting and payroll records at the Minnesota plant. She organized payroll costs, including benefits, by department and analyzed expenditure records to identify tools, supplies, and other costs with individual departments. After collecting the departmental cost information, Linda interviewed the departmental managers to identify what activities the personnel in their departments performed. The following table shows the cost associated with two departments, machine setups and quality inspections, and the names of the managers of each department:

DEPARTMENT	MACHINE SETUPS	QUALITY INSPECTIONS
MANAGER	ROGER SMITH	DAVID CARLSON
Wages and benefits	$406,000	$476,000
Tools, supplies, and other costs	110,000	26,000
Initial total costs	516,000	502,000
Add: Engineer's wages	0	38,000
Revised total costs	$516,000	$540,000

Linda first interviewed Roger Smith, manager of the machine setup department, who has been with Montex Company for 26 years. Edited versions of Linda's interviews with the two managers follow:

LINDA COLLINS: How many people do you have in your department?

ROGER SMITH: I supervise eight people. We had seven until last June, but because of the high workload, we had to add Steve Swanson in the second half of last year. Steve is now a permanent worker in our department.

LINDA COLLINS: What work do they do?

ROGER SMITH: All my people are responsible for setting up the machines.

LINDA COLLINS: What drives the amount of work that they do?

ROGER SMITH: Well, setups are required each time they begin a production run. When the machine is available for the production run, our people go and set up the machine and inspect the first item produced to make sure that the machine is set up right.

LINDA COLLINS:	So the number of production runs or batches seems to drive your work, not how large a run is?
ROGER SMITH:	Yes, that is really the case. Setting up the machine takes the same time, whether we produce 60 pumps or five pumps.
LINDA COLLINS:	Do the setups for all batches take about the same amount of time?
ROGER SMITH:	No. There are big differences, depending on the product for which we have to set up the machines. Some products have very complex specifications that require about 3 hours of setup time. Other products, such as P101, are much simpler, and we can set those up in only a half hour.
LINDA COLLINS:	So the number of setup hours is perhaps the best measure of how much work the setup people perform for the manufacture of a product.
ROGER SMITH:	Yes.
LINDA COLLINS:	How many hours of setup work can your crew perform in a year?
ROGER SMITH:	Well, I expect about 1,800 hours of productive time per year from each of my people. Last year we had 7.5 workers on average, so there were a total of 13,500 hours available for setup. This year we have eight workers who will provide a total of 14,400 possible hours for setup.

Linda next interviewed David Carlson, an 18-year veteran at Montex, now in charge of the quality inspection department:

LINDA COLLINS:	How many people do you have in the quality inspection department?
DAVID CARLSON:	I have 12 people in addition to myself. Three of them are responsible for inspecting materials received from our suppliers. The remaining nine are responsible for the final inspection of all our production. I supervise all of their work, so I spend about 25% of my time on receipt inspection and 75% on final inspection.
LINDA COLLINS:	Hmm. Let me see. Our payroll records indicate that there are only 11 people reporting to you in your department.
DAVID CARLSON:	Yes, but Jon Wang from the production engineering department is now permanently assigned to me to help us with our final product inspections.
LINDA COLLINS:	(Checking her payroll records) That means I need to add another $38,000 in wages and benefits to your department and subtract it from the production engineering department. Your departmental costs, therefore, are $540,000.
DAVID CARLSON:	Yes.
LINDA COLLINS:	Let me move on. What determines the amount of work for your people who inspect material receipts?
DAVID CARLSON:	We inspect every lot of materials we receive, so I suppose it is the number of material receipts.
LINDA COLLINS:	Does the amount of inspection time depend on the size of the lot?
DAVID CARLSON:	Not unless it is an exceptionally large lot that we receive only once or twice a year. You see, we randomly inspect a fixed quantity from each batch of incoming materials. It normally takes about an hour to record, inspect, and store each lot we receive.
LINDA COLLINS:	How many lots can you receive and inspect in a year with your present staff?
DAVID CARLSON:	We can do up to 100 per week. Since the plant works 50 weeks in a year, I suppose that means that we can inspect 5,000 materials receipts in a year.
LINDA COLLINS:	What triggers the work done by your people who are responsible for the final inspection of your production?
DAVID CARLSON:	Company policy requires us to inspect every unit we produce, so it is the total number of units produced at the plant.
LINDA COLLINS:	Do all products require the same number of inspection hours?
DAVID CARLSON:	Yes. We follow the same procedures for every pump we produce.
LINDA COLLINS:	How many pumps can your crew inspect in a year?

DAVID CARLSON: We can inspect 5,000 pumps in a week, so it means that we can inspect 250,000 pumps in a year. You should realize, of course, that during some weeks when the production level is low in the plant, we do not inspect 5,000 pumps, and sometimes during peak production periods, we work overtime to get the job completed.

Required

a. Using this information, determine cost driver rates for machine setups, inspecting materials from suppliers, and inspecting units produced. Provide justification of your choice of cost drivers.
b. On viewing the computed cost driver rates, Montex managers suggested exploring the possibility of reducing inspection of materials purchased from suppliers. What advice would you give management as it pursues this option?

LO 1, 4   **4-49 *Part proliferation: role for activity-based costing***   An article in the *Wall Street Journal* by Neal Templin and Joseph B. White (June 23, 1993) reported on the major changes occurring in General Motors. Its new chief executive officer, John Smith, had been installed after the board of directors requested the resignation of Robert Stempel, the previous chief.

John Smith's North American Strategy Board identified 30 components that could be simplified for 1994 models. GM had 64 different versions of the cruise control/turn signal mechanism. It planned to reduce that to 24 versions the next year and the following year to just eight. The tooling for each one cost GM's A. C. Rochester division about $250,000. Smith said, "We've been talking about too many parts doing the same job for 25 years, but we weren't focused on it." (Note that the tooling cost is only one component of the cost of proliferating components. Other costs include the design and engineering costs for each different component, purchasing costs, setup and scheduling costs, plus the stocking and service costs for every individual component in each automobile dealership, including Booth Motors, around the United States.)

GM's proliferation of parts was mind-boggling. GM made or bought 139 different hood hinges, compared with one for Ford. Saginaw's Plant Six juggled parts for 167 different steering columns—down from 250 the previous year but still far from the goal of fewer than 40 by decade's end.

This approach increased GM's costs exponentially. Not only did the company pay far more engineers than competitors did to design steering columns, but it also needed extra tools and extra people to move parts around, and it suffered from quality glitches when workers confused one steering column with another.

Required

a. How could an inaccurate and distorted product costing system have contributed to the overproliferation of parts and components at General Motors?
b. What characteristics should a new cost system have that would enable it to signal accurately to product designers and market researchers about the cost of customization and variety?

LO 3, 4   **4-50 *Role for activity-based cost systems in implementing strategy***   Consider the case of the Cott Corporation, a Canadian private-label producer of high-quality cola beverages. Cott is attempting to get grocery retailers to stock its cola beverages as a lower-price alternative to the international brands, Coca-Cola and Pepsi-Cola. The international brands deliver directly to the retailer's store and stock their products on the retailer's shelves. Cott, in contrast, delivers to the retailer's warehouse or distribution center, leaving the retailer to move the product to the shelves of its various retail outlets. Cott offers substantially lower prices to the retailers and, in addition, is willing to work with the grocery retailer to customize the cola beverage to the retailer's specification; develop special packaging for the retailer, including labeling the beverage with the retailer's name (a practice known as *retailer branding,* such as Safeway Select Cola); offer a full variety of carbonated beverages (diet, caffeine free, multiple flavors, multiple sizes, and packaging options); and develop a marketing and merchandising strategy for the retailer for the private-label beverage.

Required

a. Consider how Cott might measure and manage activities and processes and relationships with suppliers and customers. How can Cott build cost systems to help it implement its strategy successfully?

LO 4, 9, 10   **4-51 *Financial versus management accounting: role for activity-based cost systems in privatization of government services*** The mayor of Gotham City is dissatisfied with rising costs and deteriorating quality of the services provided by the municipal workers, particularly in the transportation department: paving roads, repairing potholes, and cleaning the streets. He is contemplating privatizing these services by outsourcing the business to independent, private contractors. The mayor has demanded that before proceeding with his privatization initiative his staff develop an activity-based cost system for municipal services, declaring, "Introducing competition and privatization to government services requires real cost information. You can't compete if you are using fake money." Currently, the accounting and financial systems of Gotham City report only how much is being spent in each department by type of expenditure: payroll, benefits, materials, vehicles, equipment (including computers and telephones), and supplies.

Required

a. Before outsourcing to the private sector, why does the mayor want to develop activity-based cost estimates of the current cost of performing these municipal services?
b. After building activity-based cost models, should this information be shared with the municipal workers? Why or why not? How might the workers use the activity-based cost information?

LO 4, 5, 8, 9   **4-52 *Activity-based management, customer profitability, managing customer relationships, pricing*** Read the *Wall Street Journal* article "Survival Strategies: After Cost Cutting, Companies Turn Toward Price Increases" by Timothy Aeppel (September 18, 2002, p. A1). The article reports "an all-out search for new ways to charge more money without raising prices."

Required

a. How did Jergens, Inc., use an activity-based costing approach to justify the price for an order of odd-size metal locating fasteners?
b. What issues arose in Goodyear Tire & Rubber's pricing to distributors? What was Goodyear's response?
c. What was the outcome of Emerson Electric's decision to depart from cost-based pricing? How can a product costing system contribute to undercosting a low-volume or customized product?
d. How did Wildeck influence customers to purchase products and services that are more profitable to Wildeck? How did Wildeck respond to a competitor's lower-priced storage-rack protector? What role should a cost system play in such decisions?
e. Why was Union Pacific not concerned if it lost its less profitable customers? Will dropping unprofitable customers always lead to an immediate increase in profit?

Sales	$42,700,000	122.0%
Cost of items purchased	35,000,000	100.0%
Gross margin	7,700,000	22.0%
Personnel expense (warehouse, truck drivers)	2,570,000	7.3%
Warehouse expenses (excluding personnel)	2,000,000	5.7%
Freight	450,000	1.3%
Delivery truck expenses	200,000	0.6%
Order entry expenses	840,000	2.4%
General and selling expenses	1,600,000	4.6%
Interest expense	120,000	0.3%
Net income before taxes	$(80,000)	(0.2)%

Source: Robert S. Kaplan.

LO 1, 2, 4, 5, 6, 7, 8   **4-53** *Time-driven activity-based costing, activity-based management*
Midwest Office Products[2]

John Malone, general manager of Midwest Office Products (MOP), was concerned about the financial results for calendar year 2003. Despite a sales increase from the prior year, the company had just suffered the first loss in its history (see summary income statement in Exhibit 4-12).

Midwest Office Products was a regional distributor of office supplies to institutions and commercial businesses. It offered a comprehensive product line ranging from simple writing implements (such as pens, pencils, and markers) and fasteners to specialty paper for modern high speed copiers and printers. MOP had an excellent reputation for customer service and responsiveness.

Warehouse personnel at MOP's distribution center unloaded truckload shipments of products from manufacturers, and moved the cartons into designated storage locations until customers requested the items. Each day, after customer orders had been received, MOP personnel drove fork-lift trucks around the warehouse to accumulate the cartons of items and prepare them for shipment.

MOP ordered supplies from many different manufacturers. It priced products to its end-use customers by first marking up the purchased product cost by 16% to cover the cost of warehousing, order processing, and freight; then it added another 6% markup to cover the general, selling, and administrative expenses, plus an allowance for profit. The markups were determined at the start of each year, on actual expenses in prior years and general industry and competitive trends. Midwest adjusted the actual price quoted to a customer based on long-term relationships and competitive situations, but pricing was generally independent of the specific level of service required by that customer, except for desktop deliveries.

Typically, MOP shipped products to its customers using commercial truckers. Recently, MOP had introduced a desktop delivery option in which Midwest personnel personally delivered supplies directly to individual locations at the customer's site. Midwest had leased four trucks and hired four drivers for the desktop delivery service. Midwest charged a price premium (up to an additional 5% markup) for the convenience and savings such direct delivery orders provided to customers. The company believed that the desktop delivery option would improve margins and create more loyal customers in its highly competitive office supplies distribution business.

Midwest had introduced electronic data interchange (EDI) in 1999, and a new Internet site in 2000, which allowed customer orders to arrive automatically so that clerks would not have to enter

---

[2] Copyright © 2004 President and Fellows of Harvard College. Harvard Business School Case 9-104-073. This case was prepared by Professor Robert S. Kaplan as the basis for class discussion rather than to illustrate either effective or ineffective handling of an administrative situation. Reprinted by permission of Harvard Business School.

data manually. Several customers had switched to this electronic service because of the convenience to them. Yet Midwest's costs continued to rise. Malone was concerned that even after introducing innovations such as desktop delivery and electronic order entry, the company could not earn a profit. He wondered about what actions he should take to regain profitability.

Distribution Center: Activity Analysis

Malone turned to his controller, Melissa Dunhill and director of operations, Tim Cunningham for help. Tim suggested:

> If we can figure out, without going overboard of course, what exactly goes on in our distribution center, maybe we can get a clearer picture about what it costs to process orders and serve our customers.

Distribution center manager, Wilbur Smith, spoke with Melissa and Tim about the operations at the center:

> All we do is store the cartons, process the orders, and get them ready to ship to customers, either by commercial freight or using the desktop delivery option.

Wilbur described some details of these activities:

> The amount of warehouse space we need and the people to move cartons in and out of storage and get them ready for shipment just depends on the number of cartons. All items have about the same inventory turnover so space and handling costs are proportional to the number of cartons that go through the facility.
> We use commercial freight for normal shipments, and the cost is based more on volume than on anything else. Each carton we ship by commercial carrier costs about the same, regardless of the weight or distance. Of course, any carton that we deliver ourselves, through our new desktop delivery service, avoids the commercial shipping charges but does use our trucks and drivers.

The team talked with one of the truck drivers doing desktop deliveries:

> An average delivery time takes about three hours. But delivery times can be as short as 30 minutes for nearby customers, and up to eight hours for delivery to a distant customer. We also spend different times once we arrive at a customer's site. Some customers have only a single dropoff point while others require us to deliver individual cartons to different locations at their site.

Melissa and Tim next checked on the expenses of entering and validating customer order data at the distribution center. The order entry expenses included the data processing system, the data entry operators, and supervisors. They spoke with Hazel Nutley, a data entry operator at Midwest for 17 years.

> All I do is key in the orders, line by line by line. I start by entering the customer ID and validating our customer information. Beyond that, the only thing that really matters is how many order lines I have to enter. Each line item on the order has to be entered separately. Of course, any order that comes in through the EDI system or Internet page sets up automatically without any intervention from me. I just do a quick check to make sure the customer hasn't made an obvious error, and that everything looks correct. This validity check takes about the same time for all electronic orders; it doesn't depend on the number of items ordered.

Melissa and Tim collected information from company data bases and learned the following:

- The distribution centers processed 80,000 cartons in 2003. Of these, 75,000 cartons were shipped by commercial freight. The remaining 5,000 cartons were shipped under the desktop delivery option. Midwest made 2,000 desktop deliveries during the year (the average desktop delivery was for 2.5 cartons).

- People felt that handling, processing and shipping 80,000 cartons per year was about the capacity that could be handled with existing resources of people and space.
- The total compensation for truck drivers was $250,000 per year. Each driver worked about 1,500 hours per year doing the desktop delivery service. This was also the maximum time available from each truck, after subtracting maintenance and repair time.
- Midwest employed 16 order-entry operators. The $840,000 of order-entry costs in Midwest's income statement included the salaries, fringe benefits, supervision, occupancy, and equipment costs for the operators.
- With vacations and holidays, each operator worked about 1,750 hours per year. But allowing for breaks, training, and other time off, the order-entry supervisor believed that operators provided about 1,500 hours per year of productive work.
- Operators required about 9 minutes (0.15 hours) to enter the basic information on a manual customer order. Beyond this basic setup time for a manual order, operators took an additional 4.5 minutes (0.075 hours) to enter each line item on the order. The operators spent an average of 6 minutes (0.10 hours) to verify the information on an electronic order.
- Some customers paid their invoices within 30 days, while others took 90 to 120 days to pay. Midwest had recently taken out a working capital loan to help finance its growing accounts receivables balance. The current interest rate on this loan was 1% per month on the average loan balance.

Understanding Order Costs and Profitability

Melissa looked through recent orders and found five that seemed representative of those received during the past year (see Exhibit 4-13). The orders all involved cartons containing merchandise costing about $500 to acquire from manufacturers to which the normal 22% markup had been realized. Orders requiring direct delivery had an additional 4 to 5% surcharge. While each of these orders had been priced in the standard way for cost recovery and profit margins, Melissa wondered what profits Midwest Office Products had really earned on each of these orders.

Required

a. Based on the interviews and the data in the case, estimate the following:
   (1) The cost of processing cartons through the facility
   (2) The cost of entering electronic and manual customer orders

Exhibit 4-13
Midwest Office Products: Five Orders

ORDER	1	2	3	4	5
Price	$610	$634	$6,100	$6,340	$6,100
Acquisition cost	500	500	5,000	5,000	5,000
Number of cartons in order	1	1	10	10	10
Number of cartons shipped commercially	1	0	10	0	10
Desktop delivery time (hours)	—	4	—	4	—
Manual order	No	Yes	No	Yes	Yes
Number of line items in order	1	1	10	10	10
Electronic order	Yes	No	Yes	No	No
Payment period (months)	1	4	1	4	4

Source: Robert S. Kaplan.

(3) The cost of shipping cartons on commercial carriers

(4) The cost per hour for desktop deliveries

b. Using this cost driver information, calculate the cost and profitability of the five orders in Exhibit 4-13. Compare these costs and profitability to those calculated by Midwest's existing costing system.

c. Explain the difference in profitability of the five orders calculated by the activity-based costing system and the company's existing cost system.

d. On the basis of your analysis, what actions should John Malone take to improve Midwest's profitability?

LO 1, 2, 4, 5, 6, 10 **4-54 *Time-driven activity-based costing, activity-based management*** Sippican Corporation (A)[3]

The decline in our profits has become intolerable. The severe price cutting in pumps has dropped our pre-tax margin to less than 2%, far below our historical 15% margins. Fortunately, our competitors are overlooking the opportunities for profit in flow controllers. Our recent 10% price increase in that line has been implemented without losing any business.

Robert Parker, President of Sippican Corporation

Robert Parker was discussing operating results in the latest month with Peggy Knight, his controller, and John Scott, his manufacturing manager. The meeting among the three was taking place in an atmosphere tinged with apprehension because competitors had been reducing prices on pumps, Sippican's major product line. Since pumps were a commodity product, Parker had seen no alternative but to match the reduced prices to maintain volume. But the price cuts had led to declining company profits, especially in the pump line (summary operating results for the previous month, March 2006, are shown in Exhibits 4-14 and 4-15).

Exhibit 4-14
Sippican Corporation: Operating Results (March 2006)

Sales		$1,847,500	100%
Direct labor expense		351,000	
Direct materials expense		458,000	
Contribution margin		$1,038,500	56%
Manufacturing overhead			
Machine-related expenses	$334,800		
Setup labor	117,000		
Receiving and production control	15,600		
Engineering	78,000		
Packaging and shipping	109,200		
Total manufacturing overhead		654,600	35%
Gross margin		383,900	21%
General, selling and administrative expenses		350,000	19%
Operating income (pretax)		$33,900	1.8%

Source: Robert S. Kaplan.

---

[3] Copyright © 2006 President and Fellows of Harvard College. Harvard Business School Case Case 9-106-058. This case was prepared by Professor Robert S. Kaplan as the basis for class discussion rather than to illustrate either effective or ineffective handling of an administrative situation. Reprinted by permission of Harvard Business School.

Exhibit 4-15
Product
Profitability
Analysis
(March 2006)

	VALVES	PUMPS	FLOW CONTROLLERS
Direct labor cost[a]	$12.35	$16.25	$13.00
Direct material cost	16.00	20.00	22.00
Manufacturing overhead (at 185%)	22.85	30.06	24.05
Standard unit costs	$51.20	$66.31	$59.05
Target selling price	$78.77	$102.02	$90.85
Planned gross margin (%)	35%	35%	35%
Actual selling price	$79.00	$70.00	$95.00
Actual gross margin	$27.80	$3.69	$35.95
Actual gross margin (%)	35%	5%	38%

[a]Direct labor costs were charged at $32.50 per hour. The average daily compensation for days worked was $195 per day ($3,900 per month divided by 20 working days per month). The hourly rate was calculated by dividing $195 by the 6 hours per day available for productive work.

Source: Robert S. Kaplan.

Sippican supplied products to manufacturers of water purification equipment. The company had started with a unique design for valves that it could produce to tolerances that were better than any in the industry. Parker quickly established a loyal customer base because of the high quality of its manufactured valves. He and Scott realized that Sippican's existing labor skills and machining equipment could also be used to produce pumps and flow controllers, products that were also purchased by its customers. They soon established a major presence in the high-volume pump product line and the more customized flow controller line.

Sippican's production process started with the purchase of semi-finished components from several suppliers. It machined these parts to the required tolerances and assembled them in the company's modern manufacturing facility. The same equipment and labor were used for all three product lines, and production runs were scheduled to match customer shipping requirements. Suppliers and customers had agreed to just-in-time deliveries, and products were packed and shipped as completed.

Valves were produced by assembling four different machined components. Scott had designed machines that held components in fixtures so that they could be machined automatically. The valves were standard products and could be produced and shipped in large lots. Although Scott felt several competitors could now match Parker's quality in valves, none had tried to gain market share by cutting price, and gross margins had been maintained at a standard 35%.

The manufacturing process for pumps was practically identical to that for valves. Five components were machined and then assembled into the final product. The pumps were shipped to industrial product distributors after assembly. Recently, it seemed as if each month brought new reports of reduced prices for pumps. Sippican had matched the lower prices so that it would not give up its place as a major pump supplier. Gross margins on pump sales in the latest month had fallen to about 5%, well below the company's planned gross margin of 35%.

Flow controllers were devices that controlled the rate and direction of flow of chemicals. They required more components and more labor, than pumps or valves, for each finished unit. Also, there was much more variety in the types of flow controllers used in industry, so many more production runs and shipments were performed for this product line than for valves. Sippican had recently raised flow controller prices by more than 10% with no apparent effect on demand.

Sippican had always used a simple cost accounting system. Each unit of product was charged for direct material and labor cost. Material cost was based on the prices paid for components under annual purchasing agreements. Labor rates, including fringe benefits, were $32.50 per hour,[4] and were charged to products based on the standard run times for each product (see Exhibit 4-16). The company had only one producing department, in which components were both machined and assembled into finished products. The overhead costs in this department were allocated to products as a percentage of production-run direct labor cost. Currently, the rate was 185%. Since direct labor cost had to be recorded anyway to prepare factory payroll, this was an inexpensive way to allocate overhead costs to products.

Knight noted that some companies didn't allocate any overhead costs to products, treating them as period, not product, expenses. For these companies, product profitability was measured at the contribution margin level—price less all variable costs. Sippican's variable costs were only its direct material and direct labor costs. On that basis, all products, including pumps, would be generating substantial contribution to overhead and profits. She thought that perhaps some of Sippican's competitors were following this procedure and pricing to cover variable costs.

Knight had recently led a small task force to study Sippican's overhead costs since they had now become much larger than the direct labor expenses. The study had revealed the following information:

1. A setup had to be performed each time a batch of components had to be machined in a production run. Each component in a product required a separate production machine to run the raw material or purchased part to the specifications for the product. Workers often operated several of the machines simultaneously once they had set up the machine. Because of the large number of setups, Sippican had dedicated about 25% of its production work force to focus exclusively on setups. Some production workers did not operate any machines; they performed only manual assembly work. Their assembly time per product was included in the direct labor hour estimates for each product.

   Sippican operated two $7\frac{1}{2}$-hour shifts each weekday. Each shift employed 45 production and assembly workers, plus 15 setup workers. Workers received two 15-minute breaks each day. They received an average of 30 minutes per day for training and education activities, and all the workers—production, assembly, and setup—spent 30 minutes each shift for preventive maintenance and minor repair of the machines.

Exhibit 4-16
Product Data

PRODUCT LINES	VALVES	PUMPS	FLOW CONTROLLERS
Materials per unit	4 components	5 components	10 components
	2 at $2 = $4	3 at $2 = $6	4 at $1 = $4
	2 at $6 = 12	2 at $7 = 14	5 at $2 = 10
			1 at $8 = 8
Materials cost per unit	$16	$20	$22
Direct labor per unit	0.38 DL hours	0.50 DL hours	0.40 DL hours
Machine hours per unit	0.5	0.5	0.3
Setup hours per run	5	6	12

Source: Robert S. Kaplan.

---

[4] The full compensation, including fringe benefits, for direct and indirect employees (other than engineers) was $3,900 per month. Employees worked an average of 20 days per month (holidays and vacations accounted for the remaining 2–3 days per month).

2. The company had 62 machines for component processing. These machines were generally available for the six hours per shift that production workers were actively engaged in production or setup activities on the machines. Sippican leased the machines. Each machine's operating expenses were about $5,400 per month, including lease payments, supplies, utilities, and maintenance and repairs.

3. The receiving and production control departments employed four people over the two shifts. These personnel ordered, processed, inspected, and moved each batch of components for a production run. It took a total of 75 minutes for all the activities required to get one batch of components ordered, received and moved to a machine for processing. This time was independent of whether the components were for a long or a short production run, or whether the components were expensive or inexpensive.

4. The work in the packaging and shipping area had increased during the past couple of years as Sippican increased the number of customers it served. Each shipment took 50 minutes to prepare the packages and labels, independent of the number or types of items in the shipment, plus eight minutes per item to bubble wrap and pack in the carton, whether the item was a valve, pump, or flow controller. The packaging and shipping area employed 14 people in each of the two shifts (28 in total).

   Employees in the receiving, production control, packaging, and shipping departments worked a $7\frac{1}{2}$-hour shift that included two 15-minute breaks per day, and 30 minutes, on average, for training and education.

5. Sippican employed eight engineers for designing and developing new product varieties. Engineers' total compensation was $9,750 per month. Much of their time was spent modifying flow control products to conform to customer requests. Engineers worked $7\frac{1}{2}$-hour shifts. After breaks, training, education, and professional activities, engineers supplied about 6 hours of productive work per shift.

Knight's team had collected the data shown in Exhibit 4-17 based on operations in March 2006. The team felt that this month was typical of ongoing operations.

Required

a. Given some of the apparent problems with Sippican's cost system, should executives abandon overhead cost assignment to products entirely and adopt a contribution margin approach in which manufacturing overhead cost is treated as a period expense? Why or why not?

b. Calculate the practical capacity and the capacity cost rates for each of Sippican's resources: production and setup employees, machines, receiving and production control employees, shipping and packaging employees, and engineers.

Exhibit 4-17
Monthly Production and Operating Statistics (March 2006)

	VALVES	PUMPS	FLOW CONTROLLERS	TOTAL
Production (units)	7,500	12,500	4,000	24,000
Machine hours (run time)	3,750	6,250	1,200	11,200
Production runs	20	100	225	345
Setup hours (labor and machines)	100	600	2,700	3,400
Number of shipments	40	100	200	340
Hours of engineering work	60	240	600	900

Source: Robert S. Kaplan.

c. Using these capacity cost rates and the production data in Exhibits 4-16 and 4-17, calculate revised costs and profits for Sippican's three product lines. What difference does your cost assignment have on reported product costs and profitability? What causes any shifts in cost and profitability?

d. Could this approach be extended to service companies and to companies much larger and more complex than Sippican? What would be the barriers and difficulties with implementing time-driven activity-based costing in practice?

e. On the basis of the revised cost and profitability estimates, what actions should Sippican's management team take to improve the company's profitability?

LO 1, 2, 4, 5, 6, 10   **4-55 *Traditional activity-based costing, activity-based management*** Glenn Morris Plumbing and Heating Systems[5] general manager, Carla Hudson, pushed her chair back from her desk and sighed. Things were not going well and seemed to be getting worse. Profit margins had been slipping for several years and Carla had just spoken to her accountant who indicated that initial projections suggested that, for the first time, GMPHS would show a loss in operations of over $100,000, as summarized in Exhibit 4-18.

GMPHS competed in markets where competitors that offered undifferentiated products (goods or services) had to meet market prices for what they provided. Therefore, there was little room on the pricing side for these competitors to increase their product or service prices.

GMPHS already had all the business it could handle and, in fact, was turning business away because of a lack of capacity. To remedy this, Carla was adding staff as quickly as possible. However, GMPHS had an outstanding reputation for quality. Carla maintained this reputation by only hiring apprentices who had graduated from a recognized technical program. She then trained them in what Carla called, the GMPHS way.

GMPHS had acquired and adapted all the newest technology to its business. This technology allowed GMPHS to provide a higher-quality service and also to use less labor time on each job. Therefore, while the overhead rates at GMPHS were higher than its competitors, reflecting the use

Exhibit 4-18
Glenn Morris Plumbing and Heating Systems Summary of Operations 2006

	INSTALLATION	HEATING AND AIR CONDITIONING	PLUMBING	WHOLESALE	TOTAL
Revenues	$1,956,000	$1,245,700	$1,260,000	$2,467,800	$6,929,500
Materials costs	1,159,866	641,628	666,306	966,300	3,434,100
Labor costs	353,734	264,372	219,294	190,700	1,028,100
Margin	$442,400	$339,700	$374,400	$1,310,800	$2,467,300
Overhead costs	98,500	45,600	146,900	457,200	748,200
Segment contribution	$343,900	$294,100	$227,500	$853,600	$1,719,100
Allocated corporate costs	330,928	198,085	193,625	252,962	975,600
Segment margin	$12,972	$96,015	$33,875	$600,638	$743,500
Unallocated corporate costs					850,000
Corporate profit before taxes					($106,500)

---

[5] © Anthony Atkinson and Gene Deszca. The authors prepared this case to provide a basis for class discussion. It is not intended to illustrate either effective or ineffective management practices. This case is heavily adapted from a case the authors originally developed for CMA Canada. Reprinted by permission of Anthony Atkinson.

of new technology, the labor hours for a particular job were lower than those of competitors. Carla had hoped this would stop the margin slide that had been going on for 4 years.

With revenues growing at a constant rate, and costs seemingly under control, Carla was perplexed by the news from the accountant that losses were looming for this year.

Background

Carla's grandfather had founded GMPHS in 1913. Originally the business had focused entirely on well drilling and plumbing. By 1930, the well drilling business had been sold and in 1930 he added a full line of heating services. By 1970, air conditioning, water-treatment systems, and air-filtration systems had been added to the company's lines of business. By 2006, GMPHS had 14 plumbing trucks, 5 heating and air conditioning trucks, and two special service vehicles that provided trenching and well cleaning services.

As part of this growing business GMPHS had become a licensed distributor and service agent for most of the products that it installed, including well pumps, heating systems, air conditioning units, air-treatment systems, and water-treatment systems. Gradually, GMPHS had developed a large wholesale business selling replacement parts or new systems to other plumbing and heating companies who were the direct competitors of GMPHS in the consumer market.

Through a combination of acquiring the rights to distribute what it considered to be the best systems and by using highly skilled and well-trained personnel, GMPHS had developed an outstanding reputation for quality. Because GMPHS consistently met the market price for its labor services, its quality reputation had always created a demand for its services that outstripped its capacity. In fact, on several occasions Carla's father, who had taken over the business from her grandfather in 1954, had considered charging a price premium over the market rates in order to capture some of the benefits of GMPHS's quality reputation. In 2002, Frank had commissioned a study which suggested that the market would support a price increase of 10% for Glenn Morris's services without a drop in demand because the market viewed Glenn Morris as a superior supplier. However, Frank had always rejected premium pricing on the grounds that the business was a community business and that charging premium prices to neighbors was inappropriate.

By 2006, GMPHS was far more than a local business. From a relatively small community of 20,000, GMPHS operated over a radius of 80 kilometers. This service circle included several communities in excess of 50,000, and the total population in its service region exceeded 200,000 people.

From early childhood Carla had wanted to work in the family business. During her high school and university years she had worked as an assistant to various professionals working in the business. As soon as she graduated with her Commerce degree, Carla returned to Glenn Morris and took up a full-time position as the dispatcher and general manager. Although Carla had no technical trade or designation, her years of working with the professionals in the business had given her a strong, detailed, and practical knowledge of the business.

Carla was less familiar with the wholesale business, which had been managed by her father's brother, Frank. Carla's father had recruited Frank into the business when a heart attack prompted Frank's retirement as a regional manager for a large furnace manufacturer.

In 2004, Carla's father was elected as a member of the provincial parliament (MPP) in Ontario, Canada. At that point, Carla was given full control of GMPHS with the stipulation that Frank was to be allowed to manage the wholesale business independently.

Carla's Acceptance

Carla's acceptance in the GMPHS varied. Among the professional staff, Carla was highly admired and respected from her years of working on job sites with many of the plumbers, electricians, and heating-system specialists.

However, Carla was not well accepted among the administrative staff. Many staff members thought that Carla, at 34, was too young and too inexperienced to take on the job of running GMPHS. Long ago, Carla's father had given many of the administrative jobs in the organization to Carla's cousins, uncles, and aunts. Carla had a low regard for their enthusiasm and emotional commitment to the organization. Carla's impression was that many of these people felt that their jobs were a form of social welfare to which they were entitled and that they felt threatened by the changes that Carla might make in the organization.

In particular, Frank was a problem. Word had filtered back to Carla from the professional staff that Frank was constantly complaining about her decisions and her ability to command respect with the administrative group. Carla knew that her father could deal with this immediately but she chose not to tell him and resolved to deal with Frank on her own.

The Core Strengths at GMPHS

Carla was observant and realized that GMPHS was suffering from a lack of focus and direction. The business was widely spread out and required the careful blending of many different disciplines. While the plumbing business was fairly traditional, technology in the heating and air conditioning business was evolving rapidly. This required constant attention to new product releases and constant recertification and retraining of the staff in that area. Carla wondered whether the effort was justified by the margins earned by that line of business. Moreover, Carla doubted whether the manager of any of the businesses really had a grasp of either the technological or the marketing skills to do a good job.

Upon reflection, Carla decided that GMPHS had two core strengths—the skill and knowledge of the professional staff and the company's reputation for high levels of quality and service. Carla resolved that anything she did would rely on these core strengths.

Acting on these beliefs, Carla invited a childhood friend, Trudy Carson, to undertake a management audit of the organization. Trudy was a highly respected consultant who specialized in diagnosing and changing organization culture. Trudy confirmed Carla's worst fears. Trudy reported that GMPHS was a tired organization. Beyond the high level of skill and technical competence of the professional staff, there was little evidence of either high skill or effort levels. In fact, Trudy reported that for the most part, the managerial staff got in the way of the professional staff that did most of the marketing and installation work—confirming Carla's suspicions of her relatives' attitude toward the business. In general, the administrative staff appeared to lack an understanding of the specific business units they managed and showed little interest in developing either the relationships or the administrative systems and supports needed to nurture bottom line performance. The clerical staff was both underqualified and underworked.

The Structure of the Business at GMPHS

While Trudy was working on her report, Carla opened another line of enquiry. Carla decided that she was going to get to the bottom of the profit drain and hired Eugene Munroe, CMA, to undertake an investigation of the business and to make appropriate suggestions to return the business to profitability. While working with the administrative staff, Eugene experienced the frostiness and lack of cooperation reported by Trudy. However, within a week of starting his engagement, Eugene was able to establish a number of indisputable facts about the business at GMPHS.

Eugene reported that the wholesale business was, relative to market opportunities, overcharging the other businesses. When the decision had been made to supply parts to other organizations, the wholesale business had been established to run independently of the other businesses. The wholesale business was charging the internal businesses retail prices for any parts they used. The internal businesses could buy these parts at wholesale prices from outside suppliers. The result was that profits that would normally be reported for the installation division, the heating and air conditioning division, and the plumbing division were being reported as profits for the wholesale business. Eugene's initial estimate was that based on whole-sale market prices, the internal price to these divisions from wholesale should be reduced by 20%.

Eugene revisited the 2002 study result that customers felt that GMPHS was undercharging for its high quality work and that a 10% price increase would have a negligible effect on demand. Eugene's conclusion was that price competition had increased since then and that a price increase should be limited to 5% to avoid any effect on demand. Eugene also indicated that competitors routinely charged for travel costs and that travel costs could be charged to customers in addition to the 5% increases without affecting demand.

Eugene determined that materials costs reported in Exhibit 4-18 were the prices billed by the wholesale division for the materials used on jobs.

Eugene concluded that the overhead costs appearing in Exhibit 4-18 were actually overhead costs that were attributable directly to the respective divisions. That is, none of these overhead costs were allocated costs. They were legitimate costs of each of the divisions and consisted primarily of depreciation on plant and equipment used exclusively by each division.

Eugene undertook a study of the $975,600 allocated corporate costs and determined that these costs were comprised of the elements identified in Exhibit 4-19.

These costs were allocated to each of the divisions in proportion to the total of materials costs and labor costs on the grounds that they reflected the use of general overhead in the business. However, upon investigation, Eugene established that the pattern of use of the overhead items creating these costs was generally not proportional to materials and labor costs.

Eugene believed, based on an initial appraisal, that shop time costs were proportional to the number of machine hours, which totalled 3,450 and were distributed 1000, 1600, 700, and 150 to installation, heating and air conditioning, plumbing, and wholesale, respectively. Equipment costs were actually direct or traceable costs since these costs reflected the depreciation on equipment that was used exclusively by each of the four divisions. These costs were distributed approximately as $156,700, $112,400, $115,400, $22,500 to installation, heating and air conditioning, plumbing, and wholesale, respectively. General warehouse costs seemed to be approximately proportional to the number of stock-keeping units and were distributed 100, 700, 600, 900 to installation, heating and air conditioning, plumbing, and wholesale, respectively.

After studying the $850,000 of unallocated corporate costs reported in Exhibit 4-18, Eugene decided that $224,600 should remain unallocated on the grounds that he classified them as basic business sustaining costs. The remaining costs Eugene believed were distributed as shown in Exhibit 4-20.

Further investigation uncovered the information shown in Exhibit 4-21.

The Heating and Air Conditioning Division

Eugene noted that there were three distinct groups of customers in the Heating and Air Conditioning Division and that there was a widespread belief that these customers provided very different profit contributions to the division. The Heating and Air Conditioning Division had three types of cus-

Exhibit 4-19
Glenn Morris Plumbing and Heating Systems: Distribution of Reported Allocated Corporate Costs

Cost Item	Amount	Driver	Driver Units
Shop time	$186,400	Machine hours	3,450
Equipment costs	$407,000	Traced (direct)	Traced
Supplies costs	$125,400	Machine hours	3,450
General warehouse costs	$256,800	SKUs	2,300

Exhibit 4-20
Glenn Morris
Plumbing and
Heating Systems:
Distribution of
Reported
Unallocated
Corporate Costs

Cost Item	Amount	Driver	Driver Units
Order taking and billing	$245,000	Number of invoices issued	11,400
Customer service	$156,800	Number of calls	7,500
Administration	$223,600	Number of calls	7,500

Exhibit 4-21
Glenn Morris
Plumbing and
Heating Systems:
Distribution of
Work Units

Cost Item	Installation	Heating and Air Conditioning	Plumbing	Wholesale
Order taking and billing	350	2,650	2,600	5,800
Customer service	1,200	3,500	2,300	500
Administration	1,200	3,500	2,300	500

tomers: commercial, industrial, and residential. The revenues reported for each customer group were $304,500, $295,600, and $645,600, respectively. The materials costs in this division were proportional to the revenues reported by each unit.

The labor costs in this division were divided into three groups. The first group comprised labor costs that were chargeable to customers. The second group of labor costs were costs relating to retraining and recertification. These costs were treated as internal costs relating to maintaining quality and were not charged to customers. The third group of labor costs were costs related to travel to the customer's location. These costs were not charged to customers so that GMPHS, which covered a wider service area than its competitors, could remain competitive. The labor cost distribution was found to be 70% chargeable, 10% retraining and recertification, and 20% travel. The chargeable labor costs were proportional to revenue. The retraining and recertification costs were distributed as follows: 35% commercial, 50% industrial, and 15% residential. The travel costs were distributed as follows: 30% commercial, 5% industrial, and 65% residential.

The overhead costs of $45,600 reported for the Heating and Air Conditioning Division in Exhibit 4-18 were assumed to be proportional to the division's shop time costs which, in turn, were proportional to machine hours which were estimated as 400, 300, and 900 for the commercial, industrial, and residential units. The equipment costs related to the three units were estimated as 40%, 45%, and 15%, respectively, of the division's equipment costs. The share of the division supplies costs was estimated as being proportional to machine hours used by each unit. The stock-keeping units attributable to the division's three units were estimated as 150, 100, and 450, respectively, and each unit was assumed to account for the division's general warehouse costs in proportion to these stock-keeping units. Customer service costs for each unit were proportional to each unit's service calls, which were 500, 1000, and 2000, respectively. Administration costs were assumed to be proportional to the customer service costs.

Required

a. Carla wondered how to use the information she had gathered and has asked you to complete the financial analysis of divisional performance begun by Eugene, including a detailed analysis of operations for each division and in total for GMPHS. Include an analysis of the profitability of the three customer groups in the Heating and Air Conditioning Division.

b. Identify what you think are the key strategic issues and operational issues. Strategic issues relate to the organization's relationship with its environment in general and its customers in particular. Operational issues relate to how things are working within the organization.

c. Recommend strategic changes Carla should implement in order to deal with the strategic issues that you identified in (b).

5

Management Accounting Information for Activity and Process Decisions

After reading this chapter, you will be able to:

➤ define sunk costs and explain why sunk costs are not relevant costs

➤ analyze make-or-buy decisions

➤ demonstrate the influence of qualitative factors in making decisions

➤ compare the different types of facilities layouts

➤ explain the theory of constraints

➤ demonstrate the value of just-in-time manufacturing systems

➤ describe the concept of the cost of quality

➤ calculate the cost savings resulting from reductions in inventories, reduction in production cycle time, production yield improvements, and reductions in rework and defect rates

Tobor Toy Company

For 50 years, the Tobor Toy Company had been producing high-quality plastic toys for children. The company's best-selling toy was a pricey mechanical toy robot that performed several functions and had some unique features; it commanded a 30% market share. In early 2006, however, Tobor experienced a large drop in sales and market share. After some investigation, this loss was attributed to a significant decrease in the quality of the product and to general delays in getting it to customers. Customers complained that the toy robots failed to perform many of their functions and simply stopped working after several days. The number of returns was astronomical.

Top management decided that the quality of the toy robot needed to be improved dramatically so that the company could regain its reputation and market share. Rumors began to surface that the quality problem was due to deterioration of equipment and an out-of-date production process.

Source: Photo courtesy S. Mark Young.

Morale among the workers was also poor. Don Pielin, senior manager of manufacturing, was asked to conduct a thorough investigation and arrive at recommendations for change and improvement.

After several weeks of study, Don and a cross-functional team of management personnel documented numerous shop floor problems:

1. A disorganized, sloppy production system in which piles of both work-in-process and raw materials inventories were scattered over the shop floor
2. A lengthy and complex flow of production
3. The use of outdated machinery

In addition, the quality of the computer chip that allowed the robot to perform its functions was found to be highly variable because only some workers focused on their jobs, and thus there were as many defective robots sent back for rework as acceptable ones. Don, who had been studying the just-in-time (JIT) manufacturing philosophy, believed that the Tobor Company could benefit greatly from implementing JIT. The JIT system seemed to have many advantages, such as streamlining the production process and improving facilities layout, eliminating waste, reducing raw and work-in-process inventories, and generally creating an environment in which producing quality products was rewarded. Further, costs would be easier to control if the company had a well-designed and well-understood production process. Don's report to top management raised several questions:

1. Should many of the existing machines, including the major injection-molding machine, be replaced?
2. What should the company do about the local vendor who produced the faulty computer chips?
3. Would it make sense to implement an entirely new production process such as JIT?

Exhibit 5-1
Tobor Toys:
Major and Minor
Rework Rates

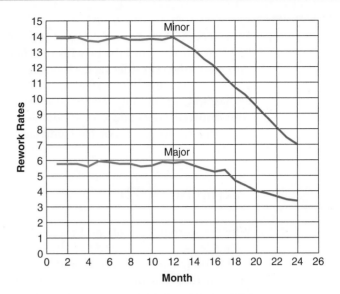

After a month of study, top management decided to implement the JIT approach. The cost of implementation and worker training amounted to $300,000. Management personnel wanted to be able to assess the return (benefits) from their investment in JIT. They were adamant that Don and his team carefully monitor the quality of products and the changes in the amount of rework. The cost of rework was part of a calculation the company made to determine what it called the *cost of quality*.

After the first year, Don plotted a graph of the rates of major rework, which required scrapping the robot, and minor rework, which included repairs such as realignment of parts and gears, as shown in Exhibit 5-1. Major rework had declined by about 2.5%, whereas the minor rework rate showed a larger decrease of 6.6%.

Don believed that improvement in yield rates should improve **cycle time**—the time it took to produce the robot from start to finish. On average, he found that cycle time had indeed decreased from 16.4 days to 7.2 days and that the work-in-process inventory had decreased from $1,774,000 to $818,000, for a savings of $956,000.

Don knew that the transition to a full JIT system would take some time, but he also wondered what the bottom-line effect on company profits would be for the year. Would the benefits of less rework, yield increases, and cycle time and inventory reductions be sufficient to offset the $300,000 implementation costs?

In this chapter, we will discuss many issues related to how management accounting information is used when making decisions. We discuss what costs are relevant for decisions and provide examples, such as how the information can be used in make-or-buy decisions. In addition to understanding what financial information is relevant for decisions, managers in today's business environment must also be well informed about the kinds of activities and processes that generate costs within their facilities. This chapter presents three types of facility designs—(1) process layouts, (2) product layouts, and (3) cellular manufacturing—all of which can be used to help organizations reduce costs. We follow this with a discussion of how organizations can reduce costs by ensuring that they focus on improving the quality of their processes. Finally, the JIT manufacturing system is presented as a system that integrates many of the ideas we discuss in the chapter.

EVALUATION OF FINANCIAL IMPLICATIONS

Managers must evaluate the financial implications of decisions that require trade-offs between the costs and the benefits of different alternatives. Financial implications are important when considering decisions such as whether to redesign an entire production process, replace existing machines, whether to purchase services such as custodial help, or to simply hire in-house custodians. Financial information about the different types of costs form the basis of decisions about the organization's activities and processes, as we saw in the case of the Tobor Toy Company.

SUNK COSTS ARE NOT RELEVANT

Whether particular costs and revenues are relevant for decision making depends on the decision context and the alternatives available. When choosing among different alternatives, managers should concentrate only on the costs and revenues that differ across the decision alternatives; these are the relevant costs/revenues. Opportunity costs by definition are also relevant costs for any decision. The costs that remain the same regardless of the alternative chosen are not considered relevant for the decision.

One category of costs that often causes confusion for decision makers consists of those incurred in the past, or sunk costs. Sunk costs are the costs of resources that already have been committed and cannot be influenced by any current action of decision. In other words, sunk costs are necessary for an activity and cannot be recovered or reversed if that activity ceases. Because sunk costs cannot be influenced by whatever alternative the manager chooses, they are not relevant to the evaluation of alternatives. One question that always arises in a discussion of sunk costs is, "Are all fixed costs sunk, and all sunk costs fixed?" The answer is no on both counts. In some instances, a fixed cost might be recoverable after the activity has ceased. As an example, consider an off-Broadway troupe that is putting on a play and who has signed a lease on a theater for 6 months. If the play is a flop and closes within a week, the fixed cost of the lease may not be sunk if the troupe can sublet the theater and recover its money. Likewise, a toy manufacturer that produces 50,000 action figures not only incurs fixed costs when making the toys but also incurs variable costs such as direct labor and direct materials. If the market for these toys becomes very soft and 30,000 of the figures are no longer saleable, the manufacturer has to consider the variable and fixed costs of production as sunk and move on. The main point is that decision makers have to think very carefully about which costs are sunk and which are not without assuming that one category of costs are always sunk.

Next we provide examples of relevant costs within a manufacturing context, but all the principles we illustrate apply equally well to any service decision.

Relevant Costs for the Replacement of a Machine

Consider the following situation. Bonner Company purchased a new drilling machine for $180,000 from USC Corporation on September 1, 2006, paying $30,000 in cash and financing the remaining $150,000 of the price with a bank loan. The loan requires a monthly payment of $5,200 for the next 36 months.

On September 27, 2006, a sales representative of another supplier of drilling machines approached Bonner Company with a newly-designed machine that had only recently been introduced to the market. Teo Machinery Company, the supplier of the new machine, offered special financing arrangements. It agreed to pay $50,000 for the old USC machine, which would serve as the down payment required for the new Teo machine. In addition, Teo would require monthly payments of $6,000 for the next 35 months.

The new Teo design relied on innovative computer chips, which would reduce the labor required to operate the machine. Bonner estimated that direct labor costs would decrease by $4,400 per month on the average if it purchased the Teo machine. In addition, the new machine would decrease maintenance costs by $800 per month because it had fewer moving parts than Bonner's current machine. The greater reliability of the machine also would allow Bonner to reduce materials scrap cost by $1,000 per month. Should Bonner dispose of the USC machine it just purchased on September 1 and buy the new machine from Teo Company? What costs are relevant for this decision?

Analysis of Relevant Costs

If Bonner Company buys the new machine from Teo Company, it will still be responsible for the monthly payments of $5,200 committed to USC on September 1. Therefore, the $30,000 that Bonner paid in cash for the USC machine and the $5,200 it is committed to pay each month for the next 36 months are sunk costs. Bonner already has committed these resources, and regardless of whether it decides to buy the new machine from Teo, it cannot avoid any of these costs. None of these sunk costs are relevant for the decision.

What costs are relevant? The 35 monthly payments of $6,000 and the down payment of $50,000 are relevant costs because they depend on Bonner's decision. In addition, labor, materials, and machine maintenance costs will be affected if Bonner acquires the new Teo machine. The expected monthly savings of $4,400 in labor costs, $1,000 in materials costs, and $800 in machine maintenance costs are relevant. The revenue of $50,000 expected on the trade-in of the old machine is also relevant because the old machine will be disposed of only if Bonner decides to acquire the Teo machine.

Exhibit 5-2 summarizes the relevant costs and revenues of this decision. In a comparison of the cost increases/cash outflows to cost savings/cash inflows, the down payment required for the new Teo machine is matched by the expected trade-in value of the USC machine. Furthermore, the expected savings in labor, materials, and machine maintenance costs each month ($6,200) are more than the monthly lease payments for the new Teo machine ($6,000). Thus, it is apparent that Bonner Company will be better off trading in the USC machine and replacing it with the Teo machine.

Exhibit 5-2
Bonner Company: Relevant Costs and Revenues

COST INCREASES AND CASH OUTFLOWS		COST SAVINGS AND CASH INFLOWS	
1. Down payment on the new Precision machine	$50,000	1. Disposal of the old Newtech machine	$50,000
2. Monthly lease payments on the Precision machine	$6,000	2. Monthly cost savings	
		Labor	$4,400
		Materials	1,000
		Maintenance	800
			$6,200

Summary of Relevant Costs

Managers must be able to identify the costs and revenues relevant for the evaluation of alternatives. Equally important, they must recognize that some costs and revenues are not relevant in such evaluations. Neither the payments that Bonner has already made on the USC machine nor the remaining monthly payments that it must continue to make are relevant for this evaluation. Both series of payments are sunk costs because the alternatives available to Bonner do not change the past cash flows or those committed in the future. We should also note that in a full analysis of this issue, we would incorporate the time value of money in the decision, but for simplicity have left this out of the analysis.

Assuming Responsibility for Decisions

On a technical level, the correct decision for Bonner Company is to dispose of the machine and replace it; however, because they are concerned about their reputations within their own organizations, not all managers would do so. Reversing a major decision made only just a month earlier makes the decision look like an error. In many circumstances, by maintaining the original course of action, the manager does not have to reveal that a better decision could have been made.

Three other factors can enter into the decision facing Bonner Company. First, if the manager does not purchase the new machine, then his or her behavior may be viewed as suboptimal in that it ensures lower productivity or performance from the old machine rather than improved performance with the new one. By not making the correct decision now, the manager may later incur the effects of a bad decision.

A second factor to consider is that if the manager admits to making an error when purchasing the old machine, that person might garner more respect from colleagues for accepting the responsibility. Finally, many decision makers have a difficult time distinguishing sunk cost business decisions from sunk cost personal decisions. In contrast to business decisions, the associated costs of previous life decisions can evoke a complex set of personal feelings. As an example, the decision to end a personal friendship or relationship is probably much more complex than the decision to replace a business asset because the personal decision takes into account one's history with an individual, with all its trials and tribulations. Unlike the case in the business decision, we do not end a friendship simply because a new friend materializes. Thus, identifying what is relevant and disentangling personal responses when dealing with business decisions are critical tasks for any business decision maker.

IN PRACTICE
Overcoming the Sunk Cost Fallacy or "Concorde Effect"

In 1962, the British and French Governments teamed up to produce a supersonic jet known as the Concorde. Both Air France and British Airways would fly the same plane but under their respective company banners. The Concorde was thought to be a marvel of engineering and could fly at 1,350 miles per hour at Mach 2 (twice the speed of sound). Initial estimates were that develop-

ment costs of the jet would be in the neighborhood of £150 to £170 million. By 1973, development costs had risen to over a billion pounds. Over the course of its long flight history (the jet was retired in October 2003), only 14 Concordes were used as passenger models. Air France and British Airways split the first nine models, but no other airline company would purchase the remaining five. As a result, only about one-third of the development costs were recovered. Rather than abandoning the Concorde, both governments continued to subsidize their operating costs of the planes. They could not cut their losses and move on. They had fallen into the sunk cost fallacy. For these reasons, the Concorde was considered an economic disaster.

Why is the sunk cost fallacy perpetuated? There are usually several types of reasons. One lies with the characteristics of individual decision makers or groups. For instance, from a psychological perspective, some individuals feel a need to justify a losing project, such as the Concorde, by escalating their commitment in the hope of turning a situation around. These individuals are seeking their own or external justification for their decisions. Other individuals are susceptible to "selective perception" in which they use all available positive information to continue to justify a project but fail to process any negative information that may lead to termination. Still others are affected by whether information is viewed in terms of gains or losses. This concept is known as "framing." When information is framed in terms of gains (for example, the glass is half full), individuals tend to be risk averse; when information is framed in terms of losses (for example, the glass is half empty), individuals tend to be risk seeking. Others engage in "impression management" and resist abandoning a losing project because they believe that giving up the project will diminish their reputation in the eyes of coworkers and superiors.

There are several ways that the sunk cost fallacy can be overcome:

Try to seek training in identifying what the sunk cost is and how it manifests itself.

Obtain opinions of others who were uninvolved in your original choice.

Determine if you would choose the same course of action that you are now on if there had been no past investment.

Recognize that even fully informed choices can result in bad outcomes. Cutting your losses does not necessarily mean that you were foolish to make the original choice. But if you don't cut your losses that true economic disaster may occur.

Source: www.aerospaceweb.org/question/planes/q0186.shtml.

Overcoming the Sunk Cost Fallacy or "Concorde Effect."

Source: www.microsoft.com/korea/games/fs2000/art/screens/concorde/concorde.jpg. Mistral Images.

MAKE-OR-BUY DECISIONS

Management accountants often supply information about relevant costs and revenues to help managers make special one-time decisions. One example is a **make-or-buy decision**. As managers attempt to reduce costs and increase the competitiveness of their products, they face decisions about whether their companies should manufacture some parts and components for their products in-house or subcontract with another company to supply these parts and components. Such make-or-buy decisions illustrate once again how to identify relevant costs and revenues.

Consider the decision faced by Ray Haradin, production manager of Sommers Motors, Inc. The company manufactures about 15% of the lamps required for its automobiles in its own plant near Schaumberg, Illinois. Steve Sommers, company president, would like to reduce costs. Steve has asked Ray to evaluate the possibility of **outsourcing** all the lamps, that is, buying them from an outside supplier instead of manufacturing them in-house. Ray obtains firm quotes from several suppliers for the four types of lamps the company manufactures in-house: standard rear lamps, standard front lamps, multicolored rear lamps, and curved side and rear lamps.

Exhibit 5-3 displays details of the two lowest quotes from outside suppliers for a representative lamp in each of the four product lines manufactured in-house. The lowest bid is lower than the total in-house manufacturing cost of each lamp. Should Ray accept the outside bid and terminate the in-house production of these products? What costs must Ray identify and consider when making this decision?

Exhibit 5-3
Sommers Motors, Inc.: Product Costs per Unit and Outside Quotes
for Four Representative Products

PRODUCT LINE	STANDARD REAR LAMP	STANDARD FRONT HALOGEN LAMP	MULTICOLORED REAR LAMP	CURVED SIDE AND REAR LAMP
Dimensions	20 cm × 6 cm	14 cm × 4 cm	14 cm × 4 cm	18 cm × 4 cm
Product number	SR214	SF120	MR314	CS418
Product costs per unit:				
Direct materials	$36	$49	$56	$58
Direct labor	22	25	24	28
Unit-related support	14	16	18	20
Batch-related support	10	16	19	22
Product-sustaining overhead	6	12	14	19
Facility-sustaining overhead	8	10	11	14
Total manufacturing costs	$96	$128	$142	$161
Bids from outside suppliers:				
Lowest	$82	$109	$140	$156
Second lowest	$88	$116	$147	$164
Annual production (units)	36,000	48,500	6,800	8,700

Avoidable Costs

To answer the previous questions, the decision maker must identify what costs are relevant for the decision. The concept of avoidable costs is useful for Ray to consider. Avoidable costs are those eliminated when a part, product, product line, or business segment is discontinued.

If Ray decides to outsource a product, Sommers Motors can avoid certain production costs. If the company purchases the standard rear lamp SR214 directly from the lowest bidder, it must pay $2,952,000 ($82 × 36,000) for it. Doing so saves the company $1,296,000 of direct material costs ($36 × 36,000). The firm also could reduce direct labor and supervisory costs and other resources contributing to unit-related support costs. As a result, it can avoid incurring $792,000 of direct labor costs ($22 × 36,000) and $504,000 of unit-related support costs ($14 × 36,000). In addition, with a suitable contraction or redeployment of resources, Sommers Motors can save $360,000 ($10 × 36,000) of batch-related support costs and $216,000 ($6 × 36,000) of product-sustaining support costs.

To decide whether facility-sustaining support costs also are avoidable requires further consideration. Sommers Motors cannot dispose of the part of the plant facility used to support the production of SR214 because most of the facility-sustaining support costs represent the prorated costs of indivisible common facilities, such as building space and machines, that cannot be eliminated without disposing of the entire machine or building. Nor can these resources be used for other productive purposes or leased to other companies that need space. Therefore, facility-sustaining support costs are unavoidable, or fixed, with respect to a decision to outsource product SR214.

It is sometimes possible to find an alternative use for the part of the facilities made available by not producing a product. Ray considered the possibility of shifting to the Schaumberg plant the other production lines manufactured in the same rented facility as the lamps. Sommers Motors could save the facility-sustaining costs for the rental facility by terminating its lease there. Such indirect savings in facility-sustaining costs for the organization are therefore relevant for the decision to outsource product SR214 because they can arise only if SR214 is outsourced. On further inquiry, however, Ray determined that it would be technically infeasible to transfer the manufacturing of the other product lines to the Schaumberg plant.

To summarize the analysis so far, if product SR214 is outsourced, Sommers Motors can avoid $3,168,000 of manufacturing costs. This is $216,000 more than the total price of $2,952,000 that Sommers Motors has to pay the outside supplier.

AVOIDABLE PRODUCTION COSTS

Direct material costs	$1,296,000
Direct labor costs	792,000
Unit-related support costs	504,000
Batch-related support costs	360,000
Product-sustaining supports costs	216,000
	$3,168,000
Cost to outside supplier	2,952,000
Increase in profits from outsourcing	$216,000

Another way to analyze the decision is to notice that avoidable costs average $88 ($36 + $22 + $14 + $10 + $6) per unit in comparison with the lowest bid of $82 per unit to outsource product SR214. Therefore, Sommers Motors stands to gain $6 per unit, or $216,000 ($36,000 × $6) overall, and it can apparently lower its costs by buying the parts rather than making them.

Qualitative Factors

Are these quantitative estimates of costs and revenues the only relevant considerations for Ray before he decides to outsource SR214? In fact, for most such decisions, several additional factors that are more qualitative in nature need to be considered for such decisions.

A question naturally arises about the permanence of the lower price: Has this supplier chosen to lowball the price to get a foot in the door? If so, after Sommers Motors discontinues the production of SR214 at its Schaumberg plant and lays off its workers there, will the supplier raise the price for subsequent orders? The reputation of the selected outside supplier is clearly a strong influence on the decision.

Even more important is the reliability of the supplier in meeting the required quality standards and in making deliveries on time. Poor performance on either of these dimensions can result in considerable costs elsewhere for the organization, especially if the outsourced component is critical to the final product. (The same type of qualitative considerations are also important when Tobor Toy Company considers the poor-quality computer chip it has been receiving from its supplier.) Lack of availability of the component or a high reject rate can lead to idling of assembly lines and unnecessary delays in meeting customer delivery schedules. Poor quality also creates customer dissatisfaction.

Therefore, many companies have adopted the practice of certifying a small set of suppliers who are dependable and consistent in supplying high-quality items as needed. They provide these certified suppliers with incentives, such as quick payments and guaranteed total purchase volumes, so that the suppliers will comply with strict quality and delivery schedules.

In many industries, technological innovation is an important determinant of competitive advantage. For example, Teijin Electronics Corporation has identified several different technologies that are critical to its business in the next 20 years. It relies on certified suppliers for many of the components of its products, but it has a corporate policy to produce in-house all components that use one of these critical technologies. This policy enables Teijin's research and development staff to experiment, learn, innovate, and implement these critical technologies in-house so that it can retain its leadership and control over innovations in important areas. If it depended on its supplier for innovation, then those benefits also would be available to the supplier's other customers, who could be competitors of Teijin.

FACILITY LAYOUT SYSTEMS

In addition to understanding the relevant costs for many decisions that change the nature of activities and processes, managers must consider the entire operations process within a facility. In this section we discuss the three general types of facility designs: (1) process layouts, (2) product layouts, and (3) cellular manufacturing.

Regardless of the type of facility design, a central goal of the design process is to streamline operations and thus increase the operating income of the system. One method that can guide this process for all three designs is the theory of constraints

(TOC). This theory maintains that operating income can be increased by carefully managing the bottlenecks in a process. A bottleneck is any condition that impedes or constrains the efficient flow of a process; it can be identified by determining points at which excessive amounts of work-in-process inventories are accumulating. The buildup of inventories also slows the cycle time of production.

The TOC relies on the use of three measures: (1) the throughput contribution; (2) investments, and (3) operating costs. The throughput contribution is the difference between revenues and direct materials for the quantity of product sold; investments equal the materials costs contained in raw materials, work-in-process, and finished goods inventories; and operating costs are all other costs, except for direct materials costs, that are needed to obtain throughput contribution. Examples of operating costs are depreciation, salaries, and utility costs.

The TOC emphasizes the short-run optimization of throughput contribution. Since proponents of the theory view operating costs as difficult to alter in the short run, activity-based costing (ABC) analyses of activities and cost drivers are not conducted. This limits the usefulness of the theory for the longer run. In theory, however, there is no reason why TOC and ABC cannot be used together.

Process Layouts

To understand why inventories stockpile in conventional processing systems and thus increase cycle time, we must understand the conventional way that factory or office facilities are organized. In a process layout, all similar equipment or functions are grouped together. Process layouts exist in organizations in which production is done in small batches of unique products. The product follows a serpentine path, usually in batches, through the factories and offices that create it. In addition to these long production paths, process layouts are also characterized by high inventory levels because it is necessary to store work in process in each area while it awaits the next operation. Often a product can travel for several miles within a factory as it is transformed from raw materials to finished goods.

For example, the process associated with a loan application at a bank may occur as follows: The customer goes to the bank (a moving activity). The bank takes the loan application from the customer (a processing activity). Loan applications are accumulated (a storage activity) and passed to a loan officer (a moving activity) for approval (both a processing and an inspection activity). Loans that violate standard loan guidelines are accumulated (a storage activity) and then passed (a moving activity) to a regional supervisor for approval (a processing activity). The customer is contacted when a decision has been made (a processing activity), and if the loan is approved, then the loan proceeds are deposited in the customer's account (a processing activity).

In most banks, work in process stockpiles at each of the processing points or stations. Loan applications may be piled on the bank teller's desk, the loan officer's desk, and the regional supervisor's desk. Work-in-process inventory, such as bank loan applications, accumulates at processing stations in a conventional organization for three reasons:

1. Handling work in batches is the most obvious cause of work-in-process inventory in a process layout system. Organizations use batches to reduce setting up, moving, and handling costs; however, batch processing increases the inventory levels in the system because at each processing station all items in the batch must wait while the designated employees process the entire batch before moving all parts in the batch to the next station.

2. If the rate at which each processing area handles work is unbalanced—because one area is slower or has stopped working because of problems with equipment, materials, or people—work piles up at the slowest processing station. Such scheduling delays create another reason why inventory levels increase in a process layout system.

3. Since supervisors evaluate many processing area managers on their ability to meet production quotas, processing station managers try to avoid the risk of having their facility idle. Many managers deliberately maintain large stocks of incoming work in process so that they can continue to work even if the processing area that feeds them is shut down. Similarly, to avoid idling the next processing station and suffering the resulting recriminations, managers may store finished work that they can forward to supply stations further down the line when their stations are shut down because of problems.

Some organizations have developed innovative approaches to eliminating many of the costs relating to moving and storing, which are significant non-value-added costs associated with process layout systems. Exhibit 5-4 illustrates the system that Gannett Corporation, the largest U.S. newspaper publisher, has developed. Gannett uses computers and electronic communication in its electronic pagination process to eliminate the physical movement of work in process, thus reducing both cycle time and costs.

Exhibit 5-4
Gannett Corporation: Using Technology to Reduce Costs in a Process Layout System

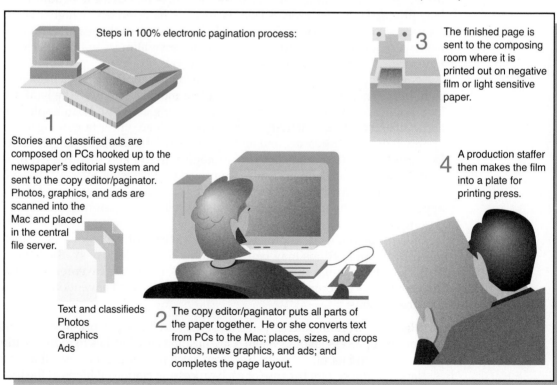

Steps in 100% electronic pagination process:

1 Stories and classified ads are composed on PCs hooked up to the newspaper's editorial system and sent to the copy editor/paginator. Photos, graphics, and ads are scanned into the Mac and placed in the central file server.

Text and classifieds
Photos
Graphics
Ads

2 The copy editor/paginator puts all parts of the paper together. He or she converts text from PCs to the Mac; places, sizes, and crops photos, news graphics, and ads; and completes the page layout.

3 The finished page is sent to the composing room where it is printed out on negative film or light sensitive paper.

4 A production staffer then makes the film into a plate for printing press.

Product Layouts

In a **product layout**, equipment is organized to accommodate the production of a specific product; an automobile assembly line or a packaging line for cereal or milk, for example, is a product layout. Product layouts exist primarily in companies with high-volume production. The product moves along an assembly line beside which the parts to be added to it have been stored. Placement of equipment or processing units is made to reduce the distance that products must travel.

Product layout systems planners often can arrange for raw materials and purchased parts to be delivered directly to the production line where and when they are needed. Suppose that an assembly line is scheduled to handle 600 cars on a given day. The purchasing group knows that these 600 automobiles require 2,400 regular tires and 600 spare tires. Under ideal conditions, the purchasing group will arrange delivery of small batches of these tires to the assembly line as frequently as they are needed. However, because each batch of tires from the supplier incurs some batch-related ordering, transportation, and delivery costs, planners may arrange for a few days' worth of tires to be delivered at a time.

IN PRACTICE

ABC Versus TOC: Will Ever the Twain Meet?

Proponents of activity-based costing (ABC) and the Theory of Constraints (TOC) have been engaging in a somewhat heated debate for a number of years. While proponents on each side are passionate, TOC and ABC have complementary features. What do you think? Below is a side-by-side summary of some of the differences in assumptions between the two approaches:

ASSUMPTIONS	THEORY OF CONSTRAINTS	ACTIVITY-BASED COSTING
Objective	Maximize profit via throughput maximization. TOC is not a product costing system. Proponents argue that product costing focuses management's attention locally and does not allow them to understand how the entire throughput process in their organization works.	Produce accurate and relevant information for decision making by tying actual resources consumed to cost objects. Managers need such information to make decisions regarding products, services and customers.
Capacity resources	After capacity has been set, managers will not adjust operating expenses quickly, if at all.	Assumes that managers can alter capacity resources.
Behavior of labor cost and operating expenses	Assumes these costs are fixed and will not eliminate skilled labor.	Assumes that all resources in the short-run are essentially variable and thus able to be reassigned based on activity analysis.
Process improvements	Focus is on increasing throughput by eliminating bottlenecks and reducing cycle time of products going through the bottleneck.	Determines which activities and processes are adding value, which are not, and which need improvement.
Profit improvement	Products to manufacture are determined based on their TOC margin and cycle time on the bottleneck.	Product mix and volume decisions are made from a longer-term perspective taking into account the product, channel, and customer profitability mix.
Planning horizon for product mix and volumes	Short-term oriented and assumes that most costs, except for raw materials, are sunk costs.	Long-term oriented and assumes that decisions will be made about less profitable products, channels, and customers.

Source: Gary Cokins, "TOC vs. ABC: Friends or Foes?," *ABC Technologies Monograph*. 1998. Reprinted by permission of Gary Cokins, garyfarms@aol.com.

Proponents of ABC versus those of TOC engage in an arm's length struggle for domination.

Source: Chris Windsor/Getty Images, Inc.–Photodisc.

Consider the work in process in a cafeteria setting. People pass by containers of food and take what they want. Employees organize the food preparation activities so that the containers are refilled just as they are being emptied—not one unit at a time. For example, the cook does not make and replace one bowl of soup at a time because the batch-related setup costs of making soup in this fashion will be prohibitively expensive. Reducing setup costs, however, allows for the reduction of batch sizes (the size of the containers) along the line. This reduces the level of inventory in the system and, therefore, costs. It also improves quality while increasing customer satisfaction. The ultimate goal is to reduce setup costs to zero and to reduce processing time to as close to zero as possible so that the system can produce and deliver individual products just as they are needed.

CELLULAR MANUFACTURING

The third approach to facilities layout, cellular manufacturing, refers to the organization of a plant into a number of cells so that within each cell all machines required to manufacture a group of similar products are arranged in close proximity to each other. As Exhibit 5-5 illustrates, the shape of a cell is often a U shape, which allows workers convenient access to required parts. The machines in a cellular manufacturing layout are usually flexible and can be adjusted easily or even automatically to make different products. Often when cellular manufacturing is introduced, the number of employees needed to produce a product can be reduced because of the new work design. The U shape also provides better visual control of the work flow because employees can observe more directly what their coworkers are doing.

Exhibit 5-5
Cellular
Manufacturing

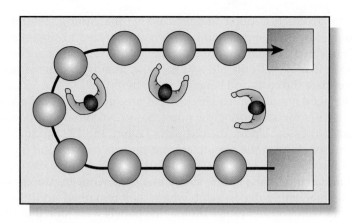

INVENTORY COSTS AND PROCESSING TIME

Inventory and Processing Time

Not only does batch production create inventory costs, but it also creates the delays associated with storing and moving inventory. These delays increase cycle times, thereby reducing service to customers. Delays can happen at any stage of the production cycle, even before manufacturing begins. For example, because of high setup costs, a manufacturer may require that a product be manufactured in some minimum batch size. If a customer order is less than the minimum batch size and if the order cannot be filled from existing finished goods inventory, then the customer must wait until enough orders have accumulated to meet the minimum batch size requirement. It may take a loan officer only 5 minutes to read and approve a loan application at the bank; however, the application may have to wait for several hours or even days before it reaches the loan officer because having a clerk run back and forth with each new loan application when it arrives is too expensive.

Inventory-Related Costs

Demands for inventory lead to huge costs in organizations, including the cost of moving, handling, and storing the work in process, in addition to costs due to obsolescence or damage. Many organizations have found that factory layouts and inefficiencies that create the need to hold work-in-process inventory also hide other problems, leading to excessive costs of rework.

For example, in batch operations, workers near the end of a process—downstream—often find batch-size problems resulting from the way workers earlier in the process—upstream—have done their jobs. When work is performed continuously on one component at a time, however, workers downstream can identify an upstream problem in that component almost immediately and correct it before it leads to production of more defective components.

Costs and Benefits of Changing to a New Layout: An Example Using Cellular Manufacturing

San Rafael Electric Corporation is a leader in the manufacturing of small electrical appliances for household and industrial use. It produces a variety of electrical valve controls at its plant in Pasadena, California. Until recently, the plant was organized into five production departments: casting, machining, assembly, inspection, and packing. Now the plant layout has been reorganized to streamline production flows and introduce cellular manufacturing. In the following sections we will take an extended look at both the old and the new, identify the benefits of the new system, and compare the costs and benefits of the two.

The plant manufactures 128 different products that have been grouped into eight product lines for accounting purposes, based on common product features and production processes. Under the old plant layout, the 128 products followed a similar sequence of steps in the manufacturing process (see Exhibit 5-6). Manufacturing of panels for valve controls occurred in large batches in the casting department. Then the manufactured panels were stored in a large work-in-process storage area located near the machining department, where they remained until the lathes and drilling machines were free. After machining, the panels were stored until they were requisitioned for assembly, during which switches and other components received from outside suppliers were placed onto each panel. Another storage area located near the assembly department was used for work in process awaiting inspection or packing, which occurred before the panels were packed for shipping. Finally, the packed valve control panels were stored in the finished goods warehouse until they were shipped to distributors and other customers.

This production flow required storage of work-in-process inventory for a long time and at several times before the beginning of the next production stage. As mentioned, manufacturing cycle time is measured as the time from the receipt of the raw materials from the supplier to the delivery of the finished goods to the distributors and customers. At San Rafael, cycle time was 28 days (5 + 1 + 9 + 1 + 1 + 4 + 1 + 2 + 1 + 3) under the old plant layout. The 4 days during which switches and other components were kept as inventory were not added to the processing time, the time expended for the product to be made, because the time spent in inventory represented parallel time with other production activities, such as work-in-process storage and machining. Therefore, the storage requirements for switches and other components did not prolong the time for the total production activity in the plant.

To evaluate how much of the old cycle time was spent in inventory, we need to know how organizations assess the efficiency of their manufacturing processes. One widely used measure is processing cycle efficiency (PCE) and is calculated as follows:

$$PCE = \text{Processing Time}/(\text{Processing time} + \text{Moving time} + \text{Storage time} + \text{Inspection time})$$

Of the 28 days required for the manufacturing cycle under San Rafael's old system, only 4 days were spent on actual processing [(1 casting) + (1 machining) + (1 assembly) + (1 packing)]. The other 24 days were spent in non-value-added activities, such as moving, storage, and inspection. The amount of time that materials spent in inventory could be as many as 24 days. The PCE formula reveals that processing time equaled 14.28% (4 ÷ 28) of total cycle time. These results are representative of many other plants that manufacture products from mechanical or electronic components. We will see shortly how the PCE changes for San Rafael after its reorganization.

Reorganization

A primary objective of the reorganization of the San Rafael plant layout was to reduce the production cycle time. Thus, the plant was reorganized into eight manufacturing cells (corresponding to the eight product lines) in addition to the casting department. Each cell focused on the manufacturing of similar products belonging to the same product line.

Exhibit 5-6
San Rafael Electric Corporation: Production Flows and Average Time Under Old Plant Layout

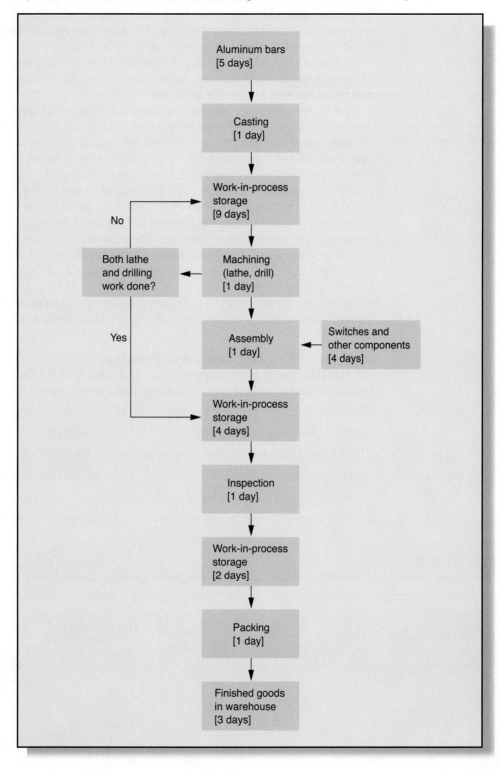

Exhibit 5-7 depicts the production flows under the new plant layout. While the casting department remains a separate department, the other four operations—machining, assembly, inspection, and packing—are now located in close proximity to each other within each manufacturing cell. Aluminum panels received from the casting department are lathe machined, drilled, and assembled in the manufacturing cells. Workers in the cells also are responsible for inspection and packing operations. Thus, material handling distances and the time required to move a panel from one process to the next are greatly reduced.

San Rafael Electric also made a transition toward JIT production. The change required that there be no work-in-process inventories among the various stages of operations in the manufacturing cells because panel production flowed immediately from lathe to drilling to assembly to inspection to packing operations. As a result of these steps, the time between operations has been greatly reduced as production is pulled from one stage to the next on the basis of orders for the finished product.

When comparing Exhibits 5-6 and 5-7, notice that San Rafael Electric Corporation did not reduce the amount of time spent on actual manufacturing when it changed the plant layout. The time spent on manufacturing operations after the change (see Exhibits 5-7) is the same as the time spent before the change (see Exhibit 5-6). However, the cycle time is reduced substantially in the new plant layout from 28 to only 12 days. Thus, PCE changes from 14.28% to 33.33% (4 ÷ 12). This significant improvement in efficiency over the previous layout comes from eliminating the need for work-in-process inventory between many of the manufacturing operations.

Analysis of Relevant Costs and Benefits

Has this change helped improve the profitability of the Pasadena plant? Edward Park, the Pasadena plant controller, identified the following costs associated with the implementation of the changes in the plant layout:

Moving machines and reinstallation	$600,000
Training workers for cellular manufacturing	+ $400,000
Total costs	$1,000,000

Edward also identified three types of benefits resulting from the plant reorganization: (1) an increase in sales because of the decrease in production cycle time,

Exhibit 5-7
San Rafael Electric Corporation: Production Flows and Average Time Under New Plant Layout

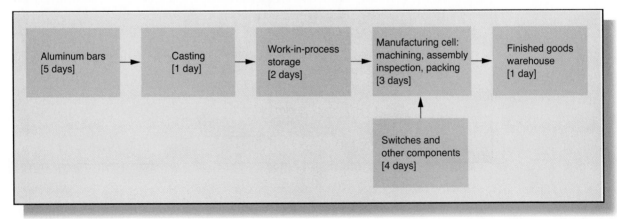

Increase in sales revenue		$880,000
Increase in costs:		
Direct materials	$245,000	
Direct labor	140,000	
Unit-related support	108,000	
Batch-related support	86,000	579,000
Net increase in profit		$301,000

(2) a reduction in inventory-related costs because of the decrease in the amount and handling of work-in-process inventory, and (3) an improvement in quality since defective processes are detected much faster (at the next processing stage), before many defective items have been produced.

Edward interviewed several production and sales managers to assess the extent of these benefits. He began with Caroline Graefe, a senior sales manager with 17 years of experience at San Rafael:

EDWARD PARK: Has the reduction in production cycle time increased sales?

CAROLINE GRAEFE: Yes, we have been able to win over many customers from our competitors because we can now quote a much shorter delivery lead time to them. Also, we have been able to retain some of our own customers because we have cut our delivery lead time. We commissioned a market research study to ascertain the impact that reduction in delivery lead time has had on our sales. On the basis of this study, our best estimate is that an increase of $880,000 in sales this year can be attributed to the change in our production cycle time. Details of estimated sales increases for individual products are also provided in this study. I think you'll find it interesting.

Edward next turned to his analyst, Kerin Cantwell, to collect the information necessary to assess the impact of the sales increase on San Rafael profits. Edward asked Kerin to determine the contribution margin for the Pasadena plant's products. She returned the next day with several detailed cost accounting reports.

KERIN CANTWELL: I've prepared a detailed analysis of the incremental costs for all our products. Here is a summary that gives the totals for all 128 products (see Exhibit 5-8). I began with the estimate of the increase in sales for each of the 128 products. Here is an example for product TL32 (see Exhibit 5-9). I multiplied the

Increase in sales	(800 units × $29 price per unit)		$23,200
Increase in costs:			
Direct materials	(800 units × $7 cost per unit)	$5,600	
Direct labor	(800 units × $4 cost per unit)	3,200	
Unit-related support	(800 units × $3 overhead per unit)	2,400	
Batch-related support	(800/100 units × $250 overhead per batch)	2,000	$13,200
Net increase in profit			$10,000

800-unit sales increase by the direct materials cost of $7 per unit, direct labor cost of $4 per unit, and unit-related support of $3 per unit. I also determined that eight additional batches are required for the increased production by using the fact that TL32 is manufactured in batch size of 100 units.

None of the product-sustaining or facility-sustaining support should increase because there are no new products added by increases in size of the plant and no additions to plant machinery. The $10,000 increase in profit is obtained by calculating the difference between the $23,200 increase in sales revenue and the $13,200 increase in costs. The summary in Exhibit 5-8 displays the totals of similar revenue and cost numbers across all of our 128 products.

EDWARD PARK: Thanks, Kerin, for all your efforts. I see that our best estimate is that the increase in sales resulting from the lower production cycle time has led to an overall increase of $301,000 in profit this year.

Edward next met with Winnie Chan, production and inventory manager at the Pasadena plant, to find out how the reduction in the level of work-in-process inventory affected the consumption of support activity resources:

EDWARD PARK: Has the change in the plant layout led to changes in the handling and storage of work-in-process inventory?

WINNIE CHAN: Yes, we have been able to make many changes. We don't need a materials-handling crew to move work-in-process inventory from lathes to drilling machines to storage areas on the shop floor. Nor do we need to move and store work-in-process inventory between the assembly, inspection, and packing stages. We did not reduce the number of materials handling workers immediately, but as work patterns stabilized a few weeks after the change in the plant layout, we reduced our materials handling crew from 14 to only eight workers.

EDWARD PARK: Were there any other changes in the workload of people performing these support activities?

WINNIE CHAN: With an almost 70% reduction in work-in-process inventory, down from $2,270,000 to $690,000, we had a corresponding decrease in inventory-related transactions. We did not require as much record keeping for the movement of materials into and out of storage. We expect to be able to reduce our shop-floor-stores staff by 75%, from four workers to only one. So far we have reassigned only one worker, but two more will be reassigned to other production-related tasks next week.

EDWARD PARK: So far we have talked about personnel. Were any other resources freed up as a result of the reduction in work-in-process inventory?

WINNIE CHAN: Yes, we need only one-third of the storage space we used earlier for work-in-process inventory. The extra space is idle at present, however, because we haven't yet found an alternative use for it. I don't believe there was any proposal to use that extra space in the 3-year facilities plan prepared last month, but eventually as production activity expands, we

EDWARD PARK: should be able to place new manufacturing cells in the space formerly used to store work-in-process inventory.

EDWARD PARK: But you don't expect any immediate benefit to arise from the availability of the extra storage space?

WINNIE CHAN: Yes, that's correct. But there is one more benefit that you shouldn't forget. When some panels are produced in large batches and stored awaiting the next stage of processing, we always find that some of them get damaged in handling, and at times some of them become obsolete because the customer no longer requires them. The change to JIT production in the manufacturing cells and the elimination of much of our work-in-process inventory have resulted in a reduction in materials scrap and obsolescence cost from 0.32% of materials cost to only 0.12%.

EDWARD PARK: Thank you, Winnie. The information you've provided will be very useful in evaluating the impact of the change in the plant layout.

Edward and Caroline sat in Edward's office to analyze the information they had collected so far. Facility-sustaining costs pertaining to plant space included building depreciation, insurance, heating, lighting, janitorial services, building upkeep, and maintenance. The support rate for this activity was $108 per square foot. However, Edward and Caroline decided that the costs associated with the extra storage space were at present a sunk cost with no cost savings yet realized from freeing up this space.

A check of the materials handling activity costs indicated that the annual wages of workers in this grade averaged $21,000, with 35% more, or $7,350 ($21,000 × 0.35), added for fringe benefits. The total materials handling cost savings, therefore, was $170,100 ($28,350 × 6) because the crew size was reduced by six workers.

In a similar fashion, Winnie determined that the annual wages of stores personnel averaged $26,400. With a 35% fringe benefit rate and an expected reduction of three workers, the total annual cost savings was $106,920 ($26,400 × 1.35 × 3).

There can be significant costs involved in financing inventories. Edward estimated the interest rate on bank loans to finance the investment in inventories to be 12% per year. The work-in-process inventory was reduced by $1,580,000 ($2,270,000 – $690,000). This reduced the cost of inventory financing correspondingly by $189,600 ($1,580,000 × 0.12).

Finally, Edward determined that the total annual materials cost was $31,000,000. If the rate of materials, scrap, and obsolescence had remained at the previous 0.32% of materials cost, this loss would have been $99,200 ($31,000,000 × 0.0032). But because of the reduction in the rate to 0.12%, the cost of materials scrap and obsolescence was reduced to only $37,200 ($31,000,000 × 0.0012). This represents a cost savings of $62,000 ($99,200 – $37,200).

Summary of Costs and Benefits

Edward then summarized the information on cost savings resulting from the change in the plant layout (see Exhibit 5-10). He estimated that annual benefits were $829,620. In comparison, the one-time costs of implementing the change were only $1,000,000. If benefits from the changed layout continue to accrue at the same rate for at least 3 more months, the total benefits will exceed the amount that San Rafael invested in the project:

$$\$829,620 \times 15/12 = \$1,037,025$$

Exhibit 5-10
San Rafael Electric Corporation: Annual Benefits Resulting from the Change in Plant Layout

Contribution from increased sales:			
Sales increase	(Exhibit 5–8)	$880,000	
Incremental manufacturing costs	(Exhibit 5–8)	(579,000)	$301,000
Cost savings from work-in-process inventory reduction:			
Cost of financing investment in work-in-process inventory		$189,600	
Cost of materials handling labor		170,100	
Cost of stores labor		106,920	
Cost of materials scrap and obsolescence		62,000	528,620
Total benefits			$829,620

In other words, the process improvements from the investment would repay the front-end cost in 1.25 years.

The San Rafael case study introduces several important concepts. We have identified several different ways in which new manufacturing practices can improve a plant's profitability. In particular, we have seen that financing is a principal inventory-related cost. It is important to consider this cost, although financing costs are often not emphasized in many traditional cost accounting systems. Streamlining manufacturing processes also reduces the demand placed on many support-activity resources. Activity analysis, therefore, is useful for assessing the potential cost savings that can be realized from more efficient product flows.

Many new manufacturing practices are designed to promote continuous improvement in manufacturing performance by enabling workers to learn and innovate. In this example, changing to a manufacturing cell layout led to improvements in production yield rates and quality and, consequently, improvements in overall plant productivity. In addition, revenues also can increase from shorter lead times to customers.

COST OF NONCONFORMANCE AND QUALITY ISSUES

The preceding example shows that cost reduction has become a significant factor in the management of most organizations. Reducing costs, however, involves much more than simply finding ways to cut product design costs by, for example, using less expensive materials. The premise underlying cost reduction efforts today is to decrease costs while maintaining or improving product quality in order to be competitive. If the quality of products and services does not conform to quality standards, then the organization incurs a cost known as the cost of nonconformance (CONC) to quality standards.

Quality may mean different things to different people. It usually can be viewed as hinging on two major factors:

1. Satisfying customer expectations regarding the attributes and performance of the product, such as in functionality and features
2. Ensuring that the technical aspects of the product's design and performance, such as whether it performs to the standard expected, conform to the manufacturer's standards

Exhibit 5-11
ISO 9000 Standards

In 1987, the International Organization for Standardization (ISO), headquartered in Geneva, Switzerland, developed the first ISO 9000 Series of Standards. These standards were revised in 1994 and again in 2000. The goal of the member nations is to develop globally recognized independent (third-party) quality system verification. Today, over 400,000 organizations have been certified worldwide. Many types of organizations are interested in becoming ISO 9000 registered in order to accomplish the following:

1. comply with external regulatory agencies,
2. meet or exceed customer requirements, or
3. implement a quality improvement program to remain competitive.

ISO 9000 contains more than 20 standards and documents. Because of the increase in the number of standards, ISO 9000:2000 was developed. ISO 9000:2000 consists of four primary standards and a greatly reduced number of supporting documents (guidance standards, brochures, technical reports, technical specifications). The major points in previous versions of the standards were integrated into the four primary standards. The four primary standards are as follows:

ISO 9000: Quality management systems—Fundamentals and vocabulary
ISO 9001: Quality management systems—Requirements
ISO 9004: Quality management systems—Guidance for performance improvement
ISO 19011: Guidance or quality and/or environmental management systems auditing (to be published)

The most significant changes in the revised ISO 9000 standards are the increased focus on top management commitment, emphasis on a process approach within the organization, and continual improvement together with enhancing satisfaction for customers and other interested parties. The overall revisions to ISO 9001 and 9004 are based on eight quality management principles based on best management practices.
Following are the eight principles:

- Customer focus
- Leadership
- Investment of people
- Process approach
- Systems approach to management
- Continual improvement
- Factual approach to decision making
- Mutually beneficial supplier relationships

The ISO 9000:2000 Standards apply to all kinds of organizations in all kinds of areas. Some of these areas include manufacturing, forestry, electronics, computing, legal services, financial services, accounting, trucking, banking, retailing, drilling, recycling, aerospace, construction, pharmaceuticals, oil and gas, petrochemicals, publishing, shipping, telecommunications, health care, hospitality, utilities, aviation, food processing, agriculture, government, education, recreation, sanitation, software development, consumer products, transportation, design, tourism, communications, biotechnology, engineering, farming, entertainment, consulting, insurance, and others.

More information can be obtained from the International Organization for Standardization (http://(www.iso.org).

Exhibit 5-12
Examples of
Quality-Related
Costs

PREVENTION COSTS	APPRAISAL COSTS
Quality engineering	Inspection/testing of incoming materials
Quality training	Maintenance of test equipment
Statistical Process control	Process control monitoring
Supplier certification	Product quality audits
Research of customer needs	
INTERNAL FAILURE COSTS	**EXTERNAL FAILURE COSTS**
Downtime due to defects	Product liability lawsuits
Waste	Repair costs in the field
Net cost of scrap	Returned products
Rework costs	Product liability recalls
	Service calls
	Warranty claims

Quality Standards

Global competition has led to the development of international quality standards. Company certification under these standards indicates to customers that management has committed their company to follow procedures and processes that will ensure the production of the highest-quality goods and services. Exhibit 5-11 presents the ISO9000 Series of Standards developed in Europe and their purposes. The exhibit also provides a sketch of the procedures that organizations need to follow if they wish to be ISO9000 certified.

Costs of Quality Control

This section focuses on how to interpret quality costs from a management accounting point of view. Companies have discovered that they can spend as much as 20% to 30% of total manufacturing costs on quality-related processes such as detection and correction of internal and external failure. The best known framework for understanding quality costs classifies them into four categories:

1. Prevention costs
2. Appraisal costs
3. Internal failure costs
4. External failure costs

Experience shows that it is much less expensive to prevent defects than to detect and repair them after they have occurred.

Prevention Costs

Prevention costs are incurred to ensure that companies produce products according to quality standards. Quality engineering, training employees in methods designed to maintain quality, and statistical process control are examples of prevention costs.

Prevention costs also include training and certifying suppliers so that they can deliver defect-free parts and materials and better, more robust product designs.

Appraisal Costs

Appraisal costs relate to inspecting products to make sure they meet both internal and external customers' requirements. Inspection costs of purchased parts and materials and costs of quality inspection on an assembly line are considered to be appraisal costs. Examples include inspection of incoming materials, maintenance of test equipment, and process control monitoring.

Internal Failure Costs

Internal failure costs results when the manufacturing process detects a defective component or product before it is shipped to an external customer. Reworking defective components or products is a significant cost of internal failures. The cost of downtime in production is another example of internal failure. Engineers have estimated that the cost of defects rises by an order of magnitude for each stage of the manufacturing process that the defect goes undetected. For example, inserting a defective $1 electronic component into a subassembly leads to $10 of scrap if detected at the first stage, $100 at the next stage, and perhaps $10,000 if not detected for two more stages of assembly.

External Failure Costs

External failure costs occur when customers discover a defect. All costs associated with correcting the problem—repair of the product, warranty costs, service calls, and product liability recalls—are examples of external failure costs. For many companies, this is the most critical quality cost to avoid. Not only are costs required to fix the problem in the short run, but customer satisfaction, future sales, and the reputation of the manufacturing organization also may be in jeopardy over the long run. Exhibit 5-12 provides examples of the quality costs in each category.

This information is compiled in a cost-of-quality (COQ) report, developed for several reasons. First, it illustrates the financial magnitude of quality factors. Often managers are unaware of the enormous impact that rework has on their costs. Second, COQ information helps managers set priorities for the quality issues and problems they should address. For example, one trend that managers do not want to see is a very high percentage of quality costs coming from external failure of a product. External quality problems are expensive to fix and can greatly harm the reputation of the product or organization producing the product. Third, the COQ report allows managers to see the big picture of quality issues and allows them to try to find the root causes of their quality problems. Fixing the problem at its root will have positive ripple effects throughout the organization, as so many quality issues are interrelated.

IN PRACTICE

Reducing Customer "Churn" by Enhancing Service Quality

One of the most daunting challenges facing service organizations is reducing customer "churn," or defection to another service provider. Many defections relate to internal quality failure on the service providers part. A recent study was conducted by *Consumer Reports* of 22,000 of its subscribers to determine what percentage of cell phone users switched providers. Results show that about 30% of those sampled churn annually. Customers churn in this industry because they do not understand complicated calling plans, experience dead spots in calling zones and dropped calls, and have problems with billing.

Source: Ken Weing art/Getty Images, Inc.

Reducing churn involves many things including using data mining to develop models of which customer segments are most likely to defect to other providers. Once these segments are identified, techniques from customer relationship management are applied to retain the customer. Recent studies have identified the key factors that influence service quality in other industries. Here are some examples:

TYPE OF SERVICE	KEY SERVICE FACTOR TO MANAGE
Credit card companies	Level of interest rates
Airlines	On-time arrival, frequent flyer program and price
Fast-food companies	Waiting time (must be under 3 minutes)
Retail banking	Waiting time (must be under 4 minutes)

Sources: ATS Network and Billing Update (February 2003) and "Rediscovering the Customer—Turning Customer Satisfaction into Shareholder Value" McKinsey Marketing Practice, 2001.

JUST-IN-TIME MANUFACTURING

A comprehensive and effective manufacturing system that integrates many of the ideas discussed in this chapter is just-in-time (JIT) manufacturing. Recall that the Tobor Toy Company implemented this system in the opening vignette to this chapter.

JIT manufacturing requires making a product or service only when the customer, internal or external, requires it. It uses a product layout with a continuous flow—one with no delays once production starts. This means there must be a substantial reduction in setup costs in order to eliminate the need to produce in batches; therefore, processing systems must be reliable.

Implications of JIT Manufacturing

JIT manufacturing is simple in theory but hard to achieve in practice. Some organizations hesitate to implement JIT because with no work-in-process inventory, a problem anywhere in the system can stop all production. For this reason, organizations

Japanese Tin Robots and the Just-in-Time Manufacturing System

The Just-In-Time (JIT) Manufacturing System, or its central principles are used today in many repetitive manufacturing firms. While a number of factors contributed to the development of JIT, only very recently has more information as to its origins been uncovered.

At the turn of the 20th Century, tin toys such as locomotives and steam ships from Germany were exported to Japan. It wasn't long before Japanese factories began to produce their own tin toys using sophisticated tin printing and punching machines. One such toy was a crude robot called Atomic Robot Man.

With the coming of World War II, tin toy production was halted since all metal was commandeered for military purposes. Because of the devastation in Japan at the end of the War no factories were operable. Put in charge of rehabilitating the Japanese Economy, General Douglass MacArthur suggested to the Japanese that they take advantage of their previous experience and make tin toys for export. As the tin toy industry was slowly rebuilding, American movies such as *Forbidden Planet* featuring Robby the Robot became popular in Japan. Combining their previous pre-war passion for Atomic Robot Man, a number of highly-skilled, but unemployed, mechanical engineers began to design new robots based on American movies.

One of the key issues was where to obtain the necessary tin for production. Initially, tin was gathered by workers who would strike deals with U.S. military bases to haul away all of their scrap. Tin was also taken directly from the streets of Japan. To this day, the battery boxes of many toy robots made during this era show tin stamped with labels from soy sauce, condensed milk, and beer cans.

Since no factories existed, tin robot designers developed a system by which robot subassemblies could be produced in very small job shops often located in people's homes. Subassemblies would be boxed and then transported to another small job shop. At that shop another subassembly would be made and added to the previous subassembly. Workers were paid on a piece rate basis for each hand movement. For instance, someone would be asked to bend down metal tabs on to the main body of a robot. The completed

Cover of Blast Off! book by S. M. Young, S. Duin, and M. Richardson (Dark Horse, 2001)
Source: Mark Young.

parts were then passed on to the next stage of production and so on until the robot was completed.

Since resources were so scarce, demand had to be carefully predicted. As is quite evident, this process is identical to the supply apparatus that forms the Japanese just-in-time (JIT) manufacturing system. By the mid-1960s, the demand for tin robots began to decline. Production in Japan turned to automobile manufacturing, but even though large factories were constructed, the small job shop system developed for the production of tin robots was still used for many small automobile components.

Source: S. Mark Young, Steve Duin, and Mike Richardson. *Blast Off! Rockets, Robots, Ray Guns and Rarities from the Golden Age of Space Toys* (Milwaukee, Org.: Dark Horse Books, 2001).

that use JIT manufacturing must eliminate all sources of failure in the system. The production process must be redesigned so that it is not prohibitively expensive to process one or a small number of items at a time. This usually means reducing the distance over which work-in-process has to travel and using very adaptable people and equipment that can handle all types of jobs.

At the core of the JIT process is a highly-trained workforce whose task is to carry out activities using the highest standards of quality. When an employee discovers a problem with a component he or she has received, it is the responsibility of that employee to call immediate attention to the problem so that it can be corrected. Suppliers must be able to produce and deliver defect-free materials or components just when they are required. In many instances, companies compete with suppliers of the same components to see who can deliver the best quality. At the end of a performance period, the supplier who performs the best will obtain a long-term contract. Preventive maintenance is also employed so that equipment failure is a rare event.

Consider how JIT manufacturing can be used at a fast-food restaurant. Some use a JIT, continuous-flow product layout, while others use batch production in a process layout. In fact, some fast-food restaurants combine both approaches into hybrid systems that use a batch approach to production and keep inventories at predefined levels. For example, the restaurant may use racks or bins to hold food ready to be sold to the customer and have employees start another batch of production when the existing inventory falls below a line drawn on the bin or rack. At off-peak times, the restaurant may produce to order.

The motivation to use the JIT approach is to improve the quality of the food and to reduce waste by eliminating the need to discard food that has been held in the bin too long. The motivation to use batch production is to sustain a certain level of inventory to reduce the time the customer has to wait for an order. As processing time and setup costs drop, the organization can move closer to JIT manufacturing and reduce the waste and quality problems that arise with batch production.

JIT Manufacturing and Management Accounting

JIT manufacturing has two major implications for management accounting. First, management accounting must support the move to JIT manufacturing by monitoring, identifying, and communicating to decision makers the sources of delay, error, and waste in the system. Important measures of a JIT system's reliability include the following benchmarks of manufacturing cycle effectiveness:

1. Defect rates
2. Cycle times
3. Percent of time that deliveries are on time

4. Order accuracy
5. Actual production as a percent of planned production
6. Actual machine time available compared with planned machine time available

Conventional production systems emphasize labor and machine utilization ratios that encourage large batch sizes and high levels of production. The result is large inventory quantities that lead to long manufacturing cycle times. Therefore, conventional labor and machine productivity ratios are inconsistent with the JIT production philosophy, in which operators are expected to produce only what is requested, when it is requested, and on time. The second implication is that the clerical process of management accounting is simplified by JIT manufacturing because there are fewer inventories to monitor and report.

JIT manufacturing has been a benefit to many organizations. Those interested in implementing this system need to remember several things. First, any significant management innovation, such as ABC or JIT, requires a major cultural change for an organization. Because the central ideas behind JIT are the streamlining of operations and the reduction of waste, many people inside companies are ill-prepared for the change. JIT also can alter the pace of work and the overall work discipline of the organization. It can cause structural changes in such areas as the arrangement of shop floors. Finally, because JIT relies on teamwork, often individuals have to subordinate their own interests to those of the team. Some employees find this difficult, especially if they have come from a work environment where they worked on a single component in relative isolation or if their personalities are not team oriented.

TOBOR TOY COMPANY REVISITED

We return now to see how Tobor Toy Company fared after its adoption of the JIT manufacturing system. Tobor succeeded in decreasing its major rework rate from 5.8% to 3.3% and its minor rework rate from 13.6% to 7.0%. Major rework required scrapping the robot. Minor rework required correcting the alignment of robot body parts or fixing the ways the gears were functioning, and it had to be done in a specially designated rework area. Minor rework did not cycle back to the beginning of the process but instead went to a different processing area where of direct labor and unit-related support costs were incurred.

As a result of the improvements in rework rates, average production cycle time was reduced by 9.2 days, from 16.4 days to 7.2 days. Average work-in-process inventory was reduced from $1,774,000 to $818,000. Don Pielin, Tobor Toy's senior manufacturing manager, now had to prepare a report for his chief executive officer detailing how these improvements had affected the company's profits.

Production Flows

Don began by obtaining the new production flowchart shown in Exhibit 5-13. He wanted to assess how the change to the JIT system was progressing. In the first step, the arms and legs of the robot were produced via an injection-molding process in plastic. To accomplish this, metal molds were designed for each component. A measured amount of polypropylene in the form of granules was fed into a horizontal heated cylinder where it was forced into a closed cold mold by a plunger. The liquid plastic entered the mold by means of a channel that led directly into the mold. Runners fed off the channel and moved the liquid plastic to each individual cavity. On cooling, the plastic took the shape of the mold. The process was designed so that each channel produced enough components for 60 robots.

Exhibit 5-13
Tobor Toy
Company:
Production
Flowchart

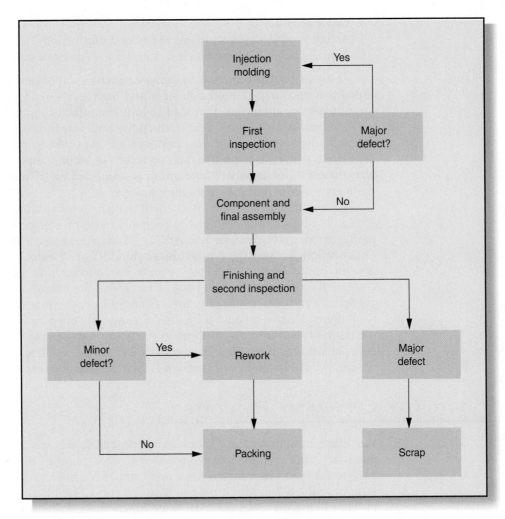

Workers now assembled the various components using the JIT manufacturing system. Other components, such as the computer chip, nylon gears, wheels, and various parts, were added as the production process continued. Although Tobor was striving to eliminate defective robots through the JIT process, achieving this goal was going to take some time. Thus, at the end of the process, any defective robots were rejected and returned for rework or scrapping, depending on the defect. Several finishing operations and inspections were performed next. Any excess plastic, or flashing, from the molding process was eliminated. The toy robot was then polished to a high gloss. During this process, each robot was inspected. A separate rework area was set aside for correcting the defects and reinserting the robots to ensure that no defects remained. Robots that passed inspection, either before or after rework, were packed and made available for shipment to customers. Don concluded that the integration of the JIT system into the overall production flow was relatively successful.

Effects on Work-in-Process Inventory

Don next turned his attention to records for work-in-process inventory. He had already found that the average work-in-process inventory decreased by $956,000 after the implementation of the JIT system. He determined from meetings with production personnel that some work-in-process inventory was still maintained between each pair of successive process stages because each batch of robots had to await the completion of work on the preceding batch. Don could find no detailed records to identify the change in work-in-process inventory. It was, however, directly influenced by the number of major and minor defects. When defect rates were high, inventory of rejected robots would build up, awaiting rework or scrap. More important, production supervisors sought to accumulate a large inventory of work in process in stages occurring after the two inspection points to enable them to keep busy when many robots were rejected. Therefore, production managers attributed the reduction in work-in-process inventory entirely to reductions in defect rates.

Effect on Production Costs

An important part of Don's analysis was an assessment of the impact that the improvement in defect rates had on production costs. Direct materials costs included the cost of the plastic content and the cost of the gears and the computer chip in the robot. The average cost of this type of chip in a robot was $58.

Don also collected information about direct labor, unit-related support, and batch-related support costs for each stage of the production process. Exhibit 5-14 includes these costs presented on a unit (robot) basis. Unit-related support costs include labor supervision and power costs. Batch-related costs for each batch of 60 robots, which include materials handling and setup of molds, are presented on a unit basis.

Don excluded product-sustaining and facility-sustaining costs from the analysis. There were no new product introductions or deletions as a consequence of the implementation of the JIT system. The installed plant machine capacity was already greater than its maximum use in recent years, and reductions in defect rates increased the surplus capacity even for the Tobor plant. The company had yet to find new products or new markets that could use this excess capacity; that is, it remained as a sunk cost.

Cost of Rework

Remembering that rework costs are considered internal failure costs, what is the cost of a major defect detected during the first inspection following the injection-molding stage? Because a robot with a major defect cannot be processed further, all incremental conversion costs already incurred on the robot are wasted, and all operations must be repeated, incurring the incremental conversion costs again. Recall from our earlier discussion that rework costs are considered internal failure costs. Don summarized the costs associated with the correction of a major defect and found that they were $42 per robot (see Exhibit 5-15).

This estimation includes unit- and batch-related support costs because more of these costs would be incurred when the entire mold-making, casting, and first-inspection operations were repeated to rectify the major defect. Because there is

Exhibit 5-14
Tobor Toy Company: Incremental Conversion Costs per Robot by Production Stages

	INJECTION MODELING	FIRST INSPECTION	COMPONENT AND FINAL ASSEMBLY	FINISHING AND SECOND INSPECTION	PACKING
Direct labor (including fringe benefits)	$14	$10	$20	$8	$6
Unit-related support	6	3	12	2	2
Batch-related support	8	1	2	1	8
Total costs	$28	$14	$34	$11	$16

Exhibit 5-15
Tobor Toy
Company: Cost
per Unit (Robot)
for the Correction
of a Major Defect

TYPE OF COST	AMOUNT
Conversion costs for injection molding:	
Direct labor	$14
Unit-related support	6
Batch-related support	8
Costs of first inspection:	
Direct labor	10
Unit-related support	3
Batch-related support	1
Total costs	$42

excess capacity at the plant, product- and facility-sustaining support costs do not increase when repeating production operations are repeated. Therefore, they were not relevant for this analysis. However, if the plant and machine capacity had already been fully utilized and there was no slack to accommodate these repeated operations, the incremental costs of acquiring the additional capacity would be a factor to consider.

Don found it somewhat easier to assess the costs of correcting minor defects, which are detected at the second inspection and do not require the rejection of the entire robot. Instead, such minor defects require additional rework operations. Therefore, the incremental costs of correcting minor defects are only the rework costs. Don did some new analyses and determined that the cost or rework per robot equaled the following:

Direct rework labor	$24
Unit-related support	+12
Total cost	$36

Because each robot is reworked independently of the batch in which it was produced, Don determined that there were no batch-related support costs. Product- and facility-sustaining support costs also were not relevant because of the excess capacity situation.

Tobor manufactures and sells 180,000 robots each year. Before implementation of the JIT system, on average, 10,440 (180,000 × 0.058) major defects and 24,480 (180,000 × 0.136) minor defects occurred each year. Now, only 5,940 (180,000 × 0.033) major defects and 12,600 (180,000 × 0.070) minor defects occur, representing a reduction of 4,500 and 11,880 defects, respectively. Therefore, the cost savings of correcting fewer defects because of the JIT system are $189,000 ($42 × 4,500) for major rework and $427,680 ($36 × 11,880) for minor rework:

	MAJOR DEFECTS	MINOR DEFECTS
Before JIT	10,440	24,480
After JIT	5,940	12,600
Reduction	4,500	11,880
Cost per correction	× $42	× $36
JIT cost reduction	$189,000	$427,680

Cost of Carrying Work-in-Process Inventory

Don turned next to the problem of evaluating the cost savings resulting from the reduction in the amount of work-in-process inventory. Interest rates on bank loans to finance the investment in inventories averaged 12.5% per year. With a reduction of $956,000 in work-in-process inventory ($1,774,000 − $818,000), the cost of financing also decreased by $119,500 ($956,000 × 0.125).

In addition, Don estimated that batch-related support costs for various production stages included a total cost of $30 per batch (of 60 robots) that pertained to activities such as work-in-process, inventory handling, and storage. With the 53.89% reduction in work-in-process inventory [100 × ($956,000 ÷ $1,774,000)], Don estimated these related costs also to decrease by about 30%, or, equivalently, by about $9 per batch ($30 × 0.30). With an annual production of 180,000 robots in 3000 batches (180,000 ÷ 60), Don expected a decrease of $27,000 in the costs of work-in-process inventory handling and storage costs ($9 × 3,000). As in the case of San Rafael Electric Corporation, however, Don's estimate of $27,000 represented the reduction in the demand for these activities because of the reduction in work-in-process inventory. Over time, these costs should decrease by this amount, but for the reduction to actually occur, the plant management must identify the personnel and other resources committed to this activity and eliminate the resources not required because of the reduction in the demand for them.

Benefits from Increased Sales

Don finally decided to evaluate whether the reduction in the production cycle time had resulted in any gains in sales. For this purpose, he met with the marketing manager, Christie Fleischer. Christie pointed out that annual sales had remained stable at around 180,000 robots for the past 3 years; however, she did believe that the improvement in the production cycle time had an impact on sales. Because of increased competition in the robot market, Christie had expected to lose sales of about 2,000 robots. But the reduction of 6.5 days in the production cycle time had permitted her to respond more aggressively to market demand by offering the robots to customers with a much shorter lead time. Chrisite believed that the shorter production cycle time led to maintaining sales of about 2,000 robots that otherwise would have been lost. As a result, Tobor had not lost any market share in this market segment.

Don determined that the average net selling price (the net of sales commission and shipping costs) for these 2,000 robots was $250. Exhibit 5-16 presents his list of the incremental costs for the production of these robots.

Notice in Exhibit 5-16 that rework costs are prorated over the good units of production. For example, incremental costs for major rework are $42 for each robot that requires rework. For every 1,000 robots produced, an average of 33 robots (1,000 × 3.3%) now require major rework. Therefore, the company obtains 967 good robots (1,000 − 33). The total incremental major rework cost for 33 robots is $1,386 ($42 × 33), which is borne by the 967 good robots at the rate of $1.43 ($1,386 ÷ 967) per good robot.

The contribution margin is estimated to be $52.86 per robot, or $105,720 in total for the 2,000 robots ($52.86 × 2,000). Without the JIT system and the consequent reduction in cycle time, this contribution from sales would have been lost.

Summary of Costs and Benefits

Exhibit 5-17 displays Don's summary of the benefits from the quality improvement program. Total estimated annual benefits of $868,900 are much greater than the one-time costs of $300,000 spent on the JIT system and worker training discussed in this chapter's opening vignette.

Exhibit 5-16
Tobor Toy
Company:
Incremental Costs
of Production per
Robot

TYPE OF COST	COST PER ROBOT
Direct materials:	
Chip	$58.00
All others	32.00
Incremental conversion costs:	
Injection molding	28.00
First inspection	14.00
Component and final assembly	34.00
Second inspection	11.00
Packing	16.00
Prorated rework costs:	
Major defects[a]	1.43
Minor defects[b]	2.71
Total incremental costs	$197.14
Average net sales price	$250.00
Contribution margin per robot	$52.86

$$^a\ \frac{33}{1,000-33} \times \$42 = \$1.43$$

$$^b\ \frac{70}{1,000-70} \times \$36 = \$2.71$$

Exhibit 5-17
Tobor Toy
Company:
Summary of
Annual Benefits
Resulting from the
JIT System

Reduction in network costs:		
Major rework	$189,000	
Minor rework	427,680	$616,680
Reduction in work-in-process inventory-related costs:		
Financing costs	119,500	
Inventory handling and storage-activity costs	27,000	146,500
Contribution from sales increases resulting from improved production cycle time		105,720
Total annual benefits		$868,900

SUMMARY

Managers evaluate the impact of managerial decisions and actions that affect the organization's activities and processes. To support decision making, they must identify the alternatives available and determine how relevant costs and revenues differ for each. As a general rule, sunk costs are not relevant costs.

Managers also must be able to evaluate the financial impact of recent activity and process decisions, such as improved plant layouts that streamline production operations. They need various types of costs and other functional information to assess the impact of decisions affecting an organization's activities and processes. Finally, detailed evaluations of implemented actions may shed light on ways to increase the benefits derived from them.

The JIT manufacturing system has many positive effects on the levels of work-in-process inventory, the cost of support activities of handling and storing work-in-process inventory, and the amounts of major and minor rework. Further, it reduces cycle times so that there are shorter lead times to fulfilling customer orders. All these changes have a very tangible and quantifiable bottom-line effect.

Kaylee Corporation, a major producer of telephone products, is considering the introduction of a videophone targeted to the business market. The proposed price is $1000 per unit. The following cost information is based on the expected annual sales level of 60,000 units for the new product:

Direct material cost	$18,000,000
Direct labor costs	12,000,000
Variable manufacturing support	6,000,000
Fixed manufacturing support	10,000,000

The average inventory levels for the videophone are estimated as follows:

Direct material	2 months of production
Work in process	2 months of production
(100% complete for materials and 50% for labor and variable manufacturing support)	
Finished goods	1 month of production

Annual inventory carrying costs, not included in these costs, are estimated to be 10%. In addition, the marketing manager estimates that the total sales revenue of the existing products will be reduced by $12,000,000 once the videophone is on the market. The average contribution margin ratio for the existing products is 30%.

1. Compute the relevant costs (revenues) for the videophone.
2. Should Kaylee introduce the new product?
3. Determine the breakeven point in units for the videophone.

The following information presents the solution to this problem.

1. Selling price per unit $1,000

   Less:

      Variable cost per unit

        Direct materials

$$\$18,000,000 \div 60,000 = \$300$$

        Direct labor

$$\$12,000,000 \div 60,000 = \$200$$

        Support

$$\$6,000,000 \div 60,000 = \$100$$

Total variable costs	−$600
Contribution margin per unit	$400

Inventory carrying value

   Direct materials

$$\$300 \times 60,000 \text{ units} \times 2/12 = \$3,000,000$$

Work in process

$$\{\$300 + [(200 + 100) \times 50\%]\} \times 60,000 \times 2/12 = \$4,500,000$$

Finished goods

$$(\$300 + 200 + 100) \times 60,000 \times 1/12 = \$3,000,000$$

Inventory carrying cost

$$(\$3,000,000 + \$4,500,000 + \$3,000,000) \times 10\% = \$1,050,000$$

Relevant costs

   Increase in contribution margin for sale of videophone

$$\$400 \times 60,000 = \$24,000,000$$

Decrease in contribution margin from cannibalization of existing sales

$$\$12,000,000 \times 30\% = \$3,600,000$$

Additional inventory carrying costs

$$\$1,050,000$$

Increase in fixed manufacturing support

$$\$10,000,000$$

2.   Increase in Kaylee's operating profit

$$\$24,000,000 - \$3,600,000 - \$1,050,000 - \$10,000,000 = \$9,350,000$$

Therefore, Kaylee should introduce the videophone

3.   Let x be the breakeven point in units

$$\$400 \times x = \$10,000,000 + \$3,600,000 + (\$300 \times x \times 2/12 + 450 \times x \times 2/12 + \$600 \times x \times 1/12) \times 0.1$$
$$\$382.5x = \$13,600,000$$
$$x = 35,556 \text{ units}$$

KEY TERMS

Appraisal costs, 229
Avoidable costs, 213
Cellular manufacturing, 218
Certified suppliers, 214
Cost of nonconformance (CONC)
  to quality standards, 226
Cost-of-quality (COQ) report, 229
Cycle time, 207
External failure costs, 229

Internal failure costs, 229
Investments, 215
Just-in-time (JIT) manufacturing, 230
Make-or-buy decision, 212
Operating costs, 215
Outsourcing, 212
Prevention costs, 228
Processing cycle efficiency, 220

Processing time, 220
Process layout, 215
Product layout, 217
Quality costs, 228
Relevant costs/revenues, 208
Sunk costs, 208
Theory of constraints, 214
Throughput contribution, 215

ASSIGNMENT MATERIALS

Questions

5-1 Why should decision makers focus only on the relevant costs for decision making? (LO 1)

5-2 Are sunk costs relevant? Explain. (LO 1)

5-3 What behavioral factors may influence some managers to consider sunk costs as being relevant in their decisions? (LO 1)

5-4 Are direct materials and direct labor costs always relevant? Explain with examples. (LO 1, 2)

5-5 Are fixed costs always irrelevant? (LO1, 2)

5-6 When are product-sustaining support costs and facility-sustaining (business-sustaining) support costs relevant? Give examples of each case. (LO 2)

5-7 Why can't we directly compare cash flows at different points in time? (LO 2)

5-8 Are avoidable costs relevant? Explain. (LO 2)

5-9 Give two examples of costs and decision contexts in which the costs are not relevant for a short-term context but are relevant for a long-term context. (LO 2)

5-10 Why are facility-sustaining (business-sustaining) support costs often not relevant for make-or-buy decisions? Give an example when facility-sustaining support costs are relevant for a make-or-buy decision. (LO 2)

5-11 What qualitative considerations are relevant in a make-or-buy decision? (LO 2, 3)

5-12 What are the opportunity costs that are relevant in a make-or-buy decision? (LO 2)

5-13 The theory of constraints relies on three measures: throughput contribution, investments, and operating costs. Define these three measures in the context of the theory of constraints. (LO 5)

5-14 What is the difference between process and product layout systems? (LO 5)

5-15 What is cellular manufacturing? (LO 4)

5-16 How is a just-in-time manufacturing system different from a conventional manufacturing system? (LO 6)

5-17 What creates the need to maintain work-in-process inventory? Why is work-in-process inventory likely to decrease on the implementation of cellular manufacturing, just-in-time production, and quality improvement programs? (LO 4, 6)

5-18 Why are production cycle time and the level of work-in-process inventory positively related? (LO 4, 6)

5-19 List two types of costs incurred when implementing a cellular manufacturing layout. (LO 4)

5-20 What are two types of financial benefits resulting from a shift to cellular manufacturing, just-in-time production, or continuous quality improvements? (LO 4, 6)

5-21 What is meant by the phrase *cost of nonconformance* in relation to quality? (LO 7)

5-22 Waste, rework, and net cost of scrap are examples of what kinds of quality costs? (LO 7)

5-23 Quality engineering, quality training, statistical process control, and supplier certification are what kinds of quality costs? (LO 7)

5-24 List three examples for each of the following quality costing categories:
(a) Prevention costs
(b) Appraisal costs
(c) Internal failure costs
(d) External failure costs (LO 7)

5-25 What is the additional cost of replacing one unit of a product rejected at inspection and scrapped? (LO 7, 8)

5-26 What is the additional cost if a unit rejected at inspection can be reworked to meet quality standards by performing some additional operations? (LO 7, 8)

5-27 What costs and revenues are relevant in evaluating the profit impact of an increase in sales? (LO 8)

5-28 "Design an accounting system that routinely reports only relevant costs," advised a management consultant. Is this good advice? Explain. (LO 1, 2, 8)

Exercises

LO 1, 3 **5-29** *Relevant and sunk costs* Don Baxter's 6-year-old Impala requires repairs estimated at $5,400 to make it roadworthy again. His friend Aaron Bloom suggested that he buy a 6-year-old Ford Escort instead for $5,400 cash. Aaron estimated the following costs for the two cars:

Costs	Impala	Escort
Acquisition cost	$24,000	$5,400
Repairs	5,400	0
Annual operating costs: gas, maintenance, insurance	2,900	1,800

Required

a. What costs are relevant and what costs are not relevant for this decision? Why?
b. What should Don do? Explain.
c. What quantitative and qualitative factors are relevant for his decision? Why?

LO 1 **5-30** *Relevant and sunk costs* Gilmark Company has 10,000 obsolete lamps carried in inventory at a cost of $12 each. They can be sold as they are for $4 each. They can be reworked, however, at a total cost of $55,000 and sold for $10 each. Determine whether it is worthwhile to rework these lamps.

LO 1 **5-31** *Relevant and sunk costs* Ideal Company's plant manager is considering buying a new grinding machine to replace an old grinding machine or overhauling the old one to ensure compliance with the plant's high-quality standards. The following data are available:

Old Grinding Machine	
Original cost	$50,000
Accumulated depreciation	40,000
Annual operating costs	18,000
Current salvage value	4,000
Salvage value at the end of 5 years	0

New Grinding Machine	
Cost	$70,000
Annual operating costs	13,000
Salvage value at the end of 5 years	0

Overhaul of Old Grinding Machine	
Cost of overhaul	$25,000
Annual operating costs after overhaul	14,000
Salvage value at the end of 5 years	0

Required

a. What costs should the decision maker consider as sunk costs?
b. List all relevant costs and when they are incurred.
c. What should the plant manager do? Why?

> LO 2   **5-32 *Make-or-buy, relevant costs***   The assembly division of Cassandra Resolution, Inc., is bidding on an order of 1,000 TV sets. The division is anxious to get this order because it has a substantial amount of unused plant capacity. The variable cost for each TV set is $600 in addition to the cost of the picture tube. The divisional purchasing manager has received two bids for the picture tube. One is from Cassandra Resolution's picture tube division. This bid is for $55 per picture tube, although its variable cost is only $42 per tube. The other is from an outside vendor for $65 per unit. Cassandra Resolution's picture tube division has sufficient unused capacity for this order.

Required

a. Determine the relevant costs for this order for the assembly division under both internal and outsourcing arrangements.
b. Determine the relevant costs for this order for Cassandra Resolution as a company under each of the sourcing arrangements.

> LO 1, 2, 3   **5-33 *Make-or-buy***   Kane Company is considering outsourcing a key component. A reliable supplier has quoted a price of $64.50 per unit. The following costs of the component when manufactured in-house are expressed on a per-unit basis:

Direct materials	$23.40
Direct labor	16.10
Unit-related support	14.70
Batch-related support	9.80
Product-sustaining support	2.20
Facility-sustaining support	6.90
Total costs	$73.10

Required

a. What assumptions need to be made about the behavior of support costs for Kane?
b. Should Kane Company outsource the component?
c. What other factors are relevant for this decision?

> LO 2   **5-34 *Make-or-buy, opportunity cost***   Premier Company manufactures gear model G37, which is used in several of its farm-equipment products. Annual production volume of G37 is 20,000 units. Unit costs for G37 are as follow:

Direct materials costs	$55
Direct labor costs	30
Variable support costs	25
Fixed support costs	15
Total costs	$125

Alternatively, Premier can also purchase gear model G37 from an outside supplier for $120 per unit. If G37 is outsourced, Premier can use the facility where G37 is currently manufactured for production of another gear—model G49. This would save Premier $113,000 in facility rental and other costs presently incurred. Should Premier make or buy G37?

LO 1   **5-35** *Relevant costs and revenues: replacement decision*   Joyce Printers, Inc., is considering replacing its current printing machines with newer, faster, and more efficient printing technology. The following data have been compiled:

CATEGORY	EXISTING MACHINES	NEW MACHINES
Original cost	$80,000	$120,000
Annual operating costs	$50,000	$ 30,000
Remaining useful life	5 years	5 years
Salvage value after 5 years	$5,000	$10,000

The existing machines can be disposed of now for $40,000. Keeping them will cost $20,000 for repair and upgrading. Should Joyce Printers keep the existing printing machines? Explain.

LO 1   **5-36** *Make-or-buy, relevant costs, opportunity cost*   Kentucky Motors has manufactured compressor parts at its plant in Pitcairn, Indiana, for the past 18 years. An outside supplier, Superior Compressor Company, has offered to supply compressor model A238 at a price of $200 per unit. Unit manufacturing costs for A238 are as follows:

Direct materials	$80
Direct labor	60
Unit-related support	26
Batch-related support	22
Product-sustaining support	8
Facility-sustaining support	17
Total costs	$213

Required

a. Should Superior Compressor's offer be accepted if the plant is presently operating below capacity?

b. What is the maximum acceptable purchase price if the plant facilities are fully utilized at present and if any additional available capacity can be deployed for the production of other compressors?

LO 6, 8   **5-37** *JIT manufacturing and cost savings*   Bogden Company introduced JIT manufacturing last year and has prepared the following data to assess the benefits from the change:

CATEGORY	BEFORE THE CHANGE	AFTER THE CHANGE
Production cycle time	68 days	30 days
Inventories	$160,000	$40,000
Total sales	$1,260,000	$1,700,000
Costs as percent of sales:		
Direct materials	30%	20%
Direct labor	22%	15%
Variable support	28%	10%
Fixed support	12%	5%

Inventory financing costs are 15% per year. Estimate the total financial benefits that resulted from the switch to JIT manufacturing operations.

5-38 *Quality cost categories*   Regarding the quality costing categories, how do prevention costs differ from appraisal costs? How do internal failure costs differ from external failure costs?

LO 7 **5-39** *Quality cost categories*   Of the four quality costing categories, which quality cost is the most damaging to the organization? Explain.

LO 4 **5-40** *Facilities layout*   How would you classify the layout of a large grocery store? Why do you think it is laid out this way? Can you think of any way to improve the layout of a conventional grocery store? Explain your reasoning. (*Hint:* Think about JIT, cycle time, and so on.)

Problems

LO 1 **5-41** *Relevant costs*   Carmen's Catering provides lunches and dinners for various groups or organizations. A new customer has approached Carmen's Catering to provide dinner for a special event featuring a well-known speaker, with estimated attendance of 100 people. Carmen suggested two different menus to the customer. The first menu would require materials and direct labor cost of $13 per meal. The second menu would require materials and direct labor cost of $16 per meal. Carmen has developed the following cost analysis for her ongoing operations:

Event-related support per event	$100
Customer-related support per event	22
Facility-sustaining support per month	2,000

Carmen has sufficient excess capacity to handle the new customer's event. Carmen would like to know the minimum price she should charge for 100 meals of the first menu or 100 meals of the second menu.

Required

a. In determining the minimum prices, what assumptions need to be made about the behavior of support costs for Carmen's Catering?
b. What other factors are relevant for this decision?
c. What prices would you recommend for the first menu or the second menu for the new customer's dinner? Provide reasons for your recommendation.

LO 1, 4, 8 **5-42** *Relevant cost and revenues: changes in facilities layout*   To facilitate a move toward JIT production, AB Company is considering a change in its plant layout. The plant controller, Anita Bentley, has been asked to evaluate the costs and benefits of the change in plant layout. After meeting with production and marketing managers, Anita has compiled the following estimates:

- Machine moving and reinstallation will cost $100,000.
- Total sales will increase by 20% to $1,200,000 because of a decrease in production cycle time required under the new plant layout. Average contribution margin is 31% of sales.
- Inventory-related costs will decrease by 25%. Currently, the annual average carrying value of inventory is $200,000. The annual inventory financing cost is 15%.

Should AB implement the proposed change in plant layout? Support your answer.

LO 2, 3 **5-43** *Make-or-buy*   Tanner Appliance Company manufactures 12,000 units of part M4 annually. The part is used in the production of one of its principal products. The following unit cost information is available on part M4:

Direct materials	$11
Direct labor	9
Unit-related support	4
Batch-related support	5
Product-sustaining support	2
Facility-sustaining support	2
Allocated corporate support	5
Total costs	$38

A potential supplier has offered to manufacture this part for Tanner Appliance for $30 per unit. If Tanner Appliance outsources the production of part M4, 50% of batch-related and 80% of product-sustaining activity resources can be eliminated. Furthermore, the production facility now being used to produce this part can be used for a fast-growing new product line that would otherwise require the use of a neighboring facility at a rental cost of $20,000 per year.

Required

a. Should Tanner Appliance purchase part M4 from the outside supplier?
b. What costs are relevant for this decision?
c. What additional factors should Tanner consider?

LO 1, 3   **5-44 *Relevant costs: replacement decision*** Anderson Department Stores is considering the replacement of the existing elevator system at its downtown store. A new system has been proposed that runs faster than the existing system, experiences few breakdowns, and as a result promises considerable savings in operating costs. Information on the existing system and the proposed new system follow:

CATEGORY	EXISTING SYSTEM	NEW SYSTEM
Original cost	$300,000	$875,000
Remaining life	6 years	6 years
Annual cash operating costs	$150,000	$8,000
Salvage value at present	$100,000	—
Salvage value in 6 years	$25,000	$100,000

Required

a. What costs are not relevant for this decision?
b. What are the relevant costs?

LO 1, 3   **5-45 *Incremental revenues and costs, special order*** Genis Battery Company is considering accepting a special order for 50,000 batteries that it received from a discount retail store. The order specified a price of $4 per unit, which reflects a discount of $0.50 per unit relative to the company's regular price of $4.50 per unit. Genis's accounting department has prepared the following analysis to show the cost savings resulting from additional sales:

COSTS	COST PER UNIT WITHOUT THE ADDITIONAL SALES (100,000 UNITS)	COST PER UNIT WITH THE ADDITIONAL SALES (150,000 UNITS)
Variable	$3.30	$3.30
Fixed	$4.20	$3.90

No additional fixed costs will be incurred for this order because the company has surplus capacity. Because the average cost per unit will be reduced from $4.20 to $3.90, Genis's president believes that a reduction in the price to $4 is justified for this order.

Required

a. Should the order for the 50,000 units at a price of $4 be accepted? What will be the impact on Genis's operating income?
b. Is the accounting department's analysis the best way to evaluate this decision? If not, what alternative method can you suggest?
c. What other considerations are important in this case? Why?

LO 1, 3 **5-46 *Relevant costs: replacement decision*** Syd Young, the production manager at Fuchow Company, purchased a cutting machine for the company last year. Six months after the purchase of the cutting machine, Syd learned about a new cutting machine that is more reliable than the machine that he purchased. The following information is available for the two machines:

CATEGORY	OLD MACHINE	NEW MACHINE
Acquisition cost	$300,000	$360,000
Remaining life	4 years	4 years
Salvage value now	$100,000	—
Salvage value at the end of 4 years	$ 4,000	$6,000

Annual operating costs for the old machine are $140,000. The new machine will decrease annual operating costs by $60,000. These amounts do not include any charges for depreciation. Fuchow Company uses the straight-line depreciation method. These estimates of operating costs exclude rework costs. The new machine will also result in a reduction in the defect rate from the current 5% to 2.5%. All defective units are reworked at a cost of $1 per unit. The company, on average, produces 100,000 units annually.

Required

a. Should Syd Young replace the old machine with the new machine? Explain, listing all relevant costs.
b. What costs should be considered as sunk costs for this decision?
c. What other factors may affect Young's decision?

LO 5 **5-47 *ABC and TOC*** Discuss the similarities and differences between activity-based costing and the theory of constraints, as well as situations in which one approach might be preferable to the other.

LO 4, 6 **5-48 *Cycle time efficiency and JIT*** Walker Brothers Company is considering installing a JIT manufacturing system in the hope that it will improve its overall processing cycle efficiency. Data from the traditional system and estimates for the JIT system are presented here for their Nosun Product:

TIME CATEGORY	TRADITIONAL SYSTEM	JIT SYSTEM
Storage	4 hours	1 hour
Inspection	40 minutes	5 minutes
Moving	80 minutes	20 minutes
Processing	2 hours	75 minutes

Required

a. Calculate processing cycle efficiency (PCE) under the traditional and JIT systems for the Nosun Product.

b. Strictly based on your PCE calculations above, should Walker Brothers implement the JIT system? Explain.

LO 4, 6   **5-49**   *JIT and cellular manufacturing*   You are a manufacturing manager faced with the decision about how to improve manufacturing operations and efficiency. You have been studying both cellular manufacturing and JIT manufacturing systems. Your boss expects you to prepare a report covering the costs and benefits of each approach.

Required

Write a detailed memorandum discussing the costs and benefits of cellular manufacturing versus JIT.

LO 1   **5-50**   *Relevant costs: dropping a product*   Merchant Company manufactures and sells three models of electronic printers. Ken Gail, president of the company, is considering dropping model JT484 from its product line because the company has experienced losses for this product over the past three quarters. The following product-level operating data have been compiled for the most recent quarter:

CATEGORY	TOTAL	JT284	JT384	JT484
Sales	$1,000,000	$500,000	$200,000	$300,000
Variable costs	600,000	300,000	100,000	200,000
Contribution margin	$400,000	$200,000	$100,000	$100,000
Fixed costs:				
Rent	$50,000	$25,000	$10,000	$15,000
Depreciation	60,000	30,000	12,000	18,000
Utilities	40,000	20,000	5,000	15,000
Supervision	50,000	15,000	5,000	30,000
Maintenance	30,000	15,000	6,000	9,000
Administrative	100,000	30,000	20,000	50,000
Total fixed costs	$330,000	$135,000	$58,000	$137,000
Operating income (loss)	$70,000	$65,000	$42,000	($37,000)

In addition, the following information is also available:

- Factory rent and depreciation will not be affected by a decision to drop model JT484.
- Quarterly utility bills will be reduced from $40,000 to $31,000 if JT484 is dropped.
- Supervision costs for JT484 can be eliminated if dropped.
- The maintenance department will be able to reduce quarterly costs by $7,000 if JT484 is dropped.
- Elimination of JT484 will make it possible to eliminate two administrative staff positions with combined salaries of $30,000 per quarter.

Required

a. Should Merchant Company eliminate JT484?

b. Merchant's sales manager believes that it is important to continue to produce JT484 to maintain a full product line. He expects the elimination of JT484 will reduce sales of the remaining two products by 5% each. Will this information change your answer to (a)? Explain.

5-51 *Quality improvement programs and cost savings*   Garber Valves Company manufactures brass valves meeting precise specification standards. All finished valves are inspected before packing and shipping to customers. Rejected valves are returned to the initial production stage to be melted and recast. Such rework requires no new materials in casting but requires new materials in finishing. The following unit cost data are available:

COSTS	CASTING	FINISHING	INSPECTION	PACKING	TOTAL
Direct materials	$225	$12	$0	$8	$245
Direct labor	84	121	24	16	245
Variable support	122	164	30	20	336
Fixed support	63	89	16	10	178
	$494	$386	$70	$54	$1,004

As a result of a quality-improvement program, the reject rate has decreased from 6.4% to 5.1%, and the number of rejects has decreased by $(6.4\% - 5.1\%) \times (10,000)$ units. Improvements in reject rates have also led to a decrease in work-in-process inventory from $386,000 to $270,000. Inventory carrying costs are estimated to be 15% per year. Estimate the annual cost savings as a result of the quality improvement.

5-52 *Relevant costs: introducing a new product, breakeven point*   Macready Company is considering introducing a new compact disc player model at a price of $105 per unit. Macready's controller has compiled the following incremental cost information based on an estimate of 120,000 units of sales annually for the new product:

Direct materials cost	$3,600,000
Direct labor cost	$2,400,000
Variable manufacturing support	$1,200,000
Sales commission	10% of sales
Fixed cost	$2,000,000

The average inventory levels for the new product are estimated as follows:

Raw materials	2 months of production
Work in process (100% complete for materials and 50% complete for labor and variable manufacturing support)	1 month of production
Finished goods	2 months of production

Annual inventory carrying costs not included in the variable manufacturing support listed earlier are estimated to be 12% of inventory value. In addition, the sales manager expects the introduction of the new model to result in a reduction in sales of the existing model from 300,000 to 240,000 units. The contribution margin for the old product is $20 per unit.

Required

a. Determine the total impact on Macready's profit from the introduction of the new product.
b. Should Macready introduce the new product? Explain.
c. Determine the breakeven point (in units) for the new product. Assume that sales of the old product decrease by one unit for every two-unit increase in the sales of the new product.

LO 2, 3   **5-53** *Make-or-buy*   Beau's Bistro has a reputation for providing good value for its menu prices. The desserts, developed by the pastry chef, are one of the distinctive features of the menu. The pastry chef has just given notice that he will relocate to another city in a month and has volunteered to share some of the dessert recipes with the next pastry chef. Beau has been concerned about the Bistro's declining profits but is reluctant to raise prices because of the competition he faces. He decided this was an opportune time to consider outsourcing dessert production. Beau solicited bids for dessert production and delivery and is evaluating two bids as well as the alternative of hiring a new pastry chef who would make the desserts in-house. The first bid is from a gourmet dessert provider who would fill the Bistro's current dessert demand for $5,500 per month and would periodically introduce new gourmet desserts. The second bid is from a dessert provider who would provide high-quality, traditional desserts to fill Bistro's current demand (in terms of servings) for $5,000 per month. Beau has identified the following costs per month if the desserts are made in-house:

Ingredients	$500
Pastry chef labor	3,500
Assistants' labor	1,500
Direct support	200
Total	$5,700

Required

  a. What qualitative factors are relevant for this decision?
  b. Would you advise Beau to outsource dessert production? Provide reasons for your decision.

LO 2, 3   **5-54** *Outsourcing, ethics*   Hollenberry, Inc., is a successful mail-order catalog business with customers worldwide. The company's headquarters is in a small town some distance from any major metropolitan area. Sales have grown steadily over the years, and the call center facilities are currently inadequate for the sales volume. Management is deciding on whether to outsource the call center operations to a company specializing in such operations. If the call center is outsourced, most of the current employees would lose their jobs because they do not wish to relocate to the new call center location, close to a major metropolitan area. Many of the employees have been with Hollenberry for over 20 years. Regardless of where the call center is located, customers will call a toll-free phone number. If the call center is outsourced, however, more multilingual operators would be available. Hollenberry has identified the following costs of operating the call center in-house:

Labor	$650,000
Building rent	60,000
Phone charges	35,000
Other support costs	42,000

If the call center is outsourced, the related office equipment would be sold to the new call center operations for $20,000. The equipment was originally purchased at a cost of $100,000. The building will no longer be rented, and call center employees will have the opportunity to transfer to the outside call center, in which case their salaries will be paid by the outside call center. The other support costs are associated with maintaining the building and office equipment for the current call center.

If Hollenberry outsources the call center and the same number and pattern of calls occur next year, Hollenberry will pay the new call center firm $700,000 for the year.

Required

a. What costs are relevant for the decision on outsourcing the call center?
b. What qualitative factors are important in this decision?
c. What should Hollenberry do? Provide reasons for your recommendation.

LO 4   **5-55** *Cellular manufacturing and processing cycle efficiency*   Ray Brown's company, Whisper Voice Systems, is trying to increase its processing cycle efficiency (PCE). Because Ray has a very limited budget, he has been searching for a way to increase his PCE by using cellular manufacturing. One of Ray's manufacturing managers, Maria Lopez, has been studying cellular manufacturing and claims that with minimal cost that includes downtime in the operation, she can rearrange existing machinery and workers and improve PCE. Ray is quite skeptical about this and decides to allow Maria to rearrange a small part of his operation. For Ray to be satisfied, he has stated that PCE must increase by 12%. PCE data before and after the rearrangement are as follows:

TIME CATEGORY	BEFORE REARRANGEMENT	AFTER REARRANGEMENT
Inspection	30 minutes	15 minutes
Moving	45 minutes	10 minutes
Processing	70 minutes	30 minutes
Storage	55 minutes	20 minutes

Does the change in PCE meet Ray's requirement? Why or why not?

LO 3, 4   **5-56** *Facilities layout*   One aspect of facilities layout for McDonald's is that when customers come into the building, they can line up in one of several lines and wait to be served. In contrast, customers at Wendy's are asked to stand in one line that snakes around the front of the counter and to wait for a single server.

Required

a. What is the rationale for each approach?
b. Which approach do you favor from (1) a customer's perspective and (2) management's perspective? Explain.

LO 3, 7   **5-57** *Quality of customer service*   Read "Everyone Likes to Laud Serving the Customer; Doing It Is the Problem," by Carol Hymowitz (*Wall Street Journal*, February 27, 2006, B1).

Required

a. According to the article, what measures are commonly used to evaluate customer service representatives, and what measure(s) should be used?

b. Explain how the prevention, appraisal, and external failure aspects of the cost-of-quality framework might be applied to customer service processes. In your response, include a discussion of which of the three aspects companies should focus on and illustrate how evaluation measures may affect performance in customer service processes.

LO 3, 7   **5-58** *Quality costing: balancing category costs*   Managers concerned with improving quality sometimes have a difficult balancing act, given the four types of quality costs they have to manage. As a new manager, you are trying to figure out a strategy for managing $2 million of quality costs; your total quality costs cannot exceed 4% of sales.

Required

You need to decide how much should go into each of the four quality-cost categories. How would you go about allocating these costs? What trade-offs would you have to make as you allocate the costs?

LO 7   **5-59** *Preparing a cost-of-quality report*   The following information shows last year's quality-related costs for the Renwal Company:

ITEM	AMOUNT
Quality engineering	$500,000
Warranty claims	2,345,000
Product liability lawsuits	4,500,000
Research of customer needs	75,000
Maintenance of test equipment	350,000
Returned products	1,200,000
Rework costs	1,200,000
Quality training	125,000
Process control monitoring	1,000,000
Inspection of and testing of incoming materials	400,000
Repair costs in the field	850,000
Statistical process control	250,000
Product recalls	2,000,000
Waste	700,000
Net cost of scrap	635,000
Product quality audits	475,000
Downtime due to defects	125,000
Supplier certification	90,000

Total sales for the year were $100,000,000.

Required

a. Prepare a cost-of-quality report grouping costs into prevention, appraisal, internal failure, and external failure. Also show costs as a percent of sales.

b. Interpret the data and make recommendations to Renwal's management.

5-60 *Preparing a cost-of-quality report*   The following data have just been gathered on last year's quality-related costs at the Ideal Company:

COST CATEGORY	AMOUNT
Product recalls	$ 325,000
Downtime due to defects	600,000
Warranty claims	420,000
Inspection of and testing of incoming materials	300,000
Product liability lawsuits	500,000
Process quality audits	350,000
Rework costs	2,000,000
Quality training	150,000
Process control monitoring	350,000
Repair costs in the field	375,000
Statistical process control	300,000
Waste	900,000
Net cost of scrap	1,500,000
Supplier certification	350,000
Quality engineering	200,000
Returned products	380,000

Total sales last year were $75,000,000.

Required

a. Prepare a cost-of-quality report grouping costs into prevention, appraisal, internal failure, and external failure. Also show costs as a percentage of sales.

b. Interpret the data and make recommendations to Ideal's management.

Cases

LO 1, 3   **5-61** *Relevant costs and revenues; marketing channels*   Diamond Bicycle Company manufactures and sells bicycles nationwide through marketing channels ranging from sporting goods stores to specialty bicycle shops. Diamond's average selling price to its distributors is $185 per bicycle. The bicycles are retailed to customers for $349.

After several years of high sales, Diamond's sales in the past 3 years have slumped to 160,000 bicycles per year, which is only 70% of its manufacturing capacity. Diamond expects the demand for its products to remain the same in the next few years.

Premier Stores, a nationwide chain of discount retail stores, has recently approached Diamond to manufacture bicycles for Premier to sell. Premier has offered to purchase 40,000 bicycles annually for a 3-year period at $125 per bicycle. It is not willing to pay a higher price because it plans to retail the bicycles at only $200. Diamond has not previously sold bicycles through any marketing channel other than specialty stores.

Mike Diamond is the chief executive officer of Diamond Bicycle. Although Premier's offer is well below Diamond's normal price, Mike is interested in the offer because Diamond has considerable surplus capacity. He has been supplied with the following variable product cost information:

Direct materials costs	$50
Direct labor costs	30
Variable manufacturing support costs	25
Total costs	$105

The direct materials cost includes $2 for embossing Premier's private label on the bicycle. Fixed support costs total $2,000,000 annually. Diamond also pays its sales staff a 10% commission but will not need to pay any salesperson for the special sale to Premier. Average inventory levels for Premier's offer are estimated as follows:

TYPE OF INVENTORY	INVENTORY LEVEL
Raw materials	1 month of production
Work in process	1.5 months of production (100% complete for materials and 50% complete for other variable manufacturing costs)
Finished goods	0.5 months of production

Annual inventory carrying cost is estimated to be 10% of the inventory carrying value based on variable costs. Premier's offer requires Diamond to deliver the bicycles to Premier's regional warehouse so that Premier can have ready access to an inventory of bicycles to meet fluctuating market demand. Diamond estimated that about 5% of Diamond's present sales will be lost if Premier's offer is accepted because some customers will comparison shop and find the same quality bicycle available at a lower price in Premier's stores.

Required

a. Should Mike Diamond accept Premier's offer?

b. What strategic and other factors should be considered before Mike makes a final decision?

LO 1, 2, 3, 7 **5-62 *Relevant costs, qualitative factors, cost-of-quality framework, ethics*** Kwik Clean handles both commercial laundry and individual customer dry cleaning. Kwik Clean's current dry-cleaning process involves emitting a pollutant into the air. In addition, the commercial laundry and dry cleaning produces sediments and other elements that must receive special treatment before disposal. Pat Polley, Kwik Clean's owner, is concerned about the cost of dealing with increasingly stringent laws and environmental regulations. Recent legislation requires Kwik Clean to reduce the amount of its air pollution emissions.

To reduce pollution emissions, Polley is considering the following two options:

- *Option 1.* Invest in equipment that would reduce emissions through filtration. The equipment would involve a large capital expenditure but would bring Kwik Clean into compliance with current regulations for emissions.
- *Option 2.* Invest in a new dry-cleaning process that would eliminate current air pollution emissions, partly through using a solvent different from the one currently used. This option would require an even larger capital expenditure than option 1, but the new equipment would reduce some operating costs. Moreover, Kwik Clean might be able to market its environmentally-safer process to increase business.

In evaluating the two options and current operations, Polley has enumerated the following items:

1. The price and quantity of solvent used in current operations (and option 1).
2. The price and quantity of the new solvent that would be used in option 2.
3. The purchase cost of new equipment for option 1 and for option 2.
4. The cost of removing old equipment and installing new equipment under option 2.
5. The purchase price of the filtration equipment in option 1 as well as the useful life of the equipment.
6. The purchase price of the current equipment and its remaining useful life.
7. The salvage value of the current equipment, which would be sold under option 2.
8. Polley's salary and fringe benefits.

9. Labor costs for current operations (and option 1) and option 2; labor costs would be lower under option 2 than under option 1.
10. Training costs associated with the new equipment in option 2.
11. Legal fees paid to handle paperwork associated with hazardous waste liabilities connected with the sediments produced when cleaning commercial laundry by the current operations. The same sediments would be produced with the equipment in option 2.
12. Storage and disposal costs associated with the sediments produced when cleaning commercial laundry.
13. Insurance for the equipment and workers. Under option 2, insurance fees would be reduced from the current level.

Polley was concerned about recent events publicized locally. A newspaper article reported that the Occupational Safety and Health Administration fined one of Polley's competitors several thousand dollars for unsafe employee working conditions related to handling solvents. Another business incurred a very expensive cleanup for accidental hazardous waste leakage that contaminated the soil. The leakage received major attention in the local television and radio news broadcasts and was headlined in the local newspapers.

Required

a. Which costs are relevant to Polley's decision between option 1 and option 2?
b. What qualitative factors is Polley likely to consider in making the decision between option 1 and option 2?
c. Explain how the cost-of-quality framework of prevention, appraisal, internal failure, and external failure might be applied to operations with environmental pollution, where *failures* are defined as accidental spillage or leakage of hazardous wastes or as illegal levels of pollutants. On which of the four cost-of-quality categories would you advise Polley to focus her attention?

LO 1, 8   **5-63 Relevant costs: replacement decision**   Rossman Instruments, Inc., is considering leasing new state-of-the-art machinery at an annual cost of $900,000. The new machinery has a 4-year expected life. It will replace existing machinery leased 1 year earlier at an annual lease cost of $490,000 committed for 5 years. Early termination of this lease contract will incur a $280,000 penalty. There are no other fixed costs.

The new machinery is expected to decrease variable costs from $42 to $32 per unit sold because of improved materials yield, faster machine speed, and lower direct labor, supervision, materials handling, and quality inspection requirements. The sales price will remain at $56. Improvements in quality, production cycle time, and customer responsiveness are expected to increase annual sales from 36,000 units to 48,000 units.

The variable costs stated earlier exclude the inventory carrying costs. Because the new machinery is expected to affect inventory levels, the following estimates are also provided. The enhanced speed and accuracy of the new machinery are expected to decrease production cycle time by half and, consequently, lead to a decrease in work-in-process inventory level from 3 months to just 1.5 months of production. Increased flexibility with these new machines is expected to allow a reduction in finished goods inventory from 2 months of production to just 1 month. Improved yield rates and greater machine reliability will enable a reduction in raw materials inventory from 4 months of production to just 1.5 months. Annual inventory carrying cost is 20% of inventory value.

Category	Old Machine	New Machine
Average per unit cost of raw materials inventory	$12	$11
Average per unit cost of work-in-process inventory	25	20
Average per unit cost of finished goods inventory	46	36
Variable cost per unit sold	42	32

Required

a. Determine the total value of annual benefits from the new machinery. Include changes in inventory carrying costs.

b. Should Rossman replace its existing machinery with the new machinery? Present your reasoning with detailed steps identifying relevant costs and revenues.

c. Discuss whether a manager evaluated on the basis of Rossman's net income will have the incentive to make the right decision as evaluated in (b).

LO 4 **5-64 *Customer service processes, non-value-added activities*** Daniel Morris purchased a 42-inch plasma television, manufactured by TVCO, from a local electronics store that permits customers to return defective products within 30 days of purchase. Approximately 45 days after Daniel's purchase, the TV began to malfunction periodically. Because Daniel could not return the TV to the local store, he turned to the warranty information and found that the warranty included picking up the approximately 100-pound TV from the owner's home, repairing the TV, and delivering the repaired TV to the owner's home. TVCO's customer service process for handling warranty repairs is as follows:

1. The customer calls Customer Service (CS) to request authorization of the TV repair.
2. CS requests the customer to mail or fax the receipt, TV model number, and serial number.
3. On receipt of the information, CS locates a nearby repair shop to perform the repair.
4. CS forwards the repair request to the Warranty Department (WD) for approval.
5. On approval, WD informs CS so that CS can inform the customer and fax authorization for the repair to the approved repair shop.
6. The customer contacts the designated repair shop to arrange for the TV pickup. The repair shop picks up the TV.
7. The repair shop diagnoses the problem and orders parts.
8. On receipt of the parts, the shop repairs the TV and delivers it to the customer.
9. If the TV cannot be repaired, TVCO replaces the defective TV with a new one.

Accordingly, Daniel called CS to request authorization to repair the TV and faxed the receipt, TV model number, and serial number to CS. CS located a repair shop (RS1) 30 miles from Daniel's city of Anytown. On obtaining WD's approval, CS faxed authorization for the repair to the approved repair shop. Daniel contacted RS1 to arrange for the TV pickup, but RS1 refused to pick up the TV, stating that Daniel's location is too far away. After several more phone calls to CS, with wait times before talking to a CS representative ranging from 25 to 45 minutes, CS, authorized another repair shop, RS2. RS2 picked up the TV, and Daniel informed RS2 that he planned to move to Othertown in 2 weeks and therefore hoped the TV could be repaired by then. RS2 did not look at the TV until Daniel called 8 days later to check on progress. RS2 then diagnosed the problem and contacted TVCO for parts for the repair and was told that parts would not be available for several weeks. Because of his impending move to another city, Daniel requested RS2 to return the TV to him, thinking that he would get the TV repaired in Othertown.

After moving to Othertown, Daniel again called CS to request authorization for the TV repair. After several phone calls with sizable wait times before talking to CS, and several miscommunications between CS and WD that led Daniel to talk to a supervisor, CS located RS3 in Othertown. However, RS3 was backlogged and would not pick up the TV for at least a week. RS3 picks up only on weekdays during regular working hours. Moreover, the technician would not look at the TV for at least 10 days after the TV arrived in the shop. Given the length of time that had now passed since Daniel's first contact with CS, Daniel found this situation unacceptable, so he called CS and asked to talk to a supervisor. The supervisor suggested other approved stores for the repair.

Daniel found RS4, which was willing to pick up the TV at a day's notice and diagnoses problems as soon as possible so that parts can be ordered. Daniel called CS to arrange for authorization, and CS promised to call back soon. After a week with no response, Daniel called CS and was told that WD refused to authorize RS4 to perform the repair because WD thought Daniel still lived in Anytown and RS4 was too far from Anytown. Daniel called the supervisor again, and after a week the supervisor arranged for authorization for RS4 to do the repair. RS4 picked up the TV; by now, more than 2 months had passed since Daniel first contacted CS, and RS4 could not provide a definite date for completion of the repair. However, as promised, RS4 diagnosed the problem shortly after the TV arrived in the shop and ordered the apparently appropriate part. Disappointingly, changing the part did not correct the problem. TVCO suggested that RS4 try changing another part but could not provide an estimated date of arrival for the part. After Daniel's further phone calls, TVCO agreed to exchange the defective TV for a new one. By this time, more than 3 months had passed since Daniel first contacted CS.

Required

a. Assuming that TVCO has a performance measurement system for CS, what measures do you think the company is using to evaluate CS performance?

b. What measures reflect what the customer is concerned about?

c. What changes in the warranty service approval process might improve the process from the customer's perspective?

d. Compare how RS3 and RS4 have designed their repair process and explain to RS3 how it can reduce the time spent on non-value-added activities.

LO 4 **5-65** *Facilities layout, value-added activities* Woodpoint Furniture Manufacturing produces various lines of pine furniture. The plant is organized so that all similar functions are performed in one area, as shown in Exhibit 5-18. Most pieces of furniture are made in batches of 10 units.

Raw materials are ordered and stored in the raw materials storage area. When an order is issued for a batch of production, the wood needed to complete that batch is withdrawn from the raw materials storage area and taken to the saw area. There the wood is sawed into the pieces that are required for the production lot.

The pieces are then transferred to the sanding and planing area, where they are stored awaiting processing in that area. When the machines are free, any sanding or planing is done on all the pieces in the batch. Any pieces that are damaged by the planing or sanding are reordered from the saw area. The other pieces in the lot are set aside in a storage area when pieces have to be reordered from the saw area.

When all the pieces have been sanded or planed, the pieces are then transferred to the assembly area, where they are placed in a large bin to await assembly. Pieces are withdrawn from the bin as

Exhibit 5-18
Woodpoint Furniture Manufacturing

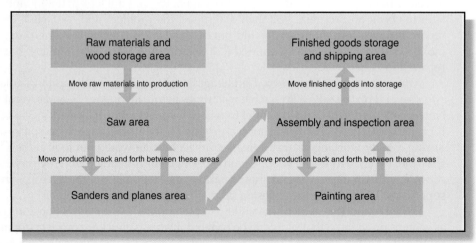

assembly proceeds. Defective pieces are returned to the saw or sand and plane area, where they are remanufactured.

As assembly proceeds or when assembly is completed, depending on the product, any required painting or staining is done in the painting area. Pieces to be stained or painted are transferred back and forth on a trolley between the assembly and paint areas. The paint department has a storage area for pieces awaiting painting. Whenever assembly is halted to await pieces that have been sent for painting and staining, the rest of the pieces in that batch are put into the storage bin to await the return of the stained or painted pieces.

When assembly is completed, the product is checked by the quality inspector. Any defective products are returned to the appropriate department for rework. When the product is approved, it is packaged and put into final storage to await an order by the customer.

Required

    a. Chart the process (that is, specify, from start to finish, the activities used) to make furniture in Woodpoint Furniture Manufacturing. Which activities do you think add value from the customer's perspective?

    b. What performance indicators do you think are critical in evaluating the performance of this manufacturing operation from the standpoint of customers and the company?

LO 4   **5-66 *Facilities layout, identifying value-added activities*** Consider Exhibit 5-19, which summarizes the activities at the former Bethlehem Steel Corporation's Sparrows Point plant. The blast furnaces make the iron that is refined into steel. The basic oxygen furnaces and open-hearth furnaces refine the iron into steel. The mix of iron, scrap, and alloys used to make the steel and the characteristics of the furnace determine the steel's properties, which include formability, strength, toughness, hardenability, and corrosion resistance. The continuous slab caster uses the steel from the basic oxygen furnace to make slabs of steel. The steel from the open-hearth furnace is poured into ingot molds for cooling.

When it has cooled and hardened, the steel ingot, weighing between 11,000 and 80,000 pounds, is removed from the mold and stored. When required, the ingots are reheated and moved to the blooming or slabbing mills, which transform the ingots into blooms (square or rectangular shapes) or slabs (wide and flat shapes), depending on the final product that the ingot will be used to make. This operation also improves the properties of the steel. The billet mill reduces blooms into 4-inch-square billets that are shipped to the rod mill, which produces coils of rod that are then transformed into finished items such as wire. Plates are rolled from reheated slabs in the plate mill. The plates must be cut on all sides to the desired dimensions after rolling. Slabs are also used to make strip steel, which is either made into some final products directly or subjected to finishing operations to make steel sheet or tinplate.

Required

    a. What do you think is critical to the customer in making a steel purchasing decision?

    b. Do you see any activities in this process that do not add value from the customer's perspective?

    c. What performance indicators in this process might be important for the company to monitor?

LO 4, 7   **5-67 *Customer service processes, non-value-added activities*** Precision Systems, Inc.[1] Precision Systems, Inc. (PSI) has been in business for more than 25 years and has generally reported a positive net income. The company manufactures and sells high-technology instruments (systems). Each product line at PSI has only a handful of standard products, but configuration

---

[1] *Source*: Institute of Management Accountants, *Cases from Management Accounting Practice, Volume 12.* Adapted with permission.

Exhibit 5-19
From Modest Beginnings to Quality Steel Products

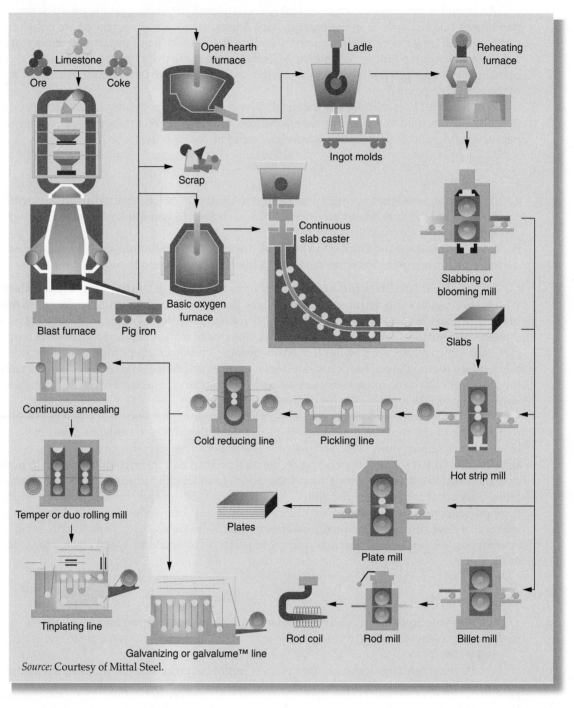

Source: Courtesy of Mittal Steel.

changes and add-ons can be accommodated as long as they are not radically different from the standard systems.

Faced with rising competition and increasing customer demands for quality, PSI adopted total quality management (TQM) in 1989. Many employees received training and several quality initiatives were launched. Like most businesses, PSI concentrated on improvements in the manufacturing function and achieved significant improvements. However, little was done in other departments.

In early 1992, PSI decided to extend TQM to its order entry department, which handles the critical functions of preparing quotes for potential customers and processing orders. Order processing is the first process in the chain of operations after the order is received from a customer. High-quality output from the order entry department improves quality later in the process, and allows PSI to deliver higher quality systems both faster and cheaper, thus meeting the goals of timely delivery and lower cost.

As a first step, PSI commissioned a cost of quality (COQ) study in its order entry department. The study had two objectives:

- to develop a system for identifying order entry errors,
- to determine how much an order entry error costs.

PSI's Order Entry Department

PSI's domestic order entry department is responsible for preparing quotations for potential customers and taking actual sales orders. PSI's sales representatives forward requests for quotations to the order entry department, though actual orders for systems are received directly from customers. Orders for parts are also received directly from customers. Service-related orders (for parts or repairs), however, are generally placed by service representatives. When PSI undertook the COQ study, the order entry department consisted of nine employees and two supervisors who reported to the order entry manager. Three of the nine employees dealt exclusively with taking parts orders, while the other six were responsible for system orders. Before August 1992, the other six were split equally into two groups: One was responsible for preparing quotations, and the other was responsible for taking orders.

The final outputs of the order entry department are the quote and the order acknowledgement or "green sheet." The manufacturing department and the stockroom use the green sheet for further processing of the order.

The order entry department's major suppliers are (1) sales or service representatives; (2) the final customers who provide them with the basic information to process further; and (3) technical information and marketing departments, which provide configuration guides, price masters and similar documents (some in printed form and others on-line) as supplementary information. Sometimes there are discrepancies in the information available to order entry staff and sales representatives with respect to price, part number, or configuration. These discrepancies often cause communication gaps between the order entry staff, sales representatives, and manufacturing.

An order entry staff provided the following example of lack of communication between a sales representative and manufacturing with respect to one order.

If the sales reps. have spoken to the customer and determined that our standard configuration is not what they require, they may leave a part off the order. [In one such instance] I got a call from manufacturing saying when this system is configured like this, it must have this part added. . . . It is basically a no charge part and so I added it (change order #1) and called the sales rep. and said to him, "Manufacturing told me to add it." The sales rep. called back and said, "No [the customer] doesn't need that part, they are going to be using another option . . . so they don't need this." Then I did another change order (#2) to take it off because the sales rep. said they don't need it. Then manufacturing called me back and said "we really need [to add that part] (change order #3). If the sales rep. does not want it then we will have to do an engineering special and it is going to be another 45 days lead time. . . ." So, the sales rep. and manufacturing not having direct communication required me to do three change orders on that order; two of them were probably unnecessary.

A typical sequence of events might begin with a sales representative meeting with a customer to discuss the type of system desired. The sales representative then fills out a paper form and faxes it or phones it in to an order entry employee, who might make several subsequent phone calls to the sales representative, the potential customer, or the manufacturing department to prepare the quote properly. These phone calls deal with such questions as exchangeability of parts, part numbers, current prices for parts, or allowable sales discounts. Order entry staff then keys in the configuration of the desired system, including part numbers, and informs the sales representative of the quoted price. Each quote is assigned a quotation number. To smooth production, manufacturing often produces systems with standard configurations in anticipation of obtaining orders from recent quotes for systems. The systems usually involve adding on special features to the standard configuration. Production in advance of orders sometimes results in duplication in manufacturing, however, because customers often fail to put their quotation numbers on their orders. When order entry receives an order, the information on the order is re-entered into the computer to produce an order acknowledgement. When the order acknowledgement is sent to the invoicing department, the information is reviewed again to generate an invoice to send to the customer.

Many departments in PSI use information directly from the order entry department (these are the internal customers of order entry). The users include manufacturing, service (repair), stockroom, invoicing, and sales administration. The sales administration department prepares commission payments and tracks sales performance. The shipping, customer support (technical support), and collections departments (also internal customers) indirectly use order entry information. After a system is shipped, related paperwork is sent to customer support to maintain a service-installed database in anticipation of technical support questions that may arise. Customer support is also responsible for installations of systems. A good order acknowledgement (i.e., one with no errors of any kind) can greatly reduce errors downstream within the process and prevent later nonvalue-added costs.

Cost of Quality

Quality costs arise because poor quality may—or does—exist. For PSI's order entry department, poor quality or nonconforming "products" refer to poor information for further processing of an order or quotation (see Exhibit 5-20 for examples). Costs of poor quality here pertain to the time spent by the order entry staff and concerned employees in other departments (providers of information, such as sales or technical information) to rectify the errors.

Class I Failures

Class I failure costs are incurred when nonconforming products (incorrect quotes or orders) are identified as nonconforming before they leave the order entry department. The incorrect quotes or orders may be identified by order entry staff or supervisors during inspection of the document. An important cause of Class I failures is lack of communication. Sample data collected from the order entry staff show that they encountered more than 10 different types of problems during order processing (see Exhibit 15-20 for examples). Analysis of the sample data suggests that, on average, it takes 2.3 hours (including waiting time) to rectify errors on quotes and 2.7 working days for corrections on orders. In determining costs, the COQ study accounted only for the time it actually takes to solve the problem (i.e., excluding waiting time). Waiting time was excluded because employees use this time to perform other activities or work on other orders. The total Class I failure costs, which include only salary and fringe benefits for the time it takes to correct errors, amount to more than 4% of order entry's annual budget for salaries and fringe benefits (see Exhibit 5-21).

Class II Failures

Class II failure costs are incurred when nonconforming materials are transferred out of the order entry department. For PSI's order entry department, "nonconforming" refers to an incorrect order acknowledgement as specified by its users within PSI. The impact of order entry errors on final (external) customers is low because order acknowledgements are inspected in several departments, so most errors are corrected before the invoice (which contains some information available on the order acknowledgement) is sent to the final customer. Corrections of the order entry errors do not guarantee that the customer receives a good quality system, but order entry's initial errors do not then affect the final customer. Mistakes that affect the final customer can be made by individuals in other departments (e.g., manufacturing or shipping).

Exhibit 5-20
Examples of Failures

1. Incomplete information on purchase order
2. Transposition of prices on purchase order
3. More than one part number on order acknowledgment when only one is required
4. Incorrect business unit code (used for tracking product line profitability) on the order acknowledgment
5. Freight terms missing on the purchase order
6. Incorrect part number on order acknowledgment
7. Incorrect shipping or billing address on the order acknowledgment
8. Credit approval missing (all new customers have a credit approval before an order is processed)
9. Missing part number on order acknowledgment
10. Customer number terminated on the computer's database (an order cannot be processed if customer number is missing)
11. Incorrect sales tax calculation on the order acknowledgment
12. Part number mismatch on purchase order

Exhibit 5-21
Estimated Annual Failure Costs (as a percentage of order entry's annual salary and fringe benefits budget)

	ORDER ENTRY	OTHER DEPARTMENTS	TOTAL COSTS
Class I failure costs			
Quotations	1.1%	0.4%	1.5%
Orders	0.9%	1.7%	2.6%
Total Class I failure costs	2.0%	2.1%	4.1%
Class II failure costs			
Order acknowledgments	2.6%	4.4%	7.0%
Change orders	2.6%	—	2.6%
Final customers	0.02%	0.1%	0.12%
Return authorizations	1.9%	—	1.9%
Total Class II failure costs	7.12%	4.5%	11.62%
Total failure costs	9.12%	6.6%	15.72%

Sample data collected from PSI's users of order entry department information show that more than 20 types of errors can be found on the order acknowledgement (see Exhibit 5-20 for examples). The cost of correcting these errors (salary and fringe benefits of order entry person and a concerned person from another PSI department) accounts for approximately 7% of order entry's annual budget for salaries and fringe benefits (see Exhibit 5-21).

In addition to the time spent on correcting the errors, the order entry staff must prepare a change order for several of the Class II errors. Moreover, a change order is required for several other reasons that are not necessarily controllable by order entry. Examples include: (1) changes in ship-to or bill-to address by customers or sales representatives, (2) canceled orders, and (3) changes in invoicing instructions. Regardless of the reason for a change order, the order entry department incurs some cost. The sample data suggest that for every 100 new orders, order entry prepares 71 change orders; this activity accounts for 2.6% of order entry's annual budget for salaries and fringe benefits (see Exhibit 5-21).

Although order entry's errors do not significantly affect final customers, customers who find errors on their invoices often use the errors as an excuse to delay payments. Correcting these errors involves the joint efforts of the order entry, collections, and invoicing departments; these costs account for about 0.12% of order entry's annual budget (see Exhibit 5-21).

The order entry staff also spends considerable time in handling return authorizations when final customers send their shipments back to PSI. Interestingly, more than 17% of the goods returned are because of defective shipments, and more than 49% fall into the following two categories: (1) ordered in error and (2) 30-day return rights. An in-depth analysis of the latter categories suggests that a majority of these returns can be traced to sales or service errors. The order entry department incurs costs to process these return authorizations, which account for more than 1.9% of the annual budget (see Exhibit 5-21). The total Class I and Class II failure costs account for 15.72% of the order entry department's annual budget for salaries and fringe benefits. Although PSI users of order entry information were aware that problems in their departments were sometimes caused by errors in order entry, they provided little feedback to order entry about the existence or impact of the errors.

Changes in PSI's Order Entry Department

In October 1992, preliminary results of the study were presented to three key persons who had initiated the study: the order entry manager, the vice-president of manufacturing, and the vice-president of service and quality. In March 1993, the final results were presented to PSI's executive council, the top decision-making body. Between October 1992 and March 1993, PSI began working toward obtaining the International Organization for Standardization's ISO 9002 registration for order entry and manufacturing practices, which it received in June 1993.

The effort to obtain the ISO 9002 registration suggests that PSI gave considerable importance to order entry and invested significant effort toward improving the order entry process. Nevertheless, as stated by the order entry manager, the changes would not have been so vigorously pursued if cost information had not been presented. COQ information functioned as a catalyst to accelerate the improvement effort. In actually making changes to the process, however, information pertaining to the different types of errors was more useful than the cost information.

Required

a. Describe the role that assigning costs to order entry errors played in quality improvement efforts at Precision Systems, Inc.

b. Prepare a diagram illustrating the flow of activities between the order entry department and its suppliers, internal customers (those within PSI), and external customers (those external to PSI).

c. Classify the failure items in Exhibit 5-20 into internal failure (identified as defective before delivery to internal or external customers) and external failure (nonconforming "products" delivered to internal or external customers) with respect to the order entry department. For each external failure item, identify which of order entry's internal customers (that is, other departments within PSI who use information from the order acknowledgment) will be affected.

d. For the order entry process, how would you identify internal failures and external failures? Who would be involved in documenting these failures and their associated costs? Which individuals or departments should be involved in making improvements to the order entry process?

e. What costs, in addition to salary and fringe benefits, would you include in computing the cost of correcting errors?

f. Provide examples of incremental and breakthrough improvements that could be made in the order entry process. In particular, identify prevention activities that can be undertaken to reduce the number of errors. Describe how you would prioritize your suggestions for improvement.

g. What nonfinancial quality indicators might be useful for the order entry department? How frequently should data be collected or information be reported? Can you make statements about the usefulness of cost-of-quality information in comparison to nonfinancial indicators of quality?

Chapter 6

Cost Information for Pricing and Product Planning

After reading this chapter, you will be able to:

➤ show how a firm chooses its product mix in the short term

➤ explain how a firm adjusts its prices in the short term, depending on whether capacity is limited

➤ discuss how a firm determines a long-term benchmark price to guide its pricing strategy

➤ evaluate the long-term profitability of products and market segments

High Performance Springs

"How can we make a profit if we sell at a price below costs? The cost report I've just received indicates a cost of $2.79 per pound for our 0.50-inch steel springs. If we accept Drew Pinsky's offer to buy 120,000 pounds of 0.50-inch springs at only $2.48 per pound, what benefit do we get? How can we survive in this business if we keep slashing our prices?"

Wendy Craven is the owner of High Performance Springs, a manufacturer of high-precision steel springs for industrial customers. She was meeting with Myriah Fitzgibbon, her marketing manager, and Robert Mercado, her controller, to evaluate an offer from Pinsky Corporation to purchase a large quantity of 0.50-inch springs at sharply reduced prices. Her question followed Myriah's comments about the costs and price of this product.

"Our accounting records show that the full cost of the 0.50-inch springs is $2.79 per pound, which breaks down to $1.38 of direct materials, $0.76 of direct labor, and $0.65 of manufacturing support costs. We usually mark up our products 30% over costs, which implies a markup of $0.84 and a price of $3.63 per pound for the 0.50-inch springs. This means that Pinsky is demanding a discount of $1.15 per pound, which is almost 32% off our normal price," Myriah had observed earlier.

Myriah realized that Robert's comments about the product costs and Wendy's reaction to it meant that he could not justify his proposal simply

Source: Christopher Nagy/Shutterstock.

by appealing to the value of developing a reputable firm such as Pinsky Corporation as a large customer. He had to make a case for accepting a lower price by comparing the price with the incremental costs (or revenues) of producing the springs. The incremental cost per unit of a product is the amount by which the total costs of production and sales increase when one additional unit of that product is produced and sold.

"It is true that the full cost of the 0.50-inch springs is $2.79, but that includes $0.65 of manufacturing support costs. We know that manufacturing support costs consist of rent, depreciation, insurance, heating and lighting, janitorial services, and so on. These are committed costs and will not increase if we accept Pinsky's order. So the only costs we need to consider are materials and labor, which add up to only $2.14. Even at a price of $2.48, we can earn a margin of $0.34 per pound," Myriah explained.

"Myriah is right about rent, depreciation, and insurance being committed cost," replied Robert. "But such committed costs are only 60% of our total manufacturing support at present. Support activities also include supervision, setups, and inspection, whose costs will increase if we accept the Pinsky order. Variable manufacturing costs for the 0.50-inch springs are $1.38 direct materials, $0.76 direct labor, and $0.26 variable support activity costs. This adds up to $2.40 of variable costs, so it seems we would have a contribution margin of $0.08 per pound. But that is before we consider selling and distribution costs, which will, I believe, add another $0.23 to the variable costs of the 0.50-inch springs. I figure the total variable costs to be $2.63 per pound, which is more than the offer of only $2.48 per pound."

Myriah asked, "Well, should we counter Pinsky's offer by suggesting that we would accept it for a $2.70 price? That would earn us a contribution margin of $0.07 per pound by your calculations."

Before Robert could respond, Wendy interrupted the discussion: "I'm very confused by all this talk about only variable costs. Costs are costs. I pay for rent and insurance just as I pay our workers and our suppliers. If our customers don't pay me a price that covers all our costs—both fixed and variable—I can't possibly make money in this business."

ROLE OF PRODUCT COSTS IN PRICING AND PRODUCT MIX DECISIONS

The situation at High Performance Springs exists at most firms whose managers make decisions about establishing or accepting a price for their products. Managers need to determine whether they should offer discounts for large orders or to valued customers. Understanding how to analyze product costs is important for making such pricing decisions. Even when prices are set by overall market supply and demand forces and the firm has little or no influence on product prices, management still has to decide the best mix of products to manufacture and sell. This mix has to take into account the products' market prices, costs, and margins (price less relevant costs) as well as their use of capacity resources.

Product cost analysis also is significant when a firm is deciding how best to deploy marketing and promotion resources, including how much commission (or how many other incentives) to provide the sales force for different products and how large a discount to offer off list prices. This chapter explores some of the more traditional methods of pricing and considers short- and long-run factors.

Short-Term and Long-Term Pricing Considerations

Managers must consider both the short-term and long-term consequences of their decisions. Recall that the costs of many resources committed to activities are likely to be fixed (committed) costs in the short term because firms cannot easily alter the capacities made available for many production and support activities. Consequently, for short-term decisions, it is important to pay special attention to whether surplus capacity is available for additional production or whether shortages of available capacity limit additional production alternatives.

Of special concern when evaluating a particular order is how long a firm must commit its production capacity to fill that order. The length of time is relevant because a long-term capacity commitment to a marginally profitable order may prevent the firm from deploying its capacity for more profitable products or orders, should demand for them arise in the future. Such a commitment could also force the firm to add expensive new capacity to handle future sales increases.

If production is constrained by inadequate capacity, managers need to consider whether overtime production or the use of subcontractors can help augment capacity in the short term. In the long term, managers have considerably more flexibility to adjust the capacities of activity resources to match the demand for them in producing various products. Decisions about whether to introduce new products or eliminate existing products have long-term consequences. Therefore, the emphasis here is on analyzing how such product decisions will affect the demand placed on the firm's capacity resources.

Decisions can be classified on the basis of whether the firm can influence the price of its products. If the firm is one of a large number of firms in an industry and if there is little to distinguish the products of different firms from each other, economic theory states that prices will be set by the aggregate market forces of supply and demand. Thus, no single firm can influence prices significantly by its own decisions. For example, in commodity businesses such as grains, meat, and sugar, traders in the commodity markets set prices on the basis of industry supply and demand. Similarly, if prices are set by one or more large firms leading an industry, a small firm on the fringe must match the prices set by the industry leaders. In such a situation, a small firm is a **price taker** because it chooses its product mix given the prices set in the marketplace for its products.

Exhibit 6-1
Classification
of Pricing and
Product Mix
Decisions

Decision Type	Price-Taker Firm	Price-Setter Firm
Short-term decisions	1	2
Long-term decisions	4	3

In contrast, firms in an industry with relatively little competition that enjoy large market shares and exercise leadership in that industry must decide what prices to set for their products. Firms in industries in which products are highly customized or otherwise differentiated from each other (because of special features, characteristics, or customer service) also need to set the prices for their differentiated products. Such firms are **price setters**. Once price setters announce their prices, customers place orders and production follows.

Four different situations are presented in this chapter (see Exhibit 6-1). The following section considers the short-term product mix decision of a price taker (quadrant 1 in Exhibit 6-1). An analysis of short-term pricing decisions for a price setter (quadrant 2) and an examination of long-term benchmark prices for a price setter (quadrant 3) follow. The price-taker firm is also considered, including how it evaluates the long-term profitability of its products and customers (quadrant 4).

IN PRACTICE

Does CD Pricing Affect Piracy in the Music Industry?

Since Steve Jobs, chief executive officer of Apple, opened Apple Computer's online iTunes store in 2003, more than 600 million songs have been legally downloaded. Apparently, customers believe that $0.99 is a fair price to pay for an individual song since the rate of illegal music downloading has slowed significantly. However, iTunes pricing structure may soon be changing. In May 2005, it was reported that the one-price-fits-all structure may be on its way out and that in its place a new pricing structure in which different prices would be charged for different songs could be implemented. One implication is that new popular releases may now cost more than a dollar, whereas older titles could cost less. Steve Jobs has long resisted this change

since the system is simple to use and understand and the value proposition for customers is compelling. Many industry executives, however, have made multiple arguments for flexible pricing. They argue that almost all retail businesses have different price points for different products. But they are particularly interested in boosting their revenue from digital music sales, which, aided by the sale of mobile phone ring tones, are increasing but not quickly enough to replace the continuing drops in compact disc sales. As an example, EMI, one of the major music labels, has stated that digital sales made up 4.9% of the company's sales in the past 6 months, up from 2.1% a year ago. So will increases in prices for new releases lead to more piracy?

Source: Paul Sakuma/AP Wide World Photos.

SHORT-TERM PRODUCT MIX DECISIONS: PRICE TAKERS

Production decisions by a firm with a very small market share in its industry have little impact on the overall industry supply and demand or on the prices of the firm's products. Such is the case in high-volume manufacturing industries in which the products are standardized and little chance exists to differentiate the products of one firm from those of another (for example, steel, commodity chemicals, pharmaceuticals, gypsum wall board, and low-end copier machines). The aggregate production decisions of all the firms determine prices in such industries. If a few firms dominate, their decisions influence the prices.

A small firm (or a firm with a negligible market share in this industry) behaves as a price taker. It takes the industry prices for its products as given and then decides how many units of each product it should produce and sell. If the small firm demands a higher price for any of its products, it risks losing its customers to other competing firms in the industry unless it can successfully differentiate its products by offering special features or services. Conversely, if the small firm seeks to increase its market share by asking a price lower than the industry prices, it risks a retaliatory reduction in prices from its competitors. Lowering the price might result in a price war that would make the firm—and the entire industry—worse off than if the firm had complied with industry prices. This action is particularly painful to smaller firms that have fewer resources to rely on should an unprofitable price war occur.

A price taker should produce and sell as much as it can of all products whose costs are less than its prices. Although this may appear to be a simple decision rule, two important considerations complicate matters. First, managers must decide which costs are relevant to the short-term product mix decision. Should all the product costs identified in chapter 3 be considered, or only those costs that vary in the short term? Second, in the short term, managers may have little flexibility to alter the capacities of some of the firm's resources. For example, the available equipment capacity may limit the ability of a firm to produce and sell more products whose costs are lower than its prices.

Consider Chunling Company, located in Hong Kong, which sells ready-made garments to discount stores such as Kmart and Wal-Mart. The plant manufactures five types of garments: shirts, dresses, skirts, blouses, and trousers. Exhibit 6-2 presents budgeted production for the third quarter of 2006. The exhibit also displays the minimum sales quantities of each type of garment that must be supplied under long-term contracts with various retail stores. The sales manager has estimated the maximum sales quantities shown in the last column. His estimates are based on his assessment of the number of orders that can be obtained for delivery in the third quarter of 2006.

Exhibit 6-3 shows unit costs for the five products. Direct material costs are based on estimated materials requirements and their estimated prices. Workers who cut, stitch, and pack are paid on a piece-rate basis. For example; column 2 (shirts) shows that workers are paid $1 for cutting, $0.80 for stitching, and $0.05 for packing one

Exhibit 6-2
Chunling Company: Budgeted Production in Quantities for 2006 (Quarter 3)

GARMENT TYPE	BUDGETED PRODUCTION	MINIMUM SALES	MAXIMUM SALES
Blouses	15,000	5,000	15,000
Trousers	8,000	4,000	9,000
Dresses	5,000	2,000	8,000
Skirts	10,000	6,000	16,000
Shirts	12,000	6,000	14,000
Total units	50,000	23,000	62,000

Exhibit 6-3
Chunling Company Product Costs per Unit

	SHIRTS	DRESSES	SKIRTS	BLOUSES	TROUSERS
Direct materials:					
Textile	$1.80	$6.00	$4.00	$2.00	$4.50
Supplies	0.20	0.90	0.60	0.40	0.60
Total	$2.00	$6.90	$4.60	$2.40	$5.10
Direct labor:					
Cutting	1.00	1.50	1.00	1.00	1.00
Stitching	0.80	1.80	1.00	0.80	1.00
Inspection	0.15	0.15	0.15	0.15	0.15
Packing	0.05	0.05	0.05	0.05	0.05
Total	$2.00	$3.50	$2.20	$2.00	$2.20
Manufacturing support:					
Utilities	0.03	0.03	0.03	0.03	0.03
Plant administration	0.04	0.04	0.04	0.04	0.04
Machine maintenance	0.02	0.02	0.02	0.02	0.02
Machine depreciation	0.04	0.04	0.04	0.04	0.04
Facility maintenance	0.04	0.04	0.04	0.04	0.04
Facility depreciation	0.03	0.03	0.03	0.03	0.03
Total	$0.20	$0.20	$0.20	$0.20	$0.20
Total product cost per unit	$4.20	$10.60	$7.00	$4.60	$7.50

Exhibit 6-4
Chunling
Company:
Machine Hour
Requirements

GARMENT TYPE	MACHINE HOURS PER UNIT	PRODUCTION IN UNITS	TOTAL MACHINE HOURS REQUIRED
Blouses	0.4	15,000	6,000
Trousers	0.5	8,000	4,000
Dresses	0.8	5,000	4,000
Skirts	0.5	10,000	5,000
Shirts	0.4	12,000	4,800
Total		50,000	23,800

shirt. Inspection labor costs total $7,500 per quarter and are assigned to products at the rate of $0.15 per garment. Support activity costs total $10,000 each quarter and are assigned to the 50,000 units budgeted for production at the rate of $0.20 per unit.

Production is limited by the 23,800-machine-hour capacity of the garment manufacturing machines. Exhibit 6-4 displays the number of machine hours required to produce each garment. Note the considerable differences in the required machine time, ranging from 0.4 hour for one shirt or blouse to 0.8 hour for one dress. The planned production for the third quarter of 2006 is to use all 23,800 machine hours currently available.

With these data, we can evaluate the profitability of the different products and decide the production levels for the five products that will maximize profits for the Chunling Company for the third quarter of 2006. Since Chunling is contemplating short-term adjustments to its product mix, it is necessary to determine what costs will vary with production levels in this period and then what costs will remain fixed when a change occurs in the production mix.

Clearly, the costs of direct materials and direct labor that is compensated on a piece-rate basis vary with the quantity of each garment produced. Inspectors are paid a monthly fixed salary, but they are employed as required to support the production of different garments. If production increases, Chunling may have to hire more inspectors. Therefore, inspection labor costs also vary with quantity of production of different garments.

In contrast, the costs of utilities, plant administration, maintenance, and depreciation for the machinery and plant facility will not change with a change in the product mix because the plant is operating at its full capacity. This analysis assumes that these support activity costs are fixed.

The contribution from each of the garments to the firm's profits is determined by subtracting the variable costs from the price of the product. Exhibit 6-5 displays the contribution per unit for the five products, all of which have a positive contribution margin. If its capacity were unlimited, Chunling could produce garments to fill the maximum demand for them. Capacity is constrained, however, and therefore the company must decide how best to deploy this limited resource, as will be discussed.

The total budgeted contribution of $141,600 ($12,000 + $24,000 + $22,000 + $54,000 + $29,600) for the budgeted production is obtained by multiplying the contribution per unit by the budgeted production quantity for each product and adding them (see Exhibit 6-5). The budgeted profit is $131,600 ($141,600 – $10,000 committed cost).

Notice that the contribution per unit, or price per unit less variable costs per unit, is highest for dresses ($4.80). Does that mean that dresses are the most profitable product and that Chunling should produce as many dresses as it can possibly sell? No, because in this case production is limited by the available machine capacity. The capacity is fixed in the short term, so Chunling must plan production to maximize the contribution to profit earned for every available machine hour used. Therefore, Chunling should rank the products not by their contribution per unit but by their contribution per machine hour.

Exhibit 6-5
Chunling Company: Contribution Margins

Garment Type	Shirts	Dresses	Skirts	Blouses	Trousers
Price per unit	$5.00	$15.20	$9.00	$8.00	$11.00
Variable costs per unit:					
Textiles	$1.80	$6.00	$4.00	$2.00	$4.50
Supplies	0.20	0.90	0.60	0.40	0.60
Cutting labor	1.00	1.50	1.00	1.00	1.00
Stitching labor	0.80	1.80	1.00	0.80	1.00
Inspection labor	0.15	0.15	0.15	0.15	0.15
Packing labor	0.05	0.05	0.05	0.05	0.05
Total variable costs	$4.00	$10.40	$6.80	$4.40	$7.30
Contribution per unit	$1.0	$4.80	$2.20	$3.60	$3.70
Machine hours per unit	0.4	0.8	0.5	0.4	0.5
Contribution per machine hour	$2.50	$6.00	$4.40	$9.00	$7.40
Budgeted production	12,000	5,000	10,000	15,000	8,000
Total budgeted contributions	$12,000	$24,000	$22,000	$54,000	$29,600

This plant works at full capacity to manufacture different apparel in time for the busy sales season. Since the plant capacity cannot be increased readily at short notice, the company evaluates the profitability of different products in the rank order of their contribution per machine hour.

Source: Brownie Harris/CORBIS/Bettmann.

Contribution per machine hour is obtained by dividing the contribution per unit by the number of machine hours per unit. Notice in Exhibit 6-5 that blouses have the highest contribution per machine hour ($9); therefore, Chunling should produce a total of 15,000 blouses, the maximum quantity that it can sell in the third quarter of 2006 (see Exhibit 6-2). Trousers have the next highest contribution per machine hour

Exhibit 6-6
Chunling Company: Production Quantities Required to Maximize Profits

Garment Type	Minimum Quantity	Machine Hours Required		Additional Quanitity	Machine Hours Required
Blouses	5,000	2,000	$5,000 \times 0.4$	10,000	4,000
Trousers	4,000	2,000	$2,000 \times 0.5$	5,000	2,500
Dresses	2,000	1,600	$2,000 \times 0.8$	6,000	4,800
Skirts	6,000	3,000	$6,000 \times 0.5$	3,000	1,500
Shirts	6,000	2,400	$6,000 \times 0.4$	0	0
Total	23,000	11,000			12,800

($7.40), so Chunling should produce a total of 9,000 trousers, the maximum it can sell in this quarter. Chunling should continue to decide which products to make by ranking the products by contribution per machine hour. After taking into account existing sales orders, it should make the most profitable products up to the maximum sales potential until it exhausts the entire available machine capacity.

Exhibit 6-6 displays the production quantities that maximize profits in the short term. The minimum production for the five products required under existing sales contracts requires a total of 11,000 machine hours (see column 3). This leaves a balance of 12,800 machine hours of capacity (23,800 − 11,000), which is sufficient to produce the maximum quantities of blouses, trousers, and dresses that Chunling can sell. These three products rank the highest in terms of their contribution per machine hour. The remaining capacity of 1,500 machine hours [12,800 − (4,000 + 2,500 + 4,800)] is not adequate to produce the maximum possible quantity of skirts, the next highest ranked product. This remaining capacity is sufficient for the production of only 3,000 (1,500 ÷ 0.5) additional skirts. No machine capacity remains for the production of any additional shirts, the product with the lowest contribution per machine hour.

To summarize, the available machine capacity should be allocated to the five garments shown in the final production plan in Exhibit 6-7. This production plan yields a profit of $141,500, which is $9,900 (about 7.5%) more than the $131,600 profit ($141,600 − $10,000) that Chunling would earn with the original production plan.

This example illustrates the basic principle used to make short-term product mix decisions when prices are unaffected by the quantities sold. With price predetermined, the only short-term decision faced by the manufacturer is how much of each possible product it should produce. The contribution margin per unit of the constrained resource, which is machine hours in this example, is the criterion used to decide which products are most profitable to produce and sell at the prevailing prices.

The Impact of Opportunity Costs

Consider next a variation of our analysis so far. Suppose a new customer that Chunling did not include in its earlier sales forecasts wishes to place an order for 2,000 shirts and is willing to pay a price higher than $5 each for this order. How high must the price be to make it profitable for Chunling to accept this special order?

If Chunling produces more shirts, its out-of-pocket costs will increase in the short term by the amount of the variable costs of the 2,000 shirts, but a simple comparison of the price with the variable costs shown in Exhibit 6-5 is not adequate for this decision. Because its production capacity is limited, Chunling must cut back the production of some other garment to enable it to produce 2,000 additional shirts.

Exhibit 6-7
Chunling
Company Final
Production Plan

GARMENT TYPE	PRODUCTION QUANTITY EXHIBIT 6-6: MINIMUM/ ADDITIONAL QUANTITIES	TOTAL MACHINE HOURS EXHIBIT 6-4		TOTAL CONTRIBUTION EXHIBIT 6-5 CONTIBUTION PER UNIT	
Blouses	15,000	6,000	15,000 × 0.4	$54,000	15,000 × $3.60
Trousers	9,000	4,500	9,000 × 0.5	33,300	9,000 × $3.70
Dresses	8,000	6,400	8,000 × 0.8	38,400	8,000 × $4.80
Skirts	9,000	4,500	9,000 × 0.5	19,800	9,000 × $2.20
Shirts	6,000	2,400	6,000 × 0.4	6,000	6,000 × $1.00
Total	47,000	23,800		$151,500	
Less: fixed costs				10,000	
Profit				$141,500	

Giving up the production of some profitable product results in an opportunity cost, which equals the lost profit on the garments that Chunling can no longer make.

Each shirt requires 0.4 machine hour, so the new order for 2,000 shirts requires a total of 800 machine hours (see Exhibit 6-4). To find the capacity of 800 machine hours required to produce the additional shirts, Chunling must forgo a part of the production of some other garment. How should Chunling decide which garment's production to sacrifice? Clearly, it should make the decision that minimizes the opportunity cost. Therefore, Chunling should sacrifice the product currently being produced that has the lowest contribution per unit of the constrained resources.

We know from our earlier ranking of the products that of all the products whose production exceeds the minimum required, skirts have the lowest contribution per machine hour (see Exhibit 6-5). To make the special order, Chunling must sacrifice 800 machine hours for the production of skirts. Because each skirt requires 0.5 machine hour, Chunling would be giving up producing 1,600 skirts. Each skirt contributes $2.20, so cutting back the production of 1,600 skirts causes a sacrifice of $3,520 in profits ($2.20 × 1,600).

An alternative is available for checking that the opportunity cost is $3,520. The contribution margin per machine hour is $4.40 for skirts, and a cutback of 800 machine hours of production of skirts results in a sacrifice of $3,520 of profits ($4.40 × 800).

The cost implication of producing an additional order of 2,000 shirts are now clear:

COST	PER UNIT	TOTAL
Variable cost	$4.00	$8,000
Opportunity cost	1.76	3,520
Total	$5.76	$11,520

Incremental costs (or revenues) are defined as the amount by which costs (or revenues) increase if one particular decision is made instead of another. Therefore, if Chunling does not charge a price of at least $5.76 per shirt, the incremental costs, including opportunity costs, will exceed the incremental revenues from this order, and Chunling will be worse off as a result. The lowest price that should be acceptable to Chunling is $11,520 for the order, or $5.76 per shirt.

Also notice that if the price of a shirt is $5.76, the contribution margin per machine hour is $4.40 [($5.76 − $4.00) ÷ 0.4], per the same as that for skirts, whose production is cut back. The basic principle to understand is that Chunling must earn at least as much contribution margin per machine hour on the new order as it must sacrifice on the alternative that it must give up.

SHORT-TERM PRICING DECISIONS: PRICE SETTERS

Thus far, this chapter has examined the way managers should adjust their product mix in the short term when the marketplace has determined what prices they can charge for their products. For such firms, known as price takers (see quadrant 1 of Exhibit 6-1), the relevant costs for the product mix decision are the short-run variable cost plus any opportunity cost of forgone alternatives.

In many businesses, potential customers request that suppliers bid a price for an order before they decide on the supplier with whom they will place the order. This section examines the relationship between costs and prices bid by a supplier for special orders that do not involve long-term relationships with the customer.

Consider Tudor Rose Tools and Dies Company in Cleveland, Ohio. Tudor Rose manufactures customized steel tools and dies for a wide variety of manufacturing businesses. A new customer, Pyro Industries of Ontario, has asked for a bid on a set of customized tools.

On the basis of the tool design, production engineers determine the routing through different production departments and estimate the quantity of different materials required for the order and the number of labor hours required in each department. This information is used to prepare a job bid sheet, as described in chapter 3. Then Tudor Rose uses this information and materials prices and labor wage rates to estimate the direct materials and direct labor costs displayed in Exhibit 6-8. Support activity costs are assigned to the job on the basis of activity cost drivers and the corresponding activity cost driver rates, as described in chapter 4.

The full costs for the job—that is, the sum of all direct materials, direct labor, and support activity costs—are estimated to be $28,500, consisting of $8,400 of direct materials, $9,900 of direct labor, and $10,200 of support activity costs. Setting the price of a product also means determining a markup percentage above cost, an approach known as cost-plus pricing. The markup percentage is determined by a company's desired profit margin and overall rate of return.[1] Tudor Rose has decided that rate is normally to be 40% of full costs.

Exhibit 6-8
Tudor Rose Tools and Dies: Company Job Cost Estimate

Direct materials:		
Steel		$8,400
Direct labor:		
Lathe	$2,600	
Grinding	3,200	
Machining	4,100	9,900
Manufacturing support:		
Supervision	$3,400	
Batch-related	3,700	
Facility-sustaining	3,100	10,200
Total costs		$28,500
Markup (40%)		11,400
Bid price		$39,900

---

[1] There are two traditional methods used to determine the cost base. Companies that use variable costing sum all variable costs of manufacturing and base their markup on total variable manufacturing costs. Those using full absorption costing sum all variable and fixed manufacturing costs and base their markup percentage on total manufacturing costs. The markup percentage is often determined using an algorithm based on a rate of return concept.

If Pyro Industries were a regular customer, the bid price would have been $39,900 (1.40 × $28,500). However, for this special order from a new customer, what is the minimum acceptable price? It turns out that one of the critical factors to consider is the level of available capacity.

The two distinct cases in the following sections analyze Tudor Rose's pricing decision when there is surplus machine capacity available in the short term to complete the production of the job. The cases are followed by an examination of the decision when the existing demand for Tudor Rose's services already uses all available capacity and the only way to manufacture the customized tools for Pyro Industries is by working overtime or adding an extra shift.

Available Surplus Capacity

Tudor Rose will incur direct material costs of $8,400 to produce customized tools for Pyro Industries. Tudor Rose pays direct production labor on an hourly basis; therefore, these costs will increase by $9,900 if the company accepts the Pyro order. In addition, batch-related costs will increase by $3,700 because a new production batch is needed for the customized tools. The costs of supervision and facility-sustaining support activities, however, will not increase if additional capacity of these resources is available to meet the production needs of the Pyro Industries order. Tudor Rose's incremental costs are as follows:

Direct material	$8,400
Direct labor	9,900
Batch-related support activities	3,700
Total incremental costs	$22,000

For the job to be profitable, the price that Tudor Rose should charge Pyro Industries must cover these incremental costs. In other words, the minimum

Source: Adapted from Energy Information Administration, *A Primer on Gasoline Prices (July 2001 Update)* www/eia.doe.gov. *Source*: Paul Sakuma/AP Wide World Photos.

acceptable price is $22,000 when surplus production capacity is available. This is the price at which Tudor Rose will break even on the Pyro Industries order. In practice, Tudor Rose will add a profit margin above incremental costs, and the bid price will be higher than $22,000, depending on competitive and demand conditions. In summary, when excess capacity exists, the minimum acceptable price must at least cover the incremental costs that the company will incur to produce and deliver the order.

No Available Surplus Capacity

If surplus machine capacity is not available, Tudor Rose will have to incur additional costs to acquire the necessary capacity. Tudor Rose often meets such short-term capacity requirements by operating its plant overtime, paying its supervisors overtime wages, and incurring additional expenditures for heating, lighting, cleaning, and security. In addition, more machine maintenance and plant engineering activities will be necessary, as past experience has shown that the incidence of machine breakdowns increases during the overtime shift. Under its machinery leasing contract, Tudor Rose also incurs additional rental costs for the extra use of machines when it adds an overtime shift.

Tudor Rose management estimates the amounts of incremental supervision costs (including overtime premium) for the Pyro order at $5,100 and the incremental business-sustaining costs at $5,400. Thus, the total costs are $10,500 ($5,100 + $5,400) if overtime is required to manufacture customized tools for Pyro Industries. Therefore, the minimum acceptable price in this case is $32,500 ($22,000 + $10,500). The actual price will depend on the amount of markup over the incremental costs charged by the Tudor Rose Tools and Dies Company.

The principle illustrated here is the same as that described in the previous case. The minimum acceptable price still must cover all incremental costs, but when the firm must acquire additional capacity to satisfy the order, more incremental costs are involved in the decision to accept or reject the order. In deciding whether to accept the Pyro Industries order and what price to charge for the special order, Tudor Rose must consider the appropriate incremental costs, depending on whether surplus production capacity is available. The incremental costs are the relevant costs for such short-run decisions.

LONG-TERM PRICING DECISIONS: PRICE SETTERS

Price-setter firms make long-term pricing decisions, as indicated in quadrant 3 of Exhibit 6-1. It is important to note that the relevant costs for the short-term special order pricing decision differ from the full costs of the job reported in Exhibit 6-8. Full costs include the direct materials, direct labor, and support activity costs assigned based on normal activity cost driver rates. Is there any benefit to reporting this information about full costs to managers who are responsible for the firm's pricing decisions?

In fact, most firms rely on full-cost information reports when setting prices. Typically, the accounting department provides cost reports to the marketing department, which adds appropriate markups to the costs to determine benchmark or target prices for all products normally sold by the firm.

There is economic justification for using full costs for pricing decisions in three types of circumstances:

Most of the cost of providing guest accomodations in a hotel are fixed—a hotel's incremental costs are tied mainly to linen services. Therefore, during off season in resort areas, hotels often cut their prices significantly to attract customers. Even at these lower prices, a hotel can cover its incremental costs and provide a contribution toward covering committed cost. Hotels that have peak and off-peak periods plan to recover most of their committed costs through the prices they charge peak-use customers.

Source: Mandarin Oriental Hotel Group Limited.

1. Many contracts for the development and production of customized products and many contracts with governmental agencies specify that prices should equal full costs plus a markup. Prices set in regulated industries also are based on full costs.
2. When a firm enters into a long-term contractual relationship with a customer to supply a product, it has great flexibility in adjusting the level of commitment for all resources. Therefore, most activity costs will depend on the production decisions under the long-term contract, and full costs are relevant for the long-term pricing decision.
3. The third situation is representative of many industries. Most firms make short-term adjustments in prices, often by offering discounts from list prices instead of rigidly employing a fixed price based on full costs. When demand for their products is low, firms recognize the greater likelihood of surplus capacity in the short term. Accordingly, they adjust the prices of their products downward to acquire additional business on the basis of the lower incremental costs they incur when surplus capacity is available. Conversely, when demand for their products is high, they recognize the greater likelihood that the existing capacity of activity resources is inadequate to satisfy all the demand. Thus, they adjust the prices upward on the basis of the higher incremental costs they incur when capacity is fully utilized. The higher prices serve to ration the available capacity to the highest profit opportunity.

IN PRACTICE
Choosing Telecommunications Packages

Deciding on a telecommunications package has become a major household decision. It was not that long ago that telephone providers were distinct from those who supplied cable television, and Internet access was delivered through telephone lines. Today, companies compete aggressively to provide video, telephone, and high-speed Internet services, with many service providers offering numerous bundles of services.

Pricing has also become much more complicated and consumers spend a great deal of time trying to sort out the trade-offs among all available options. For example, consider the debate concerning whether cable television is still of superior value compared to satellite television.

Proponents of cable systems state the following advantages over satellite systems:

- While it is true that all television providers carry a large number of national channels, the number of local channels remains very limited for satellite customers.
- Even though satellite systems offer high-speed Internet service, their capacities and capabilities are limited by the underlying technology and relatively slow download speed and more limited upload speed.
- Some cable providers also offer telephone and cost-saving telecommunications packages that come with one bill, something satellite TV is unable to offer at this point.

Mark Goldstein, president of International Research, an independent, strategic research organization, states, "While satellite services appear to have some price and channel advantages in the short term, including the most channels at the lowest monthly rates for their basic video packages, a number of factors also tend to favor cable."

Proponents of satellite TV state that satellite provides more channels per dollar, and over the past 5 years, cable prices have risen 35% while satellite prices have risen only 10%. Satellite television is delivered with 100% digital quality, while cable's basic and expanded basic services are all analog. Even when a customer upgrades to digital cable, the analog channels will remain analog. For example, if ESPN has an inferior picture, the picture will remain inferior even if a customer upgrades to digital. Satellite systems have greater bandwidth and can carry more total programming than many cable stations (although this is beginning to change as more cable stations go digital).

One thing is for certain: As technology improves and competition gets even fiercer, consumers will vote with their dollars as they did when they ultimately chose VHS over Beta.

Source: Adapted from International Research Center, www.researchedge.com/news.

Because demand conditions fluctuate over time, prices also fluctuate with demand conditions over time. For example, demand in the hotel industry is lower on weekends than on weekdays. Therefore, most hotels offer special weekend rates that are considerably lower than their weekday rates. Many amusement parks offer lower prices on weekdays when demand is expected to be low. Airfares between New York and London are higher in summer, when the demand is higher, than in winter, when the demand is lower. Long-distance telephone rates are lower in the evenings and on the weekends, when the demand is lower.

Although fluctuating short-term prices are based on the appropriate incremental costs, over the long term their average tends to equal the price based on the full costs that will be recovered in a long-term contract (see Exhibit 6-9). In other words, the price determined by adding on a markup to the full costs of a product serves as a benchmark or target price from which the firm can adjust prices up or down depending on demand conditions. Most firms use full cost-based prices as target prices, giving sales managers limited authority to modify prices as required by the prevailing competitive conditions.

As noted, prices depend on demand conditions. Markups increase with the strength of demand. If more customers demand more of a product, the firm is able to command a higher markup. Markups also depend on the elasticity of demand. Demand is said to be elastic if customers are very sensitive to the price—that is, if a small increase in the price results in a large decrease in the demand. Markups are smaller when demand is more elastic. Markups also fluctuate with the intensity of competition. If competition is intense, it is more difficult for a firm to sustain a price much higher than its incremental costs. (See Appendix 6-1 for a formal economic analysis of the general pricing decision.)

To see how demand elasticity affects the pricing decision, consider the decision by Jim and Barry's Ice Cream Company to increase ice cream prices from $2.40 to $2.50 per gallon. When prices increase, the company expects the demand to decline from 80,000 gallons to 75,000 gallons. The incremental cost is $1.60 per gallon of ice cream. How much will the profits increase because of this price increase?

Contribution to profits from each gallon of ice cream increases from $0.80 ($2.40 – $1.60) to $0.90 ($2.50 – $1.60) with the increase in price. The price increase has two effects on profits: (1) It increases the contribution of the units sold (called the *income effect* by economists), but (2) it also decreases the number of units sold, and therefore

Exhibit 6-9
Short-term Prices Relative to Long-term Benchmark Price

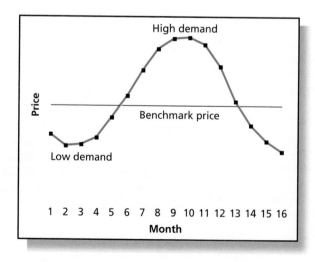

the contribution from each unsold unit is lost (called the *substitution effect* by economists). In this case, the increase in contribution is $0.10 per gallon ($0.90 − $0.80), or $7,500 ($0.10 × 75,000) for the 75,000 gallons of expected sales after the price increase. The decrease in contribution is $4,000 ($0.80 × 5,000) because of the 5,000-gallon decline in sales (80,000 − 75,000) of ice cream, which had a contribution margin of $0.80 per gallon prior to the price increase. Therefore, the net impact of the price increase on profits is an increase of $3,500 ($7,500 − $4,000).

If the demand were more elastic and sales were expected to decline by 10,000 gallons (to 70,000 gallons instead of 75,000 gallons), the higher-price markup would not be advisable. The increase in contribution of $7,000 ($0.10 × 70,000) would be more than offset by the decline of $8,000 ($0.80 × 10,000) because of the sharp decrease in sales. The price increase, therefore, would result in a net decrease of $1,000 ($7,000 − $8,000) in profits.

This example illustrates the important point that when demand is relatively inelastic, profits will usually increase when prices increase. When demand is elastic, however, the quantities sold will decrease sharply when prices increase and profits decrease.

Firms often lower markups for strategic reasons. A firm may choose a low markup for a new product to penetrate the market and win over market share from an established product of a competing firm. Many Internet businesses have adopted the strategy of setting low prices to build the business, acquire a brand name, build a loyal customer base, and garner market share. In contrast to this **penetration pricing strategy**, firms sometimes employ a **skimming price strategy**, as in the audio and video equipment industry, where initially a higher price is charged to customers who are willing to pay more for the privilege of possessing the latest technological innovations.

Companies such as Shell Oil purchase or lease offshore drilling platforms like this one with the belief that the average long-term price of oil products and the cost of alternative sources of crude oil will support its cost recovery.

Source: Simon Pedersen/ Shutterstock.

Quadrant 4 in Exhibit 6-1 represents a price-taker firm that is making long-term product mix decisions. Decisions to add a new product or to drop an existing product from the portfolio of products usually have significant long-term implications for the cost structure of a firm. Product-sustaining costs—such as product design and engineering, vendor and purchasing costs, part maintenance, and dedicated sales force costs—are relevant costs for such decisions. Batch-related costs—such as setups, materials handling, and first-item inspection (inspection of only the first few items in each batch)—also are likely to change if a change occurs in the product mix in favor of or against products manufactured in large batches.

Bear in mind, however, that managers cannot easily change the amount of resources committed for many product-sustaining and several batch-related activities in the short run. The cost consequences of either introducing a new product or deleting an existing product evolve over time because both decisions require careful implementation plans stretching over several periods. As a result, managers use the full costs of products, including the cost of using various resources to produce and sustain the product. Recall that such resources include the number of setup staff, the number of product and process engineers, and the number of quality inspectors. Managers use the costs of all resources in their product-related decisions because, in the long term, the firm is able to adjust the capacity of activity resources to match the resource levels demanded by the product quantities and mix.

Comparing product costs with their market prices reveals which products are not profitable in the long term when firms can adjust activity resource capacities to match production requirements. If some products have full costs that exceed the market price, the firm must consider several options. Although dropping these products appears to be an obvious option, it may be important to maintain a full product line to make it possible for customers to enjoy one-stop shopping for their orders. However, a comparison of the prices with costs still provides a valuable signal to managers because it indicates the net cost of the strategy to offer a full product line.

Managers also may consider other options, such as reengineering or redesigning unprofitable products, to eliminate or reduce costly activities and bring their costs in line with market prices. For example, they could improve the production processes to reduce setup times and streamline material and product flows. They also may want to explore market conditions more carefully and differentiate their products further to raise prices and bring them in line with the costs. Firms also can offer customers incentives, such as quantity discounts, to increase order sizes and thereby reduce total batch-related costs. If these steps fail and if the marketing strategy of offering such a full product line cannot justify the high net cost of such products, managers must consider a plan to phase out the products from their line. Customers also need to be shifted to substitute products still retained in the company's product line.

A caveat is in order, however. Dropping products will help improve profitability only if the managers (1) eliminate the activity resources no longer required to support the discontinued product or (2) redeploy the resources from the eliminated products to produce more of the profitable products that the firm continues to offer. Costs result from commitments to supply activity resources. Therefore, they do not disappear automatically with the dropping of unprofitable products. Only when companies eliminate or redeploy the resources themselves will actual expenses decrease.

In summary, capacity constraints are likely to be less of a concern for product mix decisions that have long-term effects because firms can adjust the level of

Congestion pricing or value pricing as it is sometimes known, is a controversial but potentially effective means to improve traffic flow and reduce congestion-related pollution. It entails using pricing in the form of fees or tolls during peak driving periods to create incentives for people to alter their travel behavior. Typically, fees are assessed electronically to eliminate delays associated with manual toll collection facilities. An inexpensive transponder is mounted to the car's windshield. Tolls are subtracted from a debit card in the transponder. For privacy, no records are kept of who travels where. All tolls can be assessed at normal driving speeds.

Congestion pricing is the same as that used in many other sectors of the economy to respond to peak-use demands. Airlines reduce their fares during off-peak periods, and the price of a hotel room increases during peak tourist seasons. Road use charges that vary with the level of congestion provide incentives to shift some trips to off-peak times, less congested routes, alternative modes, or to cause some lower-valued trips to be combined with other trips or to be eliminated. Many researchers strongly endorse road/congestion pricing as a potentially effective strategy to reduce single-operator vehicle travel while funding alternative transportation modes. Some believe that intelligent transportation system technologies, such as electronic toll collection, can facilitate such a strategy.

Value pricing is also designed to encourage ride sharing, mass transit, and less driving while improving traffic flow and reducing environmental pollution. For example, it has been estimated that pricing strategies would reduce auto emissions from four to eight times that of traditional transportation control measures.

London recently imposed an $8-per-day fee for any motorist driving into an oval cordon surrounding approximately 8 square miles of central London. Congestion pricing is being used to reduce the nightmarish motor vehicle traffic in central London. Critics of this program predicted that this would be the end of London mayor Ken Livingstone's political career. Instead of a disaster, the mayor has been hailed as a hero, and the program has been wildly successful, generating additional revenues for the city while dramatically reducing the traffic in the inner city. One group has estimated that average speeds in central London have doubled.

The London road pricing policy is one of the most significant recent efforts toward solving urban mobility problems within the context of a market economy. Basically, the London prescription is to make people pay for the convenience of their cars and

Source: De Agostini Editore Picture Library.

resources committed to most activities in the long run. As a result, a comparison of the price of a product with its activity-based costs provides a valuable evaluation of its long-run profitability.

HIGH PERFORMANCE SPRINGS REVISITED

Should High Performance Springs slash the price of its 0.50-inch springs from $3.63 per pound to $2.48 per pound to obtain business from a reputable customer, the Pinsky Corporation? Should it make a counteroffer of $2.70 instead to cover all its variable manufacturing and selling costs even though full costs amount to $2.79 per pound? How would High Performance cover the related costs if the selling price covers only the variable costs? These were some of the questions raised by Wendy Craven to her controller and marketing manager.

The concepts discussed in this chapter help us to answer these questions. Committed costs, such as product-sustaining or business-sustaining costs, can be ignored, and variable costs alone are relevant only for analyzing a short-term pricing decision for a period that is too short to adjust the company's resources. For long-term pricing decisions, the costs of many more resources are relevant because firms can adjust the supply of most resources over the long term. If firms set prices to cover only short-term variable costs, they cannot survive in the long term because the existence of costs associated with committed resources will lead to continued losses over the long term.

A case for a lower price for Pinsky could be made as a part of a penetration pricing strategy. However, High Performance Springs also must consider the reaction of both its existing customers, who may demand a lower price themselves when they learn that High Performance Springs discounts its regular prices for some customers, and its competitors, who may cut prices to respond to Precision's discounting.

SUMMARY

Managers use cost information to assist them in pricing and in product mix decisions. The manner in which they use cost information in making these decisions depends on whether the firm is a major or a minor entity in its industry. If the firm is a major entity, it would be able to influence the setting of prices. If it is a minor entity, the firm would take the industry prices as given and adjust its product mix in response to the prices it could charge. The role of cost information also depends on the time frame involved in the decision.

Business-sustaining costs are frequently relevant for long-term decisions but less often for short-term decisions.

Short-term prices are based on incremental costs that depend on the availability of activity resource capacity. If the capacity is likely to be fully utilized, the incremental costs of overtime and other means to obtain the additional required capacity are also relevant for the pricing decision. If the firm commits to a price under a long-term contract, the normal costs of all activity resources used in the manufacturing and selling of a product are relevant. Interestingly, a long-term price also can serve as a benchmark price around which actual prices may fluctuate when the firm can make short-term price adjustments, depending on the demand conditions prevailing at that point in time.

Short-term product mix decisions also require information on incremental costs that vary in the short term. If the capacity is limited for the short term, managers should use the contribution per unit of the limited capacity as the criterion to rank the products in the production plan. For long-term product mix decisions, managers rely on the full costs of products; such costs reflect the usage of the different activity resources required to design, sustain, produce, and sell the products.

Thus, the nature of the cost information required for pricing and product mix decisions depends on the time frame considered. Regardless of whether the firm is a price setter or a price taker, full cost information is more useful for long-term decisions. Short-term adjustments require information about costs that vary in the short run.

We should also note that for firms developing new, innovative products, market prices may not exist. The pricing of these products has to rely on a markup of product costs. If this is the case, product costs need to be very accurate, which meaning that an approach such as activity-based costing (discussed in chapter 5) should be used. Finally, some organizations use an approach known as target costing. Such organizations determine a target selling price and a target level of profit, and the cost to make the product—the target cost—results from the difference between the two. We will discuss this in the next chapter.

SUMMARY EXAMPLE

The following numerical example illustrates some important points discussed in this chapter. Faxtronics, Inc., is a Minnesota-based company that manufactures and sells two models (FM101 and FM102) of high-quality fax modem devices for which the following information is available:

	COSTS PER UNIT	
ITEM	FM101	FM102
Direct materials	$120	$160
Direct labor ($20 per hour)	50	80
Variable support		
($5 per machine hour)	20	40
Fixed support	20	20
Total costs per unit	$210	$300
Price per unit	$260	$400

Demand for the two models of fax modem devices has grown rapidly in recent years, and Faxtronics can no longer meet the demand with its current production capacity. At present, the monthly demand is 8,000 units for FM101 and 5,000 units for FM102. Monthly capacity is limited to 60,000 machine hours.

1. Determine the contribution margin per unit for each of the two products.
2. Determine the product mix that maximizes profits.

3. Suppose Faxtronics has received a special order from a new customer willing to buy 2,000 units of FM101 at $300 each. What is the opportunity cost associated with this order?

Should Faxtronics accept this order?

The solutions to the review problem are as follows:

1. Contribution margin per unit:

ITEM	FM101	FM102
Selling price per unit	$260	$400
Variable costs per unit		
Direct materials	$120	$160
Direct labor	50	80
Variable support	20	40
Total variable costs per unit	$190	$280
Contribution margin per unit	$ 70	$120

2. Contribution margin per unit of the scarce resource:

ITEM	FM101	FM102
Contribution margin per unit of product	$70	$120
Number of machine hours per unit	4 (20 ÷ 5)	8 (40 ÷ 5)
Contribution margin per machine hour	$17.50	$ 15.00

With capacity fully utilized, FM101 is a more profitable product because it has a higher contribution margin per unit of the scarce resource (machine hours) than FM102. Therefore, Faxtronic should first satisfy all the demand for FM101 and then use the remaining machine hours of capacity to manufacture FM102. The optimal production plan is as follows:

8,000 units of FM101
3,500 units of FM102
[60,000 − (8,000 (4)] ÷ 8

3. Faxtronics has no surplus capacity available for the production of an additional 2,000 units of FM101, which requires 8,000 (2,000 × 4) machine hours. Because FM102 has the lowest contribution margin per machine hour, Faxtronics can make available the capacity (8,000 machine hours) necessary for the special order by reducing the production of FM102 by 1,000 units

(8,000 ÷ 8). The contribution margin for these 1,000 units of FM102 is $120 per unit. Therefore, the opportunity cost to make 2000 additional units of FM101 is $120 × 1,000 = $120,000.

4.

SPECIAL ORDER COSTS	AMOUNT	CALCULATION
Variable cost	$380,000	$190 × 2,000
Opportunity cost	120,000	
Relevant cost	$500,000	
Relevant cost per unit	$250	$500,000 ÷ 2,000

Therefore, Faxtronics should accept this order because the price of $300 is higher than the relevant cost of $250 per unit. Faxtronics will enjoy increased profits by $100,000 [($300 − $250) × 2,000] by accepting the special order.

Appendix 6-1

Economic Analysis of the Pricing Decision

Quantity Decision

This chapter considered a firm's decision about setting its products' prices to maximize its profits or, more broadly, about pursuing a strategic goal such as market penetration that would maximize its long-term profits. In contrast, introductory textbooks in economics usually analyze the profit maximization decision by a firm in terms of the choice of a quantity to produce. In turn, the quantity choice determines the price of the product in the marketplace.

This appendix contains a discussion of the economic analysis of the quantity choice before examining the pricing decision and presents the quantity choice in terms of equating marginal revenue and marginal cost. **Marginal revenue** is defined as the increase in revenue corresponding to a unit increase in the quantity produced and sold. **Marginal cost** is the increase in cost for a unit increase in the quantity produced and sold. If marginal revenue is greater than marginal cost, increasing the quantity by one unit will increase profit. If marginal revenue is less than the marginal cost, it is possible to increase profit by decreasing production. Therefore, management profit is maximized by choosing the production quantity where marginal revenue equals marginal cost.

Exhibit 6-10 depicts marginal analysis. The marginal revenue curve is decreasing because additional sales quantity is generated only by lowering prices to all buyers. The average revenue curve represents the price itself because average revenue equals total revenue divided by quantity. To obtain total revenue, it is necessary to multiply the price by the quantity. Marginal cost is depicted by a horizontal line because total cost is assumed to increase at a constant rate equal to the variable cost per unit.

Exhibit 6-10
Marginal Analysis of Profit-Maximizing Quantity Choice

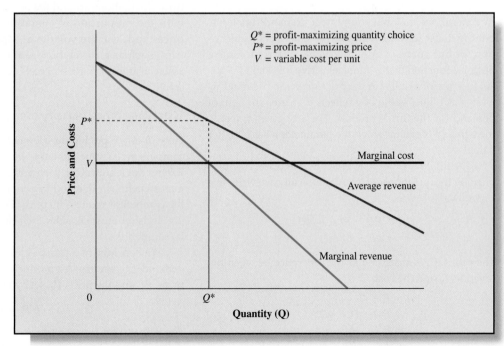

Q^* = profit-maximizing quantity choice
P^* = profit-maximizing price
V = variable cost per unit

To determine the profit-maximizing quantity, look for the intersection of the marginal revenue and marginal cost curves because marginal revenue equals marginal cost at the point of intersection. The profit-maximizing price is the average revenue corresponding to the profit-maximizing quantity.

In this analysis, the firm chooses the quantity level, and the market demand conditions determine the corresponding price. Consider next a firm that must choose a price, not a quantity, to announce to its customers. Customers then react to the price announced and determine the quantity they demand. In such a case, the analysis of the firm's pricing decision cannot be represented graphically as conveniently as in the analysis of the quantity decision previously discussed. Therefore, we shall use differential calculus to analyze the firm's pricing decision.

Pricing Decision

As discussed in chapter 2, the total costs, C, expressed in terms of its fixed and variable cost components, where f is the committed cost, v is the variable cost per unit, and Q is the quantity produced in units, are as follows:

$$C = f + vQ$$

Quantity produced is assumed to be the same as quantity demanded. The demand, Q, is represented as a decreasing linear function of the price P:

$$Q = a - bP$$

In general, we may have nonlinear demand functions, but the linear form provides a convenient characterization for our analysis. A higher value of b represents a demand function that is more sensitive (elastic) to price. An increase of a dollar in the price decreases demand by b units. A higher value of a reflects a greater strength of demand for the firm's product. For any given price, P, the demand is greater when the parameter a has a higher value.

The total revenue, R, is given by the price, P, multiplied by the quantity sold, Q. Algebraically, we write this as follows:

$$R = PQ = P(a - bP)$$
$$= aP - bP^2$$

The profit, Π, is measured as the difference between the revenue, R, and the cost, C:

$$\Pi = R - C$$
$$= PQ - (f + vQ)$$
$$= P^*(a - bP) - f - v(a - bP)$$
$$= aP - bP^2 - f - va + vbP$$

To find the profit-maximizing price, P^*, we set the first derivative of profit Π with respect to P equal to zero:

$$d\,\Pi/dP = a - 2bP + vb = 0$$

This equation implies the following:

$$P^* = (a + vb)/2b = a/2b + v/2$$

Long-Term Benchmark Prices

This simple economic analysis suggests that the price depends only on v, the variable cost per unit. Committed costs are not relevant for the pricing decision. A more complex analysis (not described here) that considers simultaneously the pricing decision and the long-term decisions of the firm to commit resources to facility-sustaining, product-sustaining, and other activity capacities indicates that the costs of these committed resources do play a role in the pricing decision. The costs of these committed activity resources appear to be committed costs in the short term, but they can be changed in the long term. The prices that a firm sets and adjusts in the short term, on the basis of changing demand conditions fluctuate around a long-term benchmark price, P^L, that reflects the unit costs of the activity resource capacities:

$$P^L = a/2b + (v + m)/2$$

Here, $m = f \div X$ is the cost per unit of normal capacity, X, of facility-sustaining activities. In this case, the degree of price fluctuations around the benchmark price increases with the proportion of committed costs. As a result, prices appear more volatile in capital-intensive industries, such as airlines, hotels, and petroleum refining, where a large proportion of costs are for facility-sustaining activities.

Competitive Analysis

How does the pricing decision change when other firms compete in the same industry with products that are similar but not identical? In such a situation, some customers may switch their demand to a competing supplier firm if the competitor reduces its price. Therefore, a firm's pricing decision must consider the prices that may be set by its competitors.

We consider two firms, A and B, and represent the demand, Q_A, for firm A's product as a function of its own price, P_A, and the price, P_B, set by its competitor:

$$Q_A = a - b\,P_A + eP_B$$

The demand for firm A's product falls by b units for each dollar increase in its own price but increases by e units for each dollar increase in the competitor's price because firm A gains some of the market demand that firm B loses.

The profit, P_A, for firm A is represented by the following:

$$\Pi_A = P_A Q_A - (f + vQ_A)$$
$$\Pi = P_A(a - bP_A + eP_B) - f - v(a - bP_A + eP_B)$$

Profit maximization requires this:

$$d\Pi_A/dP_A = a - 2bP_A + eP_B + vb = 0$$

Therefore, the profit-maximizing price $P_A{}^0$ given the other firm's price P_B is the following:

$$P_A^0 = (a + vb + eP_B) \div 2b$$

Thus, the pricing decision depends on what the competitor's price is expected to be. If the firm expects its competitor to behave as it does and expects it to choose the same price as its own, we set $P_A = P_B = P*$ in the equation $a - 2bP_A + eP_B + vb = 0$ to obtain the following:

$$a - 2bP* + eP* + vb = 0$$
$$P* = (a + vb)/(2b - e)$$

We refer to this price as the equilibrium price because, provided the other firm maintains the same price $P*$, no firm can increase its profits by choosing a different price. This analysis is based on a concept called the *Nash equilibrium*, for which its discoverer, John Nash, won the 1994 Nobel Prize in Economics.

KEY TERMS

Contribution per machine hour, 270	Incremental cost per unit, 264	Penetration pricing strategy, 279
Contribution per unit, 269	Marginal cost, 285	Price setter, 266
Cost-plus pricing, 273	Marginal revenue, 285	Price taker, 265
Full costs, 273	Markup percentage, 273	Skimming price strategy, 279

ASSIGNMENT MATERIALS

Questions

6-1 "Prices must cover both variable and fixed costs of production." Do you agree with this statement? Explain. (**LO 2, 3**)

6-2 Why is the evaluation of short-term pricing and product mix decisions different from the evaluation of long-term pricing and product mix decisions? (**LO 1, 2, 3, 4**)

6-3 What distinguishes a commodity-type business from other businesses? (**LO 1**)

6-4 What two considerations complicate short-term product mix decisions? (**LO 1, 2**)

6-5 What firms are likely to behave as price-taker firms? (**LO 1, 4**)

6-6 What firms are likely to behave as price-setter firms? (**LO 2, 3**)

6-7 "When production capacity is constrained, determine what products to make by ranking them in order of their contribution per unit." Do you agree with this statement? Explain. (**LO 1**)

6-8 "When production capacity is limited and it is possible to obtain additional customer orders, a firm must consider its opportunity costs to evaluate the profitability of these new orders." Do you agree with this statement? What are the opportunity costs in this context? (**LO 1, 2**)

6-9 What additional costs should a firm consider when making a short-term pricing decision when surplus production capacity is not available and it must employ overtime, extra shifts, subcontracting, or other means to augment the limited capacity? (**LO 1, 2**)

6-10 Should a firm consider facility-sustaining costs in making a short-run pricing decision? Give two examples to illustrate your answer. (**LO 1, 2**)

6-11 Describe three situations in which economics justifies using full costs for pricing decisions. (**LO 3**)

6-12 How do price markups over costs relate to the strength of demand, the elasticity of demand, and the intensity of competition? (LO 3)

6-13 Why do short-run prices fluctuate over time? (LO 1, 2)

6-14 What strategic reasons may influence the level of markups? (LO 3)

6-15 What options should firms consider when long-run market prices are below full costs? (LO 3, 4)

6-16 Why is full-cost information useful for long-run product mix decisions? (LO 3, 4)

Exercises

LO 2   **6-17** *Special order pricing*   Healthy Hearth specializes in lunches for the health conscious. The company produces a small selection of lunch offerings each day. The menu selections may vary from day to day, but Healthy Hearth charges the same price per menu selection because it adjusts the portion sizes according to the cost of producing the selection. Healthy Hearth currently sells 5,000 meals per month and has sufficient idle capacity to accommodate a recent special order from a government agency to provide 1,000 meals next month for senior citizens. Variable costs per meal are $3 per meal, and fixed costs total $5,000 per month. Volunteers will deliver the meals to the senior citizens at no charge. The government agency is offering to pay Healthy Hearth $3.50 per meal. What will be the impact on Healthy Hearth's operating income if it accepts this special order?

LO 2   **6-18** *Special order pricing*   McGee Corporation's Oympia plant produces a module used in automobile manufacturing. The company's practical capacity is 4,000 modules per week. The selling price is $900 per module. Production this quarter is 3,000 modules per week, and all the modules are sold each week. Demand is expected to remain steady. Total costs of production this week at the level of 3,000 modules were $300,000 of fixed costs plus $2,400,000 of variable costs.

     Suppose that a new customer's supplier has an emergency need for 1,500 modules to be delivered next week and that the plant cannot schedule overtime production. Consequently, McGee would have to give up some of its current sales to fill the new order. Total selling and administrative costs would not change if McGee accepts the order. What is the minimum price that McGee should charge for the new order?

LO 2   **6-19** *Special order pricing*   Shorewood Shoes Company makes and sells a variety of leather shoes for children. For its current mix of different models and sizes, the average selling price and costs per pair of shoes are as follows:

ITEM	AMOUNT
Price	$20
Costs:	
Direct materials	$6
Direct labor	4
Variable manufacturing support	2
Variable selling support	1
Fixed support	3
Total costs	$16

     Shoes are manufactured in batch sizes of 100 pairs. Each batch requires 5 machine hours to manufacture. The plant has a total capacity of 4,000 machine hours per month, but current month production consumes only about 80% of the capacity.

A discount store has approached Shorewood to buy 10,000 pairs of shoes next month. It has requested that the shoes bear its own private label. Embossing the private label will cost Shorewood an additional $0.50 per pair. However, no variable selling support cost will be incurred for this special order.

Determine the minimum price that Shorewood Shoes should charge for this order. What other considerations are relevant in this decision?

LO 1 **6-20 *Shelf mix decision*** Superstore is a large discount supermarket. Profits have declined, so the manager has collected data on revenues and costs for different food categories. The following data pertain to some of the frozen foods that Superstore sells. To facilitate comparisons, the manager has listed average price and cost information for each category in equivalent square-foot packages:

	ICE CREAM	JUICES	FROZEN DINNERS	FROZEN VEGETABLES
Selling price per unit (square-foot package)	$12.00	$13.00	$24.00	$9.00
Variable costs per unit (square-foot package)	$8.00	$10.00	$20.50	$7.00
Minimum square footage required	24	24	24	24
Maximum square footage allowed	100	100	100	100

The manager wants a maximum of 250 square feet devoted to the four categories in this table.

Required

a. Given the manager's constraints, and assuming that the store can sell whatever is displayed on the shelves, what shelf mix (what number of square feet for each category in the table) will maximize Superstore's contribution margin from these four categories?

b. What other factors might the manager consider in deciding on the amount of shelf space per category?

LO 1 **6-21 *Product mix decision*** Boyd Wood Company makes a regular and a deluxe grade of wood floors. Regular grade is sold at $16 per square yard, and the deluxe grade is sold at $25 per square yard. The variable cost of making the regular grade is $10 per square yard. It costs an extra $5 per square yard to make the deluxe grade. It takes 15 labor hours to make 100 square yards of the regular grade and 20 labor hours to make 100 square yards of the deluxe grade. There are 4,600 hours of labor time available for production each week. The maximum weekly sales for the regular and the deluxe model are 30,000 and 8,000 square yards, respectively. Fixed production costs total $600,000 per year. All selling costs are fixed. What is the optimal production level in number of square yards for each product?

LO 1, 4 **6-22 *Patient mix, ethics*** Willow Way Nursing Home, attempting to improve its profit, adopted a policy of welcoming only residents who are covered by private insurance or by Medicare or who have sufficient funds of their own to pay the nursing home fees. These groups of residents are clearly the most profitable for Willow Way, but a much larger number of potential residents are covered only by Medicaid, which pays a much lower fee per resident to nursing homes. Other nursing homes welcomed Medicaid patients, reasoning that having such patients covering some of the home's capacity costs was preferable to empty beds. Willow Way, however, turned away potential residents whose only coverage was through Medicaid and actively encouraged its employees to discharge current residents covered through Medicaid by paying a bonus per Medicaid resident discharged. Employees were also frequently asked to report on their efforts to discharge such residents.

Required

a. Evaluate Willow Way's approach to achieving profit for the nursing home and discuss ethical issues related to its admission and discharge policies.
b. What options are available to an employee who believes the nursing home's policies are unethical?

LO 2 **6-23** *Export order* Berry Company produces and sells 30,000 cases of fruit preserves each year. The following information reflects a breakdown of its costs:

COST ITEM	COSTS PER CASE	TOTAL COSTS
Variable production costs	$16	$480,000
Fixed production costs	8	240,000
Variable selling costs	5	150,000
Fixed selling and administrative costs	3	90,000
Total costs	$32	$960,000

Berry marks up its prices 40% over full costs. It has surplus capacity to produce 15,000 more cases. A French supermarket company has offered to purchase 10,000 cases of the product at a special price of $40 per case. Berry will incur additional shipping and selling costs of $3 per case to complete this order. What will be the effect on Berry's operating income if it accepts this order?

LO 1, 2 **6-24** *Extra shift decision* The manufacturing capacity of Ritter Rotator Company's plant facility is 60,000 rotators per quarter. Operating results for the first quarter of this year are as follows.

Sales (36,000 units at $10)	$360,000
Variable manufacturing and selling costs	198,000
Contribution margin	162,000
Fixed costs	99,000
Operating income	$63,000

A foreign distributor has offered to buy 30,000 units at $9 per unit during the second quarter of this year. Domestic demand is expected to remain the same as in the first quarter.

Required

a. Determine the impact on operating income if Ritter accepts this order. What other considerations are relevant in this decision?
b. Assume that Ritter decides to run an extra shift so that it can accept the foreign order without foregoing sales to its regular domestic customers. The proposed extra shift would increase capacity by 25% and increase fixed costs by $25,000. Determine the impact on operating income if Ritter operates the extra shift and accepts the export order. What other considerations are relevant in this decision?

LO 2, 3 **6-25** *Export order* Delta Screens Corporation is currently operating at 60% of capacity in producing 6,000 screens annually. Delta recently received an offer from a company in Germany to purchase 2,000 screens at $500 per unit. Delta has not previously sold products in Germany. Budgeted production costs for 6,000 and 8,000 screens follow:

	NUMBER OF UNITS PRODUCED	
COSTS	6,000	8,000
Direct materials	$750,000	$1,000,000
Direct labor	750,000	1,000,000
Support	2,100,000	2,400,000
Total costs	$3,600,000	$4,400,000
Full cost per unit	$600	$550

Delta has been selling its product at a markup of 10% above full cost. Delta's marketing manager believes that although the price offered by the German customer is lower than current prices, Delta should accept the order to gain a foothold in the German market. The production manager, however, believes that Delta should reject the order because the unit cost is higher than the price offered.

Required

a. Explain what causes the apparent decrease in cost from $600 per unit to $550 per unit when production increases from 6,000 to 8,000 units.

b. If the president of Delta Screens Corporation calls on you to resolve the difference in opinions, what will you recommend? Why?

LO 3   **6-26** *Pricing with elastic demand*   Sunny Valley Orchards is reevaluating the pricing of its fresh-squeezed orange juice in half-gallon containers. Variable costs per half-gallon container of fresh-squeezed orange juice are $1.50. Based on Sunny Valley's market study, the management has determined that the price per half gallon should be between $2.50 and $3. Management knows from past experience that demand is affected by price and estimates the demands shown in the following table for prices between $2.50 and $3. Considering only prices in increments of 5 cents, which price should Sunny Valley choose to maximize its contribution margin from sales of half-gallon fresh-squeezed orange juice?

PRICE PER HALF GALLON	ESTIMATED DEMAND (HALF-GALLON UNITS) AT GIVEN PRICE
$2.50	75,000
2.55	72,500
2.60	70,000
2.65	67,500
2.70	65,000
2.75	62,500
2.80	60,000
2.85	57,500
2.90	55,000
2.95	52,500
3.00	50,000

LO 3   **6-27 *Pricing and impact on demand***   Columbia Bicycle Company manufactures and sells 12 different models of bicycles. Columbia is contemplating a 5% price cut across the board for all 12 models. It expects the price cut to result in an 8% increase in the number of units sold of models M124, M126, M128, W124, W126, and W128. Columbia expects the other six models (B112, B116, B120, G112, G116, and G120) to experience a 4% increase in the number of units sold.

The following are the sales prices, variable costs, and sales volume (units) at present. Assess the impact of the price cut on Columbia's profits:

MODEL	SALES PRICE	VARIABLE COSTS	SALES VOLUME
B112	$60	$30	3,000
B116	70	33	4,500
B120	80	36	5,000
G112	60	30	4,000
G116	70	33	4,000
G120	80	36	4,000
M124	100	42	5,000
M126	120	46	5,000
M128	140	50	10,000
W124	100	42	6,000
W126	120	46	7,000
W128	140	40	6,000

LO 3   **6-28 *Pricing and impact on demand***   Andrea Kimball has recently acquired a franchise of a well-known fast-food and restaurant chain. She is considering a special promotion for a week during which there would be a $0.40 reduction in hamburger prices from the regular price of $1.09 to $0.69. Local advertising expenses for this special promotion will amount to $4,500. Andrea expects the promotion to increase sales of hamburgers by 20% and French fries by 12%, but she expects the sales of chicken sandwiches to decline by 8%. Some customers, who otherwise may have ordered a chicken sandwich, now will order a hamburger because of its attractive low price. The following data have been compiled for sales prices, variable costs, and weekly sales volumes:

PRODUCT	SALES PRICE	VARIABLE COSTS	SALES VOLUME
Hamburgers	$1.09	$0.51	20,000
Chicken sandwiches	1.29	0.63	10,000
French fries	0.89	0.37	20,000

Evaluate the expected impact of the special promotion on sales and profits. Should Andrea go ahead with this special promotion? What other considerations are relevant in this decision?

LO 3   **6-29 *Pricing using standard hours***   A major automaker collected detailed data on labor hours used by skilled technicians at its auto dealer service departments for different automobile repair jobs. The company then estimated repair times for each type of repair job and established these estimated times as standards to be used by the dealers in setting prices for the labor portion of the repair jobs. Discuss the advantages and disadvantages of this approach to pricing from the viewpoints of the auto dealer service departments and the customers.

6-30 *Dropping a product* Sanders Company recently developed an activity-based costing system and discovered that one of its products, SM5, does not cover the costs traced to it by the new cost system. Although the current sales price covers the direct material and direct labor costs, it does not cover the manufacturing support costs and customer support costs. The management team initially considered discontinuing production of SM5, but the marketing manager commented that no other local competitors produce SM5. Other than raising the price of SM5, what other actions might Sanders Company explore to increase profitability of SM5?

6-31 *Dropping a segment* George's Grill analyzes profitability of three segments: restaurant, bar, and billiards. Revenues and direct costs (variable plus fixed costs) for each segment are as follows:

	RESTAURANT	BAR	BILLIARDS
Revenue	$320,000	$150,000	$40,000
Direct costs	200,000	60,000	25,000

George, the owner, is considering converting the billiards area into an expanded bar area.

Required

a. Based on segment margin analysis (evaluating revenue minus direct costs for each segment) and ignoring remodeling costs, by how much will the bar segment margin have to increase for the grill's income to be at least as high as it is now?
b. What other considerations will George want to consider before making the decision to eliminate billards to expand the bar area?

Problems

6-32 (Appendix) Carver Company has a demand function given by this equation:

$$Q = 400 - (5 \times P)$$

where P = price and Q = quantity produced and sold. Carver Company's cost function is given by this equation:

$$C = 2,000 + (20 \times Q)$$

Determine the optimal price and the corresponding demand quantity and product unit cost.

6-33 *Product mix and overtime decisions* Excel Corporation manufactures three products at its plant. The plant capacity is limited to 120,000 machine hours per year on a single-shift basis. Direct material and direct labor costs are variable. The following data are available for planning purposes:

PRODUCT	TOTAL UNIT DEMAND FOR NEXT YEAR	SALES PRICE PER UNIT	DIRECT MATERIALS COST PER UNIT	DIRECT LABOR COST PER UNIT	VARIABLE SUPPORT COST PER UNIT	MACHINE HOURS PER UNIT
XL1	200,000	$10.00	$4.00	$2.00	$2.00	0.20
XL2	200,000	14.00	4.50	3.00	3.00	0.35
XL3	200,000	12.00	5.00	2.50	2.50	0.25

Required

a. Given the capacity constraint, determine the production levels for the three products that will maximize profits.

b. If the company authorizes overtime in order to produce more units of XL3, direct labor cost per unit will be higher by 50% because of the overtime premium. Materials cost and variable support cost per unit will be the same for overtime production as regular production. Is it worthwhile operating overtime?

LO 1, 2   **6-34 *Capacity and pricing decision*** Hudson Hydronics, Inc., is a corporation based in Troy, New York, that sells high-quality hydronic control devices. It manufactures two products, HCD1 and HCD2, for which the following information is available:

COSTS PER UNIT	HCD1	HCD2
Direct materials	$60	$75
Direct labor	80	100
Variable support	100	125
Fixed support	80	100
Total costs per unit	$320	$400
Price	$400	$500
Units sold	2,000 units	1,200 units

The average wage rate including fringe benefits is $20 per hour. The plant has a capacity of 15,000 direct labor hours, but current production uses only 14,000 direct labor hours of capacity.

Required

a. A new customer has offered to buy 200 units of HCD2 if Hudson lowers its price to $400 per unit. How many direct labor hours will be required to produce 200 units of HCD2? How much will Hudson Hydronic's profit increase or decrease if it accepts this proposal? (All other prices will remain as before.)

b. Suppose the customer has offered instead to buy 300 units of HCD2 at $400 per unit. How much will the profits increase or decrease if Hudson accepts this proposal? Assume that the company cannot increase its production capacity to meet the extra demand.

c. Answer the question in (b), assuming that the plant can work overtime. Direct labor costs for the overtime production increase to $30 per hour. Variable support costs for overtime production are 50% more than for normal production.

LO 2, 3   **6-35 *Activity-based costing and markup pricing*** Based on last year's activity, the Moose Jaw Manufacturing Company estimates the following manufacturing support costs for this year for its plant in Moose Jaw, Saskatchewan:

COST POOL	AMOUNT	ACTIVITY COST DRIVERS	RATE
Machine operations/ maintenance	$48,000	12,000 machine hours	$4.00
Supervision	45,000	$225,000 direct labor dollars	0.20
Materials handling	75,000	100,000 pounds	0.75
Quality control	66,000	550 inspections	120.00
Machine setups	75,000	250 production runs	300.00
Total	$309,000		

Moose Jaw's plant manufactures three products: A, B, and C. Data per unit are as follows:

ITEM	PRODUCT A	PRODUCT B	PRODUCT C
Direct materials	$12.00	$15.00	$18.00
Direct labor	$9.00	$15.00	$20.00
Machine hours	0.4	0.7	0.9
Pounds	4.0	5.0	7.0
Number of inspections	0.02	0.02	0.05
Number of production runs	0.01	0.01	0.02
Last year's sales price	$40.00	$57.00	$78.00
Demand at last year's prices	12,000 units	12,000 units	6,000 units
Actual production last year	10,000 units	5,000 units	5,000 units

Required

a. Determine the product costs using an activity-based costing system.
b. If Moose Jaw's target prices for each product are 25% above their respective activity-based costs, what are the target prices for products A, B, and C?
c. At present, production capacity during regular hours is limited to 12,000 machine hours. Capacity can be expanded up to 4,000 additional machine hours by using plant overtime. Overtime premium will add 50% to direct labor costs and 30% to each manufacturing support cost pool. If Moose Jaw expands its capacity by using plant overtime to provide an additional 4,000 machine hours, what will Moose Jaw's target prices be, using the 25% markup described in (b)? What issues should the company consider as it decides whether to expand capacity?

LO 1, 2 **6-36 *Capacity and product mix decision*** Barney Toy Company manufactures large and small stuffed animals. It has a long-term contract with a large chain of discount stores to sell 3,000 large and 6,000 small stuffed animals each month. The following cost information is available for large and small stuffed animals:

ITEM	LARGE	SMALL
Price per unit	$32	$21
Variable costs per unit:		
Direct material	$12	$10
Direct labor	6	2
Variable support	2	1
Fixed costs per unit	3	3
Total unit costs	$23	$16
Estimated demand (inclusive of long-term contract)	15,000	25,000

Production occurs in batches of 100 large or 200 small stuffed animals. Each batch takes a total of 10 machine hours to manufacture. The total machine hour capacity of 3,000 machine hours cannot be increased for at least a year.

Required

a. Determine the contribution margin per unit for each of the two sizes of stuffed animals.
b. Determine which size is more profitable to produce. How many units of each size should Barney produce?

c. Because of an unexpected high demand for stuffed dinosaurs, the discount store chain has requested an additional order of 5,000 large stuffed dinosaurs. It is willing to pay $37 per dinosaur for this special order. Determine the opportunity cost associated with this order.

d. Should Barney Toy Company accept the order described in (c)? Explain.

e. Suppose that the company can subcontract the production of up to 10,000 small stuffed animals to an outside supplier at a cost of $22 per animal. How many units of each size (including the special order units) should Barney produce, subcontract, and sell? What other qualitative factors should Barney consider?

LO 1, 2   **6-37 *Capacity and product mix decision*** Chang Company makes two types of wood doors: standard and deluxe. The doors are manufactured in a plant consisting of three departments: cutting, assembly, and finishing. Both labor and machine time are spent on the two products as they are worked on in each department.

In planning the production schedule for the next month, management is confronted with the facts that there is a labor shortage and that some machines must be shut down for major maintenance and repair. The following information pertains to the estimated levels of capacity of direct labor hours and machine hours available next month in the three departments:

	DEPARTMENTS		
CAPACITY AVAILABLE	CUTTING	ASSEMBLY	FINISHING
Machine hours	40,000	40,000	15,000
Labor hours	8,000	17,500	8,000

Direct labor and machine hours required per unit of each product are as follows:

	DEPARTMENTS		
PRODUCT HOURS	CUTTING	ASSEMBLY	FINISHING
Standard:			
Direct labor hours	0.5	1	0.5
Machine hours	2	2	1
Deluxe:			
Direct labor hours	1	1.5	0.5
Machine hours	3	3	1.5

The estimated demand for the next month is 10,000 units of standard doors and 5,000 units of deluxe doors. Unit cost and price information are as follows:

ITEM	STANDARD DOORS	DELUXE DOORS
Unit selling price	$150	$200
Unit costs:		
Direct materials	$60	$80
Direct labor	40	60
Variable support	10	15
Fixed support	10	5

The average wage rate is $20 per hour. Direct labor and machine availability in individual departments cannot be switched from one department to another.

Required

a. Determine whether the direct labor hour and machine hour capacities are adequate to meet the next month's demand.

b. How many units of each product should the company produce to maximize its profits?

c. Suggest alternatives the company might consider to satisfy all its customers' demands.

LO 1   **6-38 *Client mix decision***   Loren Lee, a financial planner, contacts and meets with local individuals to assist with financial planning and investments in Loren's employer's investment services company. Loren receives no fee for financial planning advice, but in addition to his salary, he receives commissions on client investments in the investment services company. Commission rates vary across different investment products. Loren's employer pays office and phone costs and also reimburses Loren for business-related travel. Satisfied clients have recommended Loren to their friends, and Loren now finds himself with more clients than he can handle in the 40 hours per week he would like to work. To analyze where to most profitably spend his time, Loren has classified his current set of customers into the three groups listed here. The hours devoted per customer include direct contact time, travel time, and research and follow-up time for the clients. Loren will introduce clients he is unable to serve to one of his colleagues.

	CUSTOMER GROUP		
	A	B	C
Average investment in company products per month	$900	$600	$200
Hours devoted per customer per month	3	1.5	0.5
Average commission percentage	6%	5%	4%
Current number of customers	20	60	120

Clients in group A are generally interested in hearing about new investment products that Loren's company is offering and will usually invest sizable amounts in new products after meeting with Loren or conversing with him on the phone. Clients in group B will also invest but generally in smaller amounts than clients in group A. Clients in group C appreciate meeting with Loren because of the excellent advice he provides in planning for retirement and other future expenses but have little discretionary income to invest. Group C clients also generally invest in products with a lower commission rate for Loren. However, Loren maintains contact with these clients because he anticipates they will become more profitable as their careers develop.

Required

a. Based on the data given, what client mix will maximize Loren's monthly commissions, assuming he works 160 hours per month?

b. What other factors should Loren consider as he makes his decisions about his client mix?

6-39 *Short-term pricing* True Image Printers, Inc., is a corporation based in Oberlin, Ohio, that sells high-quality printers in the Midwest regional market. It manufactures two products, L8011 and L8033, for which the following information is available:

	PRODUCT	
ITEM	L8011	L8033
Cost per unit:		
Direct materials	$300	$375
Direct labor	400	500
Variable support	500	625
Fixed support	400	500
Total cost per unit	$1,600	$2,000
Price	$2,000	$2,500
Units sold	400 units	200 units

The average wage rate, including fringe benefits, is $20 per hour. The plant has a capacity of 14,000 direct labor hours, but current production uses only 13,000 direct labor hours of capacity.

Required

a. A new customer has offered to buy 40 units of L8033 if its price is lowered to $2,000 per unit. How many direct labor hours will be required to produce 40 units of L8033? How much will the profit of True Image Printers increase or decrease if it accepts this proposal? All other prices will remain as before.

b. Suppose the customer has offered, instead, to buy 60 units of L8033 at $2,000 per unit. How much will the profits increase or decrease if True Image Printers accepts this proposal? Assume that the company cannot increase its production capacity to meet the extra demand.

c. Answer the question in (b), assuming instead that the plant can work overtime. Direct labor costs for the overtime production increase to $30 per hour. Variable support costs for overtime production are 50% more than for normal production.

6-40 *Bid price* (Adapted from CMA, June 1991) Marcus Fibers, Inc., specializes in the manufacture of synthetic fibers that the company uses in many products such as blankets, coats, and uniforms for police and firefighters. Marcus has been in business since 1975 and has been profitable each year since 1983. The company uses a standard cost system and applies manufacturing support costs on the basis of direct labor hours.

Marcus has recently received a request to bid on the manufacturing of 800,000 blankets scheduled for delivery to several military bases. The bid must be stated at full cost per unit plus a return on full cost of no more than 9% after income taxes. Full cost has been defined as including all variable costs of manufacturing the product, a reasonable amount of fixed support costs, and reasonable incremental administrative costs associated with the manufacturing and sale of the product. The contractor has indicated that bids in excess of $25 per blanket are not likely to be considered.

To prepare the bid for the 800,000 blankets, Andrea Lightner, cost accountant, has gathered the following information about the costs associated with the production of the blanket:

COSTS	AMOUNT
Raw materials	$1.50 per pound of fibers
Direct labor	$7.00 per hour
Direct machine costs[a]	$10.00 per blanket
Variable support	$3.00 per direct labor hour
Fixed support	$8.00 per direct labor hour
Incremental administrative costs	$2,500 per 1,000 blankets
Special fee[b]	$0.50 per blanket
Material usage	6 pounds per blanket
Production rate	4 blankets per direct labor hour
Effective tax rate	40%

[a] Direct machine costs consist of items such as special lubricants, replacement of needles used in stitching, and maintenance costs. These costs are not included in manufacturing support.
[b] Marcus recently developed a new blanket fiber at a cost of $750,000. To recover this cost, Marcus has instituted a policy of adding a $0.50 fee to the cost of each blanket using the new fiber. To date, the company has recovered $125,000. Andrea knows that this fee does not fit within the definition of full cost, as it is not a cost of manufacturing the product.

Required

a. Calculate the minimum price per blanket that Marcus Fibers, Inc., could bid without reducing the company's net income.

b. Using the full cost criterion and the maximum allowable return specified, calculate the bid price per blanket for Marcus Fibers, Inc.

c. Without prejudice to your answer to (b), assume that the price per blanket to Marcus Fibers, Inc., calculated using the cost-plus criterion specified, is greater than the maximum bid of $25 per blanket allowed. Discuss the factors that Marcus Fibers, Inc., should consider before deciding whether to submit a bid at the maximum acceptable price of $25 per blanket.

LO 1, 2 **6-41** *Product mix and special order decisions* Holmes Manufacturing Company produces three models of aquastatic controls: A17, B23, and XLT—all of which use the same basic component. The basic components are produced in department A. For model A17, the basic components are finished in department C. For both models B23 and XLT, the basic components undergo further modification in department B before being assembled in department C. Since the modifications for B23 and XLT require similar machines and labor skills, the available capacity of department B can be used for either product.

COST PER UNIT OF THE BASIC COMPONENT	
COSTS	AMOUNT
Direct materials cost	$3.80
Direct labor cost	10.00
Fixed support (allocated based on direct labor hours)	15.00
Total cost per unit	$28.80
Current production volume	4,000

	PRODUCT COSTS PER UNIT		
ITEM	A17	B23	XLT
Selling price per unit	$75.00	$120.00	$160.00
Basic component costs	$28.80	$28.80	$28.80
Direct materials costs	0	$6.00	$4.50
Direct labor costs	$9.00	$20.00	$31.00
Modification hours (department B)	0	0.5 hour	0.75 hours
Finishing hours (department C)	0.3 hours	0.3 hours	0.3 hours
Fixed support (allocated based on direct labor hours)	$9.00	$20.00	$31.00
Total cost per unit	$46.80	$74.80	$95.30
Current production volume	2,000	1,200	800

Required

a. A foreign distributor has asked Holmes to bid on a special order of 1,000 units of the basic component. There would be a special shipping charge of $3,200. The Holmes plant has excess capacity to manufacture more than 1,000 basic components, and this order would not affect sales of the other products. Determine the minimum price that Holmes could offer.

b. Determine the contribution margin per unit for each of the three products.

c. Suppose there is excess demand for all three products and the plant is currently operating at capacity. The only change that can be made is shifting workers between department B and department C. Personnel in those two departments are able to work in either area with no loss in efficiency. Determine the optimal monthly production mix of the three products. Check whether your answer changes if the price of model B23 is $140.

LO 2   **6-42 *Special order decision***   Kirby Company manufactures leather briefcases sold to wholesalers for $37.95. The plant capacity for manufacturing this product is 750,000 units annually, but normal volume is 500,000 units. The unit and total costs at normal volume follow:

TYPE OF COST	UNIT COSTS	TOTAL COSTS
Direct materials	$9.80	$4,900,000
Direct labor	4.50	2,250,000
Manufacturing support	12.00	6,000,000
Selling and administrative	6.70	3,350,000
Total costs	$33.00	$16,500,000

Manufacturing support and selling and administrative costs include both variable and fixed costs; fixed manufacturing support costs for the current year are budgeted at $4,500,000, and fixed selling and administrative costs are $2,100,000.

The company has been approached by a prospective customer who has offered to purchase 100,000 briefcases at $25 each. The customer wants the product packaged in large cartons rather than the normal individual containers and will pick them up in its own trucks. Accordingly, the variable selling and administrative costs will be lower by 60% for this order.

Required

Determine whether Kirby Company should accept this special order.

6-43 *Special order pricing, product mix decisions* (Adapted from CMA, May 1989) Purex Company produces and sells a single product called Kleen. Annual production capacity is 100,000 machine hours. It takes 1 machine hour to produce a unit of Kleen. Annual demand for Kleen is expected to remain at 80,000 units. The selling price is expected to remain at $10 per unit. Cost data for producing and selling Kleen are as follows:

Variable costs per unit:	
Direct materials	$1.50
Direct labor	2.50
Variable manufacturing support	0.80
Variable selling and distribution	2.00
Fixed costs per year:	
Fixed manufacturing support	$100,000
Fixed selling and distribution	50,000

Required

a. Purex Company has an inventory of 2,000 units of Kleen that were partially damaged in storage. It can sell these units through regular channels at reduced prices. These 2,000 units will be valueless unless sold this way. Sale of these units will not affect regular sales of Kleen. Compute the relevant unit cost for determining the minimum selling price for these units.

b. Ajax Company has offered to make and ship 25,000 units of Kleen directly to Purex Company's customers. If Purex Company accepts this offer, it will continue to produce and ship the remaining 55,000 units. Purex's fixed manufacturing support costs will decrease to $90,000. Its fixed selling and distribution costs will remain unchanged. Variable selling and distribution costs will decrease to $0.80 per unit for the 25,000 units produced and shipped by Ajax Company. Determine the maximum amount per unit that Purex Company should pay Ajax Company for producing and shipping the 25,000 units.

c. Purex Company has received a one-time special order for 5,000 units of Kleen. Acceptance of this order will not affect the regular sales of 80,000 units. Variable selling costs for each of these 5,000 units will be $1.00. Determine the minimum acceptable price for Purex Company for accepting this special order.

d. Purex Company can use its current facilities to manufacture a product called Shine. Annual production capacity of Shine, which takes 2.5 machine hours per unit to produce, is 50,000 units. The marketing department estimates that 50,000 units of Shine can be sold each year at $16 per unit. Sale of Shine will not affect the demand for Kleen. Cost data for producing and selling Shine are as follows:

Variable costs per unit:	
Direct materials	$2.50
Direct labor	4.00
Variable manufacturing support	1.20
Variable selling and distribution	3.30
Fixed costs per year:	
Fixed manufacturing support	$100,000
Fixed selling and distribution	50,000

Determine the product mix that will maximize Purex Company's profit.

6-44 *Product mix and overtime decisions*   Refer to the data for Crimson Components Company presented in Case 4-42. The following additional information is available:
- The company believes that it cannot change its selling prices.
- All manufacturing support costs described in Case 4-42 are variable costs.
- All non-manufacturing costs are fixed.
- The plant has a capacity of 80,000 casting department machine hours and 120,000 machining department machine hours on a single-shift basis.
- Estimated demand for the next year is 600,000 units of R361 and 800,000 units of R572.

Required

a. Determine the total casting department machine hours and machining department machine hours required to produce all the estimated demand for the next year. In which department is the capacity inadequate to meet estimated demand?

b. Determine the contribution margins for the two products based on your analysis for requirement (b) in Case 4-42.

c. Determine the contribution per machine hour for the department(s) in which capacity is inadequate. Given the capacity constraint(s), determine the production levels for the two products that will maximize profits.

d. Either or both of the casting and machining departments can be worked overtime. Direct labor cost per unit would be higher by 50% because of the overtime premium. Manufacturing support costs per unit would be the same for overtime production as for normal production. Is it worthwhile operating either department overtime? Explain.

6-45 *Product mix and special order decisions*   Orion Outdoors Company produces a standard model and a high-quality deluxe model of lightweight tents. Orion's workforce is organized into production teams responsible for cutting, stitching, and inspection activities. Orion has determined that its labor and support costs depend on the number of direct labor hours (cutting, stitching, and inspection), number of batches, and number of shipments. Production information is as follows:

ITEM	STANDARD MODEL	DELUXE MODEL
Direct labor time (cutting and stitching) per tent	10 minutes	15 minutes
Average batch size	60 tents	30 tents
Direct labor inspection time per batch	2 hours	2.5 hours
Average size per shipment	60 tents	10 tents
Selling price per tent	$10	$20
Materials costs per tent	$5	$11

Demand for standard and deluxe models is expected to be 6,000 and 3,000 tents, respectively. Direct labor time available for cutting, stitching, and inspection activities is 2,000 hours. The labor cost is $12 per hour, including fringe benefits, and shipping cost is $15 per shipment. Orion produces to demand and maintains no inventory on hand.

Required

a. Determine the production quantities for the two models that will maximize profits, assuming that it is not possible to change the number of available labor hours.

b. The sales manager has received an offer from Northlands Retail Company for 2,000 deluxe model tents at a price of $18.50 each. This order will be produced and shipped in batch sizes of 50 tents. Inspections for this order of deluxe model batches will take 2.5 hours per batch. Should Orion Outdoors Company accept this order if direct labor time is still restricted to 2,000 hours? What other qualitative factors should the company also consider?

LO 3   **6-46** (Appendix) Colway Company estimates the relation between the demand for its products and the price it sets, in terms of this equation where:

$$Q = \text{the quantity demanded}$$
$$P = \text{the price of the product}$$
$$Q = a - bP$$

The marketing manager, Trisha Colway, conducted a market research study last fall that indicated that $b = 500$ and $a = 8,400$ on average for the first quarter of this year.

Capacity costs are $m = \$3$ per unit, and variable costs are $v = \$8.10$ per unit. If committed capacity is exceeded, the variable costs increase to $w = \$12.70$ per unit.

Trisha determined that the long-term benchmark price is given by the following:

$$
\begin{aligned}
P^L &= \frac{a}{2b} + \frac{v+m}{2} \\
&= \frac{8,400}{2 \times 500} + \frac{\$8.10 + \$3.00}{2} \\
&= \$13.95
\end{aligned}
$$

Trisha also set the capacity level at $X = 2,150$ units.

Colway Company keeps track of demand conditions throughout the quarter. It announces a new price for each week in the Sunday newspaper based on the most current information it has on demand conditions. The following are the estimates of the demand parameter for each of the 13 weeks in the first quarter of this year:

Week T	Current Estimate of A_T	Weekly Price P_T
1	8,200	$12.25
2	8,350	?
3	8,600	?
4	8,500	?
5	8,400	?
6	8,850	?
7	8,300	?
8	8,050	?
9	8,200	?
10	8,800	?
11	8,350	?
12	7,950	?
13	8,650	?

The estimate of b remained at $b = 500$ for all 13 weeks. The short-term (weekly) price is set at this if the capacity is not exceeded by the realized demand:

$$P_t^* = \frac{a_t}{2b} + \frac{v}{2}$$

It is set at this if the capacity is exceeded:

$$P_t^* = \frac{a_t}{2b} + \frac{w}{2}$$

Note that if the price is set at this:

$$P_t^* = \frac{a_t}{2b} + \frac{v}{2}$$

the resultant demand will not exceed the capacity $X = 2{,}150$ only if this occurs:

$$Q_t = a_t - bP_t = a_t - 500\left(\frac{a_t}{1{,}000} + \frac{8.10}{2}\right) = \frac{a_t}{2} - 2{,}025$$

is less than $X = 2{,}150$, that is, if $a_t \le 8{,}350$. Similarly, if the price is set at this;

$$P_t^* = \frac{a_t}{2b} + \frac{w}{2}$$

the resultant demand will exceed the capacity $X = 2{,}150$ only if $a_t > 10{,}650$.

Required

a. Determine the weekly prices, plot them on a graph for each of the 13 weeks, and compare them with the long-term benchmark price. What is the average of the weekly prices?

b. Determine the total profit over the 13-week period. Repeat the same exercise after setting the capacity (X) at different levels ($X = 1{,}750$, $1{,}950$, $2{,}350$, and $2{,}550$). Plot the total profit on a graph against different levels of capacity that you select.

LO 2, 3, 4   **6-47 *Special order pricing***   (Adapted from CMA, December 1988) The Sommers Company, located in southern Wisconsin, manufactures a variety of industrial valves and pipe fittings that are sold to customers in nearby states. Currently, the company is operating at about 70% capacity and is earning a satisfactory return on investment.

Management has been approached by Glasgow Industries Ltd. of Scotland with an offer to buy 120,000 units of a pressure valve. Glasgow Industries manufactures a valve that is almost identical to Sommers's pressure valve. However, a fire in the valve plant of Glasgow Industries has shut down its manufacturing operations. Glasgow needs the 120,000 valves over the next 4 months to meet commitments to its regular customers. The company is prepared to pay $19 each for the valves, FOB shipping point; that is, freight and transportation insurance expenses are paid by the buyer, Glasgow Industries Ltd. Sommers's product cost for the pressure valve, based on current attainable standards, is as follows:

Direct materials	$5.00
Direct labor	6.00
Manufacturing support	9.00
Total cost	$20.00

Manufacturing support costs are applied to production at the rate of $18 per standard direct labor hour. This rate is made up of the following components:

Variable manufacturing support	$ 6.00
Fixed manufacturing support	12.00
Cost driver rate	$18.00

Additional costs incurred in connection with sales of the pressure valve include sales commissions of 5% and freight expense of $1 per unit. However, the company does not pay sales commissions on special orders that come directly to management.

In determining selling prices, Sommers adds a 40% markup to product cost. This provides a $28 suggested selling price for the pressure valve. The marketing department, however, has set the current selling price at $27 to maintain the company's market share.

Production management believes that it can handle the Glasgow Industries order without disrupting its scheduled production. The order would, however, require additional fixed manufacturing support costs of $12,000 per month in the form of supervision and clerical costs.

If management accepts the order, 30,000 pressure valves will be manufactured and shipped to Glasgow Industries each month for the next 4 months. Shipments will be made in weekly consignments, FOB shipping point.

Required

a. Determine how many additional direct labor hours would be required each month to fill the Glasgow Industries order.
b. Evaluate the impact of accepting the Glasgow Industries order on Sommers's profit.
c. Calculate the minimum unit price that Sommers's management could accept for the Glasgow Industries order without reducing its profits.
d. Identify the factors, other than price, that the Sommers Company should consider before accepting the Glasgow Industries order.

LO 1, 4   **6-48 *Product mix decisions***   (Adapted from CMA, December 1991) Bakker Industries sells three products (products 611, 613, and 615) that it manufactures in a factory consisting of four departments (departments 1 through 4). Both labor and machine time are applied to the products in each of the four departments. The machine processing and labor skills required in each department are such that neither machines nor labor can be switched from one department to another.

Bakker's management is planning its production schedule for the next several months. The community is experiencing labor shortages. Some of the machines will be out of service for extensive overhauling. Available machine and labor time by department for each of the next 6 months follows:

Monthly Capacity Availability

	DEPARTMENT			
	1	2	3	4
Normal machine capacity in machine hours	3,500	3,500	3,000	3,500
Capacity of machines being repaired in machine hours	(500)	(400)	(300)	(200)
Available machine capacity in machine hours	3,000	3,100	2,700	3,300
Labor capacity in direct labor hours	4,000	4,500	3,500	3,000
Available labor in direct labor hours	3,700	4,500	2,750	2,600

Labor and Machine Specifications per Unit of Product

PRODUCT	LABOR AND MACHINE TIME	DEPARTMENT			
		1	2	3	4
611	Direct labor hours	2	3	3	1
	Machine hours	2	1	2	2
613	Direct labor hours	1	2	0	2
	Machine hours	1	1	0	2
615	Direct labor hours	2	2	1	1
	Machine hours	2	2	1	1

The sales department's forecast of product demand over the next 6 months follows:

PRODUCT	MONTHLY SALES VOLUME
611	500 units
613	400 units
615	1,000 units

Bakker's inventory levels will not be increased or decreased during the next 6 months. The unit price and cost data valid for the next 6 months follow:

ITEM	PRODUCT		
	611	613	615
Unit costs:			
Direct material	$7	$13	$17
Direct labor:			
Department 1	12	6	12
Department 2	21	14	14
Department 3	24	0	8
Department 4	9	18	9
Variable support	27	20	25
Fixed support	15	10	32
Variable selling	3	2	4
Unit selling price	$196	$123	$167

Required

a. Determine whether the monthly sales demand for the three products can be met by Bakker's factory. Use the monthly requirement by department for machine hours and direct labor hours for the production of products 611, 613, and 615 in your calculations.

b. What monthly production schedule should Bakker Industries select to maximize its dollar profits? Support the schedule with appropriate calculations and present a schedule of the contribution to profit that would be generated by the production schedule selected.

c. What other alternatives might Bakker Industries consider so that it can supply its customers all the products they demand?

LO 1, 4   **6-49**   *Product mix decision*   (Adapted from CMA, June 1990) Sportway, Inc., is a wholesale distributor supplying a wide range of moderately priced sporting equipment to large chain stores. About 60% of Sportway's products are purchased from other companies, while the remainder of the products are manufactured by Sportway. The company has a plastics department that is currently manufacturing molded fishing tackle boxes. Sportway is able to manufacture and sell 8,000 tackle boxes annually, making full use of its direct labor capacity at available work stations. The following are the selling price and costs associated with Sportway's tackle boxes:

Selling price per box		$86.00
Costs per box:		
Molded plastic	$8.00	
Hinges, latches, handle	9.00	
Direct labor ($15 per hour)	18.75	
Manufacturing support	12.50	
Selling and administrative	17.00	65.25
Profit per box		$20.75

Because Sportway believes it could sell 12,000 tackle boxes if it had sufficient manufacturing capacity, the company has looked into the possibility of purchasing the tackle boxes for distribution. Maple Products, a steady supplier of quality products, would be able to provide up to 9,000 tackle boxes per year at a price of $68 per box delivered to Sportway's facility.

Bart Johnson, Sportway's product manager, has suggested that the company could make better use of its plastics department by manufacturing skateboards. To support his position, Johnson has a market study that indicates an expanding market for skateboards and a need for additional suppliers. Johnson believes that Sportway could expect to sell 17,500 skateboards annually at a price of $45 per skateboard. Johnson's estimate of the costs to manufacture the skateboards follows:

Selling price per skateboard		$45.00
Costs per skateboard:		
Molded plastic	$5.50	
Wheels, hardware	7.00	
Direct labor ($15 per hour)	7.50	
Manufacturing support	5.00	
Selling and administrative costs	9.00	34.00
Profit per skateboard		$11.00

In the plastics department, Sportway uses direct labor hours as the cost driver for manufacturing support costs. Included in the manufacturing support for the current year is $50,000 of factorywide, fixed manufacturing support that has been allocated to the plastics department. For each unit of product that Sportway sells, regardless of whether the product has been purchased or is manufactured by Sportway, an allocated $6 fixed support cost per unit for distribution is included in the selling and administrative cost for all products. Total selling and administrative costs for the purchased tackle boxes would be $10 per unit.

Required

To maximize the company's profitability, prepare an analysis based on the data presented that will show which product or products Sportway, Inc., should manufacture and/or purchase and that will show the associated financial impact. Support your answer with appropriate calculations.

LO 1 **6-50 *Process or sell decision*** The Troy Company manufactures electronic subcomponents that can be sold at the end of process A or can be processed further in process B and sold as special parts for a variety of electronic appliances. The entire output of process A can be sold at a market price of $2 per unit. The output of process B had been sold at a price of $5.50 for the past 3 years, but the price has recently fallen to $5.10 on most orders.

On the basis of an analysis of the product markets and costs, Toni Tobin, the vice president of marketing, thinks that process B output should be dropped whenever its price falls below $4.50 per unit. The total available capacity is interchangeable between process A and process B. She recommends that, with present prices, all sales should be process B output. Her analysis follows:

	OUTPUT OF PROCESS A
Selling price, after deducting relevant selling costs		$2.00
Costs:		
Direct materials	$1.00	
Direct labor	0.20	
Manufacturing support	0.60	1.80
Operating profit		$0.20

	OUTPUT OF PROCESS B
Selling price, after deducting relevant selling costs		$5.10
Transferred-in variable costs from process A	$1.20	
Additional direct materials	1.50	
Direct labor	0.40	
Manufacturing support for additional processing	1.20	4.30
Operating profit		$0.80

Direct materials and direct labor costs are variable. All manufacturing support costs are fixed and allocated to units produced on the basis of hours of capacity. The total hours of capacity available are 600,000. A batch of 60 units requires 1 hour for process A and 2 hours of additional processing for process B.

Required

   a. If the price of process B output for the next year is likely to be $5.10, should all sales be only the output of process B?

   b. What is the lowest acceptable price for process B output to make it as profitable as process A output?

   c. Suppose 50% of the manufacturing support costs are variable. Do your answers to (a) and (b) change? If so, how?

Cases

LO 1, 3, 4 **6-51** *Product mix decision*   Aramis Aromatics Company produces and sells its product AA100 to well-known cosmetics companies for $940 per ton. The marketing manager is considering the possibility of refining AA100 further into finer perfumes before selling them to the cosmetics companies. Product AA101 is expected to command a price of $1,500 per ton and AA102 a price of $1,700 per ton. The maximum expected demand is 400 tons for AA101 and 100 tons for AA102. The annual plant capacity of 2,400 hours is fully utilized at present to manufacture 600 tons of AA100. The marketing manager proposed that Aramis sell 300 tons of AA100, 100 tons of AA101, and 75 tons of AA102 in the next year. It requires 4 hours of capacity to make 1 ton of AA100, 2 hours to refine 1 ton of AA100 further into AA101, and 4 hours to refine 1 ton of AA100 into AA102 instead. The plant accountant has prepared the following cost sheet for the three products:

		COSTS PER TON	
COST ITEM	AA100	AA101	AA102
Direct materials:			
Chemicals and fragrance	$560	$400	$470
AA100	0	800	800
Direct labor	60	30	60
Manufacturing support:			
Variable	60	30	60
Fixed	120	60	120
Total manufacturing costs	$800	$1,320	$1,510
Selling support:			
Variable	20	30	30
Fixed	10	10	10
Total cost	$830	$1,360	$1,550
Proposed sales level	300 tons	100 tons	75 tons
Maximum demand	600 tons	400 tons	100 tons

Required

   a. Determine the contribution margin for each product.

   b. Determine the production levels for the three products under the present constraint on plant capacity that will maximize total contribution.

   c. Suppose a customer, Cosmos Cosmetics Company, is very interested in the new product AA101. It has offered to sign a long-term contract for 400 tons of AA101. It is also willing to pay a higher price if the entire plant capacity is dedicated to the production of AA101. What is the minimum price for AA101 at which it becomes worthwhile for Aramis to dedicate its entire capacity to the production of AA101?

   d. Suppose, instead, that the price of AA101 is $1,500 per ton and that the capacity can be increased temporarily by 600 hours if the plant is operated overtime. Overtime premium payments to workers and supervisors will increase direct labor and variable manufacturing support costs by 50% for all products. All other costs will remain unchanged. Is it worthwhile operating the plant overtime? If the plant is operated overtime for 600 hours, what are the optimal production levels for the three products?

LO 4 **6-52 *Pricing decision***   Refer to the data for Sweditrak Corporation presented in Case 4-47. The following additional information is now available.

The production volume budgeted for each product in weeks 47 to 52 is the same as the volume level in week 46. In early December, the company is considering subcontracting with a French company to produce 400 units of the deluxe model per week on a 4-week trial basis for $200 per unit. Accepting this purchase offer would restrict Sweditrak's own deluxe production to 50 units per week.

Required

a. Is it profitable for Sweditrak to accept this offer? (Assume the activity-based cost system is used, and use the data from weeks 45 and 46 to estimate the variable support costs.) What additional qualitative factors should Sweditrack consider in evaluating this offer?

   Suppose that Sweditrak is pleased with the quality of the trial shipment and the French company is willing to commit to produce 400 units of the deluxe model each week for the next 3 years and charge $200 per unit. Sweditrak expects the domestic demand for its two models to remain stable at 450 units per week for the next 3 years. During this 3-year period, Sweditrak can adjust the capacity of each department to any desired levels. Capacity changes will result in proportional changes in fixed costs.

b. What are the relevant costs for this long-term decision?

c. Will it be profitable for Sweditrak to accept the long-term offer?

LO 3 **6-53 *Pricing experiment***   This is a pricing experiment in which you will work with a team, using cost accounting information in pricing decisions. Each team represents one firm in a market. Each market is completely independent of other markets. Your market has four firms that use similar production technology to produce two types of hiking boots: a lightweight model (LT) and a mountaineering model (MT). Each firm faces the same demand curves where P is your price and $P1$, $P2$, and $P3$ are the other three firms' prices:

$$\text{Demand for LT} = 19{,}919 - 500 \times P + 84 \times (P1 + P2 + P3)$$
$$\text{Demand for MT} = 6{,}632 - 109 \times P + 18 \times (P1 + P2 + P3)$$

Notice that if you increase your price, your demand will fall. If, however, your competitors raise their prices, you will gain some of the market share they lose.

Your instructor will provide you a confidential cost report that you should use in your pricing decisions. No cost data should be shared with other teams.

This experiment is comprised of five periods. For each period, your firm must submit the prices at which you are prepared to sell each type of boot. Your firm operates on a just-in-time basis and produces to order. Hence, no inventory or production-quantity decisions need to be made.

The market share you obtain or the profit you make in any one period will not in any way affect your performance in subsequent periods. Your parent company has committed to remain in this market for all five periods. However, your parent company expects you to maximize profits in each period.

Bring your first set of prices to the experiment session. The prices should be specified in whole dollars only (no cents). Once you have decided on prices, enter the prices on the following pricing sheet and submit it to the instructor. The instructor will determine the quantities sold for each firm and return the pricing sheet to you with a market report (next page) containing the following information: what each firm sold, what prices each firm charged, and what the actual net income was for each firm. Then you will decide on prices for the next period.

PRICING SHEET					
FIRM: _____	MARKET: _____				
	Period 1	Period 2	Period 3	Period 4	Period 5
LT—Price					
MT—Price					

MARKET REPORT					
MARKET: _____			PRICE: _____		
Firm	Lightweight Boots		Mountaineering Boots		Net Income
	Pirce	Quantity	Price	Quantity	

Prior to the experiment session, your team should spend 2 to 3 hours understanding the cost and demand structure and thinking about how to set prices. You should also devise a strategy to adjust prices if necessary based on what you observe about your competitors' decisions and about your own and your competitors' performance in each period. Remember the purpose of this experiment is to learn about pricing in a competitive setting.

After participating in the experiment, prepare a report of no more than four typed and double-spaced pages that describe how you determined your costs and pricing rules and how competition affected your pricing. Include a statement of budget versus actual in the format shown above, together with detailed calculations of the costs of your two products.

STATEMENT OF BUDGET VERSUS ACTUAL						
FIRM: _____		MARKET: _____				
	Period 1	Period 2	Period 3	Period 4	Period 5	Total
Number of LT sold						
Price—LT						
Revenues—LT						
Number of MT sold						
Price—MT						
Revenues—MT						
Total revenues						
Estimated costs—LT						
Estimated costs—MT						
Total costs						
Estimated net income						
Actual net income						
Variance between actual and estimated net income						

LO 3, 4   **6-54 *Activity-based management, customer profitability, managing customer relationships, pricing*** Discuss Case 4-52.

Chapter

Management Accounting and Control Systems: Assessing Performance over the Value Chain

After reading this chapter, you will be able to:

➤ apply the concept of control

➤ identify the characteristics of well-designed management accounting and control systems

➤ describe the total-life-cycle costing approach to managing product costs over the value chain

➤ explain target costing

➤ compute target costs

➤ explain Kaizen costing

➤ identify environmental costing issues

➤ apply the process of benchmarking to the best practices of other organizations

Chemco International

Kaylee Young has just been appointed controller of a large chemical company. She is on the fast track, having graduated with a dual concentration in strategy and management accounting from a large southern California business school only 5 years earlier. Before going back to school, Kaylee worked as a management consultant. Her most recent job as senior manager of the manufacturing division has been challenging; however, she has performed relatively well despite the poor quality of the data coming out of the company's antiquated management accounting and control system.

Numerous problems seem to plague this system. First, managers find that cost management reports both within and across divisions are often

Source: Martin Bond/Science Photo Library/Photo Researchers, Inc.

not comparable, given the variety of ways that product costs are generated. Second, information generated by the system is focused solely on the actual manufacturing process itself and does not provide any insight into pre- and postmanufacturing costs, such as the cost of developing products or disposing of toxic waste. Since competition in the chemicals industry has increased dramatically, Kaylee wants to understand all costs related to the life cycle of his products.

On the basis of her experience as a consultant, Kaylee has decided to design a management accounting and control system that will generate relevant information. Other managers in her company are not sure whether the change is really necessary. Nevertheless, Kaylee would like to find out everything she can about how companies in her and other industries have designed their systems. She is also intrigued by how costs can be managed over their total life cycle and, in particular, wants to study how target costing and Kaizen costing can be applied in her company.

Since her company produces chemicals, she also is concerned about how to dispose of her products and what their environmental impact may be. The first step is to determine what design principles to follow. Kaylee decides to study the benchmarking process. She also has heard that another local company just completed the design of a new system, and she decides to call her counterpart at that company to see whether she can gather some benchmarking information.

WHAT ARE MANAGEMENT ACCOUNTING AND CONTROL SYSTEMS?

The preceding chapters explored different types of cost management systems and the ways the information they generate is used in a variety of decision contexts. A cost management system is one of the central performance measurement systems at the core of a larger entity known as a **management accounting and control system (MACS)**. In this chapter and the following ones, we discuss the role that MACS play in helping decision makers determine whether organization-, business-, and operational-level strategies and objectives are being met. We begin by presenting the concept of control and then delineate the technical and behavioral characteristics of a well-designed MACS. Because the design of MACS is a large topic, we have divided the discussion into two parts. This chapter will cover the technical aspects of MACS design as well as the ways managers can use benchmarking to gather information about the best practices of others who have implemented new systems. Chapter 8 will focus on the behavioral characteristics of MACS design and cover issues related to human motivation.

The technical characteristics of a well-designed MACS include the scope of the system and the relevance of the information generated. Regarding scope, many MACS measure and assess performance in only one part of the value chain—the actual production process. A major shortcoming is that pre- or postproduction costs associated with products or services are ignored. Since such costs are significant in today's business environment, not having this information puts organizations at a distinct disadvantage when trying to understand the *total-life-cycle costs* of a product or service and ways to reduce those costs.

We illustrate the advantages of considering the entire value chain by discussing three contemporary methods: *target costing, Kaizen costing,* and *environmental costing.* If well implemented, these methods can help organizations control and reduce costs effectively.

The Meaning of "Control"

Broadly speaking, a MACS generates and uses information to help decision makers assess whether an organization is achieving its objectives. The term **control** in management accounting and control refers to the set of procedures, tools, performance measures, and systems that organizations use to guide and motivate all employees to achieve organizational objectives. A system is **in control** if it is on the path to achieving its strategic objectives and deemed **out of control** otherwise.

For the process of control to have meaning and credibility, the organization must have the knowledge and ability to correct situations that it identifies as out of control; otherwise, control serves no purpose. The process of keeping an organization in control consists of five stages as shown in Exhibit 7-1:

1. *Planning* consists of developing an organization's objectives, choosing activities to accomplish the objectives, and selecting measures to determine how well the objectives were met.
2. *Execution* is implementing the plan.
3. *Monitoring* is the process of measuring the system's current level of performance.
4. *Evaluation* occurs when feedback about the system's current level of performance is compared to the planned level so that any discrepancies can be identified and corrective action prescribed.
5. *Correcting* consists of taking the appropriate actions to return the system to an in-control state.

Regardless of whether an organization makes cookies, finds job seekers work, or flies people around the world, the same basic control process applies. One key difference in the control process lies in determining the most appropriate types of performance measures used by an organization. In the following section, we discuss the characteristics that designers consider when developing a MACS.

Exhibit 7-1
The Cycle of
Control

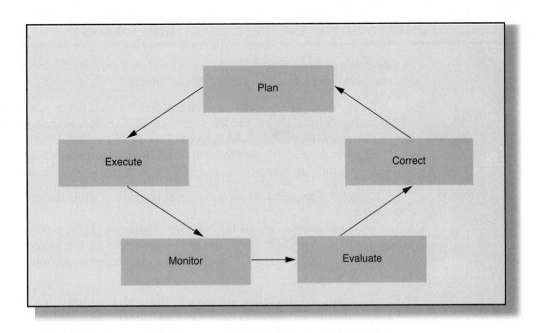

Environmental Activism: What We Do

Environmental Activism

Current Campaign

Our definition of quality includes a mandate for building products and working with processes that cause the least harm to the environment. We evaluate raw materials, invest

Enviro Internships

After many years of giving money to activists, we realized that if we could share profits, we could

As described here, organizations such as Patagonia are renowned for having both financial and social objectives such as protecting the environment.

"Our definition of quality includes a mandate for building products and working with processes that cause the least harm to the environment. We evaluate raw materials, invest in innovative technologies, rigorously police our waste and use a portion of our profits to support groups working to make a real difference. We acknowledge that the wild world we love best is disappearing. That is why those of us who work here share a strong commitment to protecting undomesticated lands and waters. We believe in using business to inspire solutions to the environmental crisis."

Source: http://www.patagonia.com.

Designers of MACS have both behavioral and technical considerations to meet. Behavioral considerations include the following:

1. Embedding the organization's ethical code of conduct into MACS design
2. Using a mix of short- and long-term qualitative and quantitative performance measures (or the Balanced Scorecard approach)
3. Empowering employees to be involved in decision making and MACS design
4. Developing an appropriate incentive system to reward performance

Chapter 8 presents these behavioral considerations. The technical side is presented here.

Technical considerations fall into two categories: (1) the relevance of the information generated, and (2) the scope of the system. The relevance of information is measured by four characteristics. The information must be accurate, timely, consistent, and flexible.

1. **Accurate.** As discussed throughout this text, inaccurate information is not relevant or useful for decision making because it is misleading. Designers have to develop a system that leads to the most accurate information possible, subject to a cost-benefit trade-off. For example, more accurate product costs can be obtained by using systems that trace costs more directly from support activities to products.

2. **Timely.** Accurate information that is late is also of little use for decision making. The MACS must be designed so that the results of performance measurement are fed back to the appropriate units in the most expedient way possible. The proliferation of high-speed computers, local area networks, and many other forms of technology make the process of providing feedback a real-time possibility in many, if not all, systems.

3. **Consistent.** Designers must structure the MACS to provide a consistent framework that can be applied globally across the units or divisions of an entity. Consistency means that the language used and the technical methods of producing management accounting information do not conflict within various parts of an organization. For example, if two divisions use different costing systems, it is more difficult to understand and compare results across divisions. If one division of an organization uses activity-based costing principles and another division, especially one that is very similar in goals and function to the first, uses volume-based overhead allocation methods, then the information system does not meet the consistency criterion. Consider the difficulties that would arise if divisions classified the same expense differently, that is, if fringe benefits of workers were classified as direct labor expenses in one division but as indirect labor expenses in another.

4. **Flexible.** MACS designers must allow employees to use the system's available information in a flexible manner so that they can customize its application for local decisions. If flexibility is not possible, an employee's motivation to make the best decision may be lessened for the decision at hand, especially if different units engage in different types of activities. For example, if one division of a company located in Pasadena undertakes new product development and another division in Monterey performs final assembly, each division probably will have different data needs and may use different cost drivers in making its decisions. The performance measures for managing new product development in Pasadena will be quite different from the factors that the Monterey assembly division must use to manage effectively. A well-designed MACS should be able to accommodate the local needs of each division. If

not, inaccurate ad hoc local systems may develop, leading to poor decisions and confusion between the company's division and upper management.

The scope of the MACS must be comprehensive and include all activities across the entire value chain of the organization. For example, historically, many MACS measure and assess performance in only one part of the value chain—the actual production or throughput process. In this case, the performance of suppliers, the design activities, and the postproduction activities associated with products and services are ignored. Without a comprehensive set of information, managers can make only limited decisions.

The Value Chain

The *value chain* is defined as a sequence of activities that should contribute more to the ultimate value of the product than to its cost. Products produced by an organization rely on different activities of the organization and use different resources along the value chain depending on their specifications. Essentially, all products flow through the value chain, which begins with research, development, and engineering and then moves through manufacturing and continues on to customers. Depending on the product, customers may require service and will either consume the product (a chocolate bar) or dispose of it after it has served its intended purpose (chemical solvents).

Total-Life-Cycle Costing

As products move along the value chain they accumulate costs. Total-life-cycle costing (TLCC) is the name we give to the process of managing all costs along the value chain as shown in Exhibit 7-2. A TLCC system provides information for managers to understand and manage costs through a product's design, development, manufacturing, marketing, distribution, maintenance, service, and disposal stages. It is also known as managing costs "from the cradle to the grave."

Deciding how to allocate resources over the life cycle usually is an iterative process. Initially, a company may decide to spend more on design to reduce the costs of all other subsequent product-related (upstream) costs, such as manufacturing, and service-related costs. At a later time, the company may determine how to reduce those initial design costs as well. Opportunity costs play a heightened role in a TLCC perspective because it is possible to develop only a limited number of products over a particular time period.

Consider the following situation. Managers of the Pinsky Company have been developing a new concept for a product they believe will revolutionize their business.

Exhibit 7-2
Cycle Comprising the Total-Life-Cycle Costing Approach

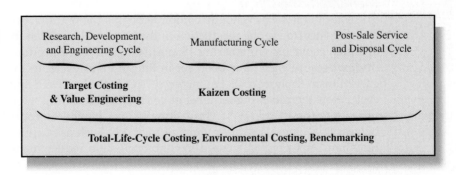

Their initial research suggests to them that they can manufacture the product at a reasonably low cost, especially given the new technology that they have just acquired. They begin to consider how they can reorganize their operation to accommodate the production of the new product. Because they have only some preliminary ideas about the feasibility of product design, they approach their research development and engineering (RD&E) division for further investigation. The report from the RD&E group tells them that the product can be produced, but the cost of developing prototypes is 20 times more than the average prototype cost. RD&E confirms, however, that the actual cost to manufacture the product after the first year will be reasonably low as Pinsky gains experience with the new technology.

Thus, the initial life-cycle cost of the product may be quite high, but the manufacturing cost will be relatively low. With this new information, managers of the division now have to determine whether they should forge ahead with new product development from an overall company perspective and given their analysis of opportunity costs.

Numerous life-cycle concepts, such as research development and engineering and postsale service and disposal, have emerged in various functional areas of business. Although each concept is useful within its respective area, a TLCC perspective integrates the concepts so that they can be understood in their entirety. From the manufacturer's perspective, total-life-cycle product costing integrates these functional life-cycle concepts: research development and engineering, manufacturing, and postsale service and disposal. Let us look at each.

Research Development and Engineering Cycle

The **research development and engineering (RD&E)** cycle has three stages:

1. *Market research*, where emerging customer needs are assessed and ideas are generated for new products
2. *Product design*, in which scientists and engineers develop the technical aspects of products
3. *Product development*, in which the company creates features critical to customer satisfaction and designs prototypes, production processes, and any special tooling required

By some estimates, 80% to 85% of a product's total life costs are committed by decisions made in the RD&E cycle of the product's life. **Committed costs** are those that a company knows it will have to incur at a future date. Decisions made in this cycle are critical because an additional dollar spent on activities that occur during this cycle can save at least $8 to $10 on manufacturing and postmanufacturing activities, such as design changes or service costs.

Manufacturing Cycle

After the RD&E cycle, the company begins the **manufacturing cycle**, in which costs are incurred in the production of the product. Usually at this stage, there is not as much room for engineering flexibility to influence product costs and product design because they have been set in the previous cycle. In Exhibit 7-3, the lower curve illustrates how costs are incurred over both the RD&E and the manufacturing cycle. Note the much higher level of costs incurred during the manufacturing cycle relative to the RD&E cycle. Traditionally, this is where product costing plays its biggest role. Operations management methods, such as facilities layout and just-in-time manufacturing (discussed in chapter 5), help reduce manufacturing life-cycle product costs. Over the past decade, in an effort to reduce costs, companies have used

Exhibit 7-3
Total Life-Cycle
Costing:
Relationship
Between
Committed
Costs and
Incurred Costs

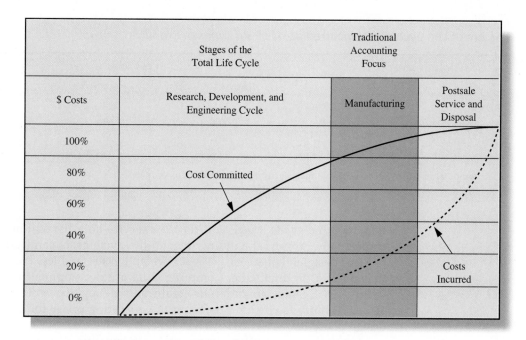

$ Costs	Stages of the Total Life Cycle	Traditional Accounting Focus	
	Research, Development, and Engineering Cycle	Manufacturing	Postsale Service and Disposal

(chart showing *Cost Committed* curve rising from 0% to 100% and *Costs Incurred* dashed curve rising later, with gridlines at 100%, 80%, 60%, 40%, 20%, 0%)

management accounting methods such as activity-based cost management to identify and reduce non-value-added activities.

Postsale Service and Disposal Cycle

The third cycle is the postsale service and disposal cycle. Although the costs for service and disposal are committed in the RD&E stage, the actual service cycle begins once the first unit of a product is in the hands of the customer. Thus, this cycle overlaps with the manufacturing cycle. The service cycle typically consists of three stages:

1. Rapid growth from the first time the product is shipped through the growth stage of its sales
2. Transition from the peak of sales to the peak in the service cycle
3. Maturity from the peak in the service cycle to the time of the last shipment made to a customer, disposal occurs at the end of a product's life and lasts until the customer retires the final unit of a product

Disposal costs often include those associated with eliminating any harmful effects associated with the end of a product's useful life. Products whose disposal could involve harmful effects to the environment, such as nuclear waste or other toxic chemicals, can incur very high costs.

A breakdown of costs for each of the functional life cycles will differ, depending on the industry and specific product produced. Exhibit 7-4 illustrates four types of products and how the organizations that produce them incur costs over the respective total life cycle of each product.[1]

Exhibit 7-4 shows the variation of costs within the cycles. For example, the manufacturing cost of the commercial aircraft company is approximately 40% of

---

[1] The information in Exhibit 7-4 comes from interviews conducted by Shields and Young in M. D. Shields and S. M. Young, "Managing Product Life Cycle Costs: An Organizational Model," *Journal of Cost Management*, Fall 1991, 39–52.

Exhibit 7-4
Percent of Life-Cycle Costs Incurred across Four Types of Products

STAGE OF LIFE CYCLE	TYPE OF PRODUCT			
CYCLE	COMBAT JETS	COMMERCIAL AIRCRAFT	NUCLEAR MISSILES	COMPUTER SOFTWARE
RD&E	21%	20%	20%	75%[a]
Manufacturing	45%	40%	60%	[a]
Service and disposal	34%	40%	20%	25%
Average length of life cycle	30 years	25 years	2 to 25 years	5 years

[a]For computer software, both RD&E and manufacturing are often tied directly together.

total incurred costs. RD&E and postsale service and disposal incur 20% and 40%, respectively. An understanding of total-life-cycle costs can lead to cost-effective product designs that are easier to service and easier and less costly to dispose of at the end of a product's life. Computer software development requires much time in the RD&E stage in order to create and debug the software. It often costs 100 times more to correct a defect in the operating phase for software than in the design phase.

The following section discusses target costing—a management accounting method of cost reduction that has its focus in the design stage of a product's life cycle but that also considers all aspects of the value chain and explicitly recognizes total-life-cycle costs.

TARGET COSTING

Target costing is a method of profit planning and cost management that was developed in Japan in the 1960s. The goal of target costing is to reduce the costs of products in the RD&E stage of a product's total life cycle rather than the more costly way of trying to reduce them during the manufacturing stage. Target costing is a relevant example of how a well-designed MACS can be used for strategic purposes and how critical it is for organizations to have a system in place that considers performance measurement across the entire value chain.

COMPARING TRADITIONAL COST REDUCTION TO TARGET COSTING

Traditional Cost Reduction

Traditional cost reduction in the United States is significantly different from target costing. As shown in Exhibit 7-5, column 1 on page 321, the traditional costing method begins with market research into customer requirements followed by product specification. Companies then engage in product design and engineering and obtain prices from suppliers in a sequential fashion. At this stage, product cost is not a significant factor in product design. After the engineers and designers have determined product design, they estimate product cost (C_t), where t indicates numbers derived under traditional thinking. If the estimated cost is considered to be too high, then it may be necessary to modify the product design. To find the desired profit margin (P_t), it is necessary to subtract the estimated cost from the expected selling

Exhibit 7-5

A Comparison of the Process of Traditional U.S. and Japanese Cost-Reduction Methods

TRADITIONAL U.S. COST REDUCTION	JAPANESE TARGET COSTING
Market research to determine customer requirements ⇩	Market research to determine consumer needs and price points ⇩
Product specification ⇩	Production specification and design ⇩
Design ⇩	Target selling price (S_{tc}) (and target product volume)
Engineering ⇩	
Supplier pricing ⇩	−
ESTIMATED COST (C_t) (if too high, return to design phase) Desired profit margin (P_t) =	Target profit (P_{tc}) =
	TARGET COST (C_{tc}) ⇩
	Value engineering Supplier pricing pressure
Expected selling price (S_t) − Estimated cost (C_t)	(Both value engineering and pressure of suppliers to reduce cost are applied as a result of the target costs for each component)
⇩	⇩
Manufacturing ⇩	**Manufacturing** ⇩
Periodic cost reduction	Continuous cost reduction

price (S_t). The profit margin is the result of the difference between the expected selling price and the estimated production cost.[2] This relationship is expressed in the following equation:

$$P_t = S_t - C_t$$

In another widely used traditional approach, the cost-plus method, an expected profit margin (P_{cp}) is added to the expected product cost (C_{cp}), where *cp* indicates numbers derived from the cost-plus method. Selling price (S_{cp}) becomes simply the sum of these two variables. In equation form, this relationship is expressed as follows:

$$S_{cp} = C_{cp} + P_{cp}$$

In both traditional methods, product designers do not attempt to achieve a particular cost target.

In target costing, both the sequence of steps and the way of thinking about determining product costs differ significantly from traditional costing (see Exhibit 7-5, column 2). Although the initial steps—market research to determine customer requirements and product specification—appear similar to traditional costing, there are some notable differences. First, marketing research under target costing is not a single event as it often is under the traditional approach. Rather, the approach is *customer driven*, with customer input obtained continually throughout the process.

---

[2] Robin Cooper developed the structure for comparing costs in this manner in "Nissan Motor Company, Ltd.: Target Costing System," Harvard Business School Case #9-194-040.

Second, a method known as concurrent design and engineering is used to help design costs out of the product before manufacturing begins. This approach is particularly effective since we know that 80% to 85% of a product's total-life-cycle costs are committed during the RD&E cycle (review Exhibit 7-3). Third, target costing uses the total-life-cycle concept by making it a key goal to minimize the cost of ownership of a product over its useful life. Thus, not only are costs such as the initial purchase price considered, but so are the costs of operating, maintaining, and disposing of the product.

After these initial steps, the target costing process becomes even more distinctive. In the next step, price-led costing is used. With this approach, a target selling price (S_{tc}) and target product volume are chosen on the basis of the company's perceived value of the product to the customer. The target profit margin (P_{tc}) results from a long-run profit analysis often based on return on sales (net income ÷ sales). Return on sales is the most widely used measure because it can be linked most closely to profitability for each product. The target cost (C_{tc}) is the difference between the target selling price and the target profit margin. (Note that tc indicates numbers derived under the target costing approach.) This relationship for the target costing approach is shown in the following equation:

$$C_{tc} = S_{tc} - P_{tc}$$

Once the target cost has been set, the company must determine target costs for each component. The value engineering process includes examination of each component of a product to determine whether it is possible to reduce costs while maintaining functionality and performance. In some cases, product design may change, materials used in production may need replacing, or manufacturing processes may require redesign. For example, a product design change may mean using fewer parts or reducing specialty parts if more common components can be used. Several iterations of value engineering usually are needed before it is possible to determine the final target cost.

Two other differences characterize the target costing process. First, throughout the entire process, cross-functional product teams made up of individuals representing the entire value chain—both inside and outside the organization—guide the process. For example, it is not uncommon for a team to consist of people from inside the organization (such as design engineering, manufacturing operations, management accounting, and marketing) and representatives from outside the organization (including suppliers, customers, distributors, and waste disposers).

A second difference is that suppliers play a critical role in making target costing work. If there is a need to reduce the cost of specific components, firms will ask their suppliers to find ways to reduce costs. Companies may offer incentive plans to suppliers who come up with the largest cost reduction ideas. Others, however, have begun to use an approach known as supply chain management. Supply chain management develops cooperative, mutually beneficial, long-term relationships between buyers and suppliers. The benefits are many. For example, as trust develops between buyer and supplier, decisions about how to resolve cost reduction problems can be made with shared information about various aspects of each other's operations. In some organizations, the buyer may even expend resources to train the supplier's employees in some aspect of the business, or a supplier may assign one of its employees to work with the buyer to understand a new product. Such interactions are quite different from the short-term, antagonistic relationships that are characteristic of a traditional buyer–seller relationship.

A Target Costing Example

How does target costing actually work in practice?[3] We illustrate the target costing process with an example using hypothetical company, Kitchenhelp, Inc.

Among other products, Kitchenhelp manufactures coffeemakers. Market research has identified eight features of a coffeemaker that are important to customers:

1. Coffee tastes and smells like espresso.
2. The unit is easy to take apart and clean.
3. Capacity is at least 6 cups.
4. The coffeemaker looks nice.
5. The unit has a clock timer to start automatically at a designated time.
6. The grinder performs well with different kinds of coffee beans.
7. The coffeemaker keeps the coffee warm after making it.
8. The unit automatically shuts off after a designated time period.

These customer requirements become the basis for the engineering design of the coffeemaker. Engineers must ensure that the product encompasses all the features that are important to customers. Assume that Kitchenhelp's coffeemaker currently costs $50 to manufacture. Management has decided that the cost of the coffeemaker has to be reduced.[4] In order to reduce costs, cost analysis and value engineering have to be conducted on each of the coffeemaker's components.

Cost Analysis

For Kitchenhelp, cost analysis involves determining what components of the coffeemaker (heating element, control panel, or grinder) to target for cost reduction and then assigning a cost target to each of these components. Cost analysis also focuses on the interaction between components and parts. Often a reduction in the cost of one component is more than offset by a cost increase elsewhere. For example, decreasing the cost of the outer shell of the coffeemaker by making it smaller may increase the costs of the control panel, electronic circuitry, and heating element. Cost analysis requires five subactivities:

1. **Developing a list of product components and functions.** Cost reduction efforts start by listing the various product components and identifying the functions that they perform and their current estimated cost. The initial product design and cost estimates provide this information. The list tells us what components and functions are needed to satisfy customer requirements and what it might cost to provide these functions. Exhibit 7-6 shows a diagram of the various components of the proposed coffeemaker.

2. **Doing a functional cost breakdown.** Each of the various parts and components of the coffeemaker performs a specific function. The next step is to identify that function and to estimate the cost. The functional cost breakdown is shown in Exhibit 7-7. For example, the function of the brew basket is to grind and filter coffee. The current estimated cost is $9 for the basket, which represents 18% of the total manufacturing cost for this product. To keep the example simple, we have combined several functions and components for the coffeemaker. At a detail level, the brew basket or the

---

[3] We thank Shahid Ansari, Jan Bell, Tom Klammer, and Carol Lawrence for allowing us to use this example from their book *Target Costing* (Boston: Houghton Mifflin, Company 2004).

[4] To simplify the example, we assume that selling, general, and administrative costs stay the same, although in practice these costs can change as well.

Exhibit 7-6
Major Components of Kitchenhelp's Proposed Coffeemaker

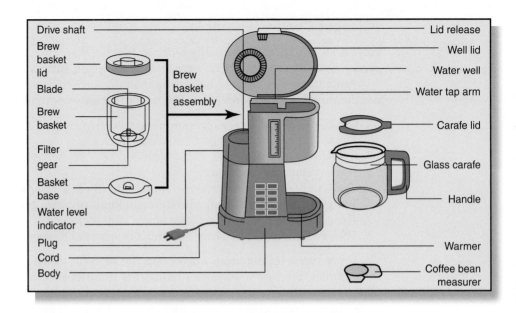

Exhibit 7-7
Functional Cost Breakdown for Kitchenhelp's Coffeemaker

		Cost	
Component	Function	Amount	Percent
Brew basket	Grinds and filters coffee	$9	18%
Carafe	Holds and keeps coffee warm	2	4
Coffee warmer	Keeps coffee warm	3	6
Body shape and water well	Holds water and encasement	9	18
Heating element	Warms water and pushes it	4	8
Electronic display panel	Controls grinder/clock settings	23	46
Total		$50	100%

electronic control panel will be broken into several subcomponents. The total for all components is $50.

3. **Determining relative ranking of customer requirements.** Engineers view a product in terms of its functions, often counter to the customer's view. Recall that Kitchenhelp had identified eight features that were important to its customers. The engineer's view of a product as functions must be reconciled with a customer's view of a product as a set of features. We must relate product functions to features that customers want. To do this, we first assess the relative importance that customers place on the various features. A formal survey of prospective customers asking them to rank the importance of these eight features can be used to rank customer requirements. An assumed ranking for each feature, based on a survey result, is shown in Exhibit 7-8. The importance ranking is based on a 5-point Likert scale. A score of 5 means that the feature is very important, and a score of 1 indicates that it is very unimportant. For example, taste and smell of coffee is the most important feature, and multiple grinder setting is the least.

The last column of Exhibit 7-8 converts the raw scores for the importance of features into a relative ranking of features (5 + 4 + 2 + 3 + 4 + 1 + 3 + 3 = 25). Each function's score is then expressed as a percentage of this total score of 25.

Exhibit 7-8
Customer Feature Ranking for Kitchenhelp's Coffeemaker

CUSTOMER REQUIREMENTS	CUSTOMER RANKING		RELATIVE RANKING
	1 NOT IMPORTANT	5 VERY IMPORTANT	IN PERCENT
Coffee tastes and smells like espresso		5	20%
Coffeemaker is easy to clean		4	16
Looks nice	2		8
Has 6+ cup capacity		3	12
Starts automatically at designated time		4	16
Works well with different coffee beans	1		4
Keeps the coffee warm		3	12
Automatically shuts off		3	12
Total			100%

For example, coffee taste has a score of 5 out of 25. The relative ranking, therefore, is 5/25 = 20%. This means that of the total value a customer derives from this coffeemaker, 20% comes from the way the coffee tastes.

4. **Relating features to functions.** The relative rankings of features must be converted into an importance ranking for each function. Since components carry out the functions of a product and are the key design parameters, this step relates customer rankings to the components that best meet that particular requirement. A tool called a quality function deployment (QFD) matrix is typically used for systematically arraying information about these three variables—features, functions (components), and competitive evaluation—in a matrix format.

The QFD matrix is a useful tool for target costing because it highlights the relationships among competitive offerings, customer requirements, and design parameters. A typical QFD matrix for Kitchenhelp's coffeemaker is shown in Exhibit 7-9. The QFD matrix summarizes the information about product functions from Exhibit 7-7 with customer rankings from Exhibit 7-8. It adds two other pieces of information that are collected in the market research phase: the correlation between a component or design parameter and customer requirements and information about how customers evaluate competitor offerings on these same features.

The matrix shows that the requirement that coffee tastes like espresso has a high correlation with the design of the brew basket and the heating element. Similarly, how many cups the coffeemaker can hold is correlated to the water well and carafe size. It also shows that taste, the most important feature to a customer, is currently rated at 3 for Kitchenhelp and 2 for its competitor. This tells Kitchenhelp that while it is ahead of the competition, it still is far from what the customer would like to see as far as taste goes. On appearance, the competition obviously has a better-looking product, with a rating of 5. However, the customer ranking for this feature is 2, which suggests that it is not worth spending too many resources in improving the appearance of the coffeemaker.

5. **Developing relative functional rankings.** The QFD matrix provides valuable information that allows us to convert feature rankings into functional or component rankings. This is critical because customers think in terms of features, but products are designed in terms of functions and components. To do this, we need one other piece of

Exhibit 7-9
A QFD Matrix For Kitchenhelp's Coffeemaker

COMPONENTS OR FUNCTIONS → CUSTOMER REQUIREMENTS ↓	BREW BASKET	CARAFE	COFFEE WARMER	BODY/ WATER WELL	HEATNG ELEMENT	DISPLAY PANEL	COMPARISON COMPETITOR VS. OUR PRODUCT 1 2 3 4 5	CUSTOMER FEATURE RANKING
Tastes/smells like espresso	▲				▲		■ □	5
Easy to clean	●	●		▲			□ ■	4
Looks nice				▲		▲	□ ■	2
Has 6+ cup capacity		▲		▲			■ □	3
Starts automatically on time						▲	□ ■	4
Works with different beans	○					▲	■ □	1
Keeps the coffee warm		●	▲				■ □	3
Automatic shutoff						▲	□ ■	3

Correlation of design parameters and customer requirements:
▲ = Strong correlation
● = Moderate correlation
○ = Weak correlation

Comparative competitor rankings:
■ = Competitor ranking
□ = Our ranking

Exhibit 7-10
Kitchenhelp Coffeemaker—Percent Contribution of Each Component to Customer Requirements

COMPONENTS → CUSTOMER REQUIREMENTS ↓	BREW BASKET	CARAFE	COFFEE WARMER	BODY/ WATER WELL	HEATING ELEMENT	DISPLAY PANEL	RELATIVE FEATURE RANKING
Tastes/smells like espresso	$50\% \times 20 = 10$				$50\% \times 20 = 10$		20%
Easy to clean	$30\% \times 16 = 4.8$	$10\% \times 16 = 1.6$		$60\% \times 16 = 9.6$			16
Looks nice				$60\% \times 8 = 4.8$		$40\% \times 8 = 3.2$	8
Has 6+ cup capacity		$50\% \times 12 = 6$		$50\% \times 12 = 6$			12
Starts automatically on time						$100\% \times 16 = 16$	16
Has multiple grinder settings	$5\% \times 4 = 0.2$					$95\% \times 4 = 3.8$	4
Keeps the coffee warm		$20\% \times 12 = 2.4$	$80\% \times 12 = 9.6$				12
Automatic shutoff						$100\% \times 12 = 12$	12
Converted component ranking	15.0	10.0	9.6	20.4	10.0	35.0	100%

information: the percentage contribution of each component to a customer feature. This information is shown as a general correlation in Exhibit 7-9. Engineers have to convert this correlation data into specific contribution percentages. Such a breakdown for our coffeemaker is shown in Exhibit 7-10 and interpreted as follows. The feature "tastes and smells like espresso" is a function of the brew basket and heating element design (you can verify this from Exhibit 7-9). Engineers feel that both of these components contribute equally to this "taste" feature. Thus, they assign each component a 50% contribution to taste. The relative value ranking of the "taste" feature is 20%. Therefore, since both components contribute equally, we assign each of the two components a value ranking of 10%. The last row of Exhibit 7-10 adds the value contributions of a component to all features to arrive at *that component's approximate value to a customer*. The brew basket is now said to have a value of 15% to a customer, the carafe has a value of 10%, and so on. Note that the last row and last column add up to 100%. They are simply different views of customer values. The column represents the value of features, and the row represents the value of components.

Conduct Value Engineering

Value engineering is an organized effort directed at analyzing the functions of the various components for the purpose of achieving these functions at the lowest overall cost without reductions in required performance, reliability, maintainability, quality, safety, recyclability, and usability. For example, the purpose or function of a heating element is to bring water temperature to a specified level. Value engineering asks how this function of raising water temperature to 110 degrees can be achieved in 3 minutes at a lower cost. It analyzes both product and manufacturing process design and reduces cost by generating ideas for simplifying both. Value engineering is at the core of target costing. It consists of the following two subactivities:

1. **Identifying components for cost reduction.** Choosing which components to select requires computing a value index. This is the ratio of the value (degree of importance) to the customer and the percentage of total cost devoted to each component. For the coffeemaker, the value information is in the last row of Exhibit 7-10, and the relative cost information is in the last column of Exhibit 7-7. Both of these quantities are expressed as percentages. Exhibit 7-11 shows the computation for the value index and its implications for cost reduction. Components with a value index less than 1 are candidates for value engineering. Components with high value are candidates for enhancement since we are spending too little for a feature that is important to the customer. These components present an opportunity to enhance the product. Cost and relative importance are plotted in Exhibit 7-12.

The optimal value zone in Exhibit 7-12 indicates the value band in which no action is necessary. The optimal value zone is based on experience and opinions of target costing team members. The zone is usually wider at the bottom of the value index chart, where low importance and low cost occur, and narrower at the top, where features are imporant and cost variations are larger. The area of the graph above the optimal value zone indicates components that are candidates for cost reduction. Items below the zone are candidates for enhancement.

Exhibit 7-11
Value Index for Kitchenhelp's Coffeemaker

COMPONENT OR FUNCTION	COMPONENT COST (% OF TOTAL) (EX. 7-7)	RELATIVE IMPORTANCE (EX. 7-10) (IN %)	VALUE INDEX (COL 3 ÷ 2)	ACTION IMPLIED
Brew basket	18	15.0	0.83	Reduce cost
Carafe	4	10.0	2.50	Enhance
Coffee warmer	6	9.6	1.60	Enhance
Body shape and water well	18	20.4	1.13	O.K.
Heating element	8	10.0	1.25	Enhance
Electronic display panel	46	35.0	0.76	Reduce cost
	100%	100%		

Exhibit 7-12
Value Index Chart
for Kitchenhelp's
Coffeemaker

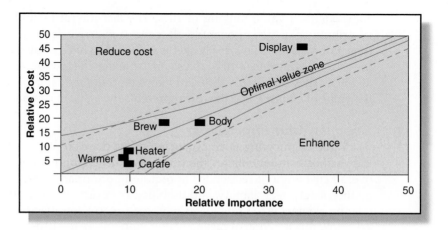

Exhibit 7-13
Kitchenhelp
Coffeemaker:
Electronic Display
Panel Value
Engineering Ideas
to Reduce Cost

Panel Subcomponent	Cost Reduction Idea
Power supply	**Reduce** wattage—more than needed in current design.
Flexible circuit	**Eliminate** flexible circuit. Use wiring harness
Printed wire board	**Standardize** board specifications. Use mass-produced unit.
Clock timer	**Combine** with printed wire board.
Central processor chip	**Substitute** standard 8088 chip instead of custom design.
Heater connector	**Rearrange** layout of board to heater connection.

2. **Generating cost reduction ideas.** This requires creative thinking and brainstorming. In this activity, decision makers try to determine what can be reduced, eliminated, combined, substituted, rearranged, or enhanced to provide the same level of functionality from a component at less cost. Exhibit 7-13 lists some sample cost reduction ideas that Kitchenhelp may consider to reduce the cost of the electronic display panel, the prime target for cost reduction identified by the value index. Perhaps reducing the number of parts, simplifying the assembly, and not overengineering the product beyond what a customer needs will lower cost. Finally, testing and implementing ideas is the last activity within value engineering. Promising ideas are evaluated to ensure that they are technically feasible and acceptable to customers.

Concerns About Target Costing

Although target costing has some obvious advantages, some studies of target costing in Japan indicate that there are potential problems in implementing the system, especially if focusing on meeting the target cost diverts attention away from the other elements of overall company goals.[5] Following are some examples:

1. **Lack of understanding of the target costing concept.** For many in the West, target costing is not a mainstream concept. Without a clear understanding of the benefits, many senior executives reject the idea.

---

[5] See M. Sakurai, "Past and Future of Japanese Management Accounting," *Journal of Cost Management*, fall, 1995, 1–14 and Y. Kato, G. Boer, and C. W. Chow, "Target Costing: An Integrated Management Process," *Journal of Cost Management*, spring 1995, 39–51.

In the early 1990s, Mercedes-Benz wanted to develop a new line of SUVs, the Mercedes-Benz M-Class. Production began in 1997 at the Tuscaloosa plant in Alabama. Mercedes decided to use target costing to help them define costs before they were committed. Mercedes relied on a number of customer, design, product, and marketing clinics before manufacturing the product and determined that safety, comfort, economy, and styling were the four key characteristics that customers were concerned about. Engineers determined that the key components for the automobile were the chassis, transmission, air conditioner, electrical system, and other systems.

Using an approach very similar to the one discussed in the Kitchenhelp coffeemaker, Mercedes determined the relationships among customer requirements and engineering components. Following is an illustration of how the final value index for the Mercedes-Benz M-Class might look. The value index shows that both the chassis and the air conditioner can be enhanced, while the transmission, electrical system, and other systems' costs can be reduced.

Component or Function	Component Cost (% of total)	Relative Importance (%)	Value Index	Action Implied
Chassis	20	33	1.65	Enhance
Transmission	25	20	0.80	Reduce cost
Air conditioner	5	7	1.40	Enhance
Electrical systems	7	6	0.86	Reduce cost
Other systems	43	35	0.81	Reduce cost

Source: Professor Thomas L. Albright, "Use of Target Costing in Developing the Mercedes-Benz M Class" (class presentation, University of Alabama).

2. **Poor implementation of the teamwork concept.** Teamwork and trust issues can lead to significant problems in implementing target costing. In some cases, companies put excessive pressure on subcontractors and suppliers to conform to schedule and reduce costs. This can lead to alienation and/or failure of the subcontractor. Sometimes design engineers become upset when other parts of the organization are not cost conscious; they argue that they exert much effort to squeeze pennies out of the cost of a product while other parts of the organization (administration, marketing, and distribution) are wasting dollars. Thus, many organizations must adapt to the level of teamwork, trust, and cooperation that has to exist for the target costing to be successful.

3. **Employee burnout.** Employees in many Japanese companies working under target costing goals experience burnout because of the pressure to meet the target cost. Burnout is particularly evident for design engineers.

4. **Overly-long development time.** Although the target cost might be met, development time may increase because of repeated value engineering cycles to reduce costs, ultimately leading to the product coming late to market. For some types of products, being 6 months late may be far more costly than having small cost overruns.

Companies may find it possible to manage many of these factors, but organizations interested in using the target costing process should be aware of them before immediately attempting to adopt this cost reduction method. The behavioral components of MACS design and, in particular, the need to motivate but not burn out employees have to be considered carefully. (We will discuss these issues more fully in chapter 8.) Despite these criticisms, target costing can provide engineers and managers the greatest leverage to reduce product costs in a critical part of the product life cycle.

Target costing has been in use in Japanese firms for many years. A survey conducted by Kobe University in Japan showed that of those responding, 100% of transportation equipment manufacturers, 75% of precision equipment manufacturers, 88% of electrical manufacturers, and 83% of machinery manufacturers stated that they used target costing.[6] The impetus for such widespread use was diminishing efficiency gains realized in production from using the just-in-time manufacturing system. The Japanese believed that further gains in both manufacturing and service costs could be made if they shifted the focus on cost reduction to the RD&E cycle.[7]

In the United States, target costing has gained momentum as a management method; however, it is not only a method of cost control but also a comprehensive approach to profit planning and cost management. Companies such as Boeing, Eastman Kodak, and DaimlerChrysler have adopted target costing in parts of their businesses, and, in particular, target costing has been applied successfully at Texas Instruments.[8]

Target costs have already been determined for these vehicles before they reach this stage of the manufacturing process.

Source: Jim Pickerell/PictureQuest.

[6] See Kato et al., *"Target Costing."*

[7] See R. Cooper and R. Slagmulder, *Target Costing and Value Engineering* (Portland, Ore: Productivity Press, 1997).

[8] See J. Dutton and M. Ferguson, "Target Costing at Texas Instruments," *Journal of Cost Management*, fall 1996, 33–38.

KAIZEN COSTING

Kaizen costing is similar to target costing in its cost-reduction mission, except that it focuses on reducing costs during the manufacturing stage of the total life cycle of a product. *Kaizen* is the Japanese term for making improvements to a process in small, incremental amounts rather than through large innovations. Kaizen's incremental approach is appropriate since products are already in the manufacturing process, making it difficult to make large changes to reduce costs.

Kaizen costing is tied into the profit-planning system.[9] In the Japanese automobile industry, for example, an annual budgeted profit target is allocated to each plant. Each automobile has a predetermined cost base that is equal to the actual cost of that automobile in the previous year. All cost reductions use this cost base as their starting point.

The *target reduction rate* is the ratio of the target reduction amount to the cost base. This rate is applied over time to all variable costs and results in specific target reduction amounts for materials, parts, direct and indirect labor, and other variable costs. Then management makes comparisons of actual reduction amounts across all variable costs to the preestablished targeted reduction amounts. If differences exist, variances for the plant are determined. Kaizen costing's goal is to ensure that actual production costs are less than the cost base. However, if the cost of disruptions to production is greater than the savings due to Kaizen costing, then it will not be applied.[10] Exhibit 7-14 illustrates one example of determining the total amount of Kaizen costs across multiple plants in a Japanese automobile plant.

Exhibit 7-14
Computing Kaizen Costs for Plants

Cost savings in Japanese automobile plants involve reducing both committed (fixed) and flexible (variable) costs. Since fixed costs are believed necessary for growth, the main emphasis is on reducing variable costs.

In this example, the total amount of Kaizen costs in all plants determined in a Kaizen planning meeting is designated as C in the formulas that follow:

Amount of actual cost per car in the last period (A)	=	Amount of actual cost in the last period	÷	Actual production in the last period
Estimated amount of actual cost for all plants in this period (B)	=	Amount of actual cost per car in the last period (A)	×	Estimated production in this period
Kaizen cost target in this period for all plants (C)	=	Estimated amount of actual cost for all plants in this period (B)	×	Target ratio of cost decrease to the estimated cost

The target ratio of cost decrease to the estimated cost is based on attaining the target profit for the year.

The Kaizen cost target for each plant is determined in the following manner:

Assignment ratio (D)	=	Costs controlled directly by each plant	÷	Total amount of costs controlled directly by plants
Total kaizen cost for each plant	=	Kaizen cost target in this period for all plants (C)	×	Assignment ratio (D)

The amount of Kaizen cost for each plant is subdivided to each division and subdivisions as cost reduction goals.

---

[9] This discussion is based on research by Y. Monden and J. Lee, "How a Japanese Auto Maker Reduces Costs," *Management Accounting*, August 1993, 22–26.

[10] See R. Cooper, *When Lean Enterprises Collide* (Boston: Harvard Business School Press, 1995).

Comparing Traditional Cost Reduction to Kaizen Costing

The Kaizen costing system is quite distinct from a traditional standard costing system in which the typical goal is to meet the cost standard while avoiding unfavorable variances. Under Kaizen costing, the goal is to achieve cost reduction targets that are continually adjusted downward. Variance analysis under a standard cost system usually compares actual to standard costs. Under the Kaizen costing system, variance analysis compares the target costs with actual cost reduction amounts. Kaizen costing operates outside the standard costing system, in part because standard costing systems in Japan are oriented toward complying with financial accounting standards.

Another key difference between standard and Kaizen costing has to do with the assumptions about who has the best knowledge to improve processes and reduce costs. Traditional standard costing assumes that engineers and managers know best because they have the technical expertise and can determine procedures that workers are required to perform according to preset standards and procedures. Under Kaizen costing, workers are assumed to have superior knowledge about how to improve processes because they actually work with manufacturing processes to produce products. To facilitate the process, information on actual costs must be shared with front line employees, which is a significant change for many companies. Thus, another central goal of Kaizen costing is to give workers the responsibility and control to improve processes and reduce costs. Exhibit 7-15 summarizes the differences in philosophy between standard costing and Kaizen costing methods.

Concerns About Kaizen Costing

Kaizen costing also has been criticized for the same reasons as that target costing has been criticized: The system places enormous pressure on employees to reduce every conceivable cost. To address the problem, some Japanese automobile companies use a grace period in manufacturing just before a new model is introduced. This period, called a *cost-sustainment period*, provides employees with the opportunity to learn any new procedures before the company imposes Kaizen and target costs on them.

Exhibit 7-15
Comparison of Standard Costing and Kaizen Costing

STANDARD COSTING CONCEPTS	KAIZEN COSTING CONCEPTS
Cost control system concept	Cost reduction system concept
Assumes stability in current manufacturing processes	Assumes continuous improvement in manufacturing
Goal is to meet cost performance standards	Goal is to achieve cost reduction standards
STANDARD COSTING TECHNIQUES	KAIZEN COSTING TECHNIQUES
Standards are set annually or semiannually	Cost reduction targets are set and applied monthly, and continuous improvement (Kaizen) methods are applied all year long to meet targets
Cost variance analysis involves comparing actual to standard costs	Cost variance analysis involves target Kaizen costs versus actual cost reduction amounts
Cost variance investigation occurs when standards are not met	Investigation occurs when target cost reduction (Kaizen) amounts are not attained
WHO HAS THE BEST KNOWLEDGE TO REDUCE COSTS?	WHO HAS THE BEST KNOWLEDGE TO REDUCE COSTS?
Managers and engineers develop standards as they have the technical expertise	Workers are closest to the process and thus know best

Another concern has been that Kaizen costing leads to incremental rather than radical process improvements. This can cause myopia as management tends to focus on the details rather than the overall system.

ENVIRONMENTAL COSTING

In today's business environment, environmental remediation, compliance, and management have become critical aspects of enlightened business practice. The impact of this change on MACS design and practice is that all parts of the value chain—and thus many kinds of costs—are affected by environmental issues. Environmental costing involves selecting suppliers whose philosophy and practice in dealing with the environment match those of buyers, disposing of waste products during the production process, and incorporating postsale service and disposal issues into cost management systems and overall MACS design.

Controlling Environmental Costs

Perhaps the best way to control and reduce environmental costs is to use the activity-based costing method developed in chapter 4. First, the activities that cause environmental costs must be identified. Second, the costs associated with the activities must be determined. Third, these costs must be assigned to the most appropriate products, distribution channels, and customers. As in all types of MACS, it is only when managers and employees become aware of how the activities in which they engage generate environmental costs that they can control and reduce them.

Environmental costs fall into two categories: explicit and implicit. *Explicit costs* include the direct costs of modifying technology and processes, costs of cleanup and disposal, costs of permits to operate a facility, fines levied by government agencies, and litigation fees. *Implicit costs* are often more closely tied to the infrastructure required to monitor environmental issues. These costs are usually administration and legal counsel, employee education and awareness, and the loss of goodwill if environmental disasters occur.

Some organizations have begun to take environmental costing seriously. Toshiba has been a pioneer in environmental accounting, introducing the concept in 1999. Environmental accounting provides information to support Toshiba's environmental management initiatives. Exhibit 7-16 illustrates Toshiba's model for weighing both environmental costs and benefits using a framework that assesses internal and external

Exhibit 7-16
Environmental Accounting as an Environmental Management Tool

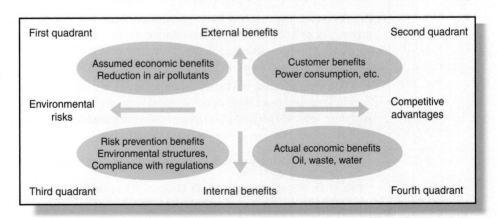

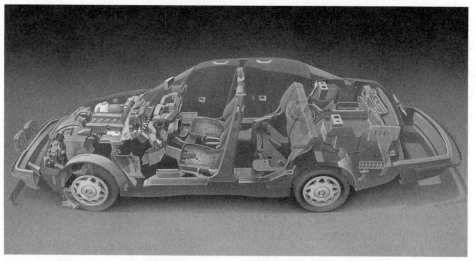

BMW uses parts made of recycled plastics (blue) and parts that can be recycled (green). So-called green manufacturing and potential legislation for companies to take back used components illustrate decision making based on the total-life-cycle costing concept.

Companies can reuse, refurbish, or dispose of a product's components safely and reduce total-life-cycle product costs.

Source: BMW of North America, LLC.

benefits, environmental risks, and competitive advantages. Toshiba states that the measurement of benefits is still in its infancy but that progress is being made.[11]

BENCHMARKING

In the opening vignette, Kaylee Young wanted to change her antiquated MACS to one that would generate relevant information over the entire value chain of her organization.[12] She investigated what other organizations had done to change their MACS. Her research and discussions with another local firm provided her with much information, as discussed next.

Organizations interested in a new management accounting method usually choose one of three ways to learn about and adopt a method:

1. The first is to bring in outside consultants to implement a particular method. Outside consultants can be effective but costly.

2. A second approach is for organizational members to develop their own systems internally with little or no assistance from outside consultants. Although this approach can be satisfying, it can be highly costly and time consuming, especially if the organization fails in its first few attempts at change.

3. The third approach, known as benchmarking, requires that organizational members first understand their current operations and approaches to conducting business and then look to the best practices of other organizations for guidance on improving.

---

[11] This information was obtained from Toshiba's Web site; http://www.toshiba.co.jp/env/en/management/account.htm.

[12] This section is based on research by D. Elnathan, T. Lin, and S. M. Young, "Benchmarking and Management Accounting: A Framework for Research," *Journal of Management Accounting Research*, Vol. 8, 1996, 37–54.

Benchmarking is a way for organizations to gather information regarding the best practices of others. It is often highly cost effective, as organizations can save time and money by avoiding the mistakes that other companies have made or by not reinventing a process or method that other companies have already developed and tested. Thus, selecting appropriate benchmarking partners (discussed later in this chapter) is a critical aspect of the process. The benchmarking process typically consists of five stages that include several organizational/diagnostic, operational, and informational factors. We present each stage here by listing its key factors. Exhibit 7-17 depicts the benchmarking process.

Stage 1: Internal Study and Preliminary Competitive Analyses

In this stage, the organization decides which key areas to benchmark for study, such as the company's activities, products, or management accounting methods. Then the company determines how it currently performs on these dimensions by initiating

Exhibit 7-17
Stages of the Benchmarking Process

STAGES OF THE BENCHMARKING PROCESS	FACTORS TO CONSIDER
Stage 1: Internal study and preliminary competitive analyses	Preliminary internal and external competitive analyses Determine key areas for study Determine scope and significance of the study

Stage 2: Developing long-term commitment to the benchmarking project and coalescing the benchmarking team	*Developing long-term commitment to the benchmarking project:*
	   Gain senior management support
	   Develop a clear set of objectives
	   Empower employees to make change
	 Coalescing the benchmarking team:
	   Use an experienced coordinator
	   Train employees

Stage 3: Identifying benchmarking partners	Size of partners Number of partners Relative position within and across industries Degree of trust among partners

Stage 4: Information-gathering and-sharing methods	*Type of benchmarking information:*
	   Product
	   Functional (process)
	   Strategic (includes management accounting methods)
	 Method of information collection:
	   Unilateral
	   Cooperative
	   Database
	   Indirect/third party
	   Group
	 Determine performance measures
	 Determine the benchmarking performance gap in relation to performance measures

Stage 5: Taking action to meet or exceed the benchmark	Comparisons of performance measures are made

Scientific Progress and the Reduction of Enviromental Costs: The Case of Chromium in Groundwater

The toxic effects of chemical chromium-6 (hexavalent chromium) found in groundwater at hazardous waste sites were brought to the public attention by Julia Roberts in her portrayal of environmental crusader Erin Brockavich. Chromium is an odorless, hard gray metal that is able to take a very high polish. The metal is extremely resistant to corrosion and is used in steel production and as a protective in automotive accessories, such as car bumpers. Chromium is not found in nature but is the result of interactions with other compounds.

Chromium becomes hexavalent chromium when it interacts with water.

Geologists at the University of Illinois at Urbana–Champaign have now developed a new method for determining the rate at which the suspected carcinogen naturally breaks down into a less toxic form. The results will help engineers assess when a major cleanup is necessary and hence provide decision makers with more accurate information by which to assess environmental and total-life-cycle costs.

Source: Adapted from Julie Foster, "Knowing When to Get the Chrome Out," *Business Week* March 25, 2002, p8. 43.

Julia Roberts (portraying Erin Brokovich) tests groundwater for the presence of chromium-6, a highly toxic chemical.
Source: Bob Marshak/Picture Desk, Inc./Kobal Collection.

both preliminary internal competitive analyses using internal company data and preliminary external competitive analyses using, for example, industry comparisons of quality from publications such as *Consumer Reports* or reports from J. D. Powers and Associates. Both types of analyses will determine the scope and significance of the study for each area. Another key factor to remember is that these analyses are not limited only to companies in a single industry. Thus, for example, although Kaylee Young works in the chemical industry, she could do competitive analyses in any type of organization.

Stage 2: Developing Long-Term Commitment to the Benchmarking Project and Coalescing the Benchmarking Team

In this stage, the organization must develop its commitment to the benchmarking project and coalesce a benchmarking team. Because significant organizational change, such as adopting a TLCC approach, can take several years, the level of commitment to benchmarking has to be long term rather than short term. Long-term commitment requires (1) obtaining the support of senior management to give the benchmarking team the authority to spearhead the changes, (2) developing a clear set of objectives to guide the benchmarking effort, and (3) empowering employees to make change.

The benchmarking team should include individuals from all functional areas in the organization. Developing a target costing system, for example, would benefit from a TLCC perspective, which requires employees from many functional areas. An experienced coordinator is usually necessary to organize the members' team and develop training in benchmarking methods. Lack of training often will lead to the failure of the implementation.

Stage 3: Identifying Benchmarking Partners

The third stage of benchmarking includes identification of partners—willing participants who know the process. Some critical factors are as follows:

1. Size of the partners
2. Number of partners
3. Relative position of the partners within and across industries
4. Degree of trust among partners

Size

The size of the benchmarking partner will depend on the specific activity or method being benchmarked. For example, if an organization wants to understand how a huge organization with several divisions coordinates its suppliers, then the organization would probably seek another organization of similar size for benchmarking. However, size is not always an important factor. For example, DaimlerChrysler Corporation, a huge corporation, studied L. L. Bean's warehousing method of flowcharting wasted motion. As a result, Chrysler implemented a method that led to significant changes in the ways that its workers were involved in organizational problem solving.

Number

Initially, it is useful for an organization to consider a wide array of benchmarking partners. However, organizations must be aware that as the number of partners increases, so do issues of coordination, timeliness, and concern over proprietary information disclosure. Researchers argue that today's changing business environment is likely to encourage firms to have a larger number of participants because increased competition and technological progress in information processing increases benchmarking benefits relative to costs.

Relative Position Within and Across Industries

Another factor is the relative position of the organization within an industry. In many cases, industry newcomers and those whose performance on leading indicators has declined are more likely to seek a wider variety of benchmarking partners than those who are established industry leaders. Those who are industry leaders may benchmark because of their commitment to continuous improvement.

Degree of Trust

From the benchmarking organization's point of view, developing trust among partners is critical to obtaining truthful and timely information. Most organizations, including industry leaders, operate on a quid pro quo basis, with the understanding that both organizations will obtain information they can use.

Stage 4: Information Gathering and Sharing Methods

Two dimensions relating to information gathering and sharing emerge from the literature: (1) the type of information that benchmarking organizations collect, and (2) methods of information collection.

Type of Information

There are three broad classes of information on which firms interested in benchmarking can focus. *Product benchmarking* is the long-standing practice of carefully examining other organizations' products. *Functional* (process) *benchmarking* is the study of other organizations' practices and costs with respect to functions or processes, such as assembly or distribution. *Strategic benchmarking* is the study of other organizations' strategies and strategic decisions, such as why organizations choose one particular strategy over another. Since management accounting methods have become an integral part of many organizations' strategies, benchmarking of these methods would occur as part of the management accounting function.

Methods of Gathering Information

Management accountants play a key role in gathering and summarizing information used for benchmarking. There are two major methods of information collection for benchmarking. The most common can be described as unilateral (covert) benchmarking, in which companies independently gather information about one or several other companies that excel in the area of interest. Unilateral benchmarking relies on data that companies can obtain from industry trade associations or clearinghouses of information. A second method is cooperative benchmarking, which is the voluntary sharing of information through mutual agreements. The major advantage of cooperative benchmarking is that information sharing occurs both within and across industries. Cooperative benchmarking has three subcategories: database, indirect/third party, and group.

Companies that use database benchmarking typically pay a fee and in return gain access to information from a database operator. The database operator collects and edits the information prior to making it available to users. In most cases, there is no direct contact with other firms, and the identity of the source of the data often is not revealed. The database method has the advantage of including a large amount of information in one place; however, insights regarding what the data mean for the firm and how to use the information often are not available.

Indirect/third-party benchmarking uses an outside consultant to act as a liaison among firms engaged in benchmarking. The consultant supplies information from one party to the others and handles all communications. Often the consultant participates in the selection of partners. Since the members may be competitors, they pass information through a consultant so that members remain anonymous. This approach requires that the sources of the information remain confidential.

Participants using group benchmarking meet openly to discuss their methods. They coordinate their efforts, define common terminology, visit each other's sites, and generally have a long-run association. Typically, firms that engage in cooperative benchmarking abide by a code of conduct that they agree on prior to the study. As in most interactions, direct contact offers the opportunity for better understanding of the other parties involved and usually is the most effective benchmarking method. This method also is the most costly to implement; therefore, firms must evaluate the cost-benefit trade-offs.

After the information-gathering process is complete, the participants conducting the benchmarking study determine a benchmarking (performance) gap by comparing their organization's own performance with the best performance that emerges from the data. The performance gap is defined by specific performance measures on which the firm would like to improve. Performance measures may include reduced defectives, faster on-time delivery, increased functionality, or reduced life-cycle product costs. Other, more qualitative measures may include better employee decisions concerning ways to work or solve problems, increased motivation and satisfaction, and improved cooperation and coordination among work groups and employees.

Financial gains such as reduced product costs usually occur as a result of addressing the relevant nonfinancial measures involved. Since most financial gains may take a significant amount of time to be felt, organizations should monitor the nonfinancial variables in the short term. Simply judging the effects of a benchmarking effort in the short term on the basis of financial indicators may lead to premature abandonment of what has been learned during the benchmarking project.

Stage 5: Taking Action to Meet or Exceed the Benchmark

In the final stage, the organization takes action and begins to change as a result of the benchmarking initiative. After implementing the change, the organization makes comparisons to the specific performance measures selected. In many cases, the decision may be to perform better than the benchmark to be more competitive. The implementation stage, especially the change process, is perhaps the most difficult stage of the benchmarking process, as the buy-in of organizational members is critical for success.

SUMMARY

This chapter is the first of two on management accounting and control system design for strategic purposes. Management accounting and control systems encompass many of the performance measure systems in an organization, including its cost management system. The concept of control refers to the set of procedures, tools, performance measures, and systems that organizations use to guide and motivate all employees to achieve organizational objectives. We also identify the technical characteristics of well-designed management accounting and control systems, which include two categories: the relevance of the information and the scope of the system. Four characteristics—accuracy, timeliness, consistency, and flexibility—measure the relevance of the information over the organization's entire value chain.

We present the total-life-cycle costing concept as a method that accumulates product costs over the entire value chain. In today's business environment, managing cost and other performance variables over the entire value chain has become of paramount importance to competing. Three methods relating to total-life-cycle costing include target costing, Kaizen costing, and environmental costing. Target costing and environmental costing begin in the research development and engineering stage of the value chain. Using these methods provides organizations with the ability to control and reduce costs at all other stages of the value chain. Kaizen costing is an approach that can be used during the manufacturing process. It enables organizations to make small improvements in products during the production stage. The chapter concludes with a discussion of how managers can use benchmarking to aid them in understanding the best practices of others and ultimately how to apply what they learn to their own organizations.

KEY TERMS

Benchmarking, 334
Benchmarking (performance) gap, 339
Committed costs, 318
Concurrent design and engineering, 322
Control, 314
Cooperative benchmarking, 338
Cross-functional product teams, 322
Database benchmarking, 338
Environmental costing, 333
Group benchmarking, 339
In control, 314

Indirect/third-party benchmarking, 338
Kaizen costing, 331
Management accounting and control system, 314
Manufacturing cycle, 318
Out of control, 314
Postsale service and disposal cycle, 319
Price-led costing, 322
Quality function deployment (QFD) matrix, 325
Relevance of information, 316

Research development and engineering cycle, 318
Scope of the MACS, 317
Supply chain management, 322
Target cost, 322
Target costing, 320
Total-life-cycle costing, 317
Unilateral (covert) benchmarking, 338
Value engineering process, 322
Value index, 327

ASSIGNMENT MATERIALS

Questions

7-1 What does *control* refer to in the context of a management accounting and control system? (LO 1)

7-2 What are the five steps involved in keeping an organization in control? (LO 1)

7-3 What two broad technical considerations must designers of management and control systems address? (LO 2)

7-4 What four components should management accounting and control systems designers consider when addressing the relevance of the system's information? (LO 2)

7-5 What is the total-life-cycle costing approach? Why is it important? (LO 3)

7-6 What are the three major cycles of the total-life-cycle costing approach in a manufacturing situation? (LO 3)

7-7 What is the difference between committed costs and incurred costs? (LO 3)

7-8 What are the three stages of the research development and engineering cycle? (LO 3)

7-9 What is the postsale service and disposal cycle? (LO 3)

7-10 What is target costing? (LO 4)

7-11 What are the two essential elements needed to arrive at a target cost? (LO 4)

7-12 What is a quality function deployment matrix, and how does it relate to value index computations for target costing? (LO 4)

7-13 What is value engineering? (LO 4)

7-14 In which stage of the total life cycle of a product is target costing most applicable? (LO 4)

7-15 What roles do cross-functional teams and supply chain management play in target costing? (LO 4)

7-16 What is Kaizen costing? (LO 5)

7-17 When is a cost-variance investigation undertaken under Kaizen costing? (LO 5)

7-18 Why is it said that a Kaizen costing system operates "outside the standard costing system?" (LO 5)

7-19 What are some examples of explicit and implicit environmental costs? (LO 6)

7-20 What is benchmarking, and why is it used? (LO 7)

7-21 What are the five stages of the benchmarking process? (LO 7)

7-22 What are the three broad classes of information on which firms interested in benchmarking can focus? Describe each. (LO 7)

7-23 What stage of the benchmarking process is the most important for benchmarking management accounting methods? Why? (LO 7)

7-24 What are the two general methods of information gathering and sharing when undertaking a benchmarking exercise? (LO 7)

7-25 What are the three types of sharing and gathering information under the cooperative form of benchmarking? (LO 7)

7-26 What is a benchmarking (performance) gap? (LO 7)

Exercises

LO 1 **7-27** *Achieving objectives* Eni Corporation's mission statement includes the following: "Our mission is to continuously improve the company's value to shareholders, customers, employees, and society." Interpret how each of Eni Corporation's stakeholder groups may interpret "the company's value" in the mission statement and, given each group's interpretation, how it may be measured for each group.

LO 2 **7-28** *Achieving relevance in MACS design* Identify the four components that MACS designers should consider when addressing the relevance of the system's information and explain why each component is important.

LO 3 **7-29** *Total-life-cycle costing* Explain how the total-life-cycle costing approach differs from traditional product costing.

LO 3 **7-30** *Benefits of total-life-cycle costing* Explain the benefits of using a total-life-cycle costing approach to product costing.

LO 3 **7-31** *Problems with traditional accounting focus* What is the traditional accounting focus in managing costs over the total life cycle of a product? What is the problem with this focus?

LO 3 **7-32** *Costs committed versus costs incurred* Review Exhibit 7-3, showing the relationship between committed costs and incurred costs over the total life cycle of a product. Explain what the diagram means and what the implications are for managing costs.

LO 3 **7-33** *Postsale and disposal cycle* When does the disposal phase of the postsale and disposal cycle of a product begin and end?

LO 4 **7-34** *Target costing* Explain how target costing differs from traditional cost reduction methods.

LO 4 **7-35** *Target costing equation* Express the target costing relationship in equation form. How does this equation differ from the two other types of traditional equations relating to cost reduction? Why is this significant?

LO 4 **7-36** *Value engineering* What is the relationship between value engineering and target costing?

LO 4 **7-37** *Target costing profitability measure* What is the profitability measure most widely used to develop the target profit margin under target costing?

LO 4 **7-38** *Target costing calculations* Refer to the Kitchenhelp Coffeemaker example in the chapter. Suppose that Exhibits 7-7 and 7-8 remain the same but that engineers developed different numerical correlations, shown below, for the QFD matrix in Exhibit 7-9.

	COMPONENTS OR FUNCTIONS					
CUSTOMER REQUIREMENTS	BREW BASKET	CARAFE	COFFEE WARMER	BODY/WATER WELL	HEATING ELEMENT	DISPLAY PANEL
Tastes/smells like expresso	0.7				0.3	
Easy to clean	0.5	0.1		0.4		
Looks nice		0.1		0.5		0.4
Has 6+ cup capacity		0.5		0.5		
Starts automatically on time						1
Has multiple grinder settings	0.1					0.9
Keeps the coffee warm		0.2	0.8			
Automatic shutoff						1

Required

a. Prepare an exhibit similar to Exhibit 7-10 showing percentage contributions of each component to customer requirements.

b. Prepare a value index exhibit similar to Exhibit 7-11. Which components are candidates for cost reduction?

LO 4   **7-39 Implementing target costing**   What are potential problems in implementing a target costing system from a behavioral point of view?

LO 5   **7-40 Kaizen versus standard costing**   What factors differentiate Kaizen costing from standard costing?

LO 5   **7-41 Target costing versus Kaizen costing**   What is the major difference between target costing and Kaizen costing?

LO 5   **7-42 Kaizen costing: knowledge**   According to the Kaizen costing approach, who has the best knowledge to reduce costs? Why is this so?

LO 5   **7-43 Kaizen meaning**   What do the terms *Kaizen* and *Kaizen costing* mean? In which stage of the total life cycle of a product is Kaizen costing most applicable? Why?

LO 5   **7-44 Kaizen costing**   Under what condition will the cost savings due to Kaizen costing not be applied to production?

LO 6   **7-45 Activity-based costing for environmental costs**   How can a firm use activity-based costing to help control and reduce environmental costs?

LO 7   **7-46 Benchmarking partners**   What are the key factors in identifying benchmarking partners? Explain why these factors are important.

LO 7   **7-47 Benchmarking a target costing system**   As a manager asked to benchmark another organization's target costing system, on what factors would you gather information? Why?

LO 3   **7-48 Total-life-cycle costing**   Consider the following situation: Your manager comes to you and says, "I don't understand why everyone is talking about the total-life-cycle costing approach to product costing. As far as I am concerned, this new approach is a waste of time and energy. I think we should just stick to what we know, and that is the traditional approach to product costing."

Required

Write a memorandum critiquing your manager's view. In the memo, discuss the benefits of adopting the total-life-cycle costing approach.

LO 3 **7-49 Total-life-cycle costing versus traditional methods** Gregoire Grant is a traditional manufacturing manager who is concerned only with managing costs over the manufacturing cycle of the product. He argues that since traditional accounting methods are focused on this cycle, he should not bother with the RD&E cycle because it is separate from his area of manufacturing.

Required

Write an essay discussing Gregoire's views. What types of structural and functional changes in organizations may be necessary to help Gregoire overcome his traditional view?

LO 4 **7-50 Target costing: unit cost** Calcutron Company is contemplating introducing a new type of calculator to complement its existing line of scientific calculators. The target price of the calculator is $75; annual sales volume of the new calculator is expected to be 500,000 units. Calcutron has a 15% return-on-sales target.

Required

Compute the unit target cost per calculator.

LO 4 **7-51 Target costing: return on sales** Stacy Yoo, president of Caremore, Inc., an appliance manufacturer in Seattle, Washington, has been trying to decide whether one of her product-line managers, Bill Mann, has been achieving the companywide return-on-sales target of 45%. Stacy has just received data from the new target costing system regarding Bill's operation. Bill's sales volume was 300,000 appliances with an average selling price of $500 and expenses totaling $90 million.

Required

Determine whether Bill's return-on-sales ratio has met the companywide target. Has Bill done a good or a poor job? Explain.

LO 4 **7-52 Target costing: implementation issues** Pierre LeBlanc, manager of Centaur Corporation, is thinking about implementing a target costing system in his organization. Several managers have taken him aside and have expressed concerns about implementing target costing in their organization.

Required

As an expert in target costing, you have been called in to discuss these concerns and offer advice on overcoming them. Write a memorandum discussing common concerns that managers have about target costing. In the memo, state how you would remedy these concerns.

LO 4 **7-53 Traditional cost reduction versus target costing** Traditional cost reduction in the United States differs significantly from the Japanese method of target costing.

Required

Discuss the similarities and differences in the process by which cost reduction under both systems occurs. Be specific in your answer.

LO 5 **7-54 Kaizen costing: behavioral issues** Kaizen costing is a method that many Japanese companies have found effective in reducing costs.

Required

From a behavioral point of view, answer these questions:

a. What are the biggest problems in using Kaizen costing?
b. How can managers overcome these problems?

LO 4, 7   **7-55 Benchmarking**   As a manager interested in learning more about target costing, you are contemplating three approaches to obtaining the best information possible. The first is to bring in an outside consultant; the second is to develop your own system inside your organization with little to no outside assistance; and the third is to engage in a benchmarking project with several other firms.

Required

Critique each of these approaches, discussing their pros and cons. On what basis will you select your approach to learning about target costing? Explain.

LO 4   **7-56 Target costing versus traditional cost reduction methods**   According to this chapter, the target costing and traditional cost reduction methods approach the relationships among cost, selling price, and profit margin quite differently.

Required

Write an essay that illustrates how the target costing and traditional cost reduction methods differ, using the appropriate symbols and equations. In addition to the equations, describe how the processes differ in deriving costs.

LO 4   **7-57 Target costing and service organization**   Imagine that you are the manager of a large bank. Having heard about a management accounting method called *target costing,* you are wondering whether it can be applied to the banking industry. In particular, you are trying to determine how to benchmark other organizations to gain more information.

Required

a. Can target costing be applied to the banking industry? To what products or services can target costing be applied?
b. Devise a benchmarking plan for the bank. Your plan should include which banks to benchmark with and the kinds of information sought.

LO 5   **7-58 Standard costing versus Kaizen costing**   Many companies are interested in adopting a Kaizen costing approach to reducing costs. However, they are not sure how their current standard costing system will fit with the Kaizen costing approach.

Required

How do the standard costing system and the Kaizen costing system differ? Can the two systems coexist? Explain.

LO 5   **7-59 Kaizen costing versus standard costing**   Your organization, located in Worthington, Ohio, is contemplating introducing Kaizen costing to help with cost reduction. As someone who has an understanding of management accounting, you have been asked for your opinion. Specifically, some of your colleagues are wondering about the differences between standard costing and Kaizen costing.

Required

Write a report discussing the following:

a. The similarities and differences between standard costing and Kaizen costing

b. Under what conditions Kaizen costing can be adapted to U.S. organizations

LO 7   **7-60** *Benchmarking: field exercise with other students*   Assume that you are an average student who has a desire to be one of the best students in class. Your professor suggests that you benchmark the working habits of the best student in the class. You are somewhat skeptical but decide to take on the challenge.

Required

How would you go about this benchmarking exercise? In answering this question, describe the process that you would undertake in benchmarking the best student, the factors that you would be trying to study, and how you would implement changes to your working habits.

LO 7   **7-61** *Benchmarking: field exercise in a company*   Benchmarking a product, process, or management accounting method takes a great deal of time and effort. Companies have many choices when it comes to conducting a benchmarking study. For example, in following the five stages of the benchmarking process, companies have to decide how to proceed, who to select as benchmarking partners, and what information they are willing to share and to gather.

Required

Locate a company in your local community that has engaged in a benchmarking study. Try to arrange a visit to the company (perhaps through your professor, relative, or friend) in order to talk to employees who have been involved in the benchmarking effort. Using the five-stage process, critique the approach that this company followed. What are the similarities and differences between what this company did and the process described in this chapter? Be specific about the procedures that were used and the variables that were assessed. Finally, what were the results of the benchmarking exercise at this company? Was it a success or a failure? Why?

Cases

LO 5,6   **7-62** *Environmental costs, activity-based costing, Kaizen costing*   Bevans Co. makes two products, product X and product Y. Bevans has produced product X for many years without generating any hazardous wastes. Recently, Bevans developed product Y, which is superior to product X in many respects. However, production of product Y generates hazardous wastes. Because of the hazardous wastes, Bevans now must deal with hazardous waste disposal, governmental environmental reports and inspections, and safe handling procedures.

Bevans Co. uses a cost driver rate based on machine hours to assign manufacturing support costs to its two products. Because of concerns about the accuracy of the product costing system, Joel Dempsey, the controller, undertook an activity-based costing analysis of the manufacturing support costs. The resulting cost information is summarized in the following table:

	Product X	Product Y
Direct costs (material plus labor)	$9,000,000	$4,000,000
Unit-level support	$2,000,000	$1,000,000
Batch-level support	$15,000,000	$20,000,000
Product-level support	$5,000,000	$8,000,000
Environmental support	—	$14,000,000
Total machine hours	10,000,000	6,000,000
Number of units	100,000,000	40,000,000

Required

    a. Compute product costs per unit for products X and Y using the current cost driver rate based on machine hours for manufacturing support costs.

    b. Compute product costs per unit for products X and Y using the activity-based costing figures provided in the table.

    c. Explain the reasons for the differences in cost for each product using the two cost systems. (You may wish to compute unit-level support, batch-level support, product-level support, and environmental support costs per unit.)

    d. Bevans has been selling products X and Y at a price equal to 1.5 times the product cost computed using the machine-hour-based cost driver rate for manufacturing support costs. Compute these prices and provide recommendations to Bevans' management concerning profit improvement through pricing changes and cost reduction through manufacturing improvements.

    LO 6   **7-63 *Explicit and implicit environmental costs***   Refer to Case 5-62, which describes Kwik Clean's environmental costs.

Required

    a. Identify explicit and implicit environmental costs that Pat Polley has listed.

    b. Should Polley identify any other environmental costs?

    c. Prepare a memo to Polley explaining how an activity-based costing approach can help her control and reduce Kwik Clean's environmental costs.

    LO 4   **7-64 *Target costing***   Mercedes-Benz All Activity Vehicle (AAV).[13]

INTRODUCTION

During the recession beginning in the early 1990s, Mercedes-Benz (MB) struggled with product development, cost efficiency, material purchasing, and problems in adapting to changing markets. In 1993, these problems caused the worst sales slump in decades, and the luxury carmaker lost money for the first time in its history. Since then, MB has streamlined the core business, reduced parts and system complexity, and established simultaneous engineering programs with suppliers.

In their search for additional market share, new segments, and new niches, MB started developing a range of new products. New product introductions included the C-Class in 1993, the E-Class in 1995, the new sportster SLK in 1996, and the A-Class and M-Class All Activity Vehicle (AAV) in 1997. Perhaps the largest and most radical of MB's new projects was the AAV. In April 1993, MB announced it would build its first passenger vehicle–manufacturing facility in the United States. The decision emphasized the company's globalization strategy and desire to move closer to its customers and markets.

Mercedes-Benz United States International used function groups with representatives from every area of the company (marketing, development, engineering, purchasing, production, and controlling) to design the vehicle and production systems. A modular construction process was used to produce the AAV. First-tier suppliers provided systems rather than individual parts or components for production of approximately 65,000 vehicles annually.

---

[13] Institute of Management Accountants, *Cases from Management Accounting Practice, Volume 15*. Adapted with permission. The case author wishes to express his gratitude to Ola Kallenins, Johnathan DeHart, Jason Hoff, Henrik Jonsson, Iosef Pfau, and Günther Thuss of Mercedes-Benz for their generous contributions to the development of this case

THE AAV PROJECT PHASES

The AAV moved from concept to production in a relatively short period of time. The first phase, the concept phase, was initiated in 1992. The concept phase resulted in a feasibility study that was approved by the board. Following board approval, the project realization phase began in 1993, with production commencing in 1997. Key elements of the various phases are described next.

Concept Phase, 1992–1993

Team members compared the existing production line with various market segments to discover opportunities for new vehicle introductions. The analysis revealed opportunities in the rapidly expanding sports utility vehicle market that was dominated by Jeep, Ford, and GM. Market research was conducted to estimate potential worldwide sales opportunities for a high-end AAV with the characteristics of a Mercedes-Benz. A rough cost estimate was developed that included materials, labor, overhead, and one-time development and project costs. Projected cash flows were analyzed over a 10-year period using net present value (NPV) analysis to acquire project approval from the board of directors. The sensitivity of the NPV was analyzed by calculating "what-if" scenarios involving risks and opportunities. For example, risk factors included monetary exchange rate fluctuations, different sales levels due to consumer substitution of the AAV for another MB product, and product and manufacturing cost that differed from projections.

On the basis of the economic feasibility study of the concept phase, the board approved the project and initiated a search for potential manufacturing locations. Sites located in Germany, other European countries, and the United States were evaluated. Consistent with the company's globalization strategy, the decisive factor that brought the plant to the United States was the desire to be close to the major market for sports utility vehicles.

Project Realization Phase, 1993–1996

Regular customer clinics were held to view the prototype and to explain the new vehicle concept. These clinics produced important information about how the proposed vehicle would be received by potential customers and the press. Customers were asked to rank the importance of various characteristics, including safety, comfort, economy, and styling. Engineers organized in function groups designed systems to deliver these essential characteristics. However, MB would not lower its internal standards for components, even if initial customer expectations might be lower than the MB standard. For example, many automotive experts believed that the superior handling of MB products resulted from manufacturing the best automobile chassis in the world. Thus, each class within the MB line met strict standards for handling, even though these standards might exceed customer expectations for some classes. MB did not use target costing to produce the lowest-price vehicle in an automotive class. The company's strategic objective was to deliver products that were slightly more expensive than competitive models. However, the additional cost would have to translate into greater perceived value on the part of the customer.

Throughout the project realization phase, the vehicle (and vehicle target cost) remained alive because of changing dynamics. For example, the market moved toward the luxury end of the spectrum while the AAV was under development. In addition, crash test results were incorporated into the evolving AAV design. For these reasons, MB found it beneficial to place the design and testing team members in close physical proximity to other functions within the project to promote fast communication and decision making. Sometimes new technical features, such as side air bags, were developed by MB. The decision to include the new feature on all MB lines was made at the corporate level because experience had shown that customers' reactions to a vehicle class can affect the entire brand.

Production Phase, 1997

The project was monitored by annual updates of the NPV analysis. In addition, a 3-year plan (including income statements) was prepared annually and reported to the headquarters in Germany. Monthly departmental meetings were held to discuss actual cost performance compared with standards developed during the cost estimation process. Thus, the accounting system served as a control mechanism to ensure that actual production costs would conform to target (or standard) costs.

TARGET COSTING AND THE AAV

The process of achieving target cost for the AAV began with an estimate of the existing cost for each function group. Next, components of each function group were identified with their associated costs. Cost reduction targets were set by comparing the estimated existing cost with the target cost for each function group. These function groups included the following: doors, sidewall and roof, electrical system, bumpers, power train, seats, heating system, cockpit, and front end. Next, cost reduction targets were established for each component. As part of the competitive benchmark process, MB bought and tore down competitors' vehicles to help understand their costs and manufacturing processes.

The AAV manufacturing process relied on high-value-added systems suppliers. For example, the entire cockpit was purchased as a unit from a systems supplier. Thus, systems suppliers were part of the development process from the beginning of the project. MB expected suppliers to meet established cost targets. To enhance function group effectiveness, suppliers were brought into the discussion at an early stage in the process. Decisions had to be made quickly in the early stages of development.

The target costing process was led by cost planners who were engineers, not accountants. Because the cost planners were engineers with manufacturing and design experience, they could make reasonable estimates of costs that suppliers would incur in providing various systems. Also, MB owned much of the tooling, such as dies to form sheet metal, used by suppliers to produce components. Tooling costs are a substantial part of the one-time costs in the project phase.

Index Development to Support Target Costing Activities

During the concept development phase, MB team members used various indexes to help them determine critical performance, design, and cost relationships for the AAV.[14] To construct the indexes, various forms of information were gathered from customers, suppliers, and their own design team. Although the actual number of categories used by MB was much greater, Table 1 illustrates the calculations used to quantify customer responses to the AAV concept. For example, values shown in the "importance column" resulted from asking a sample of potential customers whether they consider each category extremely important when considering the purchase of a new MB product. Respondents could respond affirmatively to all categories that applied.

To gain a better understanding of the various sources of costs, *function groups* were identified together with target cost estimates. (MB also organizes teams called function groups whose role is to develop specifications and cost projections.) As shown in Table 2, the relative target cost percentage of each function group was computed.

Table 1
Relative Importance Ranking by Category

Category	Importance	Relative Percentage
Safety	32	41%
Comfort	25	32
Economy	15	18
Styling	7	9
Total	79	100%

---

[14] All numbers have been altered for proprietary reasons; however, the tables illustrate the actual process used in the development of the AAV.

Table 3 summarizes how each function group contributes to the consumer requirements identified in Table 1. For example, safety was identified by potential customers as an important characteristic of the AAV; some function groups contributed more to the safety category than others. MB engineers determined that chassis quality was an important element of safety (50% of the total function group contribution).

Table 4 combines the category weighting percentages from Table 1 with the function group contribution from Table 3. The result is an importance index that measures the relative importance of each function group across all categories. For example, potential customers weighted the categories of safety, comfort, economy, and styling as .41, .32, .18, and .09, respectively. The rows in Table 4 represent the contribution of each function group to the various categories. The importance index for the chassis is calculated by multiplying each row value by its corresponding category value and summing the results: $(.50 \times .41) + (.30 \times .32) + (.10 \times .18) + (.10 \times .09) = .33$.

As shown in Table 5, the target cost index is calculated by dividing the importance index by the target cost percentage by function group. Managers at MB used indexes such as these during the

Table 2
Target Cost and Percentage by Function Group

FUNCTION GROUP	TARGET COST	PERCENTAGE OF TOTAL
Chassis	$x,xxx	20%
Transmission	x,xxx	25
Air conditioner	xxx	5
Electrical system	xxx	7
Other function groups	x,xxx	43
Total	$x,xxx	100%

Table 3
Function Group Contribution to Customer Requirements

FUNCTION GROUP	CATEGORY			
	SAFETY	COMFORT	ECONOMY	STYLING
Chassis	50%	30%	10%	10%
Transmission	20	20	30	
Air conditioner		20		5
Electrical system	5		20	
Other function groups	25	30	40	85
Total	100%	100%	100%	100%

Table 4
Importance Index of Various Function Groups

FUNCTION GROUP	CATEGORY				IMPORTANCE INDEX
	SAFETY .41	COMFORT .32	ECONOMY .18	STYLING .09	
Chassis	.50	.30	.10	.10	.33
Transmission	.20	.20	.30		.20
Air conditioner		.20		.05	.07
Electrical system	.05		.20		.06
Other function groups	.25	.30	.40	.85	.35
Total	1.00	1.00	1.00	1.00	

Table 5
Target Cost Index

INDEX FUNCTION GROUP	(A) IMPORTANCE INDEX	(B) % OF TARGET COST	(C) A/B TARGET COST INDEX
Chassis	.33	.20	1.65
Transmission	.20	.25	.80
Air conditioner	.07	.05	1.40
Electrical system	.06	.07	.86
Other function groups	.35	.43	.81
Total		1.00	

concept design phase to understand the relationship of the importance of a function group to the target cost of a function group. Indexes less than 1 may indicate a cost in excess of the perceived value of the function group. Thus, opportunities for cost reduction consistent with customer demands, may be identified and managed during the early stages of product development. Choices made during the project realization phase were largely irreversible during the production phase because approximately 80% of the production cost of the AAV was for materials and systems provided by external suppliers.

The AAV project used a streamlined management structure to facilitate efficient and rapid development. The streamlined MB organization produced an entirely new vehicle from concept to production in 4 years. Using the target costing process as a key management element, MB manufactured the first production AAV in 1997.

Required

a. What is the competitive environment faced by MB as it considers launching the AAV?
b. How has MB reacted to the changing world for luxury automobiles?
c. Using Cooper's cost, quality, and functionality chart,[15] discuss the factors on which MB would have to compete with other automobile producers, such as Jeep, Ford, and GM.
d. How does the AAV project link with MB's strategy in terms of market coverage?
e. Explain the process of developing an importance index for a function group or component. How can such an index guide managers in making cost reduction decisions?
f. How does MB approach cost reduction to achieve target costs?
g. How do suppliers factor into the target costing process? Why are they so critically important to the success of the MB AAV?
h. What role does the accounting department play in the target costing process?

---

[15] Robin Cooper, *When Lean Enterprises Collide* (Boston: Harvard Business School Press, 1995).

Chapter 8

Motivating Behavior in Management Accounting and Control Systems

After reading this chapter, you will be able to:

➤ discuss the four key behavioral considerations in the design of a management accounting and control system

➤ explain the human resources model of management

➤ discuss task and results control methods

➤ apply the ethical control framework to decisions

➤ discuss the links between different incentive systems and performance

---

Chemco International: Behavioral Considerations

As we saw in chapter 7, Nathaniel Young has been developing the technical side of the new management accounting and control system (MACS) that he plans to implement. At a management briefing, a senior vice president mentioned to him that several managers and their employees were expressing concerns about the proposed changes to the MACS. They wanted to know how the system was designed, whether their performance would be assessed differently, and whether their compensation plans would be altered. They also were uncertain about how the new MACS would alter the organizational work culture and help achieve organizational strategies.

As he was listening to the discussion, Nathaniel realized that he had committed a major error in his approach—he had not involved enough key people in system design. He wanted to achieve several goals with the new MACS. First, he wanted to design a system whose operation on a day-to-day basis was consistent with the company's ethical and cultural norms of

These employees are discussing their organization's performance in comparison to their initial plans. *Source*: Ron Chapple/Getty Images–Photodisc.

behavior. Second, because the previous system had relied myopically on narrow, short-term financial goals, he wanted to encourage broader thinking for all employees through the use of multiple performance measures. In particular, he wanted to encourage a work environment that fostered creativity. Third—and this is where he had really faltered—he wanted to make sure that people were motivated to work at the company. To this end, he had thought about various types of compensation systems to reward superior performance, but he had not considered asking more employees to participate in overall system design. Was it too late to involve them and get their valuable input?

MANAGEMENT ACCOUNTING AND CONTROL SYSTEMS

Chapter 7 presented the technical characteristics of a well-designed management accounting and control system (MACS) and illustrated how these characteristics increase the organization's ability to adapt its measurement systems to changing information needs. However, because human interests and motivation can vary significantly, a major role for control systems is to motivate behavior congruent with the desires of the organization.

This chapter turns to the second set of characteristics related to MACS design. To recap, chapter 7 enumerated four major behavioral considerations:

1. Embedding the organization's ethical code of conduct into MACS design
2. Using a mix of short- and long-term qualitative and quantitative performance measures (or the Balanced Scorecard Approach)

3. Empowering employees to be involved in decision making and MACS design
4. Developing an appropriate incentive system to reward performance

Nathaniel Young's dilemma at the beginning of this chapter highlights a key issue that plagues major companies. Although many managers want to do what is best for their companies, they often try to implement new systems without considering the behavioral implications and consequences of a MACS. Unless they pay careful attention to these factors, goal congruence may not occur, motivation could be low, and, worst of all, employees may be encouraged to engage in dysfunctional behavior.

Note, however, that these four characteristics do not simply arise by accident in every MACS. Rather, companies that have a MACS often subscribe to a particular worldview of the role of management that we label the *human resource management model of motivation*. The development of this view is discussed next, followed by a detailed discussion of the four characteristics.

THE HUMAN RESOURCE MANAGEMENT MODEL OF MOTIVATION

One of the earliest attempts at understanding the role of management, developed at the turn of the twentieth century, was the scientific management school. The underlying philosophy was that most people found work objectionable, that individuals cared little for making decisions or exercising creativity on the job, and that money was the driving force behind performance. Management believed that employees should follow highly-detailed, prescribed procedures and that behavior should be monitored and controlled very carefully through time and motion studies.

The human relations movement was the next significant step in the development of managerial views on motivation. This movement recognized that people had needs that went well beyond performing a simple repetitive task at work and that financial compensation was only one aspect of what workers desired. Employees wanted respect, discretion over their jobs, and a feeling that they contributed something valuable to their organization. The human relations movement was the impetus for developing ways to improve morale and job satisfaction and the overall quality of working life.

Perhaps the most contemporary management view of motivation is the human resources model of motivation (HRMM). Based on initiatives to improve the quality of working life and the strong influence of Japanese management practices, HRMM introduces a high level of employee responsibility for and participation in decisions in the work environment. The central assumptions of HRMM are that organizations operate under a *system of beliefs* about the values, purpose, and direction of their organization (see chapter 1); that people find work enjoyable; and that people desire to participate in developing objectives, making decisions, and attaining goals in their work environment. Individuals are motivated by both financial and nonfinancial means of compensation. This model also assumes that employees have a great deal of knowledge and information about their jobs, the application of which will improve the way they perform tasks and benefit the organization as a whole. Individuals are assumed to be highly creative, ethical, and responsible, and they desire opportunities to effect change in their organizations.

The human resource model is the basis of the presentation of the four behavioral considerations in MACS design that follows. Next, the organization's ethical code of conduct is discussed.

The Organization's Ethical Code of Conduct and MACS Design

The concept of a *boundary system* or a set of standards relating to acceptable behavior was introduced in chapter 1. At the center of many boundary systems is a set of ethical principles, and thus a well-designed MACS should incorporate the principles of an organization's code of ethical conduct to guide and influence behavior and decision making. Ethics is a discipline that focuses on the investigation of standards of conduct and moral judgment. A MACS design that incorporates ethical principles can provide decision makers with guidance as they face ethical dilemmas. Recent scandals in corporate America have greatly heightened the need for a renewed emphasis on ethical judgment and decision making.

Management accountants often play a significant role in MACS design. Their behavior and decision making are guided by the organization's code of ethical conduct and the ethical standards of their professional association, the Institute of Management Accountants (IMA). For example, holders of the title *certified management accountant* (the certification granted by the IMA) are required to be competent and to always maintain confidentiality, integrity, and objectivity.

The ethical framework embedded in system design is extremely important because it will influence the behavior of all users. The key user group—managers—interacts a great deal with the MACS. Often managers are subject to intense pressures from their job circumstances and from other influential organizational members to suspend their ethical judgment in certain situations. These pressures include the following:

1. Requests to tailor information to favor particular individuals or groups
2. Pleas to falsify reports or test results
3. Solicitations for confidential information
4. Pressures to ignore a questionable or unethical practice

To incorporate ethical principles into the design of a MACS and help managers deal effectively with the previous situations, system designers might attempt to ensure the following:

1. That the organization has formulated, implemented, and communicated to all employees a comprehensive code of ethics (This is often accomplished through the organization's beliefs system, as discussed in chapter 1.)
2. That all employees understand the organization's code of ethics and the boundary systems that constrain behavior (Chapter 1 noted that boundary systems are designed to specify what actions are appropriate and which must never be taken.)
3. That a system in which employees have confidence exists to detect and report violations of the organization's code of ethics

Avoiding Ethical Dilemmas

Most organizations attempt to address ethical considerations and avoid ethical dilemmas by developing a code of ethics. Although no universal hierarchy of ethical principles exists, five categories capture the broad array of ethical considerations: legal rules, societal norms, professional memberships, organizational or group norms, and personal norms.

This hierarchy is listed in descending order of authority. For example, an action that is prohibited by law should be unacceptable by society, by one's profession, by the organization, and then by each individual. However, an action that is legally and socially acceptable, such as strategically underestimating product costs, may be professionally unacceptable and, in turn, unacceptable to the organization and its employees. Unfortunately, any hierarchy of this sort has a number of gray areas, but it nevertheless provides general guidelines for understanding and dealing with ethical problems that arise.

This ethical hierarchy provides a set of constraints on a decision. In this scheme, ethical conflicts occur when one system of values diverges from a more fundamental system. For example, suppose that the organization's code of ethics commits it to meeting only the letter of the law regarding disclosure of a product defect in one of its manufactured goods that could prove hazardous to consumers. However, a broader societal expectation is that organizations should be aggressive in identifying and disclosing potential product defects. An individual decision maker dealing with this situation may face an ethical conflict when the organizational code of ethics implies doing nothing about the defect since there is no definitive evidence of a product problem. In such cases, broader societal expectations would imply that disclosure is necessary because there is persistent evidence of a problem.

Dealing with Ethical Conflicts

Organizations that formulate and support specific and unambiguous ethical codes can create an environment that will reduce ethical conflicts. One step in avoiding ambiguity or misunderstanding is to maintain a hierarchical ordering of authority, which means that the organization's stated code of ethics should not allow any behavior that is either legally or socially unacceptable. Because most professional codes of ethics reflect broad moral imperatives, such as loyalty, discretion, and competence, an organization would create public relations problems for itself if its stated code of ethics conflicted with a professional code of ethics.

Another critical variable that can reduce ethical conflicts is the way that the chief executive and other senior managers behave and conduct business. If these individuals demonstrate exemplary behavior, other organizational members will have role models to emulate. Organizations whose leaders exhibit unethical behavior cannot expect their employees to behave according to high ethical standards.

In some cases, when organizations develop a formal code of ethics, they can create the potential for explicit ethical conflicts with the code itself to arise. The conflicts that appear most in practice are those between the law and the organization's code of ethics, between the organization's practiced code of ethics and common societal expectations, and between the individual's set of personal and professional ethics and the organization's practiced code of ethics. Any conflicts that remain relate primarily to personal values and norms of behavior that were acceptable prior to the adoption of the organization's new code of ethics but that are now in question.

Conflicts Between Individual and Organizational Values

People bring personal codes of ethics with them into an organization. If the organization's code of ethics is more stringent than an individual's code, conflicts may arise. However, if adherence to the organization's ethical code is required and enforced, it is possible to diminish ethical conflicts if, as part of the employment contract, the individual is asked and expected to pursue a more stringent code of ethics. Another possible (and probably more desirable) outcome is that individuals may raise their own ethical standards without conflict.

Does Cheating at Golf Lead to Cheating at Other Things?

Would it surprise you to learn that many Fortune 500 chief executive officers (CEOs) cheat at golf?

According to Chad Struer, whose company, USA Diligence, is hired to investigate the honesty of start-up companies, about a third of the CEOs he has played golf with are cheats. "They're used to having things their way," Struer says. "He who holds the gold makes the rules."

In a recent survey, commissioned by Starwood Hotels and Resorts, 82% of 401 high-ranking corporate executives admit to being less than honest on the golf course. An informal survey of a dozen CEOs polled by *USA Today* reveals that they sometimes bend the rules on the course when they play. Behavior such as improving lies, hitting mulligans, and shaving strokes is not uncommon.

Are there consequences for this behavior? Jeff Harp, former president of Summit National Bank in Fort Worth, Texas, states that he has denied loans after seeing CEOs cheat at golf. Since he is in the business of trying to assess honesty, he feels that if one can cheat at golf, one can cheat on a loan application. However, there may be a bigger societal issue.

Ken Siegel, an organizational psychologist who has been interviewing executives for 25 years, says that executives who cheat and lie and then deny it may be deluding themselves and others. "They lose the ability to distinguish what is honest and what is not," Siegel says. "Lies are getting bigger and bigger. We're seeing this played out everywhere now, from Tyco to Enron."

Source: Eyewire Collection/Getty Images–Photodisc.

Source: Adapted from Del Jones, "Cheating at Golf Is Par for the Course for CEOs," *Salt Lake City Tribune*, June 30, 2002.

Difficult issues may arise when the individual's personal code of ethics prohibits certain types of behavior that are legal, socially acceptable, professionally acceptable, and acceptable to the organization. Potential for conflicts in such situations will arise when the action that is unacceptable to the individual is desirable to the organization. As an example, an employee may have deep religious objections to conducting business in any form on a holy day. Working for an organization may require that the person, under these circumstances, do things that he or she finds unacceptable. In this case, the individual is confronted with a personal choice. Unfortunately, the employee may have little institutional support in this situation but can lobby within or outside the organization to prohibit working on a holy day. This tactic may be effective, or the affected employee may choose not to work for that organization, depending on what he or she values most. As a practical matter, employees faced with ethical conflicts must make sure to document the events and discussions and list the parties involved so that a case can be made.

Conflicts Between the Organization's Stated and Practiced Values

In some cases, employees will observe management or even senior management engaged in unethical behavior, such as management fraud. This type of conflict is the most difficult because the organization is misrepresenting its ethical system, forcing the employee to make a choice between going public with the information or keeping it quiet. In this setting, the employee is in a position of drawing attention to the problem by being a whistle-blower, which many have found to be a lonely and unenviable position. In many instances, though, whistle-blowers have chosen personal integrity over their loyalty to an organization.

Experts who have studied this problem advise that the individual should first ensure that the facts are correct and that a conflict does exist between the organization's stated ethical policy and the actions of its employees in practice. Second, by speaking with superiors, the individual should determine whether this conflict is institutional or whether it reflects the decisions and actions of only a small minority of employees. Faced with a true conflict, the individual has several choices, including the following:

1. Point out the discrepancy to a superior and refuse to act unethically. This may lead to dismissal, the need to resign from the organization, or the experience of suffering hidden organization sanctions.
2. Point out the discrepancy to a superior and act unethically. The rationale for this choice, which is incorrect, is that the employee believes that this affords protection from legal sanctions.
3. Take the discrepancy to a mediator in the organization if one exists.
4. Work with respected leaders in the organization to change the discrepancy between practiced and stated ethics.
5. Go outside the organization to publicly resolve the issue.
6. Go outside the organization anonymously to resolve the issue.
7. Resign and go public to resolve the issue.
8. Resign and remain silent.
9. Do nothing and hope that the problem will dissolve.

Although most experts recommend following alternative 4 on this list, it is beyond the scope of this chapter to discuss the efficacy of any of these alternatives other than to mention that there are circumstances that can make any of them appropriate. If the organization is serious about its stated code of ethics, it should have an effective ethics control system to ensure and provide evidence that the organization's stated and practiced ethics are the same. Part of this control system should include a means for employees to point out inconsistencies between stated practices and ethics without fear of retribution. For example, some organizations rely on an ombudsman, while others rely on the internal audit function or an external auditor. Any organization that does not provide a system to protect employees in these situations either is not taking its code of ethics seriously or has an inadequate ethics control system.

The Elements of an Effective Ethical Control System

To promote ethical decision making, management should implement an ethical control system. The elements of this ethical control system should include the following:

1. A statement of the organization's values and code of ethics written in practical terms, along with examples so that the organization's employees can relate the statement to their individual jobs.
2. A clear statement of the employee's ethical responsibilities for every job description and a specific review of the employee's ethical performance as part of every performance review.
3. Adequate training to help employees identify ethical dilemmas in practice and learn how to deal with those they can reasonably expect to face.
4. Evidence that senior management expects organization members to adhere to its code of ethics. This means that management must do the following:
   - Provide a statement of the consequences of violating the organization's code of ethics
   - Establish a means of dealing with violations of the organization's code of ethics promptly, ruthlessly, and consistently with the statement of consequences
   - Provide visible support of ethical decision making at every opportunity
   - Provide a private line of communication (without retribution) from employees directly to the chief executive officer, chief operating officer, head of human resource management, or someone else on the board of directors
5. Evidence that employees can make ethical decisions or report violations of the organization's stated ethics (be the whistle-blower) without fear of reprisals from superiors, subordinates, or peers in the organization. This proof usually takes the form of an organization mediator who has the authority to investigate complaints, wherever they lead, and to preserve the confidentiality of people who report violations.
6. An ongoing internal audit of the efficacy of the organization's ethical control system.

Steps in Making an Ethical Decision

Formal training is part of the process of promoting ethical decision making. After gathering the facts relating to a particular decision and evaluating the alternative courses of action, the decision maker can eliminate possible courses of action that are ethically unacceptable. The decision model in Exhibit 8-1 is one approach to eliminating unacceptable alternatives.

In summary, the organization's code of ethics is integral to MACS design. Both designers and users of the system should remember this fact and rectify any deviations from the code of ethics that the system explicitly or implicitly promotes.

Motivation and Congruence

In addition to fostering ethical behavior and decision making, a central issue in MACS design is how to motivate appropriate behavior at work. When designing jobs and specific tasks, system designers should consider the following three dimensions of motivation:

1. Direction, or the tasks on which an employee focuses attention
2. Intensity, or the level of effort the employee expends
3. Persistence, or the duration of time that an employee will stay with a task or job

Exhibit 8-1
Decision Model for Resolving Ethical Issues

1. **Determine the Facts–What, Who, Where, When, How**

   What do we know or need to know, if possible, that will help us define the problem?

2. **Define the Ethical Issue**
   - List the significant stakeholders
   - Define the ethical issues

   Identify precisely what the ethical issue is, for example, conflict involving rights, questions over limits of disclosure obligation, and so on.

3. **Identify Major Principles, Rules, Values**

   Determine key principles such as integrity, quality, respect for persons, societal benefits, and costs.

4. **Specify the Alternatives**

   List the major alternative courses of action, including these that represent some form of compromise or point between simply doing or not doing something.

5. **Compare Values and Alternatives**

   Determine if there is one principle or value (or a combination) that is so compelling that the proper alternative is clear, for example, correcting a defect that is almost certain to cause loss of life.

6. **Assess the Consequences**

   Identify short- and long-term positive and negative consequences for the major alternatives. The common short run focus on gains or losses needs to be measured against long-run considerations.

7. **Make Your Decision**

   Balance the consequences against your primary principles or values and select the alternative that best fits.

Consistent with theories of individual motivation, careful attention to motivation is a key step for the organization and its employees to align their respective goals; this alignment is known as achieving goal congruence.[1] The alignment of goals occurs as employees perform their jobs well and are helping to achieve organizational objectives; they are also attaining their own individual goals, such as obtaining promotions, earning financial bonuses, or advancing their careers in other ways.

In a frictionless world, as employers and employees align their goals, employers could simply rely on the concept of employee self-control, in which employees monitor and regulate their own behavior and perform to their highest levels. Even if goals are aligned, however, different types of tasks require different levels of skill, precision, responsibility, initiative, and uncertainty. In most situations, managers try to establish systems that they do not have to personally monitor on a regular basis. The hope is that if these systems are well designed, the manager has much more time to attend to other concerns. These are called diagnostic control systems. These are feedback systems that monitor organizational outcomes and correct any deviations from predetermined performance standards. Typically, there is little debate about the nature of the system, and the systems tend to run in a routine fashion.

However, if a large degree of strategic uncertainty offers threats and opportunities that could alter the operating assumptions of a business, managers have to spend

---

[1] See two-factor theory by F. Herzberg, "One More Time: How Do You Motivate Employees?," *Harvard Business Review*, January–February 1968, 53–62; expectancy theory by V. Vroom, *Work and Motivation* (New York: John Wiley & Son's, 1964); and goal-setting theory by E. Locke and G. Latham, *A Theory of Goal Setting and Task Performance* (Upper Saddle River, N.J.: Prentice Hall, 1990).

As technology has proliferated in the workplace, a number of new ethical questions regarding work behavior have surfaced. See how your responses to these questions in this *Wall Street Journal* Workplace-Ethics Quiz compare to national survey data, which appears at the end of the quiz.

Office Technology

1. Is it wrong to use company e-mail for personal reasons?
   _ Yes   _ No

2. Is it wrong to use office equipment to help your children or spouse do schoolwork?
   _ Yes   _ No

3. Is it wrong to play computer games on office equipment during the workday?
   _ Yes   _ No

4. Is it wrong to use office equipment to do Internet shopping?
   _ Yes   _ No

5. Is it unethical to blame an error you made on a technological glitch?
   _ Yes   _ No

6. Is it unethical to visit pornographic Web sites using office equipment?
   _ Yes   _ No

Gifts and Entertainment

7. What's the value at which a gift from a supplier or client becomes troubling?
   _ $25 _ $50 _ $10

8. Is a $50 gift to a boss unacceptable?
   _ Yes   _ No

9. Is a $50 gift FROM the boss unacceptable?
   _ Yes   _ No

10. Of gifts from suppliers: Is it OK to take a $200 pair of football tickets?
    _ Yes   _ No

11. Is it OK to take a $120 pair of theater tickets?
    _ Yes   _ No

12. Is it OK to take a $100 holiday food basket?
    _ Yes   _ No

13. Is it OK to take a $25 gift certificate?
    _ Yes   _ No

14. Can you accept a $75 prize won at a raffle at a supplier's conference?
    _ Yes   _ No

Truth and Lies

15. Due to on-the-job pressure, have you ever abused or lied about sick days?
    _ Yes   _ No

16. Due to on-the-job pressure, have you ever taken credit for someone else's work or idea?
    _ Yes   _ No

ANSWERS TO ETHICS QUIZ

Following are the responses based on national cross-sectional survey data of employees at large companies gathered by the Ethics Officer Association, Belmont, Massachusetts, and the Ethical Leadership Group, Wilmette, Illinois. How do your answers compare? Are you surprised?

1. 34% said personal e-mail on company computers is wrong
2. 37% said using office equipment for schoolwork is wrong
3. 49% said playing computer games at work is wrong
4. 54% said Internet shopping at work is wrong
5. 61% said it's unethical to blame your error on technology
6. 87% said it's unethical to visit pornographic sites at work
7. 33% said $25 is the amount at which a gift from a supplier or client becomes troubling, while 33% said $50, and 33% said $100
8. 35% said a $50 gift to the boss is unacceptable
9. 12% said a $50 gift from the boss is unacceptable
10. 70% said it's unacceptable to take the $200 football tickets
11. 70% said it's unacceptable to take the $120 theater tickets
12. 35% said it's unacceptable to take the $100 food basket

much more time monitoring the decisions and actions of their subordinates. Such a system is called an interactive control systems.[2] Unlike diagnostic systems, interactive systems force a dialogue among all organizational participants about the data coming out of the system and what action to take.

Task and Results Control Methods

At the core of diagnostic and interactive systems are two common methods of control: task control and results control.

Task Control

Task control is the process of finding ways to control human behavior so that a job is completed in a prespecified manner. Task control can be separated into two categories: preventive control and monitoring. In preventive control, much, if not all, of the discretion is taken out of performing a task because of the precision required or the nature of the materials involved. For example, tasks that require very careful handling, such as making silicon wafers, or those that use precious metals, such as gold, often are controlled carefully or are performed by machines or computers. This is to say not that machines are infallible but rather that the degree of error is probably less than that experienced with humans. Naturally, as the accomplishment of a task requires increasingly greater judgment, the building of preventive control systems becomes more difficult.

Monitoring means inspecting the work or behavior of employees while they are performing a task. Monitoring can be accomplished using listening devices or through surveillance. For example, all of us have experienced the situation in which a (sometimes annoying) phone message tells us that the conversation we are about to have with a company representative may be "monitored to ensure quality control." Since monitoring, or listening in to a conversation in this case, is often done randomly, the employee does not know when it will occur and thus will be disciplined to act in a consistent, professional manner at all times. Monitoring also can be accomplished using surveillance. For example, cameras or "eyes in the sky" are used to observe the actions and behaviors of croupiers at gambling casinos.

Monitoring, however, can have its negative consequences. Some employees feel that being monitored causes them unnecessary stress. These same employees

---

[2] See R. Simons, *Levers of Control* (Boston: Harvard Business School Press, 1995).

believe that monitoring also undermines the level of trust between employers and employees.

Task control is most appropriate in the following situations:

1. When there are legal requirements to follow specific rules or procedures to protect public safety, such as in the manufacture of prescription drugs and critical aircraft components and in the operation of nuclear power generation facilities.
2. When employees handle liquid assets (or other precious assets) to reduce the opportunity for temptation and fraud.
3. When the organization can control its environment and eliminate uncertainty and the need for judgment. In such instances, the organization can develop specific rules and procedures that employees must follow.

Results Control

Rather than directly monitoring and directly controlling tasks, results control systems focus on measuring employee performance against stated objectives. For results control to be effective, the organization must have clearly defined its objectives, communicated them to appropriate organization members, and designed performance measures consistent with the objectives. For example, salespeople are often evaluated on the basis of the volume of sales they made during a specific time interval. The organization sets standards of performance against which the actual results of an employee's performance are compared. For another example, consider a business unit head who must improve her organization's financial performance relative to a prespecified target.

Most organizations require that employees who handle cash provide a cash register receipt to each customer—and some, such as McDonald's back this up by promising customers a free meal or a discount if a receipt is not provided. Requiring that the customer receive a cash receipt requires entering the sale into the cash register's memory, which, in turn, ensures that all incoming cash receipts are recorded—a form of task control that relies on prevention.

Source: Joseph Sohm/Corbis–NY.

In some instances, task and results controls are used in tandem. As mentioned, phone calls by company salespeople often are monitored to control behavior; however, in addition, these same salespeople often have a weekly sales quota to reach. This is particularly true of salespeople from major long-distance carriers.

Results control is most effective in the following situations:

1. When organization members understand the organization's objectives and their contribution to those objectives
2. When organization members have the knowledge and skill to respond to changing situations by taking corrective actions and making sound decisions
3. When the performance measurement system is designed to assess individual contributions so that an individual can be motivated to take action and make decisions that reflect his or her own and the organization's best interests

Central to the design of results control systems is the development of a performance measurement system that fully reflects the multiple objectives and goals of an organization. This issue is discussed in the following section.

USING A MIX OF PERFORMANCE MEASURES

The Need for Multiple Measures of Performance

The old saying "What gets measured gets done" indicates that the ways in which organizations and individuals measure performance send signals to all employees and stakeholders about what the organization considers as its priorities. If organizations choose performance measures without careful consideration, noncongruent behavior can occur. For example, suppose a firm sets up a performance evaluation system that rewards a vendor only on the basis of on-time delivery of a product. In all likelihood, on-time delivery will be the variable on which the vendor's employees will focus. Since this evaluation would not consider the quality of the goods sent, vendors who supply the merchandise may sacrifice quality for the sake of meeting promised delivery dates, or they may quote excessively long lead times to ensure that deliveries are not late. Either action could work to the long-term detriment of the organization and the vendor.

Department store managers have discovered that when salespeople are compensated using sales quotas, their attention is focused on selling as much expensive merchandise as possible. Employees faced with such a situation initially may find that their sales volume is increasing, but as the competition for customers develops, the work environment may become hostile as salespeople dispute about customers or sales. Another consequence of relying solely on commissions as a motivating tool is that other aspects of the sales function, such as straightening merchandise or restocking shelves, may become lower priorities. Also, customers may return merchandise that has been oversold to them.

Non–Goal-Congruent Behavior

Occasionally, employees are so motivated to achieve a single goal that they engage in non–goal-congruent or dysfunctional behavior. For example, consider a company whose single performance measure is whether employees attain their sales quotas.

Using multiple rather than single performance measures helps this flight attendant focus on several dimensions of customer service than on one dimension alone.

Source: Stewart Cohen/www.indexopen.com.

If an employee is worried about being fired and if there are no other ways to demonstrate good performance, the employee might alter his or her actions specifically in an attempt to manipulate a performance indicator through job-related acts. This is known as gaming the performance indicator. As an example, a salesperson might ask his coworker to give him credit for the colleague's sales bookings, or the salesperson may have his friends come into the store, buy merchandise, and return it 30 days later. The salesperson might engage in data falsification by knowingly altering sales booking records in his or her favor. Data falsification is considered illegal, and the accounting profession has recently witnessed the dire consequences of employees engaged in such activities.

Another form of non–goal-congruent behavior is smoothing, a form of earnings management that occurs when individuals acclerate or delay the preplanned flow of data without altering the organization's activities. For example, a manager who is close to meeting a performance target, such as a net income or ROI number, may decide to defer expenses incurred in the current period to a future period. Similarly, the manager may attempt to book future revenues into the current period to increase net income. Over the long term, such behavior will led to the same bottom-line financial outcomes, but the cost to the organization is that it does not have a clear picture of performance for a defined time period. Excessive amounts of smoothing are probably the result of inappropriate standards or a poorly conceived reward system.

In addition to setting up boundary systems so that employees have a clear understanding of what is considered appropriate and inappropriate behavior, organizations also can design performance measurement systems that encourage the desired behavior. One possibility is to use multiple performance measures that reflect the complexities of the work environment and the variety of contributions that employees make. In many of today's manufacturing and service environments, employees or associates are being cross trained to perform a variety of tasks. For example, at the General Motors Saturn plant, employees are organized into self-managed work teams that follow a product's manufacture from beginning to end. Thus, organizations have an opportunity to design multiple measures to assess the work that is actually being done. Using multiple performance measures also will cause employees to recognize the various dimensions of their work and to be less intent on trying to maximize their performance on a single target at the expense of other aspects of their jobs.

Using a Mix of Performance Measures

In addition to using multiple performance measures, MACS designers have to expand their views of the kinds of performance measures to use. For example, only within the past few years have managers become aware of the need for measures of quality, speed to market, cycle time, flexibility, complexity, innovation, and productivity. Historically, some of these measures, such as quality, were in the hands of industrial engineers, while others, such as speed to market or flexibility, were not measured at all.

Managers should keep in mind other new organizational realities. Faced with increasing competitive pressures, many organizations have begun to move away from traditional hierarchical organizations with many layers of management, referred to as *tall organizations*, to those with fewer and fewer layers, or *flat organizations*. General Electric, for example, has reduced its hierarchical structure significantly. As the barriers between functional areas such as engineering design, manufacturing, accounting, finance, and marketing are eliminated, employees are working increasingly in cross-functional teams.

Another significant corresponding change is the use of *business process reengineering*, in which designers begin with a vision of what organizational participants would like their process or product to look like or how they would like it to function and then radically redesign it. Such an approach is significantly different from starting with an existing product or process and then making slight incremental changes. Further, reengineering design changes have led to the need for new informational requirements and measures related to the costs and benefits of innovation. Thus, new measures of performance must take into account group-level performance measures and cross-functional business process measures, not just departmental efficiency and spending measures.

The traditional focus of performance measures in management accounting has been on quantitative financial measures such as cost and profit rather than quantitative nonfinancial and qualitative measures. Examples of quantitative nonfinancial measures include yield, cycle time, schedule adherence, number of defectives, market share, and customer retention. Variables such as the image of a product or service, the level of caring of the staff in a hospital, or the reputation of a company are examples of qualitative variables. While they may be more subjective than quantitative variables, many qualitative variables can now be assessed using psychometric methods developed in the behavioral sciences. Customer satisfaction, for example, is a qualitative measure, which can now be quantified by using psychological scales. Clearly, measures such as customer satisfaction and employee morale are crucial for both the short- and the long-term success of any organization. In chapter 9 we provide a comprehensive approach to performance measurement known as the Balanced Scorecard, which overcomes many of the problems and concerns discussed in this section.

EMPOWERING EMPLOYEES TO BE INVOLVED IN MACS DESIGN

Empowering employees in MACS design requires two essential elements: allowing employees to participate in decision making and ensuring that employees understand the information they are using and generating.

Participation in Decision Making

Organizations often do not realize that their greatest asset is the people they employ. Encouraging participation has a twofold benefit for organizations. First, research has suggested that employees who participate in decision making evince greater feelings of morale and job satisfaction. In many instances, these heightened feelings translate into increased productivity as employees begin to feel that they have some ownership and control over what they do at work.

Second, except in highly automated industries, people (not machines) still perform the major portion of work and have superior information and understanding in regard to how work is best accomplished and, consequently, how to improve products and processes. For example, employees in the Sydney branch of ANZAC Company will know more about the way their branch functions than will central headquarters located in Melbourne. Therefore, MACS designers should strongly consider enlisting the participation of the Sydney employees. The same concept applies within a division. Assembly-line operators usually know more about the process on which they work than their managers do. Research has shown that participation and communication between local and central offices and between superiors and subordinates result in the transmission of critical information to which central management would otherwise not have access.

Education to Understand Information

The second critical element of empowering employees is to ensure that they understand the information they use and on which they are evaluated. Many executives believe that only managers need to understand the information generated by the MACS. Recently, it has become evident to many managers that employees at all levels must understand the organization's performance measures and the way they are computed in order to be able to take actions that lead to superior performance. For example, if employees do not understand how their actions affect a variable such as cycle time (the time it takes for a product or service to be produced or performed from start to finish), they will not know how to alter their actions to improve cycle time performance. If employees in a manufacturing plant are performing unnecessary actions on an assembly line or are idle, for example, the cycle time performance of their group will be affected. Similarly, at the point of service, or the point where organizational employees interact with customers, delays in the processing of claims also will increase cycle time.

Consider an airline whose intent is to improve its public image. From time to time, some airlines ask customers to fill out a customer satisfaction survey. If flight attendants have not been educated regarding how each of their actions (such as being rude or slow to produce service) directly affects customer satisfaction, the airline has failed to do its part to ensure satisfactory performance of one of its key indicators for flight attendants. This is also true in many other types of service organizations. In restaurants or department stores, customers often become frustrated with the level of service. For example, assigning waitpersons in a restaurant to too many tables can cause them to forget customer requests, or if they have annoying personal habits or are extremely clumsy, customers remember the negative experience and may not return. Consider a department store in which sales personnel may be too pushy, too difficult to find for service, or arrogant. A customer may become irritated with such an experience and vow never to shop at that store again.

Unless restaurant owners and department store managers educate their employees about how their actions affect customer perceptions of service quality and repeat business, the energy devoted to improving customer satisfaction is wasted. Studies have shown that, on average, five times as many customers who are dissatisfied with a product or service tell other people about their experience than do customers who are satisfied with a product or service. Thus, the reputation of organizations that offer a poorly produced product or a poorly delivered service can be ruined rather quickly. In general, poor or nonresponsive service by employees who have direct contact with customers is usually evidence of poor management, poor training, and poor education rather than an indicator that the employee is not a good worker.

For MACS to function well, employees have to be constantly reeducated as the system and its performance measures change. Without continuous updating of everyone's education, companies cannot be leaders or even players in international markets. In the United States, lack of training is a severe problem. For example, some studies have shown that U.S. employees receive only one-tenth the training of Japanese employees. Thus, U.S. management cannot expect its employees to be globally competitive if management does not supply them with the necessary training. Ultimately, the concept of continuous education should become so ingrained in employees that continually mastering new skills becomes a job requirement. Organizations that foster such an environment have been labeled *learning organizations*.

DEVELOPING APPROPRIATE INCENTIVE SYSTEMS TO REWARD PERFORMANCE

The final behavioral consideration in MACS design is to consider the most appropriate reward systems to further motivate employees. The following presentation begins with a focus on both intrinsic and extrinsic rewards and continues with a discussion of the many types of financial reward systems that organizations use. A number of different theories of human motivation exist, including expectancy theory, agency theory, and goal-setting theory. Each theory stresses different aspects of motivation. Because the debate regarding these theories is so extensive, readers must decide to which theory they subscribe.[3]

Organizations use both intrinsic and extrinsic rewards to motive employees. Intrinsic rewards are those that come from within an individual and reflect satisfaction from doing the job and from the opportunities for growth that the job provides. In some cases, intrinsic rewards reflect the nature of the organization and type of work one is performing. For example, volunteering at a day care center offers no financial compensation but instead provides the volunteer with the feeling or reward that he or she is helping children learn. Even in jobs where people are financially compensated, one of management's most challenging tasks is to design jobs and develop an organizational environment and culture that lead employees to derive intrinsic rewards just by working. Organizations also hope that through the hiring process they can find a good match between a specific type of job and a specific individual. Because of how intrinsic rewards are derived, manufacturing accounting information has no effect on them.

Based on assessed performance, extrinsic rewards are any rewards that one person provides to another to recognize a job well done. Examples of commonly used extrinsic rewards are meals, tips, cash bonuses, stock bonuses, and recognition in

---

[3] Readers are referred to S. E., Bonner, and G. B. Sprinkle, "The Effects of Monetary Incentives on Effort and Task Performance: Theories, Evidence, and a Framework for Research," *Accounting, Organizations, and Society,* May/July 2002, 303–45.

newsletters and on plaques. Extrinsic rewards reinforce the notion that employees have distinguished themselves from the organization. Many people believe that extrinsic rewards also reinforce the common perception that the wage compensates the employee for a minimally acceptable effort and that the organization must use additional rewards or compensation to motivate the employee to provide additional effort.

Choosing Between Intrinsic and Extrinsic Rewards

Many compensation experts believe that organizations have not made enough use of intrinsic rewards. They claim that, given proper management leadership, intrinsic rewards may have motivational effects as strong as or even stronger than extrinsic rewards. The issue of the effectiveness of intrinsic and extrinsic rewards is a topic of heated debate in the management literature. Some argue that people who expect to receive a reward for completing a task or for doing that task successfully do not perform as well as those who expect no reward at all. Others argue that, although this result holds true over a wide range of tasks, people, and rewards, the result is strongest when the job requires creative skills. For some, pay may not be a motivator. This argument is built around the idea that the preoccupation with extrinsic rewards undermines the effectiveness of reward systems and that the design of organizations and jobs should allow employees to experience intrinsic rewards.

The issue remains unresolved. However, one thing is clear: Most organizations have ignored and continue to ignore the role of intrinsic rewards in motivation and blindly accept the view that only financial extrinsic rewards motivate employees. Many people believe that financial extrinsic rewards are both necessary and sufficient to motivate superior performance. Both systematic and anecdotal evidence suggests, however, that financial extrinsic rewards are not necessary to create effective organizations and that performance rewards do not necessarily create them. Whether nonfinancial extrinsic and intrinsic rewards are more or less effective than financial extrinsic rewards in motivating behavior is an unresolved matter. However, both nonfinancial extrinsic and intrinsic rewards have a role to play in most organizations.

Beyond the debate about the relative effectiveness of intrinsic and extrinsic rewards, some people argue that incentive compensation programs in any form are unacceptable. They suggest that organizations must strive to be excellent to survive in a complex and competitive world. Thus, superior and committed performance is necessary for all employees in organizations and is part of the contract of employment, not something that merits additional pay.

Conversely, a large number of organizations rely on extrinsic monetary rewards to motivate performance. Since employees often engage in social comparisons of how they are performing at work, extrinsic monetary rewards are a tangible indicator of how well one is doing relative to others. These organizations base their reward systems to a large extent on information and measures provided by management accounting systems. The remainder of this section focuses on the kinds of extrinsic rewards that are most commonly used in organizations.

Extrinsic Rewards Based on Performance

Incentive compensation, or pay-for-performance systems, are reward systems that provide monetary (extrinsic) rewards based on measured results. Pay-for-performance systems base rewards on achieving or exceeding some measured performance. The underlying philosphy of this system is based on the adage "You get what you measure and reward." Thus, organizations need performance measurement systems that gather relevant and reliable performance information. The reward can be based on absolute performance, performance relative to some plan, or performance relative to that of some comparable group. Measures of absolute performance include the following:

1. The number of acceptable quality units produced (such as a piece-rate system)
2. The organization's results (such as profit levels or an organization's Balanced Scorecard measures of customer or employee satisfaction, quality, and rate of successful new product introductions)
3. The organization's share price performance (such as stock option plan)

Examples of rewards based on relative performance are those tied to the following:

1. The ability to exceed a performance target level (such as paying a manager for accomplishing his or her goals under budget or paying a production group a bonus for beating a benchmark performance level)
2. The amount of a bonus pool (such as sharing in a pool defined as the organization's reported profits less a stipulated return to shareholders)
3. The degree to which performance exceeds the average performance level of a comparable group

Occasionally, compensation policy can be affected by government regulations. For example, since 1994, for the purpose of computing taxable income, most organizations in the United States cannot claim as an expense the portion of any employee's salary that exceeds $1 million. This will certainly (1) reduce the use of salary and perquisites (such as company cars and club memberships), and (2) increase the use of variable pay based on performance.

Effective Performance Measurement and Reward Systems

Following are the six attributes of a measurement system that must be in place in order to motivate desired performance:

1. **The employees must understand their jobs and the reward system and believe that it measures what they control and contribute to the organization.** This attribute ensures that the employee perceives the reward system as fair and predictable. If employees do not understand their jobs or how to improve their measured performance, a reward system based on performance measures is ineffective. In this case, employees perceive no relationship between effort and performance and, ultimately, outcomes. Similarly, if the reward system is complex, employees are unable to relate perceived performance improvements to changes in outcomes, and the motivational effect of the reward system will be lost.

Additionally, if the reward system does not measure employees' controllable performance, they conclude that measured performance is independent of their efforts, and again the incentive effect of the reward system is lost. Specifying and developing a clear relationship among effort, performance, and result and ensuring that all employees understand this relationship is a critical management role. Therefore, the centerpiece of incentive compensation systems is the performance measurement system, which becomes the focus of the employees' attention. The decisions that employees make in pursuing the performance measures that ultimately provide valued personal outcomes move the organization toward achieving its goals if the performance measures are aligned with the organization's goals.

2. **Related to the first attribute, designers of the performance measurement system must make a careful choice about whether it measures employees' inputs or outputs.** In general, the greatest alignment between employees' and the organization's interests is provided when the performance measurement system monitors and rewards employee outputs that contribute to the organization's success. However, outputs often reflect circumstances and conditions that are beyond the employee's control, and when they do, the perceived link between individuals' efforts and measured results is reduced, thereby decreasing the motivation provided by the reward system. Under circumstances when outcome measurement is problematic, organizations often choose to monitor and reward inputs (such as employee learning, demonstrated skill, and time worked). For example, in some manufacturing organizations, employees can take on-site night classes to increase their skills. Once these classes are completed and the new skills mastered, the employees are moved to a higher wage level. The choice of the mix of performance measures and the decision about whether those measures are input based, output based, or a combination of measures make up one of the most difficult tasks in the design of performance measurement and compensation systems.

3. **The elements of performance that the performance measurement system monitors and rewards should reflect the organization's critical success factors.** This attribute ensures that the performance system is relevant and motivates intended performance that matters to the organization's success. Moreover, the performance measurement system must consider all facets of performance so that employees do not sacrifice performance on an unmeasured element for performance on an element that the reward system measures. This is the role and purpose of measuring and rewarding employees across a set of balanced and comprehensive measures, as proposed in the Balanced Scorecard. For example, if a supervisor tells a telephone operator that productivity (such as the number of help requests handled per shift) is important, the operator may sacrifice the quality and courtesy offered to customers in order to handle as many questions as possible.

4. **The reward system must set clear standards for performance that employees accept.** Standards help employees assess whether their skills and efforts create results that the performance measurement system captures and reports as outcomes. This attribute determines employees' beliefs about whether the performance system is fair. If performance standards are either unspecified or unclear to employees, the relationship between performance and outcome is ambiguous and thereby reduces the motivational effect of the performance reward system.

5. **The measurement system must be calibrated so that it can accurately assess performance.** This attribute ensures that the performance measurement system establishes a clear relationship between performance and outcome.

6. **When it is critical that employees coordinate decision making and other activities with other employees, the reward system should reward group rather than individual performance.** Many organizations now believe that, to be effective, employees must work well in teams. These organizations are replacing evaluations and rewards based on individual performance with rewards and evaluations based on group performance.

In most organizations, pay is more than simply what is required to keep an employee from leaving the organization. Pay is part of the complex bundle of factors that motivate people to work in the organization's best interests. Therefore, organizations must consider pay issues within the larger context of motivation.

Conditions Favoring Incentive Compensation

Not all organizations are suited to incentive compensation systems. Centralized organizations require most of the important operating decisions to be made in the head office. Such organizations are unsuited to incentive compensation systems for their frontline employees because employees in these organizations are expected to follow rules and have no authority to make decisions. In fact, it is more appropriate to call compensation systems in these organizations *enforcement systems* because employment continues only if people follow the rules and standard operating procedures. Here the task of the management accountant is to design internal control systems and conduct internal audits to verify that people are following rules and procedures.

Incentive compensation systems work best in organizations in which employees have the skill and authority to react to conditions and make decisions. We previously discussed organizations that face continually changing environments—ones in which it is either impractical or impossible to develop standard operating procedures to deal with these changing conditions. Such organizations can develop incentive compensation systems to motivate employees to identify changes in the environment, to apply their skills and knowledge accordingly, and to make decisions that best reflect the organizations' goals.

When the organization has empowered its employees to make decisions, it can use incentive compensation systems to motivate appropriate decision-making behavior. In these organizations, the focus of control changes from telling people what to do to asking employees to use their skills and delegated authority to do their best to help the organization achieve its stated objectives.

Incentive Compensation and Employee Responsibility

The incentive compensation system must focus primarily on outcomes that the employee controls or influences. Consider an incentive compensation plan that rewards the performance of a production worker only when the sales department meets its sales target. Assuming that the worker is responsible only for the amount of resources used in the production of a product and its quality, it would be demotivating to base the employee's compensation on a sales target because the sales department, and not the production department, controls the level of sales.

Employees' incentive compensation should reflect the nature of their responsibilities in the organization. Employees whose roles are to plan, coordinate, and control day-to-day activities should receive rewards based on their ability to manage these daily operations effectively and to make the best short-term use of available resources. Their rewards should be tied to short-term controllable performance measures, such as efficiency and the ability to meet customer quality and service requirements. Employees whose roles are to plan long-term projects, such as building new facilities or acquiring significant capital equipment, should be rewarded on the basis of the long-term growth or improvement in the organization's operations that results from their strategic choices. These rewards should be based on the organization's performance compared with its stated objectives. In some cases, rewards also can be based on how an organization's performance compares with other, similar organizations. This mix of rewarding both short- and long-term outcomes is consistent with the goals of the Balanced Scorecard approach discussed in the next chapter.

This team of Unocal employees earned a team bonus for designing a system to reduce the time taken to perform the annual maintenance on a natural gas liquids plant from 8 days to 3.5 days. The faster turnaround saved Unocal maintenance costs and reduced the amount of lost production time. Asked to describe his reaction to the reward, the employee shown to the far right seemed to derive more satisfaction from having his views "listened to and acted on" than from the monetary reward. The satisfaction expressed by this employee is a form of intrinsic reward related to satisfaction from a job that provides an opportunity for thinking and contribution.

Source: Alan Whitman/Unocal

Rewarding Outcomes

Another consideration in the design of effective incentive compensation systems is the manner in which performance is measured. Incentive compensation schemes tie rewards to the outputs of employee performance rather than to such inputs as their level of effort. Moreover, incentive compensation based on outcomes requires that organization members understand and contribute to the organization's objectives.

However, rewards can be based on inputs in three instances:

- When it is impossible to measure outcomes consistently
- When outcomes are affected by factors beyond the employee's control
- When outcomes are expensive to measure

Input-based compensation measures the time, knowledge, and skill level that the employee brings to the job, with the expectation that the unmeasured outcome is correlated with these inputs. Many organizations use some form of knowledge-based remuneration. This type of remuneration bases the rate of pay on an employee's training and job qualifications, which can be upgraded by on-the-job training. The employee's compensation is the product of the number of hours worked (time input) and the hourly rate (a reflection of the deemed level of skill input). Organizations use knowledge-based pay to motivate employees to continuously upgrade their job skills, thereby allowing them to receive a higher base pay.

Managing Incentive Compensation Plans

Considerable evidence indicates that organizations have mismanaged incentive compensation plans, particularly those for senior executives. Many articles have appeared in influential business periodicals arguing that executives, particularly executives of U.S. corporations, have been paid excessively for mediocre performance.

Experts debate whether compensation systems motivate goal-seeking behavior and whether they are efficient, that is, whether they pay what is needed and no more. Some studies show a positive correlation between executive compensation and shareholder wealth. Other studies report finding no correlation (or even a negative one) between organization performance and executive compensation. Until recently, shareholder value was decreasing downward, while executive compensation was climbing higher. Some believe it is particularly inappropriate for companies to continue operating compensation systems in which executive rewards bear no relation to corporate performance.

Despite economic data showing an association between executive compensation and company performance, many professionals still argue that the amounts are excessive and reflect high status rather than good performance. The issue of fairness has also surfaced. Surveys indicate that, on average, chief executive officers in the United States earn 300 times the amount of the lowest-paid employee. In Japan, however, the relationship is only 30 times the lowest-paid worker. That these questions are raised reflects perceptions of unfairness and a degree of cynicism that average people feel about the role of incentive compensation in organizations.

Types of Incentive Compensation Plans

The most common incentive compensation plans are cash bonuses, profit sharing, gain sharing, stock options, performance shares stock, stock appreciation rights, participation units, and employee stock ownership plans. These different plans pose varying challenges for the management accounting system.

We can group compensation plans into two broad categories: (1) those that rely on internal measures, invariably provided by the organization's management accounting system, and (2) those that rely on performance of the organization's share price in the stock market.

Management accountants get involved in the first group of plans—those that revolve around rewards based on performance that the organization's management accounting system monitors and reports. Most employees who participate in financial incentive plans take the plans very seriously. These people are both interested in and concerned about the performance measurement system that monitors and reports the performance measures used to compute and distribute financial rewards. Many practicing management accountants have found that the most contentious debates arise from issues relating to performance measurement used for financial rewards. Therefore, management accountants take the matter of developing performance measures for financial reward systems very seriously.

Organizations use many other forms of stock-related incentive compensation plans, including performance shares stock, stock appreciation rights, participation units, and employee stock ownership plans that are beyond the scope of issues in management accounting. These plans provide incentive compensation to the participants when the stock price increases. The idea behind such plans is to motivate employees to act in the long-term interests of the organization by engaging in activities that increase the organization's market value. Therefore, all these plans assume that stock markets will recognize exceptional behavior in the form of increased stock prices.

Cash Bonus

A **cash bonus** plan—also called a *lump-sum reward, pay for performance*, or *merit pay*—pays cash on the basis of some measured performance. Such a bonus is a one-time award that does not become part of the employee's base pay in subsequent years.

Cash bonuses can be fixed in amount and triggered when measured performance exceeds the target, or they can be proportional to the level of performance relative to the target. They can be based on individual or group performance, and they can be paid to individuals or groups.

For example, in the late 1980s, General Motors eliminated automatic salary increases based on increases in the cost of living and replaced them with a pay-for-performance system that rewarded managers based on their results. Managers were required to group their employees into four groups: high performers (the top 10%), good performers (the next 25%), average performers (the next 55%), and low performers (the last 10%). Supervisors used these groupings to award merit pay and to enforce salary differences based on assessed performance.

Profit Sharing

Profit sharing is a cash bonus calculated as a percentage of an organization unit's reported profit. Profit sharing is a group incentive compensation plan focused on short-term performance.

All profit-sharing plans define what portion of the organization's reported profits is available for sharing, the sharing formula, the employees who are eligible to participate in the plan, and the formula for each employee's share.

Many profit-sharing plans are based on residual income, now called *economic value added*. In such plans, the reported profit will be reduced by some percentage (say 15%) of the shareholders' investment in the organization. This allotment provides the shareholders with the required return on their investment. The resulting pool is shared between employees and shareholders on some fractional basis, such as 40% for employees and 60% for shareholders. The plan also may specify a limit on the total amount of profits that can be distributed to employees. In addition, the profit-sharing plan specifies how it will distribute the money in the pool to each employee: Some

Source: National Geographic Image Collection.

Many companies are beginning to shy award from granting pay raises for good performance; instead, they are handing out larger cash bonuses. The bonus structure is also expanding to include employees down to the clerical and production levels as opposed to the traditional method of providing bonuses only to executives. Some companies award bonuses in an egalitarian fashion; if the company hits an established production or profit goal, then everyone gets a bonus. Others use a more meritocratic approach and pay out bonuses differentially to people in the same job on the basis of their performance.

A recent study by Hewitt Associates shows that companies are expecting to offer pay raises of about 3.4% to 3.7% for 2005, depending on an employee's position in the heirarchy. These raise levels are some of the lowest ever recorded by Hewitt over the 28 years it has been recording the data. A key reason for the change is that companies want to keep their fixed costs low, and raising someone's salary is a permanent cost that a company must contend with for years. Bonuses, however, are optional from year to year, allowing companies more control over their expenses.

Source: J. Opdyke, "Getting a Bonus Instead of a Raise," *Wall Street Journal*, December 29, 2004, D1–D2.

plans provide equal distribution; others distribute the bonus pool on the basis of the employee's performance relative to individual performance targets.

In the performance compensation approach, employees receive a performance score that reflects how well they achieved specific performance goals for that year. The employee's score divided by the total scores of all employees in the profit-sharing agreement is the individual's share of the pool total. Some profit-sharing plans distribute rewards to each employee in an amount proportional to the base wage or salary because the plans' designers believe this reflects the employee's contribution to the overall result.

Profit-sharing plans require a number of contributions from the organization's accounting systems in general and from the management accounting system in particular. First, the organization must prepare a means to calculate profits. This process usually is monitored and attested to by an external auditor. Second, when a deduction is to be made from the pool that is based on the owners' investment, the management accounting system must provide a measure of invested capital. Third, when the profit sharing is based on some measured level of performance (for example, a composite score that reflects the employee's ability to meet a set of performance targets), the management accounting system must provide the underlying measures of performance and the overall performance score.

Gain Sharing

Gain sharing is a system for distributing cash bonuses from a pool when the total amount available is a function of performance relative to some target. For example, employees in a designated unit receive bonuses when their performance exceeds a performance target. Gain sharing is a group incentive, unlike the pay-for-performance cash bonus, which is an individual reward. In its usual form, gain sharing provides for the sharing of financial gains in organizational performance. The gain-sharing plan usually applies to a group of employees within an organization unit, such as a department or a store. It uses a formula to specify the amount and distribution of the rewards and a base period of performance as the benchmark for comparing subsequent performance. This benchmark is not changed unless a major change occurs in process or technology. When performance exceeds the base period performance, the gain-sharing plan pays a bonus pool.

Gain sharing promotes teamwork and participation in decision making. It requires that employees have the skills to participate and that the organization encourages participation. Consider these companies that have used gain sharing effectively:

- The Herman Miller Company, a furniture manufacturer that is frequently rated as one of the 10 best-managed U.S. corporations, has used a gain-sharing plan for many years. The company also uses a strategy of employee involvement that supports and enhances the motivational effect of the gain-sharing plan.
- Grumman Corporation developed a performance bonus plan for the crew in its Long Life Vehicle project that it used in conjunction with its Grumman Quality program. Employees focused on processes that involved rework, scrap, and excessive maintenance costs. Half the savings from improved performance were divided equally among the crew members working on the project.

The three most widely used gain-sharing programs are improshare, the Scanlon plan, and the Rucker plan.

1. Improshare (improved productivity sharing) determines its bonus pool by computing the difference between the target level of labor cost given the level of production and the actual labor cost (the direct labor efficiency variance; see chapter 10 for details). The plan specifies how the difference will be shared between the shareholders and the employees and how to calculate the amount distributed to each employee.

2. The Scanlon plan is based on the following formula, computed using the data in some base period:

Base ratio = Payroll costs/Value of goods or services produced

For example, if in the base period payroll costs are $25 million and the deemed value of production or service is $86 million, the base ratio would be 0.29 ($25 million ÷ $86 million). In any period in which the ratio of labor costs to the value of production or service is less than the base ratio, the deemed labor savings are added to a bonus pool. Therefore, continuing the previous example, if actual payroll costs were $28 million in a period when the deemed value of production was $105 million, the amount added to the bonus pool would be as follows:

$$\text{Amount added to bonus pool} = (\text{Value of production this period} \times \text{Base ratio}) - \text{Actual payroll costs}$$
$$= (\$105,000,000 \times 0.29) - \$28,000,000$$
$$= \$2,450,000$$

When labor costs are more than the base ratio, some organizations deduct the difference from the bonus pool. Periodically, usually once a year, the pool is apportioned between the company and the employees in the pool using the plant ratio, which is often 50%/50%.

3. The Rucker plan is based on the following formula, which reflects the data from a representative period:

Rucker standard = Payroll costs/Production value

where production value is measured as net sales – inventory change – materials and supplies used. As in the Scanlon plan, the idea of the Rucker plan is to define a baseline relationship between payroll costs and the value of production and then to reward workers who improve efficiency. Efficiency is measured as lowering the ratio of payroll costs to the value of production. When actual costs are less than the Rucker standard, the employees receive a bonus.

For gain-sharing plans to work, they must reflect performance levels that are reasonable. As might be expected, management and the employees who are subject to these plans often have very different ideas about what is fair. Management usually seeks tighter standards or targets, and employees want the opposite. These plans require that management, the management accountant, and employees participate in seeking the performance level that will serve as the standards or benchmarks for the plans. Many management accountants relish their role as the honest brokers between management and the employees who are subject to these plans.

The people who designed gain-sharing plans believed, from the beginning, that monthly or even weekly performance awards are best because they provide rapid feedback and, therefore, additional motivation, as rewards reinforce the desired type of behavior. While rapid feedback may improve the motivational effect of rewards (expectancy), short-cycle feedback can put strains on the organization's management accounting system when the need for recording and accruing labor costs increases both the cost and potential for error in the management accounting system.

Since gain-sharing plans are team-based rewards, they have the associated problem that some team members may not be doing their fair share and could earn rewards based on the work of others. For example, students often complain about group projects, particularly when they cannot choose their own groups, because someone in the group often refuses to do or is incapable of doing the work. Students, like employees, are often uncomfortable about disciplining, or reporting, their peers. The early proponents of gain sharing recognized this phenomenon and observed that for gain sharing to work, the organization culture must promote cohesive relationships within the group and between the group and management.

In addition, corporate culture has a significant effect on the potential of gain-sharing plans. These programs rely on employee commitment and involvement. Therefore, a corporate culture that respects employees, encourages their involvement, and actively supports employee learning and innovation reinforces the motivational potential of a gain-sharing program.

Like all incentive programs, gain-sharing programs work best when they are simple to understand and monitor. A test of this attribute is whether employees can do the math to compute their own bonuses. In addition, such programs should be perceived as fair, as being directly affected by employee performance, and as being conducive to promoting teamwork.

Gain-sharing plans usually rely on performance measures reported by an organization's management accounting system, which plays a primary supporting role in the gain-sharing process. Most gain-sharing plans focus on management accounting measures relating to labor costs and the relationship of actual labor cost to some standard, or budgeted, level of labor cost. Therefore, the key issues in performance measurement relate to measuring labor costs accurately and consistently and to having the ability to establish a cost standard that is perceived as fair.

Stock Options and Other Stock-Related Compensation Plans

Judging by the published remarks of compensation experts, stock options are the most widely known, misused, and maligned approach to incentive compensation. A **stock option** is the right to purchase a unit of the organizations stock at a specified price, called the *option price*.

A common approach to option pricing is to set the option price at about 105% of the stock's market price at the time the organization issues the stock option. This method is intended to motivate the employee who has been granted the stock option to act in the long-term interests of the organization, thereby increasing the value of the firm so that the market price of the stock will exceed the option price. For this reason, compensation system designers usually restrict stock options to senior executives because they believe that these people have the greatest effect on increasing the market value of the organization. Others have argued, however, that operations staff, as they carry out short-term operating plans, can make significant and sustainable process improvements. This would provide the organization with a competitive advantage, thereby increasing the organization's market value.

The critics of stock option plans have argued that organizations have been too generous in rewarding senior executives with stock options. For example, the organization may issue a senior executive many thousands of stock options with an option price that is very near (or even below) the market price at the time the stock option is issued. This is an implementation issue, not a fundamental defect of stock options. Some critics have argued, however, that stock price increases often reflect general market trends that have nothing to do with the performance of the individual organization. For this reason, many incentive compensation experts have argued that the stock option price should be keyed to the performance of the organization's shares relative to the performance of the prices of comparable shares. In this case, the stock option would be valuable only if the organization's share price increases more rapidly than the share prices of comparable organizations. Since management accountants are often involved in studies or systems that rely on external benchmarks, organizations sometimes delegate the role of developing the appropriate performance standards for relative stock option plans to a team that includes a management accountant.

In general, the use of employee stock ownership plans assumes that employees will work harder when they have an ownership stake. Avis, the automobile rental company, used an employee stock ownership plan to improve employee motivation, resulting in both higher sales and a higher margin on sales. Salomon Brothers, a Wall Street investment house, provided huge bonuses for high-performing employees during the 1980s and early 1990s. For example, one bond trader was paid a $23 million bonus in 1990. Reacting to this, Salomon Brothers' largest shareholder, Warren Buffett, whom *Forbes* magazine identified as the wealthiest person in the United States in 1993 and who was interim chairman at the time, indicated that he wanted Salomon Brothers employees to earn rewards through owning shares, not by free riding on the

IN PRACTICE

The New Accounting Rules for Stock Options: The Case of SFAS 123 (R)

In December 2004, the Financial Accounting Standards Board (FASB) issues Statement on Financial Accounting Standards 123(R)—Share-Based Payment. This statement requires significant changes in the accounting for stock options in that it requires companies to measure employee-based options at fair value, eliminates the so-called intrinsic approach used in APB No. 25, remeasures options at each reporting date, simplifies the accounting for modification of terms or conditions, and requires estimation of forfeitures.

This statement was issued to address the concerns of users and critics, to improve comparability of financial information, to simplify U.S. GAAP, and to align more closely with international accounting standards. The effective date for firms to comply was July 1, 2005.

Source: Adapted from FASB Pronouncement 123 (R) Stock-Based Payment, Financial Accounting Standards Board. http:// www.fasb.org/st/summary/stsum123r.shtml.

This employee is part of a gain-sharing plan at Georgia-Pacific, a paper products manufacturer. The plan pays employees cash bonuses based on productivity improvements. A motivationally desirable feature of the Georgia-Pacific gain-sharing plan is that it pays these productivity bonuses even when the company's net income is negative.

Source: John Chiasson/Liaison Agency, Inc.

owners' investment. To align the interests of the firm's employees and its shareholders and provide for more reasonable performance rewards, Buffett, through the Salomon Brothers Compensation Committee, developed an incentive plan that paid employees up to half their pay in company stock, issued at below-market prices, but that could not be sold for at least 5 years after issue. However, Buffett failed to weigh a consideration that is vital in designing any compensation plan, namely, how other investment banking firms were compensating their employees. While some people applauded the rationality of Buffett's plan, many employees left the firm to join other investment banking firms that were using compensation practices similar to the ones abandoned at Salomon Brothers. These departures precipitated a crisis that eventually led to the scrapping of the new plan.

SUMMARY

In the opening vignette to this chapter, Nathaniel Young thought he had not been careful enough to involve employees in designing his new MACS. He wondered about the kinds of behavioral characteristics that he needed to manage.

This chapter outlines four key behavioral characteristics that make up a well-designed MACS. The choice of the four characteristics is based largely on an acceptance of the human resources model of human motivation. Understanding these

characteristics should provide Nathaniel guidance for designing his new MACS.

The first is embedding the organization's ethical code of conduct into MACS design. At the core of a well-designed MACS is the organization's ethical code of conduct. Ethical codes of conduct help organizations deal with ethical dilemmas or conflicts between individuals and organizational values and those that exist between the organization's stated and practiced values. The elements of an effective ethical control system are presented together with a specific decision model that can be applied when attempting to resolve ethical issues.

Organizations spend a lot of time determining how to motivate employees. One way is to align the goals of employees with those of the organization. However, even if goals are aligned, organizations cannot always rely on employee self-control to achieve targeted performance. In many instances, organizations must set up task or results control systems. Task control uses either preventive control devices or relies on monitoring, whereas results control focuses on comparing actual results to desired performance. Development and use of the right kinds of performance measures are tied directly into the second behavioral characteristic, which involves using a mix of short- and long-term qualitative and quantitative performance measures. This is the Balanced Scorecard approach.

The Balanced Scorecard is the first systematic attempt to design a performance measurement system that translates an organization's strategy into clear objectives, measures, and initiatives. The scorecard is built around four perspectives: the financial perspective, the customer perspective, the internal business perspective, and the learning and growth perspective. For each of these, specific performance measures are developed. Having such perspectives allows an organization to manage itself in a balanced fashion, as no particular perspective gets overemphasized at the expense of the others.

The third characteristic is empowering employees to be involved in decision making and MACS design. This characteristic acknowledges that people are the organization's greatest asset. Providing a voice through participation has a twofold benefit. First, participation in decision making has been shown to increase employee morale, commitment to a decision, and job satisfaction. Second, by allowing employees to participate, the organization is able to gather information about jobs and processes from the individuals who are closest to those jobs and processes. Such information provides managers with insights that they would not normally be able to obtain simply by performing cursory inspections of how people are working. Continuing to educate employees in the information they are using and being evaluated on is another critical aspect of employee involvement. For example, without a clear understanding of how their actions translate into a score on a performance measure, employees are left without direction and may take actions detrimental to the organization.

Both intrinsic and extrinsic rewards are used by organizations to motivate employees. However, intrinsic rewards come from inside an individual and may simply be the result of an employee liking a specific job. Organizations try to hire individuals who will match a particular job and thus be intrinsically motivated. However, even if intrinsic motivation exists, many organizations still rely on extrinsic rewards, such as financial incentives, for motivational purposes.

Developing an appropriate incentive system to reward performance is the fourth characteristic. This chapter discussed the characteristics of an effective performance measurement system and the most common ways of rewarding results, including cash bonus, gain sharing, and stock options.

KEY TERMS

Balanced Scorecard, 365
Cash bonus, 374
Data falsification, 364
Diagnostic control systems, 359
Earnings management, 364
Employee self-control, 359
Ethical control system, 358
Extrinsic rewards, 367
Gain sharing, 375
Gaming the performance
  indicator, 364

Goal congruence, 359
Human relations movement, 353
Human resources model
  of motivation, 353
Improshare, 376
Incentive compensation, 368
Interactive control
  systems, 361
Intrinsic rewards, 367
Monitoring, 361
Motivation, 353

Pay-for-performance systems, 368
Preventive control, 361
Profit sharing, 374
Results control, 362
Rucker plan, 376
Scanlon plan, 376
Scientific management
  school, 353
Smoothing, 364
Stock option, 377
Task control, 361

Questions

8-1 What are the four major behavioral considerations in MACS design? (LO 1)

8-2 What is the scientific management view of motivation? (LO 2)

8-3 What is the human relations movement view of motivation? (LO 2)

8-4 What is the human resources model view of motivation? (LO 2)

8-5 What are the four requirements of ethical conduct by which certified management accountants have to abide? (LO 4)

8-6 What are some choices that individuals can make when ethical conflicts arise? (LO 4)

8-7 What is an ethical control system, and what are its key elements? (LO 4)

8-8 What are the three key dimensions of motivation? (LO 3)

8-9 What is goal congruence? (LO 3)

8-10 How do diagnostic control systems differ from interactive control systems? (LO 3)

8-11 How does task control differ from results control? (LO 3)

8-12 List and explain the two categories in task control. (LO 3)

8-13 List three quantitative financial measures of performance in a manufacturing organization of your choice. (LO 3)

8-14 List three quantitative financial measures of performance in a service organization of your choice. (LO 3)

8-15 List three quantitative nonfinancial measures of performance in a manufacturing organization of your choice. (LO 3)

8-16 List three quantitative nonfinancial measures of performance in a service organization of your choice. (LO 3)

8-17 List three qualitative measures of performance. (LO 3)

8-18 What is meant by gaming a performance indicator? (LO 3)

8-19 What is data falsification? (LO 3)

8-20 What is an example of earnings management or smoothing?

8-21 What are two essential elements in employee empowerment? (LO 5)

8-22 What is an intrinsic reward? (LO 5)

8-23 What is an extrinsic reward? (LO 5)

8-24 What is incentive compensation? (LO 5)

8-25 What are the six attributes of effective performance measurement systems? (LO 5)

8-26 What type of organization is best suited to incentive compensation? Why? (LO 5)

8-27 What is a cash bonus? (LO 5)

8-28 What is profit sharing? (LO 5)

8-29 What is gain sharing? (LO 5)

8-30 What is a stock option plan? (LO 5)

Exercises

LO 2   **8-31** *Managerial approaches to motivation*   How do the scientific management, human relations, and human resource schools differ in their views on human motivation?

LO 4   **8-32** *Characteristics of a MACS: ethical issues*   List and describe the hierarchy of ethical considerations.

LO 4   **8-33** *Characteristics of a MACS: ethical issues*   What should a person do if faced with a conflict between his or her values and those of the organization?

LO 4   **8-34** *Characteristics of a MACS: ethical issues*   What should a person do if the organization's stated values conflict with practiced values? What are the individual's choices? Why do you think such conflicts exist?

LO 3   **8-35** *Choosing an approach to control*   Think of any setting in need of control. Explain why you think that task control or results control would be more appropriate in the setting that you have chosen. Do not use an example from the text.

LO 3   **8-36** *Characteristics of a MACS: multiple performance measures*   What is the advantage of having multiple measures of performance?

LO 3   **8-37**   *Understanding performance measurement*   Why is it important that people understand what performance is measured, how performance is measured, and how employee rewards relate to measured performance?

LO 3   **8-38**   *Controllable performance*   Why should performance measurement systems and rewards focus on performance that employees can control?

LO 3   **8-39**   *Tailoring performance measurement to the job*   In a company that takes telephone orders from customers for general merchandise, explain how you would evaluate the performance of the company president, a middle manager who designs the system to coordinate order taking and order shipping, and an employee who fills orders. How are the performance measurement systems similar? How are the performance measurement systems different?

LO 3, 5   **8-40**   *Characteristics of a MACS: rewards*   Can goal congruence be increased if rewards are tied to performance? Explain.

LO 3   **8-41**   *Non–goal-congruent behavior*   What distinguishes data falsification from gaming activities?

LO 3   **8-42**   *Non–goal-congruent behavior*   List some methods of gaming performance indicators.

LO 3   **8-43**   *Non–goal-congruent behavior*   Can you think of instances when gaming behavior is appropriate in an organization?

LO 5   **8-44**   *Characteristics of a MACS: participation*   What are the advantages for the individual in being able to participate in decision making in the organization, and what are the advantages for the organization in allowing the individual to participate in decision making?

LO 5   **8-45**   *The nature of intrinsic and extrinsic rewards*   Do you believe that people value intrinsic rewards? Give an example of an intrinsic reward that you would value and explain why. Why are extrinsic rewards important to people? If you value only extrinsic rewards, explain why.

LO 5   **8-46**   *Choosing what to reward*   Explain when one would reward outcomes or outputs, reward inputs, or use knowledge-based pay.

LO 5   **8-47**   *Choosing the reward level*   You work for a consulting firm and have been given the assignment of deciding whether a particular company president is overpaid both in absolute terms and relative to presidents of comparable companies. How would you undertake this task?

LO 5   **8-48**   *Using cash bonuses*   When should an organization use a cash bonus?

LO 5   **8-49**   *Using profit sharing*   When should an organization use profit sharing?

LO 5   **8-50**   *Using gain sharing*   When should an organization use gain sharing?

LO 5   **8-51**   *Using stock options*   When should an organization use stock options?

LO 5   **8-52**   *Rewarding group performance*   How would you reward a group of people that includes product designers, engineers, production personnel, purchasing agents, marketing staff, and accountants whose job is to identify and develop a new car? How would you reward a person whose job is to discover a better way of designing crash protection devices in cars? How are these two situations similar? How are they different?

Problems

LO 1   **8-53**   *MACS design motivation*   Explain why an understanding of human motivation is essential to MACS design.

LO 1   **8-54**   *Behavioral considerations in MACS design*   List the four key behavioral considerations in MACS design and explain the importance or benefits of each.

LO 4   **8-55**   *Ethics quiz*   Refer to the *Wall Street Journal* Workplace-Ethics Quiz in the In Practice box on page 360. Discuss reasons why individual respondents might feel justified answering as they did.

LO 4 **8-56 *Ethics*** Suppose you are the chief executive officer of a manufacturing firm that is bidding on a government contract. In this situation, the firm with the lowest bid will win the contract. Your firm has completed developing its bid and is ready to submit it to the government when you receive an anonymously sent packet containing a competitor's bid that is lower than yours. If your firm loses the bid, you may need to lay off some employees, and your profits will suffer. What are some possible options in this situation, what are the possible consequences, and what would you do?

LO 4 **8-57 *Characteristics of MACS design: ethical issues*** During data collection for the transition from an old management accounting system to a new activity-based cost management system, you see a manager's reported time allotments. You know that the data supplied by the manager are completely false. You confront the manager, and she states that she is worried that if she reports how she actually spends her time, her job will be altered, and it will also be found out that she is really not performing very well. She implores you not to tell anyone because she has needed to take time off to care for her chronically ill parents and needs the pay to help cover her parents' medical expenses. What actions should you take? Explain.

LO 3 **8-58 *Approaches to control*** Cite two settings or jobs where each of the following approaches to control would be appropriately applied. Identify what you feel is the definitive characteristic of the setting that indicates the appropriateness of the approach to control that you have identified:
(a) Preventive control
(b) Monitoring
(c) Results control

LO 1, 3 **8-59 *Characteristics of MACS: types of information*** Under what circumstances should both quantitative and qualitative performance measures be used to evaluate employee, work-group, and divisional performance? Provide examples to support your answer.

LO 1, 3 **8-60 *Evaluating system performance*** Suppose that you are the manager of a production facility in a business that makes plastic items that organizations use for advertising. The customer chooses the color and quantity of the item and specifies what is to be imprinted on the item. Your job is to ensure that the job is completed according to the customer's specifications. This is a cutthroat business that competes on the basis of low price, high quality, and good service to the customer. Recently you installed a just-in-time manufacturing system. How may you evaluate the performance of this system given the characteristics of your organization?

LO 5 **8-61 *Characteristics of MACS design: participation and education*** Explain how participating in decision making and being educated to understand information received in an organization contribute toward employee empowerment in MACS design.

LO 5 **8-62 *Characteristics of MACS design: rewards*** What are some pros and cons of tying an individual's pay to performance?

LO 5 **8-63 *Designing reward structures*** Answer the following two questions about the organization units:
* What behavior should be rewarded?
* What is an appropriate incentive compensation system?
  (a) A symphony orchestra
  (b) A government welfare office
  (c) An airline complaint desk

(d) A control room in a nuclear power–generating facility

(e) A basketball team

LO 5   **8-64** *Designing a compensation plan*   Suppose that you are the owner/manager of a housecleaning business. You have 30 employees who work in teams of three. Teams are dispatched to the homes of customers where they are directed by the customer to undertake specific cleaning tasks that vary widely from customer to customer.

Your employees are unskilled workers who are paid an hourly wage of $9. This wage is typical for unskilled work. Turnover in your organization is quite high. Generally, your best employees leave as soon as they find better jobs. The employees that stay are usually ones who cannot find work elsewhere and have a poor attitude.

The hourly rate charged customers per team hour is $40. That is, if a team spends 1.5 hours in a customer's home, the charge is $60.

You want to develop an incentive system to use in your organization. You would like to use this incentive system to motivate good employees to stay and motivate poor workers either to improve or to leave. What type of system would you develop? If the system relies on any measurements, indicate how you would obtain these measurements.

LO 5   **8-65** *Motivating desired performance*   DMT Biotech is a biotechnology research and development company that designs products for the needs of life science researchers. The company consists of an administrative unit, a research laboratory, and a facility used to develop prototypes of and produce new products. The major costs in this company are the salaries of the research staff, which are substantial.

In the past, the research scientists working at DMT Biotech have been rewarded on the basis of their proven scientific expertise. Salaries of these research scientists are based on the level of education achieved and the number of research papers published in scientific journals. At a recent board of directors meeting, an outside director criticized the research and development activities with the following comments:

> There is no question that we have the most highly trained scientists in our industry. Evidence of their training and creativity is provided by the number of research publications they generate. However, the knowledge and creativity are not translating into patentable inventions and increased sales for this company. Our organization has the lowest rate of new product introduction in our industry, and we have one of the largest research and development teams. These people are too far into basic research, where the rewards lie in getting articles published. We need these people to have more interest in generating ideas that have commercial potential. This is a profit-seeking organization, not a university research laboratory.

Required

a. Assuming that the director's facts are correct, do you agree that this is a problem?

b. The board of directors has ordered the president of DMT Biotech to increase the rate of new products and the time devoted to new product development. How should the president go about this task?

LO 5   **8-66** *Profit-sharing plan at Hoechst Celanese*   Hoechst Celanese, a pharmaceutical manufacturer, has used a profit-sharing plan, the Hoechst Celanese Performance Sharing Plan, to motivate employees. To operationalize the plan, the Hoechst Celanese executive committee set a target earnings from operations (EFO). This target was based on the company's business plans and the economy's expected performance. The performance sharing plan also used two other critical values: the earnings from operations threshold amount and the earnings from operations stretch target. The targets for 1994 are shown here:

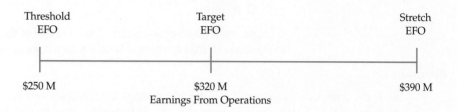

The plan operates as follows. If earnings from operations fall below the threshold value, there is no profit sharing. If earnings from operations lie between the threshold amount and the target, the profit-sharing percentage is prorated between the threshold award of 1% and the target payment of 4%. For example, if earnings from operations were $285 million, the profit-sharing percentage would be 2.5%:

$$\text{Profit-sharing percentage} = 1\% + \{3\% \times [(285 - 250)/(320 - 250)]\} = 2.5\%$$
$$\text{Profit-sharing pool} = 2.5\% \times \$285{,}000{,}000 = \$7{,}125{,}000$$

If earnings from operations are between the target and the stretch target, the profit-sharing percentage is prorated between the target payment of 4% and the stretch-sharing payment of 7%. For example, if earnings from operations were $350 million, the profit-sharing percentage would be 5.29%, and the profit-sharing pool would be $18.5 million:

$$\text{Profit-sharing percentage} = 4\% + \{3\% \times [(350 - 320)/(390 - 320)]\}$$
$$= 5.28571\%$$
$$\text{Profit-sharing pool} = 5.28571\% \times \$350{,}000{,}000 = \$18{,}500{,}000$$

If earnings from operations equal or exceed the stretch target level, the profit-sharing pool would be $27.3 million:

$$\text{Profit-sharing pool} = 7\% \times \$390{,}000{,}000 = \$27{,}300{,}000$$

Required

a. List, with explanations, what you think are desirable features of the Hoechst Celanese Performance Sharing Plan.
b. List, with explanations, what you think are the undesirable features of the Hoechst Celanese Performance Sharing Plan.
c. The EFO for 1994 was $332 million. Compute the size of the profit-sharing pool.
d. In 1995, the Performance Sharing Plan parameters were threshold EFO—$420 million; target EFO—$490 million; and stretch EFO—$560 million. What do you think of the practice of raising the parameters from one year to the next?

LO 5   **8-67** *Profit sharing*   Peterborough Medical Devices makes devices and equipment that it sells to hospitals. The organization has a profit-sharing plan that is worded as follows:

> The company will make available a profit-sharing pool that will be the lower of the following two items:
>
> 1. 40% of income before taxes in excess of the target profit level, which is 18% of net assets, or
> 2. $7 million
>
> The individual employee is paid a share of the profit-sharing pool equal to the ratio of that employee's salary to the total salary paid to all employees.

Required

a. If the company earned $45 million of earnings before taxes and had net assets of $100 million, what would be the amount available for distribution from the profit-sharing pool?
b. Suppose that Marg Watson's salary was $68,000 and that total salaries paid in the company were $25 million. What would Marg's profit share be?
c. What do you like about this profit-sharing plan?
d. What do you dislike about this profit-sharing plan?

LO 5   **8-68** *Gain sharing*   Sakura Snack Company manufactures a line of snack foods, such as cheese crackers, granola bars, and cookies. The production workers are part of a gain-sharing program that works as follows: A target level of labor costs is set that is based on the achieved level of production. If the actual level of labor costs is less than the target level of labor costs, the difference is added to a cumulative pool that is carried from year to year. If the actual level of labor costs exceeds the target level, the amount of the excess is deducted from the cumulative pool.

   If the balance of the pool is positive at the end of any year, the employees receive half the balance of the pool as part of a gain-sharing plan, and the balance of the pool is reset to zero. If the balance of the pool is negative at the end of any year, the employees receive nothing, and the negative balance is carried to the following year.

   In any year when the target level of costs exceeds the actual level of costs, the target level for the following year is based on the actual level of cost performance in the previous year.

Required

a. Suppose that the target level of performance is set using the following labor use standards: (1) 0.20 labor hour per case of snack food A, (2) 0.15 labor hour per case of snack food B, (3) 0.25 labor hour per case of snack food C, and (4) 0.10 labor hour per case of snack food D.

   During the last year, production levels of snacks A, B, C, and D were 200,000 cases, 220,000 cases, 130,000 cases, and 240,000 cases, respectively. The company used 110,000 labor hours during the year, and the average cost of labor was $16 per hour. What is the amount available for distribution to employees under this gain-sharing program, assuming no prior balance in the pool?
b. What do you like about this program?
c. What do you dislike about it?

LO 5   **8-69** *Scanlon plan*   Knox Company manufactures consumer products such as cleansers, air fresheners, and detergents. During a recent quarter, the value of the products made was $50 million, and the labor costs were $3 million. The company has decided to use a Scanlon plan with this quarter being used to establish the base ratio for the plan.

The formula is to be applied quarterly with differences, positive or negative, added to the bonus pool. The pool is to be distributed on a 35%/65% basis between the employees and the company at the end of the fourth quarter.

The following production and cost levels were recorded during the first year of the plan's operation:

Quarter	Production Value	Payroll Costs
1	$45,000,000	$2,475,000
2	60,000,000	3,480,000
3	55,000,000	3,575,000
4	48,000,000	2,832,000

Required

a. How much would be distributed to the employees at the end of the year?
b. What assumptions does the Scanlon plan make about the behavior of payroll costs?
c. What formula should be used to determine each employee's share?
d. Management proposes to adjust the base ratio using the lowest ratio experienced in any year. Do you think this is a good idea?

LO 4 **8-70 *Characteristics of MACS design: ethical issues***   You are a management accountant working in the controller's office. Rick Koch, a very powerful executive, approaches you in the parking lot and asks you to do him a favor. The favor involves falsifying some of his division's records on the main computer. The executive states that if you do not do as he asks, he will have you fired. What do you do? Explain.

LO 5 **8-71 *Choosing what to reward***   During the late 1970s, Harley-Davidson, the motorcycle manufacturer, was losing money and was very close to bankruptcy. Management believed that one of the problems was low productivity and, as a result, asked middle managers to speed up production. The employees who made the motorcycles were told that the priority was to get the motorcycles made and shipped on schedule, which was usually very tight. Middle managers were judged by their ability to meet shipment schedules.

Required

a. What is the rationale that would lead to a desire to speed production in the face of increasing costs and declining productivity?
b. What type of behavior do you think this performance measurement system would create in the sense of the priorities that middle management would establish for the production process?
c. What type of problems would this performance measurement system create?
d. How, if at all, would you modify this system?

LO 5 **8-72 *Characteristics of MACS design: participation versus imposition***   Denver Jack's is a large toy manufacturer. The company has 100 highly trained and skilled employees who are involved with six major product lines, including the production of toy soldiers, dolls, and so on. Each product line is manufactured in a different city and state. Denver Jack has decided to make all the production decisions for the toy lines himself, including which products to eliminate. The managers of each toy line believe he is making a mistake.

Required

What are the pros and cons of Denver Jack's approach?

LO 5   **8-73 *Evaluating a compensation plan***   Beau Monde, Inc., a manufacturer and distributor of health and beauty products, made the following disclosure about its compensation program:

> Our compensation philosophy is based on two simple principles: (1) We pay for performance, and (2) management cannot benefit unless our shareholders benefit first.
>
> Executive compensation at Beau Monde consists of three elements: base salary, bonus, and stock awards. Frankly, we see base salaries and the underlying value of restricted stock as what you have to pay to get people in the door—capacity-related costs, if you will. Incentives, in the form of annual cash bonuses and gains tied to increases in the price of our stock, are the performance drivers of our pay equation—the variable costs.
>
> The first element is base salary. Our philosophy is to peg salary levels at median competitive levels. In other words, we pay salaries that are sufficient to attract and retain the level of talent we require.
>
> The second element of our executive compensation is our bonus plan. This plan is based on management by objectives. Each year, the compensation committee approves objectives and performance measures for the corporation, our divisions, and our key individual managers. At year end, bonuses are paid on the basis of measurable performance against these objectives.
>
> The third element of our executive compensation program is stock incentives, namely, restricted stock and stock options.
>
> Our restricted stock program is very straightforward. Stock option grants are made each year at market value. Our options vest over time periods of 2 to 6 years to encourage long-term equity holding by management.
>
> In 1998, we instituted an innovative stock incentive plan called the Stock Option Exchange Program. Under this program, management can purchase stock options by exchanging other forms of compensation, such as the annual bonus or restricted stock, for the options. The price charged for the options is determined by an independent investment banker using pricing mechanics.
>
> Our compensation committee is made up entirely of independent outside directors. We have no interlocking directorates, in which I serve on the compensation committee of one of my director's companies and he or she serves on mine. The compensation committee uses outside advisers chosen independently to ensure that recommendations are fair to all shareholders.

Required

Evaluate this incentive compensation plan.

LO 5   **8-74 *The mix of salary and commission***   Belleville Fashions sells high-quality women's, men's, and children's clothing. The store employs a sales staff of 11 full-time employees and 12 part-time employees. Until recently, all sales staff were paid a flat salary and participated in a profit-sharing plan that provided benefits equal to about 5% of wages. Recently, the manager and owner of Belleville Fashions announced that in the future all compensation would be commission based. The initial commission rate was set equal to the rate that would have caused the actual wage bill based on the old system to be equal to what the wage bill would have been under the commission system. Profit sharing was discontinued.

Required

a. What do you think of this change?
b. Describe some of the reactions that the owner might hear from the sales staff when announcing this change.
c. Do you think that the method of determining the commission rate was appropriate?
d. Describe what you think will happen under the new system.

LO 5 **8-75 *Salary and job responsibilities*** Marie Johnston, the manager of a government unemployment insurance office, is paid a salary that reflects the number of people she supervises and the number of hours that her subordinates work.

Required

a. What do you think of this compensation scheme? What incentives does this compensation scheme provide to Marie?
b. What would you recommend as an appropriate performance measurement and reward system?

LO 5 **8-76 *Distributing a bonus pool*** Four broad approaches to distributing the proceeds of a bonus pool in a profit-sharing plan are listed here:

1. Each person's share is based on salary.
2. Each person receives an equal share.
3. Each person's share is based on position in the organization (larger payments to people at higher levels).
4. Each person's share is based on individual performance relative to some target.

Required

a. Give two reasons to support each alternative.
b. Give two reasons to oppose each alternative.
c. Pick the alternative that you think is best and support your choice with an argument of no more than 100 words.

Cases

LO 1, 3 **8-77 *Characteristics of MACS design: types of information*** Chow Company is an insurance company in Hong Kong. Chow hires 55 people to process insurance claims. The volume of claims is extremely high, and all claims examiners are kept extremely busy. The number of claims in which errors are made runs about 10%. If a claim has an error, it must be corrected by the claims examiners. After looking at the data, Judy Choy, senior manager of the division, was not satisfied with the volume of claims processed. She instructed Anne Wu, the manager, to motivate the claims examiners to work faster. Judy believes that the claims examiners are working as fast as they possibly can. She is also concerned that, by working faster, the examiners will make more errors.

Required

a. How should Anne Wu handle this situation?
b. On what performance measures is the organization relying?
c. What performance measures should the organization use?

LO 4 **8-78 *Ethical control frameworks*** In December 2002, *Time* magazine named Cynthia Cooper, Coleen Rowley, and Sherron Watkins as its Persons of the Year. Cynthia Cooper was vice president of internal audit for WorldCom and informed the firm's audit committee that the firm had improperly treated billions of dollars as capital expenditures rather than properly treating them as period expenses. Coleen Rowley was an FBI attorney who wrote a 13-page memo describing deficiencies in the FBI. Sherron Watkins was vice president at Enron and informed chairman Kenneth Lay of her serious concerns about Enron's financial reporting. Select one of the two accounting-related situations (WorldCom or Enron) to answer the following questions on the basis of the *Time* magazine Person of the Year articles or other articles.

Required

a. How did Cooper and Watkins become aware of financial reporting problems within their companies?

b. Which of the nine alternatives listed on page 357 (or other variation) did Cooper or Watkins take? How did the public become aware of their concerns?

c. What pressures did Cooper or Watkins face to suspend their ethical judgments or drop their concerns? Who would have benefited if Cooper or Watkins had dropped their concerns?

d. What information is reported in the article about WorldCom's or Enron's code of ethics, communication of the code, and system of reporting violations of the code?

e. What role did personal norms play in Cooper's and Watkins's decisions to report the problems they had discovered?

f. What consequences did Cooper and Watkins face for reporting the problems?

g. If you had been in Watkins's or Cooper's place, what would you have done?

LO 5   **8-79 *Compensation tied to Balanced Scorecard, degree of difficulty of target achievement*** [4] In the mid-1990s, Mobil Corporation's Marketing and Refining (M&R) division underwent a major reorganization and developed new strategic directions. In conjunction with these changes, M&R developed a Balanced Scorecard around four perspectives: financial, customer, internal business processes, and learning and growth.[5] Subsequently, M&R linked compensation to its Balanced Scorecard metrics. To illustrate, all salaried employees in M&R's Natural Business Units received the following percentages of their competitive market salary:

	POOR PERFORMANCE WITHIN INDUSTRY	AVERAGE PERFORMANCE WITHIN INDUSTRY	PERFORMANCE BEST IN INDUSTRY
Base pay	90%	90%	90%
Award based on corporate performance on financial metrics	1–2%	3–6%	10%
Award based on performance on Balanced Scorecard metrics for the M&R division and business unit	0%	5–8%	20%
Total pay as percentage of market salary	91–92%	98–104%	120%

The Balanced Scorecards included numerous metrics. M&R's financial metrics included return on capital employed and profitability, and customer metrics included share of targeted segments of consumers and profitability of dealers. Internal business process metrics included safety and quality indices. Finally, learning and growth metrics included an index of employees' perceptions of the work climate at M&R.

Business units developed their own Balanced Scorecards. In addition to choosing targets for scorecard metrics, the business units chose percentage weights that determined how much the

---

[4] Adapted from "Mobil USM&R (A): Linking the Balanced Scorecard," Harvard Business School Case #9-197-025.

[5] The Balanced Scorecard is discussed in detail in chapter 9.

achieved scorecard measures would contribute to the bonus pool displayed in the table. These percentage weights were required to sum to 100%. Furthermore, in connection with the award for performance on the business unit Balanced Scorecard metrics, the business units assigned a performance factor, that is, a "degree of difficulty" of target achievement for each target. The performance factors are similar in concept to those in diving or gymnastic competitions where performance scores depend on the difficulty of the attempted dive or gymnastic routine. The performance factors underwent review by peers, upper management, and the employees whose evaluation and compensation depended on the performance factors. The performance factors ranged from 1.25 (for best-in-industry performance) to 0.7 for poor performance. A target corresponding to average industry performance rated a 1.0 performance factor.

Required

a. What are the advantages and concerns in linking compensation to a Balanced Scorecard generally?

b. Evaluate M&R's approach to linking compensation to multiple measures (Balanced Scorecard measures), including its system of assigning degrees of difficulty to achieving targets. In your response, consider the process that is involved in developing the compensation scheme.

Chapter 9

The Balanced Scorecard

After reading this chapter, you will be able to:

➤ understand why managers need a Balanced Scorecard to measure and manage intangible assets for value creation

➤ appreciate the role of strategy maps in visualizing the cause-and-effect linkages between outcomes in the financial and customer perspectives and the drivers of those outcomes: the value proposition, critical processes, human resources, information technology, and organization capital

➤ translate mission, vision, and strategy statements into a Balanced Scorecard

➤ understand how to develop a coherent set of Balanced Scorecard objectives, measures, and targets

➤ explain why key performance indicator scorecards are not necessarily Balanced Scorecards

➤ design a Balanced Scorecard for nonprofit and public sector organizations

➤ describe how to use the Balanced Scorecard to implement strategy

➤ recognize common pitfalls in implementing the Balanced Scorecard and suggest ways to avoid the pitfalls

---

Metro Bank

Mike Hancock, chief executive officer of Metro Bank, pondered how he could reposition the retail bank to a new strategic direction. Historically, retail banking had emphasized efficiency in processing transactional products, such as checking accounts, saving accounts, and consumer loans. Banking was simple in the highly regulated environment that constrained competition on interest rates offered to consumers, prevented competition from banks outside Metro's geographic area, and prevented nonbanking institutions from offering demand and time deposit accounts. Banking, however, was completely different today. The deregulation of interest rates had led to increased competition among banks and thrift institutions,

Source: Chuck Savage/CORBIS.

which now had to offer high interest rates to attract and retain consumers' deposits. Relaxed geographical restrictions had allowed banks in neighboring states to open branches in Metro's banking area, and many nonbanking institutions, such as Merrill Lynch, were offering money market accounts and mutual funds that let consumers earn market rates on their funds and still enjoy check-writing privileges. Metro's operating expenses, such as rental and lease expenses for branch office space and salaries for branch personnel, were continuing to increase. In addition, technological advances that enabled consumers to bank electronically had compelled Metro to make large investments at a time when revenue growth had slowed and margins on interest-based products (deposits and loans) were decreasing.

Hancock wanted to transform the bank from depending exclusively on the income from interest rate spreads of traditional retail banking products (deposits and consumer and commercial loans) to earning fees by providing a wider range of financial products and services to customers with high net worth and high disposable income. The senior executive team had created a new mission for the retail bank: "We will provide superior service to our targeted (high net worth and high disposable income) customers." Hancock wanted the bank to develop and customize new financial products such as annuities, investment products, and technology-based payment services that would meet these customers' financial needs. Branch personnel would do fewer deposits, withdrawals, and check-cashing transactions and instead would do more higher-value interactions with customers to sell and support the new products and services. The bank would partner with other financial service providers, such as insurance companies and brokerage firms, to offer a one-stop financial supermarket for customers who would provide the greatest opportunities for increasing profits. With a broader product and service line and excellent knowledge of its customer base, the bank would then be able to find ways to develop new relationships with its most desirable customers and expand the bank's business with them.

Hancock felt that his biggest problems in transforming Metro Bank were how to communicate the new strategy to the bank's more than 8,000 employees and how to motivate them to help the bank succeed. While Metro's executive team had all agreed to the new mission statement, Hancock believed it was too broad to provide adequate guidance to employees' day-to-day activities in hundreds of branches throughout the metropolitan area. Currently, the only reports at Metro Bank and its branches were the monthly company and branch income statements and balance sheets. Performance measures focused solely on deposit growth and operating cost reductions. While these reports and measures had been fine for executing Metro's previous strategy, which was focused on transactional accounts, Hancock felt that Metro Bank needed a much more comprehensive and strategic set of performance measures to communicate the new customer-focused strategy, to guide resource allocation in accordance with the strategy, for monthly reporting about whether the new strategy was working, and for aligning employee objectives and compensation to successful strategy implementation.

Chapter 1 described the financial control systems used by industrial-age companies such as General Motors and DuPont. Managers of these companies used only financial measures, such as operating profits and return on investment, to evaluate the performance of divisions and as the basis for allocating capital to them. Chapter 8 described additional roles for performance measurement systems, such as to motivate and evaluate the performance of individual employees and to help employees improve the performance of processes they control. For these purposes, companies need performance measurement systems that include nonfinancial as well as financial measures. The keen interest in designing effective performance measurement systems arises from the management dictum that "if you can't measure it, you can't manage it."

Performance measurement systems perform multiple roles:

- Communicate the company's strategic objectives
- Motivate employees to help the company achieve its strategic objectives
- Evaluate the performance of managers, employees, and operating units
- Help managers allocate resources to the most productive and profitable opportunities
- Provide feedback on whether the company is making progress in improving processes and meeting the expectations of customers and shareholders

The challenge is to find the right mix of financial and nonfinancial measures to perform these multiple tasks. Financial measurements alone may have been adequate for early twentieth-century industrial-age companies that competed by making effective investments in physical assets and managing well their financial assets and liabilities. Companies today, however, succeed by creating distinctive value from their intangible assets as well as their physical and financial assets. An organization's intangible assets include the following:

- Loyal and profitable customer relationships
- High-quality processes
- Innovative products and services
- Employee skills and motivation
- Databases and information systems

Financial measurements cannot measure the performance of these intangible assets except in a highly aggregate and delayed fashion. Nonfinancial measurements help to communicate, motivate, and evaluate their current drivers of performance.

The management accounting literature describes several performance measurement frameworks,[1] including those introduced by national and international quality management programs: the Malcolm Baldrige National Quality Program for performance excellence[2] and the EFQM Excellence model.[3] In this chapter, rather than provide a survey of the many existing performance measurement models, we will select one, the Balanced Scorecard (BSC), which one of the book's authors has helped to develop. The Balanced Scorecard is a general and flexible approach to performance measurement; surveys indicate that 60% to 70% of companies around the world report they use some version of this approach. And the Balanced Scorecard has been adapted to work in public sector and nonprofit enterprises as well. A distinguishing feature of the Balanced Scorecard is that it provides a framework that selects financial and nonfinancial performance measures from the company's strategy. The measures include, but are not restricted to, measures of operating, quality, and process improvements.

THE BALANCED SCORECARD

The Balanced Scorecard measures organizational performance across four different but linked perspectives that are derived from the organization's vision, strategy, and objectives:[4]

- *Financial.* How is success measured by our shareholders?
- *Customer.* How do we create value for our customers?
- *Process.* At which processes must we excel to satisfy our customers and shareholders?
- *Learning and growth.* What employee capabilities, information systems, and organizational capabilities do we need to continually improve our processes and customer relationships?

---

[1] References on organizational performance measurement include Richard L. Lynch and Kelvin F. Cross, *Measure Up! How to Measure Corporate Performance* (Cambridge, Mass.: Blackwell Business, 1995); Robert S. Kaplan and David P. Norton, *The Balanced Scorecard: Translating Strategy into Action* (Cambridge, Mass.: Harvard Business School Press, 1996); and Andy Neely, *Business Performance Measurement: Theory and Practice* (Cambridge, UK; Cambridge University Press, 2002).

[2] http://www.quality.nist.gov/Business_Criteria.htm.

[3] http://www.efqm.org/Default.aspx?tabid=35.

[4] No theorem exists that four perspectives are necessary and sufficient for an effective balanced scorecard, but most implementing organizations have found four to be the right number for describing their strategy. Some organizations have added a fifth perspective to highlight particularly important aspects of their strategy, such as suppliers, employees, community involvement, or, for nonprofit organizations, social impact. Few have used fewer than four without sacrificing critical aspects of their strategy.

The Balanced Scorecard enables companies to track financial results while simultaneously monitoring, with nonfinancial measures, how they are building their capabilities—with customers, with their processes, and with their employees and systems—for future growth and profitability.

As a simple example of how the Balanced Scorecard measures and links performance across its four perspectives, consider the partial scorecard produced by a small manufacturing company that wins business on the basis of low-cost, high-quality products that it consistently delivers on-time to its customers. The company's most important financial metric is return on investment, which it places in its financial perspective (see the following diagram). The company expects to generate increased revenues for improving its return on investment financial measure by retaining and expanding sales to existing customers. Therefore, it includes measures in the customer perspective for percentage of repeat customers and the growth in sales with existing customers. The company believes that customers highly value on-time delivery of orders. Thus, improved on-time delivery performance is expected to lead to increased customer loyalty, which in turn will lead to higher financial performance. So both customer loyalty metrics and on-time delivery are incorporated into the scorecard's customer perspective.

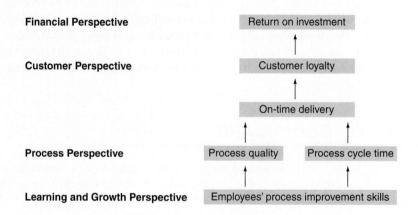

The financial and customer measures represent the "what" of strategy, that is, what the company wants to accomplish with its two most important external constituents: shareholders and customers. The process perspective describes "how" the strategy will be executed; it identifies the processes that are most important to meet the expectations of shareholders and customers. For example, short cycle times and high-quality production processes are necessary to achieve exceptional on-time delivery. Therefore, measures of quality, such as defect rates and yields, and process cycle time, or the time required to convert raw materials into finished products, are identified as process metrics. Measures for the fourth perspective arise from asking another "how" question: How will employees obtain the skills and knowledge to be able to improve the quality and cycle times of the company's production processes? The company recognizes that its production workers must be well trained in process improvement techniques. Therefore, a measure of employees' skills and capabilities in process improvement is included within the learning and growth perspective.

This simple example shows how an entire chain of cause-and-effect relationships among performance measures in the four Balanced Scorecard perspectives tells the story of the business unit's strategy. The scorecard measures identify and make explicit the hypotheses about the cause-and-effect relationships between outcome measures (e.g., return on investment and customer loyalty) in the financial and customer perspectives and the performance drivers of those outcomes—such as zero defect processes, short cycle-time processes, and skilled, motivated employees—that are measured in the process and learning and growth perspectives,.

Exhibit 9-1 provides another example of performance measures linked across the four perspectives of a Balanced Scorecard. Lowcost Airlines competes by offering low prices and on-time arrivals to its passengers. The left side shows a diagram of the cause-and-effect relationships across the four perspectives that describe a key element of Lowcost's strategy: how it can make money even at low prices by being efficient and low cost in its operations. The high-level financial measures are net income and return on assets. Lowcost has also identified two additional financial metrics, revenue growth and asset utilization (fewer planes), that drive its high-level financial metrics. If Lowcost can get more utilization from its most expensive resources (airplanes and flight crews), it can earn higher revenues without having to spend more on these resources.

The company hopes to attract more passengers (and, therefore, revenues) by offering the lowest prices and the most reliable departure and arrival times in the industry. It reflects these objectives in the customer perspective and measures them by prices compared to competitors and by on-time departures and arrivals, again benchmarked against industry competitors. A key process that contributes both to the on-time departure customer metric and the asset utilization financial metric is the ground-turnaround process. Lowcost uses two measures for this critical process: the average time its planes spend on the ground between flights and the percentage of flights that depart the gate on time. By reducing the time its planes spend on the

Exhibit 9-1
Illustrative Example for Lowcost Airlines

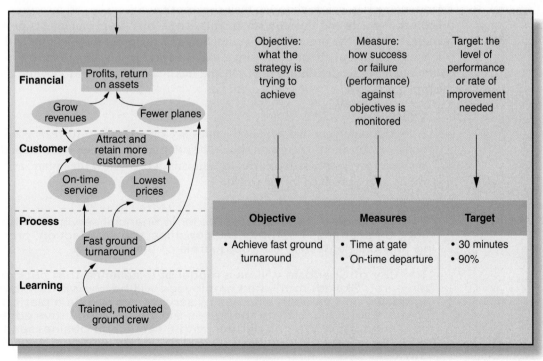

ground, Lowcost enables its planes to depart on time (meeting a key customer expectation) and get better utilization of its most expensive resources—airplanes and flight crews—enabling Lowcost to earn profits even at prices that are the lowest in the industry (a key financial objective). In the learning and growth perspective, Lowcost has an objective to train and motivate ground crews for fast ground turnarounds, much like the training of the pit crew for a race car in the Indianapolis 500 that can change four tires in less than 15 seconds.

Lowcost tells the story of its strategy through the cause-and-effect relationships among performance measures in the four Balanced Scorecard perspectives. It believes that by improving the training and motivation of its ground crews, it will achieve faster ground turnaround, satisfying customers through on-time departures; fast ground turnaround also leads to higher utilization of expensive resources (aircraft and flight crews), yielding one or two extra flights per day with them. The higher resource utilization enables Lowcost to charge the lowest prices in the industry, another feature attractive to its targeted customers, while earning profits sufficient to deliver an attractive return on shareholder investment. The various measures in Lowcost's Balanced Scorecard include desired outcomes in the financial and customer perspectives—high return on investent, increased revenues, lower cost per passenger mile flown, and increased market share and customer satisfaction—as well as the drivers of these outcomes in the process and learning and growth perspectives—fast turnaround times and high employee capabilities and motivation.

With this introduction to the Balanced Scorecard framework, we can now delve more deeply into developing performance measures in each of the four perspectives that link to the enterprise's strategy.

VISION, MISSION, AND STRATEGY

Many enterprises, before choosing their performance objectives and measures, create vision statements and mission statements. These high-level statements provide a general sense of the organization's direction and purpose; they inspire and often motivate employees about the positive role the enterprise wants to play in society. Although the exact definitions of vision and mission can vary, the following provide helpful guidelines:

VISION
A concise statement that defines the mid- to long-term (3- to 10-year) goals of the organization. The vision should be external and market oriented and should express—often in colorful or visionary terms—how the organization wants to be perceived by the world.

Examples
"We will become the respected leader in financial services with a focus on seamless customer relationships and satisfaction, producing financial returns in the top quartile of the industry."

"The City of Charlotte will be a model of excellence that puts its citizens first. Skilled, motivated employees will be known for providing quality and value in all areas of service. We will be a platform for vital economic activity that gives the city a competitive edge in the marketplace. We will partner with citizens and businesses to make the city a community of choice for living, working, and leisure activities."

MISSION

A concise, internally focused statement of how an organization expects to compete and deliver value to customers. The mission often states the reason for the organization's existence, the basic purpose toward which its activities are directed, and the values that guide employee's activities.

Examples

Ben & Jerry's is dedicated to the creation and demonstration of a new corporate concept of linked prosperity. Our mission consists of three interrelated parts:

Product: To make, distribute, and sell the finest-quality all-natural ice cream and related products in a wide variety of innovative flavors made from Vermont dairy products.

Economic: To operate the company on a sound financial basis of profitable growth, increasing value for our shareholders, and creating career opportunities and financial rewards for our employees.

Social: To operate the company in a way that actively recognizes the central role that business plays in the structure of society by initiating innovative ways to improve the quality of life of a broad community—local, national, and international.

The mission of the City of Charlotte is to ensure the delivery of quality public services that promote the safety, health, and quality of life of its citizens. Organizations identify and respond to community needs and focus on the customer through the following:

- Creating and maintaining effective partnerships
- Attracting and retaining skilled and motivated employees
- Using strategic business planning

Such vision and mission statements set the general direction for the organization. They should help shareholders, customers, and employees understand what the company is about and what it intends to achieve. These statements, however, are far too vague to guide day-to-day actions and resource allocation decisions. Companies can make their statements more operational when they define a **strategy** of how the vision and mission will be achieved. The strategy literature is uncommonly diverse. Different scholars and practitioners have very different definitions about what strategy is and how it should be defined.[5] Michael Porter, a founder and leader of the strategy field, argues that strategy is about selecting the set of activities in which an organization will excel to create a sustainable difference in the marketplace.[6] The sustainable difference can be to deliver greater value to customers than competitors or to provide comparable value at lower cost than competitors. He states, "Differentiation arises from both the choice of activities and how they are performed." Specific examples of such strategies are presented later in this chapter as part of a discussion of the value proposition the organization selects to deliver to its customers.

---

[5] See, for example, Henry Mintzberg, Bruce Ahlstrand, and Joseph Lampel, *Strategy Safari: A Guided Tour Through the Wilds of Strategic Management* (New York: Simon & Schuster, 1998), and Pankaj Ghemawat, "Competition and Business Strategy in Historical Perspective," *Business History Review,* spring 2002, 37–74.

[6] Michael Porter, "What Is Strategy?" *Harvard Business Review,* November–December 1996, 61–78.

Objectives, Measures, and Targets

Once the company's vision, mission, and strategy have been established, the senior management team selects performance measurements to provide the needed specificity that makes vision, mission, and strategy statements even more meaningful and actionable for all employees. The process of building a Balanced Scorecard should start not with measures but with word statements, called *objectives*, that describe what the company is attempting to accomplish. For example, the left-hand side of Exhibit 9-1 uses words to describe the objectives in each perspective. Objectives are typically written as action phrases—a verb followed by an object—and also may include the means and the desired results. Following are typical objectives found in the four Balanced Scorecard perspectives:

- Increase revenues through expanded sales to existing customers (financial)
- Become service oriented (customer)
- Achieve excellence in order fulfillment through continuous process improvements (process)
- Align employee incentives and rewards with the strategy (learning and growth)

While only a short summary of each objective may appear in each oval of a linkage diagram, such as on the left side of Exhibit 9-1, the company's Balanced Scorecard would typically contain a more extensive (three- to five-sentence) description, as we will subsequently illustrate as we work through the Metro Bank example.

Measures describe how success in achieving an objective will be determined. Measures provide specificity and reduce the ambiguity that is inherent in word statements. Take, for example, an objective to deliver a product or service to a customer on time. The definition of "on time" can differ between supplier and customer. A manufacturer may consider an item on time if it ships the item within a week of the delivery commitment date. A company like Toyota, however, which operates just-in-time production processes with essentially no inventory of materials or purchased parts, measures an order to be on time only if it arrives within an hour of the scheduled delivery time. Toyota is not interested in whether the vendor shipped the item on time; it wants the item to arrive at its factory site on time. Only by specifying exactly how an objective, such as on-time delivery, is measured can a company eliminate ambiguity between suppliers and customers about the definition of "on-time." The selected measure also provides a clear focus to employees on how their improvement efforts will be evaluated. Thus, measurement is a powerful tool for communicating clearly and without ambiguity about what the company means in its word statements of strategic objectives, mission, and vision.

Once the objectives have been translated into measures, managers select targets for each measure. A target establishes the level of performance or rate of improvement required for a measure. Targets should be set to represent excellent performance, much like the par scores on a golf course. The targets, if achieved, should position the company as one of the best performers in its industry. Even more important would be to choose targets that create distinctive value for customers and shareholders. Lowcost has chosen 30 minutes at the gate and 90% on-time departures as its targets for its "fast ground turnaround" process measures. These values represent best-in-industry performance.

By comparing current performance to the target performance, employees and managers can determine whether the company is achieving its desired level of performance. Thus, performance measures serve multiple purposes: communication, clarification, motivation, feedback, and evaluation. Since performance measures play such important roles, they should be chosen carefully. The Balanced Scorecard framework enables managers to select objectives and measures, derived from their strategy, that are linked together in a chain of cause-and-effect relationships.

THE STRATEGY MAP AND BALANCED SCORECARD

The development of strategic objectives and measures across the four Balanced Scorecard perspectives should follow a logical progression. First, identify the long-run financial objectives, the ultimate destination for the strategy. Then, in the customer perspective, select the targeted customers for the new strategy and the objectives for the value proposition offered to attract, retain, and grow the business with the customers. In the process perspective, select objectives that create and deliver the customer value proposition and also improve productivity and efficiency, key drivers of several financial measures. Finally, identify the employee skills, information needs, and company culture and alignment that would drive improvement in the critical processes. Companies represent these linkages with a picture called a strategy map, which illustrates the causal relationships among the objectives in the four Balanced Scorecard perspectives. Companies generally start their Balanced Scorecard projects by building a strategy map that contains the word statements of their strategic objectives in the four perspectives and the linkages among them.

A general template for constructing strategy maps is shown in Exhibit 9-2. At first, this diagram may seem intimidating, but we will work sequentially through the four Balanced Scorecard perspectives starting with financial at the top and concluding with the learning and growth objectives that are the foundation for any strategy. After describing how to choose objectives for the four perspectives, we provide a specific example of how Metro Bank, the company featured in the chapter-opening vignette, built its strategy map and Balanced Scorecard.

Financial Perspective

The Balanced Scorecard's financial perspective contains objectives and measures that represent the ultimate success measures for profit-maximizing companies. Financial performance measures, such as operating income and return on investment, indicate whether the company's strategy and its implementation are delivering increases in shareholder value. The company's financial performance improves through two basic approaches: *revenue growth* and *productivity* (see Exhibit 9-3).

One source of revenue growth is to deepen relationships with existing customers, such as selling them additional products and services beyond the first product or service they purchase. For example, banks can attempt to get their checking account customers to also use the bank for credit cards, mortgages, and car loans. Companies also generate revenue growth by introducing new products, selling to new customers, and expanding operations into new markets. For example, amazon.com now sells CDs and electronic equipment, not just books, Mobil encourages its customers to buy from the station's convenience store in addition to purchasing

Exhibit 9-2
The Complete Balanced Scorecard Strategy Map

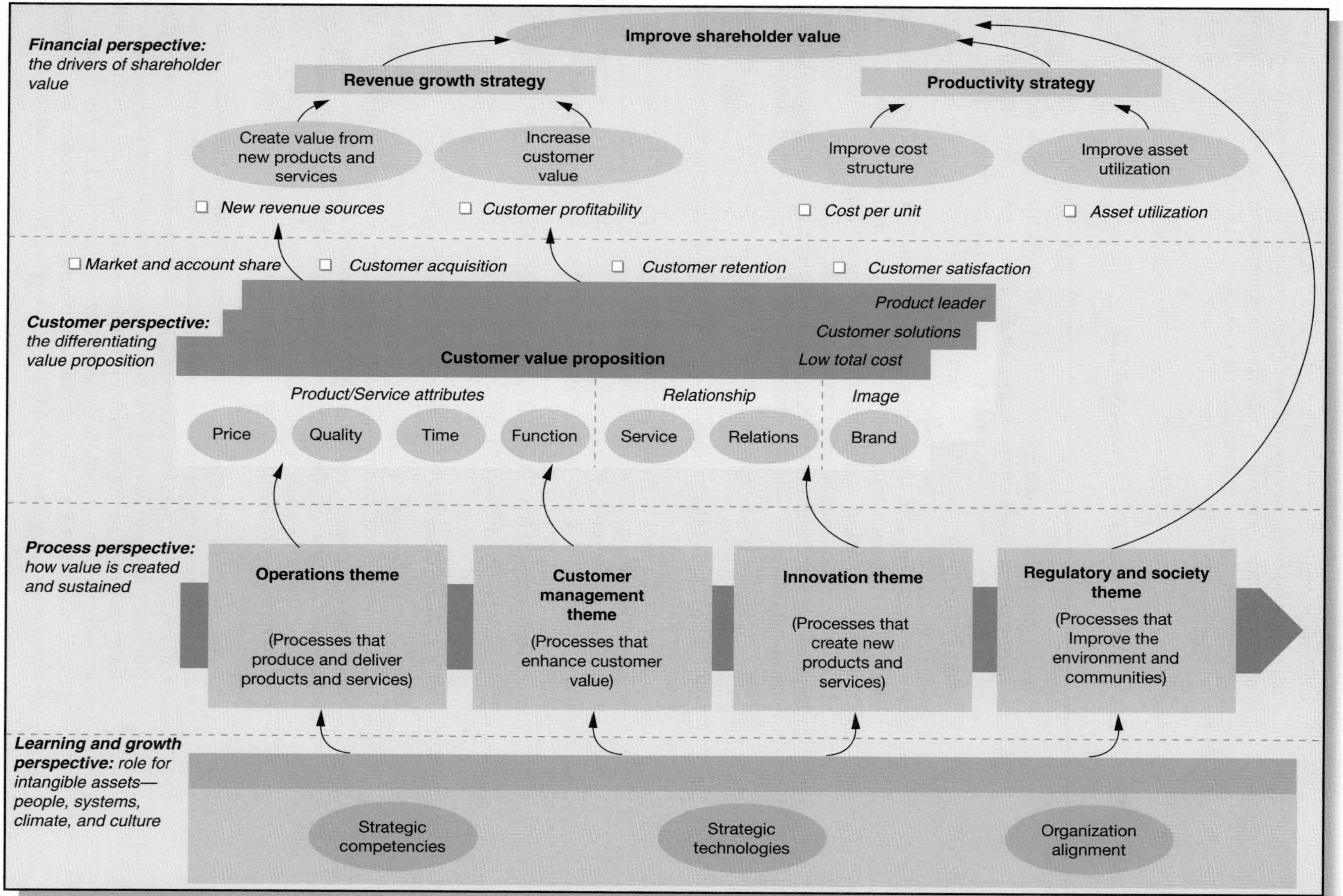

Financial perspective:
the drivers of shareholder value

Improve shareholder value

Revenue growth strategy

Productivity strategy

Create value from new products and services

Increase customer value

Improve cost structure

Improve asset utilization

☐ New revenue sources
☐ Customer profitability
☐ Cost per unit
☐ Asset utilization

☐ Market and account share
☐ Customer acquisition
☐ Customer retention
☐ Customer satisfaction

Customer perspective:
the differentiating value proposition

Customer value proposition

Product/Service attributes | Relationship | Image

Price | Quality | Time | Function | Service | Relations | Brand

Low total cost
Customer solutions
Product leader

Process perspective:
how value is created and sustained

Operations theme
(Processes that produce and deliver products and services)

Customer management theme
(Processes that enhance customer value)

Innovation theme
(Processes that create new products and services)

Regulatory and society theme
(Processes that Improve the environment and communities)

Learning and growth perspective: role for intangible assets— people, systems, climate, and culture

Strategic competencies

Strategic technologies

Organization alignment

Exhibit 9-3
Financial Perspective Objectives

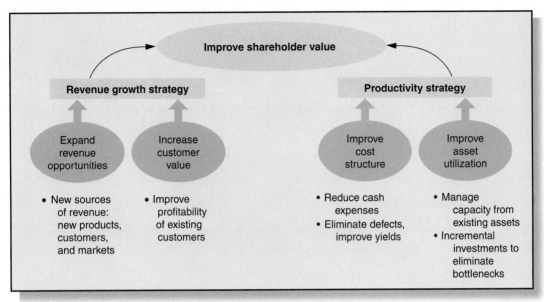

gasoline, Staples sells to small businesses as well as retail customers, and Wal-Mart expands from its domestic U.S. base into international markets.

The second component for enhancing financial performance, productivity improvements, also occurs in two ways. First, companies reduce costs by lowering direct and indirect expenses. Such cost reductions enable a company to produce the same quantity of outputs while spending less on people, materials, energy, and supplies. Second, by utilizing their financial and physical assets more efficiently, companies reduce the working and fixed capital needed to support a given level of business. For example, companies can reduce the inventory levels required to support a given level of sales by implementing just-in-time production processes. They can support a higher level of sales with the same investment in plant and equipment by reducing unexpected shutdowns and unscheduled downtime on equipment.

In summary, four financial subobjectives typically drive a company's overall financial performance: increase revenues and margins with existing customers; expand sales with new customers, products, and markets; reduce the unit costs of producing products and services; and enhance asset utilization.

Customer Perspective

The customer perspective should describe how company intends to differentiate itself from competitors to attract, retain, and deepen relationships with targeted customers. The customer perspective should reflect the heart of the strategy; it should contain specific objectives and measures for the strategy's customer value proposition—the combination of product attributes, service, and customer relationship it will offer to meet targeted customers' needs better than competitors. Success in the customer perspective should lead to improvement in the financial perspective objectives for growth in revenues and profits.

Exhibit 9-4
Common
Customer
Outcome
Objectives

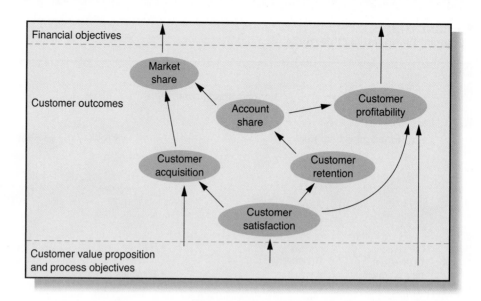

The customer perspective of the Balanced Scorecard typically starts by including several common measures of the successful outcomes from a well-formulated and implemented strategy. These can be drawn from the following list (see Exhibit 9-4):[7]

- Customer satisfaction
- Customer retention
- Customer acquisition
- Customer profitability
- Market share
- Account share

The causal chains in Exhibit 9-4 suggest a relationship among these common measures. That is, customer satisfaction leads to customer loyalty (retention) and, through word of mouth, the acquisition of new customers. As customer loyalty expands, the company increases the share of the customer's business (account share) it captures. With increases both in new customers and in the business done with existing customers, the company's market share should increase. Next, retention of customers should lead to increases in customer profitability since retaining a customer typically costs much less than acquiring new or replacement customers. Companies will not use all six of these common measures; typically, it would identify between two or three of them as most important to track.

Since virtually all organizations try to improve the common customer measures, these measures by themselves do not describe a strategy. The measures become associated with a strategy only when managers apply them to the customer segments

---

[7] *Market share* refers to the percentage of a company's sales to total industry sales. *Account share* measures the company's proportion of a given customer or group of customer's purchases in a given category. For example, a retail clothing store measures that it supplies, on average, 13% of the clothing purchased by its customers. A fast-food outlet might supply 40% of a family's fast food purchases or 2% of its total food consumption.

in which they choose to compete. A strategy typically identifies specific customer segments that the company has identified as its target audience for growth and profitability. For example, Wal-Mart appeals to price-sensitive customers who value the retailer's low prices. Neiman-Marcus, on the other hand, targets customers with high disposable incomes who are willing to pay more for high-end merchandise. Price-sensitive customers with low disposable income are not likely to be satisfied with the shopping experience at a Neiman-Marcus store, while wealthy individuals will be disappointed with the fashion, fabric, and style of clothing offered at Wal-Mart as well as the amenities and salesperson attention they receive at this discounted retail outlet. Therefore, Wal-Mart should measure customer satisfaction, loyalty, and market share only with its price-sensitive customers, while Neiman-Marcus would apply these same measures only to segments that feature customers with high disposable incomes.

Beyond identifying the segments for measuring these generic customer outcomes, a company must also identify the objectives and measures for the value proposition it offers its customers. The value proposition is the unique mix of product, price, service, relationship, and image that a company offers its targeted group of customers. The value proposition, the core of a company's strategy, should communicate what it will deliver to its customers better or differently from its competitors.

For example, companies as diverse as Southwest Airlines, Dell Computers, Wal-Mart, McDonald's, and Toyota have been extremely successful by offering their customers the "best buy" or *lowest total cost* in their category. The measurable objectives for a low-total-cost value proposition should emphasize attractive prices—relative to competitors, excellent and consistent quality for the product attributes offered, good selection, short lead times, and ease of purchase.

Another value proposition, followed by companies such as Sony, Mercedes, and Intel, emphasizes *product innovation and leadership*. These companies command prices far above the average in their industry because of the superior performance of their products. The objectives for this value proposition emphasize the particular features and functionalities of the products that leading-edge customers value and are willing to pay more to receive. The objectives could be measured by speed, accuracy, size, power consumption, or other performance characteristics that exceed the performance of competing products and that are valued by important customer segments. Being the first to market with new features and functionality is another objective for such product leadership companies.

A third type of value proposition stresses the provision of *complete customer solutions*. Good examples of companies successfully delivering this value proposition are Goldman Sachs and IBM. For this value proposition, customers should feel that the company understands them and is capable of providing them with customized products and services that meet their unique preferences and needs. IBM offers its targeted customers complete solutions that are tailored to each organization's needs for consulting, hardware, software, installation, field service, training, and education. Companies offering such a customer-solutions value proposition stress objectives relating to the completeness of the solution (selling multiple, bundled products and services), exceptional service both before and after the sale, and the quality of the relationship between the company and its customers.

Exhibit 9-5 displays the value proposition objectives for these three different customer value propositions. By developing objectives and measures that are specific to its value proposition, a company translates its strategy into tangible measures that all employees can understand and work toward improving.

Exhibit 9-5
Examples of Different Customer Value Propositions

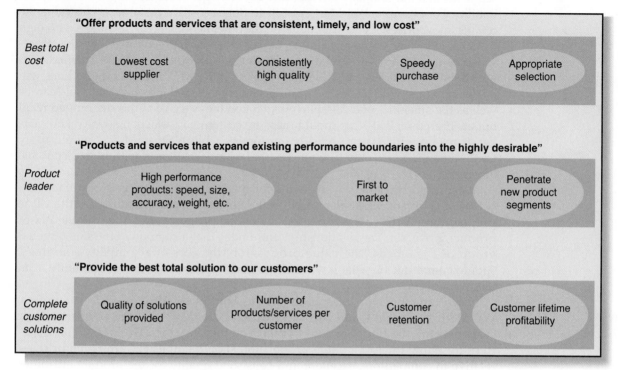

Process Perspective

The financial and customer objectives and measures reflect the outcomes—satisfied shareholders and loyal customers—from a successful strategy. Once the company has a clear picture of *what* it intends to deliver to its shareholders and customers, it can determine the *how* of its strategy, which are the key processes that accomplish the following:

- Produce and deliver the value proposition for customers
- Achieve the productivity improvements for the financial objectives

The process perspective identifies the critical operating, customer management, innovation, and regulatory and social processes in which the organization must excel to achieve its customer, revenue growth, and profitability objectives (see Exhibit 9-6).

Operating processes are the basic, day-to-day processes that produce products and services and deliver them to customers. Operating processes include the following:

- Acquiring raw materials from suppliers
- Producing finished goods and services
- Distributing finished goods to customers

Managers can choose performance objectives and measures from each of these three operating processes. Effective supplier processes enable the company to receive competitively priced, defect-free products and services that are delivered on-time.

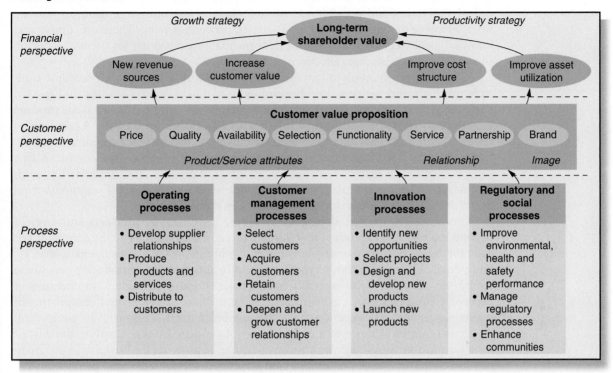

Exhibit 9-6
Strategic Processes

Financial perspective

Growth strategy — **Long-term shareholder value** — *Productivity strategy*

- New revenue sources
- Increase customer value
- Improve cost structure
- Improve asset utilization

Customer perspective

Customer value proposition

Price · Quality · Availability · Selection · Functionality · Service · Partnership · Brand

Product/Service attributes — *Relationship* — *Image*

Process perspective

Operating processes	Customer management processes	Innovation processes	Regulatory and social processes
• Develop supplier relationships • Produce products and services • Distribute to customers	• Select customers • Acquire customers • Retain customers • Deepen and grow customer relationships	• Identify new opportunities • Select projects • Design and develop new products • Launch new products	• Improve environmental, health and safety performance • Manage regulatory processes • Enhance communities

Production processes convert inputs, such as purchased materials, into outputs that the company sells to customers. For a service company, the production processes deliver the services used by customers. Excellence in production processes generally involves improving their cost, quality, and process times. Finally, the company's strategy might require excellence in the processes for distributing finished products and services to customers. The appendix to this chapter provides examples of typical objectives and measures used by companies to describe their supplier relationships, production processes, and distribution processes.

Customer management processes expand and deepen relationships with targeted customers. We can identify four sets of customer management processes:

- Select customers
- Acquire customers
- Retain customers
- Grow business with customers

Customer selection involves identifying the target populations for which the company's value proposition is most desirable. The outcome from a good customer selection process is a set of customer characteristics—such as income, wealth, age, family size, or lifestyle for consumer companies or price-sensitive, early adopting, or technically sophisticated for business customers—that defines an attractive customer segment for the company.

Customer acquisition relates to generating leads, communicating to potential customers, choosing entry-level products, pricing the products, and closing the sale.

Customer retention requires excellent service and response to customer requests. Companies operate customer service and call center units to respond to requests about orders, deliveries, and problems. Customers may defect from organizations that are not responsive to requests for information and problem solving. Therefore, timely and knowledgeable service units are critical for maintaining customer loyalty and reducing the likelihood of customer defections.

Customer growth involves managing the relationship effectively, crossselling multiple products and services, and becoming known as a trusted adviser and trusted supplier to the customer. For example, a company can differentiate its basic product or service by providing additional features and services after the sale. A commodity chemical company was able to differentiate its basic product by providing a service that picked up used chemicals from customers and reprocessed the chemicals in a central location for disposal or reuse in an efficient process that conformed to environmental and safety regulations. This service relieved many small customers from performing expensive environmental processes themselves.

Customer growth can also occur by selling the customer products and services beyond the entry-level product that initially brought the customer to the company. For example, banks now try to market insurance, credit cards, money management services, and personal loans of various types—especially automobile, educational, and home equity—to customers who currently have a basic checking account. Manufacturers of expensive equipment such as medical imaging devices, elevators, and computers sell maintenance, field service, and repairs that minimize the downtime of the equipment. As a customer buys more of a complete set of services from a supplier, the cost of switching to alternative suppliers becomes higher, so growing the business in this manner also contributes to customer retention and higher lifetime customer profitability.

The appendix to this chapter presents typical objectives and measures for these four customer management processes.

Innovation processes develop new products, processes, and services, often enabling the company to penetrate new markets and customer segments. Successful innovation drives customer acquisition, loyalty, and growth, in turn leading to enhanced operating margins. Without innovation, a company's value proposition can eventually be imitated, leading to competition solely on price for its undifferentiated products and services.

Managing innovation includes four important subprocesses:

- Identify opportunities for new products and services
- Manage the research and development portfolio
- Design and develop the new products and services
- Bring the new products and services to market

Product designers and managers *generate new ideas* by extending capabilities of existing products and services, applying new discoveries and technologies, and learning from the suggestions of customers. Once ideas for new products and services have been generated, managers must decide which projects to fund.

Managers must select a *research-and development portfolio of projects*, which could include projects done entirely with internal resources, those done collaboratively in a joint venture, those licensed from another organization, or those outsourced entirely. The output from the evaluation process is an aggregate project plan that defines the portfolio of projects the organization is investing in, the specific objectives to be achieved by the collection of projects, the resources required, and the mix between internal and external sources.

The *design and development process*, the core of product development, brings new concepts to market. A successful design and development process culminates with a product that has the desired functionality, is attractive to the targeted market, and can be produced with consistent quality and at a cost that enables satisfactory profit margins to be earned. In addition to these demanding specifications for the output it delivers, the design and development process has to meet its own targets for completion time and development cost.

At the conclusion of the product development cycle, the project team *brings the new product to market*. In this final phase, the company starts commercial production at low volume levels to ensure that its production processes and those of suppliers can consistently produce and deliver the product. Also, the marketing and sales staffs begin to sell the new product to customers. As customer orders increase and the supply and production processes stabilize, the production process is ramped up further. Ultimately, the development project concludes when the company achieves targeted levels of sales and production at specified levels of product functionality, quality, and cost.

Some typical objectives and measures for the four innovation processes are presented in the appendix.

Regulatory and social processes make up the final process group. Companies must continually earn the right to operate in the communities and countries in which they produce and sell. National and local regulations—on the environment, employee health and safety, and hiring and employment practices—impose standards on companies' practices. At a minimum, to avoid shutdowns or expensive litigation, companies must comply with all regulations related to business practices. Many companies, however, seek to go beyond complying with the minimal standards established by regulations. They wish to perform better than the regulatory constraints so that they develop a reputation as an employer of choice in every community in which they operate.

Companies manage and report their regulatory and social performance along several critical dimensions:

- Environment
- Health and safety
- Employment practices
- Community investment

Investing in the environment and in communities need not be for altruistic reasons alone. First, an excellent reputation for performance along regulatory and social dimensions assists companies in attracting and retaining high-quality employees, thereby making human resource processes more effective and efficient. Second, reducing environmental incidents and improving employee safety and health improves productivity and lowers operating costs. Third, companies with outstanding reputations generally enhance their image with customers and with socially conscious investors. These linkages to enhance human resource, operations, customer, and financial processes illustrate how effective management of regulatory and community performance can drive long-term shareholder value creation.

Some of the data for regulatory measures already exist to comply with national reporting requirements. Companies should decide which, among the myriad of measures that describe their environmental, health, safety, employment, and community performance, are most critical for their strategy. Some typical examples of strategic objectives and measures for regulatory and social processes are presented in the appendix.

In developing their Balanced Scorecard, managers identify which objectives and measures, in the four process groups, are the most important for their strategies. See, for example, the choices made by Metro Bank, as described later in this chapter. Companies following a product leadership strategy would stress excellence in their innovation processes. Companies following a low-total-cost strategy must excel at operating processes. Companies following a customer-solutions strategy will emphasize their customer management processes.

Even with an emphasis on one of the four process groups, companies must still follow a balanced strategy and invest in improving processes in all four groups. Typically, the financial benefits from improving strategic processes occur within different time frames. Cost savings from improvements in *operational processes* deliver quick benefits (within 6 to 12 months) to productivity objectives in the financial perspective. Revenue growth from enhancing *customer relationships* accrues in the intermediate term (12 to 24 months). *Innovation processes* generally take longer to produce customer and revenue and margin improvements (24 to 48 months). The benefits from *regulatory and social processes* also typically take longer to capture as companies avoid litigation and shutdowns and enhance their image as employers and suppliers of choice in all communities in which they operate. Achieving overall process excellence generally requires that companies have objectives and measures for improving processes in all four process groups so that the benefits, from each set of processes, phase in over time.

Exhibit 9-7
Learning and Growth Perspective Provides the Foundation for the Strategy

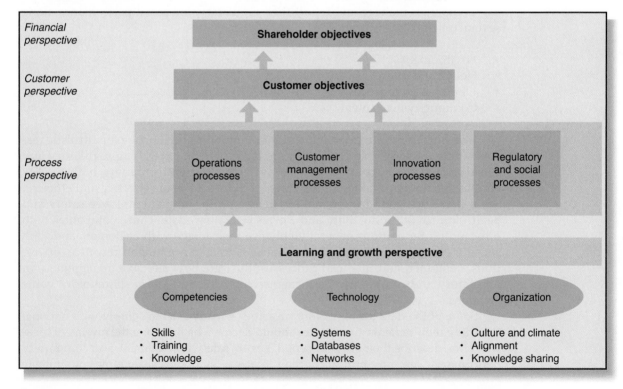

Learning and Growth Perspective

The fourth perspective of the Balanced Scorecard, learning and growth, identifies the objectives for the people, systems, and organizational alignment that create long-term growth and improvement. The process objectives identify the key processes that the organization must excel at for its strategy to be successful. The learning and growth objectives emphasize the employee capabilities and skills, technology, and organizational alignment that will drive improvement in these critical processes (see Exhibit 9-7). The learning and growth objectives direct management's attention to the required investments to improve the skills of their employees, the information technology and systems, and the organizational alignment to the company's strategic objectives. It is in the learning and growth scorecard perspective that executives mobilize their intangible assets—human resources, information technology, and organizational culture and alignment—to drive improvement in the processes most important for implementing their strategy. The following describes typical objectives for the three components in the learning and growth perspective:

Human Resources
- *Strategic competency availability.* The company's employees have the appropriate mix of skills, talent, and know-how to perform activities required by the strategy.

Information Technology
- *Strategic information availability.* The company's information systems and knowledge applications are adequate to support the strategy.

Organization Culture and Alignment
- *Culture and climate.* Employees have an awareness and understanding of the shared vision, strategy, and cultural values needed to execute the strategy.
- *Goal alignment.* Employee goals and incentives are aligned with the strategy at all organization levels.
- *Knowledge sharing.* Employees and teams share best practices and other knowledge relevant to strategy execution across departmental and organizational boundaries.

In general, for companies to develop their learning and growth objectives and measures, managers examine the process objectives in the third Balanced Scorecard perspective and determine the following:

- Employee capabilities, knowledge, and skills
- Information systems and databases
- Employee culture, alignment, and knowledge sharing

These are required to perform the strategic processes in an outstanding manner. Specific examples of learning and growth measures can be found in the Metro Bank example shown in the next section.

STRATEGY MAP AND BALANCED SCORECARD AT METRO BANK

The Metro Bank executive team met several times over a 4-week period and eventually agreed on the strategy map shown in Exhibit 9-8. Over the course of several more weeks, the team described the objectives in more detail and selected measures for the Balanced Scorecard that would accompany the strategy map. We describe the process next.

Exhibit 9-8
Metro Bank's Strategy Map

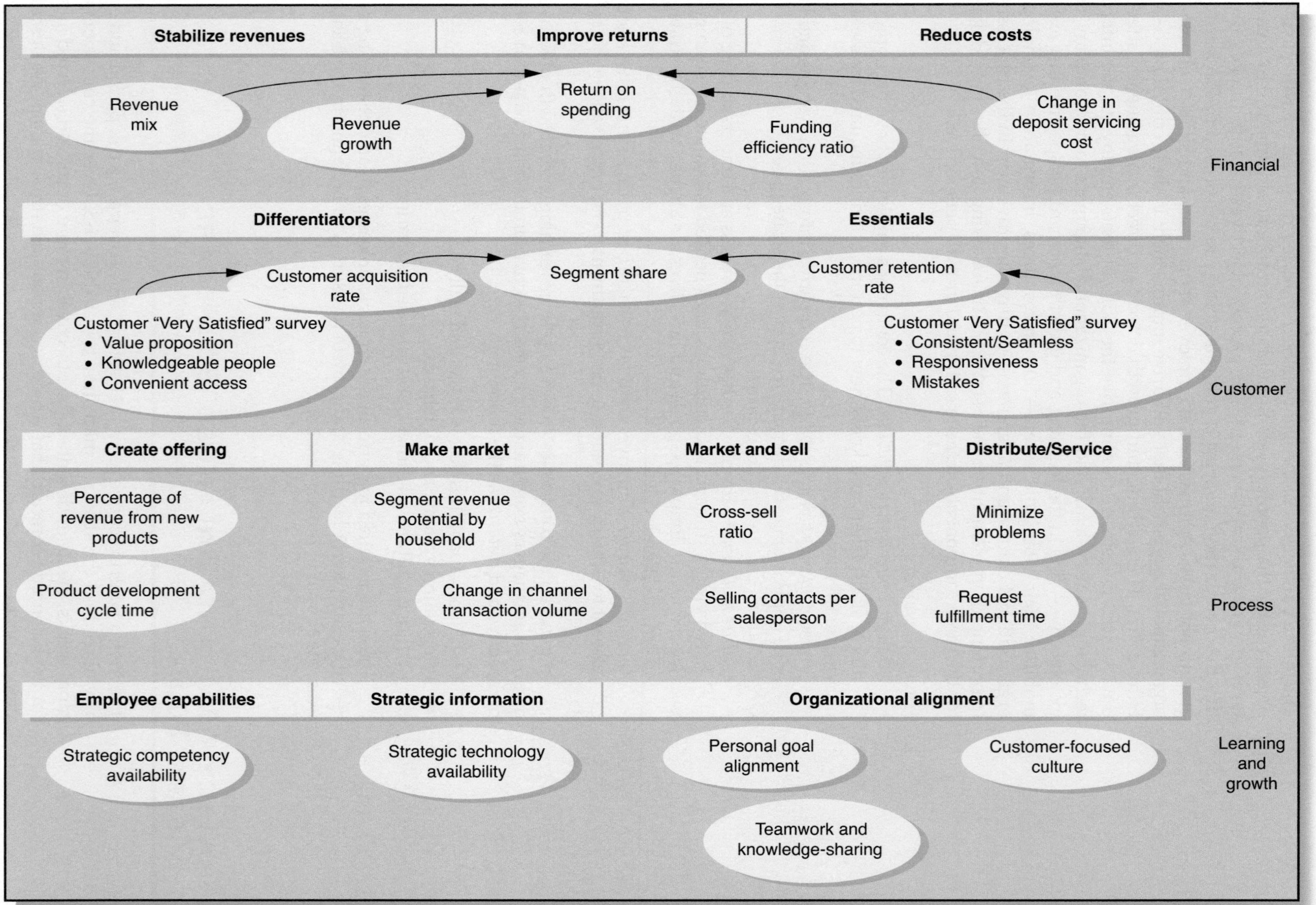

Financial

Stabilize revenues | Improve returns | Reduce costs

Revenue mix — Revenue growth — Return on spending — Funding efficiency ratio — Change in deposit servicing cost

Customer

Differentiators | Essentials

Customer acquisition rate
Customer "Very Satisfied" survey
- Value proposition
- Knowledgeable people
- Convenient access

Segment share — Customer retention rate
Customer "Very Satisfied" survey
- Consistent/Seamless
- Responsiveness
- Mistakes

Process

Create offering | Make market | Market and sell | Distribute/Service

Percentage of revenue from new products
Product development cycle time

Segment revenue potential by household
Change in channel transaction volume

Cross-sell ratio
Selling contacts per salesperson

Minimize problems
Request fulfillment time

Learning and growth

Employee capabilities | Strategic information | Organizational alignment

Strategic competency availability

Strategic technology availability

Customer-focused culture
Personal goal alignment
Teamwork and knowledge-sharing

Financial Perspective

Metro Bank's senior executives decided, as its overarching financial objective, to aim for improving its return on spending—net income divided by operating expenses. They described this objective as follows:

Improve return on spending. Return on spending (ROS) reflects our ability to create wealth with the company's funds. ROS will align our expense outlays with the revenue generated. By aligning our spending with high value and high return on activities, we will increase the return we achieve on dollars spent.

The executive team then crafted three supporting financial objectives, as described here:

Revenue mix. We will move away from a dependence on net interest income by broadening and selling our portfolio of fee-based products to cover a greater portion of our expense base. Changing our mix toward more fee-based business will cushion Metro from the risks of the interest rate cycle.

Revenue growth. We will grow our revenue streams by redefining our core businesses and increasing the number of valuable customers. We will retain and acquire valuable customers and broaden high-margin relationships with them through crossselling of existing products and the sale of new products and services.

Reduce costs. By becoming more streamlined and efficient, we will focus resources and help to achieve higher profitability. We will eliminate expenses that do not lead to revenue generation, improve productivity, and streamline and redesign key business processes.

Once the executive team had decided on Metro's financial objectives, it selected measures for each of these objectives as shown in the following table:

FINANCIAL OBJECTIVE	FINANCIAL MEASURE
Return on spending	• Net income/expense dollars
Revenue mix	• Percentage of revenues from fee-based services
Revenue growth	• Percentage increase in year-to-year revenues
Reduce costs	• Percentage reduction in cost of servicing checking and savings accounts

Customer Perspective

The bank's executive team realized that they were following a customer-solutions strategy that featured building long-term relationships with targeted customers to whom the bank could sell multiple financial products and services, including financial planning and advice. Metro's project team chose a high-level customer objective to increase market share with customers in three targeted segments, defined by income, wealth, and proclivity for using banking products and services. Metro Bank expected to *acquire* new customers in these segments by offering an attractive value proposition, which it described as follows:

We will differentiate ourselves through employees capable of recognizing customer needs and possessing the knowledge to proactively satisfy them. A greater knowledge of Metro's product and service offerings will help our customers better fulfill their banking needs. This knowledge, along with crossselling, consultative skills, and a supporting operating structure, will satisfy a greater proportion of our customers' financial needs.

Metro selected a second customer objective: to retain existing customers by offering consistent excellent service, giving customers access to banking services or information 24 hours a day, and performing consistently and seamlessly in the eyes of the customer.

Now that it had defined its targeted customers and the value proposition to offer them, the executive team selected the measures shown here:

CUSTOMER OBJECTIVE	CUSTOMER MEASURE
Share of segment	Metro Bank's percentage of customers in targeted segments
Acquire new customers	Number of new Metro Bank customers in targeted segments
Value proposition for new customers	Survey of new customer satisfaction, including feedback on • Metro's value proposition, • employee knowledge and capabilities, and • convenient access
Retain existing customers	Customer retention rate in targeted segments
Provide consistent/seamless service	Survey of existing customers on • quality; • availability; • responsiveness; and • errors and defects

Process Perspective

Now that the executive team had defined its financial and customer measures, it could select objectives and measures for the process perspective. The bank's executive team developed the following objectives and measures:

Operating Processes

Distribute and service. Achieve service excellence with our people and systems, providing customers with the best reliability, availability, and responsiveness and no defects or errors. Service excellence is the key to maintaining existing relationships and a prerequisite to attracting valuable new customers.

Customer Management Processes

Make the market. Identify the needs of customer segments who represent high current profitability and future economic potential. Understand the risk of each and how Metro Bank can sustain differentiation with these target customers.

Market and sell. Crosssell our products and services through organized, knowledgeable, consultative, and proactive employees. We must listen to our customers, educate them about our products, and communicate to them how our products can meet their financial needs. To perform these activities, our salespeople must have a high level of systematic and regular contact with our customers and employ professional sales management practices.

Innovation Processes

Create offering. Create profitable, innovative financial service products that are among the first to market, easy to use, and convenient to our targeted customers.

The team selected the measures in the following table for each process objective:

Process Objectives	Process Measures
Distribute and service	• Number of customer complaints
	• Response time to customers' requests
Make the market	• Revenue potential per household in targeted segments
	• Profitability by segment
Market and sell	• Cross-sell ratio; or the percentage of customers who use more than one product or service
	• Selling contacts per salesperson
	• New revenue per salesperson
Create the offering	• Product development cycle time
	• Percentage of revenue from new products and services

Learning and Growth Perspective

The executive team now addressed the most difficult task: selecting the learning and growth objectives and measures that would support the achievement of the process, customer, and financial objectives already defined. After extensive deliberation and coaching, particularly from the bank's human resources and information technology experts, the executive team identified the following learning and growth objectives as critical for the success of its new strategy:

Employee capabilities. Build our marketing, sales, and customer service competencies to accomplish our aggressive revenue generation targets. First, our people need the competency to crosssell our products and services. They need an ability to recognize customer needs, the initiative to proactively solicit business, and superior consultative selling skills. Second, our people need a broader knowledge of our product portfolio and financial markets to support their cross-selling activities.

Strategic information. The ability to extract, process, and use information holds the key to competitive advantage for our new strategy. We must harvest and disseminate information on our processes, products, and customers. We must improve the utility, access, ease of use and timeliness of information.

Alignment and culture. Performance management systems are key to communication and to motivating and rewarding employees for behavior that supports the Balanced Scorecard business objectives. We will align incentive plans to Balanced Scorecard objectives to encourage behavior toward our business vision. We will focus our resources to align our capital, expense, and personnel decisions with strategic priorities. Allocating resources where the return is highest and has the greatest alignment with strategic priorities will enable us to operate more predictably and profitably.

To illustrate how to move from these somewhat general word statements of learning and growth objectives to actual measures, consider one of the process objectives for the bank's new strategy—market and sell—which includes the crossselling of the bank's multiple products and services to customers. The human resources executive at Metro Bank, responsible for developing the human capital required to support the strategy, identified three employee capabilities as fundamental to this process: solution selling and relationship management skills, product-line knowledge, and professional certification as a financial planner. The measure for this objective was the gap between the desired state—having 100% of employees who performed the market and sell process with the requisite skills—and the current state—the percentage of employees who currently had the skills to perform this process at the desired performance level.

Assume that 100 financial planners are required to execute this aspect of the strategy. Through a set of programs for hiring, training, and development, a group of 40 individuals had reached a level of proficiency to execute the cross-selling objective. Metro Bank used rigorous testing to determine that these individuals had reached that level of proficiency. Since 100 individuals are required to execute the strategy but only 40 have reached the requisite level of proficiency, the measure of strategic competency availability for this piece of the strategy is only 40%.

The bank's information technology (IT) department was responsible for selecting specific objectives for the availability of strategic technologies, networks, data, and knowledge to support the strategy. The IT managers identified three technology priorities for the market and sell process: a financial planning model, an integrated customer file, and Web-enabled access by customers. IT managers could measure the gap between the desired state of technology deployment and the current state—the strategic technology availability—and develop action plans to close the gap, much like the human resources measurement of strategic competency availability.

Metro Bank's executive team also established three objectives for organizational alignment for the employees who would perform the market and sell:

1. A culture based on partnerships with customers.
2. Alignment of employees' personal objectives to cross-selling objectives.
3. Improved teamwork to promote best practice sharing on cross-selling approaches. Performance measures were developed on the basis of surveys and interviews to assess the scores on these three organizational alignment objectives.

These three objectives would be measured through a semiannual survey of employees.

Metro Bank now had a complete Balanced Scorecard of objectives and measures that described its new strategy and that could be used to communicate the strategy to all employees as the basis for resource allocation in new information technology, training of employees, setting of departmental and personal goals, and periodic reviews of organization and individual employee performance.

IN PRACTICE
Media General Implements a Convergence Strategy

Media General, a southeastern U.S. media company with 7,500 employees, had revenues in 2004 of $900 million. The company had a history of somewhat haphazard growth until 1990, when it embarked on a massive transformation, shedding old businesses and acquiring others to refocus on its historic roots in the Southeast.

The company embarked on a new convergence strategy that would create synergy by exploiting the strengths of its three divisions: newspapers, TV, and interactive media. The goal was to coordinate different media in a given market to provide quality information in the way that each does best. The concentration of the three related properties would also enable Media General to offer advertisers a high-quality audience to which they could direct integrated multimedia advertising packages.

The chief executive officer used the Balanced Scorecard to help implement his convergence strategy since the strategy required strong teamwork, communication, and cooperation across previously independent and competitive business lines. The learning and growth perspective in the corporate strategy map included an objective to train sales personnel to sell new multimedia packages to advertisers. Another learning and growth objective was to "promote a culture of change and employee empowerment" to help employees understand the benefits of working as a single regional Media General team rather than thinking, within a silo, as employees of a newspaper, a TV station, or a Web page.

A process objective was to "develop and deliver superior content," signaling how the newsrooms from all three divisions should work together to jointly develop stories and increase local awareness of Media General's brand. A customer objective was to deliver integrated multimedia content for local advertisers to get their message out to the public and generate more consumer traffic to their places of business.

One financial objective was to increase revenue through the purchase of the new multimedia/multimarket packages by existing advertisers as well as revenues from new advertisers acquired through convergence offerings.

Once Media General had developed the enterprise strategy map and Balanced Scorecard, each of the properties in the three divisions developed its

individual scorecard. These scorecards reflected the balance between the convergence priorities on the corporate scorecard and each division's local business situation.

Multimedia advertising packages contributed to a 42.5% revenue gain in the interactive media division. The publishing division was second in the nation in its peer group of newspapers in total revenue growth, and the interactive media division increased revenues by 60%. Broadcast revenues increased more than 38% in 2004. Media General's stock price from the time of the initial rollout of the BSC in 2001 to mid-2004 increased by 82%, far outperforming both its industry and general stock market indices.

Source: Company presentations and documents.

KEY PERFORMANCE INDICATOR SCORECARDS

Some organizations, unlike Metro Bank, do not start their performance measurement process by clearly describing their strategy and building their strategy map. Instead, they identify *key performance indicators* (KPIs), classify them into the four basic scorecard perspectives, and declare that they now have a Balanced Scorecard. KPIs typically are common measures, such as customer satisfaction, quality, cost, and employee satisfaction and morale, that are certainly worth striving to achieve but don't reflect a company's unique strategy. KPI scorecards also arise when an organization expands its compensation system to reward executives for a broader set of performance than simply short-term financial results. For example, the organization might include measures of environmental performance, safety, and employee diversity in the calculation of an executive's compensation so that the executive will pay attention and attempt to improve performance along those added dimensions. Such expanded coverage is probably desirable but not as powerful as selecting measures for compensation that can be linked back to the strategy and that will drive successful strategy implementation.

For example, consider one financial service organization that articulated the four Ps for its Balanced Scorecard:

1. Profits
2. Portfolio (size of loan volume)
3. Process (percentage of processes meeting ISO (International Organization for Standardization standards)
4. People (meeting diversity goals in hiring)

Although this scorecard is more balanced than its previous one, which used only financial measures, comparing the four-P measures to a strategy map like that in Exhibit 9-2 or Exhibit 9-8 reveals the major gaps in the measurement set. The four-P scorecard has no customer measures and only a single measure each in the process perspective and learning and growth perspectives. This KPI scorecard has no role for information technology (strange for a financial service organization), no linkages from the process measure (ISO process certification) to a customer value proposition or to a customer outcome, no linkage from the learning and growth measure (diverse workforce) to improving a process (such as achieving ISO certification), and no linkage to a customer or financial outcome.

KPI scorecards are most helpful for departments and teams in which a strategic program already exists at a higher level. In this way, the diverse indicators enable individuals and teams to define what they must do well to contribute to higher-level goals. However, unless the link to strategy is clearly established, KPI scorecards will lead to local but not global or strategic improvements.

Balanced scorecards should not be just collections of financial and nonfinancial measures organized into four (or five) perspectives. The best Balanced Scorecards reflect the strategy of the organization. A good test is whether one can understand the strategy by looking only at the strategy map and scorecard. Many organizations, especially those that create key performance indicator scorecards, fail this test.

IN PRACTICE
Mellon Europe

Jack Klink, newly appointed in 2001 as chief executive officer of Mellon Europe, a specialist in asset servicing and asset management, faced the challenge of aligning the company's multiple business lines across Europe. Executives were focused on their individual businesses and had little sense of corporate-level priorities. Klink realized that the Balanced Scorecard could help Mellon Europe articulate and execute its strategy, which came to be known as "One Mellon" in which Mellon's 14 business lines and 10 shared service units throughout Europe would be aligned to a common strategy. The company adopted the concept, which included a customer objective for "shared services to provide superior knowledge, value, and service to their customers at a reasonable cost" and for the business units to "consistently deliver on the 'Mellon Promise.'" A process perspective emphasized "leveraging synergies to make One Mellon greater than the sum of its parts, through an integrated, stable, scalable model." Among the synergies were for each business to cross sell products of other Mellon Europe business lines to its clients.

During 2002 and 2003, a core BSC team—consisting of the firm's chief administrative officer, an external consultant, and an internal consulting team—helped to cascade the corporate-level scorecard to business lines and shared services units, such as human resources and information technology.

The company established a Strategic Performance Forum that met quarterly to discuss one theme from the Mellon Europe strategy map and scorecard. Two members of the company's executive team led a discussion on the selected theme, raising two or three critical strategy-related concerns. Actions steps were assigned, and accountability was established. These quarterly meetings sharpened the focus of business leaders on strategic objectives. More cross-unit collaboration and problem solving followed, along with a heightened commitment to strategy execution. Klink described the impact of the Balanced Scorecard at Mellon Europe:

> The BSC has introduced a structure to our strategy execution such that there is now increased ownership and accountability of initiatives across the business. We are also less emotional about agreeing on strategic priorities because we can see the organizational cause-effect model more clearly. This is incredibly motivating for senior managers who, in turn are motivating their staff by ensuring that the link between personal goals and strategic objectives is clear.

Mellon Europe's annual revenues grew 21% from 2002 to 2003 and nearly 30% in 2004, exceeding its target contribution to parent company's total revenues. Despite this growth, shared services costs have not increased since the introduction of the Balanced Scorecard.

Source: "Mellon Europe, a Balanced Scorecard Hall of Fame Profile" (Balanced Scorecard Hall of Fame Report: 2005, Harvard Business School Publishing, 2005).

APPLYING THE BALANCED SCORECARD TO NONPROFITS AND GOVERNMENT ORGANIZATIONS

Nonprofit and government organizations (NPGOs) can also develop performance measurements within the Balanced Scorecard framework. Prior to the development of the Balanced Scorecard, the performance reports of NPGOs focused only on financial measures, such as funds appropriated, donations, expenditures, and operating expense ratios. NPGOs, however, cannot be measured primarily by their financial performance. Certainly, they must monitor their spending and operate within financial constraints, but their success has to be measured by their effectiveness in providing benefits to constituents, not by their ability to raise money, be efficient, or balance their budgets. The use of nonfinancial measures enables NPGOs to assess their performance with constituents.

Many NPGOs, however, encountered difficulties in developing their initial Balanced Scorecard. First, they learned that they didn't have a clear strategy. Some had "strategy" documents that ran upward of 50 pages. Some had a "strategy" that consisted of a lengthy list of planned programs and initiatives but never mentioned the outcomes the programs and initiatives they were intended to achieve. To apply the Balanced Scorecard, an NPGO's thinking has to shift from what it plans *to do* to what it intends *to accomplish*, a shift from activities to outcomes. Otherwise, any new scorecard will be just a list of key performance indicators of operational performance, not a system to communicate and implement its strategy.

The Nature Conservancy (TNC) is an example of an NPGO that had some excellent performance indicators, but these were not initially linked to its strategy. TNC's mission is to preserve biodiversity, the variety of life, and the natural processes of plants and animals. Its strategy to achieve the mission was to protect the habitats that plants and animals, particularly rare species, needed to survive. For years, TNC operated with two basic performance measures: dollars raised and acres of land acquired to keep in a natural, pristine condition. The dollars and acres performance measures set the agenda for all employees, the board, and donors, and the organization was apparently successful according to these two measures. During the 1990s, revenues grew at an 18% annual compounded rate, and the number of acres protected more than doubled during this period. Yet TNC's management team reluctantly concluded that its recent success in raising money and protecting acres had not necessarily contributed to its fundamental mission of conserving biodiversity. A gap existed between its mission and the measures that employees and constituents had worked so hard to improve. The management team eventually led a process that created a set of measures better balanced across outcomes and performance drivers and linked to its organizational mission.[8] The new measures led TNC to trade some of its large acreage for much smaller land plots felt to be more valuable for preserving important species.

Since financial success is not their primary objective, NPGOs cannot use the standard architecture of the Balanced Scorecard strategy map where financial objectives are the ultimate, high-level outcomes to be achieved. NPGOs generally place an objective related to their *social impact* and *mission*—such as reducing poverty, school dropout rates, or the incidence or consequences from particular diseases

---

[8] J. Sawhill and D. Williamson, "Mission Impossible: Measuring Success in Nonprofit Organizations," *Nonprofit Management & Leadership*, 11, 3, spring 2001, 371–86.

A novel Balanced Scorecard application was at the heart of New Profit, Inc. (NPI), a venture capital philanthropic fund. Vanessa Kirsch, founder of NPI, wanted to create a performance framework for the nonprofit sector. Kirsch and her general partners actively managed a portfolio of social enterprises that met the fund's investment strategy, including the following:

- *Scalable organizations.* The basic model of this could be expanded to increase their social impact and lead to self-sufficiency.
- *Performance-based design.* Fund dispersal would depend on organizations achieving mutually agreed-on benchmarks based on measurable performance criteria.

NPI helped each portfolio organization in which it invested develop its own Balanced Scorecard to define and evaluate performance. One NPI executive said; "The scorecard aligns all our stakeholders for creating social innovation and social returns."

NPI also created a Balanced Scorecard for itself. The financial perspective had objectives about raising adequate capital and operating funds and using them in an efficient and sustainable manner. For the customer perspective, the team identified the investors in the fund as the primary customers and featured investor satisfaction as an important outcome measure.

The NPI team decided that portfolio organizations warranted their own perspective, labeled *social impact,* that would capture the benefits to society from the funded organizations. The success of the portfolio organizations was central for investor satisfaction.

Beyond its role in managing its own internal operations and its relationships with portfolio organizations, Kirsch used the Balanced Scorecard as the primary communication tool with NPI's board of directors and donors. One board member commented; "The BSC allows the board to be updated about what is happening across the organization, factoring in a breadth of issues ranging from those of the balance sheet to the softer aspects involving people and their knowledge."

For potential investors, Kirsch used the Balanced Scorecard of NPI and its portfolio organizations to illustrate a highly attractive product-leadership value proposition. An early investor enthusiastically endorsed the concept and made a significant financial commitment and a promise to give more on the basis of performance: "Do well and you will get more."

Source: R. Kaplan and J. Elias, "New Profit, Inc.," Harvard Business School Case #100-052.

or eliminating discrimination—at the top of their scorecard and strategy map. A nonprofit or public sector agency's mission represents the accountability between it and society as well as the rationale for its existence and ongoing support. The measured improvement in an NPGO's social impact objective may take years to become noticeable, which is why the measures in the other perspectives provide the short- to intermediate-term targets and feedback necessary for year-to-year control and accountability.

NPGOs also modify the private-sector scorecard framework by expanding the definition of who is the customer. Donors or taxpayers provide the financial resources—they pay for the service—while another group, the citizens and beneficiaries, receive the service. Who is the customer, the one paying for the service or the one receiving the service? Many NPGOs treat both as their customers. They place a funder (taxpayer/donor) perspective and a recipient perspective at the top of their Balanced Scorecards (see Exhibit 9-9). With these changes, NPGOs—as wideranging in focus as a local opera company, the Royal Canadian Mounted Police, and the U.S. Army—have developed Balanced Scorecards that described their strategy and used them to communicate mission and strategy more clearly to employees and constituents.

Exhibit 9-9
The Balanced Scorecard Model for Public Sector and Nonprofit Organizations

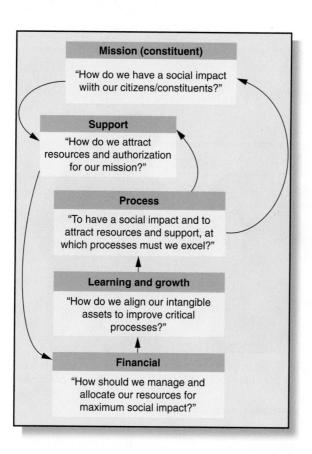

Mission (constituent)
"How do we have a social impact with our citizens/constituents?"

Support
"How do we attract resources and authorization for our mission?"

Process
"To have a social impact and to attract resources and support, at which processes must we excel?"

Learning and growth
"How do we align our intangible assets to improve critical processes?"

Financial
"How should we manage and allocate our resources for maximum social impact?"

IN PRACTICE

Royal Canadian Mounted Police

The Royal Canadian Mounted Police has 23,000 employees and a $3 billion annual budget. The RCMP operates at four levels—international; national; provincial (eight provinces and three territories); and local (192 municipalities, 175 communities, and 556 aboriginal communities). At the turn of the century, the RCMP faced several challenges. It was overspending its budget, creating significant concern in the Canadian Treasury Board, yet its resources were still not adequate for the policing environment of the twenty-first century. A new RCMP commissioner, G. Zaccardelli, felt passionately about improving management; he had a vision that the RCMP could become the world's best policing force. Even with his strong centralized leadership and vision, however, Zaccardelli faced the challenge of getting all RCMP units, scattered across an enormous land mass, to fall in with corporate-level priorities.

A senior-level project team launched a process to build a Balanced Scorecard that would translate the RCMP mission ("safe homes and safe communities")

into something operational that could be understood by the highly motivated but also very tactical police officers throughout Canada. The heart of the strategy for delivering on the mission was contained within a set of five overarching corporate-level strategic themes that formed part of the BSC's process perspective and went beyond day-to-day policing activities:

- Reduce the threat and impact of organized crime.
- Reduce the threat of terrorist activity in Canada and abroad.
- Reduce and prevent youth involvement in crime, both as offenders and as victims.
- Support international operations and initiatives.
- Produce safer and healthier aboriginal communities.

The five themes required national-level strategic coordination. Accordingly, the RCMP developed a separate strategy map for each, with its own initiatives, targets, and measures. Each theme was assigned

An RCMP employee, far from the Ottowa headquarters, is pleased to learn from the RCMP strategy map how his local actions can contribute to enterprise strategic objectives.

Source: Company documents, used with approval.

a senior RCMP executive owner, who organized periodic meetings of local and national managers to review progress against the theme's targets. Once the strategy maps and scorecards for the corporate-level strategy and for the five strategic themes were completed, the cascading process to local units could commence. Each local divisional unit selected up to ten RCMP objectives for their strategies that customized the high-level themes to the specific realities of their operations. In addition, the local strategy maps incorporated the division's normal policing responsibilities.

The process promoted cooperation and integration among previously independent local, provincial, and national policing units, allowing them to share lessons learned and best practices. Three years after launching the Balanced Scorecard initiative, the RCMP was enjoying large increases in citizen support and satisfaction for its performance.

Source: R. S. Kaplan and D. P. Norton, "How to Implement Your Strategy Without Disrupting Your Organization," *Harvard Business Review*, March 2006, 100–109.

MANAGING WITH THE BALANCED SCORECARD

The strategy map describes and the Balanced Scorecard measures the enterprise's strategy. This, however, is just the start of the journey to performance improvement. Management must take several additional steps to translate the strategy into action. Perhaps most important, executives must communicate the strategy to all employees since, ultimately, employees are the ones who must implement the strategy. People cannot help implement a strategy that they are not aware of or do not understand.

Communication takes various forms; one rule of thumb is that to gain understanding, you must communicate to people seven times seven different ways.

Companies use senior executive talks, brochures, newsletters, videotapes, company intranets, supervisor one-on-ones, and orientation and training programs to explain the balanced scorecard to each employee.

Once all employees understand the strategy of their operating units, divisions, and corporation, managers ask them to develop personal objectives in light of the broader priorities. Their personal objectives should be chosen so that, if achieved, the objectives will contribute to one or more components of higher-level balanced scorecards. Companies have been surprised with the outcomes from this process. Individuals find new ways to do their jobs and identify areas outside their normal responsibilities in which they can contribute. Most organizations link *incentive compensation* to the balanced scorecard, typically after managing with the scorecard for a year. The executives must be confident that they are using sensible measures, have valid and reliable data collection processes to support the measures, and have measures not easily manipulated. Once they become confident about their measures and data, they turn the powerful compensation lever on. One executive remarked;

> People got that scorecard out and did the calculations to see how much money they were going to get. We could not have got the same focus on the scorecard if we didn't have the link to pay.

Information and reporting systems change. In the past, only the executive team would see the overall performance of the organization. Many organizations now go further by making performance on the various indicators on the Balanced Scorecard available to everyone through Web-based software. This enables all employees to see how the strategy is working and where problems are occurring and provides a mechanism for them to make suggestions for how to improve performance.

THE TECHNOLOGICAL EDGE
Business Intelligence Software

Most companies collect a large amount of data from their business operations. To keep track of that information, a business would need to use a wide range of software, such as Excel, Access, and different database applications for various departments throughout their organization. Using multiple software programs makes it difficult to retrieve information in a timely manner and to perform analysis of the data.

The term *business intelligence* (BI) represents the tools and systems that play a key role in the strategic planning process of the corporation. These systems allow a company to gather, store, access, and analyze corporate data to aid in decision making. Generally these systems provide business intelligence in the areas of customer profiling, customer support, market research, market segmentation, Balanced Scorecards, product profitability, statistical analysis, and inventory and distribution analysis, to name a few.

More than 20 companies, including SAP, Oracle, SAS, Cognos, and Hyperion, now offer certified Balanced Scorecard solutions within their BI applications (see http://www.bscol.com/bsc_online/technology/certified/). Microsoft joined this group in 2005 when it delivered its new server-based Business Scorecard Manager. The new application leverages the power of the Microsoft Office System to help organizations build, manage, and use scorecards and key performance indicators and perform deep analysis—within a collaborative environment. Business Scorecard Manager gives companies a broad view of business opportunities through which employees can better understand business challenges, effectively shape solutions, and quickly execute on their objectives. Decisionmaking happens across all levels of an organization, and empowering employees with powerful BI solutions can help them have greater impact.

Source: Adapted from (http://msdn.microsoft.com/isv/technology/bss/default.aspx; February. 16, 2006).

To keep the enterprise focused on strategy implementation, executives make the Balanced Scorecard the basis of the agenda for their monthly meetings. In this way, a broad spectrum of managers, from various functions and different business units, can discuss on a regular basis the recent performance on the strategic measures and develop ideas about how to improve performance. They can propose new initiatives, review employee suggestions, and reallocate resources to deal with new issues that have emerged.

The executive team should also institute a formal process for learning and adapting the strategy. The Balanced Scorecard and strategy map make explicit the cause-and-effect linkages in the hypotheses underlying the strategy. As reporting systems begin providing feedback on actual results, management can test these hypotheses. Most companies test the hypotheses qualitatively, reviewing causal linkages at meetings where managers discuss and refine the programs being used to drive service quality and customer retention. A few do the testing formally, using statistical correlations between measures on the scorecard to determine the sign and magnitude of the effects from, for example, employee empowerment programs to improved processes and increased customer satisfaction.

Managers also schedule meetings to search for new strategic opportunities that aren't currently on their scorecards. Ideas and learning emerge continually from within the organization. Rather than waiting for next year's budget cycle, the priorities and the scorecards are updated immediately. Instead of being an annual event, strategy formulation, testing, and revision become a continual process.

In summary, to capture the benefits from their new performance measurement system, companies must also institute processes to communicate, report, review, and adapt their strategies throughout the year. Companies that align these various management processes and systems to their strategies enjoy the greatest success from their performance measurement systems.

PITFALLS OF THE BALANCED SCORECARD

Not all companies, however, have been successful in building Balanced Scorecards. Several factors can lead to problems when building a performance measurement and management system around the Balanced Scorecard. Some companies use too few measures—only one or two measures per perspective—in their scorecards. A scorecard with too few measures doesn't depict enough of the company's strategy and doesn't represent a balance between desired outcomes and the performance drivers of those outcomes. Or, conversely, some companies include too many measures, incorporating more than 100 measures, so that managers' attention is so diffused that they pay insufficient attention to those few measures that can make the greatest impact.

Some companies do not link the correct drivers in the process and learning and growth perspectives to the desired outcomes in the financial and customer perspectives. For example, a company's strategy may call for creating innovative solutions for its customers, but the measures in its Balanced Scorecard process perspective focus exclusively on operational improvements.

A poor scorecard design, however, is not the biggest threat to successful Balanced Scorecard implementation. When too few or too many measures are present or they are not the right measures, these design defects can be recognized and fixed. The biggest threat is a poor organizational process for developing and implementing the scorecard. For example, some companies use their Balanced Scorecard only as a checklist for operational improvements or to expand the compensation system to include nonfinancial measures. For these companies, the commitment to organizational learning diminishes as well, and design flaws can go undetected.

Building and embedding a new measurement and management system into an organization is complicated and susceptible to at least four pitfalls.

1. *Senior management is not committed.* By far, the largest source of failures occurs when the Balanced Scorecard project is led by or gets delegated to a middle-management project team. Often the impetus for a new performance measurement system arises from the quality group or the finance function. Individuals in these groups see the limitations from attempting to manage with only financial measures and want the organization to adopt a performance measurement system that is more closely tied to operations, not just financial results. They manage to get approval from senior management to explore a new measurement system, but senior management treats this as a local, operational project and has not understood the need for the measurement system they use to change. Ultimately, the lack of understanding and commitment among the senior management team to using the new performance measurement system to communicate and drive the strategy will undermine the success of any such project, led my middle managers.

The senior management team must be actively involved in the Balanced Scorecard project for several reasons. First, few middle managers understand the strategy for the entire organization. They depend on senior management to articulate the organization's strategy. If senior management is not actively engaged in the project, new measurements will focus on local operational improvements and not be a comprehensive system that senior executives can use to manage the successful implementation of their strategy.

Second, in most companies, only the senior management team is empowered to make the decisions necessary for an effective strategy. Lacking comprehensive knowledge and authorization to make decisions about the organization's overall strategy, a middle-management team would likely not produce a Balanced Scorecard that represents the strategy of the organization.

Third, the emotional commitment of senior management is as important as their knowledge and authority. When senior managers have invested hours deciding on the targeted customer segments, selecting the value proposition that they will deliver better than competitors, and identifying the cause-and-effect relationships that link the measures across the four Balanced Scorecard perspectives, they also build an emotional commitment to the strategy, to the scorecard that articulates the strategy, and to the ongoing management processes to implement and improve the strategy. Without that emotional commitment from senior management, the project soon languishes, and the benefits from the new measurement and management system are never realized.

2. *Scorecard responsibilities don't filter down.* In some companies, senior executives feel that only they need to know and understand the strategy. They fail to share the strategy and scorecard with middle managers and with lower-level employees on the front lines and in back offices. A successful Balanced Scorecard implementation, while requiring commitment from the senior management team, must involve more than them. The executive team must communicate the Balanced Scorecard to everyone in the organization so that all employees learn about the strategy and how they can contribute to its successful implementation.

3. *The solution is overdesigned, or the scorecard is treated as a one-time event.* Some failures have occurred when the project team allowed "the best to be the enemy

of the good." These teams wanted to have the perfect scorecard. They did not want to launch the scorecard until they were sure they had exactly the right measures as well as valid data for every measure on the scorecard. The teams believed they would have only one opportunity to launch the scorecard, and they wanted it to be the best it could possibly be. So they spent months refining the measures, improving data collection processes, and establishing baselines for the scorecard measures. Eighteen months after the start of the Balanced Scorecard project, management had yet to use it in any meetings or to support their decision processes. When interviewed, several executives at these companies responded, "I think we tried the Balanced Scorecard last year, but it didn't last." The problem was not that it didn't last. It had never begun!

All Balanced Scorecards start with some new measures for which no data currently exist. Sometimes, up to one-third of the measures are not available in the first few months, especially for measures relating to employee skills, information technology availability, and customer loyalty. Managers should initiate new data collection processes for the missing measures and still use the scorecard for their review and resource allocation processes, even without specific data on the new measures.

As the data become available, managers will have an even better basis for their discussions and decisions. However, the management system should be dynamic, and the objectives, the measures, and the data collection processes can be modified over time on the basis of organizational learning.

4. *The Balanced Scorecard is treated as a systems or consulting project.* Some of the most expensive Balanced Scorecard failures have occurred when companies implemented a Balanced Scorecard as a systems project rather than as a management project. The companies apparently believed they could acquire their new measurement systems from a software provider or from outside consultants. These failures usually occurred when an outside consulting organization, particularly one that specialized in installing large information systems, convinced someone in the company to hire them to install a Balanced Scorecard management system. The consultants spent the next 12 to 18 months and several million dollars automating all existing data collection systems to provide a generalized executive information system on managers' desktops. The executive information system enabled managers to access any existing piece of data or to sort through the extensive database many different ways. Yet hardly anybody used the new system. Automating and facilitating access to the thousands (or millions) of data observations collected in a company does not lead to a Balanced Scorecard.

Automation of existing data would never identify the critical measurements of an organization's strategy not currently being measured at all (recall the missing measurement problem in the preceding pitfall). Also, giving managers more convenient access to an organization's database is much different than having a structured strategy map, with cause-and-effect linkages, for the relatively few (20 to 30) measures that represent the strategic variables that most affect the organization's performance to achieve its strategy.

Most important, consider the first pitfall. By delegating the scorecard to an outside consulting and systems integration firm, the process of engaging the senior management team in a strategic dialogue has been completely bypassed. The scorecard must start with a management process, not with a process to acquire a new system.

None of these pitfalls is insuperable. In fact, companies and government agencies around the world have introduced this new performance management system and enjoyed considerable success. Some of the best examples are described at the Web site of the Balanced Scorecard Hall of Fame (http://www.bscol.com/hof). The Hall of Fame enterprises had strong leadership from the top that saw the benefits from developing a measurement system based on the strategy. The leaders used the scorecard to communicate strategic objectives and measures to all employees and subsequently aligned employees' personal goals and incentives to improvements in scorecard measures. The executives used scorecard results as the agenda for periodic management meetings so that senior management continually discussed how to improve the implementation of their strategy. For these organizations, the Balanced Scorecard was no longer just a performance measurement system; it had become the basis for how they led and managed the company, and it helped them deliver dramatic improvements in performance for shareholders and customers.

EPILOGUE TO METRO BANK

Mike Hancock, chief executive officer of Metro Bank, reflected on how he would use his new strategy map, description of strategic objectives, and Balanced Scorecard measures to communicate the new strategy to Metro's 8,000 employees. He knew that he would soon have to align all employees' objectives to the bank's strategic measures.

The biggest transformation would have to occur in the learning and growth perspective—to reskill thousands of branch employees and supply them with ready access to customer information. In the past, the bank had emphasized efficient processing of customer transactions for demand and time deposit accounts. Now employees had to become skilled and credible in marketing and selling a broad array of financial products and services. Metro Bank executives recognized that a multiyear program would be required for its frontline employees to obtain these capabilities that would transform them from routine processors of customer requests into proactive, trusted, and valued financial counselors. Ted Franklin, chief planning officer, reflected on this:

> In the past, we found it hard to get and maintain focus on our infrastructure, things like information systems and employee training and skills. We talked about their importance, but when quarterly earnings targets applied financial pressure, these were the first spending programs to get sacrificed. Now, with our measures of strategic information availability and strategic job coverage on the Balanced Scorecard, people can see the linkages between improving these capabilities and achieving our long-term financial goals. The Balanced Scorecard keeps senior management focused on these infrastructure investments, and these investments can be sustained even in a highly constrained environment for corporate spending.

Hancock was greatly concerned by the following incident that he had recently witnessed:

> A well-dressed, confident, apparently high-income customer walked into a Metro branch bank. She told the bank employee that she had just changed to a more responsible, higher-paying job with a new employer. She wanted to know how she could have payroll checks from her new employer deposited directly into her checking account. The employee took out a form that she filled out with the customer. The customer left with the form that she could give to her company's human resources department that authorized the direct deposit of her payroll check. The customer left with her request satisfied within 15 minutes.

Hancock realized that the employee likely thought that this was a "good" transaction. The employee had been responsive to the customer's request. Hancock saw this event, however, as a strategic disaster! The bank had just lost out on a major opportunity. The employee, by responding to the customer's immediate request, had now made it possible for this targeted, high-income customer never to come back to the bank again. The request for direct deposit of a payroll check was clearly tied to a major inflection point in this customer's income and, perhaps, lifestyle. Hancock wished that the bank employee had used the opportunity to get a more complete personal financial profile of the customer, including the following information:

- Own or rent a house or apartment?
- Automobiles: how many, how old?
- Credit and charge cards: how many, which?
- Annual income
- Household assets and liabilities
- Insurance
- Children: how many, how old?

Such a profile could have provided the information for the bank employee to suggest a much wider array of financial products and services—for example, credit card, consolidating personal loan, home equity loan, investments, mutual funds, insurance policies, home mortgage, car loans, savings plans for college, and student loan programs—in addition to the particular financial transaction that brought the customer into the bank: the direct deposit of a payroll check.

Before the financial profile could have been used effectively, however, it was necessary for the bank employee to have been trained in all the potential product and service offerings and to have acquired the skills to match particular products and services to the needs of the individual customer. Hancock could now understand the major human resource investments that the bank would have to make to upgrade the skills of all branch employees to the new strategy (as well as the investments in new information technology) so that every contact between a bank employee and a customer could be an opportunity to expand the bank's relationship with the customer. In addition, the culture of the bank had to change from efficient transactions processing to providing solutions and high-end services to the bank's most important customers. The Balanced Scorecard had clearly set the path for future investments in the bank's intangible assets.

SUMMARY

Information-age companies succeed by investing in and managing their intangible assets. As organizations invest in acquiring the new capabilities provided by these assets, their success cannot be motivated or measured by the traditional financial accounting model. This financial model, developed for trading companies and industrial-age corporations, measures events of the past, not the investments in the capabilities that provide value for the future.

One of the popular performance measurement systems, the Balanced Scorecard, integrates measures derived from strategy. While retaining financial measures of past performance, the Balanced Scorecard introduces the drivers of future financial performance. The drivers—found in the customer, process, and learning and growth perspectives—are selected from an explicit and rigorous translation of the organization's strategy into tangible objectives and measures. The benefits from the scorecard are realized as the organization integrates its new measurement system into management processes that communicate the strategy to employees, align employees' individual objectives and incentives to successful strategy implementation, and integrate the strategy with ongoing management processes: planning, budgeting, reporting, and management meetings. A new performance measurement and management system has its greatest impact when the executive team leads these transformational processes.

Appendix 9-1

Examples of Balanced Scorecard Objectives and Measures

In this appendix, we list some typical objectives and measures for the process objectives of a Balanced Scorecard.

1. Supplier relationship objectives and measures

SUPPLIER OBJECTIVES	MEASURES
Lower cost of acquiring materials	• Activity-based cost of acquiring materials (includes cost of ordering, receiving, inspecting, storing, and moving materials) • Cost of purchasing as percentage of total purchase price
Achieve just-in-time supplier capability	• Lead time from order to receipt • On-time delivery percentage • Percentage of late orders • Percentage of orders delivered directly to production process by suppliers
Develop high-quality supplier capability	• Part-per-million defect rates from suppliers • Percentage of defects, incoming orders • Percentage of suppliers qualified to deliver without incoming inspection • Percentage of perfect orders received

Achieve excellent supplier relationships	• Supplier scorecard, with ratings on
	   ○ Cost
	   ○ Quality
	   ○ Delivery
	   ○ Flexibility
	• Percentage of strategic partnerships established with suppliers

2. Production process objectives and measures

PRODUCTION PROCESS OBJECTIVES	MEASURES
Lower cost of producing products and services	• Activity-based cost of key operating processes • Cost per unit of output (for organizations producing homogeneous outputs) • Marketing, selling, distribution, and administrative expenses as a percentage of total costs
Continuously improve processes	• Number of processes with substantial improvements • Part-per-million defect rates • Yield percentage • Scrap and waste percentage • Cost of inspection and testing • Total cost of quality (cost of prevention, appraisal, internal failure, external failure)
Improve process responsiveness	• Cycle time (from start of production until product completed) • Process time (the time product is actually being processed)[9] • Process efficiency: ratio of process time to cycle time
Improve fixed asset utilization	• Percentage of capacity utilization • Equipment reliability; percentage of time available for production • Number and percentage of breakdowns • Flexibility; range of products/ services that processes can produce and deliver

---

[9] *Cycle time* is the total time required from the start of production to completion of outputs. *Process time* represents the time actually required for processing, excluding waiting, movement, and setup times. For example, the cycle time for mortgage approval could be 28 days but with only 40 minutes of actual processing time during the 28-day time period.

3. Distribution objectives and measures

DISTRIBUTION OBJECTIVES	MEASURES
Deliver products and services responsively to customers	• Lead times from order to delivery
	• Time from completion of product/service until ready for use by customer
	• On-time delivery percentage
Lower cost of serving customers	• Activity-based cost of storage and delivery to customers
	• Percentage of customers reached via low-cost-to-serve channels, such as switching customers from manual and telephone transactions to electronic transactions
Enhance quality	• Percentage of items delivered with no defects
	• Number and frequency of customer complaints

4. Customer selection objectives and measures

CUSTOMER SELECTION OBJECTIVES	MEASURES
Understand customer segments	• Profit contribution by segment
Screen unprofitable customers	• Percentage of unprofitable customers
Target high-value customers	• Number of relationships with targeted customers
Manage the brand	• Customer survey on brand awareness and preference

5. Customer acquisition objectives and measures

CUSTOMER ACQUISITION OBJECTIVES	MEASURES
Communicate value proposition	• Brand awareness
Acquire new customers	• Percentage of leads converted
	• Cost per new customer acquired
	• Lifetime value (estimated) of new customers acquired
Conduct marketing campaign to attract new customers	• Customer response rate to campaigns

6. Customer services objectives and measures

CUSTOMER SERVICE OBJECTIVES	MEASURES
Respond to customer feedback and complaints	• Time for customer to resolve concern or complaint
	• Percentage of customer queries not satisfied by initial respondent
	• Quality ratings from targeted customers
Provide service excellence	• Service levels, by channel

7. Customer growth objectives and measures

CUSTOMER GROWTH OBJECTIVES	MEASURES
Cross sell customer	• Number of products per customer
Enhance postsales value to customer	• Revenue/margin from postsales services
	• Number of value-added services available to customers

8. Innovation process objectives and measures

INNOVATION PROCESS OBJECTIVES	MEASURES
Anticipate future customer needs	• Time spent with key customers learning about future opportunities and needs
	• Number of new projects launched based on client input
Actively manage the product portfolio for superior innovation	• Technology ranking: independent, peer review of current technology capabilities
	• Net present value of products in project pipeline
Manage the project portfolio	• Number of patents; number of patent citations
	• Project yield: percentage of projects advancing through product development pipeline
	• Number of projects entering each phase of product development process
Reduce development cycle time	• Number of projects delivered on time
	• Total time elapsed: from initial concept to time product produced for market
Manage development cycle cost	• Actual versus budgeted spending on projects at each development stage
Effective production of new products	• Revenue and margins from new products
	• Manufacturing cost of new products: actual versus targeted
	• Number of defects or returns from customers
	• Consumer satisfaction or complaints about new products launched

9. Regulatory and social process objectives and measures

REGULATORY AND SOCIAL PROCESS OBJECTIVES	MEASURES
Improve environmental performance	• Number of environmental incidents, such as an unexpected discharge of air, water, or solid waste • Water emissions • Air emissions • Solid waste production and disposal • Energy and resource consumption
Improve health and safety performance	• Number of OSHA-recordable cases per 100 employees • Lost workdays per 100 employees or per 200,000 hours worked
Improve employment practices	• Percentage of women and minorities by job position
Enhance communities	• Dollars invested in local communities • Number of employee days volunteered in communities • Number of partnerships with community nonprofit organizations

KEY TERMS

Balanced Scorecard, 395
Customer management processes, 407
Customer perspective, 396
Financial perspective, 396
Innovation processes, 408

Learning and growth perspective, 396
Measures, 400
Mission statements, 398
Objectives, 395
Operating processes, 406
Process perspective, 396

Regulatory and social processes, 409
Strategy, 399
Strategy map, 401
Targets, 400
Value proposition, 401
Vision statements, 398

ASSIGNMENT MATERIALS

Questions

9-1 What is a Balanced Scorecard? (LO 1)

9-2 What are the four measurement perspectives in the Balanced Scorecard? (LO 1)

9-3 Explain why the growing importance of intangible assets complements growing interest in the Balanced Scorecard. (LO 1)

9-4 What is a strategy map? (LO 2)

9-5 Define and explain the role of measures, objectives, and targets, in the Balanced Scorecard strategy map. (LO 2, 3, 4)

9-6 Compare and contrast the definitions of an organization's vision and mission. (LO 3)

9-7 What is this chapter's concept of strategy? (LO 3)

9-8 What are the two basic approaches to improving a company's financial performance? (LO 2)

9-9 Describe two broad approaches that companies can use to generate additional revenues. (LO 2)

9-10 Describe two broad approaches that companies can use to improve productivity. (LO 2)

9-11 Why does attempting to improve customer measures such as customer satisfaction, customer retention, customer profitability, and market share not necessarily constitute a strategy? (LO 2, 3)

9-12 Describe the best-buy or lowest-total-cost value proposition and provide your own example of a company that has successfully implemented this value proposition. (LO 2)

9-13 Describe the product innovation and leadership value proposition and provide your own example of a company that has successfully implemented this value proposition. (LO 2)

9-14 Describe the complete-customer-solutions value proposition and provide your own example of a company that has successfully implemented this value proposition. (LO 2)

9-15 Explain how a Balanced Scorecard approach is helpful in identifying critical processes and evaluating the processes. (LO 2)

9-16 All of a Balanced Scorecard's measures for processes should be fully controllable by people who perform the work in the processes.

Do you agree with this statement? Explain. (LO 2)

9-17 What four categories of processes are useful in developing the process perspective measures for a Balanced Scorecard? (LO 3, 4)

9-18 What are operating processes, and what three broad areas are included in the operating processes part of the Balanced Scorecard's process perspective? (LO 3, 4)

9-19 What are the four sets of customer management processes that are part of the Balanced Scorecard's process perspective? (LO 3, 4)

9-20 How are innovation processes in the process perspective linked to the Balanced Scorecard's customer and financial perspectives? (LO 3, 4)

9-21 What four important subprocesses does managing innovation include? (LO 3, 4)

9-22 What are some critical dimensions along which to measure regulatory and social processes in the operating processes part of the Balanced Scorecard's process perspective? (LO 3, 4)

9-23 Discuss the number of measures that might typically be included in each of the Balanced Scorecard's four perspectives. (LO 4)

9-24 What is the nature of the objective(s) that non-profit and government organizations are likely to put at the top of their Balanced Scorecard and strategy maps? (LO 6)

9-25 What are four common pitfalls in developing a Balanced Scorecard? (LO 8)

Exercises

LO 2, 4　9-26 *Balanced Scorecard measures, lowest-total-cost value proposition*　Identify an organization with the best-buy or lowest-total-cost value proposition and suggest at least two possible measures within each of the four Balanced Scorecard perspectives.

LO 2, 4　9-27 *Balanced Scorecard measures, innovation-and-leadership value proposition*　Identify an organization with the product-innovation-and-leadership value proposition and suggest at least two possible measures within each of the four Balanced Scorecard perspectives.

LO 2, 4　9-28 *Balanced Scorecard measures, complete-customer-solutions value proposition*　Identify an organization with the complete-customer-solutions value proposition and suggest at least two possible measures within each of the four Balanced Scorecard perspectives.

LO 2, 4　9-29 *Balanced Scorecard measures, environmental and safety dimensions*　Discuss the accuracy of the following statement: "The Balanced Scorecard approach is incomplete because it does not include measures on environmental performance and measures of employee health and safety."

LO 4　9-30 *Number of measures*　Respond to the following statement: "It is impossible for an organization to focus on 25 to 30 different measures that result if each of the four Balanced Scorecard perspectives includes as few as four to seven measures."

LO 5　9-31 *Balanced Scorecard and key performance indicators*　Respond to the following statement: "Our organization has key performance indicators that measure financial and nonfinancial performance, including customer satisfaction, product and service quality, cost, revenues, and employee satisfaction. We therefore have a Balanced Scorecard approach."

LO 6　9-32 *Balanced Scorecards for non-profit and governmental organizations*　Explain how a Balanced Scorecard for a non-profit or governmental organization typically differs from for-profit Balanced Scorecards.

LO 7　9-33 *Performance measurement or management system*　Discuss whether the Balanced Scorecard approach is a performance measurement system, a management system, or both.

LO 7　9-34 *Strategy and the budgeting process*　Explain how organizations might use the Balanced Scorecard to link strategy to the budgeting process.

Problems

9-35 *Designing a Balanced Scorecard* Consider the manager of a store in a fast-food restaurant chain. Construct a Balanced Scorecard to evaluate that manager's performance.

9-36 *Developing a Balanced Scorecard within a university* Develop a Balanced Scorecard that the dean or director of your school may use to evaluate the school's operations. Be specific and indicate the purpose of each Balanced Scorecard measure.

9-37 *Balanced Scorecard for governmental or non-profit organization* Organizations in the public and non-profit sector, such as government agencies and charitable social service entities, have financial systems that budget expenses and monitor and control actual spending. Choose a government agency or nonprofit organization and describe the various perspectives the agency or organization should include in its Balanced Scorecard. What objectives and measures should be included in each perspective, and how might they be linked?

9-38 *Pitfalls in Balanced Scorecard implementation* BC Company attempted to build a Balanced Scorecard by fitting the company's objectives and financial and nonfinancial performance measures into the four Balanced Scorecard perspectives. Explain why this approach may not lead to a well-developed Balanced Scorecard.

9-39 *Pitfalls in Balanced Scorecard implementation* ED Company's chief executive officer (CEO) wanted his company to develop a Balanced Scorecard. He gave considerable thought to who should lead the development, and he selected the head of the information technology group because the Balanced Scorecard would obviously involve collecting information leading to the needed measurements. Comment on potential problems with the CEO's approach.

9-40 *Relationship of the Balanced Scorecard to activity-based costing* Explain how an activity-based costing model can be linked to a Balanced Scorecard approach.

9-41 *Balanced Scorecard or activity-based costing* Suppose an organization has not implemented either activity-based costing or a Balanced Scorecard but believes both would be valuable for the organization. However, management is currently willing to undertake only one major change initiative. Advise management on the decision between implementing an activity-based costing model or a Balanced Scorecard.

Cases

9-42 *Compensation tied to Balanced Scorecard, degree of difficulty of target achievement* Discuss Case 8-79.

9-43 *Implementing the Balanced Scorecard* Either by visiting a Web site or from a description in a published article, find a description of the implementation of a Balanced Scorecard.

Required

a. Document in detail the elements (objectives, measures, and targets) of the Balanced Scorecard.
b. Identify the purpose of each Balanced Scorecard element.
c. Describe, if the facts are available, or infer, if the facts are not available, how the Balanced Scorecard elements relate to the organization's strategy.
d. Evaluate the Balanced Scorecard by indicating whether you agree that the choice of Balanced Scorecard performance measures is complete and consistent with the organization's plan and stakeholder set.

LO 2, 3, 4, 6   **9-44** *Designing a Balanced Scorecard for a city*   The vision and mission statements for the City of Charlotte, North Carolina, appear on pages 398 and 399. The city's senior administrative staff, after much debate, selected the following five strategic focus areas in which the city should try to excel:[10]

- Community safety (evolved from an initial focus on crime)
- Transportation
- City within a city (evolved from an initial focus on attacking poverty to a focus on strengthening the many diverse neighborhoods in the city's core districts)
- Restructuring government
- Economic development

Required

Develop a Balanced Scorecard for the City of Charlotte. Explain in detail your choice of what appears at the top of your proposed strategy map. Bear in mind that the city's Balanced Scorecard need not include every important service.

LO 2, 3, 4   **9-45** *Designing a Balanced Scorecard*   Wells Fargo's 2001 annual report (p. 16) states that the company's vision is "to satisfy all our customers' needs, offer them sound financial advice and help them succeed financially." Similarly, the 2002 annual report (p. 16) states that the vision is "to earn all our customers' business." Both annual reports list the following 10 areas of strategic initiatives that the company has been benchmarking itself against for several years:

1. Investments, Trust, Brokerage and Insurance
2. Going for "Gr-eight"! (Increase the average number of products per customer to eight)
3. Doing It Right for the Customer
4. 100 Percent Bank and Mortgage/Home Equity Cross-Sell
5. Wells Fargo Cards in Every Wallet
6. When, Where, and How
7. Information-Based Marketing
8. Be Our Customers' Payments Processor
9. Outstanding Customers
10. People as a Competitive Advantage

Required

The 2001 and 2002 annual reports provide some specific measures within the initiatives. Based on the annual reports and any other information you are able to find, develop a Balanced Scorecard for Wells Fargo that will help it achieve its vision and monitor its performance on the strategic initiatives.

LO 2, 3, 4   **9-46** *Designing a Balanced Scorecard for a pharmaceutical company*   Chadwick, Inc.: The Balanced Scorecard (Abridged)[11]

The "Balanced Scorecard"[12] article seemed to address the concerns of several division managers who felt that the company was over-emphasizing short-term financial results. But the process of getting agreement on what measures should be used proved a lot more difficult than I anticipated.

Bill Baron, Comptroller of Chadwick, Inc.

---

[10] R. S. Kaplan, "City of Charlotte (A)," Harvard Business School Case 9-199-036 (1999).

[11] Copyright © 1996 President and Fellows of Harvard College. Harvard Business School Case 9-196-124. This case was prepared by Professor Robert S. Kaplan as the basis for class discussion rather than to illustrate either effective or ineffective handling of an administrative situation. Reprinted by permission of Harvard Business School.

[12] Robert S. Kaplan and David P. Norton, "The Balanced Scorecard: Measures that Drive Performance," *Harvard Business Review*, January–February 1992, 71–79.

COMPANY BACKGROUND

Chadwick, Inc. was a diversified producer of personal consumer products and pharmaceuticals. The Norwalk Division of Chadwick developed, manufactured and sold ethical drugs for human and animal use. It was one of five or six sizable companies competing in these markets and, while it did not dominate the industry, the company was considered well-managed and was respected for the high quality of its products. Norwalk did not compete by supplying a full range of products. It specialized in several niches and attempted to leverage its product line by continually searching for new applications for existing compounds.

Norwalk sold its products through several key distributors who supplied local markets, such as retail stores, hospitals and health service organizations, and veterinary practices. Norwalk depended on its excellent relations with the distributors who served to promote Norwalk's products to end users and also received feedback from the end users about new products desired by their customers.

Chadwick knew that its long-term success depended on how much money distributors could make by promoting and selling Norwalk's products. If the profit from selling Norwalk products was high, then these products were promoted heavily by the distributors and Norwalk received extensive communication back about future customer needs. Norwalk had historically provided many highly profitable products to the marketplace, but recent inroads by generic manufacturers had been eroding distributors' sales and profit margins. Norwalk had been successful in the past because of its track record of generating a steady stream of attractive, popular products. During the second half of the 1980s, however, the approval process for new products had lengthened and fewer big winners had emerged from Norwalk's R&D laboratories.

RESEARCH AND DEVELOPMENT

The development of ethical drugs was a lengthy, costly, and unpredictable process. Development cycles now averaged about 12 years. The process started by screening a large number of compounds for potential benefits and use. For every drug that finally emerged as approved for use, up to 30,000 compounds had to be tested at the beginning of a new product development cycle. The development and testing processes had many stages. The development cycle started with the discovery of compounds that possessed the desirable properties and ended many years later with extensive and tedious testing and documentation to demonstrate that the new drug could meet government regulations for promised benefits, reliability in production, and absence of deleterious side effects.

Approved and patented drugs could generate enormous revenues for Norwalk and its distributors. Norwalk's profitability during the 1980s was sustained by one key drug that had been discovered in the late 1960s. No blockbuster drug had emerged during the 1980s, however, and the existing pipeline of compounds going through development, evaluation and test was not as healthy as Norwalk management desired. Management was placing pressure on scientists in the R&D lab to increase the yield of promising new products and to reduce the time and costs of the product development cycle. Scientists were currently exploring new bio-engineering techniques to create compounds that had the specific active properties desired rather than depending on an almost random search through thousands of possible compounds. The new techniques started with a detailed specification of the chemical properties that a new drug should have and then attempted to synthesize candidate compounds that could be tested for these properties. The bio-engineering procedures were costly, requiring extensive investment in new equipment and computer-based analysis.

A less expensive approach to increase the financial yield from R&D investments was to identify new applications for existing compounds that had already been approved for use. While some validation still had to be submitted for government approval to demonstrate the effectiveness of the drug in the new applications, the cost of extending an existing product to a new application was much, much less expensive than developing and creating an entirely new compound. Several valuable suggestions for possible new applications from existing products had come from Norwalk salesmen in the field. The salesmen were now being trained not only to sell existing products for approved applications, but also to listen to end users who frequently had novel and interesting ideas about how Norwalk's products could be used for new applications.

MANUFACTURING

Norwalk's manufacturing processes were considered among the best in the industry. Management took pride in the ability of the manufacturing operation to quickly and efficiently ramp up to produce drugs once they had cleared governmental regulatory processes. Norwalk's manufacturing capabilities also had to produce the small batches of new products that were required during testing and evaluation stages.

PERFORMANCE MEASUREMENT

Chadwick allowed its several divisions to operate in a decentralized fashion. Division managers had almost complete discretion in managing all the critical processes: R&D, production, marketing and sales, and administrative functions such as finance, human resources, and legal. Chadwick set challenging financial targets for divisions to meet. The targets were usually expressed as Return on Capital Employed (ROCE). As a diversified company, Chadwick wanted to be able to deploy the returns from the most profitable divisions to those divisions that held out the highest promise for profitable growth. Monthly financial summaries were submitted by each division to corporate headquarters. The Chadwick executive committee, consisting of the chief executive officer, the chief operating officer, two executive vice presidents, and the chief financial officer met monthly with each division manager to review ROCE performance and backup financial information for the preceding month.

THE BALANCED SCORECARD PROJECT

Bill Baron, Comptroller of Chadwick, had been searching for improved methods for evaluating the performance of the various divisions. Division managers complained about the continual pressure to meet short-term financial objectives in businesses that required extensive investments in risky projects to yield long-term returns. The idea of a Balanced Scorecard appealed to him as a constructive way to balance short-run financial objectives with the long-term performance of the company.

Baron brought the article and concept to Dan Daniels, the President and Chief Operating Officer of Chadwick. Daniels shared Baron's enthusiasm for the concept, feeling that a Balanced Scorecard would allow Chadwick divisional managers more flexibility in how they measured and presented their results of operations to corporate management. He also liked the idea of holding managers accountable for improving the long-term performance of their division.

After several days of reflection, Daniels issued a memorandum to all Chadwick division managers. The memo had a simple and direct message: Read the Balanced Scorecard article, develop a scorecard for your division, and be prepared to come to corporate headquarters in 90 days to present and defend the divisional scorecard to Chadwick's Executive Committee.

John Greenfield, the division manager at Norwalk, received Daniel's memorandum with some concern and apprehension. In principle, Greenfield liked the idea of developing a scorecard that would be more responsive to his operations, but he was distrustful of how much freedom he had to develop and use such a scorecard. Greenfield recalled:

> This seemed like just another way for corporate to claim that they have decentralized decision-making and authority while still retaining ultimate control at headquarters.

Greenfield knew that he would have to develop a plan of action to meet corporate's request but lacking a clear sense of how committed Chadwick was to the concept, he was not prepared to take much time from his or his subordinates' existing responsibilities for the project.

Exhibit 9-10
Norwalk Pharmaceutical Division: Business Strategy

1. Manage Norwalk portfolio of investments
   - Minimize cost to executing our existing business base
   - Maximize return/yield on all development spending
   - Invest in discovery of new compounds
2. Satisfy customer needs
3. Drive responsibility to the lowest level
   - Minimize centralized staff overhead
4. People development
   - Industry training
   - Unique mix of technical and commercial skills

The next day, at the weekly meeting of the Divisional Operating Committee, Greenfield distributed the Daniels memo and appointed a three-man committee, headed by Divisional Controller, Wil Wagner, to facilitate the process for creating the Norwalk Balanced Scorecard. Wagner approached Greenfield later that day:

> I read the Balanced Scorecard article. Based on my understanding of the concept, we must start with a clearly defined business vision. I'm not sure I have a clear understanding of the vision and business strategy for Norwalk. How can I start to build the scorecard without this understanding?

Greenfield admitted: "That's a valid point. Let me see what I can do to get you started." Greenfield picked up a pad of paper and started to write. Several minutes later he had produced a short business strategy statement for Norwalk (see Exhibit 9-10). Wagner and his group took Greenfield's strategy statement and started to formulate scorecard measures for the division.

Required

a. How does the Balanced Scorecard approach differ from traditional approaches to performance measurement? What, if anything, distinguishes the Balanced Scorecard approach from a "measure everything, and you might get what you want" philosophy?

b. Develop the Balanced Scorecard for the Norwalk Pharmaceutical Division of Chadwick, Inc. What parts of the business strategy that John Greenfield sketched out should be included? Are there any parts that should be excluded or cannot be made operational? What are the scorecard measures you would use to implement your scorecard in the Norwalk Pharmaceutical Division? What are the new measures that need to be developed, and how would you go about developing them?

c. How would a Balanced Scorecard for Chadwick, Inc., differ from ones developed in its divisions, such as the Norwalk Pharmaceutical Division? Do you anticipate that there might be major conflicts between divisional scorecards and those of the corporation? If so, should those conflicts be resolved, and, if so, how should they be resolved?

LO 2, 3, 4   **9-47 *Designing a Balanced Scorecard strategy map for an auto parts manufacturing company*   Domestic Auto Parts**[13]
Domestic Auto Parts (DAP), a $1 billion subsidiary of a U.S. auto parts manufacturing company, manufactured and marketed original and after-market parts for automobile producers in the U.S. It distributed products directly to original equipment automakers as well as to large retail

---

[13] Copyright © 2005 President and Fellows of Harvard College. Harvard Business School Case 9-105-078. This case was prepared by Professor Robert S. Kaplan as the basis for class discussion rather than to illustrate either effective or ineffective handling of an administrative situation. Reprinted by permission of Harvard Business School.

chains. DAP was currently number four in market share in the U.S. out of nine direct competitors. Its 9% return on capital was respectable but less than that of its leading competitors.

DAP's current product line was solid, but it had not introduced new products to the market over the last three years. This had caused its projected revenues to decline and its industry position to slip. As recently as two years ago, DAP was number two in the industry, but competitors Western Auto and Just in Time Automotive had passed it, pushing DAP to number four. Western Auto had introduced higher-value products to the market with the use of technology both to manufacture products and in the parts themselves. Western's customers paid a premium price for the improved performance of the company's products.

DAP, on the other hand, had protected margins during its revenue decline by aggressively attacking costs. It succeeded in maintaining its gross and operating margin levels but at the cost of limiting plant investment and technology upgrades in manufacturing plants. It was beginning to experience maintenance problems, such as an increase in unscheduled downtime. Also, because it lacked the flexible manufacturing capabilities of competitors, it had to produce to stock rather than to order, causing inventory costs to rise to noncompetitive levels. Company management now recognized that the recent cost cutting had maintained margins in the short term but may have severely affected DAP's ability to compete in the longer term.

To help turn the company around, the parent company had recently hired a new CEO, Ellen Bright. Her job was clearly set out for her—either turn the subsidiary around in two years or close the business. The minimum requirements for continued operations were to achieve 12% return-on-capital-employed (ROCE) and a growth rate faster than the industry's so that it could regain its number one or two position among competitors.

With this directive in hand, Bright held a meeting with her executive team to explain the situation and get their input. She started the meeting by stating:

> The only way we can achieve our goal is for each of you and your departments to cooperate to improve our return on capital. Product quality has set us apart in the past. We must regain our high-quality position and grow our revenues and our contribution to the parent company.
>
> My review of the economics and the competitive situation at DAP suggests that we must do three things: we need to grow; we must be customer intimate; and, we must be operationally excellent. And we must do all three things at once to be successful.
>
> Joe [the new chief financial officer brought in by Bright], you and I have been working on the economics required to achieve our financial goals. Why don't you share our initial findings with the group?

Joe Nathan described the financial goals for the turnaround:

> Basically, I designed a simple economic model to pinpoint the critical economic drivers needed to reach our goal of a 12% ROCE. We must increase our top line revenue by 50% through innovation and customer relationships, we need to better utilize our capital assets (both current and new)—currently we are operating at 65% on old assets—and we must get to 90% utilization on an upgraded asset base. Finally, we must minimize our total cost structure—today we are operating above the average cost in our competitor group. We need to get to the lowest-cost quartile to compete. These are the key drivers needed to get to the financial results expected by the parent company. We must balance them—one against the other—to achieve our overall goal of 12% ROCE. The question is how are we going to do this? What must we do—what objectives must we set and achieve?

Ellen Bright interjected, "We are going to build a strategy to achieve each of these thrusts. I need your commitment and active contribution." She asked Michael Milton, Vice President of Manufacturing, for his perspective. Milton said:

I'll admit that we certainly need to get more creative and bring to market new and improved products. But we need to do a lot of our processes better. Supplier management and manufacturing as well as product delivery have to be better coordinated so we can effectively and efficiently get new products to the customer. We need to be on time and on spec just to get the opportunity to sell new products. Key in my mind is managing the supplier pipeline, the raw materials—there is a lot of money to be saved there.

We also need to balance our intense focus on cost cutting with the need to make investments in process improvements and new and upgraded equipment. Unscheduled downtime and the inability to make product switchovers on the manufacturing floor are killing us. Upgraded capital will both reduce our costs and help deliver consistently on time and on spec. We talk a lot about preventive maintenance, but we need to get real about it. This could save us big time in terms of costs and effectiveness. If we don't do these operational things we will have trouble convincing customers to pay a premium price for our products.

David Dillon, Head of Distribution, described the problems he faced:

At the moment, I don't have the infrastructure tools to create a first-class network of wholesalers and distributors. We need to streamline our distribution process and position ourselves as a strong business partner to attract and retain profitable customers. There are a lot of people out there with great experience and good ideas about how to achieve this, but the department is large and geographically dispersed, and there is no formal way of sharing best practices and best thinking. These steps will help us achieve our grow-revenue goal by getting products to market at a reasonable price in a reasonable time.

Mary Stewart, Vice President of Marketing and Sales, added:

Improving our distribution will be a major factor in our new customer intimacy thrust by providing the opportunity for win-win relationships with our distributor customers and enhancing our reputation for efficiency and organization.

In addition, we must position ourselves in the market—with the right customers—to be viable. We have recently studied our customer base and found an important segment of the current customer base that is profitable in both the direct and wholesale segments. In fact, 69% of our customers produce 90% of our profit. We went on to determine what these key customers want and will pay for. Both key segments, direct and wholesale, want essentially the same things. They expect us to deliver products on time and on spec. This, however, is expected from everyone in the industry. It's a hurdle that must be passed just to be considered a viable vendor. The differentiator is for a supplier to understand their needs and translate that by continuous communication and productive dialogue. They want a long-term, mutually beneficial relationship with their suppliers. They want superior, technology-sophisticated products from a supplier with a superior reputation and image in the industry. Such a supplier makes their buying decisions less risky.

Rita Richardson, Vice President of Research and Development, responded to the challenge to produce state-of-the-art technologically sophisticated products:

Well, we have some talented people in our R&D group who can produce the kind of products our customers need. But all the products in the world will not be bought without a good marketing communications effort. We need to be able to tell people what we have and how it can benefit them. We need a marketing effort that positions us as an innovator with new and enhanced products to offer. I think it might help to have some of our marketing staff spend time in the R&D department to get a feel for what's going on. Sure some reskilling may be needed to achieve our innovation goals but I think we have a solid base of R&D professionals.

Bright interjected at this point, "I think you have hit on something there, Rita. I think we all need to be more business focused and less functionally focused. The company seems to be suffering because employees know only what goes on inside their own area. This team needs to lead this cross-functional view by example—in what we say and what we do."

She closed the meeting by challenging the group even further:

> None of our objectives can be accomplished without a major commitment from all of us to build a world-class workforce. To operate as an innovator we must change the way we think in this organization. Our employees must value change not resist it. We must reskill large parts—not some—of the organization. This will require training. Training involves both time and money. To support the new workforce we will also need to provide tools to work smarter and harder. We can do this and align the organization through the use of just-in-time (JIT) technology. This commitment to people and organization is necessary to do the things we need to do to deliver customer benefits and ultimately financial returns.

Required

From the meeting of senior DAP executives, develop a strategy map of objectives, as well as potential Balanced Scorecard measures, for DAP. You can be guided by the following questions:

Financial
1. Who are the shareholders, and what do they want?
2. What are the shareholders' expectations in the following areas?
   (a) Revenue growth
   (b) Asset utilization
   (c) Cost improvement

Customer
1. Who are the customers?
2. What do the customers want? How does DAP create value for them?

Process
1. What processes are most important for creating value for DAP's shareholders and customers?
2. What are the objectives and measures for each process identified here?

Learning and Growth
1. What specific skills and capabilities do DAP's people need in order to excel at the critical processes that you identified in the process perspective?
2. What other objectives can you identify to improve the human, information, and organization capital of DAP if it is to succeed with its strategy?

Chapter 10

Using Budgets to Achieve Organizational Objectives

After reading this chapter, you will be able to:

➤ explain the role of budgets and budgeting in organizations

➤ demonstrate the importance of each element of the budgeting process

➤ explain the different types of operating budgets and financial budgets and the relationships among them

➤ describe the way organizations use and interpret budgets

➤ develop and use what-if and sensitivity analyses—budgeting tools used by budget planners

➤ compute and interpret common variances used by management accountants

➤ identify the role of budgets in service organizations and not-for-profit organizations

➤ recognize the behavioral effects of budgeting on an organization's employees

---

The Financing Crisis in Mount Pleasant

Mount Pleasant was a thriving city whose population exceeded 750,000. The residents were proud of their vibrant downtown, extensive community services, and clean and relatively crime-free environment. The city's major employers were two automobile parts manufacturing plants, a university, the headquarters of a major insurance company, and the headquarters of a major software development company. A business friendly attitude in Mount Pleasant had also supported the development and success of many small and intermediate-sized businesses.

In 2005, the projected city revenues were about $2.5 billion, of which 50% were collected from property taxes, 20% from business taxes, 20% from user fees and profits of the city-owned public utility, and 10% in grants from the federal government. The general feeling was that the city

Source: Ron Chapple/Getty Images, Inc.

council had to hold the line on tax increases, that user fees were unlikely to increase over the foreseeable future, and that grants from the federal government were unlikely to increase and, in fact, might fall because the federal government was suffering chronic deficits.

Proposed expenditures for 2006 were slightly higher at approximately $2.7 billion, of which about 60% were for education, 20% for police and fire services, 5% for recreation (parks, arenas, and classes), 4% for debt servicing, 3% for transit, 2% for road maintenance, 2% for garbage collection and processing, 1% for the library, and 3% for other services.

Mayor Sandra Moore and the city council were concerned about the projected deficit for two reasons. First, the city was not allowed to incur deficits. Second, the mayor and most of the council believed that residents expected to continue to enjoy the high level of services and quality of life currently provided in Mount Pleasant. The city's budget committee was at an impasse concerning how to deal with the difference between projected revenues and expenditures.

DETERMINING THE LEVELS OF CAPACITY-RELATED AND FLEXIBLE RESOURCES

Thus far in this book, we have focused on how costs are created by short- and long-term decisions. We called costs that varied with the activity level in the firm variable costs; costs that did not change with changes in activity levels we called fixed, or capacity-related, costs. For decisions affecting the short term, the firm's fixed costs are considered to be given and fixed. So the costs that are relevant to the firm in the short run, since they are the only ones that are controllable, are variable costs.

In this chapter, we discuss the budgeting process, which determines the planned level of most variable costs. Chapter 11 considers budgeting for fixed resources which provides the capacity to use flexible resources in the short run.

Budgeting also includes discretionary spending, such as for machine maintenance, research and development, advertising, and employee training. These discretionary costs do not supply the firm with capacity to produce, but they do provide support for the organization's strategy by enhancing its performance potential. For example, systematic maintenance increases machine reliability and lowers the lifetime costs of equipment, successful research and development increases the organization's future profit potential by developing new products, advertising increases profit potential by making products more attractive to customers, and employee training enhances employees' ability to undertake their assigned roles as expected. Once authorized, discretionary spending budgets are committed or fixed—that is, they do not vary with levels of production or service.

The Budgeting Process

The Role of Budgets and Budgeting

Most families have developed a financial plan to guide them in allocating their resources over a planning period. Usually the plan reflects spending priorities and demands, including specific spending categories such as the mortgage, utilities, property taxes, and essential items such as food and clothing. Family budgets often are the result of negotiations among parents, children, and others such as relatives and creditors reflecting their different priorities and objectives. For example, money left over after required spending on food, clothing, medicine, insurance, and shelter may go into savings or be used for other purposes; one parent may want to use most of the disposable income for a vacation, while another may want to use the money to paint the house. Within the same household, teenagers may ask their parents for help in financing the purchase of a used car. The family budget is a planning tool, but it also serves as a

Source: Alamy Images.

control on the behavior of family members by setting limits on what can be spent in each budget category. Without a budget, the family would not have a way to monitor and control its spending by categories of spending. Without such monitoring and control, a family can easily succumb to unexpected debt and severe financial difficulties.

Budgets serve the same purpose for managers within the business units of an organization and are a central part of the design and operation of management accounting systems. Exhibit 10-1 shows the central role budgets play and the relationship between planning and control. Note the distinct but linked steps for each function—three for planning and two for control.

As in households, budgets in organizations reflect in quantitative terms how to allocate financial resources to each part of an organization—each department or division or other distinct part—based on planned activities and short-run objectives of that part of the organization. For example, a bank manager may want to increase the bank's local market share, which may require a larger spending budget than the previous year's for local advertising, implementing a staff training program to improve customer service, and renovating the building to make it more appealing to customers.

Keep in mind always: A budget is a quantitative expression of the planned money inflows and outflows that reveal whether the current operating or business plan will meet the organization's financial objectives. Budgeting is the process of preparing budgets.

Budgets also provide a way to communicate the organization's short-term goals to its employees. Asking organization unit managers to undertake budgeting activities can accomplish two things: (1) reflect how well unit managers understand the organization's goals, so that they can align their activities and spending priorities with those goals, and (2) provide an opportunity for the organization's senior planners to correct misperceptions about the organization's goals. Suppose an organization recognized quality as a critical factor for its success and wanted to promote quality

Exhibit 10-1
Planning and
Control and the
Role of Budgets

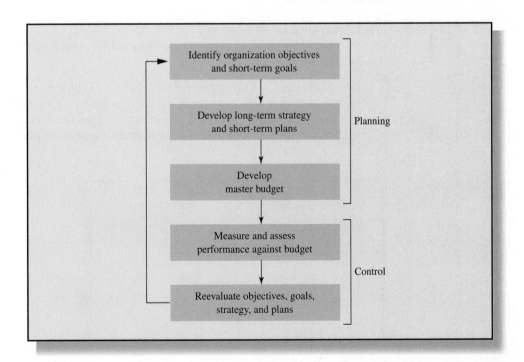

awareness among its employees. If a department prepared a budget that reflected no expenditures for employee quality training, a senior planner would recognize that the organization's goal with respect to quality had not been communicated properly to whoever should have recognized the need for quality training.

Budgeting also serves to coordinate the many activities of an organization. For example, budgets show the effect of sales levels on purchasing, production, and administrative activities and on the number of employees that must be hired to serve customers. In this sense, budgeting is a tool that promotes coordination of the organization's activities and helps identify coordination problems. Suppose the sales force plans to significantly expand sales. By comparing selling plans with manufacturing capacity, planners might discover that the manufacturing operations are unable to meet the planned increased level of sales. The kind of coordination needed can be accomplished through powerful desktop computers and software; with the computer and software, planners can simulate the effect of different decisions on the organization's financial, human, and physical resources. Simulation analysis—which is, simply, what-if analysis—helps managers choose a course of action among many alternatives by identifying a decision's consequences in a complex system with many interdependencies.

By considering interrelationships among operating activities, a budget helps to anticipate potential problems and can serve as a tool to help provide solutions to these problems. For example, canneries engage in seasonal production, consuming large amounts of cash when they build inventory during the canning season. Throughout the year, the cannery sells its inventory and recovers cash. Budgeting reflects this cash cycle, shown in Exhibit 10-2, and provides information to help the organization plan the borrowing needed to finance the inventory buildup early in the cash cycle. If budget planning suggests that the organization's sales potential exceeds its manufacturing potential, the organization can develop a plan to put more capacity in place or to reduce planned sales. It is important for managers to anticipate problems because putting new capacity in place can take several months to several years.

The Elements of Budgeting

Budgeting involves forecasting the demand for four types of resources over different time periods:

1. *Flexible resources that create variable costs.* Flexible resources can be acquired or disposed of in the short term, such as the lumber, glue, and varnish used in a furniture factory or, based on estimates of the number of automobiles to be assembled, the number of tires an automobile assembly plant needs to acquire.

Exhibit 10-2
The Cash Cycle

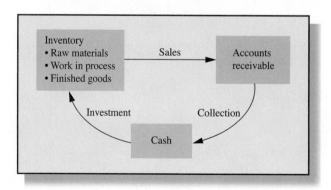

2. *Intermediate-term capacity resources that create fixed costs.* An example is forecasting the need for rental storage space that might be contracted on a quarterly, semiannual, or annual basis.
3. *Resources that, in the intermediate run and long run, enhance the potential of the organization's strategy.* These are discretionary expenditures, which include research and development, employee training, the maintenance of capacity resources, advertising, and promotion. These discretionary expenditures do not provide capacity, nor do they vary with the level of organization activity.
4. *Long-term capacity resources that create fixed costs.* An example is a new fabrication facility for a computer chip manufacturer, which might take several years to plan and build and might be used for 10 years.

The framework for budgeting in organizations is discussed in the following sections. The discussion begins with the budgeting process and leads to formulation of the master budget. Two major types of budgets make up the master budget:

1. **Operating budgets** summarize the level of activities such as sales, purchasing, and production.
2. **Financial budgets**, such as balance sheets, income statements, and cash flow statements, identify the expected financial consequences of the activities summarized in the operating budgets.

Behavioral Considerations in Budgeting

It is important to understand the behavioral issues that arise from the participants in the budget-setting process and the kinds of games that people subject to budgets sometimes play with budgets.

As demand for oil increased spectacularly in the early part of this century, the world experienced a shortage of oil refining capacity that caused huge price increases as demand outpaced supply. Planning for long-term capacity resources poses major challenges for organizations. On the one hand, long-term capacity resources create huge financial risks for organizations, since fixed costs will continue even if capacity-related resources go unused. On the other hand, organizations often cannot acquire long-term capacity quickly in response to demand surges, thereby suffering major opportunity losses if needed capacity is not available.
Source: Corbis–NY.

Game playing with budgets is inherent in the budgeting process. Budget planners solicit information from managers or employees who are in the best position to know performance potential—such as sales, production potential, and costs. This information is then incorporated into the budget that is later used to evaluate actual performance. This creates the incentive for managers to misrepresent their information—a process known as gaming the budgeting process.

For example, a production machine operator might understate the machine's production potential in order to secure a lower budget or standard for output, thus making after-the-fact evaluations of actual performance to budget look favorable. A sales manager might understate the sales potential in a region in order to have a lower target set for sales.

To avoid this potential for managers to misrepresent their information, many students of budgeting have proposed that the information that managers provide not be used later to evaluate their performance. We will return to consider behavioral issues in budgeting later in this chapter.

Budget Components

Exhibit 10-3 summarizes different components of the budget. The dotted lines from the expected financial results (boxes 11 and 12) show how the estimated financial consequences from the organization's tentative budgets can influence the organization's plans and objectives. The dotted lines illustrate a recursive process in which planners compare projected financial results with the organization's financial goals. If initial

Exhibit 10-3
The Master Budget

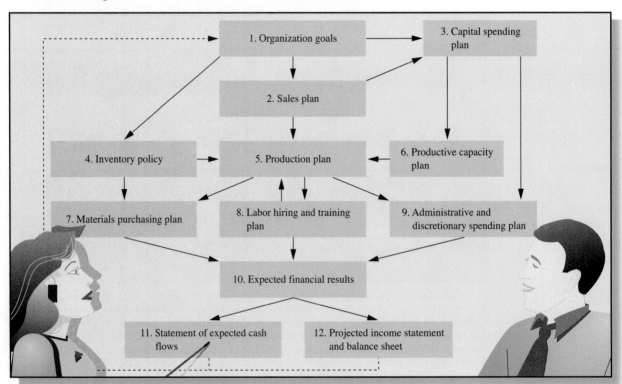

In 2004, Nokia sold 200 million cellular telephones, each consisting of approximately 300 components. Nokia relied on a sophisticated planning and logistical system to provide for a smooth and orderly acquisition and delivery of these 60 billion components.

Source: Nokia.

budgets prove infeasible (because the organization does not have the capacity to produce or sell the planned level of output) or financially unacceptable (because the proposal plan does not yield the desired target level of profits), planners repeat the budgeting cycle with a new set of decisions until the results are both feasible and financially acceptable.

The budgeting process describes the acquisition, production, selling, and logistical activities performed during the budget period. Planners can select any budget period, but they usually choose 1 year to conform to the organization's external reporting cycle. A 1-year budget period is assumed in the following discussion.

The master budget process in Exhibit 10-3 includes two broad sets of outputs: (1) the plans or operating budgets that operating personnel use to guide operations (sales plan [box 2], capital spending plan [box 3], production plan [box 5], production capacity plan [box 6], materials purchasing plan [box 7], labor hiring and training plan [box 8], and the administrative and discretionary spending plan [box 9]), and (2) the expected or projected financial results [boxes 11 and 12]. Planners usually present the expected, or projected, financial results, in three forms:

1. A statement of expected cash flows
2. The projected balance sheet
3. The projected income statement

Accountants call the projected statement of cash flows, balance sheet, and projected income statement pro forma financial statements (pro forma means provided in advance).

Operating Budgets

Operating budgets typically consist of the following six operating plans (see Exhibit 10-3):

1. The sales plan (box 2) identifies the planned level of sales for each product.
2. The capital spending plan (box 3) specifies the long-term capital investments, such as buildings and equipment, that must be made to meet activity level objectives.

3. The production plan (box 5) schedules required production.
4. The materials purchasing plan (box 7) schedules required purchasing activities.
5. The labor hiring and training plan (box 8) specifies the number of people the organization must hire or release to achieve its activity level objectives and, based on those numbers, the needed hiring, training, and counseling out policies requirements.
6. The administrative and discretionary spending plan (box 9) includes administration, staffing, research and development, and advertising.

Operating budgets specify the expected resource requirements of selling, capital spending, manufacturing, purchasing, labor management, and administrative activities during the budget period. Operations personnel use those plans represented in the operating budget to guide and coordinate the level of various activities during the budget period. At the same time, operations personnel record data from current operations that can be used to develop future budgets.

Financial Budgets

Planners prepare the projected balance sheet and projected income statement to estimate the financial consequences of investment, production, and sales plans.
Planners use the statement of projected cash flows in two ways:

1. To plan when excess cash will be generated so that it can be used to make short-term investments rather than simply holding cash during the short term.
2. To plan how to meet any cash shortages.

THE BUDGETING PROCESS ILLUSTRATED

The budgeting process can be frustrating and time consuming. Some organizations invest thousands of hours over many months to prepare the budget documents just described. We will illustrate an entire budgeting process with a simplified yet comprehensive exercise that covers many of the budgeting elements that we have just described.

Oxford Tole Art, Buoy Division

Oxford Tole Art sells high-quality wood and metal objects, new and antique, painted by the owner, Gael Foster. Until recently, each object was unique and Gael did all the work herself. Two years ago, Gael developed a new product line that she intended to sell in larger volumes because she wanted to expand her business. The new products are two models of painted fishing buoys: Santa, a buoy painted to look like Father Christmas, and Danny Buoy, a buoy painted to look like an Irish fisherman. Gael set up a new operation for this new product: Oxford Tole Art, Buoy Division (hereafter called Oxford Tole Art). Gael did the planning for this operation and hired a manager, April Cheung, to handle the daily operations of the new business.

The production process begins when Gael purchases used fishing buoys from local fishers for $2.25 each. An artist sands the used buoys to remove old paint and debris and applies a base coat of primer paint. When the base coat is dry, the artist hand paints the image of the Santa or the fisherman onto the buoy. Once the image dries, the artist applies a finishing coat of varnish. When the varnish dries, the artist wraps the finished buoy in packing material and inserts it into a specifically designed mailing container that Oxford Tole Art ships directly to the customer.

Oxford Tole Art has two types of customers: retail and dealer. Retail orders arrive by mail and are prepaid. The retail price per unit, including packing and shipping charges, is $80. If capacity exceeds retail demand, Gael sells to dealers at the lower per unit price of $55. Because dealers will buy other products from other suppliers, Gael loses dealer orders that she is not able to fill immediately.

Sales to dealers are on account; stated terms call for the dealers to pay the full amount of the invoice within 30 days of billing. Receipts from dealers, however, are often delinquent. Typically only 30% of dealers pay in the month following the sale, 45% pay in the second month following the sale, 20% day in the third month following the sale, and 5% of sales to dealers are never collected.

Oxford Tole Art hires local area artists to paint the buoys. Because of local employment conditions, Oxford Tole Art must hire artists for periods of 3 months. The artists receive a fixed monthly salary of $2,000 and work a maximum of 160 hours per month. April, the Oxford Tole Art manager, makes staffing decisions at the start of each quarter, beginning January 1. The total time to sand, apply the base coat, paint, and pack each buoy is 0.8 labor hour.

Paint costs $3.15 for each buoy. Other manufacturing costs, including sandpaper, brushes, varnish, and other supplies, amounts to $2.75 per buoy. Packing materials cost $1.95 per buoy, and shipping by courier costs $7.50 per buoy. Oxford Tole Art purchases for cash all flexible resources in the month they are needed.

Oxford Tole Art rents space in a local industrial park where the artists work on the buoys. The 1-year lease stipulates that rent is to be paid quarterly and in advance. Oxford Tole Art can rent production space of several sizes that would provide area for producing the following monthly capacities in buoys: 600, 800, 1,000, and 1,200. The quarterly rents for each of these units are $3,600, $4,800, $6,000, and $7,200, respectively. All production takes place to order, and Oxford Tole Art acquires supplies only as needed.

Shop Space Type	Shop Capacity (Number of Buoys)	Quarterly Rent
A	600	$3,600
B	800	4,800
C	1,000	6,000
D	1,200	7,200

Insurance, heating, lighting, and business taxes are $20,000 per year, and advertising expenses amount to $40,000 per year. April Cheung receives $30,000 per year to supervise the operation, manage the raw materials acquisitions, handle all the order taking and billing, and do the accounting.

All operating expenses are incurred and paid in equal monthly installments.

Realized sales for October, November, and December 2005 and forecasted demand for 2006 appear in Exhibit 10-4. Based on this forecasted demand, Gael and April have decided to rent an 800-capacity unit for 2006 and hire two painters in the first quarter, two painters in the second quarter, one painter in the third quarter, and three painters in the fourth quarter.

Gael plans to withdraw $20,000 from the company at the start of each 6-month period for a total of $40,000 per year as her compensation for acting as owner and planner. She also wants to maintain the entire firm's cash in a separate bank account for her business with a minimum cash balance of $5,000 (see Exhibit 10-5). She has arranged a $50,000 line of credit with her bank to provide her with short-term funds for the company. At the start of each month, the bank charges interest at the rate of 1% on the outstanding balance of the line of credit as of the end of the previous month. The bank pays interest at the rate of 0.6% on any cash in excess of $5,000 held

Exhibit 10-4
Oxford Tole Art:
Forecasted Unit
Demand,
2005–2006

| | DEMAND | | |
MONTH	RETAIL	DEALER	TOTAL
October 2005*	275	510	785
November 2005*	420	425	845
December 2005*	675	175	850
January 2006	100	375	475
February 2006	105	400	505
March 2006	95	425	520
April 2006	115	350	465
May 2006	75	300	350
June 2006	60	250	310
July 2006	50	300	350
August 2006	55	325	380
September 2006	75	300	375
October 2006	150	300	450
November 2006	290	350	640
December 2006	350	400	750

*Actual

Exhibit 10-5
Oxford Tole Art:
Proposed Balance
Sheet, January
2006

Cash	$5,000	Owner's equity	$34,948
Accounts receivable	29,948		
Total assests	$34,948	Total liabilities and owner's equity	$34,948

in the account. The bank pays interest on the first day of each month based on the balance in the account at the end of the previous month.

Demand Forecast

An organization's goals provide the starting point and the framework for evaluating the budgeting process (see Exhibit 10-3, box 1). At Oxford Tole Art, the goals are to produce high-quality products and to be profitable. To assess the plan's acceptability, Gael compares the tentative operating plan's projected financial results with the organization's financial goals.

As shown in Exhibit 10-3, the budgeting process is influenced strongly by the demand forecast, which is simply an estimate of sales demand at a specified selling price. Organizations develop demand forecasts in many ways. Some use market surveys conducted either by outside experts or by their own sales staff. Other organizations use statistical models to generate demand forecasts from trends and forecasts of economic activity in the economy and the relation of past sales patterns to this economic activity. Other companies simply assume that demand will either grow or decline by some estimated rate over previous demand levels.

Regardless of the approach used to develop the demand forecast, the organization must prepare a sales plan for each major line of goods or services. The sales plan provides the basis to acquire the necessary factors of production, such as labor, materials, production capacity, and cash. Production plans are sensitive to the sales plan; therefore, most organizations develop budgets on computers so that planners can readily explore the effects of changes in the sales plan on production plans.

Choosing the amount of detail to present in the budget involves making trade-offs. A greater level of detail in the forecast improves the chances that the budgeting process will identify potential bottlenecks and problems by specifying the exact timing of production flows in the organization. However, forecasting and planning in great detail for each item among thousands of items in production can be extremely expensive and overwhelming to compute. Most organizations rely on the judgment of their production planners to strike a balance between the need for detail and the cost and practicality of detailed scheduling. Planners do this by grouping products into pools so that each product in a given pool places roughly equivalent demands on the organization's resources so that planning is simplified. Because Oxford Tole Art has one product, a painted buoy with only two variations, its budget can be detailed and comprehensive. Organizations with many products and services may choose, however, to budget at a more aggregated level, such as by product line. For example, production in a plant making headache capsules might budget by the product line rather than by individual stock-keeping units.

The Production Plan

Planners match the completed sales plan with the organization's inventory policy and capacity level to determine a production plan (Exhibit 10-3, box 5). The plan identifies the required production in each of the interim periods making up the annual budget period. Budget periods, such as a year, may have interim periods comprised of days, weeks, or months, depending on the information needs of the people managing the acquisition, manufacturing, selling, and distribution activities.

Planners use the inventory policy (Exhibit 10-3, box 4) and the sales plan (Exhibit 10-3, box 2) to develop the production plan (Exhibit 10-3, box 5). Therefore, the inventory policy is critical and has a unique role in shaping the production plan. Some organizations have a policy of producing goods for inventory and attempt to keep a predetermined, or target, number of units in inventory at all times. This inventory policy often reflects a level production strategy that is characteristic of an organization with highly skilled employees or equipment dedicated to producing a single product. A level production strategy reflects a lack of flexibility. Highly skilled production workers cannot be used to do various jobs in the organization; therefore, they must be kept busy in the job they know. Similarly, dedicated equipment that can be used for only one job must be kept busy to justify its expense. In such organizations, monthly sales draw down the inventory levels, and the production plan for each month attempts to restore inventory levels to their target levels.

Other organizations have an inventory policy of producing for planned sales in the next interim period within the budget period. Organizations moving toward a just-in-time inventory policy produce goods to meet the next interim period's demand as an intermediate step along the path to moving to a full just-in-time inventory system in which only an order can trigger production, as does Toyota. Each interim period becomes shorter and shorter until the organization achieves just-in-time production. In this setting, the inventory target is the level of next week's or next month's planned sales, and the scheduled production is the amount required to meet the inventory target. Implementing a just-in-time inventory policy requires flexibility among employees, equipment, and suppliers and a production process that has little potential for failure. In organizations using a just-in-time inventory strategy, demand

Pioneered by Toyota Motor Company, just-in-time manufacturing is a system where suppliers deliver parts to a factory just and only when they are needed. Just-in-time manufacturing systems provide huge reductions in inventory-related costs, such as storage and obsolescence. Just-in-time manufacturing systems require sophisticated and reliable coordination between customers and their suppliers.

Source: Alamy Images.

drives the production plan directly—that is, the production in each interim period equals the next interim period's planned sales. This is the inventory policy that Oxford Tole Art uses (Exhibit 10-3, box 4).

Developing the Spending Plans

Once planners have identified a feasible production plan, they can make tentative resource commitments. The purchasing group prepares a materials purchasing plan to acquire the raw materials and supplies that the production plan requires (Exhibit 10-3, box 7). Materials purchasing plans are driven by the cycle of the organization's production plans (which may be hourly, daily, weekly, monthly, or even longer) and the suppliers' production plans. The organization's production plans notify suppliers of the quantity of materials they should supply and when those materials must be delivered. Because sales plans and production plans change during the year, the organization and its suppliers must be able to quickly adjust their plans based on information received during the operating period. For example, a manufacturer of a fashion item might find that demand is far outpacing expectations and supply. The manufacturer would have to signal to its suppliers that it will require more raw materials. At some point, however, the production and materials supply plans have to be locked in place and no additional changes made. For example, commitment to a production schedule in a large automotive assembly plant happens about 8 weeks before production takes place. This provides suppliers and the assembly plant managers the time to put raw materials supply in place and schedule the production.

The personnel and production groups prepare the labor hiring and training plan (Exhibit 10-3, box 8). This plan works backward from the date when the personnel are needed to develop hiring and training schedules that will ensure the availability of these personnel. This plan can include both expansion and contraction activities. For example, when an organization is contracting, it will use retraining plans to redeploy employees to other parts of the organization or will develop plans to discharge employees from the organization. The discharge plans for laid-off employees may include retraining and other activities to help them find new jobs. Because discharging employees reflects moral, ethical, and legal issues and may involve high severance costs, many organizations attempt to avoid layoffs unless no other alternative can be found.

Other decision makers in the organization will prepare an administrative and discretionary spending plan that summarizes the proposed expenditures on such activities as research and development, advertising, and training (Exhibit 10-3, box 9). Discretionary expenditures provide the infrastructure required by the proposed production and sales plan. Discretionary, as used here, means the actual sales and production levels do not drive the amount spent; rather, the senior managers in the organization determine the amount of discretionary expenditures. Once determined, however, the amount to be spent on discretionary activities becomes fixed for the budget period because it is unaffected by product volume and mix.

If a fast-food restaurant plans to make 3,000 hamburgers during some budget period, it knows the quantity of materials it will use because there is a physical, or engineered, relationship among ingredients such as meat, buns, condiments, packages, and the number of hamburgers made. However, no direct physical, or engineered, relationship exists among the number of hamburgers sold and the discretionary amounts spent on items like advertising and employee training.

Finally, the appropriate authority in the organization approves the capital spending plan for putting new productive capacity in place (Exhibit 10-3, box 3). Because capital spending projects usually involve time horizons longer than the period of the operating budget, a long-term planning process rather than the 1-year cycle of the operating budget drives the capital spending plan. The spending plans for material, labor, and support resources are based on a forecast of the activities the organization must complete to achieve the production targets identified in its production plan. As the planning period unfolds and time reveals the actual production requirements, production planners make commitments to detailed production schedules and the required related purchasing requirements.

Choosing the Capacity Levels

At Oxford Tole Art, the following three types of resources determine the monthly production capacity:

1. *Flexible resources that the organization can acquire in the short term, such as paint and packing supplies.* If suppliers either do not deliver these resources or deliver unacceptable resources, production may be disrupted. This problem was not identified as an issue for Oxford Tole Art, but it is a practical concern for many organizations. Organizations such as Wal-Mart spend a great deal of time and money developing supplier relationships so that they will receive zero-defect materials and purchase inventory if and only when needed.

2. *Capacity resources, such as painters, that the organization must acquire for the intermediate term.* Between July 1 and September 30, Oxford Tole Art plans to employ one painter. Because each painter works 160 hours per month and because each buoy requires 0.8 hour to complete, the monthly capacity provided by intermediate-term activity decisions between July 1 and September 30 is 200 ($=160/0.8$) units.

Wal-Mart's vaunted logistics system was clearly evident in September 2005, when the company delivered much needed goods to the survivors of hurricane Katrina in the southern United States. *Source:* Chris Hondros/Getty Editorial.

3. *Capacity resources, such as building a factory, that the organization must acquire for the long term.* Gael plans to rent a shop that provides a monthly capacity of 800 units. Gael faces a simple setting with a relatively short commitment period. Other organizations may take several years to acquire long-term capacity that may last for 10 years or longer, and the cost is justified only if it is used that long. Consider the amount of time an oil company takes to build an oil refinery or the time that a municipality needs to build a hospital. Capacity resources are expensive and are called *committed* because they are the same regardless of how much of the facility is used and because the level of capacities and fixed costs are very difficult to change in the short term. Therefore, capacity resources impose financial risk on the organization.

As indicated in Exhibit 10-6, the nature of the resources determines whether they are short term, intermediate term, or long term. Many organizations develop sophisticated approaches to choose a production plan that balances the use of short-term, intermediate-term, and long-term capacity to minimize committed resource idle time. For example, the size and number of service areas in a bank represent the capacity available for use during any period provided by long-term building decisions. The level of long-term capacity chosen reflects the organization's assessment of its long-term growth trend. For Oxford Tole Art, which is renting capacity, long-term capacity is defined by the lease stipulations, which equals 1 year. If Oxford Tole Art were building this capacity, its long-term capacity would be defined by the time needed to plan and build the facility.

The number of full-time staff employed by a bank determines the long-term capacity available for the intermediate term. For example, if the plan were to acquire capacity that the organization could use increasingly as sales grew, the intermediate-term capacity decisions would put in place other elements that require

Exhibit 10-6
Summary of
Capacity Types
and Commitment
Time

TERM	TYPE OF CAPACITY ACQUIRED	EXAMPLES
Flexible resources required in short term (less than several weeks)	Provides the ability to use existing capacity	Raw materials, supplies, casual labor
Committed resources acquired for the intermediate term (several weeks to six months)	General purpose capacity that is transferrable among organizations given time	Employees, general-purpose equipment, specialty raw materials
Committed resources acquired for the long-term (more than six months)	Special purpose capacity that is customized for the organization's use	Buildings, special-purpose equipment

intermediate-term commitments. These would include defining the number of people and banking equipment necessary to allow the bank to use its long-term capacity. The intermediate-term capacity decision reflects the longer of either the duration needed to put intermediate-term capacity in place or the duration of the contracting period for intermediate-term capacity. For Oxford Tole Art, this is the contracting period for artists, which is 3 months.

The number of part-time or temporary staff employed by a bank determines its capacity on a day-to-day basis. Such short-term capacity decisions reflect the cyclical demands that the bank may face daily, weekly, monthly, or annually. The short-term capacity decision reflects the time needed to put short-term capacity in place. For Oxford Tole Art, this is the time that suppliers require for delivery, which is assumed to be nearly instantaneous. However, if Oxford Tole Art had to order and wait for supplies, it would become very important to plan acquisitions so that in the very short term, such as hourly, Oxford Tole Art would not have to stop production while it waited for supplies to arrive. In this sense, supplies provide the short-run capacity to use longer-term capacity.

Organizations use many different approaches to plan capacity, and it is important to understand how production planners choose capacity levels. The process that Oxford Tole Art used was to choose a level of shop capacity (either 600, 800, 1,000, or 1,200 units) and then to hire the number of painters in each quarter that, given the forecasted demand and chosen shop capacity, provided the highest level of expected profits.

The resource-consuming activities for Oxford Tole Art can be classified into three groups that are common to most organizations:

1. *Activities that create the need for resources and, therefore, resource expenditures in the short term.* For Oxford Tole Art, these short-term activities include the purchasing, preparation, painting, packing, and shipping of buoys. Acquiring the resources for these short-term activities requires expenditures that vary directly with the production levels because the inventory policy is to produce only to order.
2. *Activities undertaken to acquire capacity for the intermediate term.* For Oxford Tole Art, this is the quarterly acquisition of painting capacity, that is, hiring the painters to paint the buoys.
3. *Activities undertaken to acquire or support capacity needed for the long term.* For Oxford Tole Art, this includes annually choosing the level of shop capacity, the level of advertising, the manager and manager's salary, and expenditures for such items as insurance and heat.

Planners classify activities by type because they plan, budget, and control short-, intermediate-, and long-term expenditures differently. Analysts evaluate short-term activities by considering efficiency: Did we accomplish this task with the fewest possible resources and effectiveness? Did we achieve what we set out to accomplish? They also ask questions such as the following:

1. Is this expenditure necessary to add to the product value perceived by customers?
2. Can the organization improve how it performs this activity?
3. Would changing the way this activity is done provide more satisfaction to customers?

Analysts evaluate intermediate- and long-term activities by using efficiency and effectiveness considerations and asking questions such as these:

1. Are alternative forms of capacity available that are less expensive?
2. Is this the best approach to achieve our goals?
3. How can we improve the capacity selection decision to make capacity less expensive or more flexible?

Choosing the capacity plan—making the commitments to acquire intermediate- and long-term capacity—commits the firm to its intermediate- and long-term expenditures. Choosing the production plan—that is, choosing the level of the short-term activities—fixes the short-term expenditures that the budget summarizes.

Handling Infeasible Production Plans

Although the relationship between planning and production at Oxford Tole Art are simple, the company's planning process reflects how planners use forecasted demand to plan activity levels and provide required capacity. If planners find the tentative production plan infeasible because projected demand exceeds available capacity, they must make provisions to acquire more capacity or reduce the planned level of production. For example, if the labor market is tight and Oxford Tole Art can hire only two artists between January and June, Gael would have to revise her capacity and production plans to reflect this constraint.

Interpreting the Production Plan

Exhibit 10-7 summarizes the production plan that Oxford Tole Art has developed for 2006. The three factors that drive planning are the following:

1. Demand, which is the quantity customers are willing to buy at the stated price
2. The capacity levels chosen
3. Production output quantity

Oxford Tole Art starts no production until it receives an order. Therefore, production is the minimum of total demand and production capacity. In equation form, we write this in general form as follows:

Production = Minimum (total demand, production capacity)

Exhibit 10-7
Oxford Tole Art: Demand, Capacity, and Sales Data, 2006

	JAN.	FEB.	MARCH	APRIL	MAY	JUNE	JULY	AUG.	SEPT.	OCT.	NOV.	DEC.
Retail demand	100	105	95	115	75	60	50	55	75	150	290	350
Dealer demand	375	400	425	350	300	250	300	325	300	300	350	400
Total demand	475	505	520	465	375	310	350	380	375	450	640	750
Shop capacity	800	800	800	800	800	800	800	800	800	800	800	800
Painting capacity	400	400	400	400	400	400	200	200	200	600	600	600
Production capacity	400	400	400	400	400	400	200	200	200	600	600	600
Total units made and sold	400	400	400	400	375	310	200	200	200	450	600	600
Retail units made and sold	100	105	95	115	75	60	50	55	75	150	290	350
Dealer units made and sold	300	295	305	285	300	250	150	145	125	300	310	250

The general form can be applied to Oxford Tole Art:

Production capacity = Minimum (shop capacity, painting capacity, supplies capacity)

Remember that for Oxford Tole Art,

Total demand = Retail demand + Dealer demand

In Oxford Tole Art's case, the production capacity is the minimum of the long-term capacity (the productive capacity of the shop), the intermediate-term capacity (the painting capacity provided by hiring artists), and the short-term capacity (the capacity provided by the short-term acquisition of materials). For example, in August the retail demand is 55 units and the dealer demand is 325 units, totaling 380 units. The shop capacity is 800 units, and the painting capacity is 200 units. Therefore, production capacity, which is the minimum of the shop capacity and painting capacity, is 200 units. Planned production and sales of 200 units represents the minimum of total demand (380 units) and production capacity (200 units).

The Financial Plans

Once the planners have developed the production, staffing, and capacity plans, they can prepare a financial summary of the tentative operating plans. The financial results for Oxford Tole Art implied by the production plan developed in Exhibit 10-7 appear in the following exhibits:

- Exhibit 10-8 presents the cash flows expected from the production and sales plan.
- Exhibits 10-9 and 10-10 summarize the projected balance sheet and income statement, respectively, expected as a result of the production and sales plans. (These are examples of the elements in boxes 11 and 12 in Exhibit 10-3.)

Planners use the projected balance sheet as an overall evaluation of the net effect of operating and financing decisions during the budget period and the income statement as an overall test of the profitability of the planners' proposed activities. To keep it simple, this example ignores taxes. Taxes are part of the budgeting and cash flow estimation process of all organizations.

Exhibit 10-8
Oxford Tole Art Cash Flow Forecast 2006

CASH INFLOWS	JAN.	FEB.	MARCH	APRIL	MAY	JUNE	JULY	AUG.	SEPT.	OCT.	NOV.	DEC.
Retail sales	$8,000	$8,400	$7,600	$9,200	$6,000	$4,800	$4,000	$4,400	$6,000	$12,000	$23,200	$28,000
Dealer collections												
1 month	$2,887	$4,950	$4,868	$5,033	$4,703	$4,950	$4,125	$2,475	$2,392	$2,062	$4,950	$5,115
2 months	10,519	4,331	7,425	7,301	7,549	7,054	7,425	6,188	3,713	3,589	3,094	7,425
3 months	5,610	4,675	1,925	3,300	3,245	3,355	3,135	3,300	2,750	1,650	1,595	1,375
Total cash inflows	$27,016	$22,356	$21,818	$24,834	$21,497	$20,159	$18,685	$16,363	$14,855	$19,301	$32,839	$41,915
Cash outflows												
Flexible resources:												
Buoys	$900	$900	$900	$900	$844	$698	$450	$450	$450	$1,013	$1,350	$1,350
Paint costs	1,260	1,260	1,260	1,260	1,181	977	630	630	630	1,418	1,890	1,890
Other manufacturing costs	1,100	1,100	1,100	1,100	1,031	853	550	550	550	1,238	1,650	1,650
Packing costs	780	780	780	780	731	605	390	390	390	878	1,170	1,170
Shipping costs	3,000	3,000	3,000	3,000	2,813	2,325	1,500	1,500	1,500	3,375	4,500	4,500
Committed resources:												
Painters' salaries	$4,000	$4,000	$4,000	$4,000	$4,000	$4,000	$2,000	$2,000	$2,000	$6,000	$6,000	$6,000
Shop rent	4,800	0	0	4,800	0	0	4,800	0	0	4,800	0	0
Manager's salary	2,500	2,500	2,500	2,500	2,500	2,500	2,500	2,500	2,500	2,500	2,500	2,500
Other shop costs	1,667	1,667	1,667	1,667	1,667	1,667	1,667	1,667	1,667	1,667	1,667	1,667
Advertising costs	3,333	3,333	3,333	3,333	3,333	3,333	3,333	3,333	3,333	3,333	3,333	3,333
Interest paid	0	163	127	95	81	48	17	208	177	160	231	145
Total cash outflows	$23,340	$18,703	$18,667	$23,435	$18,181	$17,006	$17,837	$13,228	$13,197	$26,382	$24,291	$24,205
Net operating cash flow this month	**$3,676**	**$3,653**	**$3,151**	**$1,399**	**$3,316**	**$3,153**	**$848**	**$3,135**	**$1,658**	**$−7,081**	**$8,548**	**$17,710**
Financing operations												
Opening cash	$5,000	$5,000	$5,000	$5,000	$5,000	$5,000	$5,000	$5,000	$5,000	$5,000	$5,000	$5,000
Cash withdrawn	−20,000	0	0	0	0	0	−20,000	0	0	0	0	0
Cash available	−11,324	8,653	8,151	6,399	8,315	8,155	−14,152	8,134	6,658	−2,079	13,548	22,710
Opening loan	0	16,324	12,671	9,520	8,121	4,806	1,652	20,803	17,669	16,010	23,089	14,541
Borrowing made	16,324	0	0	0	0	0	19,152	0	0	7,079	0	0
Borrowing repaid	0	3,653	3,151	1,399	3,315	3,155	0	3,134	1,658	0	8,548	14,541
Ending loan	16,324	12,671	9,520	8,121	4,806	1,652	20,803	17,669	16,010	23,089	14,541	0
Ending cash	$5,000	$5,000	$5,000	$5,000	$5,000	$5,000	$5,000	$5,000	$5,000	$5,000	$5,000	$8,168

Exhibit 10-9
Oxford Tole Art
Projected Balance
Sheet December
31, 2006

Cash	$8,168		
Accounts receivable	27,445	Owner's equity	$35,613
Total assets	$35,613	Total liabilities and owner's equity	$35,613

Exhibit 10-10
Oxford Tole Art
Projected Income
Statement
December 31,
2006

Revenue		$279,134
Flexible resources expenses:		
Buoys	$10,204	
Paint	14,285	
Other suppliers	12,471	
Packing	8,843	
Shipping	34,013	$79,816
Contribution margin		$199,318
Committed resource expenses:		
Painters' salaries	$48,000	
Shop rent	19,200	
Other shop costs	20,000	
Manager's salary	30,000	117,200
Other expenses:		
Advertising	$40,000	
Interest paid	1,452	41,452
Net income		$40,666

Understanding the Cash Flow Statement

The cash flow statement in Exhibit 10-8 is organized into three sections:

1. *Cash inflows* from retail cash sales and collections of dealer receivables.
2. *Cash outflows* for flexible resources that are acquired and consumed in the short term (buoys, paint, other supplies, packing, and shipping) and cash outflows for capacity resources that are acquired and consumed in the intermediate term and long term (painters, shop rent, manager's salary, other shop costs, interest paid, and advertising costs). The difference between cash inflows from revenues and cash outflows from expenditures is called the net cash flows from operations.
3. *Results of financing operations.*

For each month, the format of the cash flow statement is as follows:

Cash inflows − Cash outflows = Net cash flow

In January, for example, ending cash was as follows:

Ending cash = Operating cash flow + Opening cash + Effects of financing operations
= $3,676 + $5,000 + [−$20,000 + $16,324] = $5,000

To understand the derivation of the numbers in Oxford Tole Art's cash flow statement, study the numbers for July to ensure that you can follow the calculations.

Cash Inflows Section

Recall that the pattern of collections at Oxford Tole Art is as follows:

1. Retail orders are paid for with the order at a retail price per unit of $80.
2. Sales to dealers for $55 per unit are on account with a typical collection pattern being 30% in the month following the sale, 45% in the second month following the sale, 20% in the third month following the sale, and 5% never collected.

Therefore, in July, Oxford Tole Art will collect (1) all the retail sales for July, (2) 30% of the dealer sales from June, (3) 45% of the dealer sales from May, and (4) 20% of the dealer sales from April. Exhibit 10-11 summarizes these July collections.

Cash Outflows Section

Exhibit 10-12 summarizes the cash outflow numbers for July. Since Oxford Tole Art pays cash for flexible resources, this equation applies for each flexible resource purchased:

$$\text{Cash outflow} = \text{Units of flexible resource purchased} \times \text{Price per unit of flexible resource}$$

For expenditures on capacity resources—that is, resources acquired in the intermediate or longterm—the following equation applies for each resource:

$$\text{Cash outflow} = \text{This month's expenditure for that capacity resource}$$

Exhibit 10-11
Oxford Tole Art: Summary of Cash Collections, July 2006

ITEM	CALCULATION
Retail sales from July (see Exhibit 10-7)	50 × $80 = $4,000
30% of June dealer sales*	30% × 250 × $55 = 4,125
45% of May dealer sales	45% × 300 × $55 = 7,425
20% of April dealer sales	20% × 285 × $55 = 3,135
Total	$18,685

*Sales equals units sold multiplied by the selling price of $55 per unit.

Exhibit 10-12
Oxford Tole Art: Cash Outflow Calculations, July 2006

ITEM	AMOUNT	FORMULA	CALCULATION
Flexible resources			
Buoy cost	$450	July production × Price per buoy	200 × $2.25
Paint cost	630	July production × Paint cost per buoy	200 × $3.15
Other supplies cost	550	July production × Other supplies cost per buoy	200 × $2.75
Packing costs	390	July sales × Packing cost per buoy	200 × $1.95
Shipping costs	1,500	July sales × Shipping cost per buoy	200 × $7.50
Committed resources:			
Painters' salaries	$2,000	Number of painters in July × Monthly salary	1 × $2,000
Shop rent	4,800	Units of capacity × Capacity cost per unit	800 × $6
Manager's salary	2,500	Annual salary ÷ 12	$30,000 ÷ 12
Other shop costs	1,667	Annual other costs ÷ 12	$20,000 ÷ 12
Interest paid	17	June ending loan balance × 1%	$1,652 × 1%
Advertising costs	3,333	Annual advertising ÷ 12	$40,000 ÷ 12

Exhibit 10-13
Format of
Financing Section
of Cash Flow
Statement

	Net cash flow from operations	848
+	Opening cash	15,000
±	Cash invested or withdrawn[*]	−20,000
±	Cash provided or used in issuing or retiring stock or debt	0
=	Cash available before short-term financing	−14,152
±	Cash used or provided by short-term financing	19,152
=	Ending Cash	5,000

[*]In the case of a private business such as Oxford Tole Art, this refers to the capital transactions by the owner.

Financing Section

The financing section of the cash flow statement summarizes the effects on cash of transactions that are not a part of the normal operating activities. This section includes the effects of issuing or retiring stock or debt and buying or selling capital assets. Exhibit 10-13 shows a common format used in the financing section of the cash flow statement with the corresponding numbers for July. Note that the format of the financing section of the cash flow statement is as follows:

Net operating cash flow + Opening cash ± Cash from financing activities
= Ending cash

The major sources and uses of cash in most organizations are (1) operations, (2) investments or withdrawals by the owner in an unincorporated organization, (3) long-term financing activities related to issuing or retiring stock or debt, and (4) short-term financing activities.

Short-term financing often involves obtaining a line of credit, secured or unsecured, with a financial institution. The line of credit allows an organization to borrow up to a specified amount at any time. The line of credit is secured if the organization has pledged an asset that the financial institution can seize if the borrower defaults on any of the bank's requirements. The financial institution sets a limit on the line of credit, and the borrower, in the example of Oxford Tole Art, pays the specified interest at specified periods, such as monthly, on the outstanding balance borrowed. See the ending loan row in Exhibit 10-8 and note that Oxford Tole Art's line of credit balance varies between $0 and $23,089 during the year, well within the limit of $50,000 that Gael negotiated with the bank.

The format of the financing section of the cash flow statement in Exhibit 10-8 for Oxford Tole Art does not follow the format used in Exhibit 10-13. The financing section of Oxford Tole Art's cash flow statement provides information about the line-of-credit balance. Many organizations include the line-of-credit information in the cash flow statement because financial statement readers should be aware of the limits that can potentially constrain operations.

Using the Financial Plans

Oxford Tole Art's cash flow statement, shown in Exhibit 10-8, contains a short-term financing plan that suggests that, if events unfold as expected, Oxford Tole Art's cash balance increases only modestly during the year because of the $40,000 withdrawal that Gael will make from the business. Therefore, the company will use its line-of-credit agreement heavily. It will be borrowing from the bank for 11 of the 12 months in the year.

Organizations can raise money from outsiders by borrowing from banks, issuing debt, or selling shares of equity. A cash flow forecast helps an organization identify if and when it will require external financing. The cash flow forecast also shows whether any projected cash shortage will be temporary or cyclical, which can be met by a line-of-credit arrangement, or whether it will be permanent, which would require either or all of a long-term loan from a bank, further investment by the current owners, or investment by new owners. Based on the information provided by the cash flow forecast, organizations can plan the appropriate mix of external financing to minimize the long-run cost of capital.

The projected income statement and balance sheet provide a general assessment of the operating efficiencies at Oxford Tole Art. If Gael feels that these projected results are unacceptable, she must take steps to change the organizational processes that create the unacceptable results. For example, if the employees consistently use more quantities of any factor of production than competitors use, such as paint, labor, or capacity, Gael should attempt to modify procedures and, therefore, resource use to be able to compete profitably with competitors.

Suppose April has studied the projected financial results in the initial budget plans and has decided that the 14.6% profit margin on sales ($40,666 ÷ $279,134 from Exhibit 10-10) is too low. April has reached this conclusion because Oxford Tole Art is in the craft industry, in which competitors often duplicate attractive products quickly, resulting in short periods of product profitability. After determining that this profit margin on sales is too low, the manager may develop a marketing program or a cost reduction program to improve the cost/revenue performance at Oxford Tole Art.

Using the Projected Results

The operating budgets, like the production plan, hiring plan, capital spending plan, and purchasing plan for materials and supplies, provide a framework for developing expectations about activity levels in the upcoming period. Planners also use the operating budgets to test the feasibility of production plans. As the budget period unfolds, production and operations schedulers will make more accurate forecasts and base their production commitments on them. Thus, planners use the budget information to accomplish the following:

1. *Identify broad resource requirements.* This helps develop plans to put needed resources in place. For example, April can use the activity forecast to plan when the organization will have to hire and train temporary help.
2. *Identify potential problems.* This helps to avoid problems or to deal with them systematically. For example, April can use the statement of operating cash flows to identify when the business will need short-term financing from its bank. This will help April negotiate with a bank lending officer for a line of credit that is both competitive and responsive to Oxford Tole Art's needs. The forecasted cash flows also will identify when the buoy business will generate cash that Gael can invest in other business opportunities.
3. *Compare projected operating and financial results.* These comparisons within an organization serve as a measure for comparison with the operating and financial results of competitors. Such a comparison to plan can be used as a test of the efficiency of the organization's operating processes. The differences between planned and actual costs at Oxford Tole Art will focus April's

attention on understanding whether the plans were unrealistic or whether the execution of a sound business plan was flawed. This signals the need for improved planning, better execution, or both.

WHAT-IF ANALYSIS

The cost volume profit analysis discussed in chapter 2 provided insights into how revenues, costs, and profits respond to changes in the quantity of product made and sold. However, that analysis assumed a constant product mix. Now, powerful desktop computers and electronic spreadsheet software make it possible to consider product mixes (and much more) so that managers can evaluate alternative strategies.

Using a computer for the budgeting process, managers can explore the effects of alternative marketing, production, and selling strategies. For example, at Oxford Tole Art, April may consider raising prices, opening a retail outlet, or using different employment strategies. Such alternative proposals can be evaluated in a what-if analysis.

April may ask, "What if I decrease prices on my retail products by 5% and then sales increase by 10%? What will happen to my profits?" The answer: Oxford Tole Art profits will fall from $40,666 to $39,103. (This revised profit number was found by inserting the revised price and demand schedule in the spreadsheet that was used to prepare the original budget figures.) Therefore, this proposed price adjustment is undesirable.

April may also wonder, "What if retail sales would increase by 50% if Oxford Tole Art opened a retail outlet that would cost $40,000 per year to operate (including all costs). The retail outlet orders would be shipped by courier to the customer's

In very competitive markets, competitors need to anticipate the actions of competitors. Organizations can explore the financial and operational implications of responding to competitor initiatives using what-if analysis.

Source: Richard Levine/Alamy Images.

address. What would happen to my profits?" In this case, Gael would use the same shop capacity; the painters hired in the year's four quarters would be three, two, two, and four, respectively; and projected profit would increase to $56,553.

The structure and information required to prepare the master budget can be used easily to provide the basis for what-if analysis. (It took only several seconds to answer April's questions using the spreadsheet developed to prepare the Oxford Tole Art cash flow forecast. This spreadsheet is available from this text's Web site for you to try what-if analysis on your own.)

Evaluating Decision-Making Alternatives

Suppose April is considering renting a machine to automatically sand the buoys and apply the primer coat. The capacity of the machine is 1,300 buoys per month. This machine will reduce the painting time per buoy from 0.8 to 0.5 hour but will increase other shop costs from $20,000 to $35,000. The reduction in painting time per buoy allows Oxford Tole Art to reduce the number of painters needed for any level of scheduled production.

Exhibit 10-14 shows the revised estimated income statement reflecting the rental of the sanding and priming machine. Renting this machine will increase projected net income from the original level of $40,666 to $57,490, a 41% increase of $16,824.

Sensitivity Analysis

What-if analysis is only as good as the model used to represent what is being evaluated. The model must be complete, it must reflect relationships accurately, and it must use accurate estimates. A model that is incomplete, fails to reflect relationships accurately, or uses unreasonable estimates will not provide good estimates of a plan's results. If the model is complete and reflects capacity, cost, and revenue relationships accurately, the remaining issue is the accuracy of the data used. Planners test planning

Exhibit 10-14
Oxford Tole Art:
Projected Income
Statement,
December 31,
2006

Revenue		$326,943
Flexible resources expenses:		
Buoys	$12,263	
Paint	17,168	
Other suppliers	14,988	
Packing	10,628	
Shipping	40,875	$95,920
Contribution margin		$231,023
Committed resource expenses:		
Painters' salaries	$48,000	
Shop rent	19,200	
Other Shop costs	35,000	
Manager's salary	30,000	132,200
Other Expenses:		
Advertising	$40,000	
Interest paid	1,332	41,332
Net income		$57,490

models by varying the model estimates. Suppose one machine represents a bottleneck for manufacturing operations. Then the productivity (output per hour) of that machine is a key estimate for the production plan. The production planner could test the effect of errors in the estimate of the machine's productivity on the production plan by varying the productivity number by 10% or 20% above and below the estimate used in the planning budget.

If small forecasting errors of an estimate used in the production plan change the plan, we say that the model is sensitive to that estimate. If the performance consequences (for example, profits) from a bad estimate are severe, planners may want to invest time and resources to improve the accuracy of their estimates. For example, suppose an organization has the production capacity to accept only one of two possible orders. Order 1 promises revenues of $1,000,000 and expected costs of $750,000. Order 2 promises revenues of $800,000 and has costs of $600,000. Based on this information, order 1—with an expected profit of $250,000—looks like a better prospect than order 2, which has a profit of $200,000. Note that the profit associated with order 1 is uncertain, while the profit associated with order 2 is certain. Suppose that, with further investigation, planners decide that the costs associated with order 1 could be anywhere between $720,000 and $780,000. This would not affect the decision because even if the worst costs are realized for order 1, profits will still be $220,000 and more than the $200,000 associated with order 2. However, if the costs associated with order 1 could be anywhere between $680,000 and $820,000, certain circumstances (when costs are more than $800,000) after the fact will have planners wishing they had accepted order 2. This is an example of sensitivity analysis.

Sensitivity analysis is the process of selectively varying a plan's or a budget's key estimates for the purpose of identifying over what range a decision option is preferred. In the preceding example, order 1 is preferred if its costs are $800,000 or less. Sensitivity analysis enables planners to identify the estimates that are critical for the decision under consideration. For example, the labor that Oxford Tole Art needs to make each product is an important factor in its planning budget. Small changes in the estimate of this factor, which is the key productive resource, produce large changes in the projected or planned profit. If Oxford Tole Art can develop a process or can redesign the product so that labor time needed to make a buoy would be reduced by 10%, from 0.8 to 0.72 hour per buoy, projected profit would increase 31% from $40,666 to $53,229. This is a signal to April that designing and running the manufacturing process so that the artists can work as efficiently as possible are critical to the success of her business.

COMPARING ACTUAL AND PLANNED RESULTS

To understand results, such as production and financial outcomes, organizations use variance analysis to compare planned or budgeted results in the master budget with actual results.

Variance Analysis

Budgets are prepared for specific periods so that managers can compare actual results for the period with the planned results for that period. **Variance analysis** has many forms and can result in complex measures, but, as shown in Exhibit 10-15, its

Exhibit 10-15
Comparison of
Actual Cost to
Budgeted Cost
to Identify the
Variance

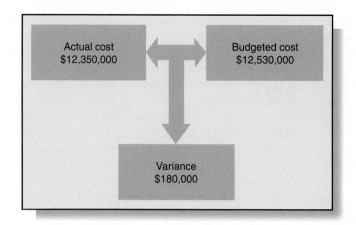

basis is very simple—an actual cost or actual revenue amount is compared with a target cost or target revenue amount to identify the difference, which accountants call a **variance**. For example, the accountant might compute the cost of labor that went into making an aircraft and compare that cost with the planned cost of labor for making that aircraft. A variance represents a departure from what was budgeted or planned. What caused the variance and the size of a variance will trigger an investigation to determine its cause and what should be done to correct that variance.

Budgeted, or planned, costs can come from three sources:

1. *Standards established by industrial engineers*, such as cost of steel that should go into an automobile door based on the door's specifications
2. *Previous period's performance*, such as the average cost of steel per door that was made in the last budget period
3. *A performance level achieved by a competitor*—usually called a *benchmark* and based on best-in-class results—such as the cost of steel per comparable door achieved by a competitor who is viewed as the most efficient

The financial numbers used in variance analysis for flexible resources are the product of a price and a quantity component:

Planned, or budgeted, amount = Standard price per unit × Budgeted quantity

while

Actual amount = Actual price per unit × Actual quantity

Variance analysis explains the difference between planned costs and actual costs by evaluating differences between standard prices and actual prices and budgeted quantities and actual quantities. Accountants focus separately on prices and quantities because in most organizations one department or division is responsible for the acquisition (thereby determining the actual price) of a resource and a different department uses (thereby determining the quantity of) the resource.

A variance is a signal that is part of a control system for monitoring results, and thus variances provide a signal that operations did not go as planned. Supervisory personnel use variances as overall checks on how well the people who are managing day-to-day operations are doing what they should be doing. When compared to the performance of other organizations engaged in comparable tasks, variances show the effectiveness of the control systems that operations people are using.

Basic Variance Analysis

Variance analysis helps managers understand the source of the differences—the variances—between actual costs and budgeted costs. If managers learn that specific actions they took on some jobs helped lower the actual costs of these jobs, they can pursue further cost savings by repeating those actions on similar jobs in the future. If they can identify the factors causing actual costs to be higher than expected, managers may be able to take the necessary actions to prevent those factors from recurring in the future. If they learn that cost changes are likely to be permanent, they can update their cost information when bidding for future jobs.

We will now study a specific example that illustrates the nature and role of variances.

Canning Cellular Services

Canning Cellular Services (CCS) is a national provider of cellular phone services. Cellular services are highly competitive, and, as in any competitive industry, CCS depends on cost control to be profitable. For this reason CCS has undertaken a major study of its costs to understand the behavior of its costs and to provide a continuing basis for cost reduction. The two major costs in the cellular business are equipment costs and personnel costs.

As part of its effort to control personnel costs, CCS has documented in euros (€) the costs associated with connecting a new customer and estimated it to be €95.50. Exhibit 10-16 reports the results of the study, which identified three relevant costs: direct materials costs, direct labor costs, and support costs.

The *direct materials costs* relate to the welcoming package provided to each new customer. This package defines the range and nature of the various cellular services offered by CCS.

The *direct labor costs* include two components: One is the cost of the salesperson, who describes the various services available and writes up the sales contract. On average, the salesperson spends 0.5 hour with each new customer and is paid €25 per hour. The other component is the cost of the sales staff employees who activate new cellular telephones by calling the control center and providing electronic

Exhibit 10-16
Canning Cellular Services: Total Cost per Activated Customer

	UNIT	COST/UNIT	TOTAL COST
Direct material:			
Welcoming package	1.00	€25.00	€25.00
Direct labor:			
Sales staff	0.50	25.00	12.50
Technical staff	0.25	40.00	10.00
Support cost:			
Data processing	0.20	15.00	3.00
System activation	0.15	300.00	45.00
Total cost per activated customer			€95.50

serial numbers and such customer-related information as names, addresses, and payment details. This requires 0.25 hour of time per phone, and sales staff are paid €40 per hour.

The support costs are comprised of two components. One is the salaries of the data processing staff who enter customer-related information into the CCS customer database. This information is used for billing and advertising purposes. On average, it takes 0.20 hour to enter the information for each customer, and the data processing clerks are paid €15 per hour. The other component is the system activation cost. This includes the cost of the computing and data processing systems that support the process of entering each new customer into the system and activating the customer on the system. On average, the activation process takes 0.15 hour on the computer, and the cost of computer time is estimated at €300 per hour.

Based on these cost estimates and the projected addition of 1 million new customers during fiscal 2006, CCS developed the estimate of costs for the upcoming year (see Exhibit 10-17.)

The document summarizing these costs—variously referred to as budgeted costs, estimated costs, projected costs, target costs, or forecasted costs, but all identify the same costs—is called the *master budget*. Note that the budgeted costs of €95,500,000 depend on the following:

1. The projected volume of activity, which in this example is 1 million customers
2. The standards for the quantity of each of the budgeted items
3. The standards for the cost per unit of each of the budgeted items

If any of these items differ from the forecasted amount, the actual total costs will differ from the master budget total.

First-Level Variances

Several weeks after the 2006 year end, the company comptroller forwarded to the manager of new customer accounts the summary shown in Exhibit 10-18, which displays the first-level variances for different cost items. The first-level variance for a cost item is the difference between the actual costs and the budget or planned costs for that cost item. By convention, variances are computed by subtracting budget costs from actual costs. Therefore, variances are "favorable," or "F," if the actual costs are less than estimated master budget costs—that is, if the variance is negative. "Unfavorable," or "U," variances arise when actual costs exceed estimated budget costs—that is, when the variance is positive. In this example, the first-level cost variance for sales staff, for example, is €2,350,000 unfavorable.

Exhibit 10-17
Canning Cellular Services; Master Budget

	Units/Customer Use	Cost/Unit	Total Cost
Direct material:			
Welcoming package	1.00	€25.00	€25,000,000
Direct labor:			
Sales staff	0.50	25.00	12,500,000
Technical staff	0.25	40.00	10,000,000
Support cost:			
Data processing	0.20	15.00	3,000,000
System activation	0.15	300.00	45,000,000
Total customer-related costs			€95,500,000

Exhibit 10-18
Canning Cellular Services: Summary of First-Level Variances

	MASTER BUDGET	ACTUAL COSTS	DIFFERENCE
Direct material:			
Welcoming package	€25,000,000	€29,700,000	€4,700,000
Direct labor:			
Sales staff	12,500,000	14,850,000	2,350,000
Technical staff	10,000,000	10,890,000	890,000
Support cost:			
Data processing	3,000,000	3,960,000	960,000
System activation	45,000,000	42,900,000	−2,100,000
Total customer-related costs	€95,500,000	€102,300,000	€6,800,000

Sharon Mackenzie, the manager of new customer accounts, was surprised by the report because she had directed her staff to undertake specific initiatives related to employee training and equipment improvement, both intended to reduce costs. Not only had costs not decreased, but they had increased by €6,800,000, which was significant. There was no explanation in this exhibit to help Sharon understand what went wrong. Therefore, Sharon demanded an explanation for why costs had not decreased following the cost-cutting initiatives.

Decomposing the Variances

Following up on Sharon's demand, the financial group prepared Exhibit 10-19 and forwarded it to her. Fred Liang, the CCS comptroller, explained to Sharon that Exhibit 10-19 uses a **flexible budget**, in which the forecast in the master budget is adjusted for the difference between planned volume and actual volume. Therefore, the flexible budget reflects a cost budget or forecast based on the level of volume that is actually achieved rather than the planned volume—and it is the planned volume that underlies the master budget. Fred referred Sharon to Exhibit 10-19, which provides the details of the flexible budget calculations. A cost difference between a

Exhibit 10-19
Canning Cellular Services: Master Budget, Flexible Budget, and Actual Results Summary

	MASTER BUDGET 1,000,000			FLEXIBLE BUDGET 1,100,000			ACTUAL RESULTS 1,100,00		
	U/C	COST	TOTAL	U/C	COST	TOTAL	U/C	COST	TOTAL
Direct material:									
Welcoming package	1.00	€25.00	€25,000,000	1.00	€25.00	€27,500,000	1.00	€27.00	€29,700,000
Direct labor:									
Sales staff	0.50	25.00	12,500,000	0.50	25.00	13,750,000	0.45	30.00	14,850,000
Technical staff	0.25	40.00	10,000,000	0.25	40.00	11,000,000	0.22	45.00	10,890,000
Support cost:									
Data processing	0.20	15.00	3,000,000	0.20	15.00	3,300,000	0.24	15.00	3,960,000
System activation	0.15	300.00	45,000,000	0.15	300.00	49,500,000	0.12	325.00	42,900,000
Total customer-related costs			€95,500,000			€105,050,000			€102,300,000

master budget and flexible budget is a planning variance because it reflects the difference between planned activity and actual activity. Planning variances arise entirely because the planned volume of activity was not realized. Therefore, based on the result that 1.1 million new customers were added instead of the planned 1 million, the projected, or budgeted, level of costs is now €105,050,000.

Sharon immediately noted three facts in Exhibit 10-19:

1. The number of actual customers exceeded the number of customers used to forecast costs.
2. The actual unit cost of four of the five items in the budget exceeded the standard unit cost used to develop the forecast.
3. The per-unit use of both labor items and one of the two support costs was lower, reflecting the results of the process improvements that Sharon had commissioned. The per-unit use of the other support item was higher, but only because midway through the year Sharon had developed a more comprehensive form that required more input for new customers.

Sharon asked the finance group to isolate the effects of these various price and use variances.

Planning and Flexible Budget Variances

In response, the finance group provided Sharon with the additional information shown in Exhibit 10-20. Fred explained that the differences between the flexible budget and the actual results—the flexible budget variances—reflect variances from the budget level of costs adjusted for the actual level of activity. He further explained that since the flexible budget identifies the budgeted level of costs for the activity levels achieved, Sharon's focus should be on these variances to determine whether the cost-cutting activities had been successful. Because the total flexible budget variance was −€2,750,000—a favorable variance—overall costs were lower than the budgeted costs for the achieved level of activity. Fred pointed out to Sharon that the planning variance and flexible budget variance are called second-level variances, which together add up to the first-level variance.

Sharon was pleased with this information but still concerned. She pointed out to Fred that these flexible budget variances reflect both quantity variances—the difference

Exhibit 10-20
Canning Cellular Services: Second-Level Variance Summary

	MASTER BUDGET	PLANNING VARIANCE	FLEXIBLE BUDGET	FLEXIBLE BUDGET VARIANCE	ACTUAL RESULTS
Direct material:					
Welcoming package	€25,000,000	€2,500,000	€27,500,000	€2,200,000	€29,700,000
Direct labor:					
Sales staff	12,500,000	1,250,000	13,750,000	1,100,000	14,850,000
Technical staff	10,000,000	1,000,000	11,000,000	−110,000	10,890,000
Support cost:					
Data processing	3,000,000	300,000	3,300,000	660,000	3,960,000
System activation	45,000,000	4,500,000	49,500,000	−6,600,000	42,900,000
Total customer-related costs	€95,500,000	€9,550,000	€105,050,000	€−2,750,000	€102,300,000

between the planned and the actual use rates per unit of output—and price variances—the difference between the planned and the actual price per unit of the various cost items. Sharon asked Fred to prepare an exhibit that would highlight the incremental effects of quantity differences and the incremental effects of price variances.

QUANTITY AND PRICE VARIANCES FOR MATERIAL AND LABOR

Direct material flexible budget variances and direct labor flexible budget variances can be decomposed further into efficiency variances—also called quantity variances—and rate variances—also called price variances. We can refer to these as third-level variances because together they explain the flexible budget component of the second-level variance. In Exhibit 10-20, the amount of direct materials used equals the volume of production achieved (1.1 million units produced, that is, customers served) multiplied by the actual use rate, which was 1, giving an actual quantity of direct materials use of 1.1 million. The flexible budget allowance is the volume of production achieved (1.1 million customers) multiplied by the planned or target quantity use rate, which was 1, giving a planned, or budgeted, quantity of direct materials of 1.1 million.

Material Quantity and Price Variances

The material quantity variance can be calculated from the following relationship:

$$\text{Quantity variance} = (AQ - SQ) \times SP$$
$$= (1,100,000 - 1,100,000) \text{ units} \times €25 \text{ per unit}$$
$$= 0$$

where

AQ = actual quantity of materials used
SQ = standard quantity of materials allowed for the production level achieved
SP = estimated or standard price of materials

The material price variance for direct materials is calculated using the following relationship:

$$\text{Price variance} = (AP - SP) \times AQ$$
$$= (€27 - €25) \text{ per unit} \times 1,100,000 \text{ units}$$
$$= €2,200,000 \text{ (Unfavorable)}$$

where

AP = actual price of materials
SP = estimated or standard price of materials
AQ = actual quantity of materials used

We have now decomposed the total variance for the cost of the welcoming package, which is the direct material in this example, into a material quantity variance and a material price variance. When we add these two third-level variances together (€0 + €2,200,000 U), we obtain the total flexible budget variance for direct materials (€2,200,000 U).

The logic of decomposing the variances is easily verified by adding together the algebraic formulas for material quantity and price variances. The sum of the decomposed variances is as follows:

$$\text{Sum of decomposed variances} = \text{Quantity variance} + \text{Price variance}$$
$$= [(AQ - SQ) \times SP] + [(AP - SP) \times AQ]$$
$$= (AQ \times SP) - (SQ \times SP)$$
$$+ (AP \times AQ) - (SP \times AQ)$$
$$= (AP \times AQ) - (SQ \times SP)$$
$$= \text{Actual cost} - \text{Budgeted cost}$$
$$= \text{Flexible budget variance}$$

What does this variance and its decomposition tell Sharon, who is the manager ultimately responsible for these costs? They tell her that the quantity used was consistent with the number of customers, no more and no less. They also tell her that the cost of €27 per unit exceeded the standard, or budgeted, cost of €25 per unit. Perhaps this cost increment reflected changes in the welcoming package or perhaps additional costs billed by the supplier. Given the magnitude of the variance—€2, or 8% of the target cost—Sharon would follow up to determine its cause. However, it is important to point out that as a good manager, Sharon might already be well aware of the variance and its cause and that the value of the variance analysis is to confirm its amount.

Material Quantity and Price Variances: A General Approach

Many people find that a graphical approach to variance analysis makes calculating variances easier. To implement the graphical approach, we need to define one more variable, PQ, the actual quantity of raw materials purchased. This additional variable allows one to handle situations where the amount of raw materials purchased

In factories where labor is a large component of total cost, management monitors labor use closely to identify opportunities for improving efficiency and to identify situations where more labor was used than planned.
Source: Jim Pickerell/The Stock Connection.

Exhibit 10-21
Materials Flexible
Budget Variance
Analysis

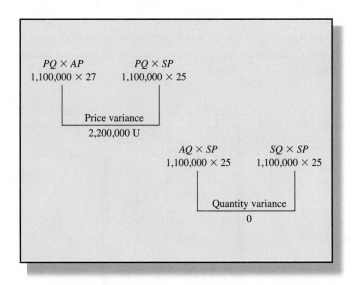

differs from the amount of raw materials used. Here are the terms that you will see in Exhibit 10-21:

Total Cost: The actual cost of the acquired raw materials = purchased quantity (PQ) × actual price (AP).
Price Adjusted Cost: The cost of acquired materials using the standard price = purchased quantity (PQ) × standard price (SP).
Price Adjusted Quantity: The cost of materials used using the standard price = quantity used (AQ) × standard price (SP).
Flexible Budget Cost: The cost of the standard quantity of materials = standard quantity (SQ) × standard price (SP).

Where the quantity acquired is the quantity used, as is the case in the CSS example, the price adjusted cost and the price adjusted quantity are equal.

Exhibit 10-21 shows the graph for the flexible budget materials variances, and Exhibit 10-22 shows another approach to represent these variances.

Efficiency and Wage Rate Variances for Direct Labor Costs

The labor cost variances are determined in a way similar to that described for material quantity and price variances. The formulas are as follows:

$$\text{Labor efficiency variance} = (AH - SH) \times SR$$
$$\text{Labor rate variance} = (AR - SR) \times AH$$

where

AH = actual number of direct labor hours
AR = actual wage rate
SH = number of direct labor hours allowed given the level of output achieved
SR = standard wage rate

Note that while it is common to use the terms *price* and *quantity* for the material variances, it is common to use the terms *rate* and *efficiency* for the comparable labor variances.

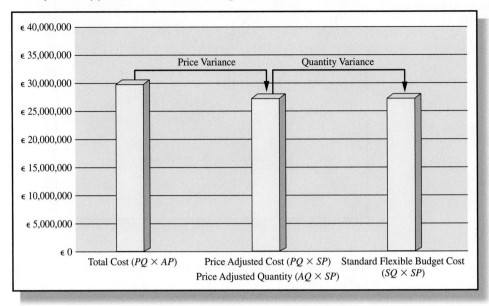

The total cost variance for labor is computed as follows:

Efficiency variance + Rate variance = $(AH - SH) \times SR + (AR - SR) \times AH$

$= (AH \times SR) - (SH \times SR) + (AR \times AH) - (SR \times AH)$

$= (AR \times AH) - (SR \times SH)$

= Actual cost − Budgeted cost

=Flexible budget variance

To compute the efficiency and rate variance for the sales staff, the total hours of sales staff used is 495,000 ($0.45 \times 1{,}100{,}000$ hours), and the total budgeted level of hours, given the achieved level of production, is 550,000 ($0.5 \times 1{,}100{,}000$ hours).

Therefore, the efficiency variance for sales staff labor cost is as follows:

Efficiency variance = $(AH - SH) \times SR$

$= (495{,}000 - 550{,}000) \times €25$

$= -€1{,}375{,}000$ (Favorable)

The efficiency efforts commissioned by Sharon evidently paid off in terms of fewer hours used of sales staff time than planned for the achieved level of income, resulting in cost savings of €1,375,000.

The price or rate variance for sales staff labor is as follows:

Rate variance = $(AR - SR) \times AH$

$= (€30 - €25)$ per hour $\times$ 495,000 hours

$= €2{,}475{,}000$ (Unfavorable)

In other words, for the number of hours worked, the sales staff was paid €2,475,000 more than was planned when the master budget was developed. This increase might reflect a corporate-wide wage adjustment that is beyond Sharon's control, or perhaps it reflects the hiring of more skilled and qualified sales staff that was responsible for the favorable efficiency variance. These facts would be established by an investigation, which would be triggered by a variance this size.

Exhibit 10-23 shows another way to show flexible resource variances visually. As required, the sum of the rate variance and the efficiency variance equals the total flexible budget variance for sales staff costs. Total flexible budget variance for sales staff cost = –€1,375,000 + €2,475,000 = €1,100,000 (Unfavorable)

Efficiency and Wage Rate Variances for Direct Labor Costs: A General Approach

Following are the terms we need to use the graphical approach to analyze the flexible budget variances for direct labor costs:

Total Cost: The actual cost of direct labor = actual labor hours (*AH*) × actual labor rate (*AR*).

Price Adjusted Quantity: The cost of direct labor quantity using the standard price = actual labor hours (*AH*) × standard labor rate (*SR*).

Flexible Budget Cost: The cost of the standard quantity of labor = standard labor hours (*SH*) × standard labor rate (*SR*).

Exhibit 10-24 shows the graph for the flexible budget labor variances, and Exhibit 10-25 shows another approach to representing these variances visually.

Detailed Analysis of Support Activity Cost Variances

What about support costs? Support costs can reflect variable, or fixed, costs. The quantity of fixed costs may not change from period to period, but the spending on them may fluctuate. Engineers can travel, take courses, vacation, quit, and be replaced with someone else. Thus, it is possible and desirable to monitor spending variances on capacity-related resources, even when one cannot monitor efficiency variances that will show up as changes in used and unused capacity.

Exhibit 10-23
Decomposing the Direct Labor Cost Variance

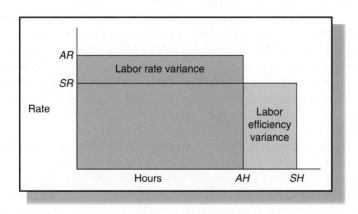

Exhibit 10-24
Direct Labor Flexible Budget Variance Analysis

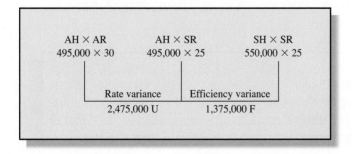

Exhibit 10-25
A Graphical Approach to Flexible Budget Labor Variance Analysis

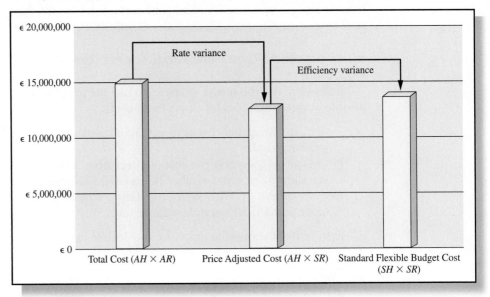

What about variable support costs? Such support costs reflect behind-the-scenes operations that are proportional to the volume of activity but are not directly a part of the product or service provided to the customer. For example, an indirect support cost in a factory would be the wages paid to employees who move work in process around the factory floor as the product is being made.

At CCS, these support costs reflect (1) the time and cost of the equipment and personnel who input customer data each time a new customer is added to the CCS customer file, and (2) the time and cost of equipment and personnel each time a new customer is activated on the computers that control access to the cellular system.

An investigation by Sharon revealed that the cost of the data processing staff had two components: a wage rate and a system access charge incurred when the data processor was accessing the system. These cost components are summarized in Exhibit 10-26.

The actual hourly clerical wage is €10, and for each hour the clerk works, the database is, on average, accessed for 0.1 hour. The system access fee is €50. This yields a total cost of €15 per data processing clerk hour. When an aggregate rate per hour is constructed in this way, the rate variance will reflect both the amount and the cost of the components used to compute the rate. With this understanding of how the rate was computed for a flexible support item, cost analysis can be used to investigate the variance associated with a support cost item.

Exhibit 10-26
Canning Cellular Services: Clerical Budgeted Cost per Hour

	UNITS	RATE	TOTAL
Clerical wage	1	€10.00	€10.00
Computer access time	0.1	50.00	5.00
Total cost per hour			€15.00

Exhibit 10-27
Canning Cellular
Services Technical
Staff Budgeted
Hourly Cost
Calculation

	Units	Rate	Total
Technical staff	1	€40.00	€40.00
Computer access time	0.5	520.00	€260.00
Total cost per hour			€300.00

Exhibit 10-28
Canning Cellular
Services Actual
Calculation of
Technical Staff
Cost per Hour

	Units	Rate	Total
Technical staff	1	€55.00	€55.00
Computer access time	0.45	600.00	€270.00
Total cost per hour			€325.00

Exhibit 10-29
Canning Cellular Services

Analysis of System Activation Flexible Budget Variance	
Due to labor use	$[(1,100,000 \times 0.12 \times 1) - (1,100.000 \times 0.15 \times 1)] \times €40 = €1,320,000$ F
Due to labor rate	$1,100,000 \times 0.12 \times 1 \times (€55 - €40) = €1,980,000$ U
Due to additional computer use	$[(1,100,000 \times 0.12 \times 0.45) - (1,100,00 \times 0.15 \times 0.5)] \times €520 = €12,012,000$ F
Due to additional access rate	$1,100,000 \times 0.12 \times 0.45 \times (€600 - €520) = €4,752,000$ U

In view of the size of the variance associated with system activation costs, Sharon directed Fred to analyze its source. Exhibit 10-27 summarizes the calculation used to develop the €300 hourly charge for the hourly activation rate, which has two components. One component reflects the wage paid to the sales staff, which is €40 per hour. The other component is the system access fee, which is charged at the rate of €520 per hour of access. On average, the sales staff accesses the activation system for half an hour for each hour worked, yielding the blended rate of €300 per hour, which was used in developing the budget.

Investigation yielded the information in Exhibit 10-28 to explain the actual access fee. Note that the actual rate differs from the budget rate for three reasons: (1) The wage paid to the sales staff was €15 higher than the budgeted rate, (2) the computer access time per hour worked by sales staff was lower than budgeted, and (3) the rate for computer access time was higher than budgeted.

These three elements, combined with the data in Exhibit 10-19, allow Fred to develop the information in Exhibit 10-29, which explains the total flexible budget variance for system activation support costs.

SALES VARIANCES

We have studied how management accountants factor cost variances into different components in order to signal to management where costs deviated from the plan or target amounts. What about revenues? To illustrate a common approach to variance analysis for sales, consider Danny's Bagel Barn.

In the food industry, organizations pay for raw materials such as meat, fish, or vegetables that are processed into salable products. A commonly used variance used in these industries is the yield variance, which is the ratio of the weight or value of product produced to the weight or value of raw materials purchased. In professional services industries, such as accounting, consulting, or law firms, managers often evaluate performance using a labor yield variance, which is the ratio of the value or amount of hours charged to clients to the value or amount of hours paid. In both the materials and labor cases, the idea is to monitor how well the organization is using a major component of total costs.

Source: Alamy Images.

Danny sells three types of bagels: regular, superior, and deluxe, which are priced at $0.40, $0.55, and $0.70, respectively. Exhibit 10-30 displays the sales budget that Danny prepared for July.

During July, Danny experienced intense sales competition from Maggie's Bagel Factory on his regular and superior bagel lines. Danny cut his prices for those two lines. Even with the price cut, Danny sold fewer regular bagels than planned. However, the price cut on the superior bagels resulted in higher than planned sales. Exhibit 10-31 summarizes the July results.

Danny notes that revenues where $550 higher than planned ($10,650 − $10,100) and would like to know how the price changes and volume changes each contributed to this difference between planned and actual results.

Exhibit 10-30
Danny's Bagel Barn Planned Sales for July

| | PRODUCTS | | | | | | |
| | REGULAR | | SUPERIOR | | DELUXE | | |
	DATA	% TOTAL	DATA	% TOTAL	DATA	% TOTAL	TOTAL
Unit Price	$0.40		$0.55		$0.70		
Unit Sales	10,000	50.00%	6,000	30.00%	4,000	20.00%	$20,000
Total	$4,000		$3,300		$2,800		$10,100

Exhibit 10-31
Danny's Bagel Barn Actual Sales for July

| | REGULAR | | SUPERIOR | | DELUXE | | |
	DATA	% TOTAL	DATA	% TOTAL	DATA	% TOTAL	TOTAL
Unit price	$0.35		$0.50		$0.80		
Unit sales	9,000	42.86%	7,000	33.33%	5,000	23.81%	21,000
Total	$3,150		$3,500		$4,000		$10,650

Management accountants undertake the reconciliation between actual and planned sales revenue in two steps. The first step isolates the effect of sales volume differences, and the second step isolates the effect of sales price differences.

Sales Volume Effects

In a firm with multiple products, volume-related revenue differences can arise in two ways:

1. Because the mix (the percentage of the total comprised of each product's sales) was different than planned. This is called the **sales mix variance**, and *for each product,* the sales mix variance is computed as follows:

   Actual total sales units of all products × (Actual sales mix percentage of this product − Planned sales mix percentage of this product) × Planned revenue per unit of this product

   Here is the sales mix variance for each of the products:

   Regular: 21,000 × (.4286 − .5000) × $0.40 = −$600 (unfavorable). (Note that now we are dealing with revenues, so a negative variance is unfavorable.) This means that because sales of the regular bagel made up less than the planned percentage of total sales, revenues of $600 were lost on this product.
   Superior: 21,000 × (.3333 − .3000) × $0.55 = $385 (favorable). This means that because sales of the superior bagel made up more than the planned percentage of total sales, revenues of $385 were gained on this product.
   Deluxe: 21,000 × (.2381 − .2000) × $0.70 = $560 (favorable). This means that because sales of the deluxe bagel made up more than the planned percentage of total sales, revenues of $560 were gained on this product.

2. Because the volume of sales was different than planned. This is called the **sales quantity variance** and *for each product,* the sales quantity variance is computed as follows:

   (Actual total sales units of all products − Planned total sales units of all products) × Planned sales mix percentage of this product × Planned revenue per unit of this product

   Here is the sales quantity variance for each of the products:

   Regular: (21,000 − 20,000) × .5000 × $0.40 = $200 (favorable). This means that because of the overall increase in sales, if the regular bagel's sales mix percentage had remained as planned, then an increase in sales revenues of $200 would have been realized on this product.

Superior: $(21{,}000 - 20000) \times .3000 \times \$0.55 = \$165$ (favorable). This means that because of the overall increase in sales, if the regular bagel's sales mix percentage had remained as planned, then an increase in sales revenues of $200 would have been realized on this product.

Deluxe: $(21{,}000 - 20{,}000) \times .2000 \times \$0.70 = \$140$ (favorable). This means that because of the overall increase in sales, if the regular bagel's sales mix percentage had remained as planned, then an increase in sales revenues of $140 would have been realized on this product.

Sales Price Effects

The sales volume and sales mix variances explain the difference between planned and actual revenues because of volume-related effects. What remains to consider is the effect on revenues of differences between actual and planned selling prices. This is the sales price variance.

For each product, the sales price variance is computed as follows:

$$\text{Actual number of units sold} \times (\text{Actual price per unit} - \text{Planned price per unit})$$

Here are the sales price variance calculations:

Regular: $9{,}000 \times (0.35 - .40) = -\$450$ (unfavorable). This means that because Danny was unable to sell the regular bagels at the planned price of $0.40 per unit, $450 of revenues were lost on the 9,000 units of sales.

Superior: $7{,}000 \times (.50 - .55) = -\$350$ (unfavorable). This means that because Danny was unable to sell the superior bagels at the planned price of $0.55 per unit, $350 of revenues were lost on the 7,000 units of sales.

Deluxe: $5{,}000 \times (.80 - .70) = \$500$ (favorable). This means that because Danny was able to sell the deluxe bagels at a price that exceeded the planned price of $0.70 per unit, $500 of revenues were gained on the 5,000 units of sales.

Exhibit 10-32 summarizes the sales variances for Danny's July operations. Note that, as required, the total of the variances equals the difference between the actual and planned revenues ($10,650 - $10,100).

Exhibit 10-32
Danny's Bagel
Barn Sales
Variance
Summary

	PRODUCTS			
	REGULAR	SUPERIOR	DELUXE	TOTAL
Price variance	−$450	−$350	$500	−$300
Sales mix variance	−600	385	560	345
Sales quantity variance	200	165	140	505
Total	−$850	$200	$1,200	$550

THE ROLE OF BUDGETING IN SERVICE AND NOT-FOR-PROFIT ORGANIZATIONS

We have focused on the role of budgeting in manufacturing organizations up to this point. Budgeting serves a slightly different but equally relevant role in natural resource companies, service organizations, and not-for-profit (NFP) organizations such as charitable organizations and government agencies. As in manufacturing organizations, budgeting helps nonmanufacturing organizations perform their planning function by coordinating and formalizing responsibilities and relationships and communicating the expected plans. Exhibit 10-33 summarizes the focus of the budgeting process in manufacturing, natural resource, service, and NFP organizations.

In the natural resources sector, the focus is on balancing demand with the availability of natural resources, such as minerals, fish, or wood. Because the natural resource supply often constrains sales, success requires managing the resource base effectively to match resource supply with potential demand.

In the service sector, the focus is on balancing demand and the organization's ability to provide services, which is determined by the level and mix of skills in the organization. Although the service sector often uses machines to deliver products to customers, most operations remain labor paced—that is, they operate at a pace dictated by their human operators. Therefore, people rather than machines usually represent the capacity constraint in the service sector. Planning in the service sector must consider the time needed to put skilled new people in place as sales increase. Planning is critical in high-skill organizations, such as in a consulting business, because people capacity is expensive and services cannot be inventoried when demand falls below capacity.

In NFP organizations, the focus of budgeting has been to balance revenues raised by taxes or donations with spending demands. In government agencies, planned cash outflows, or spending plans, are called appropriations. Appropriations set limits on a government agency's spending. Governments worldwide are facing increased pressures to eliminate deficits without raising tax revenues. Therefore, many governments are looking for ways to eliminate unnecessary expenditures and to make necessary expenditures more efficient rather than just ensuring that government agencies do not spend more than they have been authorized to spend. As part of the planning process, these agencies must establish priorities for their expenditures and improve the productivity with which they deliver services to constituents.

Periodic and Continuous Budgeting

The basic budgeting process described in this chapter involves many organizational design decisions, such as the length of the budget process, the basic budget spending assumptions, and the degree of top management control.

Exhibit 10-33
Focus of Budgeting in Different Organizations

ORGANIZATION TYPE	MAIN FOCUS OF BUDGETING PROCESS
Manufacturing	Sales and manufacturing activities
Natural resource	Sales, resource availability, and acquisition
Service	Sales activities and staffing requirements
NFP	Raising revenues and controlling expenditures

The budget process described for Oxford Tole Art is performed on an annual budget cycle or, generally, a periodic budget cycle. Gael, the owner, prepares budgets periodically for each planning period. Although planners may update or revise the budgets anytime during the budget period, periodic budgeting is typically performed once per budget period.

In a continuous budget cycle, as one budget period—usually a month or a quarter—passes, planners drop the current budget period from the master budget and add a future budget period in its place. Therefore, if Oxford Tole Art used continuous budgeting with a 1-year cycle, April would drop 1 month from the beginning of the budget period and add a month to the end of the budget period as each month passes, at the same time making any changes in the estimates of the original months 2 through 12 that appear appropriate given new information that arrived during period 1. For example, at the end of February 2006, April would drop February 2006 from the budget and add February 2007.

The length of the budget period used in continuous budgeting reflects the competitive forces, skill requirements, and technology changes that the organization faces. The budget period must be long enough for the organization to anticipate important environmental changes and adapt to them and yet short enough to ensure that estimates for the end of the period will be reasonable and realistic. Advocates of periodic budgeting argue that continuous budgeting takes too much time and effort and that periodic budgeting provides virtually the same benefits at a lower cost. Advocates of continuous budgeting argue that it keeps the organization planning and assessing and thinking strategically year-round rather than just once a year at budget time.

CONTROLLING DISCRETIONARY EXPENDITURES

Organizations use three general approaches to budget discretionary expenditures for items such as spending on research and development:

1. Incremental budgeting
2. Zero-based budgeting
3. Project funding

Each has benefits relative to the others.

Incremental Budgeting

Incremental budgeting bases a period's expenditure level for a discretionary item on the amount spent for that item during the previous period. If the total budget for discretionary items increases by 10%, each discretionary item is allowed to increase 10%. This basic model has variations. For example, if the total spending on all discretionary items is allowed to increase by 10%, all discretionary spending may experience an across-the-board increase of 5%, and the remaining 5% increase in total spending may be allocated to discretionary items based on merit, such as a high level of performance on an existing project that can be expanded, or based on need, such as a promising new project.

Some people have criticized incremental budgeting because it does not require justification of the organization's goals for discretionary expenditures. Incremental budgeting includes no provision to reduce or eliminate expenditures as the organization changes, nor does it have a mechanism to provide disproportionate support to discretionary items that will yield substantial benefits.

Zero-Based Budgeting

Zero-based budgeting (ZBB) requires that proponents of discretionary expenditures continuously justify every expenditure. (Note: ZZB is inappropriate for budgeting costs that vary in proportion to production, such as the amount of wood used in a furniture factory, since by their nature they are inevitable once the manufacturing decision is made.) For each planning period, in ZBB, the starting point for each budget line item is zero.

ZBB arose, in part, to combat indiscriminate incremental budgets, which are based on a percentage adjustment of the previous period's budget. Because incremental budgeting requires very little thought, it often results in misallocation of resources. Proponents also proposed ZBB to control projects that, once activated, take on a life of their own and resist going out of existence, such as a government department that is created for one purpose and is not disbanded when that purpose has been achieved or is no longer required.

Under ZBB, planners allocate the organization's scarce resources to the spending proposals they think will best achieve the organization's goals. While this seems logical, the zero-based approach to planning discretionary expenditures is controversial. This approach to project budgeting has been used primarily to assess government expenditures. In profit-seeking organizations, ZBB has been applied only to discretionary expenditures, such as research and development, advertising, and employee training.

Traditionally, ZBB ideas do not apply to engineered costs—that is, short-term costs that have an identifiable relationship with some activity level. Engineered costs are controlled by measuring and using reports of the amounts of resources consumed by operating activities and by the cost variances described earlier. However, even for engineered costs, ZBB could be effective when combined with the reengineering approach. For example, reengineering a product or process involves developing a vision of how a product should perform or how a process should work independently of current conditions. It is possible to use ZBB as a tool to provide baseline costs to new products or processes.

Project Funding

Critics of ZBB complain that it is expensive because it requires so much employee time to prepare. These critics have proposed an intermediate solution between the two extremes of ZBB and incremental budgeting to mitigate the disadvantages of each. The intermediate solution is called *project funding* and is a proposal for discretionary expenditures with a specific time horizon or sunset provision. Projects with indefinite lives, which are sometimes called *programs*, should be continuously reviewed to ensure that they are living up to their intended purposes.

Advocates of discretionary expenditures state their requests as project proposals that include project duration and cost for each period during a project's life. Planners approve no discretionary spending for projects that have indeterminate lengths or indeterminate spending amounts. If the planners approve the project, they agree to provide the level of support requested in the plan. Requests to extend or modify the project must be approved separately. The advantage of providing sunset provisions is that they strike a balance between the high cost resulting from the need for close scrutiny and continuous justification provided by ZBB and the much lower cost of incremental budgeting.

EXTENDING THE FLEXIBLE BUDGETING PROCESS: ACTIVITY-BASED BUDGETING

A recent approach to budgeting is activity-based budgeting, which is based on activity-based costing (chapter 4). Activity-based budgeting uses knowledge about the relationships between the quantity of production units and the activities required to produce those units to develop detailed estimates of activity requirements underlying the proposed production plan. The two main benefits of activity-based budgeting are (1) that it identifies situations when production plans require new capacity—both physical capacity and capacity in people resources—to deliver much of the support and service activities in organizations, and (2) that it provides a more accurate way to project future costs.

The following simple example illustrates the insights provided by activity-based budgeting. Paris Packing Components manufactures three products. Exhibit 10-34 summarizes the revenue, variable cost, and capacity consumption data for each of the three products.

For example, each unit of product A consumes four activity units in moving, eight activity units in fabricating, and three activity units in assembly.

Exhibit 10-35 summarizes expectations regarding total revenues, variable costs, and capacity consumption given the production plan for the upcoming period, which is to produce 6,000 units of product A, 4,000 units of product B, and 5,000 units of product C. The activity information not only allows a projection of the production cost that will be allocated to production (the actual cost incurred, which will be the budgeted amount, will equal the total units of capacity for each capacity resource multiplied by its rate) but also projects the demand on capacity for the production plan. If any of the proposed uses of capacity of the current production plan exceeds the capacity available, the organization will have to either take steps to expand capacity or find a production plan whose capacity use does not exceed availability.

Exhibit 10-34
Paris Packing Components: Product Line Summary

	PRODUCT A		PRODUCT B		PRODUCT C	
	UNITS	$/UNIT	UNITS	$/UNIT	UNITS	$/UNIT
Revenue		$1,900		$2,500		$2,600
Variable costs:						
Materials		$125		$140		$210
Components		230		260		290
Supplies		35		40		60
Shipping		60		70		110
Contribution margin		$1,450		$1,990		$1,930
Support activities and costs:						
Moving at $35	4	$140	6	$210	9	$315
Fabricating at $110	8	880	7	770	9	990
Assembly at $85	3	$255	9	765	6	510
Unit profit contribution		$175		$245		$115

Exhibit 10-35
Paris Packing Components: Master Budget

	PRODUCT A		PRODUCT B		PRODUCT C	
	UNITS	$	UNITS	$	UNITS	$
Revenue	6,000	$11,400,000	4,000	$10,000,000	5,000	$13,000,000
Variable costs:						
Materials		$750,000		$560,000		$1,050,000
Components		1,380,000		1,040,000		1,450,000
Supplies		210,000		160,000		300,000
Shipping		360,000		280,000		550,000
Contribution margin		$8,700,000		$7,960,000		$9,650,000
Support activities and costs:						
Moving at $35	24,000	$840,000	24,000	$840,000	45,000	$1,575,000
Fabricating at $110	48,000	5,280,000	28,000	3,080,000	45,000	4,950,000
Assembly at $85	18,000	1,530,000	36,000	3,060,000	30,000	2,550,000
Total profit contribution		$1,050,000		$980,000		$575,000

MANAGING THE BUDGETING PROCESS

Who should manage and oversee the budgeting process? Many organizations use a budget team, headed by the organization's budget director, sometimes the controller or the chief financial officer, to coordinate the budgeting process. The budget team usually reports to a budget committee, which generally includes the chief executive officer, the chief operating officer, and the senior executive vice president. The composition of the budget committee reflects the role of the budget as the planning document that reflects and relates to the organization's strategy and objectives. The danger of using a budget committee is that it may signal to other employees that budgeting is something relevant only for senior management. Senior management must take steps to ensure that the organization members affected by the budget do not perceive the budget and the budgeting process to be beyond their control or responsibility.

BEHAVIORAL ASPECTS OF BUDGETING

Because of the human factor involved in the entire process, budgets often do not develop in a smooth, frictionless manner. How do people try to affect the budget, and, in turn, how do budgets affect people's behavior? These questions have led social scientists to undertake extensive studies about the human factors involved in budgeting.

Whether developing a family budget, a budget for a small company like Oxford Tole Art, or a budget for a major multinational company, it is important to be aware that the ways in which people interact with budgets are essentially the same. This section presents two related behavioral issues in budgeting:

1. *Designing the budget process:* How should budgets be determined, who should be involved in the budgeting process, and at what level of difficulty should the

budget be set to have the greatest positive influence on people's motivation and performance?

2. *Influencing the budget process:* How do people try to influence or manipulate the budget to their own ends?

Designing the Budget Process

Where do the data that planners use to prepare the master budget and supporting plans come from? How should budgets be determined, and who should be involved in the budgeting process?

Three common methods of setting budgets are authoritative, participative, and consultative.

Authoritative Budgeting

Authoritative budgeting occurs when a superior informs subordinates what their budget will be without requesting input. The benefit to the organization is that the process is straightforward and efficient—it allows superiors to assign budgets and promotes overall coordination among subunits in the organization because it is done from a single perspective. Managers who want to impose a budget in a top-down manner often want control and have authoritarian aspects to their personalities. One disadvantage of imposing budgets is that superiors usually have less information about the process being budgeted than the subordinate. In authoritative budgeting situations, the superior indicates the goals to the subordinates and subordinates who have high aspirations for the coming year regarding new goals may become frustrated and debilitated. A second problem is the lack of motivation and commitment to the budgeted goals because of the lack of employee participation in establishing the budget. Worse yet, if the superior sets high goals and provides only a small budget for resource spending, motivation can decrease significantly, and individuals and the organization can fail to attain their goals.

Research shows that the most motivating types of budgets are those that are tight, that is, those with targets that are perceived as ambitious but attainable. Companies such as Boeing and General Electric have implemented what are known as *stretch targets*. In the past, both companies used an incremental approach in which targets from the previous year were increased slightly. Stretch targets exceed previous targets by a significant amount and usually require an enormous increase in a goal over the next budgeting period. *Stretch budgeting* means that the organization will try to reach much higher goals with the current budget. The rationale is that stretch targets push an organization to its limits. The thinking is that only in this manner will companies completely reevaluate the ways in which they develop and produce products and services. While some employees thrive in this type of environment, the pace of work and the difficulty of achieving stretch targets can frustrate many and cause others to quit their jobs. Further, whereas employees may be able to push themselves very hard to meet the stretch target in the short run, they may not be able to sustain a high level of effort in every subsequent period. Organizations need to make sure that they provide resources and a plan so that employees believe that stretch targets are achievable.

Participative Budgeting

Participative budgeting is an approach to budget setting that uses a joint decision-making process in which all parties agree about setting the budget targets. Allowing employees to participate in decision making provides an opportunity for them to use information that they develop through their training or experience on the job to jointly set their goals and negotiate the level of their budgets. Participation has many benefits for employees, such as greater feelings of commitment to the budget and, therefore, a higher level of motivation to attain goals and keep within the budget. Research on participative budgeting has shown that employees generally feel greater job satisfaction and higher morale because they feel greater control over their jobs. In some instances, higher levels of performance can result. Allowing participation offers an additional benefit for management because it often induces subordinates to reveal their private information, reveals data about how well they can perform their jobs, or allows the introduction of new ideas that may help improve existing processes. As a result of discussing the budget jointly, subordinates indirectly reveal this information and their level of aspiration to management. It then can be incorporated into the planning process.

Consultative Budgeting

Consultative budgeting occurs when managers ask subordinates to discuss their ideas about the budget but no joint decision making occurs. Instead, the superior solicits the subordinates' ideas and determines the final budget alone. For many large organizations in which complete participation is impractical, consultation is the norm. A variant of the consultative form of budgeting may occur when subordinates believe their input will be used directly in setting the budget—even though their superior really has no intention of considering their input. This process is called pseudoparticipation and can have a debilitating effect on subordinates if they find out that the superior was insincere.

Influencing the Budget Process

Clearly, the budgeting process is neither simple nor mechanical. It highlights the need for interactions about resource allocation, organizational goals, and human motivation and performance. In large organizations, as in families, budgets represent the outcomes of negotiations among individuals. Some individuals will do all they can to increase the size of their budgets because they believe a large budget is a symbol of power and control.

Although the budget is used as a tool for planning, coordinating, and resource allocation, it also serves to measure performance and serves ultimately to control and influence behavior. In addition, many managers have their incentive compensation tied directly to budget and goal attainment. When incentives and compensation are tied to the budget, some managers engage in behavior that is dysfunctional to their organizations. Managers have been known to play budgeting games in which they attempt to manipulate information and targets to achieve as high a bonus as possible. One well-known way that managers engage in budgeting games is through the participation process.

Participation has provided employees the opportunity to affect their budgets in ways that may not always be in the best interests of the organization. For example, subordinates might ask for more resources than they need to accomplish their budget objectives. This results in a misallocation of resources for the organization as a whole. Another risk is that subordinates will distort information by claiming that they are not as efficient or effective at what they do as they really are, thereby attempting to lower management's expectations of their performance. Subordinates may want some additional cushion in performance requirements in case there is an unforeseen change in the work environment that detrimentally affects resources or impairs their ability to meet the budget. If subordinates succeed in this type of negotiation, they will find it easy to meet or exceed their budgeted objectives. Again the organization suffers because it is not obtaining the most accurate information available to assess and thereby improve its operations. Both these acts—requiring excess resources and distorting performance information—fall under the heading of creating **budget slack**.

Consider a manager who is worried that a supplier will be unwilling to sell raw materials at a historically budgeted price. The manager may decide to increase the allowance requested for purchasing raw materials, which would build slack into this budget line item. The request leads to the assignment of excess resources for this purpose and, hence, fewer resources for other purposes. Other distortions can arise from arbitrary increases in resource requests because the resulting established standard costs for products will be incorrect. Further, subordinates are also concerned about standards or budgets that are too difficult to attain: If their bonuses are based on attaining a budget, they will opt for an easier budget. To counter the problem of low target setting, management may design an incentive system that provides higher levels of bonuses based on attaining higher targets.

Budgeting games can never be eliminated, although some organizations have devised methods to decrease the amount of budget slack. They can use an iterative process to formulate the budget, for example, developing a very lengthy budgeting cycle that may last as long as a year. Then subordinate managers submit a preliminary budget, which is modified by senior management and sent back to subordinate managers for modification. The modifications usually require justification in painful detail for each line item. This process continues for several iterations until senior managers are convinced that they have eliminated as much slack as possible from the subordinate manager's budget. The other benefit of this approach is that by the time both parties agree to the budget, everyone has developed a strong commitment to it. This commitment gives everybody involved the confidence that they can achieve their goals for the coming year.

Criticisms of the Traditional Budgeting Model: The Beyond Budgeting Roundtable

A number of organizations—for example, the Beyond Budgeting Roundtable at CAM-I (Computer Aided Manufacturing International)—and people have been very critical of the traditional budgeting process described in this chapter. These critics argue that the traditional budgeting process does the following:

1. Reflects a top-down approach to organizing that is inconsistent with the need to be flexible and adapt to changing organization circumstances
2. Focuses on controls (such as meeting the target budget) rather than focusing on helping the organization achieve its strategic objectives
3. Causes resource allocations to be driven by politics rather than strategy—that is, political power in the organization drives resource allocations rather than the strategic needs that drive traditional budgeting

As an alternative, these critics make a number of proposals including the following:

1. Using traditional budgeting to plan the resource requirements implied by production plans
2. Tying budgeting to strategic initiatives by including provisions for strategic expenditures, such as new product development, employee training, and process improvements in budgets

3. Abandoning the use of variances to assess performance and using variances instead to identify the need for process improvements
4. Using multidimensional performance measures, such as those in the balanced scorecard, to evaluate the performance of individuals or units on the basis of their contribution to the organization's ability to achieve strategic results, such as quality improvements, lowered costs, and improved customer service

EPILOGUE TO THE FINANCING CRISIS IN MOUNT PLEASANT

Sandra, the mayor of Mount Pleasant, instructed Shawn Dawson, the senior analyst in the finance group, to develop a budget that reflected the nature and type of costs facing the municipality. The result is shown in Exhibit 10-36. The projected shortfall was $200 million ($2.7 billion – $2.5 billion), and Shawn's role was to identify ways to eliminate this projected shortfall.

Shawn began by identifying the revenue elements and cost elements in the municipal budget. After a detailed investigation, each cost element was divided into three groups:

- *Committed costs*, which were costs that were contractually committed and could neither be reduced nor varied. These costs totaled $2,340,630,000.
- *Discretionary costs*, which were costs that could be reduced by eliminating the programs or activities that created them. These costs totaled $294,570,000.
- *Reengineering or redesign program costs with a costreduction potential*, which totaled $64,800,000 and had, on average, a 2-year payback period—that is, their costs would be recovered in 2 years by the savings they generated. Therefore, the net effect in the current year of implementing these costreduction programs would be to increase cash outflows by $64,800,000.

Armed with this analysis, Shawn had an informal meeting with most of the members of the city council. Since the costreduction activities would create additional costs before their savings were realized, it was evident to Shawn that the immediate problem was to choose which discretionary expenditures would have to be cut in the short run, and he communicated this to the council members. The council members were strongly divided not only about which programs to cut but also about the principle of whether any programs should be cut.

The councilors agreed that tax increases on residential properties were out of the question. Residential property taxes were above the average for comparable communities, and earlier election promises indicated no increases for at least 3 years. The councilors agreed to a modest increase in business taxes because these taxes were below the average for communities with comparable services to businesses. In addition, a study of licenses issued for construction and new retail businesses indicated that there would be a natural increase in business taxes resulting from planned expansions that would come online in the next year. The result was that the forecast for business tax collections was increased by 5%, or $25 million.

The councilors instructed Shawn and his group to look into increasing revenues from user fees and from the municipally owned power company. Shawn's senior analyst, Karen Brown, indicated that a moderate price increase was possible and would generate about $30 million in additional revenues. Moreover, the utility could sell off excess equipment, which would generate cash inflows of about $10 million.

These changes would cover the short-run costs of the cost-reduction programs, leaving the benefits to be enjoyed in future years. This left Shawn to resolve the original $200 million deficit.

Exhibit 10-36
Mount Pleasant: Budget Analysis

REVENUES			
Property taxes	50%		$1,250,000,000
Business taxes	20%		500,000,000
User fees	20%		500,000,000
Grants	10%		250,000,000
Total			2,500,000,000
EXPENDITURES			
Education	60%		1,620,000,000
Committed	85%	$1,377,000,000	
Discretionary	12%	194,400,000	
Cost reduction potential	3%	48,600,000	
Policing and fire services	20%		540,000,000
Committed	90%	486,000,000	
Discretionary	8%	43,200,000	
Cost reduction potential	2%	10,800,000	
Recreation	5%		135,000,000
Committed	77%	103,950,000	
Discretionary	22%	29,700,000	
Cost reduction potential	1%	1,350,000	
Dept servicing	4%		108,000,000
Committed	100%	108,000,000	
Discretionary	0%	0	
Cost reduction potential	0%	0	
Transit	3%		81,000,000
Committed	94%	76,140,000	
Discretionary	5%	4,050,000	
Cost reduction potential	1%	810,000	
Road maintanance	2%		54,000,000
Committed	72%	38,880,000	
Discretionary	27%	14,580,000	
Cost reduction potential	1%	540,000	
Garbage collection	2%		54,000,000
Committed	96%	51,840,000	
Discretionary	1%	540,000	
Cost reduction potential	3%	1,620,000	
Library	1%		27,000,000
Committed	75%	20,250,000	
Discretionary	24%	6,480,000	
Cost reduction potential	1%	270,000	
Other services	3%		81,000,000
Committed	97%	78,570,000	
Discretionary	2%	1,620,000	
Cost reduction potential	1%	810,000	
Total			2,700,000,000
Total committed costs	$2,340,630,000		
Total discretionary costs	$294,570,000		
Total committed and discretionary	$2,635,200,000		
Cost reduction potential	$64,800,000		
Total costs	$2,700,000,000		

Recognizing that the current budget numbers were projections of the costs incurred in the most recent 2 years—a form of incremental budgeting—Shawn instructed his staff to study those costs. The following facts emerged:

1. Police and fire expenditures had been significantly higher in the past 2 years because of major capital expenditures. Like most municipalities, Mount Pleasant did its accounting on a cash flow basis rather than an accrual basis. This analysis suggested that projected expenditures for police and fire services were likely overstated by $30 million. There was no evidence that this type of effect on costs was evident in any other expenditure class.

2. Following the rule of thumb to look for opportunities to reduce costs in the area where most expenditures were made, Shawn studied the education budget. This study confirmed what Shawn already suspected: The cost per student enrolled in the public school system in Mount Pleasant was significantly higher than in any comparable community. Through modest increases in class size and the creation of split campuses at two schools, Shawn identified savings of about $60 million.

Finally, Shawn's staff investigated the federal government grant proposal. Analysis suggested that there had been significant underpayments of these grants, which were based on legislation. The town's solicitor indicated that these underpayments were between $20 million and $30 million. Shawn took the midpoint of $25 million as his estimate of what was owed.

Shawn was still about $85 million short of his cost-reduction target ($200 million − $30 million − $60 million − $25 million) and concluded that there were no more cost savings possible from scrutinizing current operations or recasting projections. Shawn advised the city council that the next step would have to be either to reconsider raising residential taxes or to start cutting into discretionary expenditures. The proposal to increase residential tax expenditures was again flatly rejected, and the council was preparing to debate which discretionary expenditures would be eliminated.

In this regard, the council approved a motion that Shawn hire a consultant to survey community attitudes concerning which programs to eliminate. A consensus quickly developed to eliminate several programs whose costs totaled $55 million, leaving $30 million of cost cuts on the table.

The council now turned to the political process of deciding which discretionary programs would be eliminated to achieve these target cuts. Shawn was told that the council wanted to use ZBB to prioritize the discretionary cost spending in order to target the remaining cost cuts.

SUMMARY

This chapter discussed how organizations use budgets to plan what they are going to do during a budget period—which is usually 1 year—to allocate resources to various projects, and to monitor progress toward achieving financial objectives.

We saw that there are two types of budgets: operating budgets describe the various activities (for example, hiring people, acquiring machinery and raw materials, producing, and distributing) that the organization plans to undertake during the budget period, while financial budgets describe the expected financial consequences (in particular, cash flows and expected profits) of those planned activities.

Budgeting, the process of preparing budgets, allows the organization to evaluate whether prospective plans are feasible and have the potential to achieve the organization's objectives. When done properly, budgeting coordinates activities toward achieving the organization's objectives and provides a means of involving organization members in the budgeting process and through this involvement increasing employee commitment to achieving the budget objectives.

Oxford Tole Art: Buoy Division provided an extended illustration of the budgeting process and showed how organizations commit to and budget for variable costs (such as raw materials and paint) and short- and long- term fixed costs (such as painters and production facilities).

The chapter discussed what-if analysis, a modeling tool that explores the effects on scheduled activities and financial results as key assumptions (such as employee productivity, materials costs, or product prices) are changed. We saw that what-if analysis allows decision makers to determine how sensitive plans are to the underlying assumptions, which, in turn, may suggest either contingency planning or additional investment to make estimates more accurate.

The chapter described variance analysis—which involves comparing actual results to planned results and, when the variance (the difference between the planned and actual results) is deemed significant, undertaking an investigation to determine its cause. In this sense, a variance is like a warning signal—it signals that someone was not as expected but not what or why—that requires investigation.

The chapter discussed some different approaches to the traditional budgeting model illustrated by Oxford Tole Art. Whereas periodic budgeting involves developing a budget for each budget period, continuous budgeting involves rolling the budget forward each month. So, for example, as January of this year is completed, a budget for January of next year is added to the budget. In this way the budget period is continuously maintained.

A common approach to budgeting, often found in governments, is incremental budgeting. In this approach, this year's budget is based on an incremental adjustment of last year's budget. For example, each budget unit is told to increase sales by 10% or to cut costs by 5%. Most students of budgeting consider this approach to be practical but ineffectual since it does not recognize the specific and differential opportunities facing different units in the organization. For example, one division may face a mature and declining market for its products and find it difficult to maintain let alone increase its sales, while another product division may be competing in an expanding market where sales increases come relatively easily. Asking both divisions to increase sales by 10% does not reflect the differential opportunities facing the two divisions.

Accountants monitor and evaluate discretionary expenditures (such as advertising, research and development, and employee training) differently than expenditures that are tied to and driven by acquisition, production, and distribution activities where activity measures and outcomes are readily measured. Because it is very difficult to measure the outcome of discretionary expenditures (for example, how do we measure the effect on profits of advertising), accountants usually control these expenditures through spending budgets that are often tied to sales (for example, research and development will be 5% of sales). As we saw, this type of control does not evaluate whether the money is being well spent, and accountants continue to search for ways to measure the benefits of discretionary expenditures.

Because budgets are developed and implemented through people, we must consider the effects that budgets and budgeting have on people and how people affect budgets and budgeting. Research suggests that involving those subject to budgets in the budgeting process increases their commitment to the budget if people believe that they are contributing to the setting of targets and standards. In this regard, research also suggests that stretch targets, which are targets deemed difficult but achievable by the people subject to the target, are the most effective in motivating performance levels.

Finally, the chapter considered some alternatives to, and complaints about, traditional budgeting. The concern is that organizations often prepare budgets slavishly and then tie performance to achieving budgeted performance. Some people believe that this approach inhibits both organization flexibility and innovation (better to achieve the budget than be innovative by redirecting funds to another project). In summary, most organizations continue to use some form of budgeting to plan, allocate resources, and coordinate organization activities. There are well-known limitations associated with budgeting that continue to be addressed by modifications, such as those described in this summary and in the chapter, to the traditional budgeting model.

KEY TERMS

ASSIGNMENT MATERIALS

Questions

10-1 What is a budget? (LO 1)

10-2 What is the difference between flexible and capacity-related resources? (LO 1)

10-3 A student develops a spending plan for a school semester. Is this budgeting? Why? (LO 1)

10-4 How does a family's budget differ from a budget developed for an organization? (LO 1)

10-5 What is a production plan? Give an example of one in a courier company. (LO 2, 3)

10-6 What is the difference between operating and financial budgets? (LO 3)

10-7 Would a labor hiring and training plan be more important in a university that is hiring faculty members, or a municipal government office that hires casual workers to do unskilled work? Why? (LO 2,3)

10-8 What is the relationship between a demand forecast and a sales plan? (LO 4)

10-9 What is a demand forecast? Why is it relevant in budgeting? (LO 4)

10-10 Is employee training an example of a discretionary expenditure? Why? (LO 4)

10-11 What does a capital spending plan do? (LO 4)

10-12 What is an example of a capacity-related expenditure? (LO 4)

10-13 Are food costs in a university residence cafeteria a variable cost or a capacity-related fixed cost? Briefly explain. (LO 4)

10-14 Are materials always a flexible resource? Why? (LO 4)

10-15 What is a line of credit? How is it useful to a small organization? (LO 4)

10-16 What are three broad uses for budget information? (LO 4)

10-17 What are the similarities and differences between what-if and sensitivity analysis? (LO 5)

10-18 What is a variance? How is a dashboard warning light that indicates low oil pressure like a variance? (LO 6)

10-19 How does analysis of reasons for variances between actual and estimated costs help managers? (LO 6)

10-20 What is a flexible budget? (LO 6)

10-21 How are first, second, and third levels of variance analysis related? (LO 6)

10-22 Why is it useful to decompose a flexible budget variance into a price variance and an efficiency (quantity) variance? (LO 6)

10-23 "If more experienced workers work on the job than planned in developing the labor standards, the labor efficiency variance is likely to be favorable, but the labor rate variance is likely to be unfavorable." Do you agree with this statement? Explain. (LO 6)

10-24 What effect will the purchase and use of cheaper, lower-quality materials likely have on price and quantity (efficiency) components of both materials and labor variances? (LO 6)

10-25 What two steps are taken to reconcile the difference between actual and planned sales revenue? (LO 6)

10-26 What is an appropriation? Give an example of one in a university. (LO 7)

10-27 What is a periodic budget? (LO 4)

10-28 You are planning your expenditures for the upcoming school semester. You assume that this year's expenditures will equal last year's plus 2%. What approach to budgeting are you using? (LO 4)

10-29 You are willing to donate to worthy organizations. However, you believe strongly that each request for a donation should be evaluated on the basis of its own merits. You would not feel bad in any year if you donated nothing. What approach to budgeting are you using? (LO 4)

10-30 What are the two interrelated behavioral issues in budgeting? (LO 8)

10-31 What are the three most common methods of setting the budget? (LO 8)

10-32 What is the most motivating type of budget with respect to targets? (LO 8)

10-33 What is a stretch target? (LO 8)

10-34 What is budget slack? (LO 8)

10-35 What are some criticisms of the traditional budgeting model? (LO 1, 4)

Exercises

LO 2, 3 **10-36** *Budgeting information* Consider a company that sells prescription drugs. It has salespeople who visit doctors and hospitals to encourage physicians to prescribe its drugs. The company sells to drugstores. Salespeople are evaluated based on the sales in their territories. For each, income is a salary plus a bonus if actual sales exceed planned sales. To plan operations, this company needs to develop estimates of total sales. Where should it get this information?

LO 1, 4, 8 **10-37** *Budgeting and planning* Some people say that budgets are great for planning but not for control. What do you think they mean? Do you agree with this sentiment? Explain.

LO 1, 4, 7 **10-38** *Budgeting: types of resources in a university* For a university, identify a cost that you think is controllable in the short term and explain why. Identify a cost that you think is controllable in the intermediate term and explain why. Identify a cost that you think is controllable in the long term and explain why. What does this cost structure imply about the university's flexibility in responding to changing student demands and enrollment?

LO 1, 2, 3, 4 **10-39** *Financial budgets* Many managers consider the pro forma financial statements to be the most important product of the master budgeting process. Why do you think they believe this?

LO 1, 2, 4, 7 **10-40** *Consulting company: types of resources* Budgeting allows an organization to identify broad resource requirements so that it can develop plans to put needed resources in place. Use an example to illustrate why this might be valuable in a consulting company that provides advice to clients.

LO 1, 2, 3, 4 **10-41** *Canning company: budgeting process* Budgeting allows an organization to identify potential problems so that plans can be developed to avoid these problems or to deal with them systematically. Give an example of how budgeting might serve this role in a company that buys vegetables and cans them.

LO 3, 4 **10-42** *Financial budgets: cash flows* Monthly cash budgets of inflows and outflows are an important part of the budgeting process in most organizations. In the course of preparing a cash budget, the organization must estimate its cash inflows from credit sales. Suppose that in response to projected cash shortfalls, the organization decides to speed its collections of credit sales. What effect can this have on the organization?

LO 1, 3, 4 **10-43** *Machine shop: comparing financial and operational results* Budgeting allows an organization to compare its projected operating and financial results with those of competitors as a general test of the efficiency of the organization's operating processes. Explain how this might be valuable for a machine shop that does custom machining work for its customers.

LO 5 **10-44** *What-if-analysis* Jeren Company is considering replacing its existing cutting machine with a new machine that will help reduce its defect rate. Relevant information for the two machines includes the following:

COST ITEM	EXISTING MACHINE	NEW MACHINE
Monthly fixed costs	$32,000	$40,000
Variable cost per unit	$44	$40
Sales price per unit	$55	$55

Required

a. Determine the sales level, in number of units, at which the costs are the same for both machines.
b. Determine the sales level in dollars at which the use of the new machine results in a 10% profit on sales (profit/sales) ratio.

LO 2, 3, 5 **10-45** *Sensitivity analysis* Sensitivity analysis is an important component of any budgeting exercise. Which estimates do you think will be most crucial in developing a master budget? Why?

LO 5, 7 **10-46** *Sensitivity analysis: cost cutting* A university faced with a deficit reacts by cutting resource allocations to all faculties and departments by 8%. Do you think this is a good approach to budgeting? Why?

LO 6 **10-47** *Variance analysis, material, and labor* The following information is available for Mandalay Company:

Actual	
Materials:	12,000 pounds purchased at $2.50 per pound; used 10,500 pounds
Direct labor:	1,800 hours at $12 per hour
Units produced:	500
Standard	
Materials:	20 pounds per unit at a price of $2.20 per pound
Direct labor:	4 hours per unit at a wage rate of $10 per hour

Required

a. Determine the material price variance and material quantity variance.
b. Determine the direct labor rate variance and direct labor efficiency variance.

LO 6 **10-48** *Variance analysis, material and labor* Pharout Company uses a standard cost system. Job 822 is for the manufacturing of 500 units of the product P521. The company's standards for one unit of product P521 are as follows:

QUANTITY		PRICE
Direct material	5 ounces	$2 per ounce
Direct labor	2 hours	$10 per hour

The job required 2,800 ounces of raw material costing $5,880. An unfavorable labor rate variance of $250 and a favorable labor efficiency variance of $100 also were determined for this job.

Required

a. Determine the direct material price variance for job 822 based on the actual quantity of materials used.
b. Determine the direct material quantity variance for job 822 based on the actual quantity of materials used.
c. Determine the actual quantity of direct labor hours used on job 822 based on the actual quantity of materials used.
d. Determine the actual labor costs incurred for job 822.

10-49 *Variance analysis, material and labor*   Each unit of job Y703 has standard requirements of 5 pounds of raw material at a price of $100 per pound and 0.5 hour of direct labor at $12 per hour. To produce 9,000 units of this product, job Y703 actually required 40,000 pounds of the raw material costing $97 per pound. The job used a total of 5,000 direct labor hours costing a total of $60,000.

Required

a. Determine the material price and material quantity variances for job Y703.
b. Assume that the materials used on this job were purchased from a new supplier. Would you recommend continuing with this new supplier? Why or why not?
c. Determine the direct labor rate and direct labor efficiency variances.

10-50 *Standard costs versus actual costs for materials*   Assembly of product P13 requires one unit of component X, two units of component Y, and three units of component Z. Job J372 produced 220 units of P13. The following information pertains to material variances for this job, analyzed by component:

	COMPONENT		
	X	Y	Z
Price variance	160 U	120 F	192 U
Quantity variance	168 U	100 U	84 F

The actual material prices were $0.30 more, $0.20 less, and $0.50 more per unit for components X, Y, and Z, respectively, than their standard material prices per unit.

Required

a. Determine the number of materials units consumed of each type of component.
b. Determine the standard materials price per unit of each type of component.

10-51 *Master and flexible budgets*   An organization plans to make a product in batches of 25,000 units. Planned production is 1,000,000 units, and actual production is 1,125,000 units. What are the planned (master budget) number of batches and the flexible budget number of batches?

10-52 *Method of designing the budget*   How does participation in the budgeting process differ from consultation?

10-53 *Budget slack*   What are the pros and cons of building slack into the budget from (1) the point of view of the employee building in slack, and (2) from a senior manager's point of view?

10-54 *Budgeting games*   What are budgeting games, and why do employees engage in them?

Problems

10-55 *Operating budgets: production plan*   Borders Manufacturing is developing a sales and production plan as part of its master budgeting process. Following are the projected monthly sales, which occur uniformly during each month, for the upcoming year:

Borders Manufacturing
Projected Monthly Sales

Month	Unit Sales
January	8,742
February	9,415
March	7,120
April	8,181
May	7,942
June	9,681
July	2,511
August	2,768
September	2,768
October	2,283
November	1,542
December	1,980
January	8,725

Production for each month equals one-half of the current month's sales plus one-half of the next month's projected sales. Develop the production plan for Borders Manufacturing for the upcoming year.

LO 2, 3, 4 **10-56 *Operating budgets: labor hiring and production plan*** Mira Vista Planters provides reforestation services to large paper products companies. It must hire one planter for every 10,000 trees that it has contracted to plant each month. New employees are hired in the month needed, on the first day of the month. An employee must receive 1 week of evaluation and training before being profitably employed and therefore works three out of four weeks in the month hired. For every five prospective employees who enter training, three are deemed suitable for employment. When cutbacks occur, employees are laid off on the first day of the month. Every employee laid off receives severance pay equal to 1 week's salary, which is on average $400, regardless of how long the layoff will last. Laid-off employees inevitably drift away, and new hires must be trained.

The company has been offered the following contracts for the upcoming year. Each monthly contract is offered on an accept or reject basis; that is, if a monthly contract is accepted, it must be completed in full. Partial completion is not acceptable. The revenue per tree planted is $0.20.

Mira Vista Planters
Monthly Tree Planting Contracts

Month	Trees
January	8,692
February	5,765
March	8,134
April	34,400
May	558,729
June	832,251
July	1,286,700
August	895,449
September	733,094
October	203,525
November	29,410
December	9,827

Required

Prepare a labor plan for the upcoming year, indicating the following for each month:

a. Whether you feel the company should accept or reject the proposed planting contract.

b. How many people will be hired for training. (Recall that an employee is not available for planting during the week of training and that only three of the five employees accepted for training can be hired.)

c. How many people will be laid off. The organization will have two trained employees on January 1.

LO 2, 3, 4   **10-57** *Operating budgets: materials purchasing plan*   Pasadena Chemical Company manufactures a wide range of chemical compounds. One of the most difficult compounds is a cleaning solvent made from an expensive and volatile raw material, tetrax, that is often in short supply. The company uses 1 liter of tetrax for every 100 liters of cleaning solvent it makes.

Tetrax costs $560 per liter and must be stored in space leased in a special warehouse. The storage cost including all related costs is $2 per liter per day stored. The chemical is unstable, and the loss on average is 1% of the volume stored per day. The cleaning compound can also be made from monax, which costs $1,000 per liter. Because of the prohibitive cost of monax, however, Pasadena avoids using it unless it is absolutely necessary.

The three existing tetrax suppliers have been unreliable. For this reason, Pasadena has refused to begin production of the cleaning compound. Recently, a new supplier joined the field and guarantees the supply of tetrax under three conditions: (1) Customers must be prepared to take weekly deliveries of tetrax, (2) the weekly order must be for precisely the same quantity each week, and (3) the contract must cover 1 year. If these conditions are met, the supplier will replace any undelivered tetrax with monax.

Because the cleaning compound itself is also volatile, users demand the product when they are ready for it and no sooner. Suppliers carefully estimate the amount of cleaner they require and will not accept less than the ordered amount.

Following are the contracted cleaning compound sales for next year:

Pasadena Chemical Company
Cleaning Solvent Product

MONTH	UNIT SALES	MONTH	UNIT SALES
January	41,203	July	41,889
February	48,077	August	42,107
March	53,646	September	47,488
April	60,038	October	49,638
May	46,332	November	49,942
June	50,508	December	37,593

Required

a. Set up a spreadsheet for this problem. The spreadsheet should allow you to compute the total cost of a contract with the new supplier. This total cost includes purchase price, storage cost, and the cost, if necessary, of any monax that would be purchased. Set up the spreadsheet to allow you to easily vary the purchase quantity of tetrax. To simplify the problem, make the following assumptions:

- The loss each month is 1% times the number of days in the month times the sum of (1) the average of the opening and ending inventory (before the loss), and (2) one-half the batch size.
- The cost of carrying inventory each month is two times the number of days in the month times the sum of (1) the average of opening and closing inventory (after the loss), and (2) one-half the batch size.
- Production takes place 7 days per week.
- January, March, July, and November have 35 days each; the rest of the months of the year have 28 days each.

b. What is the best weekly quantity to contract for purchase from the new supplier?

LO 2, 3, 7   **10-58**   *Operating budgets: labor hiring plan*   Strathfield Motel is planning its operations for the upcoming tourist season. The motel has 60 units. The following table presents the average number of daily rentals expected for each of the 12 weeks of the tourist season.

     The motel hires housekeeping staff on a weekly basis. Each person can clean 15 rooms per day. Employees must be hired for the entire week at a wage of $400 per employee per week. Because of the motel's location in a midsize city, trained people are always available to work on short notice.

     The motel does not own its linen and towels but rents them from a rental agency in a nearby city. The rental contract must be signed for a 4-week period and for a fixed amount of linen and towels. Therefore, the motel must sign three contracts for the 12-week tourist season. The contract provides the linen required for each room for $3 per night.

Strathfield Motel
Average Number of Daily Rentals

WEEK	AVERAGE UNITS RENTED	WEEK	AVERAGE UNITS RENTED
1	46	7	55
2	48	8	55
3	54	9	50
4	60	10	45
5	60	11	37
6	60	12	30

Required

Prepare a weekly budget for the hotel showing the following:
a. The number of housekeeping staff to employ
b. The number of linen and towel units to contract

LO 2,3   **10-59**   *Financial budgets: expense budget*   During the school year, the Homebush School band arranges concert dates in many communities. Because only part of the school's travel expenses are covered by the concert admission fees, the band raises money to help defray its operating expenses through events in the local community such as car washes.

     To estimate its expenses for the upcoming year, the band's manager has estimated the number of concert dates for each of the school months, September through May. For each concert, the manager estimates hotel costs of $900, food costs of $480, bus rental costs of $600, and other costs of $200.

The following table presents the number of planned concerts during the upcoming year:

Homebush School Band
Scheduled Concerts

Month	Scheduled Concerts	Month	Scheduled Concerts
September	3	February	4
October	4	March	2
November	5	April	5
December	8	May	7
January	3		

Prepare a monthly schedule estimating the band's travel expenses.

LO 2, 3, 7 **10-60** *Financial budgets: cash inflows*   Worthington Company makes cash (20% of total sales), credit card (50% of total sales), and account (30% of total sales) sales. Credit card sales are collected in the month following the sale, net a 3% credit card fee. This means that if the sale is $100, the credit card company's fee is $3, and Worthington receives $97. Account sales are collected as follows: 40% in the first month following the sale, 50% in the second month following the sale, 8% in the third month following the sale, and 2% never collected.

The following table identifies the projected sales for the next year:

Worthington Company
Projected Sales

Month	Sales	Month	Sales
January	$12,369,348	July	$21,747,839
February	15,936,293	August	14,908,534
March	13,294,309	September	11,984,398
April	19,373,689	October	18,894,535
May	20,957,566	November	21,983,545
June	18,874,717	December	20,408,367

Pepare a statement showing the cash expected each month from the collections from these sales.

LO 2, 3 **10-61** *Operating budgets: materials purchasing plan*   Masefield Dairy is preparing a third-quarter budget (July, August, and September) for its ice cream products. It produces five brands of ice cream, and each uses a different mix of ingredients. Its suppliers deliver ingredients just in time, provided that they are given 2 months' notice. The following table indicates the units of weight or volume of each type of ingredient required per unit of each product:

Masefield Dairy
Required Ingredients

Ingredients	Product A	B	C	D	E
Ingredient 1	1	2	1	1	1
Ingredient 2	2	0	3	1	4
Ingredient 3	0	1	2	4	0
Ingredient 4	1	3	0	2	2
Ingredient 5	0	2	1	0	2
Ingredient 6	3	1	3	0	1

The following table summarizes the estimated unit sales for each product in each of the months in the third quarter:

Masefield Dairy
Estimated Unit Sales

PRODUCT	JULY	AUGUST	SEPTEMBER
A	194,675	162,033	129,857
B	104,856	98,375	76,495
C	209,855	194,575	170,654
D	97,576	75,766	55,966
E	47,867	39,575	20,958

Prepare a monthly purchases budget for the ice cream ingredients.

LO 2, 3, 7   **10-62** *Financial budgets: wages and expense budgets*   Nathaniel's Motor Shop does major repair work on automobile engines. The major cost in the shop is the wages of the mechanics. The shop employs nine mechanics who are paid $750 for working a 40-hour week. The work week consists of 5 days of 8 hours. Employees actually work 7 hours each day because they are given 1 hour of breaks each day. They are highly skilled and valued by their employer, so these mechanics are paid whether or not there is work available for them to do. They are also paid $30 for every overtime hour or partial overtime hour they work.

The machine shop industry estimates that for every mechanic hour actually worked in a shop like this, the employee consumes about $25 of variable support items, such as lubricants, tool parts, and electricity.

The motor shop estimates that the following work will be available each week during the next 10 weeks:

Nathaniel's Motor Shop
Estimated Work

WEEK	HOURS OF WORK	WEEK	HOURS OF WORK
1	255	6	280
2	330	7	260
3	300	8	300
4	285	9	340
5	325	10	355

Develop a weekly budget of mechanic wages and variable support costs.

LO 2, 3   **10-63** *Financial budgets: cash outflows*   Country Club Road Nurseries grows and sells garden plants. The nursery is active between January and October each year. During January, the potting tables and equipment are prepared. The potting and seeding are done in February. In March and April, the plants are cultivated, watered, and fertilized. May and June are the peak selling months. July, August, and September are the peak months for visiting customers in their homes to provide them with advice and help solve their problems. During October, the equipment and buildings are secured for the winter months, and in November and December, full-time employees take their paid holidays, and the business is closed.

The nursery employs 15 full-time staff and, depending on the season, up to 20 part-time staff. The full-time staff members are paid an average salary of $2,700 per month and work 160 hours per month.

The part-time staff members are paid $10 per hour. Because the nursery relies on local students for part-time work, there is no shortage of trained people willing to work the hours that are available. The ratio of full-time employee hours worked to part-time employee hours worked is as follows: January, 5:1; February, 5:1; March, 3:1; April, 3:1, May, 1:1; June, 1:1; July, 1:1; August, 1:1; September, 2:1; and October, 4:1. Because part-time students are used mainly for moving and selling activities, their work creates very little incremental support costs.

Fixed costs, other than wages, associated with this operation are about $55,000 per month. The cost drivers in this operation are the activities that the full-time employees undertake. These cost drivers are proportional to the hours worked by the full-time employees. The variable costs depend on the season and reflect the common employee activities during that season. Average variable costs per employee hour worked are as follows: January, $15; February, $15; March, $15; April, $15; May, $5; June, $5; July, $20; August, $20; September, $20; and October, $10. These variable costs include both support items such as power and water and direct items such as soil and pots. Assume that all expenses are paid in the month they are incurred.

On the basis of the information provided, determine the cash outflows for the upcoming year.

LO 2, 3 **10-64 *Master budget*** Adams Company, a merchandising firm that sells one product, estimates it will sell 12,000 units of its product at $60 per unit in December. The company has prepared other information to prepare a budget for December, as shown here:

Merchandise inventory, December 1	2,000 units
Desired merchandise inventory for December 31	3,000 units
Cost per unit of merchandise purchases	$40
Selling and administrative expenses	$200,000
Cash balance, December 1	$30,000
November sales	$600,000

- The company estimates that 60% of each month's sales are collected in the month of sale and that the remaining 40% is collected in the month after sale.
- The $200,000 of selling and administrative expenses includes $40,000 of depreciation.
- The company pays for half of merchandise purchases during the month of purchase and pays the remainder during the month following purchase. Estimated merchandise purchases for November are $340,000.
- All other out-of-pocket expenses are paid for in cash.

Required

a. How many units of merchandise will Adams budget to purchase in December? What is the dollar amount of Adams's budgeted merchandise purchases for December?
b. Prepare a budgeted income statement for the month ended December for Adams Company.
c. Prepare a statement of estimated cash flows for the month ended December for Adams Company.

LO 2, 3, 7 **10-65 *Operating budgets: labor hiring plan*** Shadyside Insurance Company manages a medical insurance program for its clients. Employees of client firms submit claims for reimbursement of medical expenses. Shadyside processes these claims, checks them to ensure that they are covered by the claimant's policy, notes whether the claimant has reached any limit on coverage, computes any deductible, and issues a check for the claimant's refund.

Three types of clerks work in the claims processing department: supervisors, senior clerks, and junior clerks. The supervisors are paid $42,000 per year, the senior clerks are paid $37,000 per year, and the junior clerks are paid $32,000 per year. For every 150,000 claims processed per year, Shadyside plans to use one supervisor, six junior clerks, and two senior clerks.

Last year, the company processed 2 million medical claims and employed 14 supervisors, 30 senior clerks, and 83 junior clerks.

Required

a. Compute the excess costs or cost savings relating to the claims processing staff.
b. How would you interpret these results? What additional information would you ask for if you were making a determination of the clerical group's processing efficiencies?

LO 3, 4, 5   **10-66 *Budgeted profit, what-if analysis***   The Monteiro Manufacturing Corporation manufactures and sells folding umbrellas. The corporation's condensed income statement for the year ended December 31, 2006 follows:

Sales (200,000 units)		$1,000,000
Cost of goods sold		600,000
Gross margin		400,000
Selling expenses	$150,000	
Administrative expenses	100,000	250,000
Net profit (before income taxes)		$150,000

Monteiro's budget committee has estimated the following changes for 2007:

30% increase in number of units sold
20% increase in material cost per unit
15% increase in direct labor cost per unit
10% increase in variable indirect cost per unit
5% increase in indirect capacity-related costs
8% increase in selling expenses, arising solely from increased volume
6% increase in administrative expenses, reflecting anticipated higher wage and supply price levels

Any changes in administrative expenses caused solely by increased sales volume are considered immaterial.

As inventory quantities remain fairly constant, the budget committee considered that for budget purposes any change in inventory valuation can be ignored. The composition of the cost of a unit of finished product during 2006 for materials, direct labor, and manufacturing support, respectively, was in the ratio of 3:2:1. In 2006, $40,000 of manufacturing support was for fixed costs. No changes in production methods or credit policies were contemplated for 2007.

Required

a. Compute the unit sales price at which the Monteiro Manufacturing Corporation must sell its umbrellas in 2007 in order to earn a budgeted profit of $200,000.
b. Unhappy about the prospect of an increase in selling price, Monteiro's sales manager wants to know how many units must be sold at the old price to earn the $200,000 budgeted profit. Compute the number of units which must be sold at the old price to earn $200,000.
c. Believing that the estimated increase in sales is overly optimistic, one of the company's directors wants to know what annual profit is likely if the selling price determined in (a) is adopted but the increase in sales volume is only 10%. Compute the budgeted profit in this case.

10-67 *Budget preparation, breakeven point, what-if analysis with multiple products (Adapted from CPA, May 1993)* The following budget information for the year ending December 31, 2006, pertains to Rust Manufacturing Company's operations:

	PRODUCT		
BUDGET ITEM	ACE	BELL	TOTAL COSTS
Budgeted sales in units	200,000	100,000	
Selling price per unit	$40	$20	
Direct materials cost per unit	$8	$3	
Direct labor hours per unit	2	1	
Depreciation			$200,000
Rent			$130,000
Other manufacturing support costs			$500,000
Selling costs			$180,000
General and administrative costs			$40,000

The following information is also provided:

1. Rust has no beginning inventory. Production is planned so that it will equal the number of units sold.
2. The cost of direct labor is $5 per hour.
3. Depreciation and rent are fixed costs within the relevant range of production. Additional costs would be incurred for extra machinery and factory space if production is increased beyond current available capacity.
4. Rust allocates depreciation proportional to machinery use and rent proportional to factory space. Budgeted usage is as follows:

Depreciation item	Ace	Bell
Machinery	70%	30%
Factory space	60%	40%

5. Other manufacturing support costs include variable costs equal to 10% of direct labor cost and also include various fixed costs. None of the miscellaneous capacity-related fixed manufacturing support costs depend on the level of activity, although support costs attributable to a specific product are avoidable if that product's production ceases. Other manufacturing support costs are allocated between Ace and Bell on the basis of a percentage of budgeted direct labor cost.
6. Rust's selling and general administrative costs are committed in the intermediate term.
7. Rust allocates selling costs on the basis of a number of units sold at Ace and Bell.
8. Rust allocates general and administrative costs on the basis of sales revenue.

Required

a. Prepare a schedule, using separate columns for Ace and Bell, showing budgeted sales, variable costs, contribution margin, fixed costs, and pretax operating profit for the year ending December 31, 2006.
b. Calculate the contribution margin per unit and the pretax operating profit per unit for Ace and for Bell.
c. Calculate the effect on pretax operating profit resulting from a 10% decrease in sales and production of each product.
d. What may be a problem with the above analysis?

LO 5   **10-68** *Breakeven analysis, what-if analysis*   The Herschel Candy Company produces a single product: a chocolate almond bar that sells for $0.40 per bar. The variable costs for each bar (sugar, chocolate, almonds, wrapper, and labor) total $0.25. The total monthly fixed costs are $60,000. Last month, bar sales reached 1 million. However, the president of Herschel Candy Company was not satisfied with its performance and is considering the following options to increase the company's profitability:

1. Increase advertising
2. Increase the quality of the bar's ingredients and simultaneously increase the selling price
3. Increase the selling price with no change in ingredients

Required

a. The sales manager is confident that an intensive advertising campaign will double sales volume. If the company president's goal is to increase this month's profits by 50% over last month's, what is the maximum amount that can be spent on advertising that doubles sales volume?
b. Assume that the company increases the quality of its ingredients, thus increasing variable costs to $0.30 per bar. By how much must the selling price per unit be increased to maintain the same breakeven point in units?
c. Assume next that the company has decided to increase its selling price to $0.50 per bar with no change in advertising or ingredients. Compute the sales volume in units that would be needed at the new price for the company to earn the same profit as it earned last month.

LO 5   **10-69** *Breakeven point, what-if analysis*   Premier Products, Inc., is considering replacing its existing machine with a new and faster machine that will produce a more reliable product and will turn around customer orders in a shorter period. This change is expected to increase the sales price and fixed costs but not the variable costs:

Cost Item	Old Machine	New Machine
Monthly fixed costs	$120,000	$250,000
Variable cost per unit	14	14
Sales price per unit	18	20

Required

a. Determine the breakeven point in units for the two machines.
b. Determine the sales level in units at which the use of the new machine will achieve a 10% target profit-to-sales ratio.
c. Determine the sales level in units at which profits will be the same for either the old or the new machine.
d. Which machine represents a lower risk of incurring a loss? Explain why.
e. Determine the sales level in units at which the profit-to-sales ratio will be equal with either machine.

LO 5   **10-70** *What-if-analysis*   Tenneco, Inc., produces three models of tennis rackets: standard, deluxe, and pro. Following are the sales and cost information for 2006:

Item	Standard	Deluxe	Pro
Sales (in units)	100,000	50,000	50,000
Sales price per unit	$30	$40	$50
Variable manufacturing cost per unit	$17	$20	$25

Fixed manufacturing support costs are $800,000, and fixed selling and administrative costs are $400,000. In addition, the company pays its sales representatives a commission equal to 10% of the price of each racket sold.

Required

a. If the sales price of deluxe rackets decreases 10%, its sales are expected to increase 30%, but sales of standard rackets are expected to decrease 5%, as some potential buyers of standard rackets will upgrade to deluxe rackets. What will be the impact of this decision on Tenneco's profits?

b. Suppose that Tenneco decides to increase its advertising by $50,000 instead of cutting the price of deluxe rackets. This is expected to increase sales of all three models by 2% each. Is this decision advisable?

c. The incentive created by sales commissions has led Tenneco's sales force to push the higher-priced rackets more than the lower-priced ones. Is this in the best interest of the company?

LO 5 **10-71** *Breakeven point, what-if analysis* The following information pertains to Torasic Company's budgeted income statement for the month of June 2006:

Sales (1,200 units at $250)	$300,000
Variable cost	150,000
Contribution margin	$150,000
Fixed cost	200,000
Net loss	($50,000)

Required

a. Determine the company's breakeven point in both units and dollars.

b. The sales manager believes that a $22,500 increase in the monthly advertising expenses will result in a considerable increase in sales. How much of an increase in sales must result from increased advertising in order to break even on the monthly expenditure?

c. The sales manager believes that an advertising expenditure increase of $22,500 coupled with a 10% reduction in the selling price will double the sales quantity. Determine the net income (or loss) if these proposed changes are adopted.

LO 5 **10-72** *Breakeven point, what-if analysis* Air Peanut Company manufactures and sells roasted peanut packets to commercial airlines. Following are the price and cost data per 100 packets of peanuts:

Estimated annual sales volume = 11,535,700 packets	
Selling price	$35.00
Variable costs:	
Raw materials	$16.00
Direct labor	7.00
Manufacturing support	4.00
Selling expenses	1.60
Total variable costs per 100 packets	$28.60
Annual fixed costs:	
Manufacturing support	$192,000
Selling and administrative	276,000
Total fixed costs	$468,000

Required

a. Determine Air Peanut's breakeven point in units.

b. How many packets does Air Peanut have to sell to earn $156,000?

c. Air Peanut expects its direct labor costs to increase by 5% next year. How many units will it have to sell next year to break even if the selling price remains unchanged?

d. If Air Peanut's direct labor costs increase by 5%, what selling price per 100 packets must it charge to maintain the same contribution margin to sales ratio?

LO 6   **10-73**   *Variance analysis*   The Sudbury, South Carolina, plant of Saldanha Sports Company has the following standards for its soccer ball production:

Standards:	
Material (leather) per soccer ball	0.25 yard
Material price per yard	$16
Direct labor hours per soccer ball	0.20 hour
Wage rate per direct labor hour	$10 per hour
Variable support cost rate	$15 per direct labor hour
Actual results for October:	
Used 13,000 yards of raw material, purchased for $205,150	
Paid for 8,240 direct labor hours at $9.50 per hour	
Incurred $131,840 of variable support costs	
Manufactured 40,000 soccer balls	

Required

Determine the following variances for October:

a. Total direct material cost variance

b. Total direct labor cost variance

c. Total variable support cost variance

d. Direct material price variance

e. Direct material quantity variance

f. Direct labor rate variance

g. Direct labor efficiency variance

h. Variable support rate variance

i. Variable support efficiency variance

LO 6   **10-74**   *Variance analysis*   The North Point plant of Englehart Electronics Company has the following standards for component C93:

Standards:	
Material	2 units of material B
Material price	$10 per unit of B
Direct labor	1 hour
Wage rate	$10 per direct labor hour
Variable support cost rate	$25 per direct labor hour
Actual results for May:	
Used 4,200 units of B, purchased at $9.75 per unit of B	
Paid for 2,000 direct labor hours at $11 per hour	
Incurred $48,000 of variable support costs	
Manufactured 2,000 units of component C93	

Determine the following variances for May:

a. Total direct material cost variance
b. Total direct labor cost variance
c. Total variable support cost variance
d. Direct material price variance
e. Direct material quantity variance
f. Direct labor rate variance
g. Direct labor efficiency variance
h. Variable support rate variance
i. Variable support efficiency variance

LO 6 **10-75** *Standard versus actual costs* For each of the following two jobs manufacturing two different products, determine the missing amounts for items (a) through (h):

ITEM	JOB 321	JOB 322
Units produced	200	(e)
Standards per unit:		
Material quantity	5 pounds	(f)
Material price	$2 per pound	$3 per pound
Labor hours	2 hours	3 hours
Labor rate	$15 per hour	$12 per hour
Actual consumption:		
Material quantity	(a)	1,000 pounds
Material cost	$2,000	(g)
Labor hours	(b)	(h)
Labor cost	(c)	$5,800
Variance:		
Material quantity	(d)	$100 F
Material price	$50 U	$500 F
Labor efficiency	$100 F	$50 U
Labor rate	$60 U	$200 F

LO 4, 6 **10-76** *Variance analysis, material and labor* Trieste Toy Company manufactures only one product, Robot Ranger. The company uses a standard cost system and has established the following standards per unit of Robot Ranger:

	STANDARD QUANTITY	STANDARD PRICE	STANDARD COST
Direct materials	3.0 pounds	$12 per pound	$36.00 per unit
Direct labor	1.2 hours	15 per hour	18.00 per unit

During November, the company recorded the following activity:

1. The company produced 6,000 units.
2. A total of 21,000 pounds of material were used, purchased at a cost of $241,500.
3. The company employs 40 persons to work on the production of Robot Ranger. These employees worked an average of 160 hours at an average rate of $16 per hour.

The company's management wishes to determine the efficiency of the activities related to the production of Robot Ranger.

a. For direct materials used in the production of Robot Ranger, compute the direct material price variance and the direct material quantity variance.

b. The direct materials were purchased from a new supplier who is eager to enter into a long-term purchase contract. Would you recommend that Trieste sign the contract? Explain.

c. For direct labor employed in the production of Robot Ranger, compute the direct labor rate variance and the direct labor efficiency variance.

d. In the past, the 40 persons employed in the production of Robot Ranger consisted of 16 experienced workers and 24 inexperienced assistants. During November, the company experimented with 20 experienced workers and 20 inexperienced assistants. Would you recommend that Trieste continue the new labor mix? Explain.

LO 6, 7 **10-77** *Variance analysis, hospital (Adapted from* **CMA,** *June 1989)* Mountain View Hospital has adopted a standard cost accounting system for evaluation and control of nursing labor. Diagnosis-related groups (DRGs), instituted by the U.S. government for health insurance reimbursement, are used as the output measure in the standard cost system. A DRG is a patient classification scheme that perceives hospitals to be multiproduct firms where inpatient treatment procedures are related to the numbers and types of patient ailments treated. Mountain View Hospital has developed standard nursing times for the treatment of each DRG classification, and nursing labor hours are assumed to vary with the number of DRGs treated within a time period.

The nursing unit on the fourth floor treats patients with four DRG classifications. The unit is staffed with registered nurses (RNs), licensed practical nurses (LPNs), and aides. Following are the standard nursing hours and salary rates:

FOURTH-FLOOR NURSING UNIT STANDARD HOURS			
DRG CLASSIFICATION	RN	LPN	AIDE
1	6	4	5
2	26	16	10
3	10	5	4
4	12	7	10

STANDARD HOURLY RATES	
RN	$12
LPN	8
Aide	6

Following are the results of operations for the fourth-floor nursing unit for the month of May:

	ACTUAL NUMBER OF PATIENTS
DRG 1	250
DRG 2	90
DRG 3	240
DRG 4	140
	720

	RN	LPN	AIDE
Actual hours	8,150	4,300	4,400
Actual salary	$100,245	$35,260	$25,300
Actual hourly rate	$12.30	$8.20	$5.75

The accountant for Mountain View Hospital calculated the following standard times for the fourth floor nursing unit for May:

DRG Classification	No. of Patients	Standard Hours/DRG RN	Standard Hours/DRG LPN	Standard Hours/DRG AIDE	Total Standard Hours RN	Total Standard Hours LPN	Total Standard Hours AIDE
1	250	6	4	5	1,500	1,000	1,250
2	90	26	16	10	2,340	1,440	900
3	240	10	5	4	2,400	1,200	960
4	140	12	7	10	1,680	980	1,400
					7,920	4,620	4,510

The hospital calculates labor variances for each reporting period by labor classification (RN, LPN, aide). The variances are used by nursing supervisors and hospital administration to evaluate the performance of nursing labor.

Required

Calculate the total nursing labor variance for the fourth floor nursing unit of Mountain View Hospital for May, indicating how much of this variance is attributed to the following for each class of hospital workers:
a. Labor efficiency
b. Rate differences

LO 6   **10-78** *Variance analysis*   Asahi USA, Inc., based in Denver, Colorado, is a subsidiary of a Japanese company manufacturing specialty tools. Asahi USA employs a standard cost system. Following are the standards per unit of one of its products, tool KJ79. This tool requires as direct materials a special chrome steel.

	Standard Quantity	Standard Price	Standard Cost
Direct materials	8 pounds	$18 per pound	$144
Direct labor	2.5 hours	$8 per hour	20
			$164

During November, Asahi USA started and completed job KJX86 to manufacture 1,900 units of tool KJ79. It purchased and used 14,250 pounds of the special chrome steel for tool KJ79 at a total cost of $270,750. The total direct labor charged to Job KJX86 was $37,800. Job KJX86 required 5,000 direct labor hours.

Required

a. For job KJX86, compute the following and indicate whether the variances are favorable or unfavorable:

(i) direct material price variance
(ii) direct material quantity variance

(iii) direct labor rate variance

(iv) direct labor efficiency variance

b. Provide a plausible explanation for the variances.

LO 6 **10-79 *Variance analysis*** Bakery Extraordinaire sells several types of muffins and scones and also sells carrot bread loaves. Planned prices and sales quantities for February are shown here:

Planned Sales for February

	MUFFINS	SCONES	CARROT BREAD	TOTALS
Unit price	$1.35	$1.75	$2.75	
Unit sales	1,600	3,400	1,000	6,000
Total	$2,160	$5,950	$2,750	$10,860

The actual results for February are shown here:

Actual Sales for February

	MUFFINS	SCONES	CARROT BREAD	TOTALS
Unit price	$1.55	$1.60	$3.25	
Unit sales	1,400	4,500	1,300	7,200
Total	$2,170	$7,200	$4,225	$13,595

The owner would like to know how the price changes and volume changes each contributed to the $2,735 difference between planned and actual sales revenues.

Required

a. Compute the sales mix variance for each product line and explain the meaning of each variance you computed.

b. Compute the sales quantity variance for each product line and explain the meaning of each variance you computed.

c. Compute the sales price variance for each product line and explain the meaning of each variance you computed.

LO 6, 8 **10-80 *Variances and motivation*** Discuss the possible effect on human behavior of a preoccupation with variances in financial control.

LO 8 **10-81 *Methods of setting budgets*** Megan Espanoza, manager of the Wells Division of Mars, Inc., a large credit card company, recently received a memorandum describing the company's new budgeting process for the coming year. The new process requires Megan and the other division managers to submit a budget proposal outlining their operating plans and financial requirements. Management would then study the proposals and determine the budget for each division.

Required

a. What is this form of budgeting called?

b. What are the pros and cons of this approach? Explain.

LO 8 **10-82 *Methods of designing budgets*** Budgets are usually set through one of three methods: participation, authority, or consultation.

Required

Write an essay stating the circumstances under which each method is most appropriate. If you disagree with a particular method, justify your answer.

LO 8 **10-83** *Budgeting: motivational issues* Manoil Electronics manufactures and sells electronic components to electronics stores. The controller is preparing her annual budget and has asked the sales group to prepare sales estimates. All members of the sales force have been asked to estimate sales in their territory for each of the organization's 10 major products.

The marketing group is paid a salary and a commission based on sales in excess of some target level. You have discovered that the sales manager uses the sales estimates to develop the target levels at which commissions begin. Specifically, the sales manager takes the sales estimate, adds 10%, and the result becomes the sales hurdle level. If sales are less than the hurdle level, no commissions are paid. If sales are above the hurdle level, commissions are paid at varying rates.

Required

a. What is the motivation of the sales force if they know the relationship between their estimate and the target level of sales?
b. What is the likely consequence of basing the organization's budgets on these estimates?
c. If you were the controller in this situation and were responsible for both the reward system and the budgeting system, what would you do?

LO 8 **10-84** *Budget slack* Mike Shields was having dinner with one of his friends at a restaurant in Memphis. His friend, Woody Brooks, a local manager of an express mail service, told Mike that he consistently overstated the amount of resources needed in his budget requests for his division. He also told Mike that year after year he was able to obtain the budget requested. When Mike asked him why he did this, Woody replied, "It's a dog-eat-dog world out there. If I'm going to succeed and move up the ladder, I've got to perform well. Having those extra resources really helps!"

Required

Write an essay discussing Woody's point of view related to budgeting. Is he justified in his approach? Explain.

Cases

LO 2, 3, 4, 5 **10-85** *Budgeting: comprehensive problem* Judd's Reproductions makes reproductions of antique tables and chairs and sells them through three sales outlets. The product line consists of two styles of chairs, two styles of tables, and three styles of cabinets. Although customers often ask Judd Molinari, the owner/manager of Judd's Reproductions, to make other products, he does not intend to expand the product line.

The planning group at Judd's Reproductions prepares a master budget for each fiscal year, which corresponds to the calendar year. It is December 2006, and the planners are completing the master budget for 2007.

Unit prices are $200, $900, and $1,800 for the chairs, tables, and cabinets, respectively. Customers pay (1) by cash and receive a 5% discount, (2) by credit card (the credit card company takes 3% of the revenue as its fee and remits the balance in the month following the month of sale), or (3) on account (only exporters buy on account). The distribution of cash, credit card, and exporter sales is 25%, 35%, and 40%, respectively. Of the credit sales to exporters, Judd's Reproductions collects 30% in the month following the sale, 50% in the second month following the sale, and 17% in the third month following the sale, with 3% going uncollected. Judd's Reproductions recognizes the expense of cash discounts, credit card fees, and bad debts in the month of the sale.

Judd's employs 40 people who work in the following areas: 15 in administration, sales, and shipping; 2 in manufacturing supervision (director and a scheduler); 9 in manufacturing fabrication and assembly (carpenters); and 14 in manufacturing, finishing, and other areas (helpers, cleaners, and maintenance crew).

The carpenter hours required to make the parts for and assemble a chair, table, or cabinet are 0.4, 2.5, and 6, respectively. Production personnel have organized the work so that each carpenter hour worked requires 1.5 helper hours. Therefore, production planners maintain a ratio on average of 1.5 helpers for every carpenter. The company pays carpenters and helpers $24 and $14 per hour, respectively (including all benefits).

Judd's Reproductions guarantees all employees pay for at least 172 hours per month regardless of the hours of work available. When the employees are not doing their regular jobs, they undertake maintenance, training, community service, and customer relations activities. Judd's pays each employee weekly for that week's work. If an employee works 172 hours or less during the month, Judd's still pays the employee for 172 hours at his or her normal hourly rate. The company pays 150% of the normal hourly rate for every hour over 172 that the employee works during the month. Planners add new carpenters if the projected total monthly overtime is more than 5% of the total regular carpenter hours available. Judd's has a policy of no employee layoffs. Any required hiring is done on the first day of each month.

For a factory, Judd's Reproductions rents a converted warehouse that costs $600,000 per year. The company pays rent quarterly beginning January 1 of each year. Judd's pays other fixed manufacturing costs, which include manufacturing supervision salaries and amount to $480,000 annually, paid in equal monthly amounts.

The capital investment policy is to purchase, each January and July, $5,000 of machinery and equipment per carpenter employed during that month. Judd's recognizes depreciation at the rate of 10% of the year-end balance of the machinery and equipment account. Statistical studies of cost behavior have determined that supplies, variable support, and maintenance costs vary with the number of carpenter hours worked and are $5, $20, and $15 per hour, respectively.

The units of wood required for chairs, tables, and cabinets are 1, 8, and 15, respectively. Each unit of wood costs $30. The inventory policy is to make products in the month they will be sold. Two suppliers deliver raw materials and supplies as required. The company pays for all materials, supplies, variable support, and maintenance items on receipt.

Annual administration salaries, fixed selling costs, and planned advertising expenditures are $300,000, $360,000, and $600,000, respectively. Judd's Reproductions makes these expenditures in equal monthly amounts. Packaging and shipping costs for chairs, tables, and cabinets are $15, $65, and $135, respectively. Variable selling costs are 6% of each product's list price. Judd's Reproductions pays packaging, shipping, and variable selling costs as incurred.

Using its line of credit, Judd's Reproductions maintains a minimum cash balance of $50,000. All line-of-credit transactions occur on the first day of each month. The bank charges interest on the line-of-credit account balance at the rate of 10% per year. Judd's pays interest on the first day of each month on the line-of-credit balance outstanding at the end of the previous month. On the first of each month, the bank pays interest at the rate of 3% per year on funds exceeding $50,000 in the company's cash account at the end of the previous month.

Realized sales for October and November and expected sales for December 2006 appear in the following table:

Judd's Reproductions
Unit Sales 2006

ITEM	OCTOBER	NOVEMBER	DECEMBER
Chairs	900	975	950
Tables	175	188	201
Cabinets	90	102	95

Sales staff estimates the unit demand for 2007 as follows: chairs, 1,000, plus a random number uniformly distributed between 0 and 50, plus 15% of the previous month's sales of chairs; tables, 200, plus a random number uniformly distributed between 0 and 20, plus 15% of the previous months sales; and cabinets, 100, plus a random number uniformly distributed between 0 and 10, plus 15% of the previous month's sales of cabinets. This estimation process resulted in the demand forecasts and the sales plan found in the following table:

Judd's Reproductions
Projected Unit Sales 2007

MONTH	CHAIRS	TABLES	CABINETS
January	1,020	200	109
February	1,191	237	120
March	1,179	243	119
April	1,195	250	126
May	1,200	252	122
June	1,204	255	125
July	1,194	242	123
August	1,199	253	121
September	1,222	243	127
October	1,219	248	126
November	1,207	244	126
December	1,192	255	119

Planners project the Judd's Reproductions balance sheet at January 1, 2007, to be as follows:

Judd's Reproductions
Balance Sheet January 1, 2007

Cash	$50,000	Bank loan	$0
Accounts receivable	575,008		
Machinery (net book value)	360,000	Shareholder's equity	985,008
Total	$985,008	Total	$985,008

Required (Round quantities up in the problem.)

a. Prepare a sales forecast, staffing plan, production plan, estimated cash flow statement, pro forma income statement for the year ended December 31, 2007, and pro forma balance sheet at December 31, 2007.

b. The level of bad debts concerns the Judd's Reproductions controller. If Judd's insists on cash payments from exporters who would be given the cash discount, the sales staff expects that total sales to exporters in 2007 will fall by 5% (sales in 2006 will not be affected). Based on the effect of this change on profitability, is it desirable? (Round sales forecasts to the nearest unit.)

c. Ignore the changes described in (b) and return to the data in the original example. The sales staff is considering increasing the advertising budget from $600,000 to $900,000 and cutting prices by 5% beginning on January 1, 2007. This should increase sales by 30% in 2007. Based on the effect of this change on profitability, is it desirable? (Round sales forecasts to the nearest unit.)

d. Is there a criterion other than profitability that may be used to evaluate the desirability of the changes proposed in (b) and (c)? If yes, what is that criterion, and why is it important? If no, why is profitability the sole relevant criterion?

LO 4   **10-86 *Compensation tied to Balanced Scorecard, degree of difficulty of target achievement*** Discuss case 8-79.

LO 6   **10-87 *Variance and cost analysis*** Peterborough Food produces a wide range of breakfast cereal foods. Its granola products are two of its most important product lines.

Because of the complexity of the granola production process, the manufacturing area in the plant that makes these two product lines is separated from the rest of the plant and is treated as a separate

Exhibit 10-37
Peterborough Food: Granola Line Products

	LINE 1 PLAN	LINE 1 ACTUAL	LINE 2 PLAN	LINE 2 ACTUAL	TOTAL LINE 1 PLAN	TOTAL LINE 1 ACTUAL	TOTAL LINE 2 PLAN	TOTAL LINE 2 ACTUAL	TOTAL PLAN	TOTAL ACTUAL
Number of boxes	945,000	1,200,000	1,175,000	945,000						
Number of batches	189	200	235	210						
Units per batch	5,000	6,000	5,000	4,500						
Unit-related costs:										
Materials										
Grams per box	500	515	350	375						
Cost per gram	$0.0030	$0.0027	$0.0050	$0.0055	$1,417,500	$1,668,600	$2,056,250	$1,949,062	$3,473,750	$3,617,662
Packaging										
Units per box	1.0000	1.0600	1.0000	1.0405						
Cost per unit	$0.0450	$0.0420	$0.0380	$0.0410	$42,525	$53,424	$44,650	$40,314	$87,175	$93,738
Labor										
Hours per box	0.013	0.011	0.009	0.010						
Cost per hour	$18.00	$18.25	$18.00	$18.25	$221,130	$240,900	$190,350	$172,463	$411,480	$413,363
Batch-related costs:										
Materials										
Per batch	$1,200	$1,325	$1,525	$1,495	$226,800	$265,000	$358,375	$313,950	$585,175	$578,950
Labor										
Hours per batch	12	11	16	18						
Per hour	$18.00	$18.25	$18.00	$18.25	$40,824	$40,150	$67,680	$68,985	$108,504	$109,135
Product-sustaining costs										
Labor					$256,000	$287,000	$305,000	$323,000	$561,000	$610,000
Other					$2,054,000	$2,123,000	$1,927,000	$2,005,000	$3,981,000	$4,128,000
Business-sustaining costs										
Labor									$145,000	$152,000
Other									$4,560,000	$4,740,000
Total all costs					$4,258,779	$4,678,074	$4,949,305	$4,872,774	$13,913,084	$14,442,849

cost center. Exhibit 10-37 presents the activity and cost data for this cost center for the most recent quarter. The plan data in Exhibit 10-37 reflect the master budget targets for the quarter.

The factory accountant estimates that, with the increased production in line 1, the labor-related product-sustaining costs and the other product-sustaining costs for line 1 should increase by $20,000 and $100,000, respectively. The factory accountant also indicates that the decreased production in line 2 would require several quarters to be reflected in lower product-sustaining costs.

The factory accountant indicated that the labor-related business-sustaining costs and the other business-sustaining costs should increase by $0 and $140,000, respectively, given the net increase in production.

Required

Prepare a second-level and third-level variance analysis of costs for the granola line cost center. In your analysis, group costs into unit-related, batch-related, product-sustaining, and business-sustaining costs.

LO 4, 7, 8 10-88 *Budgeting: motivational issues* Nate Young is the dean of a business school. The university is under strong financial pressures, and the university president has asked all the deans to cut costs. Nate is wondering how he should respond to this request.

The university receives its operating funds from three sources: (1) tuition (60%), (2) government grants (25%), and (3) gifts and endowment income (15%). The money flows into the university's general operating fund. A management committee consisting of the university president, the three vice presidents, and the nine deans allocates funds to the individual schools. The university's charter requires that it operate with a balanced budget.

The initial allocation of funds reflects (1) fixed costs that cannot be avoided, primarily the employment costs of tenured faculty, and (2) fixed costs relating to support items, such as staff, building maintenance, and other operations costs. The balance of funds is allocated to discretionary activities, such as scholarships, program changes or additions, and sports.

The various deans compare their respective funding levels. The basis of comparison is to divide total university expenditures by the number of full-time students to get an average cost per student. Then the average cost per student is multiplied by the number of full-time students to get the target funding for each school. On average, the actual funding for the business school has been about 70% of the target funding, which is the second lowest in the university. (The lowest is the arts school.)

Because of the rapid growth of fixed faculty and administrative costs, the amount of funds allocated to discretionary activities has been declining from a historic level of about 10%. This year, the projected revenues will not even cover the projected fixed costs. In response to this development, the president has called on all deans to "do your best to reduce the level of expenditures."

The president's request has been met with skepticism by many deans, who are notorious for digging in their heels, ignoring requests for spending cuts, and then being bailed out by funds released from other activities or raised to meet the budget shortfall. Many deans believe that the departments that sacrificed and reduced their budgets would only create funds that would be used by the university to support other schools that had made little or no effort to reduce their budgets. Then these schools would be asked to make even more cuts to make up for the lack of cuts in schools that made little progress in cost reduction. On the other hand, the deans also believe that if there were no reaction to the president's initial request for cost reductions, arbitrary cutbacks would be imposed on the individual schools.

In response to this situation, Nate is wondering what to do. He knows that by increasing class sizes slightly, using some part-time instructors, and eliminating some optional courses that seldom attract many students, he can trim about $800,000 from his operating budget of $11,000,000. However, making these changes would create hardships for both the students and faculty in the business school, and given the historic relationship of the school's average funding to its target funding, Nate is wondering whether the business school should be asked to make additional sacrifices.

Nate knows that he has several alternatives:

- Do nothing, arguing that the business school is already cost effective relative to others and that it is time for others to reduce their cost structures.
- Make the cuts that he has identified but stretch them out over a number of years and stop making them if other schools are not doing their share in cutting costs.
- Make the cuts unilaterally and advise the administration that the business school budget can be reduced by about $800,000.

Required

Explain what you would do if you were Nate and why. Your explanations should include your analysis of the motivation of all schools to cut costs in an environment that traditionally has taken advantage of those who cooperate.

LO 3, 5, 7 **10-89** *Budgeting and cost drivers* Dinkum Company provides package courier services. Each afternoon its couriers pick up packages; they drive trucks operating out of local terminals. Packages are returned to the terminal and are transported to the central hub that evening. In the hub, packages are sorted during the late evening and are sent to the destination terminal overnight. The next morning couriers from the destination terminal deliver packages to the addresses.

Most of the routes that the couriers follow are fixed. Each day the couriers have both scheduled and unscheduled pickup and drop-off stops. However, studies have shown that adding an unscheduled stop to a route or picking up an additional shipment at a scheduled stop creates negligible additional costs. The key costs in terms of the courier's time, the vehicle, and the fuel costs are determined by the route itself. Therefore, most of the costs at Dinkum result from decisions that reflect the planned level of activity rather than decisions that reflect the actual volume of activity. The major exception is the sorting cost in the hubs and terminals. Because sorting labor is hired on a part-time basis as required, the sorting cost varies with the number of shipments handled.

Linda Price, the manager of the Miami terminal, is preparing an expense budget for the upcoming year. She plans to base this year's budget on the trends from the previous years. The following table shows the level of costs in the previous three years.

Dinkum Courier Company
Activity Cost Levels

Item	2004	2005	2006
Shipments handled	8,500,000	10,300,000	11,100,000
Administrative costs	$300,000	$315,000	$320,000
Truck depreciation and maintenance	$750,000	$830,000	$850,000
Courier fuel costs	$600,000	$660,000	$670,000
Courier wages	$1,750,000	$1,810,000	$1,850,000
Terminal support costs	$240,000	$280,000	$260,000
Labor costs in terminal	$120,000	$ 150,000	$170,000

Required

a. Identify what you think are the cost drivers for each of the items in this table.
b. Given the information provided, prepare an expense budget for the upcoming year, assuming that the volume of shipments handled is expected to be 14,000,000 units.

---

[1] Copyright © 2006 President and Fellows of Harvard College. Harvard Business School Case 9-106-060. This case was prepared by Professor Robert S. Kaplan as the basis for class discussion rather than to illustrate either effective or ineffective handling of an administrative situation. Reprinted by permission of Harvard Business School.

10-90 *Activity-based budgeting, Balanced Scorecard, and strategy* Sippican Corporation (B)[1]

Refer to case 4-54, the Sippican Corporation (A) case, which required time-driven activity-based costing (ABC) analysis.

Sippican's senior executive committee met to consider the implications from its time-driven ABC model. Frankly all had been shocked to learn that their apparently highest margin product line, flow controllers could actually be losing money because of its many shipments, short production runs, and heavy use of engineering time. The team contemplated action steps to restore profitability.

After some deliberation, the executive team crafted a new strategy that involved the following principles:

Improve Revenue Quality: Product Focus and Menu-Based Pricing

- Focus on core products: valves and pumps
- Increase market share in valves by offering discounts for large orders
- Reduce discounting for pumps, especially in small order sizes
- Aggressively raise prices for small orders of flow controllers

Productivity

- Reduce set-up times

Based on the new strategy, Peggy Knight developed the forecasted monthly sales and production plan shown in Exhibit 10-38. She wondered whether the shift in product mix, new pricing model, and forecasted productivity improvement in setup times would be sufficient to restore Sippican's historic margins. Sippican's machines were leased monthly and had staggered expiration times; Knight believed she could, on short notice, make 10%–15% adjustments up or down to accommodate changes in demand for machine capacity. Also, Knight felt that she had some flexibility with the size and composition of the labor force as well. The company had recently hired quite a few production employees on short-term contracts to meet the expanded demand for the newly-introduced flow controller line.

Required

a. Estimate the resource demands from Knight's forecasted sales production plan in Exhibit 10-38.
b. Prepare a pro forma product line income statement based on the new plan.
c. Comment on the magnitude of the change in profit with the new plan in relation to the change in production and sales under the previous plan.

Exhibit 10-38
Forecasted
Monthly Sales
and Production
Plan

	Valves	Pumps	Flow Controllers	Total
Forecasted price	$75	$80	$110	
Forecasted sales (units)	10,000	12,000	2,500	24,500
Number of production runs	40	40	50	130
Number of shipments	40	70	100	210
Total direct labor hours	3,800	6,000	1,000	10,800
Setup labor hours per run	4.0	4.8	9.6	
Total setup hours	160	192	480	832
Machine hours: run + setup	5,160	6,192	1,230	12,582
Engineering hours	60	240	400	700

Source: Robert S. Kaplan.

Chapter 11

Capital Budgeting: Long-Term Assets

After reading this chapter, you will be able to:

➤ recognize the nature and importance of long-term (capital) assets

➤ understand why organizations control long-lived assets and short-term assets differently

➤ use the following basic tools and concepts of financial analysis: investment, return on investment, future value, present value, annuities, and required rate of return

➤ use capital budgeting to evaluate investment proposals and recognize how the concepts of payback, accounting rate of return, net present value, internal rate of return, and economic value added relate to investing in long-term assets

➤ incorporate the effect of income taxes and inflation in evaluating investments in long-term assets

➤ use what-if, sensitivity, and basic options analyses to deal with uncertainty issues that arise in evaluating investments in long-term assets

➤ recognize and know how to include strategic considerations in long-term investment decisions

➤ use postimplementation audits to evaluate past long-term investment decisions

Dow Chemical Purchases Union Carbide

In early August 1999, Dow Chemical Company announced that it was acquiring Union Carbide Corporation for $9.3 billion. This acquisition meant that Dow Chemical became second in size in the chemical industry only to DuPont. In response to the announcement, Dow Chemical shares fell approximately 6%, and Union Carbide shares jumped approximately

Source: The Dow Chemical Company.

20%—the implication being that the market believed that Dow Chemical had overpaid for its Union Carbide shares.

The acquisition reflected a merger of two organizations with troubled pasts. Dow Chemical was still recovering from the negative image it acquired from producing napalm during the Vietnam War. Union Carbide had never recovered from the effects of a tragic chemical leak at its Bhopal, India, plant that killed an estimated 10,000 people.

Both Dow Chemical and Union Carbide manufactured primary and intermediate chemicals that were used as inputs to produce final products. This merger reflected a global trend among companies that made primary or intermediate chemical products as they sought to achieve economies of scale and rationalization of duplicated services.

Dow and Union Carbide had pursued comparable strategies to preserve sales and market share. They both concentrated on product and process refinements to produce conventional chemicals at the lowest price and actively sought new uses for these primary chemical products. Both organizations had systematically eliminated their investments in consumer products over the previous decade in order to focus on industrial chemicals. Industry analysts agreed that Dow Chemical had been more successful in narrowing its focus to concentrate on what appeared to be its distinctive competencies and in reducing its cost structure.

In a news release, Dow Chemical announced that it believed the acquisition would increase its earnings and that rationalization and reengineering would create, within 2 years, at least $500 million of annual cost savings relative to the existing cost structures of the two organizations. For example, because the two organizations had complementary products, Dow Chemical could now offer customers a more complete product line.

Most analysts accepted these claims and observed that matters could improve even more for the new Dow Chemical, since the prices of primary and intermediate chemicals were expected to rise in the years immediately following the acquisition. However, some analysts viewed the acquisition as a merger of two unattractive and unimaginative organizations.

LONG-TERM (CAPITAL) ASSETS

In considering Dow Chemical's acquisition of Union Carbide, reflect back to chapters 3 and 4, which discussed the cost of capacity resources that organizations purchase in advance and use for several years to make goods and provide services. These long-term, or capital, assets create fixed costs. The significant investment made by Dow Chemical in acquiring Union Carbide illustrates issues addressed in this chapter, including the approach that planners use to evaluate the acquisition of long-term assets that create significant cost commitments.

Cost commitments associated with long-term assets create risk for an organization because they remain even if the asset does not generate the anticipated benefits. In this sense, long-term assets reduce an organization's flexibility. Therefore, organizations approach investments in long-term assets with considerable care.

Organizations have developed specific tools to control the acquisition and use of long-term assets for three reasons:

1. Unlike flexible resources, whose level can be modified quickly in response to changes in demand, organizations usually are committed to long-term assets for an extended time. This type of commitment creates the potential for either excess or scarce capacity that, in turn, creates idle capacity costs or lost opportunities, respectively.
2. The amount of capital committed to the acquisition of capital assets is usually quite large; therefore, acquiring long-term assets creates significant financial risks for organizations.
3. The long-term nature of capital assets creates technological risk for organizations.

Capital budgeting is a systematic approach to evaluating an investment in a long-term, or capital, asset. This topic is discussed more fully later in this chapter.

INVESTMENT AND RETURN

A long-term asset is acquired and paid for before it generates benefits that last more than one year. The fundamental evaluation issue in dealing with a long-term asset is whether its future benefits justify its initial cost.

Investment is the monetary value of the assets that the organization gives up to acquire a long-term asset. **Return** is the increased future cash inflows that are attributable to the long-term asset. Investment and return are the foundations of capital budgeting analysis, which focuses on whether the increased cash flows that the organization expects the long-term asset to generate will justify the investment in that asset. The tools and methods used in capital budgeting focus on comparing investment and return or, more generally, the cash outflows and cash inflows associated with a long-term asset.

TIME VALUE OF MONEY

A central concept in capital budgeting is the time value of money. Because money can earn a return from investment, its value depends on when it is received. Like all resources, money has a cost. The cost of using money is not an out-of-pocket cost, such as the cost of buying raw materials or paying a worker; rather, it is the lost opportunity to invest the money in another investment alternative. For example, if you invest your cash in a stock, you forgo the opportunity to deposit it in a savings account and earn interest. Therefore, the problem is that investment cash is paid out now, and in return cash is received in the future. In making investment decisions, then, we must have a way to compare the cash flows that occur at different points in time.

Because money has a time-dated value, the critical idea underlying capital budgeting is that amounts of money received at different periods of time must be converted into their value on a common date to be compared.

Some Standard Notation

To simplify the discussion, the following notation is used throughout this chapter:

ABBREVIATION	MEANING
n	**Number of periods** considered in the investment analysis; common period lengths are a month, a quarter, or a year.
FV	**Future value**, or ending value, of the investment n periods from now.
PV	**Present value**, or the value at the current moment in time, of an amount to be received n periods from now.
a	**Annuity**, or equal amount, received or paid at the end of each period for n periods.
r	**Rate of return required** (or expected) from an investment opportunity; the rate of interest earned on an investment.

Future Value

Because money has time value, it is better to have money now than in the future. Having $1.00 today is more valuable than receiving $1.00 in 1 year or 5 years because the $1.00 on hand today can be invested to grow to more than $1.00 in the future.

Consider the difference between having $1.00 now and $1.00 a year from now. If you have $1.00 now, you might invest it in a savings account to earn 5% interest. After 1 year, you will have $1.05. We call this $1.05 the future value of $1.00 in 1 year when the rate of return is 5%. Thus, the future value (FV) is the amount that today's investment will be after a stated number of periods at a stated periodic rate of return.

Here is the formula for future value:

Future value of investment in 1 period = Investment $\times$ (1 + Periodic rate of return)
$$FV = PV \times (1 + r)$$

Suppose Bruce Brooks wants to borrow $10,000 to buy a used car. He plans to repay the loan in full after 1 year. If the rate of interest is 7% per year, Bruce will have to repay $10,700 at the end of the year as shown:

$$FV = PV \times (1 + r)$$
$$FV = \$10,000 \times (1.07)$$
$$FV = \$10,700$$

As another example, Frank and Rose Robinson recently inherited $15,000 from Rose's great aunt. They plan to buy a new home and will use the inheritance as a down payment on the home. However, the home will not be ready for 1 year. If the money is invested at 9% and ignoring taxes, how much will Frank and Rose have for their down payment 1 year from now? The answer is $16,350 (15,000 × 1.09). In summary, future value is the amount a present sum of money will be worth in the future, given a specified rate of interest and time period.

Multiple Periods

Because investment opportunities usually extend over multiple periods, we need to be able to compute future value over several periods. Exhibit 11-1 shows how an initial amount of $1.00 accumulates to $1.2763 over 5 years when the rate of return is 5% per year.

The calculations shown assume the following:

1. Any interest earned is not withdrawn until the end of the fifth year; therefore, interest is earned each year on both the initial investment and the interest earned in previous periods, what financial analysts call the *compound effect* of interest.
2. The rate of return is constant.

Computing Future Values for Multiple Periods

It is possible to compute the future value of an investment for multiple periods in a number of ways. These calculations assume that no interest is withdrawn until the end of the investment period.

Calculator Methods

A calculator can be used to compute future values by either sequential multiplication or exponents.

- *Sequential multiplication:* Multiply $1.00 by 1.05 five times to compute the future value of $1.00 in five periods when the rate of interest is 5% ($1.2763).
- *Exponents:* If your calculator can compute exponents, you can avoid repeated multiplication by computing $(1.05)^5$ directly.

$$\$1.00 \times 1.05 \times 1.05 \times 1.05 \times 1.05 \times 1.05 = \$1.00 \times 1.05^5$$

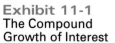

Exhibit 11-1
The Compound Growth of Interest

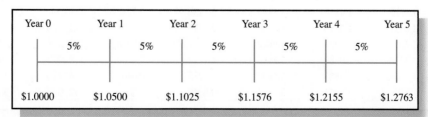

Year 0	Year 1	Year 2	Year 3	Year 4	Year 5
	5%	5%	5%	5%	5%
$1.0000	$1.0500	$1.1025	$1.1576	$1.2155	$1.2763

These calculations show that the general formula for a future value is

$$FV = PV \times (1 + r)^n$$

This formula is the multiperiod extension of the future value formula presented earlier.

Table Method

Tables provide the factors needed to compute a future value. For example, the table in Exhibit 11-2 provides the future value factor for different numbers of periods and rates of return. If you look down the 5% column and find where that column intersects with the row for five periods, you will find the value 1.2763. Multiply this factor by the amount of the initial investment to find the future value in the required number of periods at the stated rate of return:

$$FV_{\$1,\ 5\%,\ 5\ periods} = \$1 \times future\ value\ factor_{5\%,\ 5\ periods}$$
$$= \$1 \times 1.2763$$
$$= \$1.2763$$

Suppose a child's parents have just won $100,000 in a lottery. They decide to place $20,000 of this money in a trust fund for their newborn child's education. If the money is invested to earn 7% each year with all interest reinvested, the equation for future value computes the amount to which it will have accumulated after 15 years.

$$FV_{\$20,000,\ 7\%,\ 15\ periods} = \$20,000 \times future\ value\ factor_{7\%,\ 15\ periods}$$
$$= \$20,000 \times 2.7590$$
$$= \$55,180$$

Returning to a previous example, suppose that Bruce Brooks believes it will take him 3 years to accumulate enough money to repay his car loan in one lump sum. If

Exhibit 11-2
Future Value of $1

PERIOD	2%	5%	7%	10%	12%	15%	17%	20%
1	1.0200	1.0500	1.0700	1.1000	1.1200	1.1500	1.1700	1.2000
2	1.0404	1.1025	1.1449	1.2100	1.2544	1.3225	1.3689	1.4400
3	1.0612	1.1576	1.2250	1.3310	1.4049	1.5209	1.6016	1.7280
4	1.0824	1.2155	1.3108	1.4641	1.5735	1.7490	1.8739	2.0736
5	1.1041	**1.2763**	1.4026	1.6105	1.7623	2.0114	2.1924	2.4883
6	1.1262	1.3401	1.5007	1.7716	1.9738	2.3131	2.5652	2.9860
7	1.1487	1.4071	1.6058	1.9487	2.2107	2.6600	3.0012	3.5832
8	1.1717	1.4775	1.7182	2.1436	2.4760	3.0590	3.5115	4.2998
9	1.1951	1.5513	1.8385	2.3579	2.7731	3.5179	4.1084	5.1598
10	1.2190	1.6289	1.9672	2.5937	3.1058	4.0456	4.8068	6.1917
15	1.3459	2.0789	2.7590	4.1772	5.4736	8.1371	10.5387	15.4070
20	1.4859	2.6533	3.8697	6.7275	9.6463	16.3665	23.1056	38.3376
25	1.6406	3.3864	5.4274	10.8347	17.0001	32.9190	50.6578	95.3962

the interest rate is 7% per year, the lump-sum loan repayment in 3 years would be as follows:

$$FV_{\$10,000,\ 7\%,\ 3\ periods} = \$10,000 \times \textit{future value factor}_{7\%,\ 3\ periods}$$
$$= \$10,000 \times 1.2250$$
$$= \$12,250$$

Spreadsheet Method

Every computer spreadsheet program can compute future values and any of the other financial calculations that we describe in this chapter. See the first Excel spreadsheet application (ESS 1).

ESS 1: COMPUTING FUTURE VALUE

The Excel formula to compute the future value of a single payment is

$$FV\ (\text{interest rate, number of periods, payment,}$$
$$\text{present value, type})$$

where payment is the amount of the payment made each period, and type is 1 if made at the beginning of the period and 0 if made at the end. The default value is zero. The convention in signing payments and interpreting the sign of the amount returned by Excel is that a minus value is an outflow and a positive value is an inflow.

Entering the following in an Excel spreadsheet cell will compute the loan repayment amount for Bruce's loan as −$12,250.43.

$$= FV\ (0.07,3,,10000,0)$$

Compound Growth of Interest

When an amount of money is invested and left to accumulate for multiple periods, the rate of growth is compounded because interest is earned on the interest earned in previous periods. Exhibit 11-3 shows the path of compound growth for various rates of interest. Note that the rate of growth is exponential—that is, growth occurs at an increasing rate.

Present Value

An investor may expect that a proposed investment will generate benefits in the form of increased cash flow over many periods into the future. The investor must compare these cash flow benefits, or inflows, to the investment's costs, or outflows, to assess the investment. Because money has time value, all cash flows associated with an investment must be converted to their equivalent value at some common date in order for us to make meaningful comparisons between the project's cash inflows and outflows.

Although any point in time can be chosen as the common date for comparing inflows and outflows, the conventional choice is the point when the investment is undertaken. Analysts call this point *time zero,* or *period zero.* Therefore, conventional capital budgeting analysis converts all future cash flows to their equivalent value at time zero.

Exhibit 11-3
Compound
Growth for Future
Value

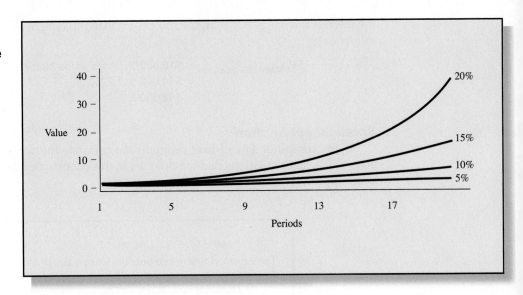

Analysts call a future cash flow's value at time zero its present value. The process of computing present value is called discounting. Recall the formula for future value:

$$FV = PV \times (1 + r)^n$$

We can rearrange this formula to compute the present value:

$$PV = \frac{FV}{(1+r)^n}$$

Or

$$PV = FV \times (1 + r)^{-n}$$

Suppose a newborn's parents want to accumulate $70,000 over 15 years for their child's education. The parents have idle cash available now to make this investment, which will earn 7% annually. To determine the amount of money they must invest now, we compute the present value of $70,000 with a rate of return of 7%. Use any of the methods described earlier to compute this value.

Calculator Methods

To compute the present value of a future amount of money, use either the sequential division or the exponential method.

- *Sequential division:* Divide $70,000 by 1.07 15 times.

  $70,000 \div 1.07 \div 1.07 \div 1.07 \div 1.07 \div 1.07 \div 1.07 \div 1.07 \div 1.07 \div 1.07$
  $\div 1.07 \div 1.07 \div 1.07 \div 1.07 \div 1.07 \div 1.07$

- *Exponents:* Evaluate the equation directly.

  $$\$70{,}000 \div (1.07)^{15}$$

Table Method

Use the appropriate factor shown in Exhibit 11-4. Exhibit 11-4 shows that the factor used to compute present value when there are 15 interest periods and a periodic interest rate of 7% is 0.3624. Therefore, we can compute the present value of this investment as follows:

$$PV = \$70,000 \times present\ value\ factor_{7\%,\ 15\ periods}$$
$$PV = \$70,000 \times 0.3624$$
$$PV = \$25,368$$

Spreadsheet Method

See ESS 2 for another Excel spreadsheet application.

ESS 2. COMPUTING PRESENT VALUE

The Excel formula to compute the present value of a single payment is

PV (interest rate, number of periods, payment, value, type)

where payment is the amount of the payment made each period, and type is 1 if made at the beginning of the period and 0 if made at the end. The default value is zero. The convention in signing payments and interpreting the sign of the amount returned by Excel is that a minus value is an outflow and a positive value is an inflow.

Entering the following in an Excel spreadsheet cell will compute the amount of the initial investment required to accumulate the target amount of $70,000 as −$25,371.22.

= PV (0.07,15,,70000,0)

The reader is reminded that the difference in the amount shown in the spreadsheet method and the table method results from rounding errors from using only four significant digits in the table method.

Exhibit 11-4
Present Value of $1

PERIOD	2%	5%	7%	10%	12%	15%	17%	20%
1	0.9804	0.9524	0.9346	0.9091	0.8929	0.8696	0.8547	0.8333
2	0.9612	0.9070	0.8734	0.8264	0.7972	0.7561	0.7305	0.6944
3	0.9423	0.8638	0.8163	0.7513	0.7118	0.6575	0.6244	0.5787
4	0.9238	0.8227	0.7629	0.6830	0.6355	0.5718	0.5337	0.4823
5	0.9057	0.7835	0.7130	0.6209	0.5674	0.4972	0.4561	0.4019
6	0.8880	0.7462	0.6663	0.5645	0.5066	0.4323	0.3898	0.3349
7	0.8706	0.7107	0.6227	0.5132	0.4523	0.3759	0.3332	0.2791
8	0.8535	0.6768	0.5820	0.4665	0.4039	0.3269	0.2848	0.2326
9	0.8368	0.6446	0.5439	0.4241	0.3606	0.2843	0.2434	0.1938
10	0.8203	0.6139	0.5083	0.3855	0.3220	0.2472	0.2080	0.1615
15	0.7430	0.4810	**0.3624**	0.2394	0.1827	0.1229	0.0949	0.0649
20	0.6730	0.3768	0.2584	0.1486	0.1037	0.0611	0.0433	0.0261
25	0.6095	0.2953	0.1842	0.0923	0.0588	0.0304	0.0197	0.0105

Thus, if the rate of return is 7%, the parents must invest $25,371 today to accumulate the $70,000 they would like to give their child for the college fund.

Decay of a Present Value

Invested amounts grow at a compound rate through time because interest is earned on interest earned in prior periods and reinvested. Similarly, a fixed amount of cash to be received at some future time becomes less valuable as (1) interest rates increase, and (2) the time period before receipt of the cash increases. Exhibit 11-5 shows the loss of present value associated with various rates of interest and future cash receipt times. Note that present value decays at a decreasing rate and that the compounding effect of interest causes the decay to be more rapid as the interest rate increases. This effect causes the decay line to be bowed even more in Exhibit 11-5 as the interest rate increases. The consequence of this decay is that large benefits expected far into the future, when interest rates exceed 10%, will have relatively little current value. This situation works against investment projects that provide benefits well into the future, so the required rate should be carefully determined. Arbitrarily high interest rates will result in many projects (particularly long-term projects) being inappropriately turned down because incorrect low values will be assigned to cash flows expected at distant points in the future.

Present Value and Future Value of Annuities

Not all investments have cash outlays at time zero and provide a single benefit at some point in the future. Most investments actually provide a series, or stream, of benefits over a specified period in the future. An investment that promises a constant amount each period over n periods is called an *n*-period annuity. For example, many lotteries are examples of an *n*-period annuity because they pay prizes in the form of an annuity that lasts, for example, for 20 years.

Project benefits received far into the future will have an insignificant present value if the interest rate is high.
Source: Galen Rowell/CORBIS Bettman.

Exhibit 11-5
Present Value
Decay

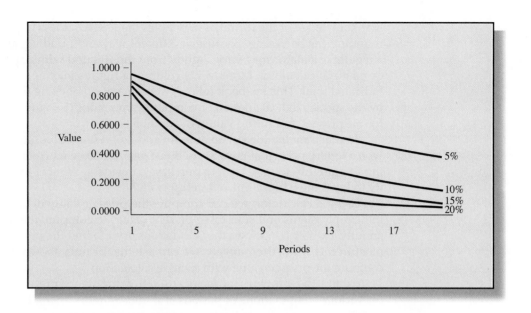

Sometimes lottery winnings are paid over time rather than immediately. Within this happens, the value of the winnings is diminished because of the time value of money.
Source: AP Wide World Photos.

Formulas and financial tables that allow analysts to compute the present value of annuities directly were produced before the widespread availability of calculators and spreadsheets. Today most annuity present value calculations are performed on calculators or computer spreadsheets that can calculate present values directly, so that knowledge of the formulas and tables themselves is less important. The issue of rounding can be vexing. Because of different ways of rounding, answers found with a regular calculator may vary slightly from those found with a spreadsheet program or financial calculator. Moreover, a column of figures may appear not to sum to the indicated total. This textbook follows the convention of using the number computed by the specialized calculation or computer. Appendix 11-1 summarizes the formulas for the present and future values of annuities.

To illustrate the idea of an annuity and its present value, suppose that you have won a lottery prize that pays $1 million a year for 20 years. You are interested in selling this annuity to raise cash to purchase a business. What is the value of this annuity today if the current rate of interest is 7%?

Using a calculator, we can compute the present value of each of the twenty $1 million payments and sum these present values to compute the present value of the annuity. Exhibit 11-6 shows the calculations used to find the present value of the payment in this way. Alternatively, we can use the formula shown in Appendix 11-1 to compute the present value with a single calculation.

Exhibit 11-7 provides the factors used to compute the present value of an annuity for various combinations of periods and interest rates. Using this table we can compute the present value of the lottery annuity as follows:

$$PV = a \times \textit{annuity present value factor}_{7\%,\ 20\ periods}$$
$$PV = \$1,000,000 \times 10.594$$
$$PV = \$10,594,000$$

Exhibit 11-6
Computing the Value of an Annuity

PERIOD	AMOUNT	PV FACTOR	PV
1	$1,000,000	0.9346	$934,579.44
2	1,000,000	0.8734	873,438.73
3	1,000,000	0.8163	816,297.88
4	1,000,000	0.7629	762,895.21
5	1,000,000	0.7130	712,986.18
6	1,000,000	0.6663	666,342.22
7	1,000,000	0.6227	622,749.74
8	1,000,000	0.5820	582,009.10
9	1,000,000	0.5439	543,933.74
10	1,000,000	0.5083	508,349.29
11	1,000,000	0.4751	475,092.80
12	1,000,000	0.4440	444,011.96
13	1,000,000	0.4150	414,964.45
14	1,000,000	0.3878	387,817.24
15	1,000,000	0.3624	362,446.02
16	1,000,000	0.3387	338,734.60
17	1,000,000	0.3166	316,574.39
18	1,000,000	0.2959	295,863.92
19	1,000,000	0.2765	276,508.33
20	1,000,000	0.2584	258,419.00
Total			$10,594,014.25

Exhibit 11-7
Present Value of an Annuity of $1

PERIOD	2%	5%	7%	10%	12%	15%	17%	20%
1	0.9804	0.9524	0.9346	0.9091	0.8929	0.8696	0.8547	0.8333
2	1.9416	1.8594	1.8080	1.7355	1.6901	1.6257	1.5852	1.5278
3	2.8839	2.7232	2.6242	2.4869	2.4018	2.2832	2.2096	2.1065
4	2.8077	3.5460	3.3872	3.1690	3.0373	2.8550	2.7432	2.5887
5	4.7135	4.3295	4.1002	3.7908	3.6048	3.3522	3.1993	2.9906
6	5.6014	5.0757	4.7665	4.3553	4.1114	3.7845	3.5892	3.3255
7	6.4720	5.7864	5.3893	4.8684	4.5638	4.1604	3.9224	3.6046
8	7.3255	6.4632	5.9713	5.3349	4.9676	4.4873	4.2072	3.8372
9	8.1622	7.1078	6.5152	5.7590	5.3282	4.7716	4.4506	4.0310
10	8.9826	7.7217	7.0236	6.1446	5.6502	5.0188	4.6586	4.1925
15	12.8493	10.3797	9.1079	7.6061	6.8109	5.8474	5.3242	4.6755
20	16.3514	12.4622	**10.5940**	8.5136	7.4694	6.2593	5.6278	4.8696
25	19.5235	14.0939	11.6536	9.0770	7.8431	6.4641	5.7662	4.9476

See ESS 3 for an Excel spreadsheet application.

ESS 3. COMPUTING PRESENT VALUE OF AN ANNUITY

The Excel formula to compute the present value of an annuity payment is

PV (interest rate, number of periods, payment, future value, type)

where payment is the amount of the payment made each period, and type is 1 if made at the beginning of the period and 0 if made at the end. The default value is zero. The convention in signing payments and interpreting the sign of the amount returned by Excel is that a minus value is an outflow and a positive value is an inflow. Entering the following in an Excel spreadsheet cell will compute the present value of an annuity of $1,000,000 per year for 20 years when the discount rate as 7% is −$10,594,014.25. That is, an outflow of this amount now will produce the 20-year annuity of $1,000,000.

= *PV* (0.07,20,1000000,,0)

Given that zero is the default value, entering the following in the Excel cell will produce the same result.

= *PV* (0.07,20,1000000)

Consider a bond with a face value of $1,000 that pays $60 in interest every 6 months for 10 years—that is, $60 per period for 20 6-month periods and a lump sum of $1,000 at the end of the tenth year. If an investor's required return were 5% per 6 month period, what would the investor be willing to pay for this bond? Exhibit 11-8 summarizes the cash flows associated with the bond.

Two components of the cash flow are associated with the bond: the periodic interest payments of $60 for 20 periods and the lump-sum payment at the end of the

Exhibit 11-8
Cash Flows Associated with a 20-Year Bond

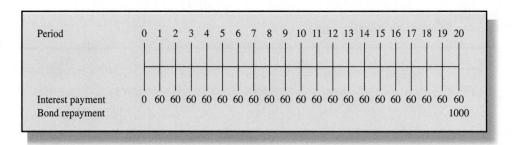

twentieth period. The following formula shows the calculation of the present value for the periodic interest payments:

$$PV = a \times \textit{annuity present value factor}_{5\%, \ 20 \ \text{periods}}$$
$$PV = \$60 \times 12.4622$$
$$PV = \$747.73$$

The following formula shows the calculation of the present value for the single lump-sum payment of $1,000 after 20 periods:

$$PV = FV \times \textit{present value factor}_{5\%, \ 20 \ \text{periods}}$$
$$PV = \$1,000 \times 0.37689$$
$$PV = \$376.89$$

Therefore, the present value of the bond is $1,124.62 ($747.73 + $376.89). The bond sells at a premium—that is, its price is greater than its face value of $1,000—because it is paying 6% interest ($60) each period when the market required interest rate is only 5%. We say that at the price of $1,124.62 the bond is sold to yield 5%.

A bond that paid only 4% interest ($40) each period would sell at a discount from its redemption value. You should be able to show that this discount is $124.62.

COMPUTING THE ANNUITY REQUIRED TO REPAY A LOAN

We often need to compute the annuity value that a current investment will generate. For example, if you agreed to repay a loan with equal periodic payments, you are selling the lender an annuity in exchange for the face value of the loan. The factor required to compute the amount of the annuity to repay a present value is simply the inverse of the present value factor for an annuity. Exhibit 11-9 shows these factors for selected periods and rates of return.

Returning to the preceding automobile purchasing example, suppose Bruce discovers that no one will lend him $10,000 to be repaid at the end of 3 years because financial institutions reduce their risk by requiring periodic loan repayments. Therefore, Bruce must make payments semiannually with a semiannual interest rate of 5%. Bruce's required semiannual payment will be $1,970 for 3 years, as shown in the following calculation:

$$a = PV \times \textit{capital recovery factor}_{5\%, \ 6 \ \text{periods}}$$
$$a = \$10,000 \times 0.1970$$
$$a = \$1,970$$

Exhibit 11-9
Annuity Required to Repay an Amount of $1

PERIOD	2%	5%	7%	10%	12%	15%	17%	20%
1	1.0200	1.0500	1.0700	1.1000	1.1200	1.1500	1.1700	1.2000
2	0.5150	0.5378	0.5531	0.5762	0.5917	0.6151	0.6308	0.6545
3	0.3468	0.3672	0.3811	0.4021	0.4163	0.4380	0.4526	0.4747
4	0.2626	0.2820	0.2952	0.3155	0.3292	0.3503	0.3645	0.3863
5	0.2122	0.2310	0.2439	0.2638	0.2774	0.2983	0.3126	0.3344
6	0.1785	**0.1970**	0.2098	0.2296	0.2432	0.2642	0.2786	0.3007
7	0.1545	0.1728	0.1856	0.2054	0.2191	0.2404	0.2549	0.2774
8	0.1365	0.1547	0.1675	0.1874	0.2013	0.2229	0.2377	0.2606
9	0.1225	0.1407	0.1535	0.1736	0.1877	0.2096	0.2247	0.2481
10	0.1113	0.1295	0.1424	0.1627	0.1770	0.1993	0.2147	0.2385
15	0.0778	0.0963	0.1098	0.1315	0.1468	0.1710	0.1878	0.2139
20	0.0612	0.0802	0.9440	0.1175	0.1339	0.1598	0.1777	0.2054
25	0.0512	0.0710	0.0858	0.1102	0.1275	0.1547	0.1734	0.2021

See ESS 4 for an Excel spreadsheet application.

ESS 4. COMPUTING THE ANNUITY REQUIRED TO REPAY LOAN

The Excel formula to compute the annuity required to repay a loan is

PMT (interest rate, number of periods, present value, future value, type)

where payment value is the amount of the loan or future value is the target amount that is to be accumulated by the annuity payments, and type is 1 if made at the beginning of the period and 0 if made at the end. The default value is zero. The convention in signing payments and interpreting the sign of the amount returned by Excel is that a minus value is an outflow and a positive value is an inflow.

Entering the following in an Excel spreadsheet cell will compute the amount that Bruce has to pay every six months for three years to repay his $10,000 loan as −$1,970.17.

= PMT (0.05,6,10000,,0)

Given that zero is the default value, entering the following in the Excel cell will produce the same result.

= PMT (0.05,6,100000)

Cost of Capital

The cost of capital is the interest rate organizations use for discounting future cash flows: The cost of capital is the return the organization must, on average, earn on its investments to meet its investors' return requirements. From a financial perspective, when the organization expects to earn less than its cost of capital from a proposed investment, it should return the funds that otherwise would be required for the proposed investment to its providers of capital. If the organization expects to earn more than its cost of capital from a proposed investment, the investment is desirable and any surplus that is earned increases the organization's (and therefore its shareowners') wealth. The cost of capital is the benchmark the organization uses to evaluate investment proposals. The organization's cost of capital reflects (1) the amount and cost of debt and equity in its financial structure and (2) the financial market's perception of the financial risk of the organization's activities. Finance courses cover in depth the way organizations compute the cost of capital used to evaluate new investments. Although several approaches are employed, the most widely used is the weighted average cost of capital method.

Weighted Average Cost of Capital Method

To illustrate, Simple Organization is financed 20% by debt with a pretax cost of 8%, 15% by preferred shares with a pretax cost of 11%, 30% by common equity with a pretax cost of 16%, and 35% by retained earnings with an estimated pretax cost of 14%. Simple's marginal tax rate is 45%. Exhibit 11-10 illustrates calculation of Simple Organization's weighted average after tax cost of capital, which is 12.23%.

Exhibit 11-10
Simple
Organization
Weighted Average
Cost of Capital

	PRETAX COST	AFTER TAX COST	WEIGHT	WEIGHTED AVERAGE
Debt	8%	8%(1 − .45) = 0.044	20%	0.0088
Preferred stock	11%	11%	15%	0.0165
Common stock	16%	16%	30%	0.0480
Retained earnings	14%	14%	35%	0.0490
Total				0.1223

The investment needed to build this facility represents a major investment of funds that creates significant committed costs. For this reason, organizations have developed special tools to evaluate capital investment proposals.
Source: George D. Lepp/Corbis Bettman.

CAPITAL BUDGETING

Capital budgeting is the approach that planners use to evaluate the desirability of acquiring long-term assets. Organizations have developed many approaches to capital budgeting. Six approaches are discussed in the following pages:

1. Payback
2. Accounting rate of return
3. Net present value
4. Internal rate of return
5. Profitability index
6. Economic value

To show how each of these methods works and alternative perspectives, each is applied to the following investment opportunity.

Shirley's Doughnut Hole

Shirley's Doughnut Hole is considering the purchase of a new automatic doughnut cooker that would cost $70,000 and last 5 years. It would expand capacity and reduce operating costs, thereby allowing Shirley's to increase profits by $20,000 per year. Shirley's cost of capital is 10%; the new cooker would be sold for $10,000 at the end of 5 years. Is this investment worthwhile? To keep the example simple, we will ignore taxes.

Payback Method

The payback method computes the number of periods needed to recover a project's initial investment. Shirley's initial investment of $70,000 is recovered midway between years 3 and 4, as Exhibit 11-11 shows. Therefore, that payback period for this project is 3.5 years.

$$\text{Payback Period} = \frac{70,000}{20,000} = 3.5$$

Many people use the payback period as a measure of the project's risk. Because the organization has unrecovered investment during the payback period, the longer the payback period, the higher the risk. Organizations compare a project's payback period with a criterion or target that reflects what the organization thinks is an appropriate level of risk.

Exhibit 11-11
Shirley's Doughnut Hole Payback Criterion

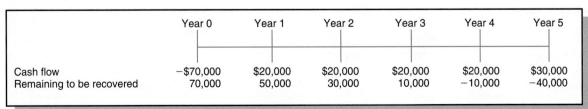

	Year 0	Year 1	Year 2	Year 3	Year 4	Year 5
Cash flow	−$70,000	$20,000	$20,000	$20,000	$20,000	$30,000
Remaining to be recovered	70,000	50,000	30,000	10,000	−10,000	−40,000

The payback method has two drawbacks:

1. It ignores the time value of money. In the Shirley's example, suppose that the cash flows resulting from the cooker were $60,000 in the first year, $0 in the second year, $0 in the third year, $20,000 in the fourth year, and $30,000 in the fifth year. This set of cash flows has the same payback period, 3.5 years, as the original alternative; however, this alternative would be more desirable because Shirley's recovers $60,000 at the end of year 1. In the first set of cash flows, Shirley's does not recover a total of $60,000 until the end of year 3. Because of the time value of money, it is always preferable to receive cash earlier. To recognize the time value of money, some organizations use the discounted payback method, which computes the payback period but uses discounted cash flows. Exhibit 11-12 shows the discounted cash flow variation of the payback method applied to the two variations of the cash flow at Shirley's. Note that the payback period for the original version of this exercise is now 4.35 years. Why is it longer than in the nondiscounted example? Because with discounting the future values that enter into the payback calculation are smaller. Note also that the payback period under the original discounted cash flow pattern is higher than under the revised discounted cash flow pattern. Why? Because in the revised pattern the cash flows occur earlier in the project life.

2. It ignores the cash outflows that occur after the payback period. Suppose there are two alternative cookers that Shirley's is considering: Cooker 1 is as described in the original example; cooker 2 has cash flows that are identical to those of cooker 1 except that its disposal value is $20,000 instead of the $10,000 disposal value for cooker 1. Based on a year-by-year comparison, cooker 2 is the better deal because in every year its cash flows are either equal or higher than those of cooker 1; however, the payback method would consider the two alternatives equal because their payback periods are both 3.5 years.

Accounting Rate of Return Criterion

Analysts compute the **accounting rate of return** by dividing a project's average accounting income by the average level of investment. Analysts use the accounting rate of return to approximate the return on investment, which is the ratio of the average income from an investment over the average investment level.

Exhibit 11-12
Shirley's Doughnut Hole

Cash Flow Version 1	YEAR 0	YEAR 1	YEAR 2	YEAR 3	YEAR 4	YEAR 5
Cash flow	−$70,000	$20,000	$20,000	$20,000	$20,000	$30,000
Present value at 10%	−$70,000	$18,182	$16,529	$15,026	$13,660	$18,628
Remaining to be recovered	$70,000	$51,818	$35,289	$20,263	$6,603	−$12,025
Payback period					= 4 + (6,603/18,628)	4.35

Cash Flow Version 2	YEAR 0	YEAR 1	YEAR 2	YEAR 3	YEAR 4	YEAR 5
Cash flow	−$70,000	$60,000	$0	$0	$20,000	$30,000
Present value at 10%	−$70,000	$54,545	$0	$0	$13,660	$18,628
Remaining to be recovered	$70,000	$15,455	$15,455	$15,455	$1,794	−$16,833
Payback period					= 4 + (1,794/18,628)	4.10

To compute the accounting rate of return, the accounting income must be computed first. Suppose Shirley's decides to depreciate the cooker so that the total amount of depreciation equals the cooker's historical cost less its salvage value. Using the straight-line method, which recognizes an equal depreciation each year, the annual depreciation is $12,000, as shown in the following equation:

$$\text{Annual depreciation} = \frac{\text{Historical cost} - \text{Salvage value}}{\text{Asset life}} = \frac{\$70,000 - \$10,000}{5} = \$12,000$$

Thus, the increased annual income related to the new cooker that Shirley's will report will be $8,000 ($20,000 − $12,000). Since all annual incomes are equal in this example, the average income will equal the annual income.

The average investment for the cooker will be $40,000, as shown in the following equation:

$$\text{Average investment} = \frac{\text{Historical cost} + \text{Salvage value}}{2} = \frac{\$70,000 + \$10,000}{2} = \$40,000$$

We can now compute the accounting rate of return for the cooker investment as follows:

$$\text{Accounting rate of return} = \frac{\$8,000}{\$40,000} = 20\%$$

If the accounting rate of return exceeds the criterion or target rate of return, the project is acceptable. Like the payback method, however, the accounting rate of return method has a drawback: By averaging, it does not consider the explicit timing of cash flows. However, this method is an improvement over the payback method in that it considers cash flows in all periods.

Net Present Value Criterion

A project's **net present value** is the sum of the present values of all its cash inflows and outflows. This is the first method we have considered that incorporates the time value of money. Following are the steps used to compute an investment's net present value:

Step 1   Choose the appropriate period length to evaluate the investment proposal. The period length depends on the periodicity of the investment's cash flows. The most common period length used in practice is 1 year, although analysts also use quarterly and semiannual period lengths.

Step 2   Identify the organization's cost of capital and convert it to an appropriate rate of return for the period length chosen in step 1.

Step 3   Identify the incremental cash flow in each period of the project's life.

Step 4   Compute the present value of each period's cash flow using the organization's cost of capital.

Step 5   Sum the present values of all the periodic cash inflows and outflows to determine the investment project's net present value.

Step 6   If the project's net present value, or residual income, is positive, the project is acceptable from an economic perspective.

In the case of Shirley's, the question is whether the 5-year annuity of $20,000 plus the single salvage payment of $10,000 after 5 years justifies the initial $70,000 investment. Let us follow our six steps to determine the net present value of Shirley's investment.

Step 1 The period length is 1 year because all cash flows are stated annually. The convention in capital budgeting is to assume, unless otherwise stated, that the cash flows occur at the end of each period.

Step 2 Shirley's cost of capital is 10% per year. Because the period chosen in step 1 is annual, no adjustment is necessary to the rate of return.

Step 3 The incremental cash flows are $70,000 outflow immediately, $20,000 inflow at the end of each year for 5 years, and $10,000 salvage at the end of 5 years. It is useful to organize the cash flows associated with a project on a timeline, as shown in Exhibit 11-13, to help identify and consider all the project's cash flows systematically.

Step 4 The present value of a 5-year annuity of $20,000, when the organization's cost of capital is 10%, is $75,816:

$$PV = a \times \textit{annuity present value factor}_{10\%,\ 5\ years}$$
$$PV = \$20,000 \times 3.7908$$
$$PV = \$75,816$$

The present value of the $10,000 salvage in 5 years, when Shirley's Doughnut Hole's cost of capital is 10%, equals $6,209:

$$PV = FV \times \textit{present value factor}_{10\%,\ 5\ years}$$
$$PV = \$10,000 \times 0.6209$$
$$PV = \$6,209$$

Step 5 The present value of the cash inflows attributable to this investment is $82,025 ($75,816 + $6,209). Because the investment of $70,000 takes place at time zero, the present value of the total outflows is $70,000. The net present value, or residual income, of this investment project is $12,025 ($82,025 − $70,000). If you refer back to the discounted payback method example in Exhibit 11-12, you will see the net present value of $12,025 excess over the amount to be recovered. This suggests—and it is indeed true—that the discounted payback method can provide the same information as the net present value method along with the payback period calculation.

Exhibit 11-13
A Timeline for Shirley's Doughnut Hole

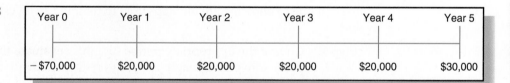

Year 0	Year 1	Year 2	Year 3	Year 4	Year 5
− $70,000	$20,000	$20,000	$20,000	$20,000	$30,000

Exhibit 11-14
Shirley's Doughnut Hole Computing Net Present Value

COST OF CAPITAL			10%
TIME	AMOUNT	PV FACTOR	PV
0	($70,000.00)	1.0000	($70,000.00)
1	20,000.00	0.9091	18,181.82
2	20,000.00	0.8264	16,528.93
3	20,000.00	0.7513	15,026.30
4	20,000.00	0.6830	13,660.27
5	30,000.00	0.6209	18,627.64
Total			$12,024.95

Step 6   Because the project's net present value is positive, Shirley's should purchase the cooker because it is economically desirable.

Exhibit 11-14 summarizes the individual cash flow calculations for the new doughnut cooker investment. See ESS 5 for an Excel spreadsheet application.

ESS 5. EXCEL SPREADSHEET APPLICATION

COMPUTING AN INVESTMENT'S NET PRESENT VALUE Excel has a built-in function to compute a project's net present value.
The function has this form:

$$NPV\ (rate, value\ 1, value\ 2, \dots, value\ n)$$

Suppose that you entered the periodic net cash flows into the following cells in an Excel spreadsheet; -70000 in cell B6, 20000 in cells B7 through B10, and 30000 in cell B11. The net present value function would be this:

$$= NPV\ (0.1,B7{:}B11) + B6$$

This will return the value of $12,024.95. Note that the function assumes that the first cash flow takes place at the end of period 1. therefore, if there is an initial investment it must be included separately in the expression.

Internal Rate of Return Criterion

The internal rate of return is the actual rate of return expected from an investment. It is the discount rate that makes the investment's net present value equal to zero. If an investment's net present value is positive, its internal rate of return exceeds its cost of capital; if an investment's net present value is negative, its internal rate of return is less than its cost of capital.

Since the net present value of Shirley's problem is positive, we know that the internal rate of return is greater than 10%. If we compute the net present value of the cash flows in Shirley's using 16%, we find that the net present value is $247. Since the net present value using 16% is still positive, we know that the internal rate of return is higher—so we will try 17%. Using 17% the net present value of the cash flows in

---

IN PRACTICE

Using Net Present Values to Evaluate a Merger

In December 2004, Sprint and Nextel announced plans to merge. The merger was to be accomplished by issuing 1.28 Sprint shares and $0.50 for each outstanding Nextel share. Since the Nextel share price at the time was $29.44 and the Sprint share price was $24.50, the exchange proposal represented a premium of about 8% over market value $(((1.28 \times 24.50) + 0.50 - 29.44)/29.44)$, totaling about $2.5 billion. Sprint executives expected that the synergies resulting from the merger would justify the premium. Sprint estimated the present value of the synergies to be $12.1 billion (later revised upward to $14.5 billion). These synergies included eliminating redundancies in network operations, improved customer service and marketing effectiveness, implementing superior Sprint technology in the Nextel customer base, and eliminating duplicated back-office functions.

Shirley's is –$1,452. So we know that the internal rate of return is less than 17%. Now we need to look on the interval between 16% and 17% to find the internal rate of return.

At this point there are two approaches we can use to converge on a value for the internal rate of return. One approach is to use simple interpolation. We know that the project's net present value falls from $247 to –$1,452, or a total of $1,699 (247 + 1,452) over the interval between 16% and 17%. So, assuming that the drop in net present value is linear over this range, the $247 drop that moves the project's net present value to zero is a point that is 0.1454 (247/1,699) along this interval. So we would estimate the internal rate of return as 16.1454% (16% + 0.1454%). It turns out that the net present value of the cash flows in Shirley's is –$4 when we use a discount rate of 16.1454%, so this is a pretty good estimate of the internal rate of return. Exhibit 11-15 summarizes these calculations.

As you might expect, spreadsheets and even some calculators can find a project's internal rate of return for you. See ESS 6 for an Excel spreadsheet application that will compute the internal rate of return as 16.143%. If you are wondering about the discrepancy between the interpolation approach and the trial-and-error approach that a spreadsheet uses to find the internal rate of return, the answer is that the decline of net present value as the discount rate changes is not linear.

ESS 6. EXCEL SPREADSHEET APPLICATION

COMPUTING AN INVESTMENT'S INTERNAL RATE OF RETURN Excel has a built-in function to compute a project's internal rate of return.

The function has this form:

IRR (value 1, value 2, . . . , value n, guess)

Suppose that you entered the periodic net cash flows into the following cells in an Excel spreadsheet: –70000 in cell B6, 20000 in cells B7 through B10, and 30000 in cell B11. The net present value function would be this:

= *IRR* (B6:B11,0.1)

The guess is your estimate of the project's internal rate of return. You can generally start with a rate like 10% or the organization's cost of capital.

This will return a value of 16.1429%. Note that the IRR function assumes that the first cash flow takes place at time zero.

Exhibit 11-15
Shirley's Doughnut Hole: Internal Rate of Return Calculation

ITEM	15.0000%	16.0000%	17.0000%	16.1454%	16.1429%
Present value of initial investment of $70,000	–$70,000	–$70,000	–$70,000	–$70,000	–$70,000
Present value of annuity of $20,000	67,043	65,486	63,987	65,264	65,268
Present value of salvage value of $10,000	4,972	4,761	4,561	4,731	4,732
Project net present value	$2,015	$247	–$1,452	–$4	$0

Because this project's 16.1429% internal rate of return is greater than the 10% cost of capital, the project is desirable.

Because a project's net present value summarizes all its financial elements, using the internal rate of return criterion is unnecessary when preparing capital budgets. Moreover, the internal rate of return criterion has some disadvantages:

1. It assumes that an organization can reinvest a project's intermediate cash flows at the project's internal rate of return, which is frequently an invalid assumption.
2. It can create ambiguous results, particularly when evaluating competing projects in situations when capital shortages prevent the organization from investing in all projects with a positive net present value and when projects require significant outflows at different times during their lives.

The net present value criterion is a superior alternative to the internal rate of return criterion and requires only one additional piece of information—the organization's cost of capital—for its calculation. However, internal rate of return is pervasive in financial markets and is widely used in capital budgeting. Exhibit 11-16 summarizes how respondents, when asked in a survey of practice in the United States, which criterion is extremely important, rated the four capital budgeting criterion discussed previously. Note that the most highly rated criterion is payback.

Profitability Index

The profitability index is a variation on the net present value method. It is used to make comparisons of mutually exclusive projects with different sizes and is computed by dividing the present value of the cash inflows by the present value of the cash outflows. A profitability index of 1 or greater is required for the project to be acceptable. Consider the two investments with the characteristics described in Exhibit 11-17.

Exhibit 11-16
Percentage of Respondents Rating Capital Budgeting Tool as Extremely Important

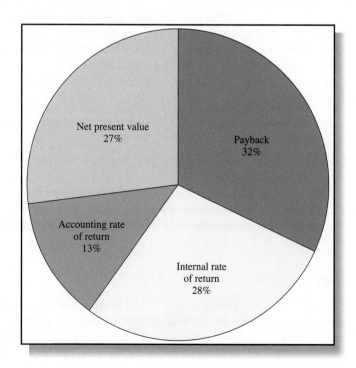

Exhibit 11-17
Profitability
Indexes
Compared

	PV Cash Inflows	*PV* Cash Outflows	Profitability Index
Project A	$50,000	$40,000	1.25
Project B	$60,000	$50,000	1.20

Advocates of the profitability index argue that project A is a better investment because it has a higher profitability index. What this means is that project A provides a higher leverage for a dollar of investment than project B. However, proponents of the net present value method argue that project B is better because it provides a greater wealth increment to the owners than project A. What this means is that the owners can create more total wealth for themselves by investing in project B. The profitability index can provide useful insights when the organization does not have enough funds to invest in all projects that have a positive net present value—which is usually the case. The net present value criterion is appropriate when the organization has enough funds to invest in all projects with a positive net present value.

Returning to Shirley's Doughnut Hole and the net present value criterion section, recall that the present value of the cash inflows was $82,025 and that the present value of the cash outflows was $70,000. Therefore, the profitability index for that project was 1.17 (82,025/70,000).

Economic Value Added Criterion

Recently, some analysts and consultants have proposed using the economic value added criterion as a way to evaluate organizational performance. Although the criterion is not directly suitable for evaluating new investments, its insights are useful.

Computing economic value added begins by using accounting income calculated according to generally accepted accounting principles (GAAP). The analyst then adjusts accounting income to correct what the proponents of economic value added consider to be its conservative bias. For example, common adjustments include capitalizing and amortizing research and development and significant product launch costs, eliminating the amortization of goodwill, adjusting for the LIFO effect on inventory valuation, and eliminating the effect of deferred income taxes. The analyst next computes the amount of investment in the organization and derives economic value added as follows:

$$\text{Economic value added} = \text{Adjusted accounting income} - (\text{Cost of capital} \times \text{Investment level})$$

The formula for economic value added is closely related to the net present value criterion. The major difference between the two criteria is that economic value added, unlike the net present value model which focuses on cash flows, begins with accounting income, which includes various accruals and allocations. This is why economic value added is more suited to evaluating an ongoing investment, for example, in a product or a division than a new investment opportunity.

Effect of Taxes

The effect of taxes on capital budgeting has been ignored so far. In practice, capital budgeting must consider the tax effects of potential investments. The exact effect of taxes on the capital budgeting decision depends on tax legislation, which is specific to each tax jurisdiction. In general, however, the effect of taxes is twofold:

Popularity of the Capital Budgeting Methods

The following chart reports some of the findings of a survey of capital budgeting practices of responding Fortune 1000 firms. For each capital budgeting method the data reports the percentage of firms indicating that particular method was always used. The data is reported for different project sizes: less than $100 million, between $100 and $500 million, and more than $500 million. Note the increased use of net present value method as the project size increases. This may reflect either the importance of the project or the size of the firm or both. Note also that for a given project size, the sum of the percentage of firms reporting that they use a capital budgeting tool exceeds 100% implying that organizations can and do use multiple tools. In fact, the data indicate that organizations' use of multiple tools increases with the project size.

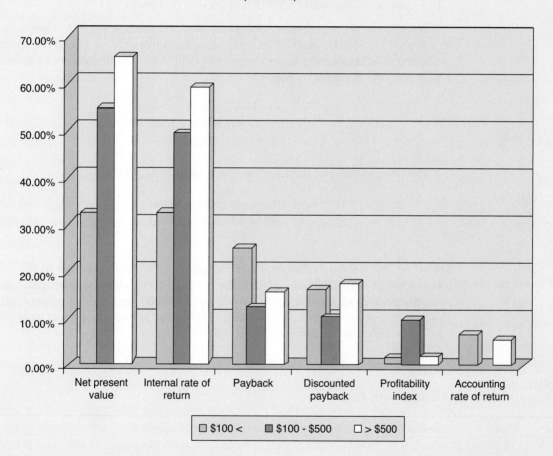

Reported Required Tool Use

Source: Patricia Ryan and Glenn Ryan, 2002, "Capital Budgeting Practices of Fortune 1000: How Have Things Changed?," *Journal of Business and Management* 8, no. 4, (2002): 359.

1. Organizations must pay taxes on any net benefits provided by an investment.
2. Organizations can use the depreciation associated with a capital investment to reduce income and offset some of their taxes. The rate of taxation and the way that legislation allows organizations to depreciate the acquisition costs of their long-term assets as taxable expenses vary.

Suppose Shirley's income is taxed at the rate of 40%. To keep things simple, suppose that the relevant tax legislation requires that Shirley's claim straight-line depreciation of its net investment—which is the historical cost less the salvage value of long-term assets—as a tax-deductible expense. If Shirley's after-tax cost of capital is 7%, is the cooker project desirable?

This analysis requires converting all pretax cash flows to after-tax cash flows. In turn, this requires knowing the amount of depreciation that will be claimed each year. Using straight-line depreciation, Shirley's Doughnut Hole will claim $12,000 depreciation each year, as noted earlier.

With this information, the after-tax cash flows attributable to this investment can be computed. Exhibit 11-18 shows these calculations.

The investment in the cooker provides two after-tax benefits:

1. A 5-year annuity of $16,800
2. A lump-sum payment of $10,000 at the end of 5 years

Because the cooker's book value at the end of 5 years is $10,000, there is no gain in selling it for $10,000. Rather, its salvage value is treated as a return of capital and is not taxed. When the organization's cost of capital is 7%, the present value of the 5-year annuity of $16,800 is $68,883:

$$PV = a \times annuity\ present\ value\ factor_{7\%,\ 5\ years}$$
$$PV = \$16,800 \times 4.1002$$
$$PV = \$68,883$$

The present value of the lump-sum payment of $10,000 is $7,130:

$$PV = FV \times present\ value\ factor_{7\%,\ 5\ years}$$
$$PV = \$10,000 \times 0.7130$$
$$PV = \$7,130$$

Therefore, the present value of the incremental inflows attributable to this investment is $76,013 ($68,883 + $7,130). Since the $70,000 investment takes place at time zero, the present value of the total outflows is $70,000, and the net present value of this investment project is $6,013 ($76,013 − $70,000). Because the project's net present value is positive, it is economically desirable.

Exhibit 11-18
Net Present Value Calculations with Taxes

Time	Cash Flow	Depreciation	Taxable Income	Tax @ 40%	Net Cash Flow	PV Factor	PV
0	($70,000)				($70,000)	1.0000	($70,000)
1	20,000	$12,000	$8,000	$3,200	16,800	0.9346	15,701
2	20,000	12,000	8,000	3,200	16,800	0.8734	14,674
3	20,000	12,000	8,000	3,200	16,800	0.8163	13,714
4	20,000	12,000	8,000	3,200	16,800	0.7629	12,817
5	20,000	12,000	8,000	3,200	16,800	0.7130	11,978
6	10,000	0	0	0	10,000	0.7130	7,130
Total							$6,013

Effect of Inflation

Inflation is a general increase in the price level. To account for the time value of money, one must discount future cash flows to the present using an appropriate discount rate. Similarly, to account for inflation, one must adjust future cash flows in order to compare dollars of similar purchasing power at time zero when the investment is made.

To do this, each cash flow is discounted by the appropriate discount rate and the expected inflation rate.

Consider the following example: Danny Company is considering investing in a new machine. The new machine will cost $125,000 and is expected to provide incremental cash flows of $50,000 per year, after consideration of all inflation and tax effects, for the next 3 years. Danny Company has a required after-tax return of 10% and expects that the rate of inflation will be 2%. The estimate of incremental cash flows reflects the effect of inflation. The planners at Danny Company want to determine the net present value, in current dollar and current purchasing power terms, of this machine. Following is the equation to compute the net present value of this project. Note that each future cash flow is divided by two factors—one factor to reflect the time value of money and another factor to reflect the purchasing power loss due to inflation. The idea is to convert all cash flows into equivalent current dollars.

$$\text{Net present value} = -\frac{125{,}000}{(1.10)^0 \times (1.02)^0} + \frac{50{,}000}{(1.10)^1 \times (1.02)^1} + \frac{50{,}000}{(1.10)^2 \times (1.02)^2}$$
$$+ \frac{50{,}000}{(1.10)^3 \times (1.02)^3} = -\$5{,}320$$

The first term in the numerator of each fraction is the adjustment needed to convert the cash flow to current dollars, and the second term in the numerator of each quotient is the adjustment to convert the cash flow to dollars of current purchasing power.

Rather than engage in this tedious two step calculation for each cash flow, we can compute the appropriate discount rate to use as follows:

Time and inflation adjusted discount rate $= (1 + \text{Cost of capital})$
$\times (1 + \text{Inflation rate}) - 1$

For Danny Company, compute the rate as follows:

Time and inflation adjusted discount rate $= (1 + \text{Cost of capital})$
$\times (1 + \text{Inflation rate}) - 1 = (1.1) \times (1.02) - 1 = 1.122 - 1 = 12.20\%$

We will now need to use a spreadsheet method since tables generally do not provide tabulated annuity and present value factors for fractional discount rates. Using the rate of 12.2% and spreadsheet calculations for Danny Company, we find that the net present value of this investment is $-5,320$ as shown in Exhibit 11-19.

Exhibit 11-19
Danny Company: After-Tax Cash Flows

	YEAR 0	YEAR 1	YEAR 2	YEAR 3	TOTAL
After-tax cash flow	−125,000	50,000	50,000	50,000	
Present value at 12.2%	−125,000	44,563	39,718	35,399	−5,320

NEW PRODUCT EVALUATION: AN EXAMPLE

Assume that you have the opportunity to invest in a new product that will have a 10-year life. The initial investment is $10 million in machinery and equipment, which will have a salvage value of $200,000 at the end of the tenth year. Your best judgment is that the product will increase profits by $2.5 million in the first year, and then incremental profits will decline by 10% per year. Your company faces a marginal tax rate of 40% and its after-tax cost of capital is 7%. Should you invest in this project?

Exhibit 11-20 summarizes the details of this example. We will now consider this investment opportunity from the perspective of the different capital budgeting criteria. In a given capital budgeting situation, an organization may use several of these approaches to evaluate an investment proposal, given that the different capital budgeting approaches can rank investment opportunities differently. For example, an organization may turn down a long-lived project with a positive net present value and a long payback period because of risk considerations. Therefore, if an organization is using several capital budgeting criteria, it must develop an individual, and therefore ad hoc, approach to determine how to make choices in situations in which different approaches provide different recommendations. Because of its problematic and ad hoc nature, dealing with approaches providing conflicting recommendations is not considered in the following discussion. Instead, we focus on the individual application of each approach.

Payback Criterion

Exhibit 11-21 summarizes the information needed to compute the payback period for this project. It shows that the investment is recovered sometime during the seventh year. Using interpolation, the payback period value is 6.52, as shown in the following equation:

$$\text{Payback period} = 6 + \frac{\$619,615}{\$1,189,162} = 6.52 \text{ years}$$

Exhibit 11-20
New Product Evaluation Example

YEAR	CASH FLOW	DEPN	TAX INC	TAX AT 40%	ACC. INC	NCF	PV FACTOR	PV
0	($10,000,000)							($10,000,000)
1	$2,500,000	$980,000	$1,520,000	$608,000	$912,000	$1,892,000	0.9346	$1,768,224
2	2,250,000	980,000	1,270,000	508,000	762,000	1,742,000	0.8734	1,521,530
3	2,025,000	980,000	1,045,000	418,000	627,000	1,607,000	0.8163	1,311,791
4	1,822,500	980,000	842,500	337,000	505,500	1,485,500	0.7629	1,133,281
5	1,640,250	980,000	660,250	264,100	396,150	1,376,150	0.7130	981,176
6	1,476,225	980,000	496,225	198,490	297,735	1,277,735	0.6663	851,409
7	1,328,603	980,000	348,603	139,441	209,162	1,189,162	0.6227	740,550
8	1,195,742	980,000	215,742	86,297	129,445	1,109,445	0.5820	645,707
9	1,076,168	980,000	96,168	38,467	57,701	1,037,701	0.5439	564,440
10	1,168,551	980,000	(11,449)	(4,580)	(6,869)	1,173,131	0.5083	596,360
Total								$114,469

Exhibit 11-21
New Product Evaluation Example Payback Criterion

YEAR	CASH FLOW	DEPN.	TAX INC.	TAX AT 40%	NCF	CUM NCF
0	($100,000,000)				($10,000,000)	($10,000,000)
1	$2,500,000	$980,000	$1,520,000	$608,000	$1,892,000	(8,108,000)
2	2,250,000	980,000	1,270,000	508,000	1,742,000	(6,366,000)
3	2,025,000	980,000	1,045,000	418,000	1,607,000	(4,759,000)
4	1,822,500	980,000	842,500	337,000	1,485,500	(3,273,500)
5	1,640,250	980,000	660,250	264,000	1,376,150	(1,897,350)
6	1,476,225	980,000	496,225	198,490	1,277,735	(619,615)
7	1,328,603	980,000	348,603	139,441	1,189,162	569,547
8	1,195,742	980,000	215,742	86,297	1,109,445	1,678,992
9	1,076,168	980,000	96,168	38,467	1,037,701	2,716,693
10	1,168,551	980,000	(11,449)	(4,580)	1,173,131	3,889,823

An organization using the payback criterion needs to decide whether it is willing to accept projects with payback periods of this length.

Accounting Rate of Return Criterion

By computing the average of the accounting income numbers in the sixth column of Exhibit 11-20, we can determine that the expected average accounting income for this investment is $388,982. The average investment level is $5,100,000, as shown in the following equation:

$$\text{Average annual investment} = \frac{\text{Initial investment} + \text{Salvage value}}{2}$$

$$= \frac{\$10,000,000 + \$200,000}{2} = \$5,100,000$$

Therefore, the accounting rate of return is 7.63%, as shown in the following equation:

$$\text{Accounting rate of return} = \frac{\text{Average accounting income}}{\text{Average investment}} = \frac{\$388,982}{\$5,100,000} = 7.63\%$$

The organization would then decide whether this accounting rate of return is acceptable.

Net Present Value Criterion

Exhibit 11-20 shows the calculation of the net present value of this project, which is $114,469. Because the net present value is positive, judged by the net present value criterion, this project should be accepted.

use the IRR function mentioned in ESS 6, or (2) by organizing the spreadsheet so that the discount rate can be varied so that the effects of its change can be easily observed.

Here is one way of organizing the spreadsheet so that either of the above approaches could be used.

Discount Rate						7%
Year	Cash Flow	Depreciation	Taxable Income	Tax at 40%	Net Cash Flow	Present Value
0	−10,000,000	0	0	0	−$10,000,000	−$10,000,000
1	2,500,000	980,000	1,520,000	608,000	1,892,000	1,768,224
2	2,250,000	980,000	1,270,000	508,000	1,742,000	1,521,530
3	2,025,000	980,000	1,045,000	418,000	1,607,000	1,311,791
4	1,822,500	980,000	842,500	337,000	1,485,500	1,133,281
5	1,640,250	980,000	660,250	264,100	1,376,150	981,176
6	1,476,225	980,000	496,225	198,490	1,277,735	851,409
7	1,328,603	980,000	348,603	139,441	1,189,162	740,550
8	1,195,742	980,000	215,742	86,297	1,109,445	645,707
9	1,076,168	980,000	96,168	38,467	1,037,701	564,440
10	1,168,551	980,000	−11,449	−4,580	1,173,131	596,360
Project net present value						$114,469
Project internal rate of return						7.28%

This spreadsheet is set up so that the upper left corner is cell A1. The discount rate is set up in cell C1 of this spreadsheet. Each of the present value calculations use the value in C1. For example, the formula for the calculation for the present value of the net cash flow in period 3 is as follows:

$$= F6/(1 + \$G\$1)^\wedge A6$$

Here, F6 is the value of the net cash flow in period 3, C1 is the discount rate, and A6 is 3 the current year. This approach involves varying the value in C1 until the project's net present value equals zero.

An alternative approach is to use the Excel IRR function. The following formula was entered into cell G15:

$$= IRR(F3:F13,0.07)$$

This formula computes the internal rate of return as 7.28%.

UNCERTAINTY IN CASH FLOWS

Capital budgeting analysis relies on estimates of future cash flows. Because estimates are not always realized, many decision makers like to know how their estimates affect the decisions they are making. Estimating future cash flows is an important and difficult task. Cash flow estimation is important because many decisions will be affected by those estimates. It is difficult because these estimates will reflect circumstances that the organization may not have previously experienced.

Most cash flow estimation is incremental, meaning that it is done by projecting previous experience. For example, based on claims from the manufacturer, a new machine might be expected to decrease costs by 10%. Many organizations assume that learning will systematically reduce the costs of a new system or process. Cash flows related to sales of a new product are often estimated based on past experiences with similar products. Whatever the forecast, it usually starts with a previous experience or makes appropriate adjustments.

High Low Method

The high low method of estimating cash flows begins by asking the planner to estimate the most likely effect of a decision, such as a cost decrease or a revenue increase, and then to estimate the highest and lowest possible values that could occur. The planner next constructs a normal distribution with a mean equal to the most likely value estimated and a standard deviation equal to the highest estimated value minus the mean, the difference divided by 3.

For example, suppose that Murphy Company is installing a new machine that is expected to improve quality and reduce product cost. The effect will be to increase revenues and decrease manufacturing costs. The planner believes that the most likely net effect will be to increase pretax cash flows by $100,000 per year; however, the planner also believes the effect could be as low as $70,000 per year or as high as $130,000. Assuming that the benefits are normally distributed, the standard deviation of the estimated distribution of benefits is $10,000 [($130,000 − $100,000)/3] because only an insignificant probability exists that an observation will be beyond three standard deviations from the mean.

Only the mean or expected value of the estimate is needed for the net present value model, but by assessing a distribution of possible outcomes, the planner can make probabilistic statements about the outcomes. In this example, if the planner believes the possible outcomes have a normal distribution with a mean of $100,000 and a standard deviation of $10,000, she might say, "I believe the probability is about 98% (.9773) that the net cash flow benefit will be at least $80,000." since only about 2% of the area under a normal distribution lies below 2 standard deviations below the mean.

Expected Value Method

In the expected value method, the planner identifies four or five possible outcomes and assigns a probability of occurring to each one such that the total probabilities assigned equals one. Then the expected value of the estimate is computed by weighting each estimate by its probability. For example, Benny Manufacturing is considering adding 100,000 units to existing capacity. Part of the process of evaluating this capacity addition is determining whether it will be used effectively. The planner has developed the estimates shown in Exhibit 11-22.

This calculation suggests that, based on the planner's underlying beliefs, average use will be 69,000 units of new capacity. This estimate would be used in the capital budgeting model to project the revenue and cost effects of the capacity addition.

Exhibit 11-22
Benny Manufacturing Probability Estimates

Use	Probability	Weight
50,000 units	0.1	5,000
60,000 units	0.3	18,000
70,000 units	0.3	21,000
80,000 units	0.2	16,000
90,000 units	0.1	9,000
Expected value		69,000

Wait and See Possibilities

Suppose employees in the research group at Fyfe Company have designed a new product. Planners estimate that the net present value of the cash flows associated with this project will be $1.9 million given its 10% cost of capital. If Fyfe Company uses the net present value criterion to evaluate investments, it would choose to implement this project.

As the senior management group is preparing to accept this project proposal, it learns that the cash flows associated with this project are actually uncertain. There is a 70% chance that the project net present value will be $4 million, the high (H) return, and a 30% chance that the project net present value will be −$3 million, the low (L) return. The expected net present value of this project is $1.9 million (70% × $4 + 30% × −$3), which was the amount that the planners used to propose project approval. However, if the senior management group at Fyfe Company evaluates projects based on the expected net present value, this project would still be acceptable with the uncertain cash flows.

Suppose the marketing vice president, who is a member of this senior management group, makes the following proposal: Fyfe Company could develop a prototype that could be tested using a consumer panel. Testing would mean that the project would be delayed for 1 year. The marketing vice president believes that the panel will allow Fyfe Company to determine with certainty whether the project will have a net present value of $4 million or −$3 million. What is the most that Fyfe Company

Exhibit 11-23
Consumer Panel Decision Tree Diagram

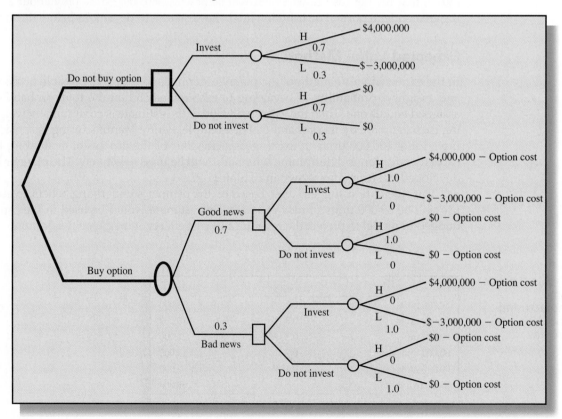

should be willing to pay for the prototype development and the consumer panel test? The value is up to $0.65 million, and the reasoning is as follows.

Based on current beliefs, which are the bases for evaluating any proposal, there is a 70% chance that the consumer panel will reveal that the project net present value will be $4 million, in which case Fyfe Company would proceed with the project. There is also a 30% chance that the consumer panel will reveal that the project net present value will be −$3 million, in which case the Fyfe Company would abandon the project. Exhibit 11-23 summarizes the decision alternatives.

Following the "Do Not Buy" consumer panel option, planners at Fyfe Company will make their decision based on their prior beliefs that the probability of the high return (H) is 70% and the low return (L) is 30%. The expected value of investing is $1,900,000 ($4 million × 70% + −$3 million × 30%), and the expected value of doing nothing is $0. Therefore, absent the consumer panel information, the best alternative is to launch the new product with an expected return of $1.9 million. Exhibit 11-24 summarizes this calculation.

Following the "Buy" consumer panel option, two possible outcomes present: good news or bad news. If the news is good, the best decision is to launch the new product with a value of $4,000,000. If the news is bad, the best decision is to abandon the new product, and that decision has an expected value of $0 because, based on the consumer panel option, planners will assess a 70% chance that the news will be good with an associated return of $4 million and a 30% chance that the news will be bad with an associated return of $0, the expected value of decision making with the

Exhibit 11-24
Consumer Panel Decision Tree Diagram with Expected Values

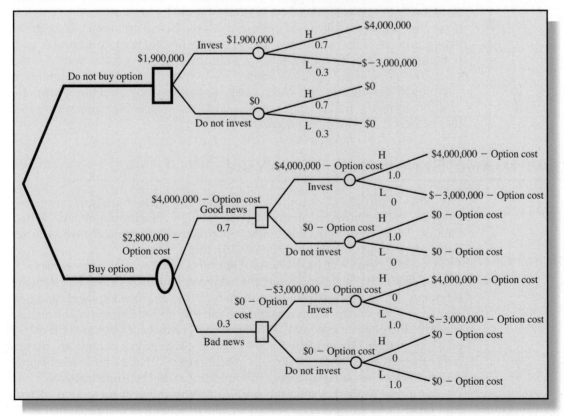

consumer panel information is $2.8 million (.7 × $4 million + .3 × $0). Note that the expected value of decision making has increased over the no information case because Fyfe Company has the option of abandoning the project if the news is bad.

Since the project would be delayed for 1 year if the consumer panel were used, the $2.8 million would have to be discounted to the present. If the discount rate is 10%, the present value of $2.8 million 1 year from now is $2.55 million ($2.8 million ÷ 1.1). Since Fyfe Company expects a return of $1.9 million without the panel information, the most it should be willing to pay for the managerial option of the consumer panel is $.65 million ($2.55 − $1.9). Thus, the value of the managerial option of delaying and using the consumer panel is $0.65 million. Exhibit 11-24 summarizes these expected values.

Consider what happens if uncertainty in the returns associated with this project, that is return volatility, increases. Maximum uncertainty occurs when each outcome is equally likely. If the probabilities that net present value is $4 million or −$3 million are both 50%, the value of the consumer panel is $1.32 million (.5 × $4 million + .5 × $0)/1.1) − (.5 × $4 million − .5 × $3 million). Similarly, if return volatility increases because the outcomes are 70% of $8 million and 30% of −$6 million, you should be able to show that the value of the consumer panel is $1.29 million. The value of the managerial option to use the consumer panel and wait increases as return volatility increases because there is no downside risk. If the consumer panel says that the product is a loser, Fyfe Company can abandon the project.

We have assumed in this example that the consumer panel predicts the project returns with certainty. This type of analysis will still work with some modifications if the customer panel alters our prior beliefs but does not predict the project returns with certainty. However, with less-than-perfect information, the value of the consumer panel information will be less than what was computed previously.

This insight of how delaying a project to acquire more information will add value for management has spawned an interest in applying options theory to investment decisions—a process called **real options analysis**. In real options analysis, the organization purchases an option that allows the option holder to purchase a real asset (a building, a project, or a machine) at a specified future point in time at a specified price. The value of the option is affected, as we saw in the previous example, by the volatility of the future value of the asset—in the previous example, the product. As volatility increases, the call option increases in value—meaning more value in delaying the decision to acquire more information.

WHAT-IF AND SENSITIVITY ANALYSIS

Two other approaches to handling uncertainty are **what-if analysis** and **sensitivity analysis**. In the Shirley's Doughnut Hole example, Shirley might ask, "What must the cash flows be to make this project unattractive?" Fortunately, we can use computer spreadsheets to answer questions like this.

Most planners today use personal computers and electronic spreadsheets for capital budgeting. The planner can set up a computer spreadsheet to make changes to the estimates of the decision's key parameters. If the analysis explores the effect of a change in a parameter on an outcome, we call this investigation a *what-if analysis*. For example, the planner may ask, "What will my profits be if sales are only 90% of the plan?" A planner's investigation of the effect of a change in a parameter on a decision rather than on an outcome is called a *sensitivity analysis*. For example, the planner may ask, "How low can sales fall before this investment becomes unattractive?"

Returning to the tax situation for Shirley's, suppose the expected incremental cash flows from the operation were only 95% of what was planned—that is, $19,000

Exhibit 11-25
Net Present Value Calculations with Taxes

TIME	AMOUNT	DEPRECIATION	TAX INCOME	TAX AT 40%	NCF	PVFACTOR	PV
0	($70,000)				($70,000)	1.0000	($70,000)
1	17,556	12,000	5,556	2,222	15,334	0.9346	14,330
2	17,556	12,000	5,556	2,222	15,334	0.8734	13,393
3	17,556	12,000	5,556	2,222	15,334	0.8163	12,517
4	17,556	12,000	5,556	2,222	15,334	0.7629	11,698
5	27,556	12,000	5,556	2,222	25,334	0.7130	18,063
Total							$1

instead of $20,000. Is the cooker still an attractive investment? The answer is yes. As shown in Exhibit 11-25, the annual cash benefits need to fall below $17,556 each year before the project becomes economically undesirable. This is a drop of 12% from the estimated amount of $20,000, which is not a big error. Therefore, the decision is sensitive to the estimated benefits.

For an example of how an organization might deal with uncertainty, consider Southport Consulting. The college and university recruiting season is approaching and Southport Consulting is thinking of hiring new consultants. Each consultant undergoes the training process that costs Southport approximately $30,000. Southport is wondering if this $30,000 cost is justified. The company treats hiring as a capital budgeting exercise. Each entry-level consultant is paid $70,000 per year, including benefits, and generates approximately $80,000 of annual net revenues (revenues less all nonsalary costs related to the revenues). The net contribution of each consultant is thus $10,000 per year.

Southport's consultants are highly prized by client organizations, and they are often hired away at higher salaries than Southport can pay and still be profitable. Consultants normally leave at the end of the year, and the probability of keeping a consultant longer than 5 years is assessed at virtually zero. Exhibit 11-26, which is based on past experience, summarizes the assessed probabilities of keeping the consultant for 1 through 5 years and indicates the present value of the benefits given the organization's cost of capital (12%).

As an exercise, verify the present value of the benefits reported in Exhibit 11-26. For example, the value given for year 3 is the present value of a 3-year annuity of $10,000 discounted at the rate of 12%. The expected net present value of the net margin contributed by the consultant is $24,762.70, which is less than the $30,000 initial hiring and training costs, suggesting that, given these circumstances, hiring a consultant is not an acceptable investment. (*Bonus:* Can you show that the minimum acceptable annual contribution by a consultant must be approximately $12,115 for the consultant to be attractive under these circumstances?)

Exhibit 11-26
Southport Consulting Present Value of Benefits

YEARS KEPT	PROBABILITY	PRESENT VALUE OF BENEFITS	WEIGHT
1	0.1	$8,928.57	$892.86
2	0.2	$16,900.51	$3,380.10
3	0.3	$24,018.31	$7,205.49
4	0.2	$30,373.49	$6,074.70
5	0.2	$36,047.76	$7,209.55
Expected net present value			$24,762.70

Increasingly, organizations are turning to simulation to identify risk in capital budgeting projects. The decision maker provides statistical or probabilistic estimates of the important parameters of the capital budgeting decision, and a computer program then simulates the performance of the project over many different trials.

For the simulation approach to be useful, the uncertainty must be complex enough so that direct application of statistical methods (such as computing project expected values) is impossible. A second requirement for simulation to be useful is that the decision maker can provide reasonable estimates of the nature and form of the uncertainty.

For a simulation of a capital budgeting project, the financial simulation will provide data, such as the minimum and maximum returns, the distribution of returns, and an estimate of the percentage of time that the project return exceeded the required rate of return. These data provide decision makers with various ways of estimating the risk associated with a project.

If you are interested in reading more about simulation in capital budgeting, do a Web search on "monte carlo simulation in capital budgeting."

STRATEGIC CONSIDERATIONS

So far, only the profits from incremental revenues or the expected cost savings offered by a long-term asset have been considered. The common benefits associated with acquiring long-term assets ignore the assets' strategic benefits such as improved product quality, improved customer service, or improved product functionality, which are of increasing importance in increasingly competitive global markets. Including strategic benefits in a capital budgeting example is controversial because such benefits are difficult to estimate and, therefore, risky to include. However, strategic benefits are, in fact, likely to be no more difficult to estimate than the profits from expected sales or expected cost savings.

Strategic benefits reflect the enhanced revenue and profit potential that derive from some attribute of a long-term asset. Usually long-term assets provide the following strategic benefits:

1. They allow an organization to make goods or deliver a service that competitors cannot—for example, by developing a patented process to make a product that competitors cannot replicate.
2. They support improving product quality by reducing the potential to make mistakes—for example, by improving machining tolerances or reducing reliance on operator settings.
3. They help shorten the cycle time needed to make the product—for example, by implementing 1-hour photo developing.

For example, Shirley's Doughnut Hole may consider investing in a new cooker that can sense when a doughnut is cooked and then eject it automatically. This cooker may offer the following benefits:

1. It may allow Shirley to hire less-skilled and lower-paid employees to work at the Doughnut Hole.
2. By compensating for ambient factors such as external temperature and humidity, the cooker may improve the consistency of cooking and, therefore, the quality of the doughnuts. As customers recognize the high quality of the doughnut, they are likely to find Shirley's doughnuts more desirable. In this situation, the

benefits from the automatic cooker can include increased sales and lower operating expenses if the competitors do not have this cooker. On the other hand, the automatic cooker can prevent an erosion of sales if Shirley's competitors also purchase it.

In either situation, acquiring the automatic cooker provides benefits to Shirley's that should be incorporated in the capital budgeting analysis. Moreover, any capital budgeting analysis should reflect the alternatives available to competitors and not simply assume that the status quo will continue indefinitely.

POSTIMPLEMENTATION AUDITS AND CAPITAL BUDGETING

After-the-fact audits can provide an important discipline to capital budgeting, which is a subjective judgmental process. Revisiting the decision to purchase a long-lived asset is called a **postimplementation audit** of the capital budgeting decision and provides many valuable insights for decision makers.

The decisions that are reached using capital budgeting models rely heavily on estimates, particularly those about the project's cash flows and its life. These estimates can come from many sources: past experience, judgment, or the experience of others, such as competitors. When estimates are used to support proposals, recognizing the behavioral implications that lie behind them is important. For example, a production supervisor who is anxious to have the latest production equipment may be optimistic to the point of being reckless in forecasting the benefits of acquiring the equipment in terms of cost reduction, quality improvement, and production-time improvements. This behavior is mitigated if people understand that, once equipment is acquired, the company will compare results with the claims made in support of the equipment's acquisition and that higher costs, including depreciation, will be assigned to products or customers produced with or served by this asset.

Many organizations fail to compare the estimates made in the capital budgeting process with the actual results. This is a mistake for three reasons:

1. By comparing estimates with results, the organization's planners can identify where their estimates are wrong and try to avoid making similar mistakes in the future.
2. By assessing the skill of planners, organizations can identify and reward those who are good at making capital budgeting decisions.
3. By auditing the results of acquiring long-term assets, companies create an environment in which planners are less tempted to inflate estimates of the cash benefits associated with their projects in order to get them approved.

BUDGETING OTHER SPENDING PROPOSALS

Organizations develop spending proposals for discretionary items that are not capital expenditure items, such as research and development, advertising, and training. Such items can provide benefits that will be realized for many periods into the future. However, financial accounting conventions relating to external reporting

(GAAP) require that discretionary expenditure items not related to capital be expensed in the periods in which they are made, even if they provide future benefits.

Despite the financial accounting treatment of discretionary expenditures, their magnitude suggests that they should be evaluated like capital spending projects when possible. The approach to analyzing a discretionary expenditure is identical to that used to decide whether to make a capital investment. Planners should estimate the discounted cash inflows (benefits) and discounted cash outflows (costs) associated with any discretionary spending project and accept the project if the net present value of the discounted cash flows is positive.

EPILOGUE TO DOW CHEMICAL PURCHASES UNION CARBIDE

This chapter on capital budgeting has provided some tools for evaluating the decision by Dow Chemical to pay $9.3 billion to acquire Union Carbide. Obviously, we do not have all the facts that senior executives at Dow Chemical used to justify their offer, but we can certainly evaluate the broad parameters of this acquisition using published financial information.

The net income reported by Union Carbide was $403 million in 1998. According to Union Carbide's 10-K filings with the Securities and Exchange Commission, the average annual net income reported by Union Carbide for the 5 fiscal years preceding the acquisition was about $586 million.

Assume that Dow Chemical has a cost of capital of 12%. The present value of a perpetual annuity of $403 million is $3.4 billion:

$$\text{Present value of a perpetuity} = \text{Annuity value/Cost of capital}$$
$$= 403/.12$$
$$= \$3.4 \text{ billion}$$

Using the more optimistic estimate for the annual annuity provided by the average income level over the past 5 years, we compute a present value of about $4.9 billion ($586/.12). For the sake of convenience and to reflect the increased potential for sales from the broader product line and perhaps the more effective management of Union Carbide's former assets by the management team of Dow Chemical, let us use the more optimistic $4.9 billion in our valuation.

In addition, Dow Chemical expects that costs of the merged entity will fall by $500 million per year because of cost rationalization. If we assume that Dow Chemical has a marginal tax rate of 40%, the after-tax amount of the savings is $300 million [$500 million × (1 − tax rate)]. Assuming that this annuity is perpetual, the present value of these cost savings is $2.5 billion ($300/.12). Therefore, we can account for a value of $7.3 billion ($4.9 + $2.5) from this acquisition, and we are left to explain $2 billion ($9.3 − $7.3), or about 22% of the acquisition price.

This seems like a large residual value to explain, but can you think of other sources from which value might accrue in this purchase? The discussion at the beginning of this chapter stated that analysts expected the income of primary chemicals to rise in the future, which would increase the value of the income stream that Dow Chemical purchased. Would costs increase as well?

One possibility to explain this gap is that Dow Chemical's cost of capital is less than 12%. Suppose Dow Chemical uses an after-tax cost of capital of 10% to evaluate its investments. In this case, the value of the income stream purchased is $5.9 billion ($586/.1), and the value of the cost savings is $3.0 billion ($300/.1), yielding a total of $8.9 billion, which is within $500 million of the purchase price.

SUMMARY

This chapter discussed and illustrated the tools that management accountants use to evaluate the acquisition and use of long-term assets (also known as capacity-related assets, long-term assets, and capital assets). Long-term assets create risk for the organization for two reasons. First, they commit the organization to a long-term use of the asset. Second, the cost of the asset is fixed at the time the asset is acquired—the cost of the asset is independent of the subsequent level of asset use. For these reasons, management accountants have developed specific tools to manage investments in long-term assets.

Money has a time value because money on hand today can be invested to return a higher future amount, and this chapter introduced the notion of the time value of money and the various financial tools that planners use to recognize the time value of money.

Of particular importance is the notion of the present value of a sum or sums of money, which is the current equivalent of future amounts to be received or paid when we recognize that, because of the time value of money, money now is worth more than money in the future.

We saw that capital budgeting is a systematic approach to evaluating the investment in a long-term asset. The chapter discussed six different approaches to capital budgeting. Surveys of practice suggest that the payback method, which does not recognize the time value of money, is likely the most widely used. The net present value method, which reflects the time value of money, is the approach most widely promoted by financial analysts and textbooks.

The chapter showed how taxes and inflation can be incorporated into the capital budgeting decision and how analysts have developed new approaches including simulation, what-if analysis, and real options analysis to deal with cash flow uncertainty. Finally, the chapter discussed why including the strategic benefits associated with the acquisition of a long-term asset is an important adjunct to the capital budgeting process.

KEY TERMS

Accounting rate of return, 538
Capital budgeting, 523, 537
Compound growth, 527
Cost of capital, 535
Discounting, 528
Economic value added, 544
Expected value method, 551
Future value, 524

High low method, 551
Inflation, 547
Internal rate of return, 541
Investment, 523
Net present value, 539
Payback method, 537
Period annuity, 530
Postimplementation audit, 557

Present value, 528
Profitability index, 543
Real options, 554
Return, 523
Sensitivity analysis, 554
Time value of money, 524
What-if analysis, 554

ASSIGNMENT MATERIALS

Questions

11-1 What is the defining feature of a long-term, or capital, asset? (LO 1)

11-2 What is capital budgeting? (LO 2)

11-3 What are the attributes of long-term assets? Why do organizations use capital budgeting to evaluate the acquisition of long-term assets? (LO 1)

11-4 What is the fundamental evaluation issue in dealing with a long-term asset? (LO 1, 2)

11-5 What is an investment? (LO 3)

11-6 What does return mean? (LO 3)

11-7 What does *time value of money* mean? (LO 3)

11-8 Is it always true that money now is worth more than the same amount of money received a year from now? (LO 3)

11-9 What is future value of a dollar amount? (LO 3)

11-10 What is the role of future value in capital budgeting? (LO 3)

11-11 What is the compounding effect of interest? (LO 3)

11-12 What is present value of a dollar amount? (LO 3)

11-13 What is the significance and role of time zero in capital budgeting? (LO 3)

11-14 What is discounting? (LO 3)

11-15 Give an example of an annuity. (LO 3)

11-16 What is the cost of capital? (LO 3)

11-17 What is the most widely used approach to computing the cost of capital for evaluating new investments? (LO 3)

11-18 What is the discount rate? (LO 3)

11-19 What does payback period mean? (LO 4)

11-20 How is accounting rate of return defined? (LO 4)

11-21 What are inflows and outflows in capital budgeting? (LO 4)

11-22 Why are incremental cash flows important in capital budgeting? (LO 4)

11-23 Why do planners compute the present value of a sum that will be received in the future? (LO 4)

11-24 What is net present value? (LO 4)

11-25 How is the idea of net present value used in capital budgeting? (LO 4)

11-26 What is internal rate of return? (LO 4)

11-27 How would you explain the idea of internal rate of return using nonfinancial terms? (LO 4)

11-28 How is profitability index defined? (LO 4)

11-29 How is economic value added computed? (LO 4)

11-30 What two major effects of taxes must be incorporated in capital budgeting decisions? (LO 5)

11-31 What is the difference between what-if analysis and sensitivity analysis? (LO 6)

11-32 What are the high low method and the expected value method of dealing with uncertainty of cash flows in capital budgeting? (LO 6)

11-33 What are two examples of possible strategic benefits provided by long-term assets? (LO 7)

11-34 Why are postimplementation audits useful? (LO 8)

Exercises

LO 1, 2   **11-35** *Explaining capital budgeting*   How would you describe capital budgeting to someone who is intelligent but knows nothing about the time value of money or the concept of a required return on an investment?

LO 1, 2   **11-36** *Quantifying intangible benefits in capital budgeting*   Suppose you work for a bank and are proposing a system that customers can access from their home computers to do their banking. Only about one-half of the estimated cost of this system can be recovered by decreased clerical time required in the banks. However, you believe that the balance of the cost will be more than made up by improved customer service that will attract more customers. How would you handle this situation in a capital budgeting exercise?

LO 3   **11-37** *Evaluating payment alternatives*   Suppose you can earn a 6-month return of 2.5% on invested cash. Which is a better deal: $1,000 at the end of 1 year or $495 at the end of 6 months and another $495 at the end of 12 months?

LO 3   **11-38** *Compounding*   Explain the notion of compounding interest using an example.

LO 3   **11-39** *Effect of compounding*   Quintin is now 22 years old and has just started a new job. He is trying to decide whether to start investing for retirement now or to wait several years. Verify that investing a fixed amount at a 10% return per year yields approximately the same total accumulation at age 52 for Quintin under the following alternatives:
(a) Invest $3 per year for 30 years, beginning now
(b) Invest $5 per year for 25 years, beginning at age 27
(c) Invest $80 per year for 5 years, beginning at age 47

LO 3   **11-40** *The rule of 72*   The "rule of 72" states that the number of periods n that it will take to double an investment whose rate of return is r percent is approximately $72/r$. That is, nr is approximately equal to 72. Verify this approximation for $r = 4, 6, 8,$ and 10.

LO 3   **11-41** *Valuing an annuity*   You have won a lottery with an advertised prize of $1,000,000. The prize is to be paid in installments of $100,000 per year for the next 10 years. Is this prize really worth $1,000,000? Explain.

LO 3   **11-42** *Choosing an annuity*   You have been offered two annuities for the same price. Annuity 1 pays $50,000 per year at the end of the year for 10 years. Annuity 2 pays $40,000 per year at the end of the year for 20 years. If your cost of capital is 10%, which of these two annuities is a better deal? Why?

LO 3   **11-43** *Effective annual interest rate*   Your credit card agreement states that interest on any outstanding balance is computed monthly and at the rate of 1.25% on the outstanding balance. What is the effective annual interest rate on this credit card account?

LO 3   **11-44** *Cost of capital determinants*   Would you expect the cost of capital to be higher for an electric utility or a genetics laboratory? Explain.

LO 3   **11-45** *Weighted average cost of capital*   McDonough Corporation is financed 25% by debt with a pretax cost of 8%, 20% by preferred shares with a pretax cost of 12%, 35% by common equity with a pretax cost of 16%, and 20% by retained earnings with an estimated pretax cost of 14%. McDonough Corporation's marginal tax rate is 40%. Calculate McDonough's weighted average cost of capital.

LO 4   **11-46** *Net present value and profitability index*   Lebar Company is considering two mutually exclusive investment alternatives. Lebar has a 10% cost of capital. Following is the cash flow information for the two alternatives:

Initial investment in equipment	$170,000	$100,000
Increase in annual cash flows	$50,000	$30,000
Life of equipment	5 years	5 years
Salvage value of equipment	0	0

   a.   Compute the net present value for each alternative and determine which alternative is more desirable using the net present value criterion.
   b.   Compute the profitability index for each alternative and determine which alternative is more desirable using the profitability index criterion.
   c.   Why do the rankings differ under the two alternatives? Which alternative would you recommend?

LO 4, 5   **11-47** *Net present value with tax effects*   Branson Manufacturing is considering purchasing a piece of equipment costing $45,000. The new equipment would create a new cash inflow of $20,000 at the end of the year for 5 years. At the end of the 5 years, the equipment would have no salvage value. The company's cost of capital is 10%, and the tax rate is 34%. Assuming the company uses straight-line depreciation for tax purposes and taking income taxes into account, what is the net present value of purchasing the new equipment?

LO 5   **11-48** *After-tax cash flows*   Simpson Corporation has taxable income of $300,000 and an income tax rate of 34%. Simpson is considering selling an asset whose original cost is $20,000, with $12,000 of it depreciated. How much total after-tax cash will be generated from the sale of the asset for $18,000?

LO 6   **11-49** *Sensitivity analysis and capital budgeting*   Suppose you are advising someone who is using capital budgeting to evaluate the purchase of a clothing store. What role might sensitivity analysis play in this evaluation?

LO 6 **11-50** *Capital budgeting and risk* Suppose you are using capital budgeting to evaluate two alternative business opportunities. Both require comparable investments and have comparable average cash flows. However, the cash flows of one business appear to be more volatile than those of the other—that is, the cash flows of this opportunity vary more about its average. Is this an important consideration in capital budgeting?

Problems

LO 2, 3, 4 **11-51** *Capital budgeting alternatives* Discuss the advantages and disadvantages of each of the following as approaches to capital budgeting:

a. Payback
b. Accounting rate of return
c. Net present value
d. Internal rate of return
e. Profitability index
f. Economic value added

LO 3 **11-52** *Valuing a bond* A company issues a bond with semiannual interest payments of $45 for 10 years and a lump-sum repayment of the $1,000 face value of the bond after 10 years. If the bond market requires 10% interest compounded semiannually for the debt issued by this company, what is the market price (present value) of this bond?

LO 3 **11-53** *Valuing zero coupon bonds* A government issues a savings bond that will pay the holder $1,000 in 10 years. (This is called a zero coupon bond.) If the bond market is now requiring 5% annual interest on government debt, what will be the issue price (present value) of this bond?

LO 3 **11-54** *Revaluing a bond* Review the data in problem 11-53. Suppose you purchase that bond. It is 1 year later, and the bond market now requires 7% interest on government debt. What will you receive for this bond if you sell it today?

LO 3 **11-55** *Accumulating a target level of wealth* Carolyn Martin, who is now 30 years old, wants to retire at age 60 with $2.5 million in an investment account. If funds can be invested to earn 12% per year compounded annually, what equal annual amount must she invest at the end of each year? What will be the required amount if the funds are invested to earn 12% per year compounded semiannually?

LO 3 **11-56** *Accumulating a retirement fund* Review the data in problem 11-55. Suppose Carolyn decides it is unrealistic to invest an equal annual amount in her retirement fund at the end of each year. Instead she decides to invest increasing amounts at the end of each year. If the amount that she invests each year is 5% more than the amount she invested in the previous year, what amount must she invest in the first year? Assume again that funds can be invested to earn 12% per year compounded annually.

LO 3 **11-57** *Value in the face of risk* Return to the data in exercise 11-42. Suppose you are 65 years old and are deciding which of the two annuities to buy. The proposal is that the annuity will cease on your death—that is, in the event of your death, the balance of the annuity you buy will not be paid to your heirs. Choose one of the two annuities and show the basis for your choice.

LO 3 **11-58** *Mortgage payments* Under the provisions of the Dominion Interest Act, revised statutes of Canada 1952, Chapter 102, Section 6, whenever any principal money or interest secured by a mortgage of real estate is, by the same, made payable on the sinking fund plan, or on any plan in which the payments of interest and principal are blended, no interest whatsover shall be chargeable unless the mortgage contains a statement showing the amounts of such principal and the rate of interest chargeable thereon, calculated yearly or half yearly not in advance.

You have negotiated a mortgage in the amount of $400,000 with the stated nominal annual interest of 6%, and the mortgage document, as required, states that the interest will be calculated half yearly and not in advance. You will be making monthly blended payments of principal and interest and the amortization period for the mortgage is 25 years. What will be your monthly payment on this mortgage?

LO 3 **11-59** *Effective annual rate* A credit term that companies sometimes offer to their trade customers is 2/10 net 30. This means that if the customer pays its account in full within 10 days, the customer can deduct 2% from the balance otherwise due. Otherwise, the full amount is due in 30 days. If we assume that customers either take the offer to pay early and remit 90% of the obligation on the tenth day or the full amount on the thirtieth day, what is the effective annual rate of interest the company is offering?

LO 3 **11-60** *Effective annual rate* Fred's Payday Loans offers to advance you $1,050 in anticipation of your semimonthly payday check totaling $1,100. In exchange for the $1,050 received now, you are to turn over the full amount of your payday check of $1,100 when you are paid in 15 days. What is the effective annual rate of interest on this loan?

LO 3 **11-61** *Buy or lease* Dana is considering whether to buy or lease a new car. The dealer's list price on the car is $28,500, and the car is expected to remain in good to excellent condition for 10 years. The dealer offers a 3-year leasing arrangement in which the lessee pays $2,000 plus $360 per month (due at the end of each month) for 35 months (the first month's payment is included in the $2,000). At the end of the 3-year lease, the lessee can purchase the car for $17,000. Assume the lessee purchases the car for $17,000 at the end of the lease.

Required

a. What is the implicit interest rate that the dealer is charging under the lease?
b. Suppose Dana is able to pay for the new car in full without borrowing. However, if he leased the car, his expected return on invested cash is 5% per year. Is Dana better off purchasing or leasing the car?

LO 3 **11-62** *Changing the payment frequency* Suppose you are buying a house and require a $200,000 mortgage. You have told the bank you want to repay your mortgage over 30 years. The bank has indicated that, whatever payment option you consider, you will be charged an effective annual interest rate of 7% on your mortgage.

Required

What will be your mortgage payment if you are required to make
a. Mortgage payments at the end of each year?
b. Mortgage payments at the end of each six months?
c. Mortgage payments at the end of each quarter?
d. Mortgage payments at the end of each month?
e. Mortgage payments at the end of each week?

Explain any relationships you see among your responses to (a) through (e).

LO 4 **11-63** *Car alternatives, quantitative and qualitative considerations* Pick two comparable cars where one is a hybrid electric vehicle and the other uses gasoline only. Search the Internet to find approximate manufacturer's suggested retail price (MSRP) and miles per gallon for each vehicle. Also determine the relevant price per gallon of gasoline in your locality.

Required

a. Suppose you drive 10,000 miles per year and your driving is in the city rather than on highways. Comparing only the MSRP and miles per gallon, how long is the payback period for the hybrid electric vehicle?

b. Suppose that in (a), your discount rate is 5%. What is the discounted payback period for the hybrid electric vehicle? Assume for simplicity that all costs are paid at the end of the relevant year.

c. What considerations besides financial comparisons might be considered in choosing between a hybrid electric vehicle and a gasoline-only vehicle?

LO 4 **11-64** *Net present value for equipment investment, unknown operating costs* Bauman Company, which has a cost of capital of 15%, is thinking of replacing an existing piece of production equipment with new equipment. The following data relate to the analysis:

	OLD MACHINE	NEW MACHINE
Future life expectancy	5 years	5 years
Current salvage value	$50,000	Not applicable
Current purchase price	Not applicable	$500,000
Salvage value in 5 years	$10,000	$125,000
Annual variable operating costs	$350,000	Unknown

What is the maximum amount of annual variable operating costs for the new machine that would make this an attractive purchase?

LO 3, 4 **11-65** *Net present value, payback, internal rate of return, and accounting rate of return* Consider the following two mutually exclusive projects, each of which requires an initial investment of $100,000 and has no salvage value. The organization, which has a cost of capital of 15%, must choose one or the other.

Cash Inflows (End of Year)

YEAR	PROJECT A	PROJECT B
1	$30,000	$0
2	30,000	20,000
3	30,000	20,000
4	30,000	50,000
5	30,000	90,000

Required

a. Compute the payback period of these projects. Using the payback criterion, which project is more desirable?

b. Compute the net present value of these two projects. Using the net present value criterion, which project is more desirable?

c. What do you think about the idea of using the payback period to adjust for risk?

d. How do you think conventional capital budgeting adjusts for a project's risk?

e. Compute the internal rate of return for each project.

f. Assuming that straight-line depreciation is used to compute income, compute the accounting rate of return for these two projects.

g. What do you think of the accounting rate of return criterion?

11-66 *Capital budgeting with taxes and strategic consideration* Ronnie's Welding uses welding equipment mounted in the bed of a pickup truck to provide on-site welding services. The expected life of his existing equipment is 5 more years, after which the equipment will be worthless and scrapped for zero salvage.

Ronnie is considering replacing his existing welding equipment. The new equipment will allow him to do jobs he must now decline and will also reduce the costs of his current jobs. The new equipment should last 5 years, reduce the operating costs associated with existing jobs by $9,000 per year, and attract new jobs that will provide incremental profits of $5,000 per year. (Assume these cash flows occur at the end of each year.) The purchase price of the new equipment is $50,000, net of what Ronnie could get from selling his old equipment. The salvage value of the new equipment would be $2,000 in 5 years. Assume that Ronnie can borrow money at 12% and that he faces a 40% marginal tax rate. Assume that for tax purposes Ronnie will depreciate the net investment (that is, purchase price less salvage value) on a straight-line basis.

Required

a. Using the net present value criterion, is this investment desirable?
b. Suppose that while he is considering this project, Ronnie discovers that the quality of the welds produced by the new machine exceeds the quality of the welds made by the old machine. Because weld quality is related to safety, Ronnie knows that this will be attractive to many of his customers. Suppose Ronnie believes that if he buys the machine and his competitors do not, the increased profits associated with the new machine will be $8,000 per year instead of the original estimate of $5,000. Is this investment desirable?
c. Ronnie knows that his competitors have access to the same trade information he does and that he cannot restrict their access to the equipment he is considering. What do you think would happen if all these competitors purchased the equipment? What do you think would happen if only one competitor purchased the equipment?

11-67 *Capital budgeting and sensitivity analysis* You work for an automobile company that is considering developing a new car. The product development costs for this new car will be $500 million per year for 3 years. During the third year of product development, the company will incur $1 billion for manufacturing setup costs. Three years after the start of product development, the company will begin making and selling cars. Production and sales will last 7 years, and each car sold will generate an incremental profit of $2,500. After 7 years, the salvage value associated with the manufacturing facilities will be $200 million. The company's cost of capital is 12%. Assume all cash flows occur at the end of the year.

Required

a. What is the minimum number of cars the company must sell during each of the 7 years of the product's life to make this investment desirable under the net present value criterion?
b. What will the minimum number of vehicles be if the company's cost of capital is 15%? (Ignore taxes when answering this question.)

11-68 *Capital budgeting and uncertainty* Jane Eby, the chief financial officer of Baden Discount Enterprises, is faced with choosing between two machines. A new machine is needed to replace an existing machine that makes plastic mop handles for one of the company's most popular products. Jane is not sure about the demand for these mops but estimates that it would not be less than 20,000 units per year or more than 30,000 units per year for the next 5 years.

The two machines are the semiautomatic and the automatic, respectively. Relative to the semiautomatic machine, the automatic machine makes the handles more quickly and makes fewer mistakes that require rework. Thus, the total cost per unit for materials and labor for mop handles made by the automatic and semiautomatic machines is not the same. The total unit cost of material and labor for mop handles is $6 on the automatic machine and $8 on the semiautomatic machine.

The automatic and semiautomatic machines cost $500,000 and $300,000, respectively, and both would last 5 years. After 5 years of use, either machine could be scrapped for a zero salvage value. This organization has a cost of capital of 12%. (Ignore the effect of taxes when answering this question.)

How should Jane choose between the two machines in this situation? Be specific. You do not have to make a specific decision about one machine or the other, but your recommendation should tell her exactly how she should make the decision.

LO 4, 5, 6   **11-69** *Capital budgeting, taxes, and inflation*   If the annual cash flows and salvage value in Exhibit 11-18 were subject to inflation at the annual rate of 4%, the cash flows would be those shown below. (Note that, under these conditions, the annual depreciation is now approximately $11,566.69 [($70,000 − $12,166.53) ÷ 5].) Assume all cash flows except for the purchase occur at the end of the year.

TIME	AMOUNT	DEPRECIATION	TAXABLE INCOME	TAX AT 40%	NET CASH FLOW
0	($70,000.00)				($70,000.00)
1	20,800.00	11,566.69	9,233.31	$3,693.32	17,106.68
2	21,632.00	11,566.69	10,065.31	4,026.12	17,605.88
3	22,497.28	11,566.69	10,930.59	4,372.23	18,125.05
4	23,397.17	11,566.69	11,830.48	4,732.19	18,664.98
5	36,499.59	11,566.69	12,766.36	5,106.55	31,393.04

However, with inflation, the required rate of return must be increased so that it will provide for both the time value of money and the purchasing power loss due to inflation. In general, the required rate of return is as follows:

$$(1 + \text{Required rate of return}) = (1 + \text{Real rate of interest}) \times (1 + \text{Inflation rate})$$
$$\text{Required rate of return} = (1 + \text{Real rate of interest}) \times (1 + \text{Inflation rate}) - 1$$
$$\text{Required rate of return} = \text{Real rate of interest} + \text{Inflation rate}$$
$$+ (\text{Real rate of interest} \times \text{Inflation rate})$$

where the real rate of interest is the return required in the absence of inflation.

Required

a. Using the appropriate required return, compute the project's net present value.
b. Why is the net present value of the project lower under conditions of inflation than it was without inflation?

LO 4, 6, 7   **11-70** *Capital budgeting and sensitivity analysis*   Ritchie's Trucking hauls logs from wood lots to pulp mills and sawmills. Ritchie now operates a single truck and is considering buying a second truck. The total required investment in the truck and trailer would be $130,000. The equipment would have a 5-year life and a salvage value of $20,000. Ritchie's cost of capital is 12%, and Ritchie faces a marginal tax rate of 35%. You can assume that for tax purposes Ritchie will depreciate the net cost (that is, purchase price less salvage value) of the new equipment on a straight-line basis.

Adding a second truck would provide two major advantages for Ritchie. First, the new equipment would allow Ritchie to accept business that he now turns down because of a lack of capacity. Ritchie expects that the net cash flow associated with this additional business is about $25,000 per year. Second, the new equipment would allow Ritchie to reduce the cost of current operations primarily by discontinuing the practice of having to pay drivers overtime. This savings would amount to approximately $10,000. Assume these last two cash flows occur at the end of the year.

Required

a. Using the net present value criterion, is the investment in the new equipment justified?
b. What is the minimum amount of annual benefit from the investment in the new equipment that will make the project acceptable?

LO 4, 6, 7 **11-71 *Capital budgeting and sensitivity analysis*** Magic Mountain Enterprises runs a ski center. Its 14 downhill runs vary in difficulty from beginner to expert. To attract more customers, Maria Jasper, the owner/manager, is considering developing cross-country ski trails. The cross-country ski trails would take 2 years to build and would cost $1,000,000 per year to build. The trails would open for business in year 3 and would generate $500,000 per year in net cash flows. Maria has a required return of 12% on all investments.

The land on which the trails would be built is leased. The lease costs are included in the $500,000 annual net cash flow calculation. The lease will expire 9 years from now, that is, after the trails have been operated for 7 years. There will be no opportunity to renew the lease, and Maria will not be compensated for any of the work done building the ski trails. Assume all cash flows occur at the end of the year.

Required

a. Compute the net present value of the decision to enter the cross-country ski business. Should the investment be made? (Ignore taxes in your analysis.)
b. What is the minimum annual net cash flow from the cross-country ski business during the 7 years of operations that would make this investment desirable?
c. What other factors would you consider in making the decision?

LO 5, 6 **11-72 *Wait and see, what-if analysis, uncertainty*** Refer to the Fyfe Company example on page 552 and analyze the effect of the independent changes described here. In addition to your computations for expected values with and without the consumer panel option and the maximum Fyfe would be willing to pay for the customer panel option, provide an intuitive explanation for the following changes in the results from the original situation.
a. A change in the discount rate to 12%.
b. A change in the probability of "good news" to 0.8. (The discount rate is 10%.)

c. A change in the probability of "good news" to 0.5. Explain why Fyfe is willing to pay the most for the customer panel option with this probability equal to 0.5. (The discount rate is 10%.)

LO 8 **11-73 *Allocating capital funds and postimplementation audit*** You are the general manager of a consumer products company. One of your major tasks is to approve new product proposals brought to you by the product managers who report to you. The product managers are primarily an aggressive lot who are eager to expand the product lines they supervise. These product managers are paid a wage, which is based in part on the number of products they supervise. In addition, they receive a bonus that is based on the amount of product sales. Each year you receive between 20 and 25 new product proposals.

Each year the appropriations committee gives you a fund you use to support new product introductions. This fund is usually in the range of $60 million. On average, each new product introduction costs about $10 million. Therefore, you can fund between five and six new product introductions each year.

Required

a. What effect do you think postimplementation audits, which compare managerial claims made during new product proposals with actual results, would have on new product proposals?
b. Do you think managers would have to be penalized for variances (differences) between planned and actual results for the postimplementation audit to have any behavioral effect? If so, how should the company structure the penalty? If not, why would penalties not be necessary?
c. Do you think the way managers are paid is appropriate? If so, why? If not, what changes would you suggest?

Cases

LO 4, 6 **11-74 *Sensitivity and what-if analysis*** Your instructor has an Excel spreadsheet for the Shirley's Doughnut Hole example used in the chapter. You will need it to answer this question. The file shows how easily capital budgeting calculations can be done on a computer. (Knowledge and judgment are required to perform capital budgeting analysis; however, the computer makes the necessary calculations easy.) This exercise shows you how quickly you can answer what-if or sensitivity analysis questions after you have set up the spreadsheet. Do not be misled by the simple nature of the problem. The procedure is the same for more complex problems.

After you retrieve this file, look at the layout of the spreadsheet. The key problem parameters are the initial investment amount in cell D4, the annual benefits in cell D5, the salvage value in cell D6, the cost of capital in cell D3, and the tax rate in cell D9. The project's net present value of $6,013 is shown in cell D10.

Required

a. Move to cell D5 and adjust the annual benefits up or down until the amount in cell D10 is zero. (This will be about $17,556; you can verify this using Goal Seek in Excel.) This is the annual benefit that just makes the project desirable. Note that $17,556 is about 88% of $20,000, the estimated value of the benefit. Therefore, the decision of whether to invest in this project is quite sensitive to our estimate of the cost savings. This causes us to focus our attention on the estimate of cost savings.

b. Put the value of $20,000 in cell D5. The net present value shown in cell D10 should again be $6,013. Now move to cell D3 and experiment with the cost of capital until the net present value in cell D10 is zero. (This will be about 9.94%; you can verify this using Goal Seek.) This is 42% more than the estimated required return of 7%, so you should consider the decision to invest in the cooker relatively insensitive to the estimate of the required return.

c. Put the value of 7% (0.07) in cell D3. Again, the net present value shown in cell D10 should again be $6,013. Now look at the project life estimate. This simple spreadsheet is not set up in a way that allows us to vary the project life easily, although if you want to, it can be done fairly easily with spreadsheet macros. Suppose you want to know if the doughnut cooker investment would be justified if the cooker lasted only 4 years. Copy the original worksheet into a new worksheet. Delete row 19. Move to the new cell A19 and enter 4. This terminates the project after 4 years. However, you must adjust the depreciation so that it is taken over 4 years instead of 5. Move to cell D8 and enter 4. This will adjust the depreciation amount. You can see that the project now has a present value of –$1,401, which means that the project is undesirable. The decision to buy the cooker is very sensitive to the estimate of the cooker's life.

This simple example gives you the idea of how to use sensitivity analysis to identify what estimates are critical to the project's acceptance or rejection and where to spend more time or money improving the accuracy of estimates used in the analysis.

Required

Suppose the required return is 9%. If everything else in the problem remains the same as in the original problem, what is the minimum amount of the annual benefits that would make the project desirable?

LO 3, 4, 5, 6, 7 **11-75** *Evaluating an investment proposal under uncertainty* Serge Martin, general manager of the hapless Hogtown Flyers, is considering the acquisition of Mario Flanagan to bolster his team's sagging fortunes. Mario has played the last two seasons in Europe, so there would be no compensation paid to another team if he is hired. Mario, a prolific scorer, is holding out for a 10-year contract with contract demands of (1) an immediate and one-time payment of $200,000 as a signing bonus, and (2) $1,000,000 in salary in the first year. Mario is demanding that his salary increase at the rate of 10% each year.

Serge figures that hiring Mario will increase ticket sales by 35,000 per year. Tickets sell for $20 per game, and total variable costs associated with each customer per game are about $5. In addition, Serge is certain that with Mario, the Flyers will get into the playoffs each year. Getting into the playoffs means sales of at least 50,000 playoff tickets, which sell for $30 each. The variable cost associated with each playoff ticket is about $5. Because the Flyers have the highest ticket prices in the league and would operate at capacity if Mario were signed, Serge does not expect these numbers to change over the life of Mario's contract.

Serge's only concern is that Mario is demanding a guaranteed contract—that is, he will be paid whether he plays or not. Serge is virtually certain that Mario will play for 7 years. However, he is uncertain of the possibilities after that but certain that ticket sales will revert to their current levels whenever Mario stops playing. Assume all cash flows except the signing bonus occur at the end of the year.

Required

a. Prepare a 10-year statement of expected cash flows associated with this opportunity.
b. Assume that the Flyer's after-tax cost of capital is 6%. Compute the net present value of this deal if Mario plays for 7 years, 8 years, 9 years, and 10 years. Assume that the Hogtown Flyers face a marginal tax rate of 40% and that any losses on the sports operations can be used to reduce the taxes on other operations.
c. What would you advise Serge to do?

LO 3, 4, 5, 6, 7 **11-76** *Evaluating a new technology*   National Courier Company picks up and delivers packages across the country and, through its relationships with couriers in other countries, provides international package delivery services. Each afternoon couriers pick up packages. In late afternoon, the packages are returned to the courier's terminal, where they are placed in bins and shipped by air to National Courier Company's hub. In the hub, these bins are emptied. The packages are sorted and put into different bins according to their destination terminal. Early the next morning, the bins arrive at the various destination terminals, where they are sorted by route, put onto trucks, and delivered.

An operations study determined that about $2 million of employee time could be saved each year by using a scanning system. Each package's bill of lading would have a bar code that the courier would scan with a handheld scanner when the package is picked up. The shipment would be scanned again as it reaches the terminal, when it leaves the terminal, when it reaches the hub, when it is placed into a bin at the hub, when it arrives at the destination terminal, when it is sorted onto a courier's truck for delivery, and when it is delivered to the customer. Each scanning would eliminate the manual and less accurate completion of a form, thereby providing courier time savings.

The total cost of the scanning system is estimated to be $10 million. It is thought to have a life of 6 years, after which the equipment will be replaced with new technology. The salvage value of the equipment in 6 years is estimated to be $500,000.

At the end of each shift, the information from all the scanners will be loaded into National Courier Company's main computer, providing the exact location of each shipment. This tracking information provides for increased security, a lower mis-sort rate, and improved service in tracing shipments that have been mis-sorted. The reduced time spent tracing missing shipments accounts for the balance of the estimated employee time savings. The marketing manager believes that the increased security and service will result in an increased contribution margin of about $1 million per year if competitors do not adopt this technology and National Courier Company does. If competitors buy this technology and National Courier Company does not, it will lose $1 million in contribution margin. If everyone buys this technology, each competitor will maintain its current sales level. Assume all cash flows except the $10 million outflow occur at the end of the year.

Required

Assume that National Courier Company will use straight-line depreciation to compute depreciation for tax purposes. If National Courier Company's marginal tax rate is 35% and it has an after-tax cost of capital of 6%, should it make this investment? Include an assessment of the effect of different assumptions about the uncertainty of technology adoption by the competitors.

Appendix 11-1

Annuity Formulas

To compute the present value of an annuity, use this formula:

$$PV = a \times \left[\frac{(1+r)^n - 1}{r \times (1+r)^n} \right]$$

To compute the amount of an annuity that will repay a present value (loan), use this formula:

$$a = PV \times \left[\frac{r \times (1+r)^n}{(1+r)^n - 1} \right]$$

Chapter 12

Financial Control

After reading this chapter you will be able to:

➤ understand and be able to explain the nature and scope of financial control and its important roles both inside and outside organizations

➤ understand why organizations decentralize decision-making responsibility, the control and motivation issues that arise from this choice, and how organizations approach these control and motivation issues

➤ understand why organizations use responsibility centers, the type of responsibility center that is appropriate in a given setting, the limitations of the responsibility center approach to evaluating performance, and what performance measures senior management uses to evaluate responsibility center performance

➤ be able to design and interpret appropriate performance measures to evaluate the performance of each type of responsibility center

➤ understand why organizations use transfer prices and the types of transfer prices that organizations use

➤ be able to determine and compute the appropriate transfer price in a particular setting

➤ understand the nature and scope of return on investment and economic value added approaches to evaluating economic performance and be able to compute return on investment and residual income measures

➤ understand the nature, scope, and limitations of financial ratio analysis and be able to compute standard financial ratios to evaluate various elements of organization performance

Nucor

There are two basic steel mill types—the integrated mill and the mini mill. Here is a description of these two types provided by http://www.environmentaldefense.org:

> Historically, steel has been produced from virgin raw materials at integrated steel mills. "Integrated" refers to a combination of three steps

Source: Scott T. Smith/CORBIS–NY.

in steel production—coke making, iron making, and steel making—in one facility

The past 20 years have seen substantial growth of "mini mills"—steel production facilities that use steel scrap, instead of iron ore and coke, as the primary raw material for making new steel.

Exhibit 12-1 shows a diagram of the steelmaking process provided by http://www.steelconstruct.com. The steps that a mini mill avoids to make steel are those in the upper left branch of the diagram. Eliminating these steps in steelmaking means that mills using scrap steel as the primary raw material can be smaller than the integrated mills—hence the name mini mills.

Traditionally, using scrap metal as the primary raw material has been the least costly method of making steel because of the relatively low cost of scrap steel and the smaller investment required in a mini mill. Since scrap steel can account for as much as 70% of the raw materials cost in a mini mill, the cost advantage of a mini mill, along with its reduced capital (building) costs, is closely tied to the cost of scrap. Moreover, since mini mills can recover steel scrap from many sources such as automobiles, stoves, and refrigerators, mini mills have lower logistical costs since they can locate closer to customers rather than being tied to locations where coal and iron are mined or where there are low cost rail or ship transportation services.

The primary disadvantage of mini mills is that because they rely on scrap rather than working with the basic raw materials of coal and iron ore, they cannot control the chemical composition of their steel as well as the integrated mills. Moreover, the mini mills cannot produce the range of specialty products that are often higher-margin products that the integrated mills produce. For these reasons, the mini mills have fewer market opportunities than the integrated mills.

Exhibit 12-1
The Steel-Making Process

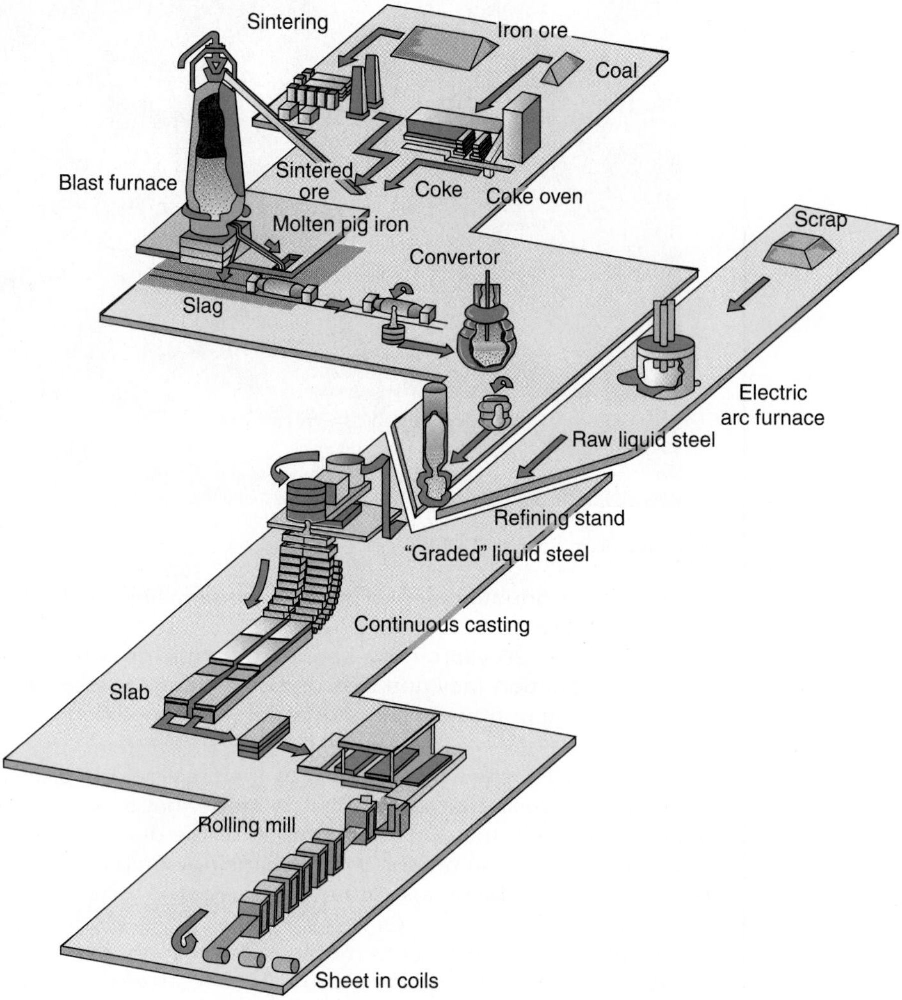

Nucor Corporation, headquartered in Charlotte, North Carolina, was one of the original proponents (and continues to be a leading proponent) of the mini mill concept. Nucor exploited its low cost producer advantage for considerable success over many years. However, the phenomenal growth in China's demand for steel in the late twentieth century and the early twenty-first century and competitive developments have created strategic concerns for Nucor. First, the increased demand for steel caused an increase in the demand for, and therefore the price of, scrap steel, reducing the relative advantage of using scrap steel as a primary input into steelmaking. Between midyear 2003 and 2004, the price of scrap steel increased more than 70% as U.S. exports of scrap steel increased dramatically (see Exhibit 12-2). The management discussion and analysis section of Nucor Corporation's annual report provided the following commentary

Source: Photos.com

Exhibit 12-2
Quarterly Average Scrap Steel Prices

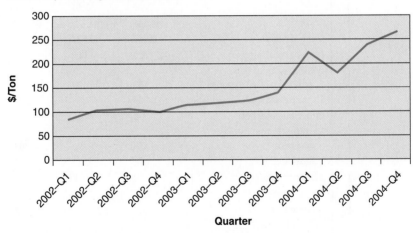

on scrap steel prices and their effect on its raw materials cost, which is the major component of cost of products sold:

In 2003, the prices of scrap steel and other raw materials surged dramatically, negatively affecting profitability. Nucor's average scrap cost per ton purchased increased $65 (57%) from December 2002 to

December 2003 and increased $99 (55%) from December 2003 to December 2004. To address this unprecedented escalation in the price of our raw materials, Nucor announced a raw materials surcharge on its products in January 2004. This surcharge has helped offset the impact of significantly higher scrap prices and has ensured that Nucor is able to purchase the raw materials needed to fill our customers' orders.

The scrap steel price increase and its decreased availability in the United States caused a number of organizations to petition the U.S. Congress to place curbs on scrap steel exports. Second, many integrated steel manufacturers began to acquire or build mini mills, creating additional competitors and therefore additional demand for scrap steel. Third, many integrated steel manufacturers began or continued a process of acquiring their own sources of coal and iron ore, thereby controlling and sometimes reducing the prices of these raw materials. These developments all contributed to reduced performance expectations for companies like Nucor with a heavy dependence on mini mills for their success. Fourth, some analysts believed that there was more long-run growth potential for specialty steel products that the mini mills could not make.

Exhibits 12-3, 12-4, and 12-5, respectively, present Nucor's annual income statements, balance sheets, and condensed cash flow statements for the years 2000–2004.

Exhibit 12-3
Nucor Corporation Income Statement, 2000–2004 (in millions)

	2000	2001	2002	2003	2004
Sales	$4,586	$4,139	$4,802	$6,266	$11,377
Cost of sales	3,666	3,531	4,025	5,632	8,746
Gross operating profit	920	608	777	633	2,631
Selling, general and administrative expense	183	139	176	165	415
Depreciation and amortization	259	289	307	364	383
Other income, net	1	16	9	7	2
Earnings before interest and taxes	478	196	303	111	1,835
Interest expense	0	22	23	27	22
Minority interest	0	0	80	24	81
Pretax income	478	174	200	60	1,731
Income taxes	167	61	68	4	610
Special income/charges	0	0	30	7	0
Total net income	311	113	162	63	1,121
Earnings per share (EPS)	$1.90	$0.73	$1.04	$0.40	$7.08

Source: Adapted from information provided at www.msn.com.

Exhibit 12-4
Nucor Corporation: Balance Sheet, 2000–2004 (in millions)

	2000	2001	2002	2003	2004
Current assets					
Cash and equivalents	$491	$462	$219	$350	$779
Receivables	350	331	484	573	963
Inventories	461	467	589	560	1,240
Other current assets	80	114	133	137	193
Total current assets	1,382	1,374	1,424	1,621	3,175
Noncurrent assets					
Property, plant, and equipment	4,025	4,227	5,094	5,331	5,694
Accumulated depreciation and depletion	1,685	1,861	2,162	2,514	2,875
Property, plant and equipment, net	2,340	2,366	2,932	2,817	2,818
Other noncurrent assets	0	20	25	55	140
Total noncurrent assets	2,340	2,386	2,957	2,872	2,958
Total assets	3,722	3,759	4,381	4,492	6,133
Current liabilities					
Accounts payable	203	189	247	330	472
Short-term debt	0	0	16	0	0
Other current liabilities	355	295	328	300	594
Total current liabilities	558	484	591	630	1,066
Noncurrent liabilities					
Long-term debt	461	461	879	904	924
Other noncurrent liabilities	260	329	371	440	515
Minority interest	312	284	217	177	173
Total noncurrent liabilities	1,033	1,074	1,467	1,521	1,612
Total liabilities	1,591	1,558	2,058	2,150	2,677
Shareholder's equity					
Common stock equity	2,131	2,202	2,323	2,342	3,456
Total liabilities and stock equity	$3,722	$3,760	$4,381	$4,493	$6,133

Source: Adapted from information provided at www.msn.com.

Exhibit 12-5
Nucor Corporation: Abbreviated Statement of Free Cash Flows (in millions)

	2000	2001	2002	2003	2004
Net cash from operating activities	$821	$495	$497	$495	$1,030
Net cash from investing activities	−410	−360	−901	−268	−535
Dividends	48	53	59	63	160
Free cash flow	$362	$82	−$464	$164	$335

Source: Adapted from information provided at www.msn.com.

THE ENVIRONMENT OF FINANCIAL CONTROL

What is meant by *financial control*? Financial control involves the use of measures based on financial information to assess organization and management performance. The focus of attention could be a product, a product line, an organization department, a division, or the entire organization. Financial control, which focuses on financial results, provides a counterpoint to the balanced scorecard view, which links financial results to their presumed drivers. In for-profit organizations, financial control looks at the drivers of profit such as the organization's ability to use its assets effectively and control costs for a given level of sales. In not-for-profit organizations, financial control looks at the organization's ability to use its resources in the most effective way to accomplish its service objectives.

In chapter 9 we explored the important role of the balanced scorecard as a means to quantify strategy and drive strategy down through the organization hierarchy. The balanced scorecard's cause-and-effect structure reflects management's assessment of what drives success in achieving organization objectives. In for-profit organizations, those objectives are invariably financial and include measures such as return on investment, earnings per share, market share growth, and profit growth.

Because external stakeholders such as investors, stock analysts, and creditors have traditionally relied on financial performance measures to assess organization potential, organizations have developed and exploited financial measures to assess performance and target areas for improvement. Recall from the balanced scorecard discussion that financial measures do not identify what is wrong, but they can provide a signal that something is wrong or, at the very least, that expectations were not met and that attention, explanation, and possibly even action are needed. For example, falling profits may reflect falling sales, which in turn may reflect customer dissatisfaction with poor quality, poor service, or high prices. Financial measures will highlight the falling profit and sales but not why—that is the role of the nonfinancial measures discussed in chapter 9.

Financial control is part of the broader topic of organization control we considered in chapters 7 and 8. Financial control is treated separately in this text because its use and tools are so pervasive in our economy.

FINANCIAL CONTROL

In chapter 10 we studied variance analysis, which is one of the oldest and most widely used forms of financial control. This chapter focuses on broader issues in financial control, including the evaluation of organization units and of the entire organization.

When managers apply financial control tools to evaluate organization units—for example, to evaluate the profitability of a product or product line—the resulting information is usually used internally and is not distributed to outsiders. Managers, particularly at General Motors during the 1920s, developed this form of internal financial control to support decentralizing decision making information in large organizations.

Outside analysts developed financial control tools to assess various aspects of organization performance, such as solvency, efficiency, and profitability. Because financial measures reflect how outsiders view the organization, these external financial control tools are relevant for management use and evaluation.

Decentralization, the process of delegating decision making authority to front line decision makers evolved for two reasons. First, as organizations became larger, it became increasingly difficult for a central decision maker, or core of decision makers, to make all organization decisions. Second, as organizations became larger and more geographically dispersed it became increasingly difficult to gather and transmit information about the organization's environment for evaluation and processing at the organization's center. Therefore decentralization was a natural development reflecting the need for large organizations to respond more quickly and effectively to important changes in their environment. In turn, decentralization was the phenomenon that prompted the development and use of internal financial control in organizations in the early 1900s.

Because of the difficulty in gathering and transmitting information quickly to a central decision maker, most highly centralized organizations are unable to respond effectively or quickly to their environments; therefore, centralization is best suited to organizations that are well adapted to stable environments. Observers of industry practice used to cite power, gas, and telephone utilities and companies such as couriers, fast-food operations, financial institutions, and natural resource industries as examples of organizations facing stable environments. A stable environment meant there were no major information differences between the corporate headquarters and the employees who were responsible for dealing with customers or running the operations that made the organization's goods and services and no changes in the organization's environment that required the organization to adapt. Therefore, there was no need for a rapid response to a changing environment or for delegation of

Wal-Mart has a very sophisticated inventory system that relies on data captured when customers pay for their purchases. This information allows Wal-Mart to respond quickly to potential stockouts and provides a good example of relying on technology rather than people to capture information at the organization's boundary.
Source: Jeff Greenberg/PhotoEdit Inc.

Standard Operating Procedures at Mercedes-Benz USA

When Mercedes-Benz built its SUV plant in Tuscaloosa, Alabama, it implemented a manufacturing system that included standard methods and procedures (SMPs). These SMPs specified the exact method in minute detail that workers must use to complete every task. No variations were permitted—effectively preventing workers from exercising any individual initiative.

decision making to local managers, and organizations could develop standard operating procedures for its well-understood environment that it expected employees to implement.

In such organizations, technology and customer requirements were well understood, and the product line consisted mostly of commodity products for which the most important attributes were price and quality. When price is critical, so is cost control. To accomplish this, organizations often develop standard operating procedures to ensure that (1) they are using the most efficient technologies and practices to promote both low cost and consistent quality, and (2) there are no deviations from the preferred way of doing things.

For example, McDonald's Corporation has honed its use of standard operating procedures almost to a science. Its kitchen layout, product design, form of raw materials, and prescribed operating procedures are all designed to keep cost low and consistency and quality high. McDonald's is not looking for a chef who wants to be creative either in preparing food or in introducing new menu items. Rather, it wants someone who can follow standardized procedures to promote consistent quality and low costs. In response to today's increasing competitive pressures and the opening up of former monopoly markets to competition, many organizations—even utilities, couriers, and financial institutions that were once thought to face stable environments—are changing the way they are organized and the way they do business. This is necessary because they must be able to change quickly in a world where technology, customer tastes, and competitors' strategies are constantly changing. McDonald's is a good example—in the face of increasing health consciousness, it was, in the years 2003–2005, experiencing franchisee losses and store closures for the first time in its history and was undertaking important changes in its menu, including introducing restaurants that stayed open 24 hours a day.

In the past, banks developed rigid and authoritarian management systems to protect assets and meet regulatory requirements. Although these systems have helped to meet such goals, in many cases they have not served well in dealing with customers. Providing high-quality customer service means remaining open in the evenings, installing automated teller machines to provide 24-hour banking services, offering online or Web-based banking that customers can access via telephone or personal computer, offering new products and services such as credit and debit cards, and responding more quickly, even immediately, to customer requests for car loans, lines of credit, and mortgages.

Being adaptive generally requires that the organization's senior management delegate or decentralize decision-making responsibility to more people in the organization. Decentralization allows motivated and well-trained organization members to identify changing customer tastes quickly and gives frontline employees the authority and responsibility to develop plans to react to these changes.

We can identify many degrees of decentralization. Some organizations restrict most decisions to senior and middle management. Others delegate important

To promote consistency, McDonald's Corporation develops a SQC (service, quality, and cleanliness) score for each store. Franchises can be terminated if a store fails to maintain an agreed SQC performance level. The SQC criteria used to evaluate the store consider performance levels and compliance with standard operating procedures. These criteria include how the customer is greeted, how much time the customer spends in line and at the counter, property cleanliness, and whether products are prepared in the prescribed manner.

decisions about how to make products and serve customers to the employees who perform these activities. The amount of decentralization reflects the organization's trust in its employees, the employees' level of skill and training, the increased risk from delegating decision making, and the employees' ability to make the right choices. It also reflects the organization's need to have people on the front lines who can make good decisions quickly.

To summarize, in decentralization, control moves from task control—where people are told what to do—to results control—where people are told to use their skills, knowledge, and creativity to achieve organization objectives. In financial control, those results are measured in financial terms. For example, a production supervisor would be asked to reduce costs by improving the manufacturing processes.

RESPONSIBILITY CENTERS AND EVALUATING UNIT PERFORMANCE

A **responsibility center** is an organization unit for which a manager is made responsible. Examples of responsibility centers include a hotel in a chain of hotels, a work station in a production line that makes computer control units, a department in a university or college, the data processing group in a government office that handles claims for payment from suppliers, a claims processing unit in an insurance company, or a shipping department in a mail-order business.

A responsibility center is like a small business, and its manager is asked to run that small business to achieve the objectives of the larger organization. The manager and supervisor establish goals for the responsibility center. Goals provide employees with focus and should therefore be specific and measurable. They also should promote both the long-term interests of the larger organization and the coordination of each responsibility center's activities with the efforts of all the others. The following section explores how this coordination is accomplished for goals that are financial.

Coordinating Responsibility Centers

For an organization to be successful, the activities of its responsibility units must be coordinated. Suppose we divided the operations in a fast-food restaurant into three groups: order taking, order preparation, and order delivery. Imagine the chaos and customer ill will that would be created if the communication links between any two of these organization groups were severed. Unfortunately, in large organizations, sales, manufacturing, and customer service activities are often disjointed, resulting in diminished performance. This need for coordination explains the interest that organizations have in enterprise resource planning systems that focus not only on

Large chains often treat their individual properties as responsibility centers. Corporate management evaluates the property managers based on either how much profit the property they manage contributes to the larger organization or based on the organization's return on investment in the property.
Source: David Young-Wolff/PhotoEdit.

integrating the organization's activities but also on linking the organization with its suppliers and customers.

Couriers, such as Federal Express, establish local stations or collector points (called terminals) from which they dispatch trucks to pick up and deliver shipments. Shipments that are bound for other terminals are sent to the Federal Express hub in Memphis, where they are sorted and redirected. The formula for success in the courier business is simple and has two key elements: (1) meeting the service commitment to the customer politely, on time, and without damage, and (2) controlling costs. The only way to achieve success is to ensure that all the pieces of the system work together effectively and to achieve these two critical elements of performance.

Suppose the management of a courier company decided that each terminal is to be treated as a responsibility center. How should the company measure the performance of each terminal, its managers, and its employees?

IN PRACTICE
The High Cost of Coordination

Many organizations invest huge amounts of money in enterprise resource planning (ERP) systems, which are complex and sophisticated computer systems that coordinate the activities of organization units. The goal of ERP systems is to smooth the flow of an order through the credit approval, scheduling, production, and shipping processes so that the customer is provided with a high level of service. Some analysts have put the average cost of an ERP system at about $15 million with one system reputedly costing $400 million. And not all ERP implementations are successful. In 2001, Sobey's, a Canadian grocery chain, reported a $60 million write-off of a failed ERP system.

First, the company can measure efficiency in each terminal. To focus on efficiency, it may measure the number of parcels picked up, sorted, or delivered per route, per employee, per vehicle, per hour, or per shift. To focus on efficiency and customer satisfaction, it may count—for productivity purposes—only those shipments that meet customer requirements, for example, on-time pickup and on-time delivery of an undamaged parcel to the right address.

Second, the organization's ability to meet its service commitment to customers in such a highly integrated operation as a courier business reflects how well the pieces fit together. The company should measure how much each group contributes to the organization's ability to meet its commitments to customers. The following are the two important elements of terminal–hub interaction for a courier:

1. The proportion of the time that the terminal meets its deadlines, that is, whether the trucks and containers are packed and ready to leave for the hub when they are required to leave (this is often called a *percent correct measure*)
2. When terminals are required to sort shipments, the number of shipments sorted to the wrong destination or that travel by the wrong mode (often called a *percent defect measure*)

Third, the company must assess its service to the customer at a more detailed level. For example, it might measure the following:

1. The number of complaints (or percentage of shipments with complaints) the terminal operations group receives
2. The average time taken by the operations group to respond to complaints
3. The number of complaints of poor or impolite service received by the company's customer service line
4. Customer satisfaction

In general, controlling the activities of responsibility centers requires measuring the nonfinancial elements of performance, such as quality and service, that create financial results in the long run. The key message is that properly chosen nonfinancial measures anticipate and explain financial results. For example, increased employee training that improves operating performance in this period should improve customer satisfaction and therefore revenues and profits in subsequent periods. Focusing on nonfinancial measures of performance such as innovation and employee morale motivates managers to avoid sacrificing long-run performance for short-run performance gains. For example, if we focus only on short-run financial performance, a manager might be motivated to reduce spending on research and development, investment in equipment to improve product quality and customer service, and employee training—thereby impairing long-run performance potential. Therefore, we must always be careful to use financial results as aggregate measures of performance and rely on nonfinancial results to identify the causes or drivers of the financial results.

Responsibility Centers and Financial Control

Organizations use financial control to provide a summary measure of how well their systems of operations control are working. When organizations use a single index to provide a broad assessment of operations, they frequently use a financial number, such as revenue, cost, profit, or return on investment, because these are the measures that describe the primary objectives of shareowners in profit-seeking organizations.

Federal Express has developed a measure called its service quality indicator (SQI) based on what it believes are nine key customer requirements. Each of these nine requirements is given a weight indicating the perceived importance of a failure of this requirement to the customer. The nine requirements and their respective weights are shown here:

Service Failure	Penalty Amount
Lost package	50
Damaged package	30
Complaint unresolved	10
Wrong day, late	10
Invoice adjustment required	3
Traces	3
Late pickup stop	3
Missing proof of delivery	1
Right day, late delivery	1

Federal Express tabulates these scores weekly and distributes them throughout the organization. Rewards to senior managers are based on these scores.

Responsibility Center Types

The accounting report prepared for a responsibility center should reflect the degree to which the responsibility center manager controls revenue, cost, profit, or return on investment. When preparing accounting summaries, accountants usually classify responsibility centers into one of four types:

1. Cost centers
2. Revenue centers
3. Profit centers
4. Investment centers

Cost Centers

Cost centers are responsibility centers in which employees control costs but do not control revenues or investment levels. Virtually every processing group in service operations (such as the cleaning plant in a dry-cleaning business, front-desk operations in a hotel, or the check-clearing department in a bank) or in manufacturing operations (such as the lumber-sawing department in a sawmill or the steelmaking department in a steel mill) is a candidate to be treated as a cost center.

Organizations evaluate the performance of cost center employees by comparing the center's actual costs with budgeted cost levels for the amount and type of work done. Therefore, cost standards and variances figure prominently in cost center reports. Moreover, because organizations often use standards and variances to assess performance, the process of setting standards and interpreting variances has profound behavioral effects on employees, particularly relating to misrepresenting performance potential and performance results.

Organizations often use cost centers to control manufacturing operations. Analysts compare the total cost of producing a product or batch of products with a budget for that level of production to help identify when the process is not working as planned.
Source: Joerg Boethling/Pete Arnold, Inc.

Other Cost Control Approaches

When an organization unit's mix of products and production levels is constant, it is possible to compare current cost levels with those in previous periods to promote an environment of continuous cost improvement. Interperiod cost comparisons can be misleading when the production mix or the production level are changing. Under such conditions, cost levels between periods are not comparable; however, when circumstances warrant, organizations are often able to plot cost levels on a graph and look for downward cost trends, which imply improved efficiencies in the processes that are creating costs.

Addressing Other Issues in Cost Center Control

Many organizations make the mistake of evaluating a cost center solely on its ability to control and reduce costs. The Federal Express example illustrates that quality, response time, the ability to meet production schedules, employee motivation, employee safety, and respect for the organization's ethical and environmental commitments are other critical measures of a cost center's performance. If management evaluates cost center performance only on the center's ability to control costs, its members may ignore unmeasured attributes of performance such as quality and customer service. Therefore, organizations should never evaluate cost centers using only the center's cost performance.

Revenue Centers

Revenue centers are responsibility centers whose members control revenues but do not control either the manufacturing or the acquisition cost of the product or service they sell or the level of investment made in the responsibility center. Examples are the appliance department in a department store, a regional sales office of a national or multinational corporation, and a restaurant in a large chain of restaurants.

Some revenue centers control price, the mix of stock on hand, and promotional activities. In such centers, revenue will measure most of their value-added activities and will indicate in a broad way how well they carried out their various activities.

Consider the activities of a gasoline and automobile service station owned by a large oil refiner. The service center manager has no control over the cost of items such as fuel, depreciation on the building, power and heating costs, supplies, and salary rates, but the manager has a minor influence, through scheduling and staffing decisions, on total labor costs. Levels of gasoline sales and repair activities determine all other costs. The service manager also has no control over the wages paid to employees: The head office staff controls them, and the central marketing staff controls all product pricing and promotional activities. The major controllable item in this service station is customer service, which distinguishes its gasoline sales and repair services from those offered in similar outlets and helps to determine the service station's sales levels.

The revenue center approach evaluates the responsibility center based only on the revenues it generates. Most revenue centers incur sales and marketing costs, however, and have varying degrees of control over those costs. Therefore, it is common in such situations to deduct the responsibility center's traceable costs, such as salaries, advertising costs, and selling costs, from its sales revenue to compute the center's net revenue.

Critics of the revenue center approach argue that basing performance evaluation on revenues can create undesirable consequences. For example, sales staff rewarded solely on sales (1) may promote or agitate for a wide product line that in turn may create excessive inventory management costs, or (2) may offer excessive customized services. In general, focusing only on revenues causes organization members to increase their use of activities that create costs to promote higher revenue levels.

Profit Centers

Profit centers are responsibility centers in which managers and other employees control both the revenues and the costs of the products or services they deliver. A profit center is like an independent business, except that senior management, not the responsibility center manager, controls the level of investment in the responsibility center. For example, if the manager of one outlet in a chain of discount stores has responsibility for pricing, product selection, purchasing, and promotion but not for the level of investment in the store, the outlet meets the conditions to be evaluated as a profit center.

Most individual units of chain operations, whether they are stores, motels, or restaurants, are treated as profit centers. It is doubtful, however, that a unit of a corporate-owned fast-food restaurant, such as Burger King, or a corporate-owned hotel, such as Holiday Inn, meets the conditions to be treated as a profit center because the head office makes most purchasing, operating, pricing, and promotional decisions. These units are sufficiently large, however, so that costs can vary because of differences in controlling labor costs, food waste, and the schedule for the facility's hours. Revenues also can shift significantly, depending on how well staff manages the property. Therefore, although these organizations do not seem to be candidates to be treated as profit centers, local discretion often affects revenues and costs enough so that they can be.

Numerous organizations evaluate units as profit centers even though the corporate office controls many facets of their operations. The profit reported by these units is a broad index of performance that reflects both corporate and local decisions. If unit performance is poor, it may reflect (1) an unfavorable condition that no one in the organization can control, (2) poor corporate decisions, or (3) poor local decisions. For these reasons, organizations should not rely only on profit center financial results for performance evaluations. Instead, detailed performance evaluations should include quality, material use (yield), labor use (yield), and service measures that the local units can control.

Investment Centers

Investment centers are responsibility centers in which the managers and other employees control revenues, costs, and the level of investment. The investment center is like an independent business. Perhaps the best example of an organization that uses investment centers is General Electric. The accompanying box provides a description of its major business units that General Electric provides on its Web site.

Since these units are so diverse, senior management uses return on investment to evaluate each of these business units and their subunits. For example GE Infrastructure includes the subbusinesses of Aviation, Aviation Financial Services (GECAS), Energy, Energy Financial Services, Oil and Gas, Rail, Water, while NBC

IN PRACTICE

Investment Centers at General Electric in 2006

GE is made up of six businesses, each of which includes a number of units aligned for growth.

GE COMMERCIAL FINANCE

GE Commercial Finance provides loans, operating leases, financing programs, commercial insurance, and an array of other products and services aimed at enabling business worldwide to grow.

GE CONSUMER FINANCE

GE Consumer Finance is a leading provider, under the GE Money brand, of credit services to consumers, retailers and automotive dealers around the world.

GE HEALTHCARE

GE Healthcare is a leader in the development of a new paradigm of patient care dedicated to detecting disease earlier and helping physicians tailor treatment for individual patients.

GE INDUSTRIAL

GE Industrial provides a broad range of products and services throughout the world, including appliances and lighting; plastics and silicones products; and equipment services.

GE INFRASTRUCTURE

GE Infrastructure is one of the world's leading providers of fundamental technologies to developing countries, including aviation, energy, oil and gas, rail, and water process technologies.

NBC UNIVERSAL

NBC Universal is one of the world's leading media and entertainment companies in the development, production and marketing of entertainment, news and information to a global audience.

Source: Courtesy of NBC Universal.

Source: General Electric Company.

Exhibit 12-6
Responsibility Center Summary

	TYPE OF RESPONSIBILITY CENTER			
FACTORS	COST CENTER	REVENUE CENTER	PROFIT CENTER	INVESTMENT CENTER
Controlled by center management	Costs	Revenues	Costs, revenues	Cost, revenues, and significant control over investment
Not controlled by center management	Revenues, investment in inventory, and fixed assets	Costs, investment in inventory, and fixed assets	Investment in inventory and fixed assets	
Measured by the accounting system	Costs relative to a budget	Revenue relative to a budget	Profit relative to a budget	Return on investment relative to a budget
Not measured by the accounting system	Performance on critical success factors other than cost	Performance on critical success factors other than revenue	Performance on critical success factors other than profit	Performance on critical success factors other than return on investment

Universal includes the subunit businesses of Network, Film, Television Stations, Entertainment Cable, Television Production, Sports/Olympic Games, and Theme Parks. These are truly diverse, and in many cases, portfolios of businesses that must be evaluated in terms of the return on investment each provides.

Exhibit 12-6 summarizes the characteristics of the various types of responsibility centers.

Evaluating Responsibility Centers

Using the Controllability Principle to Evaluate Responsibility Centers

Underlying the accounting classifications of responsibility centers is the concept of controllability. The controllability principle states that the manager of a responsibility center should be assigned responsibility only for the revenues, costs, or investments controlled by responsibility center personnel. Revenues, costs, and investments that people outside the responsibility center control should be excluded from the assessment of that center's performance. For example, the manager of a production line in a factory should be evaluated based on labor and machine hours used and not based on labor cost and machine cost because labor wage rates and machine costs were determined elsewhere in the organization. Although the controllability principle sounds appealing and fair, it can be difficult, often misleading, and undesirable to apply in practice.

A significant problem in applying the controllability principle is that in most organizations many revenues and costs are jointly earned or incurred. Consider the operations of an integrated fishing products company that is divided into three responsibility centers: harvesting, processing, and marketing and distribution. The harvesting group operates ships that go out to sea to catch various species of fish. The ships return to one of the company's processing plants to unload their catches. The plants process the fish into salable products. The marketing and distribution group sells products to customers.

As in most organizations, the activities that create the final product in this company are sequential and highly interdependent. The product must be of the right species, quality, and cost to be acceptable to the customer. The performance of the harvesting, processing, and marketing and distribution groups jointly determine the organization's success.

Evaluating the individual performance of harvesting, processing, and marketing and distribution requires the firm to consider many facets of performance. For example, it is possible to evaluate harvesting's operations by measuring its ability to do the following:

1. Catch the entire quota allowed
2. Minimize the waste and damage done to the fish caught
3. Minimize equipment failures
4. Control the costs associated with operating the ships

Similar measures can be developed for processing, and the evaluation of marketing and distribution may be based on their ability to meet delivery schedules and improve market share.

As part of the performance evaluation process, the organization may want to prepare accounting summaries of the performance of harvesting, processing, and marketing and distribution to support some system of financial control. The management accountant undertaking this task immediately confronts the dilemma of how to account for highly interrelated organization centers as if they were individual businesses. For example, costs of harvesting are easy to determine, but what are the harvesting revenues? Harvesting does not control sales or prices—its role is to catch the fish, maintain raw material and product quality, and meet the schedules determined jointly with processing and marketing and distribution.

If the company evaluates harvesting as a cost center, what about indirect organization costs, such as corporate administration, that reflect overhead resources used by the cost center? What about other important performance facets, such as maintaining quality, catching the full quota of fish, and delivering the required species of fish, when required, to the processing group? Should harvesting be asked to bear some of the costs of head office groups, such as personnel, planning, and administration, whose services it uses? If so, how should its share of the costs of those services be determined?

We could probably conclude that processing should be evaluated as a cost center, but what about the marketing and distribution group that through its general marketing efforts likely has the greatest impact on sales? What costs does this group control? It does not control harvesting and processing costs. The only costs controlled by marketing and distribution are marketing and distribution costs, which in most integrated fishing products companies are less than 10% of total costs. The harvesting group, through its ability to catch fish and maintain their quality, and the processing group, through its ability to produce quality products, are also influential in determining the organization's sales level. However, some people do not agree that the controllability principle is the best way to view performance evaluation.

Using performance measures to influence versus evaluate decisions. Some people argue that controllability is not a valid criterion to use in selecting a performance measure. Rather, they suggest that the choice of the performance measure should influence decision-making behavior.

Consider a dairy that faced the problem of developing performance standards in an environment of continuously rising costs. Because the costs of raw materials, which were between 60% and 90% of the final costs of the various products, were market determined and, therefore, thought to be beyond the control of the various product managers, managers argued that their evaluation should depend on their ability to control the quantity of raw materials used rather than the cost.

The dairy's senior management announced, however, that it planned to evaluate managers on their ability to control total costs. The managers quickly discovered that one way to control raw materials costs was to make judicious use of long-term fixed price contracts for raw materials. These contracts soon led to declining raw materials costs. Moreover, the company could project product costs several quarters into the future, thereby achieving lower costs and stability in planning and product pricing.

This example shows that managers, even when they cannot control costs entirely, can take steps to influence final product costs. When more costs or even revenues are included in performance measures, managers are more motivated to find actions that can influence incurred costs or generated revenues.

Using Segment Margin Reports

Many problems can occur when organizations treat responsibility centers as profit centers. These problems concern identifying responsibility for the control of sales and costs. In particular, this means deciding how to assign the responsibility for jointly earned revenues and jointly incurred costs. Therefore, as we now consider the form of the accounting reports that accountants prepare for responsibility centers, remember the assumptions and limitations that underlie these reports.

Despite the problems of responsibility center accounting, the profit measure is so comprehensive and pervasive that organizations prefer to treat many of their organization units as profit centers. Because most organizations are integrated operations, the first problem that designers of profit center accounting systems must confront is handling the interactions among the various profit center units.

To address this issue, consider the activities at Earl's Motors, a full-service automobile dealership organized into five responsibility centers: new car sales, used car sales, body shop, service department, and leasing. Each responsibility center has a manager responsible for the profit reported for that unit. The responsibility center managers report to Earl, using the quarterly reports format shown in Exhibit 12-7.

Exhibit 12-7
Earl's Motors Quarterly Segment Margin Report for the Period July 1 to September 30, 2006

Item	New Car Sales	Used Car Sales	Body Shop	Service Department	Lease Sales	Total
Revenue	$976,350	$1,235,570	$445,280	$685,210	$635,240	$3,977,650
Variable costs	764,790	954,850	235,450	427,400	517,360	2,899,850
Contribution margin	$211,560	$280,720	$209,830	$257,810	$117,880	$1,077,800
Other costs	75,190	58,970	126,480	185,280	46,830	492,750
Segment margin	**$136,370**	**$221,750**	**$83,350**	**$72,530**	**$71,050**	**$585,050**
Allocated avoidable costs	69,870	74,650	64,540	65,290	22,490	296,840
Income	$66,500	$147,100	$18,810	$7,240	$48,560	$288,210
Unallocated costs						325,000
Dealership profit						($36,790)

Exhibit 12-7 illustrates a common form of the segment margin report for an organization that is divided into responsibility centers. One column is devoted to each profit center. The revenue attributed to each profit center is the first entry in each column. Variable costs are deducted from revenue to determine the contribution margin, which is the contribution made by operations to cover revenue center costs that are not proportional to volume (see "Other costs" in Exhibit 12-7). Examples of these costs are equipment and buildings that the segment uses exclusively.

Next, the segment's fixed costs are deducted from its contribution margin to determine that unit's segment margin, which is the performance measure for each responsibility center. The unit's segment margin measures its controllable contribution to the organization's profit and other indirect costs. Allocated avoidable costs are the organization's administrative costs, such as personnel-related costs and committed costs for facilities. The underlying assumption is that these corporate level costs can be avoided if the unit is eliminated and the organization has time to adjust its capacity levels by selling excess facilities or by reducing the number of administrative staff. Allocated avoidable costs are deducted from the unit's segment margin to compute its income. Finally, the organization's unallocated costs (sometimes called *shutdown costs*), which represent the administrative and overhead costs

IN PRACTICE
Financial Statement Business Segment Reporting

Many countries have external reporting standards that require organizations to report the financial results for important business segments. Here is Honda Motor Co. Ltd's segment report that appeared in its 2005 financial statements. The business segment information has been prepared in accordance with the Ministerial Ordinance under the Securities and Exchange Law of Japan.

Net Sales and Operating Income by Business Segment

Years ended March 31	Yen (millions)				
	2001	2002	2003	2004	2005
Motorcycle business:					
Net sales (sales to unaffiliated customers)	¥805,304	¥947,900	¥978,095	¥996,290	¥1,097,754
Operating income	55,700	68,315	57,230	42,433	69,332
Operating income/net sales	6.9%	7.2%	5.9%	4.3%	6.3%
Automobile business:					
Net sales (sales to unaffiliated customers)	5,231,326	5,929,742	6,440,094	6,592,024	6,963,635
Operating income	315,627	512,911	551,392	438,891	452,382
Operating income/net sales	6.0%	8.6%	8.6%	6.7%	6.5%
Financial services business:					
Net sales (sales to unaffiliated customers)	169,293	201,906	237,958	242,696	255,741
Operating income	30,719	76,365	107,813	108,438	89,901
Operating income/net sales	18.1%	37.8%	45.3%	44.7%	35.2%
Power, product and other businesses:					
Net sales (sales to unaffiliated customers)	257,907	282,890	315,352	331,590	332,975
Operating income	(608)	3,611	8,092	10,382	19,305
Operating income/net sales	(0.2%)	1.3%	2.6%	3.1%	5.8%
Total:					
Net sales (sales to unaffiliated customers)	¥6,463,830	¥7,362,438	¥7,971,499	¥8,162,600	¥8,650,105
Operating income	401,438	661,202	724,527	600,144	630,920
Operating income/net sales	6.2%	9.0%	9.1%	7.4%	7.3%

incurred regardless of the scale of operations, are deducted from the total of the five profit center incomes to arrive at the dealership's profit.

Evaluating the Segment Margin Report

What can we learn from the segment margin report for Earl's Motors? First, we know that conventional accrual accounting reports a loss of $36,790 for this quarter. This loss may signal a long-term problem, or it may have been expected. Perhaps this quarter is a traditionally slow quarter, and operations in the year's other three quarters make up the deficiency. Perhaps there is a disproportionate amount of committed costs incurred in this quarter, and they will be lower in subsequent quarters.

What Do Segment Margin Statements Tell the Reader?

As we look at the statements for the individual responsibility centers at Earl's Motors, we can see that each showed a positive income. The contribution margin for each responsibility center is the value added by the manufacturing or service-creating process before the costs that are not proportional to volume.

A unit's contribution margin represents the immediate negative effect on corporate income if the unit is shut down. The unit's segment margin is an estimate of

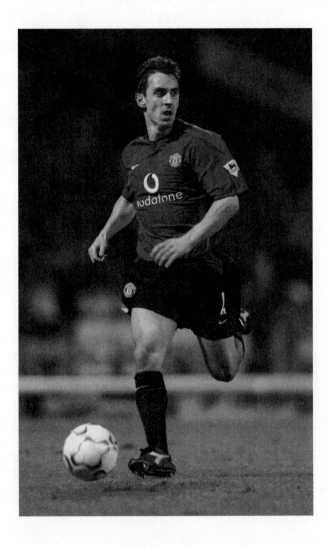

Many professional sports franchise operations may lose money from on-field activities (gate receipts less operating expenses and player salaries). However, successful franchises generate huge revenues from selling ancillaries such as clothing. Eliminating the team because it does not break even on gate receipts would eliminate the opportunity to earn profits on the ancillaries.

Source: Getty Images, Inc.

the long-term effect of the responsibility center's shutdown on the organization after the fixed capacity used by the unit is either redeployed or sold off. The unit's income is the long-term effect on corporate income after corporate-level fixed capacity is allowed to adjust. For example, if the lease sales operation is discontinued, the immediate effect is to reduce the profit at Earl's Motors by $117,880. After some period of time, however, perhaps a year or even several years, when segment level capacity has been sold off and corporate-level capacity has been allowed to adjust for this loss of activity, the estimated net effect of closing the lease operation would be to reduce corporate profits by $48,560. The difference between the unit's segment margin and income reflects the effect of adjusting for business-sustaining costs, which are committed in the short run but can be reduced in the long run as the facilities that they reflect are scaled back.

Good or Bad Numbers?

Organizations use different approaches to evaluate whether the segment margin numbers are good or bad. Following are the most popular sources of comparative information:

1. *Past performance.* Is performance this period reasonable, given past experience?
2. *Comparable organizations.* How does performance compare with similar organizations?

Evaluations include comparisons of absolute amounts, such as cost levels and revenue levels, and relative amounts, such as each item's percentage of revenue. For example, in evaluating the performance of Earl's Motors, the manager of the service department may note that variable costs are about 62% of revenue. This may compare favorably with past relationships of variable costs to revenue. By joining an industry group that provides comparative information for dealerships in similar-size communities, however, Earl's Motors may find that, on average, variable costs in automobile dealerships are only 58% of revenue. This suggests that Earl's Motors should investigate why its variable costs are higher than the industry average. Management should make similar evaluations for all cost items in this report.

Interpreting Segment Margin Reports with Caution

The segment margin statement may seem to be a straightforward and interesting approach to financial control. Segment margin statements should be interpreted carefully however, because they reflect many assumptions that disguise underlying issues.

First, like all approaches to financial control, segment margins present an aggregated summary of each organization unit's past performance. It is important to consider other facets relating to critical success factors, such as quality and service, that will affect future profits. For example, companies may use customer surveys to establish a customer satisfaction index for each department, or they might compute quality statistics that report errors or recall rates for each department.

Second, the segment margin report contains arbitrary numbers because they rest on subjective revenue and cost allocation assumptions over which there can be legitimate disagreement. (Accountants often call these arbitrary numbers *soft numbers*). Each subsequent amount shown down each column becomes less controllable by the responsibility center's manager and is affected more by the assumptions used in allocating costs. Although a unit's segment margin is assumed to be controllable, the

Exhibit 12-8
The Operation of a Typical Mobil Corporation U.S. Oil Refinery

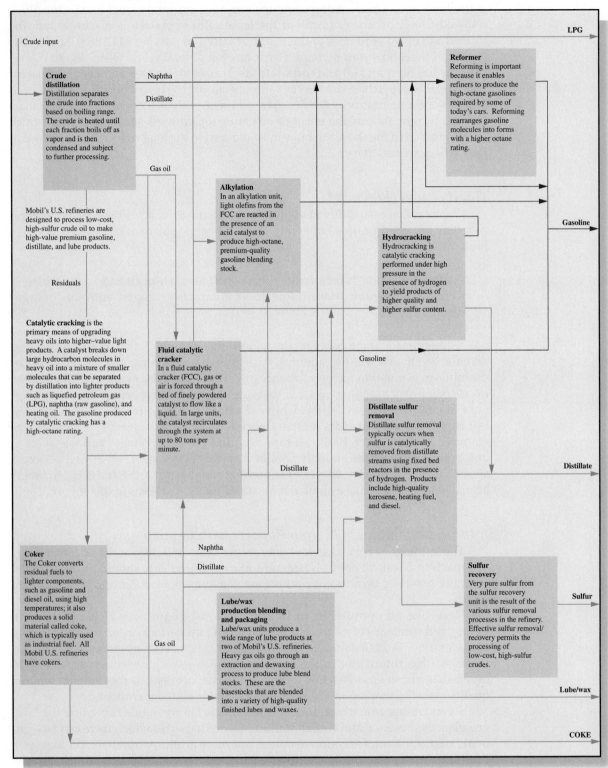

manager may have less than complete control over the costs used to compute it, and the manager may have almost no control over the costs allocated to compute the unit's income. In a typical refinery, for example, joint use of facilities creates problems when managers attempt to allocate the costs of expensive processes, such as those of the crude distillation unit, to the outputs that it produces (naphtha, distillate, gas, oil, and residuals) (see Exhibit 12-8).

Third, and perhaps most important, the revenue figures reflect important assumptions and allocations that sometimes can be misleading. These assumptions relate to the transfer pricing issue, which focuses on how the revenues the organization earns can be divided among the responsibility centers that contribute to earning those revenues.

Transfer Pricing

There are two forms of transfer pricing. One form, which we will call international transfer pricing, addresses the prices organizations charge when they transfer products and services among related organization entities that operate under different tax jurisdictions. An example is the price that an automobile company would use when it transfers an automobile made by its subsidiary in Austria to its subsidiary in Japan for sale. Since different countries tax corporate profits at different rates, companies can use international transfer prices to minimize their global tax liabilities. For this reason most countries have developed rules that put limits on the international transfer prices that organizations set and use. We will not consider international transfer pricing issues in this text since it is a topic for a course on taxation.

The second form of transfer pricing, which we will discuss in this chapter, is what we will call domestic transfer pricing. Domestic transfer pricing is the set of rules an organization uses to allocate jointly earned revenue among responsibility centers. For ease in exposition in the rest of this chapter, we will refer to domestic transfer pricing as simply transfer pricing. Transfer pricing rules can be arbitrary when a high degree of interaction exists among the individual responsibility centers. Exhibit 12-9 shows the possible interactions among the responsibility centers at Earl's Motors.

To understand the issues and problems associated with allocating revenues in a simple organization such as Earl's Motors, consider the activities that occur when a customer purchases a new car. The new car department sells the new car and takes in a used car as a trade. Then Earl's must transfer the used car to the used car department, where it may undergo repairs and service to make it ready for sale, or it may be sold externally, as in the wholesale market.

The value placed on the used car transferred between the new and used car departments is critical in determining the profits of both departments. The new car department would like the value assigned to the used car to be as high as possible because that makes its reported revenues higher; the used car department would like the value to be as low as possible because that makes its reported costs lower.

The same considerations apply for any product or service transfer between any two departments in the same organization. The rule that determines the values of the internal transfers will allocate the organization's jointly earned revenues to the individual profit centers and, therefore, will affect each center's reported profit.

In some countries, the tax authorities have responded to tax competition by getting tough with multinational firms that operate within their borders but try to take advantage of lower taxes elsewhere. When filing tax returns in a high-tax country, multinationals typically claim that they have earned as little of their profits there as they can get away with. Instead, they try to attribute as much profit as possible to their operations in low-tax countries. They do this by arranging "transactions" between their subsidiaries in the two countries and setting the "transfer price" of those transactions so that it has the desired effect on profits.

In theory, the transfer price is supposed to be the same as the market price between two independent firms, but often there is no market, so nobody knows what the market price might be. This is particularly true of firms supplying services or intangible goods. So multinationals spend a fortune on economists and accountants to justify the transfer prices that suit their tax needs.

Increasingly, firms try to restructure their operations to get their tax bills as low as possible. There are plenty of opportunities: According to the OECD (Organization for Economic Cooperation and Development), about 60% of international trade involves transactions between two related parts of multinationals. However, tax authorities are increasingly looking out for such wheezes.

Source: The Economist, January 19, 2000.

Exhibit 12-9
Earl's Motors:
Transfer Pricing
Interrelationships

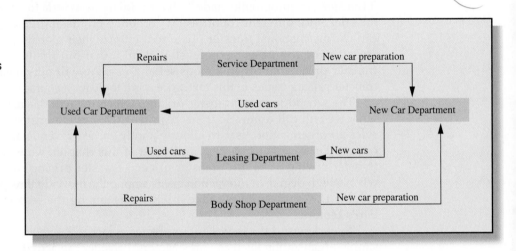

Approaches to Transfer Pricing

There are four main approaches to transfer pricing:

1. Market-based transfer prices
2. Cost-based transfer prices
3. Negotiated transfer prices
4. Administered transfer prices

It is worthwhile to recall here that the relevance and purpose of transfer prices depend on whether the transfer price has the intended effect on organization decision makers. Transfer prices can have different forms; however, *the goal of using transfer prices is always to motivate the decision maker to act in the organization's best interests.* Accountants must always remember that the primary purpose of producing management accounting numbers is to motivate desirable behavior regarding managers' planning, decision making, and resource allocation activities, not to create accounting reports that meet some aesthetic accounting criteria.

Market-Based Transfer Prices

If external markets exist for the intermediate (transferred) product or service, market-based transfer prices are the most appropriate basis for pricing the transferred good or service between responsibility centers. The market price provides an independent valuation of the transferred product or service and how much each profit center has contributed to the total profit earned by the organization on the transaction. For example, the selling division, instead of transferring the good internally, could sell it externally. Similarly, the buying division could purchase externally rather than receiving the internal transfer.

Unfortunately, such competitive markets with well-defined prices seldom exist. Consider Earl's Motors. Dealers trade used cars in well-organized markets that publish prices. A given used car could be valued using this information. The wholesale value of a used car depends, however, on its mechanical condition, which is only imperfectly observable and at a cost. In addition, the used car's value depends on its visible condition, which is a matter of subjective evaluation. Therefore, it is not clear that it is possible to easily determine an objective wholesale price for a given used car.

Some automobile dealerships avoid this problem by asking the used car manager to value any used car being taken in on trade. This value becomes the transfer price. Because people often react to risk and uncertainty by requiring a margin of safety, the used car manager may discount the perceived value of the used car to provide a margin of safety that covers the repair of any hidden problems that become evident when the car is prepared for resale. If the value is excessively low, however, the new car manager may complain that this impedes the ability of the new car department to sell new cars. Therefore, the new car manager may be given the option to shop a potential trade-in to other used car dealers or sell it at an auction to find a better price. This allows the transfer price to better reflect market forces.

Cost-Based Transfer Prices

When the transferred good or service does not have a well-defined market price, one alternative to consider is a transfer price based on cost. Some common transfer prices are variable cost, variable cost plus some percent markup on variable cost, full cost, and full cost plus some percent markup on full cost. In this context, markups, when used, are intended to provide a return for unallocated corporate-level costs and investment deemed to be supporting product production.

For example, consider a product that has a variable manufacturing cost of $5.00 and allocated fixed manufacturing cost of $3.00. Suppose that the target markup, when used, is 10%. The different possible cost based transfer prices are as follows:

Variable cost:	$5.00
Variable cost plus markup:	$5.50
Full cost:	$8.00
Full cost plus markup:	$8.80

The appropriate choice of cost-based transfer price is guided by the same criterion underlying the choice of any transfer price, namely does it provide the right incentive to profit center managers to make decisions that are in the organization's best interests?

Proponents of such types of transfer prices have arguments to support their respective choices. Economists argue, however, that any cost-based transfer price other than marginal cost (assuming that it can be computed) leads organization members to choose a lower-than-optimal level of transactions, causing an economic loss to the overall organization. For example, if the transfer price is higher than the marginal cost, the supplying unit wants to sell more than the optimal quantity and the purchasing unit wants to buy less than the optimal quantity. Because supply and demand must be equal and because no organization unit can be forced to buy or sell more than it wants, the amount that is ordered and supplied is always equal to the lesser of what is offered and what is wanted. The dilemma here, however, is that if the supplying division charges marginal cost as the transfer price and marginal costs decline with volume, the marginal cost will be less than average cost, and the supplying division will always show a loss.

Other problems arise when using cost-based transfer prices. Cost-based approaches to transfer pricing do not promote the goal of having the transfer pricing mechanism support the calculation of unit incomes. Moreover, organization units like to be treated as profit centers, not cost centers, because profit centers are considered more prestigious.

Transfer prices based on actual costs provide no incentive to the supplying division to control costs, since the supplier can always recover its costs. This is a well-known problem in government contracting and utility regulation, where prices or rates are often based on actual costs. One solution is to use a standard cost as the transfer price. Under this approach, the difference between the actual costs that a center incurs and the standard costs that are charged out become a measure of the unit's operating efficiency.

Using a cost-based transfer price assumes that the organization can compute a product's cost in a reasonably accurate way. Chapters 3 and 4 showed that developing and operating accurate costing systems present quite a challenge. People are likely to complain and become frustrated if they believe the organization is using an inaccurate costing system for transfer-pricing purposes.

A final problem with cost-based approaches is that they do not provide the proper economic guidance when operations are capacity constrained. When an organization is operating at capacity, production decisions should reflect the most profitable use of the capacity rather than cost considerations only. In this case, the transfer price should be the sum of the marginal cost and the opportunity cost of capacity, where opportunity cost reflects the profit of the best alternative use of the capacity.

One interesting approach to transfer pricing is the so-called dual rate approach, in which the receiving division is charged only for the variable costs to the point of transfer of producing the unit supplied and the supplying division is credited with the net realizable value (which equals the product's eventual final selling price less the variable costs to complete the product) of the unit supplied. To illustrate, suppose that Fyfe Company produces a product that is started in Division 1 and completed in Division 2. Division 1 incurs a variable cost of $5 to start the product, and Division 2 incurs a variable cost of $3 to complete the product, which is then sold for $20. The transfer price charged to Division 2 when the partially completed product is transferred from Division 1 is $5. The price received by Division 1 is $17. This approach to transfer pricing has the desirable effect of letting marginal cost influence the decisions of the buying division while, at the same time, giving the selling division credit for an imputed profit on the transferred good or service.

Another interesting cost-based approach charges the buying division with the target variable cost in addition to an assignment of the supplying division's committed costs. The assignment should reflect the buying division's share of the supplying division's capacity. For example, if the service department acquired capacity, expecting that 10% of its capacity would be supplied to the new car department, the new car department would receive a lump-sum assignment of 10% of the service department's capacity costs, regardless of the amount of work actually done for the new car department during the period. In this situation, the service department's income is the difference between the actual and target cost of the work it completes.

Cost-based transfer prices raise complex performance measurement, equity, and behavioral issues. Such issues are addressed more thoroughly in advanced texts.

COST ALLOCATIONS TO SUPPORT FINANCIAL CONTROL

Despite the difficulties of measuring responsibility center performance, many organizations want to develop responsibility center income statements. In effect, although revenue and cost allocation rules are arbitrary, people seem satisfied as long as the ones chosen and put in place appear to be fair and consistently applied. Organizations need to design and present responsibility center income statements so that they isolate the discretionary components included in the calculation of each center's reported income. (Exhibit 12-7 presents one possible format.)

The format shown in Exhibit 12-7 helps to identify what the center controls directly. It shows the revenue and variable costs separately from the other costs in the profit calculation, which are the indirect or joint costs that are allocated. Like the allocation of jointly earned revenues, the allocation of indirect or joint costs can cause considerable distortions and can misdirect decision making.

Many outsiders believe that, when evaluated as profit centers, the restaurants in large convention hotels report losses. However, these hotels could not provide convention services without full service restaurants.
Source: Greg Ward/Rough Guides Dorling Kindersley.

Exhibit 12-10
Shirley's Grill and Bar Responsibility Center Income Statement: Indirect Cost Allocation Based on Benefit

	RESTAURANT	BILLIARDS	BAR	TOTAL
Attributed revenue	$354,243	$32,167	$187,426	$573,836
Less segment costs	243,987	12,965	127,859	384,811
Segment margin	$110,256	$19,202	$59,567	$189,025
Less allocated costs	87,791	15,289	47,430	150,510
Segment income	$22,465	$3,913	$12,137	$38,515

Exhibit 12-11
Shirley's Grill and Bar Responsibility Center Income Statement: Indirect Cost Allocation Based on Floor Space Occupied

	RESTAURANT	BILLIARDS	BAR	TOTAL
Attributed revenue	$354,243	$32,167	$187,426	$573,836
Less segment costs	**243,987**	**12,965**	**127,859**	**384,811**
Segment margin	$110,256	$19,202	$59,567	$189,025
Less allocated costs	**60,204**	**37,627**	**52,679**	**150,510**
Segment income	$50,052	($18,425)	$6,888	$38,515

Consider the operations of Shirley's Grill and Bar, which has three operating units: a restaurant, a billiards room, and a bar (see Exhibit 12-10). The segment margin of $110,256 reported for the restaurant includes all revenues from selling food, all food costs, all costs of kitchen and serving staff, and all costs of equipment and supplies relating to the kitchen and the seating area. These revenues and costs are directly attributable to the operation of the restaurant. Indirect costs in the $87,791 allocated to the restaurant operations include depreciation and taxes on the building, advertising, and franchise fees.

In general, the restaurant's accountant can choose among many different activity bases to allocate indirect costs, for example, a responsibility center's direct costs, floor space, and number of employees. Suppose Shirley's decides to allocate indirect costs in proportion to the presumed benefit, as measured by segment margin, provided by the capacity these allocated costs reflect. Many people believe that allocating indirect costs in proportion to benefit is fair. It is a widely used criterion to evaluate an indirect cost allocation method.

The segment incomes reported in Exhibit 12-10 may seem straightforward and reasonable, but as in the case of all results involving indirect cost allocations, the numbers need careful interpretation. Suppose a cost analysis revealed the following:

1. A significant portion of total indirect costs reflects depreciation on the building.
2. Allocating building costs based on floor space is considered to be the most reasonable approach to handling building costs.
3. The amount of floor space occupied by the restaurant, billiards, and bar operations is 40%, 25%, and 35%, respectively.

Allocating costs based on floor space occupied yields the results summarized in Exhibit 12-11. Do these alternative results have any meaning? On one hand, we might argue that the indirect cost allocations based on floor space provide more meaningful economic results because the floor space allocation reflects depreciation—the major component of indirect costs, and its driver, floor space. On the other hand, even if floor space is the cost driver for indirect costs in the short term, the revised results may suggest nothing significant because the allocated depreciation cost is likely to be a committed cost that cannot be avoided in the short term.

The allocations based on floor space may imply that the contribution to profit per square foot of floor space is lowest in the billiard operation and that Shirley's should reduce the scope of the billiard operations in favor of adding more floor space to the bar or restaurant. This conclusion, however, does not necessarily follow. Suppose that without the billiard operation to attract customers, the bar sales would be cut in half. How could the responsibility center income statements reflect this? They probably cannot. With this supplementary information, it would be possible to determine the economic effect of closing the billiards operation. Conventional segment margin statements cannot capture the interactive effects of such actions.

The message here is that responsibility center income statements have to be interpreted with considerable caution and healthy skepticism. They may include arbitrary and questionable revenue and cost allocations and often disguise interrelationships among the responsibility centers.

Negotiated Transfer Price

In the absence of market prices, some organizations allow supplying and receiving responsibility centers to negotiate transfer prices among themselves. Negotiated transfer prices reflect the controllability perspective inherent in responsibility centers since each division is ultimately responsible for the transfer price it negotiates. Negotiated transfer prices—and therefore production decisions—may, however, reflect the relative negotiating skills of the two parties rather than economic considerations.

Problems arise when negotiating transfer prices because this type of bilateral bargaining situation causes the supplying division to want a price higher than the optimal price and the receiving division to want a price lower than the optimal price. When the actual transfer price is different from the optimal transfer price, the organization as a whole suffers because it transfers a smaller than best number of units between the two divisions.

Administered Transfer Price

An arbitrator or a manager who applies some transfer pricing policy sets administered transfer prices, for example, market price less 10% or full cost plus 5%. Organizations often use administered transfer prices when a particular transaction occurs frequently. However, such prices reflect neither pure economic considerations, as market-based or cost-based transfer prices do, nor accountability considerations, as negotiated transfer prices do. Exhibit 12-12 summarizes the four major approaches to transfer pricing.

Returning to the example of Earl's Motors, Earl may require that the transfer price for body shop work done for the new and used car departments will be charged out at 80% of the normal market rate. This may seem reasonable and may reflect a practical approach to dealing with the issues associated with market-based and cost-based transfer prices, but this rule is arbitrary and, therefore, provides an arbitrary distribution of revenues and costs among the body shop and the units with which it deals. Administered transfer prices inevitably create cross subsidies among responsibility centers. Subsidies obscure the economic interpretation of responsibility center income and may provide a negative motivational effect if members of some responsibility center believe that the application of such rules is unfair.

Exhibit 12-12
Summary of Transfer Pricing Approaches

APPROACH	MARKET-BASED	COST-BASED	NEGOTIATED	ADMINISTERED
MEASURE USED	MARKET PRICE	PRODUCT COST	DIRECT NEGOTIATIONS	APPLICATION OF A RULE
Advantage	If a market price exists, it is objective and provides the proper economic incentives.	This is usually easy to put in place because cost measures are often already available in the accounting system.	This reflects the accountability and controllability principles underlying responsibility centers.	This is simple to use and avoids confrontations between the two parties to the transfer-pricing relationships.
Problems	There may be no market or it may be difficult to identify the proper market price because the product is difficult to classify.	There are many cost possibilities but any cost other than the marginal cost will not provide the proper economic signal.	This can lead to decisions that do not provide the greatest economic benefits.	This tends to violate the spirit of the responsibility approach.

Transfer Prices Based on Equity Considerations

Administered transfer prices are usually based on cost; that is, the transfer price is cost plus some markup on cost or market. Thus, the transfer price is some function, such as 80%, of the market price. However, sometimes administered transfer prices are based on equity considerations that are designed around some definition of what constitutes a reasonable division of a jointly earned revenue or a jointly incurred cost.

For example, consider the situation in which three responsibility center managers need warehouse space. Each manager has undertaken a study to determine the cost for an individual warehouse that meets the responsibility center's needs. The costs are as follows: manager A—$3 million; manager B—$6 million; and manager C—$5 million. A developer has proposed that the managers combine their needs into a single large warehouse, which would cost $11 million. This represents a $3 million savings from the total cost of $14 million if each manager were to build a separate warehouse. The issue is how the managers should split the cost of this warehouse.

One alternative, sometimes called the *relative cost method*, is for each manager to bear a share of the warehouse cost that is proportional to that manager's alternative opportunity. This would result in the following cost allocations:

> Manager A's share = $11,000,000 × $3,000,000/$14,000,000 = $2,357,143
> Manager B's share = $11,000,000 × $6,000,000/$14,000,000 = $4,714,286
> Manager C's share = $11,000,000 × $5,000,000/$14,000,000 = $3,928,571

This process is fair in the sense of being symmetrical. All parties are treated equally, and each allocation reflects what each individual faces. Another approach, which reflects the equity criterion of ability to pay, is to base the allocation of cost on the profits that each manager derives from using the warehouse. Still another approach, which reflects the equity criterion of equal division, is to assign each manager a one-third share of the warehouse cost. Thus, each of the many different approaches to cost allocation reflects a particular view of equity.

Assigning and Valuing Assets in Investment Centers

When companies use investment centers to evaluate responsibility center performance, accountants confront all the problems associated with profit centers and some new problems unique to investment centers. The additional problems concern how to identify and value the assets used by each investment center. This task presents troubling questions that have no clear answers.

In determining the level of assets that a responsibility center uses, the management accountant must assign the responsibility for (1) jointly used assets, such as cash, buildings, and equipment, and (2) jointly created assets, such as accounts receivable. Once the decision makers have assigned the organization's assets to investment centers, they must determine the value of those assets. What cost should be used: historical cost, net book value, replacement cost, or net realizable value? These are all costing alternatives for which supporting arguments can be made (for a more in-depth explanation, see advanced cost accounting texts).

The culmination of the allocation of revenues, costs, and assets to operating divisions is the calculation of the division's return on investment. To consider this, we will consider the Dupont Company, one of the earliest and most prolific users of the return-on-investment criterion, which is the ratio organizations most often use to evaluate investment center performance.

Efficiency and Productivity Elements of Return on Investment

One of Dupont Company's major challenges as the organization was growing quickly in the late nineteenth century was to develop a way to manage the complex structure caused by its diverse activities and operations. At this time, most organizations were single-product operations. These organizations approached the evaluation of the investment level of the organization by considering the ratio of profits to sales and the percentage of capacity used. Dupont, however, being a multiproduct firm, pioneered the systematic use of return on investment to evaluate the profitability of its different lines of business. Dupont's approach to financial control is summarized in Exhibit 12-13. At Dupont, the actual exhibit used to summarize operations was extremely detailed and contained as many as 350 large charts that were updated monthly and permanently displayed in a large chart room in the headquarters building.

Return on investment, one of the most widely quoted and used financial ratios, is the ratio of operating income to investment. The Dupont system of financial control focused on return on investment and broke that measure into two components: a return measure that assesses efficiency and a turnover measure that assesses productivity. The following equation illustrates this idea:

$$\text{Return on investment} = \frac{\text{Income}}{\text{Investment}}$$

$$\text{Return on investment} = \frac{\text{Income}}{\text{Sales}} \times \frac{\text{Sales}}{\text{Investment}}$$

The ratio of income to sales (also called *return on sales*, or *sales margin*) is a measure of **efficiency**: it reflects the ability to control costs at a given level of sales activity. The ratio of sales to investment (often called *asset turnover*) is a measure of **productivity**: it reflects the ability to generate sales for a given level of investment.

Exhibit 12-13
The Duport Company: Return on Investment Control System

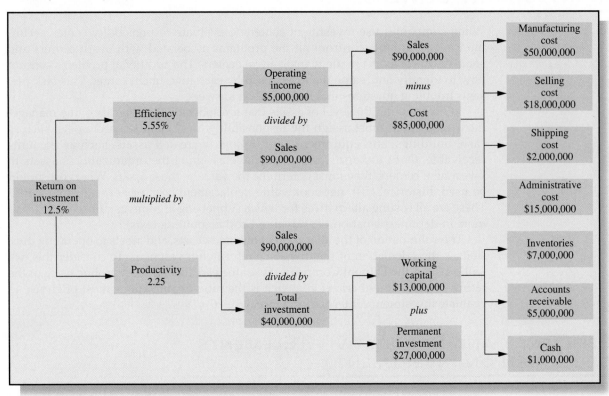

The Dupont approach to financial control develops increasingly more detailed sub-components for the efficiency and productivity measures by focusing on more detailed calculations of costs and different groups of assets. The upper portion of Exhibit 12-13 shows the efficiency measure factored into its components; and the lower portion shows the productivity measure factored into its components. For example, to determine whether each is improving, we can look at the efficiency ratio of operating income to sales and can examine the various components of costs (manufacturing, selling, shipping, and administrative), their relationship to sales, and their individual trends. It is then possible to discover where to make improvements by comparing these individual and group efficiency measures with those of similar organization units or competitors.

The productivity ratio of sales to investment allows development of separate turnover measures for the key items of investment: the elements of working capital (inventories, accounts receivable, and cash) and the elements of permanent investment (equipment and buildings). Comparisons of these turnover ratios with those of similar units or those of competitors can suggest where improvements are required.

Assessing Productivity Using Financial Control

The most widely accepted definition of productivity is the ratio of output over input. For example, if a worker produces 50 items in a 7-hour shift, the worker's productivity (often called *labor productivity*) is 7.1 (= 50 ÷ 7) units per hour. Labor-intensive industries such as consultancies, public accounting firms, hospitals, and trades organizations, monitor their labor productivity obsessively because labor costs are a big fraction of total costs.

Consultancies track and manage labor costs carefully since they are not only their major costs but these costs are often controllable. A measure consultancies often use is the ratio of labor hours billed to labor hours paid, which is effectively a productivity measure because it divides an output measure (hours billed) to an input measure (hours paid). There are many variations on this theme, but all are focused on the same objective: using resources effectively to achieve the organization's financial objectives.

Organizations develop productivity measures for all factors of production, including people, raw materials, and equipment. For example, in the fishing industry, the ratio of weight of salable final products to the weight of the raw fish is typically around 30%. This ratio of raw material in the finished product to the total quantity of raw material acquired is called *raw material productivity* or *yield*. Most organizations in the natural resource industry keep a close watch on raw material productivity because the cost of raw materials is a large proportion of total costs. For example, Weirton Steel, a U.S. steel products manufacturer, once estimated that each percentage point increase in its raw material yield was equivalent to a $4.7 million decrease in operating costs. This gives a practical example of how organizations can use a financial control number, such as raw material yield, to make inferences about how well the underlying manufacturing operations are working.

Finally, many organizations in continuous process industries, such as paper manufacturing, monitor their machine productivity ratios (output per hour or per shift of machine time). Investment in the machine represents a huge fixed cost invested in capacity, and profitability depends on how well that capacity is used. Again, a measure like machine productivity provides organizations with an effective method to relate process results and financial results.

Questioning the Return on Investment Approach

Despite its popularity, some analysts have criticized return on investment as a means of financial control. Some critics argue that the sole use of any financial measure is too narrow for effective control. They argue that the most effective approach to control is to monitor and assess the organization's critical success factors, such as quality, service, and designing and making products that customers want.

Others who accept the need for financial measures still find weaknesses with the return on investment measure. They observe that profit-seeking organizations should make investments in order of declining profitability until the marginal cost of capital of the last dollar invested equals the marginal return generated by that dollar. Unfortunately, financial control based on return on investment may not yield this result.

For example, consider a manager who is evaluated based on return on investment. Suppose that the current average return on investment is 15% and that the manager is contemplating an investment that is expected to return 12%. The manager would be motivated to decline this investment opportunity because accepting it would lower the division's total return on investment and, thus, conflict with what is in the organization's best interests. For example, if the organization's cost of capital were only 10%, the manager should accept the investment because its expected return exceeds the investment's cost of capital.

Fleet costs, such as lease payments and depreciation on aircraft, are major costs in the airline industry. For this reason, airlines focus on what the airline industry defines as load factor, which is a productivity measure. Load factor equals the ratio of seats occupied on flights divided by seats available on flights. The problem with this measure is that it can be increased dramatically by heavy discounting. For this reason, the airline industry uses another measure, passenger revenue yield per revenue passenger mile, which equals the average revenue earned per passenger mile flown. Here is an excerpt from Air Canada's 2004 financial statements summarizing some of these important use and revenue statistics for the first 3 months of fiscal 2004:

Revenue passenger miles (millions)	10,382
Available seat miles (millions)	13,215
Passenger load factor	78.6%
Passenger revenue yield per revenue passenger mile (cents)	15.6
Passenger revenue per available seat mile (cents)	12.2
Operating revenue per available seat mile (cents)	14.8
Operating expense per available seat mile (cents) (4)	14.6
Operating expense (net of cargo and other non-ASM revenue) per available seat mile (cents) (4) (5)	12.1
Average number of employees (thousands)	29.0
Available seat miles per employee (thousands)	455
Operating revenue per employee (thousands)	$67
Aircraft in operating fleet at period end	212
Average aircraft utilization (hours per day) (6)	10.7
Average aircraft flight length (miles)	1,291
Fuel price per litre (cents) (7)	43.3
Fuel litres (millions)	794

Using Residual Income

People have responded to this criticism of return on investment by creating a different investment criterion. **Residual income** equals reported accounting income less the economic cost of the investment used to generate that income. For example, if a division's income is $13.5 million and the division uses $100 million of capital, which has an average cost of 10%, residual income can be computed as follows:

$$\text{Residual income} = \text{Income} - \text{Cost of capital}$$
$$= \$13,500,000 - (\$100,000,000 \times 10\%)$$
$$= \$3,500,000$$

Like return on investment, residual income evaluates income relative to the level of investment required to earn that income. Unlike return on investment, however, residual income does not motivate managers to turn down investments that are expected to earn more than their cost of capital. Under the residual income criterion, managers are asked to do whatever they think is necessary to make residual income as large as possible. For example, recall the previous situation in which the manager faced an investment opportunity with an expected return of 12% when the cost of capital was 10%. If the project requires an investment of $100 million, the residual income if the investment is made and the expected return is realized is $2 million [$100,000,000 × (12% − 10%)]. Therefore, if rewarded based on residual income, the manager will accept this investment opportunity.

Stern Stewart, a consultancy, has developed a proprietary tool they call **economic value added (EVA®)**, which is a refinement of the residual income idea. Economic value-added adjusts reported accounting income and asset levels for what many consider the biasing effects on current results of the financial accounting doctrine of conservatism. For example, GAAP requires the immediate expensing of research and development costs; yet, when shareholder value analysis income is computed, research and development costs are capitalized and expensed over a certain time period, such as 5 years. The intent of the adjustments prescribed to compute shareholder value-added income from GAAP income is to develop an income number that better reflects the organization's long-run earnings potential. Many organizations have adopted the economic value-added criterion to evaluate their investments in product lines, divisions, even entire companies.

Organizations are beginning to use economic value added to identify products or product lines that are not contributing their share to organization return, given the level of investment they require. These organizations have used activity-based costing analysis to assign assets and costs to individual products, services, or customers. This allows them to calculate the economic value added by product, product line, or customer.

Organizations can also use economic value added to evaluate operating strategies. Quaker Foods & Beverages, a food manufacturer, used economic value added to support its decision in June 1992 to cease *trade loading*, which is the food industry's practice of using promotions to obtain orders for a 2- or 3-month supply of food from customers. Trade loading causes quarterly peaks in production and sales that, in turn, require huge investments in assets, including the inventory itself, warehouses, and distribution centers. Through higher prices, customers pay the costs of the higher inventory levels created by this cyclical pattern of inventory. An article in *Fortune* magazine[1] estimated that trade loading was primarily responsible for the $75 to $100 billion in groceries that were always in transit between manufacturers and

IN PRACTICE
Organizations Adopt Economic Value Added for Different Reasons

SPX Corporation supplies specialty service tools and original equipment components to the automotive industry. In its 1995 annual report, SPX identified the following reasons for adopting shareholder value analysis:

- It treats the interests of shareholders and management the same, encouraging SPX people to think and act like owners.
- It is easily understood and applied.
- It fits into operational improvement efforts because success requires continuous improvement of EVA®.
- It correlates closer with market value more than any other operating performance measure.
- It links directly to investor expectations through EVA® improvement targets.

- It focuses on long-term performance by using a bonus bank and predetermined improvement targets.
- It provides a common language for performance measurement, decision support, compensation, and communication.

The notion of a bonus bank, mentioned in the sixth point, is particularly interesting. In years when performance exceeds the economic value added target, two-thirds of all bonuses are set aside in a bonus bank that is carried forward and is payable only if the manager achieves economic value-added targets in subsequent years. When performance falls below target, the bonus is negative and is deducted from the bonus bank. The bonus bank turns what is nominally a short-run performance measure and reward into a longer-run measure.

---

[1] Patricia Seller, "The Dumbest Marketing Ploy," *Fortune*, October 5, 1992, pp. 88–94.

consumers and that supporting this inventory "adds some $20 billion to the $400 billion that U.S. consumers annually spend on groceries."

This economic value-added analysis suggests that even though sales levels may be reduced by the elimination of price reductions associated with trade loading, it is more profitable for the company and its trading partners to forgo the large inventories and the required warehouse space. Also, to produce food at even levels rather than in peaks reduces the level of production capacity needed. Quaker Foods & Beverages motivates managers to end trade loading by basing bonuses on efficiency and cycle times rather than on annual sales.

A measure of the increasing importance of economic value added in organizations is the seniority of people who are usually appointed to manage economic value-added implementation projects in organizations. For example, in 1995, Olin Corporation's new president and chief executive officer was heading the company's economic value-added steering team at the time of his appointment. The results of economic value added suggest interesting insights into financial control applied at all levels of the organization. However, they should be treated with caution. In order to be an effective motivational and evaluation tool, economic value-added analysis, like return on investment calculations, requires complex and potentially problematic allocations of assets, revenues, and costs to divisions, product lines, products, or customers, depending on the focus of the analysis. However, many organizations believe that these problems can be solved and that the insights provided by economic value-added analysis are well worth the effort.

THE EFFICACY OF FINANCIAL CONTROL

Although financial control is widely practiced, many people have questioned its true insights and effectiveness. Critics have argued that financial information is delayed—and highly aggregated—information about how well the organization is doing in meeting its commitments to its shareholders and that this information measures neither the drivers of the financial results nor how well the organization is doing in meeting its stakeholders' requirements, a leading indicator of future financial performance.

Financial control may be an ineffective control scorecard for three reasons:

1. Financial control focuses on financial measures that do not measure the organization's other important attributes, such as product quality, the speed at which the organization develops and makes products, customer service, the ability to provide a work environment that motivates employees, and the degree to which the organization meets its legal and social obligations to society. Because these elements and others promote the organization's long-term success, they also need to be measured and monitored. The argument is that financial control measures only the financial results and not how those results were achieved. This limitation of financial control led to the development of the balanced scorecard (discussed in chapter 9). Recall that the balanced scorecard uses a range of nonfinancial measures of performance in the area of customer requirements, process characteristics, and learning and growth to both explain and predict financial results. Therefore, the balanced scorecard provides a means of managing financial results, which is something not possible when the organization focuses exclusively on financial results since these are an aggregate measure of what happened, not why it happened.

2. Financial control measures the financial effect of the overall level of performance achieved on the critical success factors, and it ignores the performance achieved

on the individual critical success factors. For this reason, many people believe that financial control does not suggest how to improve performance on the critical success factors or on financial performance. Critics argue that, at best, financial results act only as a broad signal of how well the organization manages the tasks that create success on the critical success factors that, in turn, create financial returns. The argument is that effective control begins with measuring and managing the elements or processes that create financial returns rather than measuring the financial returns themselves. The balanced scorecard addresses this problem (as discussed in chapter 9) by focusing on both financial results (such as return on investment) and measures of process performance (such as employee skills, knowledge, and satisfaction; customer satisfaction; cycle times; the rate of process improvement and innovation; and quality) that create the financial results.

3. Financial control is usually oriented to short-term profit performance. It seldom focuses on long-term improvement or trend analysis but instead considers how well the organization or one of its responsibility centers has performed this quarter or this year. This is a result of the misuse of financial control rather than an inherent fault of financial control itself. However, the preoccupation with short-term financial results is debilitating. It motivates an atmosphere of managing short-term financial results that provides disincentives for the types of management and employee initiatives that promote long-term success, particularly in the area of investing in training, equipment, and process changes. One major reason given for taking public organizations private is to provide senior management with the opportunity to manage for long-term results rather than being forced into inappropriate concerns with short-term performance caused by financial analysts who have that preoccupation.

In summary, how should we interpret these facets of financial control? Financial control is an important tool for effective organization control. If used properly, financial results provide crucial help in assessing the organization's long-term viability and in identifying processes that need improvement. It is a tool to be supported by other tools since it is only a summary of performance.

Financial control does not try to measure other facets of performance that may be critical to the organization's stakeholders and vital to the organization's long-term success. It can, however, provide an overall assessment of whether the organization's strategies and decisions are providing acceptable financial returns. Organizations can also use financial control to compare one unit's results with another. This financial benchmarking signal indicates whether the organization's operations control systems, which seek to monitor, assess, and improve performance on the critical success factors, are operating well enough to deliver the desired financial results.

EXTERNAL FINANCIAL CONTROL: FINANCIAL RATIO ANALYSIS

For many years, analysts have used *external financial control tools* to study organizations. These external financial control tools can be divided into two broad groups.

1. Common size statements (vertical analysis)
   a. Balance sheet
   b. Income statement

2. Financial ratios
    a. Profitability
        i. Return on assets (income/total assets)
        ii. Return on common equity (income/common equity)
        iii. Basic earnings per share (income/average number of common shares outstanding)
        vi. Dividend yield ratio (dividends per share/share price)
    b. Efficiency
        i. Gross profit margin (gross operating profit/sales)
        ii. Operating profit margin (earnings before interest and taxes/sales)
        iii. Net profit margin (income/sales)
    c. Financial leverage
        i. Debt/equity ratio (total long-term debt/total equity)
        ii. Debt ratio (total debt/total assets)
    d. Liquidity
        i. Current ratio (current assets/current liabilities)
        ii. Quick ratio ([current assets – inventory]/current liabilities)
        iii. Times interest earned ([earnings before interest and taxes]/interest expense)
        vi. Free cash flow (net cash flow from operations – net cash flows from investment activities – cash dividends paid)
    e. Asset use (productivity)
        i. Accounts receivable turnover (credit sales/average accounts receivable)
        ii. Inventory turnover (cost of sales/average inventory)
        iii. Total asset turnover (sales/assets)
    f. Market Value
        i. Price earnings ratio (share price/earnings per share)
        ii. Market to book value (share price/book value per share)

These financial analysis tools are illustrated by using the data presented for Nucor Corporation at the beginning of this chapter.

The Common Size Balance Sheet

The common size balance sheet has two purposes:

1. To identify trends in a company's balance sheet components over time. For example, is working capital, as a percentage of total assets, increasing or decreasing over time?
2. To compare balance sheet components of organizations of different size in the same industry. For example, is this organization holding more debt than comparable organizations?

In a common size balance sheet, each balance sheet item on the asset side of the balance sheet is expressed as a percentage of total assets, and each item on the liabilities and shareholders' equity side of the balance sheet is expressed as a percentage of the total liabilities and shareholders' equity.

Exhibit 12-14 presents Nucor Corporation's balance sheet and common size balance sheet for the years 2000–2004.

What can we infer from the trends in Nucor Corporation's balance sheet items? Exhibits 12-15 and 12-16 summarize the trends in the various asset and liability and shareholder's equity items.

Exhibit 12-15 shows that that the asset side of the balance sheet was relatively stable until 2003, when net property plant and equipment component declined

Exhibit 12-14
Nucor Corporation: Common Size Balance Sheet (in millions)

	2000		2001		2002		2003		2004	
	$	%	$	%	$	%	$	%	$	%
Current assets										
Cash and equivalents	491	13.18%	462	12.30%	219	5.00%	350	7.80%	779	12.70%
Receivables	350	9.41%	331	8.80%	484	11.04%	573	12.74%	963	15.70%
Inventories	461	12.39%	467	12.41%	589	13.44%	560	12.47%	1.240	20.22%
Other current assets	80	2.14%	114	3.03%	133	3.02%	137	3.06%	193	3.15%
Total current assets	1,381	37.12%	1,374	36.54%	1,424	32.51%	1,621	36.07%	3,175	51.77%
Noncurrent assets										
Property, plant, and equipment	4,025	108.14%	4,227	112.43%	5,094	116.28%	5,331	118.66%	5,694	92.83%
Accumulated depreciation and depletion	1,685	45.26%	1,861	49.50%	2,162	49.35%	2,514	55.95%,	2,875	46.88%
Property, plant and equipment, net	2,340	62.88%	2,366	62.93%	2,932	66.93%	2,817	62.71%	2,818	45.95%
Other noncurrent assets	0	0.00%	20	0.53%	25	0.57%	55	1.22%	140	2.28%
Total noncurrent assets	2,340	62.88%	2,386	63.46%	2,957	67.49%	2,872	63.93%	2,958	48.23%
Total assets	3,722	100.00%	3,759	100.00%	4,381	100.00%	4,492	100.00%	6,133	100.00%
Current liabilities										
Accounts payable	203	5.46%	189	5.03%	247	5.64%	330	7.34%	472	7.69%
Short-term debt	0	0.00%	0	0.00%	16	0.37%	0	0.00%	0	0.00%
Other current liabilities	355	9.53%	295	7.85%	328	7.49%	300	6.67%	594	9.69%
Total current liabilities	558	15.00%	484	12.88%	592	13.50%	630	14.01%	1,066	17.38%
Noncurrent liabilities										
Longterm debt	461	12.37%	461	12.25%	879	20.05%	904	20.11%	924	15.06%
Other noncurrent liabilities	260	6.99%	329	8.76%	371	8.48%	440	9.79%	515	8.39%
Minority interest	312	8.39%	284	7.55%	217	4.95%	177	3.95%	173	2.83%
Total noncurrent liablities	1,033	27.75%	1,074	28.56%	1,467	33.48%	1,521	33.85%	1,612	26.27%
Total liabilities	1,591	42.74%	1,558	41.44%	2,058	46.98%	2,150	47.87%	2,677	43.65%
Shareholder's equity										
Common stock equity	2.131	57.26%	2,202	58.56%	2,323	53.02%	2,342	52.13%	3,456	56.35%
Total liabilities and stock equity	3,722	100.00%	3,760	100.00%	4,381	100.00%	4,493	100.00%	6,133	100.00%

Source: Dollar amounts adapted from www.msn.com.

proportionately rather dramatically as receivables, inventories, and cash increased. From Exhibit 12-15, we can see an increase in the net property plant and equipment account between 2001 and 2002—indicating that Nucor was buying or building capacity. After 2002, the proportionate drop in the net property, plant, and equipment account was caused by rapid growth in the inventory, cash, and receivables accounts. This pattern reflects the increase use of fixed capacity and the increase in working capital requirements caused by rapid sales growth—which, in fact, is what Nucor Corporation experienced in the years 2003–2004.

Exhibit 12-15
Nucor
Corporation:
Common Size
Asset Ratios
2000–2004

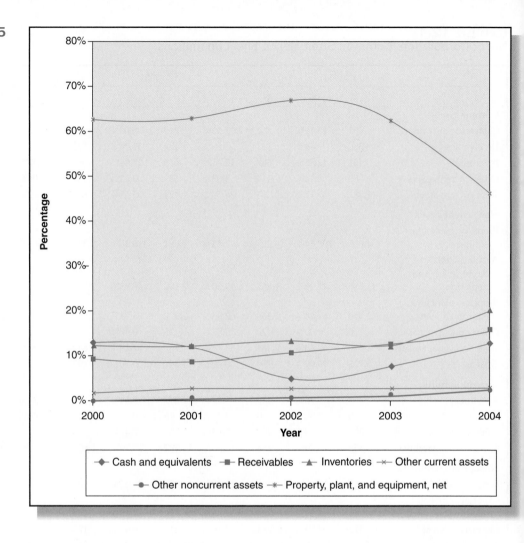

Exhibit 12-16 shows that the liability and owners equity side of the balance sheet was relatively stable with the exception of the long-term debt component. Notice the big jump in the long-term debt component in 2002. We can infer what likely happened here—debt was issued to acquire fixed assets (productive capacity) in 2002. As huge profit increases were recognized in 2003 and 2004, the owner's equity account increased dramatically, lowering the proportion of long term debt in the liabilities and owners' equity side of the balance sheet.

What do we learn from exhibits like 12-15 and 12-16? Not a lot for healthy growing companies like Nucor. However, for organizations that are in distress, we would see a worsening financial position evidenced by increases in the debt components of the liabilities and owner's equity side of the balance sheet.

The Common Size Income Statement

The common size income statement provides many valuable insights by identifying each of the organization's cost elements as a percentage of sales. Percentage of sales is used to calibrate the various income statement items with volume, for which sales serves as a proxy. This provides guidance to management and investors regarding the opportunities and potential to reduce costs. Again, it is useful to consider both the trend of these individual items through time and the comparison of these items with a competitor.

Exhibit 12-16
Nucor
Corporation:
Liability Ratios
2000–2004

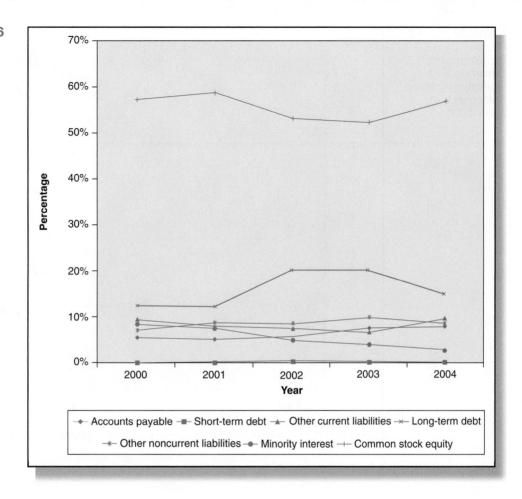

Exhibit 12-17 presents common size income statement ratios for Nucor Corporation during the years 2000–2004. Notice the downward trend of pre tax operating income as a percent of sales during the period 2000–2003, which was characteristic of oversupply and intense competition in the industry. However, steel prices exploded upward in late 2003 and 2004, and the effect on net operating income is shown by the dramatic upswing in the graph.

Profitability Ratios

Return on Assets

The return on assets ratio is a measure of the return generated by the organization's assets. This measure is independent of how the organization has financed its assets. Following is the return on assets calculation for Nucor's 2004 operations:

$$\text{Return on assets} = \frac{\text{Income}}{\text{Total assets}} = \frac{1,121}{6,133} = 18.28\%$$

This result is a huge improvement for Nucor over the years 2000–2003 inclusive and reflects the strong prices for steel in the year 2004. The industry average return on assets in 2004 was 20.9%. Nucor's return on assets was slightly lower than the industry average in 2004, indicating that, relative to the industry, Nucor did not use its assets as productively or efficiently.

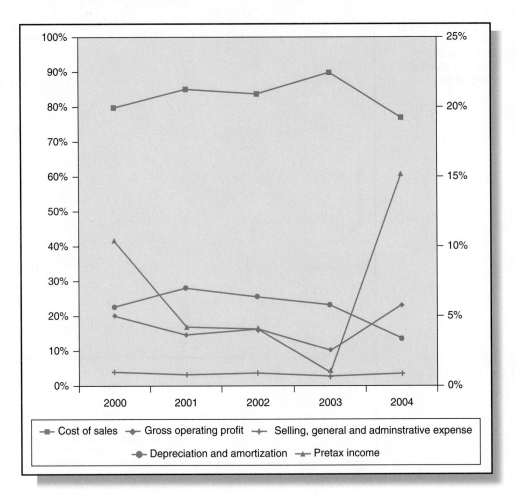

Exhibit 12-17
Nucor
Corporation:
Common Size
Operating Income
Statement,
2000–2004

Return on Common Equity

Return on common equity is a ratio that measures the return to the organization's shareholders. This measure reflects the effect of **financial leverage**, which occurs when the organization uses fixed income capital (like debt) in its capital structure. Financial leverage increases returns to the shareholders when the organization is profitable and reduces returns to the shareholders when the organization is unprofitable.

Note that return on common equity equals return on assets multiplied by the ratio of assets to common equity:

$$\text{Return on common equity} = \frac{\text{Income}}{\text{Common equity}} = \frac{\text{Income}}{\text{Total assets}} \times \frac{\text{Total assets}}{\text{Common equity}}$$

$$= \text{Return on assets} \times \frac{\text{Total assets}}{\text{Common equity}}$$

Recall that as the organization increases its use of debt, holding common equity constant, the ratio of total assets to common equity increases. Therefore, the rightmost part of the previous equation shows how using debt levers the return on assets.

Note that if the return on assets is negative, the leverage effect compounds losses in the same way that it compounds gains when return on assets is positive.

Following is the return on common equity calculation for Nucor's 2004 operations:

$$\text{Return on common equity} = \frac{\text{Income}}{\text{Common equity}} = \frac{1{,}121}{3.456} = 32.44\%$$

This is a remarkable return, again reflecting very strong steel prices. The industry average value is 50.3%, far exceeding Nucor's. This reflects two underlying circumstances: Nucor is not as efficient as the industry average (more on this later), and Nucor uses less debt to finance its operations (more on this later).

Earnings per Share

Earnings per share is perhaps one of the most widely quoted financial measures of performance. It is the monetary unit return to the investor from holding the organization's common stock. There are two types of earnings per share: basic earnings per share and diluted earnings per share.

Basic earnings per share is computed by dividing income by the weighted number of shares outstanding during the period. Nucor's basic earnings per share figures for the years 2000–2004 are shown at the bottom of Exhibit 12-3.

Here is how Nucor's basic earnings per share number was computed for 2004:

$$\text{Basic earnings per share} = \frac{\text{Income}}{\text{Average shares outstanding}} = \frac{1{,}121}{158.4} = \$7.08$$

You will also see reference in the financial press to a number called *diluted earnings per share*. This number computes the earnings per share if all outstanding financial instruments that are convertible to stock (for example, stock options and convertible debt) are exercised. Organizations are required to report fully diluted earnings per share in their annual reports, and the details of the calculations appear as notes to the financial statements.

Here is how Nucor's diluted earnings per share is computed for 2004:

$$\text{Diluted earnings per share} = \frac{\text{Income}}{\text{Average shares outstanding} + \text{Dilutive effects}}$$

$$= \frac{1{,}121}{158.4 + 1.4} = \$7.02$$

Dividend Yield Ratio

The dividend yield ratio measures the cash return on the market price of the share. This is an important measure of shareholder return for shareholders who value dividends—the other element of shareholder return being the appreciation in share value.

To compute this ratio, we need to know the amount of dividends paid per share and year-end price of the share. In 2004, the dividends paid per share were $0.47 and Nucor's share year-end closing price was $52.34. Therefore, the dividend yield is as follow:

$$\text{Dividend yield} = \frac{\text{Dividend per share}}{\text{Share price}} = \frac{0.47}{52.34} = 0.9\%$$

The industry average value is 0.6%, indicating that Nucor's dividend per share relative to its share price is higher than the industry average.

Efficiency Ratios

Gross Profit Margin

The **gross profit margin ratio** reflects the proportion of each sales dollar that variable manufacturing costs consume. For this reason, analysts use the gross profit margin as a measure of manufacturing efficiency. The gross margin residual is what is available to cover fixed manufacturing costs and all the nonmanufacturing expenditures and to pay interest and taxes. We can compute the 2004 gross profit margin for Nucor as follows:

$$\text{Gross profit margin} = \frac{\text{Gross operating profit}}{\text{Sales}} = \frac{2{,}631}{11{,}377} = 23.13\%$$

The industry average value is 29.5%. Recall that gross operating profit equals sales minus cost of sales. Cost of sales includes the cost of raw materials and labor. This means that Nucor's relative cost of raw materials and labor is higher than the industry average.

Operating Profit Margin

The **operating profit margin** computes the proportion of each sales dollar that is available to pay interest and taxes and provide a return to shareholders. The relevance of the word *operating* in the name of this ratio is that revenues or expenses that are deemed to be unusual or nonoperating items are not included in computing this ratio. We can compute the 2004 operating profit margin for Nucor as follows:

$$\text{Operating profit margin} = \frac{\text{Earnings before interest and taxes}}{\text{Sales}} = \frac{1{,}835}{11{,}377} = 16.13\%$$

The industry average value is 20.10%. Note that Nucor is operating below the industry average, but the difference here is lower than the difference in the gross profit margins. Why is this? Recall that earnings before interest and taxes equals gross operating profit minus the sum of selling general and administrative expenses and depreciation and amortization. Therefore, Nucor's use of mini mills relative to the more complex and elaborate integrated mills prevalent in the steel industry gave it a cost advantage relating to fixed manufacturing costs that mitigated some of the disadvantage caused by the combination of raw materials and labor costs.

Net Profit Margin

The **net profit margin** computes the proportion of total revenues that are available for distribution to the common shareholders. We can compute the 2004 gross profit margin for Nucor as follows:

$$\text{Net profit margin} = \frac{\text{Income}}{\text{Sales}} = \frac{1{,}121}{11{,}377} = 9.85\%$$

The industry average value is 14.7%. This means that relative to the industry average, Nucor is less efficient.

Financial Leverage

Debt/Equity Ratio

The **debt/equity ratio** is a measure of financial risk. The higher the ratio, the higher the financial risk because interest must be paid on debt regardless of the organization's profitability. We can compute the 2004 debt/equity ratio for Nucor as follows:

$$\text{Debt/equity ratio} = \frac{\text{Total long-term debt}}{\text{Total equity}} = \frac{924}{3,456} = 26.74$$

The industry average value is 44%. This means that the industry in which Nucor competes uses much higher levels of debt to finance its assets. In turn, this means that Nucor experienced a much smaller financial leverage effect, and its return on equity will be smaller for a given return on assets size and level of profits than its competitors.

Debt Ratio

Like the debt/equity ratio, the debt ratio is a measure of financial risk. It computes the proportion of total assets that are financed by debt and is, therefore, a measure of financial leverage. We can compute the 2004 debt ratio for Nucor as follows:

$$\text{Debt ratio} = \frac{\text{Total debt}}{\text{Total assets}} = \frac{2,677}{6,133} = 43.65\%$$

Liquidity

Current Ratio

The current ratio is a measure of short-run liquidity. It measures the organization's ability to cover its short-term liabilities, which are the liabilities that are due in the upcoming fiscal year. We can compute the 2004 current ratio for Nucor as follows:

$$\text{Current ratio} = \frac{\text{Current assets}}{\text{Current liabilities}} = \frac{3,175}{1,066} = 2.98$$

Although the norm for the current ratio varies from industry to industry, a value of 2 is often considered to be an appropriate target amount. The industry average value is 2.1. This means that relative to the industry average, Nucor is holding higher levels of current assets, which support income earning activities but do not provide earnings themselves.

Quick Ratio

The quick ratio, like the current ratio, is a measure of short-run liquidity. The major difference between the two ratios is that the value of inventory is excluded in the calculation of the quick ratio on the grounds that inventory cannot be easily liquidated to pay current liabilities. We can compute the 2004 current ratio for Nucor as follows:

$$\text{Quick ratio} = \frac{\text{Current assets} - \text{Inventory}}{\text{Current liabilities}} = \frac{3,175 - 1,240}{1,066} = 1.82$$

Although the norm for an appropriate current ratio varies from industry to industry, a value of 1 is often considered to be an appropriate target amount. The industry average value is 1.1, which is considerably lower than Nucor's level, again, like the current ratio, signaling relative to the industry an overinvestment in current assets.

Times Interest Earned Ratio

This is another measure of financial risk. Since interest payments are contractual and required, the times interest earned ratio provides insights into the organization's ability to meet its interest payments. We can compute Nucor's times interest earned ratio for 2004 as follows:

$$\text{Times interest earned ratio} = \frac{\text{Earnings before interest and taxes}}{\text{Interest expense}} = \frac{1,835}{22} = 83.41$$

The industry average value is 13.3. The relationship of the industry average to Nucor's value reflects Nucor's small proportionate use of debt relative to the industry average.

Since interest is paid with cash and not income, the times interest earned ratio may not be a good indicator of the organization's ability to pay interest. This creates interest in the free cash flow measure.

Free Cash Flow

Free cash flow measures the excess of cash flow generated by operations over the amount of cash required to make investments to sustain the organization and pay dividends. In effect, free cash flow represents residual or excess cash. Analysts originally viewed free cash flow as problematic since it represented funds that organizations might use speculatively. (Recall that free cash flow includes investments in profitable projects the organization needs to make to sustain itself.) However, over time, this original meaning has changed, and analysts now view free cash flow as a measure of the organization's liquidity. Using the data in Exhibit 12-5, we can compute Nucor's free cash flow for 2004 as follows:

$$\text{Free cash flow} = \text{Net cash flow from operations} - \text{Investments in capital assets} - \text{Dividends paid}$$
$$\text{Free cash flow} = 1,030 - 535 - 160 = \$335 \text{ million}$$

Asset Use

Accounts Receivable Turnover

For many organizations the investment in inventory and accounts receivable can be significant. Therefore, management's ability to minimize inventory and accounts receivable (and other elements of working capital) for a given level of sales activity enhances the organization's ability to reduce working capital and increase return on investment. However, high accounts receivable turnover numbers are not necessarily good since granting trade credit is often a sales inducement and high turnover measures for accounts receivable may signal an organization that is managing its credit terms too tightly and losing sales.

To compute the accounts receivable turnover, we need a number that is seldom provided in the organization's financial statements: amount of credit sales. For large organizations, it is safe to assume that all sales are credit sales so that the analyst replaces credit sales with sales in the numerator of the accounts receivable turnover ratio. With this in mind, we can compute Nucor's accounts receivable turnover ratio in 2004 as follows:

$$\text{Accounts receivable turnover} = \frac{\text{Sales}}{\text{Average accounts receivable}}$$

$$= \frac{\text{Sales}}{\dfrac{\text{Accounts receivable at start of year} + \text{Accounts receivable at end of year}}{2}}$$

$$= \frac{11,377}{\dfrac{573 + 963}{2}} = 14.81$$

The industry average value is 13.2, which indicates that Nucor is controlling its investment in accounts receivable better than the industry average.

Inventory Turnover

Inventory turnover is a measure of management's ability to control its investment in inventory. Since the 1980s, managements have looked at inventory as a drain on return on investment and have looked for ways to minimize inventory as a percentage of sales. Just-in-time manufacturing systems, in which inventory is received at an assembly plant just as it is needed, is the hallmark of this inventory management movement. However, just-in-time manufacturing systems need to be error free since a breakdown at any point in the system will idle the system until the breakdown is repaired. We can compute Nucor's inventory turnover ratio in 2004 as follows:

$$\text{Inventory turnover} = \frac{\text{Cost of sales}}{\text{Average inventory}}$$

$$= \frac{\text{Cost of sales}}{\dfrac{\text{Inventory at start of year} + \text{Inventory at end of year}}{2}}$$

$$= \frac{8{,}746}{\dfrac{560 + 1{,}240}{2}} = 9.72$$

The industry average value is 7.5. As with accounts receivable, the industry average inventory turnover relative to Nucor's rate indicates that Nucor is holding much lower levels of inventory, which reflects a more effective use of assets.

Organizations that face seasonal demand with inventory levels varying widely over the year use average inventory held during the year rather than year-end inventory. Note that the inventory turnover ratio uses cost of sales rather than sales in the numerator. Analysts use cost of sales rather than sales because inventory is measured at cost, and that consistency requires that cost be used in the numerator.

Total Asset Turnover

By measuring the sales generated per dollar of assets invested in the organization, total asset turnover measures management's ability to use assets effectively to generate sales. Holding too many assets will increase the capital invested in the organization and lower the return to capital. Asset use is the primary focus of the economic value measure discussed earlier. We can compute the total asset turnover measure for Nucor in 2004 as follows:

$$\text{Asset turnover} = \frac{\text{Sales}}{\text{Assets}} = \frac{11{,}377}{6{,}133} = 1.86$$

The industry average value is 2.0. The relationship of the industry average to Nucor's asset turnover shows that Nucor is using its assets less productively than the industry average.

Market Value

Price Earnings Ratio

The **price earnings ratio**, the ratio of market price to earnings per share, is one of the most widely quoted market statistics. The 2004 year-end price of Nucor's common stock was $52.34, and the 2004 earnings per share were $7.08. Therefore, the price earnings ratio is as follows:

$$\text{Price earnings} = \frac{\text{Share price}}{\text{Earnings per share}} = \frac{52.34}{7.08} = 7.39\%$$

The industry average value is 6.4. The higher price earnings ratio for Nucor means that, on average, the stock market believes that Nucor has better growth prospects than its average competitor.

Market to Book Value Ratio

The **market to book value ratio** computes the value that the market attributes to an organization as a proportion of its measured assets. We would expect this value to be more than 1 because organizations have resources, such as employees and its reputation, that do not appear on the balance sheet as assets.

Book value is taken as an approximation of the proceeds of liquidation attributable to the common shareholders. Therefore, the ratio reflects the premium over book value that the market assigns to the organization. When this ratio falls below 1, it signals that the market believes the organization's liquidation value is higher than its value as a going concern. We can compute Nucor's market value to book value ratio for 2004 as follows: share price/shareholders' equity/number of shares outstanding:

$$\text{Market to book ratio} = \frac{\text{Share price}}{\text{Book value per share}}$$

$$= \frac{\text{Share price}}{\dfrac{\text{Shareholders' equity}}{\text{Number of shares outstanding}}}$$

$$= \frac{52.34}{\dfrac{3,456}{158.4}}$$

$$2.40$$

The industry average value is 2.66, which is not significantly different from the Nucor value.

Ratio Trends

As discussed, individual price and ratio values are not meaningful in isolation. The trends of these values and their comparison to industry averages put individual firm values in context and support interpretation.

Exhibit 12-18 provides a chart developed with data adapted from http://moneycentral.msn.com that shows the common stock price performance for Nucor,

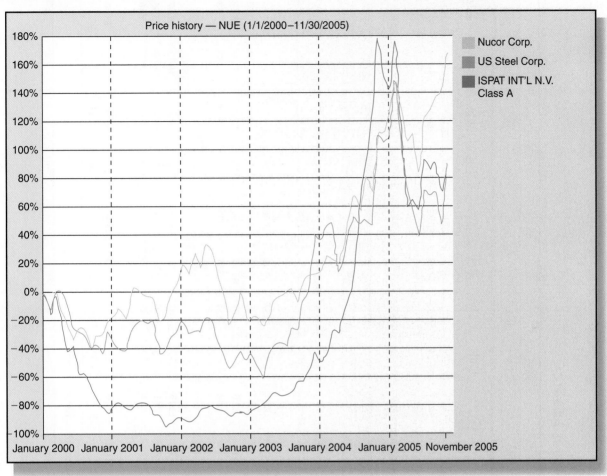

Price history — NUE (1/1/2000–11/30/2005)

Nucor Corp.

US Steel Corp.

ISPAT INT'L N.V.
Class A

US Steel Corporation, and Mittal (shown on the chart as ISPAT) which is the world's largest steelmaker.

Exhibit 12-19 provides the trend of various ratios discussed previously for the years 2000–2004 for Nucor and two major competitors, US Steel and Mittal.

For Nucor, note that almost all the profitability ratios declined over the years 2000–2003 and that 2004 saw a major profitability improvement. Similarly, the efficiency ratios were worsening over the years 2000–2003 with a major improvement in 2004. The current ratios and quick ratios were reasonably stable over the years 2000–2004, while the times interest earned ratios and free cash flow numbers followed an up-and-down pattern with major improvements in 2005. Asset use ratios showed small variances except for 2004. The price earnings ratio trend is difficult to interpret because of a stock split in 2004 that reduced the reported price earnings ratio. Note, however, the major improvement in the market to book value ratio in 2004.

Overall, 2004 was a banner year for Nucor in particular and for the steel industry in general.

Exhibit 12-19
Comparative Financial Ratios for US Steel, Nucor, and Mittal Steel, 2000–2004

Financial Ratios	US Steel					Nucor					Mittal Steel			
	2000	2001	2002	2003	2004	2000	2001	2002	2003	2004	2001	2002	2003	2004
Profitability														
Return on assets	-0.24%	-2.61%	0.75%	-5.91%	9.96%	8.35%	3.00%	3.70%	1.40%	18.28%	-5.87%	0.89%	1.17%	24.54%
Return on common equity	-1.09%	-8.70%	3.01%	-53.40%	29.06%	14.58%	5.13%	6.97%	2.68%	32.45%	-92.31%	38.28%	44.30%	80.41%
Earnings per share	-$0.33	-$2.45	$0.62	-$4.09	$9.47	$1.90	$0.73	$1.04	$0.40	$7.05	-$2.58	$0.40	$0.53	$7.31
Efficiency														
Gross profit margin	3.93%	-0.92%	11.34%	9.13%	18.25%	20.06%	14.69%	16.17%	10.11%	23.13%	4.75%	10.90%	9.15%	33.80%
Operating profit margin	1.70%	-7.86%	0.29%	-1.97%	10.23%	10.43%	4.73%	6.30%	1.77%	16.12%	-3.52%	2.90%	2.78%	27.69%
Net profit margin	-0.34%	-3.47%	0.68%	-4.95%	7.81%	6.76%	2.73%	3.37%	1.00%	9.86%	-6.95%	1.00%	1.21%	21.18%
Financial leverage														
Debt/equity ratio	116.52%	57.22%	69.39%	217.99%	36.31%	21.61%	20.92%	37.82%	38.58%	26.72%	603.85%	1579.69%	1284.56%	28.04%
Debt ratio	77.97%	69.94%	74.58%	86.06%	63.76%	42.75%	41.44%	46.98%	47.57%	43.65%	93.64%	97.68%	97.36%	69.48%
Liquidity														
Current ratio	1.95	1.65	1.78	1.46	1.58	2.48	2.84	2.41	2.57	2.98	1.19	1.27	1.06	1.54
Quick ratio	1.27	0.96	1.03	0.86	1.20	1.65	1.87	1.41	1.68	1.52	0.53	0.58	0.49	0.90
Times interest earned	NA	-3.23	0.16	-1.23	9.34	NA	8.90	13.21	4.07	81.90	-0.65	0.68	0.90	23.19
Free cash flow	-994	373	-49	-588	877	362	82	-464	164	335	168	-8	88	65
Asset use														
Accounts receivable turnover	4.57	7.57	7.44	7.65	7.89	13.10	12.15	11.79	11.87	14.82	9.95	9.24	10.73	11.07
Inventory turnover	5.98	7.00	5.98	6.61	9.64	7.95	7.61	7.63	9.80	9.72	5.31	4.99	5.97	3.66
Total asset turnover	0.70	0.75	0.87	1.19	1.28	1.23	1.10	1.10	1.39	1.85	0.84	0.89	0.97	1.16
Market value														
Price earnings ratio	NA	NA	$26.30	NA	$4.70	$11.30	$30.80	$25.50	$58.60	$5.80	NA	$5.50	$10.50	$3.40
Market book value	$0.83	$0.64	50.66	$4.18	$1.56	$1.45	$1.87	$1.39	$1.85	$2.79	$0.66	$2.14	$7.27	$42.50

Source: Ratios computed from balance sheet and income statement data adapted from www.msn.com.

Ratios and Organizations in Difficulty

Like many U.S. based airlines, AMR Corporation (American Airlines) was facing increasing financial difficulty in late 2005. Losses in 2001–2004 and a looming loss in 2005 had driven the organization to the edge of bankruptcy. Analysts attributed AMR Corporation's woes to the same factors affecting other traditional airlines in the United States: high employee-related costs caused by pension obligations and work rules, obsolete and underused aircraft fleets, and high fuel costs. Exhibit 12-20 shows some of AMR Corporation's financial ratios and their trends in the years 2000–2004.

AMR Corporation's declining financial position led some analysts to believe that bankruptcy was inevitable. Here is a commentary from one analyst:

"Yes, AMR can survive out of bankruptcy for another year or two, but it would be a pointless exercise. Its shareholders have no future, and with its current debt load, profitability is not on the horizon. With the latest bankruptcy filings, they become the only carrier left without the competitive advantage of a lean balance sheet and a lower cost bankruptcy or post-bankruptcy environment.

AMR should go for a prepackaged bankruptcy by stopping all debt payments now. It should set a negotiating deadline and offer to pay all legal fees—with incentives for all of the attorneys—if the deadline is met."*

*Source: http://www.forbes.com/columnists/investmentnewsletters/2005/09/23/amr-delta-bankruptcies-cz_rl-0923 soapbox_inl.html.

Exhibit 12-20
AMR Corporation: Key Ratios

FINANCIAL RATIOS	2000	2001	2002	2003	2004
Profitability					
Return on assets	3.14%	−5.37%	−8.34%	−4.19%	−2.64%
Return on common equity	11.45%	−32.79%	−263.64%	−2669.57%	NA
Earnings per share	$5.50	−$11.43	−$16.22	−$7.76	−$4.74
Efficiency					
Gross profit margin	52.80%	44.35%	47.75%	51.08%	48.19%
Operating profit margin	7.01%	−9.81%	−15.16%	−4.56%	−0.71%
Net profit margin	4.17%	−9.29%	−14.58%	−7.04%	−4.08%
Financial Leverage					
Debt/equity ratio	76.28%	183.03%	1286.31%	28534.78%	NA
Debt ratio	72.62%	83.64%	96.84%	99.84%	102.02%
Liquidity					
Current ratio	0.74	0.87	0.68	0.71	0.71
Times interest earned	4.37	−4.72	−4.38	−1.26	−0.17

Limitations of Financial Ratio Analysis

Financial ratio analysis provides an interesting first step in evaluating an organization's performance. However, financial ratio analysis does have some limitations:

1. Comparing an organization that is in a single line of business with an organization that is a competitor but has multiple lines of business is likely to be a meaningless comparison of unlike organizations.
2. Even though organizations might be comparable because they are in similar lines of business, they may use different accounting conventions, making ratio comparisons between the two organizations meaningless.

3. Interpreting trends in a single organization's financial ratio may be difficult because of the effect of unknown economic or competitive forces on the organization.
4. It may be difficult to determine the appropriate or acceptable value for a particular ratio, particularly if the industry is in a recession.
5. When there are strong seasonality effects, making comparisons with financial data that are a snapshot of the organization's financial activities at year end may be meaningless.
6. When organizations manipulate or misrepresent their financial information, the financial ratios drawn from these data will be misleading.
7. Like all numbers based on historical results, financial ratios look backward. It may be difficult or even meaningless to project past data to predict future performance.
8. Because they are backward looking, financial ratios ignore an organization's current strategic initiatives and may misrepresent future results of current initiatives.

Despite these limitations, analysts continue to use and interpret financial ratios. This widespread use reflects the belief that these ratios do provide important insights, particularly if combined with other information, such as that gleaned about the organization's strategic initiatives and that contained in a balanced scorecard.

EPILOGUE TO NUCOR CORPORATION: THE FUTURE AFTER 2004

After the heady days of 2004, prices and demand began to settle down in the steel industry. Beginning in late 2004 and continuing into 2005, steel prices began to soften as steel-making capacity came online in China. In 2004, China became, for the first time, a net exporter of steel. Analysts expected that steel prices would continue to decline anywhere between 15% and 40% from the peak prices in mid-2004 in the face of waning demand and continued increases in steel production capacity. Exhibit 12-21 shows the ratio of scrap steel price prices in the months indicated to the price of scrap steel in April 1994.

In addition, the period 2000–2004 had seen a major shakeout in the steel industry. Stronger manufacturers had acquired the weaker and marginal producers, creating a much more efficient and competitive industry. In the face of these developments, at the start of 2005 senior management at Nucor vowed to forge ahead by acquiring additional capacity through additions to existing plants, building new plants, and

Exhibit 12-21
Scrap Steel Price Changes (Index, April 1994)

Source: www. CRUspi.com

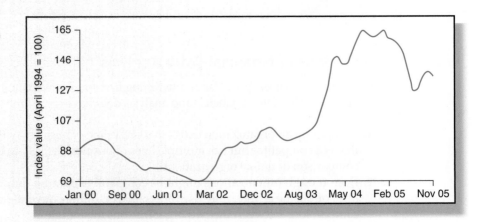

making acquisitions. In Nucor's 2005 annual report, management provided the following commentary on the uncertainty it faced:

> We recognize that uncertainty in external factors such as raw materials costs, growth rate of the economy, and the level of imports will have a significant impact on our results. In 2005, we will work towards our goal of controlling one-third of our raw materials supply.

Despite these concerns, the analysts' consensus appeared to be a good intermediate term future for Nucor. Sales growth estimates for Nucor for the years 2006–2008 inclusive were about 10%, which was slightly higher than the estimated growth rate for the industry. Earnings per share estimates provided by one investor services organization were $7.91, $6.10, and $5.80 for the years 2005–2007 inclusive. The combination of estimated sales increases with declines in earnings per share reflect an agreement that Nucor will continue to battle raw materials costs as they increase proportionately more quickly than sales—a view consistent with Nucor management's view of the effect of raw materials costs in general and scrap steel prices in particular.

SUMMARY

This chapter explored the scope and nature of financial control—an approach to evaluating operations and management that relies on financial information from internal and external perspectives.

Organizations use financial control information to evaluate how well processes and organization units are fulfilling their objectives. Chapter 10 presented how organizations use budgets and variances to evaluate operating unit and process performance. This chapter considered the different types of responsibility centers and the role of financial information in evaluating organization unit performance. When evaluating an organization unit's profit contribution, organizations use transfer prices to allocate jointly earned revenues to each of the contributing units.

This chapter also considered financial ratio analysis, a form of financial control that analysts both inside and outside the organization can use to evaluate an organization's financial performance. Analysts can use a wide range of ratios to evaluate different facets of the organization's profit performance and internal economic health.

KEY TERMS

Accounts receivable turnover, 618
Administered transfer price, 601
Common size balance sheet, 610
Common size income
  statement, 612
Controllability principle, 588
Cost centers, 584
Cost-based transfer prices, 597
Current ratio, 617
Debt ratio, 617
Debt/equity ratio, 616
Decentralization, 579
Dividend yield ratio, 615
Domestic transfer pricing, 595
Earnings per share, 615

Economic value added, 607
Efficiency, 603
Financial control, 578
Financial leverage, 614
Free cash flow, 618
Gross profit margin ratio, 616
Internal financial controls, 578
International transfer pricing, 595
Inventory turnover, 619
Investment centers, 587
Market to book value ratio, 620
Market-based transfer prices, 597
Negotiated transfer price, 601
Net profit margin, 616
Operating profit margin, 616

Price earnings ratio, 620
Productivity, 603
Profit centers, 586
Quick ratio, 617
Residual income, 606
Responsibility center, 581
Return on assets ratio, 613
Return on common equity, 614
Return on investment, 603
Revenue centers, 585
Segment margin report, 591
Times interest earned ratio, 617
Total asset turnover, 619
Transfer pricing, 595

Assignment Materials

Questions

12-1 What does financial control mean? (LO 1)

12-2 What is the difference between internal financial control and external financial control? (LO 1)

12-3 What is decentralization? (LO 2)

12-4 What does control mean in a decentralized organization? (LO 2)

12-5 What is a responsibility center? (LO 2)

12-6 What is a cost center? (LO 3)

12-7 What is the assigned responsibility in a revenue center? (LO 3)

12-8 When do organizations use profit centers? (LO 3)

12-9 What is an investment center? (LO 3)

12-10 What does the controllability principle require? (LO 4)

12-11 How do responsibility centers interact? (LO 3, 4)

12-12 What does segment margin mean? (LO 4)

12-13 What is a soft number in accounting? (LO 4)

12-14 What is a transfer price? (LO 5)

12-15 What are the four bases for setting a transfer price? (LO 5)

12-16 Why do organizations allocate revenues to responsibility centers? (LO 3, 6)

12-17 Why do organizations allocate costs to responsibility centers? (LO 3, 6)

12-18 What is return on investment? (LO 7)

12-19 How does efficiency (the ratio of operating income to sales) affect return on investment? (LO 7)

12-20 How does productivity (the ratio of sales to investment) affect return on investment? (LO 7)

12-21 What does residual income mean? (LO 7)

12-22 What are three reasons financial control alone may provide an ineffective control scorecard? (LO 1, 2)

12-23 What two broad groups of financial control tools have analysts used to study for-profit organizations? (LO 8)

12-24 What is a common size balance sheet, and what are two purposes of the common size balance sheet? (LO 8)

12-25 What is a common size income statement, and why is it useful? (LO 8)

12-26 What are the six broad groups of financial ratios? (LO 8)

Exercises

LO 2   **12-27** *Issues in decentralization*   What control problem does decentralization create in organizations?

LO 2   **12-28** *University responsibility centers*   Give an example of a responsibility center in a university.

LO 3   **12-29** *Cost centers*   Give an example of a responsibility center that is properly treated as a cost center.

LO 3   **12-30** *Revenue centers*   Give an example of a responsibility center that is properly treated as a revenue center.

LO 3   **12-31** *Investment centers*   Based on your understanding of how chains are managed, would you agree or disagree that an outlet of a large department store chain should be treated as an investment center? What about the maintenance department within that outlet? What about a single department within the store?

LO 3   **12-32** *Multinational companies and investment centers*   Many multinational companies create wholly owned subsidiaries to do business in the countries or regions where they operate. Are these wholly owned subsidiaries examples of investment centers? Explain.

LO 3   **12-33** *Responsibility centers*   Identify three responsibility centers in a fast-food restaurant and explain how they may interact.

LO 4   **12-34** *Controllability*   Based on your understanding, which of the following—costs, revenues, profits, and investment—does the manager of a cinema control?

12-35 *Computing division income*   A home services company offers renovations, as well as heating, air conditioning, and plumbing services, to its customers. Imagine that you are in the process of computing the income for the renovations division. What problems may you encounter in computing this income?

12-36 *Controllability and evaluation*   Suppose you are the manager of a fitness center that is one of many in a chain. Give one example of a cost that you control and one example of a cost you do not control. Why is it important in this setting to distinguish between costs that are controllable and costs that are not controllable?

12-37 *Controllability and motivation*   Give an example of a situation for which invoking the controllability principle would have a desirable motivational effect. Also give an example of a situation for which suspending the controllability principle would have a desirable motivational effect.

12-38 *Domestic and international transfer pricing*   Organizations might desire to use one transfer pricing system designed to support international transfer pricing and another domestic transfer pricing system designed to achieve motivational objectives. Give a reason why you think organizations would not use two transfer pricing systems—one for international tax purposes and one for motivational purposes.

12-39 *Choosing transfer prices*   How might a transfer price for logs be chosen in an organization that cuts down trees and processes the logs either in a sawmill to make lumber or in a pulp mill to make paper?

12-40 *Choosing transfer prices*   In a fishing products company, the harvesting division catches and delivers the fish to the processing division that, in turn, delivers the processed fish to the selling division to sell to customers. How can you determine the appropriate transfer price between harvesting and processing and between processing and selling?

12-41 *Using market-based transfer prices*   What is the main advantage and the main obstacle in using market-based transfer prices?

12-42 *Soft numbers*   Why did accountants develop the expression "soft number"?

12-43 *Allocating costs*   A store is divided into four departments: automotive products, home products, paint, and lumber. How would you assign the building costs, such as depreciation, to each of these departments?

12-44 *Return on investment measurement issues*   Green Company has prepared the following information for three of its divisions:

DIVISION	HISTORICAL COST OF INVESTMENTS	DIVISION OPERATING INCOME
X	$560,000	$66,500
Y	532,000	64,400
Z	350,000	43,120

Required

a. Compute each division's return on investment and residual income, assuming a 10% cost of capital.

b. Suppose the net book value of each division's investments is half of the historical cost. Using net book value as the measure of investment, compute each division's return on investment and residual income, assuming a 10% cost of capital.

c. Comment on the division rankings in (a) and (b).

d. If the division managers are rewarded on the basis of return on investment or residual income, will they find it attractive to invest in new, more costly equipment?

12-45 *Return on investment components* Alpha Company would like to examine the sales margin and asset turnover components of return on investment for three of its divisions and has accordingly prepared the following information:

DIVISION	INVESTMENT	DIVISION OPERATING INCOME	SALES
E	$575,000	$75,000	$500,000
F	700,000	91,000	542,000
G	1,000,000	176,000	763,000

Required

a. Compute each division's return on investment, sales margin, and asset turnover.
b. Comment on the divisions' relative rankings on the ratios computed in (a).

LO 7 **12-46** *Characteristic return-on-investment ratios* For-profit organizations face a requirement to earn at least a minimum-level return on investment. Some businesses rely on high ratios of income to sales; other businesses rely on high ratios of sales to investment. Give an example of each of these types of businesses and explain what this characteristic implies about the business.

LO 7 **12-47** *Productivity ratio* Give an example of why using units, rather than the value of the products produced, in the numerator of a productivity ratio may give a misleading picture of the process that produced that output.

LO 7 **12-48** *Computing residual income* A business whose investors require a return on investment of 8% reports an income of $1 million on an investment of $20 million. What is the residual income for this business?

LO 7 **12-49** *Residual income in a multiproduct company* Based on an analysis of operations, a company making sporting goods has determined that the income provided by its golf, ski, tennis, and football product lines are $3.5 million, $7.8 million, $2.6 million, and $1.7 million, respectively. The accountant believes that the investment levels in these product lines are $35 million, $50 million, $45 million, and $23 million, respectively. Use a residual income analysis to evaluate the performance of each of these product lines, assuming that the organization requires a 10% return on investment.

LO 1, 2, 8 **12-50** *Single ratio values* Give an example of why looking at a single value of a financial ratio may give either a misleading or a meaningless result.

LO 8 **12-51** *Common size statements; profitability, efficiency, and market value ratios* Cotter Company's balance sheet at December 31, 2005 and income statement for the year ended December 31, 2005 are shown here:

Cotter Company
Balance Sheet
December 31, 2005

Assets	
Current assets:	
Cash	$35,000
Marketable securities	60,000
Accounts receivable	45,000
Inventories	215,000
Prepaid expenses	45,000
Total current assets	400,000
Property, plant, and equipment, net	1,300,000
Total assets	**$1,700,000**

Liabilities and Stockholders' Equity

Liabilities:	
Current liabilities	$105,000
Long-term debt	420,000
Total liabilities	525,000
Stockholders' equity:	
Common stock, $15 par value	$150,000
Paid-in capital in excess of par	300,000
Retained earnings	725,000
Total stockholders' equity	1,175,000
Total liabilities and stockholder's equity	**$1,700,000**

Cotter Company
Income Statement
For the Year Ended December 31, 2005

Sales	$2,500,000
Cost of sales	975,000
Gross profit	1,525,000
Selling, general, and administrative expenses	945,000
Operating profit	580,000
Interest expense	38,000
Pretax income	542,000
Income taxes	216,800
Net income	$325,200

Required

a. Present the income statement and balance sheet in (monetary and) common size form.

b. Cotter Company's common stock price per share at the end of 2005 was $125, and dividends per share were $3.45. Compute the following ratios:

- Return on assets
- Return on common equity
- Basic earnings per share
- Dividend yield ratio
- Gross profit margin
- Operating profit margin
- Net profit margin
- Price earnings ratio
- Market to book value

LO 8   **12-52** *Financial leverage, liquidity, and productivity ratios*   Compute the ratios below for the financial statements in exercise 12-51:

- Debt/equity
- Debt ratio
- Current ratio
- Quick ratio
- Times interest earned
- Accounts receivable turnover (Assume all sales are credit sales and receivables are constant from year to year.)
- Total asset turnover

Problems

LO 2, 3, 4 **12-53** *Choosing responsibility center type*   For each of the following units, identify whether the most appropriate responsibility center form is a cost center, a profit center, or an investment center and why you have made that choice.
   a. A laboratory in a hospital
   b. A restaurant in a department store
   c. The computer services group in an insurance company
   d. A maintenance department in a factory
   e. A customer service department in a mail-order company
   f. A warehouse used to store goods for distribution in a large city
   g. A publishing company acquired by a diversified corporation

LO 4 **12-54** *Allocating common costs to cost centers*   You have decided to divide a factory into cost centers. How would you allocate depreciation expense on the factory building to its individual cost centers?

LO 4 **12-55** *Implementing the controllability principle*   One of the most widely accepted and longest held beliefs is the controllability principle, which says that organization units and people should be held accountable only for things that they can control.

Required

a. For any job you choose, give one example of something you should be expected to control and one example of something you should not be expected to control.
b. Can you think of an example in which making yourself responsible for something that you cannot control would promote a desirable activity?

LO 4 **12-56** *Segment margins*   Following is the information on Paragon Company's three product lines:

	Product Line		
	1	2	3
Revenue	$7,160,000	$1,900,000	$4,200,000
Variable cost percentage of sales	60%	50%	40%
Other costs	$859,200	$237,500	$693,000
Allocated avoidable corporate costs	$349,000	$156,000	$698,000
Allocated unavoidable corporate costs	$570,800	$206,500	$24,000

Required

a. Construct a segment margin statement for Paragon Company.
b. Explain why the segment margins reported for an organization unit must be interpreted carefully.

LO 4 **12-57** *Drop unprofitable segments*   Perform an Internet search on "close underperforming stores" or similar phrase to locate an example of a company that has closed unprofitable stores or other segments. Explain what issues the company considered in dropping the unprofitable segments and improving profitability of the remaining segments.

LO 5, 6 **12-58** *Transfer prices and division autonomy*   You are a government controller. A division manager being audited objects to the transfer price he is being charged by the audit group for the audit services. The manager observes,

"If I have to pay for these services, I should be allowed to buy them from an outside supplier who is prepared to offer them to me at a lower price." You have been asked to mediate this dispute. What would you do?

LO 5, 6 **12-59 *Transfer pricing and outside opportunities*** Deseronto Electronics manufactures motherboards for computers. The company is divided into two divisions: manufacturing and programming. The manufacturing division makes the board, and the programming division makes the adjustments required to meet the customer's specifications.

The average total cost per unit of the boards in the manufacturing division is about $450, and the average total cost per board incurred in the programming division is about $100. The average selling price of the boards is $700. The company is now operating at capacity, and increasing the volume of production is not a feasible alternative.

In the past, the managers of the two divisions have negotiated a transfer price. The average transfer price has been about $500, resulting in the manufacturing division recognizing a profit of about $50 per board and the programming division recognizing a profit of about $100 per board. Each of the managers receives a bonus that is proportional to the profit reported by his or her division.

Karen Barton, the manager of the manufacturing division, has announced that she is no longer willing to supply boards to the programming division. Sam Draper, the senior purchasing executive for Koala Electronics, a computer manufacturer, has indicated that he is willing to purchase, at $650 per unit, all the boards that Karen's division can supply and is willing to sign a long-term contract to that effect. Karen indicated that she offered the boards to the programming division at $625 per board on the grounds that selling and distribution costs would be reduced by selling inside. Neil Wilson, the manager of the programming division, refused the offer on the grounds that the programming division would show a loss at this transfer price.

Neil has appealed to Shannon McDonald, the general manager, arguing that Karen should be prohibited from selling outside. Neil has indicated that a preliminary investigation suggests that he cannot buy these boards for less than about $640 outside. Therefore, allowing Karen to sell outside would effectively doom Neil's division.

Required

a. What transfer price would you recommend? Why?
b. What recommendations do you have for the programming division?

LO 7 **12-60 *Return on investment*** Michelle Gutierrez, manager of the Components Division of FX Corporation, is considering a new investment for her division. The division has an investment base of $4,000,000 and operating income of $600,000. The new investment of $500,000 supports corporate strategy and is expected to increase operating income by $50,000 next year, an acceptable level of return from corporate headquarters' point of view.

Required

a. What is the current return on investment (ROI) for the Components Division?
b. What will the ROI be if Michelle undertakes the new investment?
c. Suppose Michelle's compensation consists of a salary plus a bonus proportional to her division's ROI. Is Michelle's compensation higher with or without the new investment?

d. Suggest changes to FX Corporation's management that will better align performance evaluation and compensation with corporate goals.

LO 7 **12-61** *Return on investment and residual income*   The Newburg Flyers operate a major sports franchise from a building in downtown Newburg. The building was built in 1940 at a cost of $5,000,000 and is fully depreciated so that it is shown on the company's balance sheet at a nominal value of $1. The land on which the building was built in 1940 was purchased in 1935 for $10,000 and is valued at this amount for balance sheet purposes. The franchise, which is the company's only other major investment, cost $100,000 in 1940.

The current assessed value of the building is $200,000. The assessed value of the land, which is located in a prime urban area, is $20,000,000 and reflects the net value of the property if the current building is demolished and replaced with an office and shopping complex. The current value of the franchise, assuming that the league owners would approve a franchise sale, is $50,000,000.

Required

a. Ignoring taxes in this calculation, if the team earns an income of approximately $3,000,000 per year, what is the return on investment using net book value and historical cost as the measures of investment?

b. Ignoring taxes in this calculation and assuming that the organization's cost of capital is 15%, if the team earns approximately $3,000,000 per year, what is the residual income using net book value and historical cost as the measures of investment?

LO 7 **12-62** *Problems in computing economic value added*   A bank is thinking of using economic value added to identify services that require improvement or elimination. What problems may the bank have in computing the economic value added of any of the services that it offers to its customers?

LO 7 **12-63** *Evaluating the potential of economic value added*   The owner of a chain of fast-food restaurants has decided to use economic value added to evaluate the performance of the managers of each of the restaurants. What do you think of this idea?

LO 7 **12-64** *Using residual income*   As a result of a residual income analysis, the owner of a company that makes and installs swimming pools has decided to shut down the manufacturing operations that show a negative residual income for the current year. Is this necessarily the proper response to this information?

LO 7 **12-65** *Conflicting organization and individual objectives*   Strathcona Paper rewards its managers on the basis of the after-tax return on investment of the assets that they manage—the higher the reported return on investment, the higher the reward. The company uses net book value to value the assets employed in the return on investment calculation. The company's cost of capital is assessed as 12% after taxes. The organization's tax rate is 35%.

The manager of the logistics division is faced with an opportunity to replace an aging truck fleet. The current net income after taxes of the logistics division is $7 million, and the current investment base is valued at $50 million. The current net income after taxes and the current investment base, absent any investment in new trucks, are expected to remain at their existing levels.

The investment opportunity would replace the existing fleet of trucks, which have a net book value of about $100,000, with new trucks costing about $50 million net of the trade-in allowance for the old trucks. If kept, the old trucks would last another 5 years and would have no salvage value. The new trucks would last 5 years, have zero salvage value, and increase cash flow relative to keeping the old trucks (through increased revenues and decreased operating costs) by about $16 million per year. If purchased, the new trucks would be depreciated for both accounting and tax purposes on a straight-line basis.

Required

a. From the point of view of the company, should this investment be made? Support your conclusion with net present value calculations.
b. From the point of view of the manager, should this investment be made?
c. If the manager were rewarded on the basis of after-tax residual income, would the manager want to make the investment? Show why or why not.

LO 1, 2, 3, 4   **12-66** *Strategy and control*   Many people believe that the focus of control in a successful organization reflects the strategic initiatives in the organization. For each of the following organizations, identify what you think are the three most important items assessed by the organization's financial control system and why each is important. For each organization, what critical information is not assessed by the financial control system?
     a. A company selling cable television services to its subscribers
     b. A symphony orchestra
     c. An organization selling canned soup
     d. A government agency responsible for finding jobs for its clients
     e. An auditing firm
     f. A company selling high-fashion clothing

LO 2   **12-67** *Organic and mechanistic organizations*   Researchers have defined two extreme forms of organizations. Organic organizations are highly decentralized with few rules. Most people agree that software development companies are very organic. Mechanistic organizations are highly centralized and use many rules to prescribe behavior. Most people agree that government agencies are very mechanistic.
     Do you agree with these examples? Give your own examples of each of these types of organizations, along with your reason for giving each organization the chosen classification.

LO 2, 3, 4   **12-68** *Group and individual conflict*   Think of an example of an organization in which it is important that the various functional areas be closely coordinated to promote the organization's overall success. Show how performance measures that focus solely on the performance of an individual unit could create problems in this organization.

LO 2, 3, 4   **12-69** *Coordinating divisional activities*   For many years, automobile companies were highly decentralized in terms of functions. The most obvious effect of this heavy decentralization of function was apparent when all the groups needed to work together to accomplish a goal. The highest order of integration occurs in the design of a new automobile.
     Reflecting the functional decentralization of automobile manufacturers, the traditional approach to automobile design was for the marketing group to identify a concept. The design group then created an automobile that reflected the marketing group's idea but incorporated engineering requirements and aesthetics identified by the design group. The purchasing group then identified the parts required by the design and made further

modifications to it to incorporate parts that could be made or purchased. Finally, the manufacturing group modified the design to reflect the nature and capabilities of the production process. This process took up to 4 years and usually resulted in a vehicle that was far removed from the initial design.

What was wrong here? How could the process be improved?

LO 1, 2, 3, 4   **12-70** *Choices in financial control*   Bennington Home Products sells home products. It buys products for resale from suppliers all over the world. The products are organized into groups. A few examples of these groups are floor care products, kitchen products, tool products, and paper products. The company sells its products all over the world from regional offices and warehouses in every country where it operates. Because of differences in culture and taste, the product lines and products within those lines vary widely among countries.

The regional offices have administrative staff that manage the operations, place orders to the corporate office, and undertake the usual office administrative functions, and they have sales staff that do the selling directly to stores within each region. The regional offices are evaluated as investment centers because they have responsibility for revenues, costs, and investment levels. The regional offices make suggestions for new products.

The corporate office manages the regional offices and places the orders received from the regional offices with suppliers. The corporate office does the ordering for three reasons. First, it is believed that one ordering office eliminates duplication in ordering activities. Second, it is believed that one office ordering for all the regional offices gives the organization more power when dealing with suppliers. Third, it is believed that one office can develop the expertise to find and negotiate with suppliers of unique and innovative products.

Required

a. Describe an appropriate system of financial control at the regional level.
b. Describe an appropriate system of financial control at the corporate office level.
c. Explain why the systems of financial control should or need not mesh.

LO 4   **12-71** *Assigning responsibility for uncontrollable events*   Some people and organizations believe that the discussion of controllable and uncontrollable events is distracting in the sense that it encourages finger-pointing and an excessive preoccupation with assigning blame. These observers argue that it is more important to find solutions than to identify responsibility for unacceptable or acceptable events.

Required

a. What do you think of this argument?
b. As an organization moves away from assessing and rewarding controllable performance, what changes would you expect to see in its organization structure?

LO 6   **12-72** *New product opportunities and transfer pricing*   Plevna Manufacturing makes and distributes small prefabricated homes in kits. The kits contain all the pieces needed to assemble the home. All that is required is that the builder erect the home on a foundation.

Plevna Manufacturing is organized into two divisions: the manufacturing division and the sales division. Each division is evaluated on the basis of its reported profits. The transfer price between the manufacturing division, where the kits are made, and the selling division, which sells the kits, is variable cost plus 10%, a total of about $33,000. The selling price per kit is about $40,000, and selling and distribution costs are about $5,000 per home kit.

The total costs that do not vary in proportion with volume at Plevna Manufacturing amount to about $2,000,000 per year: about $1,500,000 in manufacturing and about $500,000 in the selling division. The company is currently operating at capacity, which is dictated by the machinery in the manufacturing division. Each kit requires about 10 hours of machine time, and the total available machine time is 5,000 hours per year. Plevna Manufacturing is making and selling about 500 kits per year. Increasing the plant capacity is not a viable option in the foreseeable future.

Willie Scott is the firm's salesperson. Willie has been approached a number of times recently by people wanting to buy cottages to erect on recreational properties. The cottages would be made by modifying the existing home product. The modification process would begin with a completed home kit. The manufacturing division would then incur additional materials and labor costs of $3,000 and 3 hours of machine time to convert a home kit into a cottage kit. Willie is proposing that the company split the sales division into two divisions: home sales and cottage sales. The new divisional structure would have no effect on existing administrative, personnel, or selling costs.

Required

Suppose the new division is created. Discuss the issues in choosing a transfer price in this situation. What transfer price for each of the two products, home and cottage kits, would you recommend and why? (If you feel that the appropriate transfer price for each product can be within a range, specify the range.)

LO 7 **12-73** *General Motors and residual income* Since the firm of Stern Stewart & Co. began ranking firms on the basis of market value added, General Motors has generally been at or near the bottom of the list. Undertake an investigation to determine the circumstances that led to this ranking and whether there is any evidence that the situation is improving or getting worse.

LO 1, 7 **12-74** *Decision making with return on investment* You are the controller of a chain of dry-cleaning establishments. You are computing the return on investment for each outlet.

Outlet A, located in a city core, reported a net profit of $130,000. The land on which Outlet A is located was essentially rural when it was purchased for $100,000. Since then, the city has expanded, and the land is now located in the population center. Comparable undeveloped land in the immediate area of the outlet is worth $2,000,000. The net book value of the outlet building and equipment is $400,000. The replacement cost of the building and equipment is $1,200,000. If the outlet building, equipment, and land were sold as a going concern, the sale price would be $1,500,000. It would cost $250,000 to demolish the building and clear the property for commercial development.

Required

a. What is the return on this investment?
b. How would you decide whether this outlet should continue to be operated, sold as a going concern, or demolished and the land sold?

12-75 *Market value added, economic value added, and net income* If you look through *Fortune* magazine, you will find articles that rank organizations by market value added and economic value added. Find one such article and identify three firms: the one with the highest economic value added, the one with the highest market value added, and the one with the highest reported net income. Compare the three firms. Explain the difference in rankings. (In the event that the top-ranked firms by any two of these criteria are the same, do the same for the second-ranked firms.)

LO 8 **12-76** *Common size income statements* Osborne Company's income statements for 2004 and 2005 are shown here:

Osborne Company
Annual Income Statements (in millions)
For the Years Ended December 31, 2005 and 2004

	2005	2004
Sales	$35,000	$60,000
Cost of sales	20,000	23,000
Gross margin	15,000	37,000
Selling, general, and administrative expenses	12,000	15,000
Operating profit	3,000	22,000
Interest expense	750	420
Pretax income	2,250	21,580
Income taxes	765	7,337
Net income	$1,485	$14,243

Required

a. Present the income statements for the years ended December 31, 2005 and 2004, in monetary and common size form.
b. Discuss the changes that occurred between 2004 and 2005.

Cases

LO 2, 3, 4, 7 **12-77** *Choosing an organization structure* You are a senior manager responsible for overall company operations in a large courier company. Your company has 106 regional offices (terminals) scattered around the country and a main office (hub) located in the geographical center of the country. Your operations are strictly domestic. You do not accept international shipments.

The day at each terminal begins with the arrival of packages from the hub. The packages are loaded onto trucks for delivery to customers during the morning hours. In the afternoon, the same trucks pick up packages that are returned to the terminal in late afternoon and then shipped to the hub, where shipments arrive from the terminals into the late evening and are sorted for delivery early the next day for the terminals.

Each terminal in your company is treated as an investment center and prepares individual income statements each month. Each terminal receives 30% of the revenue from packages that it picks up and 30% of the revenue from the packages it delivers. The remaining 40% of the revenue from each transaction goes to the hub. Each terminal accumulates its own costs. All costs relating to travel to and from the hub are charged to the hub. The revenue per package is based on size and service type and not the distance that the package travels. (There are two services, overnight and ground delivery, which take between 1 and 7 days, depending on the distance traveled.)

All customer service is done through a central service group located in the hub. Customers access this service center through a toll-free telephone number. The most common calls to customer service include requests for package pickup, requests to trace an overdue package, and requests for billing information. The company has invested in complex and expensive package tracking equipment that monitors the package's trip through the system by scanning the bar code placed on every package. The bar code is scanned when the package is picked up, enters the originating terminal, leaves the originating terminal, arrives at the hub, leaves the hub, arrives at the destination terminal, leaves the destination terminal, and is delivered to the customer. All scanning is done by handheld wands that transmit the information to the regional and then central computer.

The major staff functions in each terminal are administrative (accounting, clerical, and executive), marketing (the sales staff), courier (the people who pick up and deliver the shipments and the equipment they use), and operations (the people and equipment who sort packages inside the terminal).

This organization takes customer service very seriously. The revenue for any package that fails to meet the organization's service commitment to the customer is not assigned to the originating and destination terminals.

All company employees receive a wage and a bonus based on the terminal's residual income. This system has promoted many debates about the sharing rules for revenues, the inherent inequity of the existing system, and the appropriateness of the revenue share for the hub. Service problems have arisen primarily relating to overdue packages. The terminals believe that most of the service problems relate to mis-sorting in the hub, resulting in packages being sent to the wrong terminals.

Required

a. Explain why you believe an investment center is or is not an appropriate organization design in this company.

b. Assuming that this organization is committed to the current design, how would you improve it?

c. Assuming that this organization has decided that the investment center approach is unacceptable, what approach to performance evaluation would you recommend?

LO 1, 2, 3, 4 **12-78 *Computing objectives and organization responsibility*** Baden is a city with a population of 450,000. It has a distinct organization group, called the Public Utilities Commission of the City of Baden, or Baden PUC, whose responsibility is to provide the water and electrical services to the businesses and homes in the city. Baden PUC's manager is evaluated and rewarded on the basis of the profit that Baden PUC reports.

Baden PUC buys electricity from a privately owned hydroelectric facility several hundred miles away for resale to its citizens. Baden PUC is responsible for acquiring, selling, billing, and servicing customers. The maintenance and moving of electric wires within the city are, however, the responsibility of the City of Baden maintenance department, or Baden Maintenance. Baden PUC pays Baden Maintenance for work done on its electrical wires.

Over the years, many squabbles have occurred between Baden Maintenance and Baden PUC. These squabbles have usually involved two items: complaints by customers about delays in restoring disrupted service and complaints by Baden PUC that the rates charged by Baden Maintenance are too high. However, the most recent quarrel concerns a much more serious issue.

On July 12, at about 10:30 A.M., a Baden city employee working in the parks and recreation department noticed an electrical wire that seemed to be damaged. The employee reported the problem to Baden Maintenance at about 12:15 P.M., during his lunch break. At 1:15 P.M., the report was placed on the maintenance supervisor's desk, where it was found at 2:05 P.M., when the supervisor returned from lunch. The maintenance supervisor then called the Baden PUC dispatch office to report the problem and request permission to investigate the report and make any required repairs. The request for repair was placed on the Baden PUC service manager's desk for approval at 2:25 P.M. The service manager received the message at 4:00 P.M, when he returned from a meeting. He approved the work and left a memo for a subordinate to call in the request. The request was then mistakenly called in by a clerk at 4:50 P.M. as a request for routine service and logged by the dispatcher in Baden

Maintenance. A truck was dispatched at 3:50 P.M. the following day. When the repair crew arrived at the scene, it discovered that the wire was indeed damaged and that if any of the children playing in the park had touched it, it would have caused instant death.

The incident went unreported for several days until a reporter for the *Baden Chronicle* received an anonymous tip about the episode, verified that it had happened, and reported the incident on the front page of the newspaper as an example of bureaucratic bungling. The public was outraged and demanded an explanation from the mayor, who asked the city manager to respond. The initial response from the Baden city manager that "everyone had followed procedure" only fanned the furor.

Required

a. Was what happened inevitable, given the City of Baden's organization structure? Explain.
b. Given the existing organization structure, how might this incident have been avoided?
c. How would you deal with this situation now that it has happened?
d. Would a change in the organization structure help prevent a similar situation from occurring in the future? Explain.

GLOSSARY

A

Accounting rate of return An accounting-based measure used to approximate the return on investment; computed by dividing a project's average accounting income by the investment level.

Accounts receivable turnover A measure of the organization's ability to manage its accounts receivable.

Activity-based budgeting A budgeting process that uses knowledge about the relationship between the quantity of production units and the activities required to produce those units to develop detailed estimates of activity requirements underlying the proposed production plan.

Activity-based cost (ABC) system System based on activities linking organizational spending on resources to the products and services produced and delivered to customers.

Activity-based management (ABM) The set of actions that management can take, based on the information from an activity-based cost system, to increase profitability. The actions includes making operational improvements to high-cost processes, changing product prices and product mix, and restructuring customer relationships.

Activity-based pricing Establishes a base price for a proposed customer order based on the estimated cost producing and delivering the order.

Activity cost driver rate The amount determined by dividing the activity expense by the total quantity of the activity cost driver. This rate is used to assign activity costs to individual products.

Activity cost drivers Measures that identify the linkage between activities and cost objects; they serve as quantitative measures of the output of activities.

Activity dictionary The list of the major activities performed by an organization's resources.

Appraisal costs Those costs related to inspecting materials or products to ensure that they meet both internal and external customer requirements.

Appropriations Planned and approved cash outflows, or spending plans, in government agencies.

Authoritative budgeting A budgeting process that occurs when a superior informs subordinates what their budget will be without requesting input.

Avoidable costs Those costs eliminated when a part, product, product line, or business segment is discontinued.

B

Balanced Scorecard A strategic management system that translates an organization's strategy into clear objectives, measures, targets, and initiatives organized by four perspectives.

Batch-related activities Activities triggered by the number of batches produced rather than by the number of units manufactured.

Belief systems The explicit set of statements communicated to employees of the basic values, purpose, and direction for the organization.

Benchmarking The process of studying and adapting the best practices of other organizations to improve the firm's own performance and establish a point of reference by which internal performance can be measured.

Benchmarking (performance) gap The gap between actual performance and the performance level of the organization that established the benchmark level of performance.

Bid price The price that an organization bids on a job that is open for offers. The bid price is often the estimated total job cost plus a margin.

Boundary systems Systems that prescribe organization behaviors that are unacceptable. They usually state the consequence of unacceptable behavior–for example "no employee should release customer lists to outsiders–such disclosure will result in immediate termination."

Breakeven equation

$$\text{Breakeven unit sales} = \frac{\text{Fixed costs}}{\text{Contribution margin per unit}}$$

Budget A quantitative expression of the money inflows and outflows that reveal whether the current operating plan will meet the organization's financial objectives.

Budget slack A phenomenon whereby individuals misrepresent information to secure excess resources.

Budgeting The process of preparing plans (budgets) to guide operations, and projecting the financial results.

Budgeting games Attempts by managers to manipulate information to have targets set lower so that they are more easily achieved.

Business-sustaining activities Activities required for the basic functioning of the business. These core activities are independent of the size of the organization or the volume and mix of products and customers.

C

Capacity-related costs The costs associated with capactiy-related resources.

Capacity-related resources Resources that are acquired and paid for in advance of when the work is done. Capacity-related resources provide the organization with the capacity to make or deliver goods or services.

Capital budget The management document that authorizes spending for resources, such as plant and equipment, that will have multi-year useful lifetimes.

Capital budgeting A systematic approach to evaluating an investment in a long-term, or capital, asset.

Cash bonus A payment method that pays cash based on some measured performance. Also called lump-sum reward, pay for performance, or merit pay.

Cellular manufacturing Refers to the organization of a plant into a number of cells so that within each cell, all machines required to manufacture a group of similar products are arranged in close proximity to each other.

Certified suppliers A set of suppliers who are certified by a company because they are dependable and consistent in supplying high-quality items as needed.

Channel-sustaining activities Activities that are required to maintain and sustain product distribution channels.

Committed costs Those costs that a company incurs before knowing actual production or sales volumes. Also known as capacity-related costs.

Common size balance sheet A balance sheet recast so that each balance sheet item is expressed as a percent of total assets or total liabilities and shareholders' equity. Used to compare different sized organizations.

Common size income statement An income statement recast so that each income statement item is expressed as a percent of sales. Used to compare different sized organizations.

Concurrent design and engineering A method that is used to help design costs out of the product before manufacturing begins.

Consultative budgeting A method of budget setting that occurs when managers ask subordinates to discuss their ideas about the budget but no joint decision making occurs.

Continuous budget A budget that is continuously updated as the current period is dropped from the budget and a new period is added.

Contribution margin Sales less variable cost.

Contribution per unit of scarce resource The contribution margin per unit of consumption of a constraining factor of production. For example, the contribution per machine hour.

Contribution per unit The price per unit less variable costs per unit; contribution margin per unit.

Control Refers to the set of procedures, tools, performance measures, and systems that organizations use to guide and motivate all employees to achieve organizational objectives.

Controllability principle States that the manager of a responsibility center should be assigned responsibility only for the revenues, costs, or investments controlled by responsibility center personnel.

Controlling Measuring and evaluating the performance of existing organization systems and entities to identify how each is contributing to achieving the organization's objectives.

Conversion costs Costs of labor and support activities to convert the materials or product at each process stage.

Cooperative benchmarking The voluntary sharing of information through mutual agreements.

Cost The monetary value of goods and services expended to obtain current or future benefits.

Cost centers Responsibility centers in which employees control costs but do not control revenues or investment levels.

Cost driver rate The amount determined by dividing the activity expense by the total quantity of the activity cost driver.

Cost object Something for which a cost is computed. Examples of cost objects are a product, a product line, a department, a division, and a geographical area.

Cost of capital The return that the organization must earn on its investments to meet its investors' return requirements. Also called risk-adjusted discount rate.

Cost of nonconformance (CONC) to quality standards The cost incurred when the quality of products and services does not conform to quality standards.

Cost of unused capacity The cost of unused capacity-related resources.

Cost-of-quality (COQ) report A report that details the cost of maintaining quality production processes and products.

Cost pool Each subset of total support costs that can be associated with a distinct cost driver.

Cost-plus pricing A method for setting the price of a product by a markup percentage above cost.

Cost-volume-profit analysis (CVP) A study of how costs and profits vary with changes in volume.

Cross-functional product teams Made up of individuals representing the entire value chain, both inside and outside the organization, to guide the target-costing process.

Current ratio A measure of the organization's short-run liquidity.

Customer accounting Compares the revenues and costs of dealing with a particular customer or class of customers to determine whether the customer is profitable and, if the customer is unprofitable, to provide insights into both why and how to improve the customer's profitability.

Customer management processes Processes that select, acquire, retain, and deepen relationships with targeted customers.

Customer perspective The Balanced Scorecard perspective that identifies objectives and measures for the targeted customer segments and the value proposition for customers in these segments.

Customer-sustaining activities Activities that enable the company to sell to an individual customer but are independent of the volume and mix of the products (and services) sold and delivered to the customer.

Cycle time The chronological time taken to complete an activity. For example, manufacturing cycle time is the time from start to finish taken to produce a product.

D

Data falsification The process of knowingly altering company data in one's favor.

Database benchmarking A policy in which companies usually pay a fee and in return gain access to information from a database operator.

Debt ratio A measure of financial risk, computed as total debt divided by total assets.

Debt/equity ratio A measure of financial risk, computed as total long-term debt divided by total equity.

Decentralization The process of delegating decision-making authority to front line decision makers.

Diagnostic control systems Formal information systems that managers use to monitor organizational outcomes and correct deviations from standard measures of performance.

Direct allocation method The service department cost allocation method that allocates costs directly to the production departments.

Direct cost A cost of a resource or activity that is acquired for or used by a single cost object. An example is the cost of leather used to make a leather coat.

Direct manufacturing costs Manufacturing costs that can be traced to a single cost object.

Discounting The process of computing present value.

Discretionary costs Costs that are not determined by production decisions. For example, programmed maintenance costs, research and development, advertising, and employee training expenses are discretionary costs.

E

Earnings management Methods by which managers knowingly manipulate the reporting of income.

Economic value added An estimate of the wealth increment to owners from the current years' operations; measured as adjusted accounting income minus estimated cost of capital for the investment level.

Economic value method The estimated outcome of a decision computed by weighting different possible outcomes by their probability of occurring.

Efficiency The ability to control costs at a given level of sales activity.

Efficiency (quantity) variance An estimate of the increase in costs caused by excessive use of labor or materials.

Employee self-control A managerial method in which employees monitor and regulate their own behavior and perform to their highest levels.

Environmental costing A costing system that computes the cost of the effects an organization has on the environment.

Equivalent units of production This is calculated by multiplying the number of partially completed units by the percentage of competition.

Ethical control system A management control system based on ethics used to promote ethical decision making.

Expected value method The estimated outcome of a decision computed by weighting different possible outcomes by their probability of occurring.

Expenses The costs of goods or services that have expired, that is, have been used up in the process of creating goods and services.

External failure costs Those costs incurred when customers discover a defect.

Extrinsic rewards Rewards that are given by one person to another to recognize a job well done. Examples include: money, recognition in a corporate newsletter, stock options, or congratulations.

F

Financial accounting The process of producing financial statements for external constituencies— such as shareholders, creditors, and governmental authorities.

Financial budgets Those budgets that identify the expected financial consequences of the activities summarized in the operating budgets.

Financial control A process used to assess an organization's financial success by measuring and evaluating its financial outcomes.

Financial leverage The use of fixed return financing, such as long-term debt, to increase returns to shareholders.

Financial perspective The Balanced Scorecard perspective that focuses on financial measures of an organization's success, such as various measures of profitability.

Finished goods inventory The costs of the resources for each completed job that is not yet sold.

First-level variance Difference between the actual costs and the master budget costs for individual cost items.

Fixed cost The cost that is associated with capacity-related resources. The amount of fixed costs is related to the planned rather than the actual level of activities.

Flexible budget Reflects a cost target or forecast based on the level of volume that is actually achieved.

Flexible budget variances Variances from the target level of costs adjusted for the actual level of activity.

Flexible resources Resources whose use is proportional to the amount of the resource used. An example of a flexible resource is fuel in a steel mill.

Free cash flow The excess of cash flow generated by operations over the amount of cash required to make investments to sustain the organization and pay dividends.

Full absorption costing A costing method in which all production costs become product costs.

Full costs Sum of all costs (direct materials, direct labor, and support) assigned to a product.

Future value (FV) The amount that today's investment will be after a stated number of periods at a stated periodic rate of return.

G

Gainsharing A system for distributing cash bonuses from a pool when the total amount available is a function of performance relative to some target.

Gaming the performance indicator An activity in which an employee may engage in dysfunctional behavior to achieve a single goal.

Generally accepted accounting principles (GAAP) GAAP prescribe how to determine costs for external reporting and the scope and form of external reporting.

Goal congruence The outcome when managers' and employees' goals are aligned with organizational goals.

Gross profit margin ratio Gross operating profit (that is, gross margin) divided by sales revenue; a measure of organization efficiency.

Group benchmarking A business alternative in which participants meet openly to discuss their methods.

H

Human relations movement A managerial movement that recognizes that people have needs well beyond performing a simple repetitive task at work and that financial compensation is only one aspect of what workers desire.

Human resources model of motivation (HRMM) A more contemporary managerial view that introduces a high level of employee responsibility for and participation in decisions in the work environment.

I

Improshare A gainsharing program that determines its bonus pool by computing the difference between the target level of labor cost given the level of production and the actual labor cost.

In control Refers to a system that is on a path to achieving its strategic objectives.

Incentive compensation Reward system that provides monetary rewards based on measured results. Also called pay-for-performance systems.

Incremental budgeting A budgeting process that bases a period's expenditure level for a discretionary item on the amount spent for that item during the previous period.

Incremental cost per unit The amount by which the total costs of production and sales increase when one additional unit of that product is produced and sold.

Indirect cost The cost of a resource that organizations acquire to be used by more than one cost object. An example is the wage paid to a supervisor in a factory that makes different products when the cost object is a product.

Indirect manufacturing costs Manufacturing costs that are related to more than one cost object.

Indirect/third-party benchmarking A technique that uses an outside consultant to act as a liaison among firms engaged in benchmarking.

Inflation A general increase in the price level.

Initiatives Short-term programs and action plans that will help the organization achieve the targets established for Balanced Scorecard measures.

Innovation processes Processes that develop new products, processes, and services.

Interactive control systems Formal information systems managers use to involve themselves regularly and personally in the decision activities of subordinates.

Internal failure costs The costs incurred when the manufacturing process detects a defective component or product before it is shipped to an external customer.

Internal financial control Application of financial control tools to evaluate organization units, with the resulting information used internally and not distributed to outsiders.

Internal rate of return (IRR) The actual rate of return expected from an investment.

Intrinsic rewards Those rewards that come from within an individual and reflect satisfaction from doing the job and the opportunities for growth that the job provides.

Inventory turnover A measure of management's ability to control its investment in inventory.

Investment The monetary value of the assets that the organization gives up to acquire a long-term asset.

Investment centers Responsibility centers in which the managers and other employees control revenues, costs, and the level of investment in the responsibility centers.

J

Job bid sheet A medium for estimating job costs.

Job cost sheet Medium for recording actual job costs.

Job costs The total direct material, direct labor, and support costs for a job.

Job order costing system A process that estimates the costs of manufacturing products for different jobs required for specific customer orders.

Just-in-time (JIT) manufacturing A production process method in which products are manufactured only as needed.

K

Kaizen costing A costing system that focuses on reducing costs during the manufacturing stage of the total life cycle of a product.

L

Learning and growth perspective The Balanced Scorecard perspective that identifies the objectives for employee capabilities, information systems, and organizational climate that will create longterm growth and improvement.

Life-cycle costing The process of studying cost behavior over all stages of a product's life.

Long run The period over which capacity can be adjusted.

M

Make-or-buy decision A decision in which managers must decide whether their companies should manufacture some parts and components for their products in-house or subcontract with another company to supply these parts and components.

Management accounting and control system (MACS) The larger entity of central performance measurement systems.

Management accounting systems A value-adding continuous improvement process of planning, designing, measuring, and operating both nonfinancial information systems and financial information systems that guides management action, motivates behavior, and supports and creates the cultural values necessary to achieve an organization's strategic, tactical, and operating objectives.

Manufacturing costs The cost of flexible and capacity related resources used in the factory to make a product.

Manufacturing cycle Begun after the RD&E cycle, this cycle is one in which costs are incurred in the production of the product.

Margin The difference between the revenue and the cost of a job.

Marginal cost The increase in cost for a unit increase in the quantity produced and sold.

Marginal revenue The increase in revenue for a unit increase in the quantity produced and sold.

Markup percentage See markup rate.

Markup rate The percent by which job costs are marked up.

Materials requisition note A list of materials required to begin production.

Measures Descriptions of how success in achieving Balanced Scorecard objectives will be determined.

Mission statement A concise, internally focused statement of how the organization expects to compete and deliver value to customers.

Monitoring Inspecting the work or behavior of employees while they are performing a task.

Motivation An individual's interest or drive to act in a certain manner.

Multistage process costing system A system for determining job costs in which conversion costs are applied to products as they pass through successive process stages.

N

Net present value (NPV) The sum of the present values of all the cash inflows and cash outflows associated with a project.

Net profit margin An overall measure of organization efficiency.

Nonfinancial information Information about a process (such as percent good units produced), a product (such as time taken to fill order), or a customer (such as customer satisfaction) that is not based on information developed in the financial accounting system and is relevant in monitoring the organization's performance on objectives.

O

Objectives Concise statements in each of the four Balanced Scorecard perspectives that articulate what the organization hopes to accomplish.

Operating budget The document that forecasts revenues and expenses during the next operating period including monthly forecasts of sales, production, and operating expenses.

Operating costs Costs, other than direct materials costs, that are needed to produce a product or service.

Operating processes The basic, day-to-day processes by which companies produce their products and services and deliver them to customers.

Opportunity cost The value sacrificed when the factor of production is used for a specific purpose.

Organization control The activity of ensuring that the organization is on track toward achieving its objectives.

Organizing Developing the organization systems that will develop, produce, and deliver the organization's products and the required infrastructure to support the primary production systems.

Out of control A state when a system is not on a path to achieving organizational objectives.

Outsourcing The process of buying resources from an outside supplier instead of manufacturing them in-house.

P

Participative budgeting A method of budget setting that uses a joint decision-making process in which all parties agree about setting the budget targets.

Payback method The number of periods needed to recover a project's initial investment.

Payback period The number of periods required to recover a project's initial investment.

Pay-for-performance system Reward system that provides monetary rewards based on measured results. Also called incentive compensation.

Penetration pricing strategy The act of choosing a low markup for a new product to penetrate the market and win over market share from an established product of a competing firm.

Period costs Those costs related to nonmanufacturing costs, including administrative and marketing costs.

Periodic budget A budget that is prepared for a given period, such as a quarter or a year.

Planning Includes such activities as product planning, production planning, and strategy development. By its nature, planning information is predictive and forward looking.

Planning variance The difference between the planned and flexible budget amount for some item.

Post-implementation audit The process of revisiting the decision to purchase a capacity-related resource to determine whether expectations underlying the acquisition of the resource were achieved.

Post-sale service and disposal cycle The portion of the life cycle that begins once the first unit of a product is in the hands of the customer.

Practical capacity The maximum amount of work that can be performed by resources supplied for production or service.

Present value A future cash flow's value at time zero.

Prevention costs Those costs incurred to help ensure that companies produce products according to quality standards.

Preventive control An approach to control that focuses on preventing an undesired event.

Price-led costing With this approach, a target selling price and target product volume are chosen on the basis of the company's perceived value of the product to the customer.

Price setter A firm that can determine the prices its customers will pay for its products.

Price (rate) variances The difference between the amount paid for a resource and the amount that would have been paid if the resource had been purchased at its standard price.

Price taker A firm that accepts the prices set in the marketplace for its products.

Pro forma financial statements The projected statement of cash flows, balance sheet, and income statement.

Process costing system A costing system that computes the cost of each manufacturing process used to make a product.

Process layout A production design in which all similar equipment or functions are grouped together.

Process perspective Describes how a strategy will be executed. It identifies the operating, customer management, innovation, and regulatory and social processes that are most important to meet the expectations of shareholders and customers.

Processing cycle efficiency (PCE) A measure used to assess the efficiency of a process cycle.

Processing time The time expended to complete a processing activity.

Product costs Manufacturing costs incurred to produce the volume and mix of products made during the period.

Product layout A production design in which equipment is organized to accommodate the production of a specific product.

Productivity The ratio of output to input.

Product-sustaining activities Activities that provide the infrastructure that enables the production, distribution, and sale of the product but are not involved directly in the production of the product.

Profit centers Responsibility centers in which managers and other employees control both the revenues and the costs of the product or service they deliver.

Profit sharing A cash bonus calculated as a percentage of an organization unit's reported profit; a group incentive compensation plan focused on short-term performances.

Profitability index A variation on the net present value method, computed by dividing the present value of the cash inflows by the present value of the cash outflows.

Projected or expected financial statements The forecasted balance sheet and projected income statement.

Q

Quality costs Those costs incurred on quality-related processes, including *prevention, appraisal, internal failure, and external failure.*

Quality function deployment (QFD) matrix A tool that is typically used for systematically arraying information about the variables of features, functions, and competitive evaluation in a matrix format.

Quantity (efficiency) variances The difference between the amount of a resource used and the amount allowed, given the level of production costed at the standard cost of the resource.

Quick ratio A measure of short-run liquidity.

R

Rate of return Ratio of net income to investment.

Rate (price) variance An estimate of the increase in costs caused by paying more than the standard amount per unit of direct labor or materials.

Raw materials inventory The purchase cost of materials that have not been used.

Real options analysis Analysis of the value of an option based on the volatility of the future value of the asset underlying the option.

Reciprocal allocation method A service cost allocation method that recognizes reciprocal interactions between different service departments.

Regulatory and social processes Processes that promote meeting or exceeding standards established by regulations and facilitate achievement of desired social objectives.

Relevance of information How useful information is for an organization's decision and control processes.

Relevant costs and revenues Future costs or revenues that will change as a result of a particular decision.

Research, development, and engineering (RD&E) cycle A life-cycle concept that involves market research, product design, and product development.

Residual income An accounting-based measure of the increase in shareowner wealth resulting from current operations. Measured as accounting income minus the economic cost of the investment used to generate that income.

Responsibility center An organization unit for which a manager is made responsible.

Results control The process of hiring qualified people who understand the organization's objectives, telling them to do whatever they think best to help the organization achieve its objectives, and using the control system to evaluate the resulting performance, thereby assessing how well they have done.

Return The increased cash inflows in the future that are attributable to the long-term asset.

Return on investment (ROI) The ratio of net income to invested capital.

Revenue centers Responsibility centers whose members control revenues but do not control either the manufacturing or the acquisition cost of the product or service they sell or the level of investment made in the responsibility center.

Rucker plan A form of gainsharing program.

S

Sales mix variance A difference between planned and actual revenue caused by a difference between planned and actual product mix.

Sales price variance A difference between planned and actual revenue caused by a difference between planned and actual prices for one or several products.

Sales quantity variance Computed for each product because the volume of sales was different than planned. A difference between planned and actual revenue caused by a difference between planned and actual quantity levels.

Scanlon plan A form of gainsharing program.

Scientific management school A management movement with the underlying philosophy that most people find work objectionable, that people care little for making decisions or showing creativity on the job, and that money is the driving force behind performance.

Scope of the MACS Includes the entire value chain of the organization.

Second-level variances Second level variances include both a planning variance and a flexible budget variance that sum to the first-level variance.

Segment margin report An accounting-based measure of the profit contribution of an organization unit to the overall organization.

Sensitivity analysis The process of selectively varying a plan's or a budget's key estimates for the purpose of identifying over what range a decision option is preferred.

Sequential allocation method Allocates service department costs to production departments and other service departments in a sequential order.

Service departments Departments that perform activities that support production but are not responsible for any of the conversion processes.

Short run The period over which a decision maker cannot adjust capacity.

Skimming price strategy Initially charging a higher price to customers who are willing to pay more for the privilege of possessing a product.

Smoothing The act of affecting the preplanned flow of information without altering actual behavior.

Stage 1 allocations These involve the estimation of the normal manufacturing support costs incurred in each department.

Stage 2 allocations These require the identification of appropriate cost drivers for each production department, and assign production department costs to jobs and products as they are worked on in the departments.

Stock option The right to purchase a unit of the organization's stock at a specified price, called the option price.

Strategy Describes how a company will gain competitive advantage by being different or better than its competitors. Examples of strategies include low cost, complete customer solutions, and product leadership.

Strategy map A comprehensive visual representation of the linkages among objectives and measures in the four perspectives of the Balanced Scorecard.

Stretch budgeting A method of budget setting in which the organization will try to reach much higher goals with the current budget.

Stretch target A target that exceeds previous targets by a significant amount and usually requires a large increase in effort during the next budgeting period.

Sunk costs The costs of resources that already have been committed and cannot be changed by any current action or decision; contrast with *incremental costs.*

Supply chain management A management system that develops cooperative, mutually beneficial, long-term relationships between buyers and sellers.

T

Target The level of performance or rate of improvement required for a Balanced Scorecard measure.

Target cost The difference between the target selling price and the target profit margin.

Target costing A method of cost planning used during the planning cycle to reduce manufacturing costs to targeted levels.

Task control The process of developing standard procedures that employees are told to follow.

Theory of constraints (TOC) A management approach that maximizes the volume of production through a bottleneck process.

Third-level variances Third-level variances include quantity and price variances that sum to, and therefore explain, the flexible budget variances.

Throughput contribution The difference between revenues and direct materials for the quantity of product sold.

Time-driven ABC A new ABC variant that is simple and more powerful since it requires estimating only two parameters: the cost of supplying resource capacity and the quantity of capacity consumed by each transaction, product, and customer. It enables a much simpler ABC model to capture even highly complex operations through the use of time equations.

Time equation An algebraic representation that predicts the quantity of processing time based on specific order and activity characteristics.

Time value of money The concept stating that amounts of money received at different periods of time must be converted into their value on a common date to be compared.

Total asset turnover A measure of the organization's ability to use assets effectively to generate sales.

Total-life-cycle costing (TLCC) Describes the process of managing all costs during a product's lifetime.

Transfer pricing The set of rules an organization uses to assign prices to products transferred between internal responsibility centers in order to allocate jointly earned revenue among responsibility centers.

U

Unilateral (covert) benchmarking A process in which companies independently gather information about one or several other companies that excel in the area of interest.

Unit contribution margin ratio Contribution margin per unit divided by sales revenue per unit; the fraction of each sales dollar that goes toward covering fixed costs.

Unit-related activities Activities whose volume or level is proportional to the number of units produced or to other measures, such as direct labor hours and machine hours that are themselves proportional to the amount of work done.

V

Value engineering process The process of examining each component of a product to determine whether its cost can be reduced while maintaining functionality and performance.

Value index This is the ratio of the value of a component to a customer and the percentage of total cost devoted to each component.

Value proposition Clear and short statement of competitive value that the organization will deliver to its target customers—how it will compete for, or satisfy, customers.

Variable costing A costing method in which only variable manufacturing costs are included in product costs.

Variable costs The costs of flexible resources.

Variance The difference between an actual amount and a target or planned amount.

Variance analysis A set of procedures managers use to help them understand the source of variances.

Vision statement A concise, externally focused statement that defines an organization's mid- to long-term goals and states how that organization wants to be perceived by the world. The set of selected activities in which an organization will excel to create a sustainable difference in the marketplace.

W

Weighted-average method A method used for computing equivalent units of production in process costing.

Whale curve A plot of cumulative profitability versus the number of customers, where customers are ranked from the most profitable to the least profitable. In a typical whale curve, the most profitable 20 percent of customers generate between 150 and 300 percent of the company's profits. The unprofitable customers incur losses that cumulatively bring the company's profits down to 100 percent.

What-if analysis A process of exploring the effects of changes in estimates on predictions in a financial model.

Work-in-process (WIP) inventory The costs of the resources for each job not yet completed.

Z

Zero-based budgeting (ZBB) A budgeting process that requires proponents of discretionary expenditures to continuously justify every expenditure.

Subject Index

W

Wait and *see* possibilities, 552–554
Weighted average cost of capital
method, 536
Whale curve, 155
What-if analysis, 465–467, 554–555

Z

Zero-based budgeting (ZBB), 485

Name and Company Index

A

Acorn System, 159
Airbus, 37–38
Air Canada, 606
Air France, 210
AMR Corporation, 623
ANZAC Company, 366
Apple Computer, 32, 266

B

Baring's Bank, 18
Boeing, 7, 37–38, 330
Bonner Company, 208–210
Booth Motors, 132–134
British Airways, 210
Buffet, Warren, 378–379

C

Cabinets by Design (CBD), 1–2, 8–12
Canning Cellular Services (CCS), 469–473
Carnegie, Andrew, 6
Chemco International, 312–313
Chunling company, 268–272
Clinton, Bill, 14
Cognos, 423
Craven, Wendy, 263–264

D

DaimlerChrysler, 330
Danny Company, 547
Dark Horse Comics, Inc. (DHC), 91
Dell Computers, 11, 405
Dow Chemical Company, 521–523, 558
Duin, Steve, 91
Dupont Company, 6, 394, 603–604

E

Earl's Motors, 590–593, 595, 597, 601
Eastman Kodak, 330
EMI, 266
Enron, 18
Ericson Ice Cream Company, 134–136, 150–154

F

Famous Flange Company, 88, 89–90, 93, 96–100
Federal Express, 582

Federal Standards Advisory Board (FSAB), 14–15
Financial Accounting Standards Board (FASB), 378
Fitzgibbon, Myriah, 263–264
Foster, Gael, 450–465
Fyfe Company, 33, 35, 552–554, 598

G

General Electric, 365, 587–588
General Motors, 6, 364, 374, 394, 578
Georgia-Pacific, 379
Goldman, William, 97
Goldman Sachs, 405
Goldstein, Mark, 277
Gore, Al, 14
Grumman Corporation, 376

H

Hancock, Mike, 392–394, 427–428
Hankerson, Neil, 91
Harp, Jeff, 356
Helping Hand, 106–117
Herman Miller company, 376
Hewitt Associates, 375
High Performance Springs, 263–264, 282
Homebush Glass Company, 101–105
Honda Motor Co. Ltd., 591
Hyperion, 423

I

IBM, 405
Intel, 405
International Research, 277
iTunes, 266

J

Jim and Barry's Ice Cream Company, 278–279
Jobs, Steve, 266
Johnson, Rich, 159

K

Kellogg, Jonathan, 132–134
Kemps, LLC, 157–158
Ken's Auto Service Company, 83–84, 92–96
Kidder Peabody, 18
Kirsch, Vanessa, 420
Kitchenhelp, 324–325

Klink, Jack, 418
KPMG, 16
Krock, Ray, 10

L

Livingstone, Ken, 281
Lynn's Landscaping Services, 26–28, 41–42, 43, 67–68

M

Magna Steyr, 7
Malcom Baldrige National Quality Program, 395
McArthur, Douglas, 231
McDonald's, 10, 11, 405, 580–581
Media General, 416–417
Mellon Europe, 418
Mercado, Robert, 263–264
Mercedes-Benz, 329, 405, 580
Metro Bank, 392–394, 411–417, 427–428
Microsoft Corporation, 159, 423
Mitsubishi Heavy Industries, 7
Mittal, 621–622
Mobil Corporation, 594
Moore, Sandra, 443
Mount Pleasant Plastics, 51
Multiflavor Factory, 107–108

N

Nanticoke Electric, 56–57
New Profit, Inc. (NPI), 420
Nextel, 541
Nieman-Marcus, 405
Nokia, 449
Nucor Corporation, 572–577, 610–625

O

Oracle, 159, 423
Orillia Novelty Plastics, 63–66
Oxford Tole Art, 450–452

P

Patagonia, 315
Perrier, 16
Pielin, Don, 206–207, 233–238
Pinsky Company, 317–318
Porter, Michael, 399
Pyro Industries, 273–276